Jack the Ripper

THE DEFINITIVE CASEBOOK

Ad
Cyril Whittington-Egan, the Learned Attorney,
et
Helen Margaret Zeugheer Herrmann Barrington
Progenitores meus,
et
Ad illum qui obscurae
noctis tenebras fugit

Jack the Ripper

THE DEFINITIVE CASEBOOK

RICHARD WHITTINGTON-EGAN

AMBERLEY

First published 2013

Amberley Publishing
The Hill, Stroud
Gloucestershire, GL5 4EP

www.amberleybooks.com

British Library Cataloguing in Publication Data.
A catalogue record for this book is available from the British Library.

ISBN 978 1 4456 1768 8
ISBN 978 1 4456 1786 2 (ebook)

Typesetting and Origination by Amberley Publishing.
Printed in the UK.

Contents

Acknowledgements

Res ipsa loquitur – a book of this kind necessarily owes a great deal to the authors of those books on its subject which have gone before it, and to all former investigators, students, and commentators on and around the case with which it is concerned.

I should, however, like most particularly to put on record my gratitude to those who helped me so unstintingly in the days when I was writing my first book on the subject, *A Casebook on Jack the Ripper* – Robin Odell, Donald Rumbelow, the late Tom Cullen, Stephen Knight, Joseph H. H. Gaute, Paul O'Donovan, Barrister-at-Law, Rosalind Wade, William James Dempster, F.R.C.S. and Professor Israel Donisch of the London Hospital for their expert guidance in matters relating to the human kidney.

In the course of writing this second study of the case, I have accumulated a whole new crop of debts for disinterested assistance and advice.

Above all, I am most grateful to Stewart Evans, who placed his encyclopedic knowledge and, so it seemed, total recall of the minutiae of matters relating to the Whitechapel murders at my service. He undoubtedly saved me from becoming entangled in any of the more subtle Ripper tripper-traps, which is not to say that he is to be permitted to rob me of the credit for any mistakes, which, all my own work, may have slipped through the fine meshes of the scrutineer's salvatory network.

I am indebted also to the kindness of my friends and fellow-labourers in the Whitechapel vineyard – those redoubtable Ripperian trinitarians, Paul Begg, Martin Fido, and Keith Skinner, Colin Wilson, Paul Gainey, the late Melvin Harris, and Nicholas Warren, F.R.C.S., who resolved several of my more tiresome traumata.

I owe a particular debt of gratitude to Nicholas Connell, who not only went to very considerable lengths in the matter of rescuing my original manuscript, but also contributed an enormous amount of help to me in my research.

For an assortment of good reasons I am 'very much obleeged', as old-time barristers used to say, to my friend of many years, the late Jonathan Goodman; to John Staddon; to Michael Cottrill, *ci-devant* Doge of Hay-on-Wye; and my other literary 'executors' (of difficult literary tasks and tracings) Camille Wolff, Loretta Lay, and Clifford and Marie Elmer.

In the matter of illustrations I am further and deeply indebted to Stephanie Bilton, Nicholas Connell, Stewart Evans and John Staddon.

Throughout the lengthy travail, I have been fortunate to have been able to rely upon the listening, educated ear and wise counsel of my wife, Molly.

Richard Whittington-Egan

Prologue

Jack the Ripper. The very name strikes chill, wreathed about as it is with visions of the creepy, ill-lit courts and alleyways of the Victorian East End of London, and the dreadful spectacle of the monster's deliberately laid-out handiwork, the stark, horrendously mutilated corpses of his victims.

It is surely the phantasmagoric quality of the creature who, lacking a known patronym, has been allocated the adjectival substantive Jack the Ripper, that compels the unabating and perfervid interest.

Silent as a phantom, he came and went; like Lewis Carroll's Boojum, softly and suddenly vanished away.

Had the Ripper, fleet-footed, insubstantial Jack, been 'buckled', his trial embalmed between the appropriate blood-red covers of a volume in the exemplary *Notable British Trials* series, his psychopathology expatiated upon in a learned introductory essay, the case would, no doubt, be gathering dust upon the crammed shelves of the systematic criminologists.

But he was not. It is not.

Instead, while Crippen, Cream, Wainwright, the Stauntons, and others of their ilk repine, Saucy Jacky remains fresh as new-spilt blood, talked about, speculated upon, and, every few months it seems, 'finally' and 'definitively' identified.

That being said, convention and courtesy demand of me an explanation as to what I am about in adding yet another volume to the toppling pile of Ripper books.

First then, permit me to say what I am *not* about. I am not, seduced by the growing popularity of the Hunt-the-Ripper game, proffering the breathless discovery of a brand-new suspect. I am not formulating some cherished and labyrinthine theory, compounded of believable half-truths and unbelievable coincidences, that will at last bring blinding light into hitherto dark places. I am not setting up sights to snipe joyously at the legions of my predecessors in this heavily furrowed field.

I come, not as an innovator, but as a commentator. My claim to right of hearing is based upon a familiarity with the literature and a study of the subject matter which extends over seventy-odd years. I may not in the result have achieved wisdom, but I have certainly acquired knowledge. I have moreover been fortunate in that, by an accident of time, I was in my youth afforded the opportunity of meeting and talking with a handful of those dwindling survivors – some of them then still resident in the East End – who had actually lived through that long-ago autumn of terror.

In the thirty-eight years which have so swiftly and smoothly passed, almost unnoticed, since the publication of my *Casebook on Jack the Ripper*, interest in the Whitechapel assassin has not flagged: on the contrary. What can, all these decades, these generations, on, be the fascination? Nostalgia for that which we never knew? An atmosphere?

The truth is that Ripperland, like Poppyland – which was written about by George R. Sims, the celebrated contemporary chronicler of Jack the Ripper – where in the 1880s the Norfolk idyll of Clement Scott, the 'Great Writer', and the miller's daughter, Louie Jermy, was, to deep retrospective public sentiment, enacted, are both today as much states of mind as geographical locations.[1] Both are of the East: the one, Spensarian faery East Anglia, gentle romance, vicine Overstrand; the other, daemonic, the tumultuous East End of London. Brick and mortal. Brutal tragedy in and about Whitechapel. The Stevensonian Jekyll and Hyde duality. Shades of the Great Worm of Lambton.

And yet … so have the winds and rains, the hundred and more wild Decembers, the passage of Time, the great smoother and soother, bandaged the ancient woundings, worn away the sharpest tombstone-edges of anguish, turned magically the faded sadness into a weird kind of beauty, that it is even possible, looking back from the divorce of a safe distance, to re-fashion the charnel-house horrors of old Whitechapel into a sort of Ingoldsby legends sequence, paralleling, in part, the Reverend Barham's quaint parish of tales. For here indeed be wonders and alarums and excursions and quiddities galore – Caroline Maxwell's ghost story of her matutinal vision of Mary Jane Kelly; the legend of the Curse Upon Mitre Square; the eerie tale of the magic womb candles; the scintillant cast of characters, the likes of Mrs Fiddymont, Mrs Prater, Leather Apron, Indian Harry, Pearly Poll, Dark Annie, Long Liz, Pork Butcher Isenschmidt, Clay Pipe Alice, Carrotty Nell, Harry the Hawker, and One-armed Liz – an Ingoldsbyean galaxy, and a chaplet of weird rhymes and jingles to set against the cornucopia of Barham verses:

> I'm not a butcher,
> I'm not a Yid,
> Nor yet a foreign skipper.
> But I'm your own light-hearted friend,
> Yours truly Jack the Ripper.

Moving from the landscape of imagination to the stonier townscape of Ripperian reality, we come to seedy ground in the Borough of Stepney – Whitechapel, Spitalfields, Shoreditch, Shadwell, Wapping, Limehouse, and St George's-in-the-East. It is a terrain as distinct as that demesne of Bunhill Fields, the Finsbury of Bunyan and Blake, Watts and Defoe, Wesley and Fox, an area so splendidly celebrated in the writings of Peter Ackroyd, who, incidentally, has ventured into Ripperland Marches, where Hawksmoor's Christ Church stands in Spitalfields – the spiritual defying the temporal Ten Bells – with his *Dan Leno and the Limehouse Golem*.

It is chastening to realise that, as in the *Criminologist*, spring 1990, Mason Jay points out in his article, 'The Ripper – A Layman's Theory', that this saga of entrails and ovaries, this Ripper reign of terror, lasted, as an *au courant* entity, a mere seventy-one days, and that Jack dropped out of sight for forty of them. Moreover, how low in the league table of serial killers the Ripper comes. A mere five scalps to his belt.[2]

It is no easy thing, all these years later, to convey the sensation of panic that, with each new murder, spread throughout London. Audiences emerging from the Lyceum Theatre, where they had just seen the chilling new play *Dr Jekyll and Mr Hyde*, into the road beneath the gas-flaring iron lilies of the Strand, hearing the cries of the newsboys – 'Murder! Murder! Another 'orrible Whitechapel murder' – must have felt that life was horrendously imitating art.

These same newsvendors' cries, shattering the evening somnolence of South Kensington's dignified Pembroke Square, thoroughly upset the refined sensibilities of its decorous residents, one of whom addressed himself angrily to the universe in a letter to the *Daily Telegraph*:

> Can nothing be done to prevent a set of hoarse ruffians coming nightly about our suburban squares and streets, yelling at the tops of their hideous voices … and nearly frightening the lives out of the sensitive women and children in the neighbourhood? Last evening (Wednesday) for instance, their … awful words were bawled out about nine o'clock in a quiet part of Kensington and a lady who was supping with us was so greatly distressed by these hideous bellowings that she was absolutely too unnerved to return home save in a cab, because she would have to walk about a hundred or two yards down a quiet street at the other end of her journey by omnibus.

It is doubtful if even that felicitous chronicler of the criminous, William Roughead, could have bettered the description penned by an unknown journalist of the day:

> From east to west, from north to south, the horror ran throughout the land. Men spoke of it with bated breath, and pale-lipped women shuddered as they read the dreadful details. A lurid pall rested over the densely populated district of London, and people looking at it afar off, smelt blood. The superstitious said that the skies had been of a deeper red that autumn, presaging desperate and direful deeds, and the aliens of the neighbourhood, filled with strange phantasies brought from foreign shores, whispered that evil spirits were abroad.

Hugh Kingsmill it was who, writing of the disputed authorship of Shakespeare's plays, remarked that because we have so little evidence of Shakespeare's actual existence, the plays have been the happy hunting ground for deranged minds. Would it be too fanciful, not to say offensive, to suggest something of a parallel here with the antics of some of the Ripper hunters? As A. P. Wolf writes of the host of Jack the Ripper suspects: 'An incredible 139 different candidates … A lifetime's work of false trails leading to nowhere in dusty reading rooms.'

The indefatigable Stewart Evans has rooted out yet another for us in Thurston Hopkins' *Life and Death at the Old Bailey*, published in 1935. Hopkins, after reading George Hutchinson's statement describing the man whom he allegedly saw Mary Kelly meet at the corner of Thrawl Street and take back with her to Miller's Court, summoned up his memories of the wandering poet, Ernest Dowson, whom he had known, 'and curiously enough that description fitted him down to the ground! But I could not connect a man of such extraordinary gentleness [with] committing such a dreadful series of outrages.'

The plain truth is that the evidence as regards the real identity of the ghoul who scattered the discarded tripes of his victims over the London cobbles is so slim that any conjecture will – and won't – do, can be made plausible. First select your Ripper, and then twist your facts and features to suit.

There seems to have evolved a standard format for the typical 'Ripper book'. It will generally begin with a chapter on London in the late Victorian era. The author will then proceed to rehearse interminably, and with varying degrees of inaccuracy, the sequelae of the slaughterings. Next there will be a mustering and parade of suspects, 'other men's flowers', space and time squandered, and a deal of good white paper spoilt, in the uprooting and trampling of those rival authors' blossoms. And then, usually in the last chapter, among much 'psycho-babble and reach-me-down sociology', as Christopher Wordsworth expresses it,[3] there will be embedded the name of the author's own cherished suspect. 'Whether or not we get more than a glimpse of the ghoul's coat-tails in these books, we are assured of a wild run for our money,' says Wordsworth. 'Jack remains as insubstantial as the thin air into which he vanishes, leaving the reader with a pick of surmises solemnly dressed as solutions.' It is a 'harvest of meagre fact and ripe conjecture'.

But what we *do* get are a number of unforgettable *aperçus*: for instance, Daniel Farson's vignette, in his review in the *Evening Standard* (12 September 1994) of Philip Sugden's *The Complete History of Jack the Ripper*, of how, way back in 1959, he had met a man who, as a boy, had been riding on a cart going down Hanbury Street in the early hours of that Saturday morning in 1888, and, hearing the cry 'Murder!' had jumped off and run up the passage into the backyard of No. 29. He told Farson, 'And there she was, all her entrails steamin' hot, and I'll never forget it because she had red-and-white stockings on.' The vignette of the old lady at 29 Hanbury Street selling cats' meat – for human consumption.[4] The street women, who, at night, would slip into the ramshackle horse slaughterhouses, whether in search of custom among the bloody-aproned slaughtermen, or, more sinisterly and Krafft-Ebing-ishly, at the behest of some sado-masochistic hirer for whom the death screams of the terrified, blindfolded nags salted his spasm of illicit sexual congress, or, more simply, less esoterically, merely for shelter and warmth against the night hours of a cold, bleak life.

The gallimaufry of Dickensian characters – the bricklayer's labourer, Edward Stanley, adding a little of the colour of dignity to a drab life, harmlessly posing as the Military Pensioner, whose pathetic compensatory vanity was so crudely and cruelly unmasked by the self-aggrandising coroner, Wynne E. Baxter; that perky little cockney sparrow, Catherine Eddowes,[5] she of the brand-new boots, she who described herself as 'bought *and* paid for' by her consort, John Kelly, returning sunburnt from hop-picking – at Hunton, near Maidstone – in the fields of Kent, better-fed, cheery, declaring that she knew who Jack the Ripper was, and would be able to claim the rumoured reward for the capture of the Ripper. She may or may not have been right in her vaunted knowledge. But she met him – in Mitre Square. And after that, she was beyond the telling.

The bonfires blazing across the East End on 5 November 1888, atop them not the effigy of Guy Fawkes but that of Jack the Ripper. The appalling instant, four days later, when Mary Jane Kelly, who, in fascinated horror had had her former live-in lover, Joe Barnett, read out to her from the newspaper each evening the day's quota of fresh news about the Whitechapel murders, suddenly realised what she had brought home with her … that she was alone in the room with … the monster … the Ripper. Of such dreadful epiphanies are the lingering memories of that long-ago autumn of terror compacted.

One can, of course, always find relief in playing the iconoclast game, dispelling the essential gas-lit, swirling pea-souper-wreathed shivery courts and alleyways with the disobliging truth that the Met. records chronicle an unusually clement autumn in the year 1888; there was no fog on any of the murder nights, one of the murders (that of Annie Chapman) took place in daylight, and the last of the five, cosily indoors by firelight.

Iconoclastically, it is proving possible even to question Jack's time-honoured victim score. More and more is it coming to resemble the case of the 'ten little nigger boys'.

Out goes Long Liz Stride. Then there were four.

Alex Chisholm, Stewart Evans, Paul Gainey, Paul Harrison, Bruce Paley, Peter Turnbull, A. P. Wolf and Simon Wood are all reductionists.

Alex Chisholm, in an unpublished paper, 'A Revision of History' (1966), wrote, 'Not only were the press instrumental in portraying initial murders as a series, but throughout the period they also provided the primary link between the crimes and defined the characteristics of suitable suspects.' With a reminder that murders prior to and after the canonical five 'retain their cohesion largely due to their occurrence within the period of greatest hysteria … I would query Stride's association before raising a more controversial dismissal of Mary Kelly. Again the timing and coverage of this murder seem to provide the central link, although in this instance the press may have played an even more significant role. I would contend that whoever killed Kelly, for whatever reason, need not have murdered the other victims but simply have taken advantage of the opportunity to evade detection by making the crime appear to be the work of Jack the Ripper.'

Out goes Mary Kelly. Then there were three.

Evans and Gainey step forth with the conclusion that this eliminatory concept of Chisholm's 'may finally dispose of the huge myth built around the Whitechapel murders'. Watch out, demolition men at work. They are prepared to advance that 'Tumblety murdered at least Nichols, Chapman and Eddowes, murders in which the womb appeared to be the killer's target, Kelly may or may not have been his victim'. But in the light of all the new revelations the authors concur with the possibilities explored by Alex Chisholm.

We should, Evans and Gainey believe, be seeking the East End *murderers* rather than murderer. They also say that if the police had Tumblety in custody, or under surveillance, at the time of the Kelly murder and knew that he was not responsible … he would be in the clear, for they were looking for Jack the Ripper, the killer of *five* women, and if they knew that Tumblety was not guilty of the last killing, they might well have dismissed him as responsible for the other four.

Bruce Paley and Paul Harrison are both convinced that it was Joe Barnett who killed Mary Jane Kelly. Peter Turnbull thinks that all the murders were separate transactions; that three different men killed Chapman, Eddowes and Kelly, and that Nichols and Stride were likewise despatched by different hands. The general reductionist feeling is that, like Kelly, Stride was murdered after a domestic fracas by her live-in lover, in her case, Michael Kidney.

Even now, 125 years on, discoveries can be made. Nicholas Connell has recently found a letter from the redoubtable Dr Dutton, published in the *Daily Mail* of 14 May 1929. It was addressed to the Editor and on Jack the Ripper, written in response to the advent of Leonard Matters' book.

Sir, – Living in Whitechapel (Aldgate) about the time of the Jack the Ripper murder, I took great interest in them from a medical point of view.

I did not draw the same conclusion as Mr Leonard Matters, but believe they were committed by a ship's butcher.

Having been a surgeon in the Mercantile Marine I have seen these butchers with even greater skill with the knife than many expert operating surgeons. After the murders, going home one night with a black bag in which was a Masonic apron, I was accosted by two women who shouted, 'Jack the Ripper'.

Thomas Dutton, M.D.
25, New Cavendish Street, Harley Street, W.1.

Could this, one wonders, be where Donald McCormick got the idea of drawing Dr Dutton and his alleged trilogy, *Chronicles of Murder*, and his Pedachenko theory into the story?

A word now as to the arrangement adopted in this book. The discussion is presented in six parts. In Part 1 I have set out to provide a conspectus of the views expressed and the material published from the time of the commission of the crimes in 1888 up to the year 1987. This includes the memoirs of officials and police officers, contemporarily concerned, both centrally and peripherally, with the case, the opinions of the somewhat confused medical fraternity, those of the contemporary newspapers and journals, and the views and analyses of the theoretical constructs put forward in the major literature of the first ten decades. To this are added chapters which cross, as it were, the date-line. They concern themselves with such topics as the genesis of the 'Autumn of Terror', the shaping of the Whitechapel Murderer into the legendary bogey figure of Jack the Ripper.

In Part 2 I have surveyed the many faces that have been grafted on to the Ripper. Having no interest to declare, I have found it entirely feasible to examine such passionate indictments as those levelled against personalities as varied as the epicene *fin-de-siècle* pastellist Frank Miles, the doomed, angst-ridden Ernest Dowson, the fell and pitiless Dr Thomas Neill Cream, and the halt, aged and hemiplegic Sir William Gull, with requisite dispassion.

Part 3 presents the sociological, political, sexological and psychological backgrounds obtaining to that unique period, together with a record of the points of view subscribed to by certain selected observers.

This encompassing of the wider scene must in no wise be taken to mean that the story of the comparatively few who were so tragically caught up in the black limelight is in any sense neglected.

Part 4 carries the record forward to, and beyond, the centenary year, 1988. Part 5 considers the mysterious emergence of what purports to be the diary of Jack the Ripper, the pros and cons for its claims. Part 6 deals with a temporally wide-ranging miscellany of general Ripperian topics.

In my reviewing of the writings of the multifarious Ripperine scribes and chroniclers I have tried to deal fairly with the successes and failures of those who have contributed, each his mite, to the unfolding saga. Many of their shortcomings can, indeed must, be excused on the basis of ignorance of facts that were to emerge only as further research progressed. I myself feel no shame in admitting to reconsidering some of my early views in the light of time's provision of further and better particulars.

After so lengthy an immersion, it is, I think, possible to discern and define the double bind of the Ripper fascination. In the first place, there is the straightforward appeal of the appalling puzzle. Secondly, there is the gas-lit, Holmesian period atmosphere, which invests the entire affair, and which, viewed from a comfortable distance, casts a romantic afterglow that softens the starker outlines. The whole thing has acquired the factitious cosiness of Madame Tussaud's Chamber of Horrors, engendering the permissible *frisson*, the retrospective gloat, decently separated from guilty reality. To put it another way, it is the innocent clergyman revelling in the horrid intricacies of a lurid detective novel. It all happened so long ago and far away, in another part of the forest.

An attempt by the press to increase Jack's tally is represented by the cautionary case of Fairy Fay. Fey might be a more appropriate spelling, for she is the victim who never was. Philip Sugden supplies us with her non-biography in his *Complete History* (1994). The first that he was able to trace of her alleged existence was in a broadsheet, 'Lines on the Terrible Tragedy in Whitechapel', printed at the beginning of September 1888. She is not herein actually named, merely referred to as a victim killed 'twelve months ago'. In the *Daily Telegraph* of 10 and 11 September 1888, it was stated that the Whitechapel murderer had claimed his first victim at Christmas 1887. The killing had occurred in the vicinity of Osborn and Wentworth streets. A stick or iron instrument had been viciously thrust into her body. The story, never embellished among its other multifarious ornamentations by the victim's name, appeared in the newspapers again and again over a period of sixty years. Then, in 1950, a journalist whose capacity for invention exceeded that of his capacity for truth, one Terence Robertson, in an article tastefully titled 'Madman Who Murdered Nine Women', published in *Reynolds News*, issue of 29 October 1950, gave birth to 'Fairy Fay'. He went further, furnished her with a respectable obit. She was killed on Boxing Night 1887, while taking a shortcut home from a public-house in Mitre Square, and found in a backstreet behind Commercial Road.

Philip Sugden authoritatively proclaims, 'No such event occurred. There is no reference to it in police records. No mention of it can be found in the local or national press … and a search of registered deaths at St Catherine's House reveals no woman named Fay or anything like that murdered in Whitechapel during the relevant period.' There is, he adds, no doubt that the original *Telegraph* story arose out of a confused memory of the known murder of Emma Smith, who was attacked in just such a manner in Osborn Street in the spring of 1888. 'Today writers still regularly list both Fairy Fay and Emma Smith as possible victims of Jack the Ripper,' says Sugden, 'but Fairy Fay is a phantom, born of sloppy journalism back in 1888.'

As we move further into the new millennium, two things will assuredly endure unchanging and unchanged: the ferocious stupidity and bellicosity of humankind and the impenetrable umbra of Victorian Jack's identity. We have been wandering, some of us, into wild gardens of fantasy, but the hard core that rejects the soft option must continue to press forward. There surely are many things still to be discovered, and the heartening message for the next few generations of Ripperphiles is that the Ripper files seem to be, like the categories of the tort of negligence, never closed.

When all is said and done, it is difficult, even at this stretch of time, not to feel an overwhelming sense of pity for the pathetic drabs whose small shortcomings in life were surely redeemed by the enormity of their deaths. Their petty wrongdoings were swamped in the wrong that was done to them. Retribution was out of all proportion to the original sin. They were, with the exception of Mary Kelly, ageing, ailing, alcoholic unfortunates, but they did not deserve to end up as so much butcher's meat on the cobbles of the streets they walked.

PART 1
THE SEEDING OF
THE KILLING FIELD:
THE MURDERS OF 1888

1
Genesis of a Panic

Throughout the seventy-one sanguinary days, between 31 August and 9 November 1888, of what has been somewhat picturesquely described as an 'autumn of terror', some person or persons unknown did murder and most grotesquely mutilate five prostitutes in the East End of London.

The commission of those crimes has been attributed by popular acclaim to a single individual whose true identity has been masked behind the *nom de meurtre* Jack the Ripper, and, although more than a century has elapsed since the commission of the Unknown One's deeds, the interest in speculating as to the identity of innominate Jack, far from diminishing, seems to have exponentially increased, and the putative identities of the killer to have multiplied beyond all rational expectation.

It is not proposed to enter here into a detailed description of the crimes themselves, for they are well documented in a number of works which are easily available for consultation, but it will be useful to list the dates, the names of the five generally accepted victims of the Ripper, and the locations of the killings, together with a few pertinent facts relative to each one.

Mary Ann Nichols, *née* Mary Ann Walker. aka Polly Nichols. b. Whitechapel, 26 August 1845. m. William Nichols, 1864. Children: 2 girls, 3 boys. Killed: Friday 31 August 1888, on the pavement adjacent to Buck's Row, Whitechapel. Throat cut. Buried: City of London Cemetery, Ilford.

Annie Chapman, *née* Elizabeth Anne Smith, aka Dark Annie, Mrs Sievey and Annie Siffey. b. Paddington, 1841. m. John Chapman, 1869. Children: 2 girls, 1 boy. Killed: Saturday 8 September 1888, in the backyard of 29 Hanbury Street, Spitalfields. Throat cut. Buried: Manor Park Cemetery, Forest Gate.

Elisabeth Stride. *née* Elisabeth Gustafsdotter, aka Long Liz. b. north of Gothenburg, Sweden, 27 November 1843. m. John Thomas Stride, 1869. Children: none. Co-habited with Michael Kidney 1885–88. Killed: Sunday 30 September 1888, in the passage leading into Dutfield's Yard, between Nos 40 and 42 Berner Street, Whitechapel. Throat Cut. Buried: East London Cemetery.

Catherine Eddowes, aka Kate Conway and Kate Kelly. b. Wolverhampton, 14 April 1842. Co-habited with Thomas Conway for some twenty years. Children: 1 girl, 2 boys. Co-habited with

John Kelly 1881–88. Killed: early hours of Sunday 30 September 1888, in the southern corner of Mitre Square, City of London. Throat cut. Buried: City of London Cemetery, Ilford.

Mary Jane Kelly, aka Black Mary, Fair Emma and Ginger. b. Limerick (county or town ?) *c.* 1863. m.(?) John Davis or Davies *c.* 1879. Children: none. Co-habited with Joseph Barnett 1887–88. Killed: Friday 9 November 1888, in her room at 13 Miller's Court, Dorset Street, Spitalfields. Throat cut. Buried: St Patrick's Roman Catholic Cemetery, Leytonstone.

There are, however, criminological writers who would extend the list to include:

'Fairy Fay'. Alleged victim. Killed: *circa* Christmas 1887, in the vicinity of Osborn and Wentworth streets, Whitechapel. No trace of any record of her murder has been found, and the likelihood is that the whole story is apocryphal.

Emma Elizabeth Smith. b. 1843. Widow. Children: 2. Assaulted and robbed by three men, Tuesday 3 April 1888, on Osborn Street, near Wentworth Street, Whitechapel. Died 4 April 1888, in the London Hospital. Peritonitis following vaginal wounding.

Martha Tabram, *née* Martha White, aka Martha Turner and Emma Turner. b. Southwark, 10 May 1849. m. Henry Samuel Tabram. Children: 2 boys. Co-habited with Henry Turner for some twelve years. Killed: Tuesday 7 August 1888, on the first-floor landing of George Yard Buildings, George Yard, Whitechapel. Stabbed.

Rose Mylett, aka 'Drunken Lizzie' Davis, 'Fair Alice' Downey and Catherine Millett. b. Spitalfields, 1862. m. an upholsterer named Davis. Children: 1 boy. Found dead Thursday 20 December 1888, in Clarke's Yard, between 184 and 186 Poplar High Street, Poplar. Cause of death disputed – homicidal strangulation or natural.

Alice McKenzie, aka 'Clay Pipe' Alice and Alice Bryant. b. Peterborough, 1849. Co-habited with John McCormack. Killed: Wednesday 17 July 1889, in Castle Alley, between Old Castle Street and Whitechapel High Street, Whitechapel. Throat cut.

Frances Coles, aka Carrotty Nell, Frances Coleman and Frances Hawkins. b. 1865 Killed: Friday 13 February 1891, in Swallow Gardens, a narrow passageway between Chamber Street and Rosemary Lane (now Royal Mint Street), Whitechapel. Throat cut.

In the opinion of the majority of those who have made a study of the Ripper, these additional half-dozen murders are not, with the possible exception of that of Martha Tabram, to be laid at his door.

Taking an overview of what have, rightly or wrongly, become known as the five canonical murders, it had always struck one as somewhat surprising that the populace at large should have worked themselves into such a truly heroic state of terror following the discovery of the corpse of Annie Chapman, which was, after all, preceded by only a single previous Ripper murder; that of Mary Ann Nichols.

Elucidation as regards this matter of emotional acceleration into a seemingly disproportionately early panic is supplied by Joseph C. Fisher in his *Killer among Us: Public Reactions to Serial Murder* (1997). Dr Fisher is a sociologist who can boast the advantage – or disadvantage – of having lived in two communities during the periods of their respective terrorisations by serial killers; that of the university towns of Ann Arbor and Ypsilanti, Michigan. Between August 1967 and July 1969, the so-called Ypsilanti Ripper, John Norman Collins, murdered seven young women. And in the period 1973–74, at Folly Beach, South Carolina, three teenage girls died at the hands of Richard Raymond Valenti.

Using 'contemporary newspaper reports as a window through time to observe and recapture the thoughts, feelings and actions of each community studied,' Fisher purposes an 'archival record of factual reports,' from which, amplified by the raw data of 'feature stories, editorials and letters to the editor,' it is possible to discern and describe the characteristic stages of public reaction to serial murder.

The cases selected for scrutiny are those of Albert Henry DeSalvo, the Boston Strangler, 1962–64; John Norman Collins, the Co-ed Killer, 1967–69; David Richard Berkowitz, the Son of Sam, 1976–77; Wayne Bertram Williams, the Atlanta Child Killer, 1979–81; Jeffrey Lionel Dahmer, the Milwaukee Cannibal, 1987–91; and the sixth, the classic, case is that of Jack the Ripper, the Whitechapel Murderer, 1888. There is additionally a rather more superficial examination of the case of Richard Raymond Valenti, the Folly Beach Dunes Slayer, 1973–74.

Fisher writes of the Ripper affair, 'Like so many other serial murder cases, what the public believed to be the murder count differed from the number ultimately attributed to the killer.' Of the tally of eight killings in the East End, as published in the *Pall Mall Gazette* of 10 November 1888, Fisher comments, 'The first three murders were clearly acts of isolated violence.' The first woman, unidentified by name, listed as having died at Christmas 1887, following the thrusting of an iron stake so deeply into her vagina that it fatally ruptured her internal organs, sounds disturbingly like Fairy Fay. The second murdered woman was Emma Smith, a forty-five-year-old widow, attacked in Osborn Street in the early hours of Easter Tuesday morning, 3 April 1888. She was apparently set upon by three, perhaps four, ruffians, who, although they severely beat and sexually assaulted her, did not intend murder. However, so savagely did they drive some blunt instrument, possibly a stick, up her vagina, that it ruptured the perineum, causing peritonitis. She died in the London Hospital at nine o'clock on the morning of Wednesday 4 April 1888. The third woman, Martha Turner (aka Tabram), murdered on 7 August 1888, the Tuesday after the August Bank Holiday Monday, was seen shortly before her demise in the company of two soldiers, and was later found stabbed to death in George Yard Buildings, a dagger, it was conjectured, being responsible for one of her thirty-nine puncture wounds. With the distortion of the passage of time, this has frequently – speculatively and erroneously – been stated to have been the result of the use of a bayonet. In fact, all but one of the thirty-nine wounds were thought at the time to have been inflicted by a weapon of no more ferocious a calibre than a penknife, but the injury that had penetrated the sternum, would, according to Dr Timothy Robert Killeen, who examined the body, have necessitated the use of a stronger knife or dagger.

Discounting these three as Jack's victims, Fisher says that what distinguished the Ripper murders proper was mutilation, 'gratuitous damage to the corpse secondary to death'.

By this diagnostic yardstick 'the string [of murders] began and ended in a brief two-month period, [although] in terms of public reactions, the murders extended over a full year, [and] the pace increased over the final months, when five women [victims no. 4, 5, 6, 7 and 8, counting by the *Pall Mall Gazette* abacus] were killed in ten weeks of terror; the savagery of the murders also increased, the tempo and violence causing a crescendo of anxiety in the last months of 1888'.

Fisher's brief is much wider than just the Jack the Ripper sequence; he is, as we have already noted, committed to looking at the whole serial killer phenomenon in its most extensive application temporally and spatially.

One is, indeed, constrained to ask, was Jack the Ripper a serial killer in the true sense? To quote a question and answer from *The Murder Almanac* (1992) by Richard and Molly Whittington-Egan,

What exactly is a serial killer? How does he differ from a mass murderer? Is it simply a matter of semantics? Both, surely, are multiple murderers The determining diagnostic feature has to be the psychological motivation of the killer. The mass murderer kills numbers of people for any one, or any combination of, the classic motives – gain, revenge, elimination, jealousy, conviction, which is to say killing for an idea or ideal. The serial killer kills primarily for a compulsive sexual reason, or for pure love and lust for killing; although, of course, just to make things more complicated, incidental benefits may accrue to be taken advantage of.

A further constraint is the spanner-in-works hazard that the Ripper was a true psychotic; a fifty-fifty possibility, one might think. But the plain fact is that we have not an iota of evidence to support such an assumption, and we are bound therefore by the alternative presumption.

Surveying the phenomenon as a whole, Fisher discerns a certain regularity of pattern. The invariable initial response to the realisation that there is a killer on the rampage loose among us is to seek an allaying of natural fear of the unknown, and its, perhaps unknowable, motivation, by a comforting refuge-taking in the rational.

'At the core of the fear caused by serial murder is the incomprehensibility of what is happening. The killer's motivations and actions are beyond the experience of daily life and impossible to understand … and the unknown is feared most of all.'

That explains why 'an attempt is made to find reasons for events that lie within the domain of normal behaviour. Consequently, even suspiciously abnormal occurrences are interpreted as representing the most likely, ordinary, and commonplace eventualities.'

This is, effectively, a collective defence mechanism against the horrendous potential, the twisted vastness of the might-have-been and the may-yet-be – 'the fear of personal mortality and particularly a cruel, capricious, untimely, and meaningless death'.

The primary communal invocation, then, is the power of reason.

'Victorian England prided itself on the pursuit of knowledge through the application of the scientific method', and a plethora of reassuring rationales were advanced to account for the Ripper's malfeasances. The doctrine of evolution proffered the concept of the killer's being 'an example of retrogression in the march of evolutionary improvement, an atavistic creature suffering from homicidal mania'. And the theory of Professor Moriz Benedikt of Vienna 'that the brains of murderers resemble in their conformation those of ferocious beasts [with a] special likeness to the brains of bears' was quoted.

Another notion was that the Ripper had tapped into a market where he was selling the wombs which he filched at the rate of £20 a time. The *Pall Mall Gazette*, 1 October 1888, thought to debunk this with the publication of the prevailing rates for anatomical subjects as provided by the sub-curator of the Pathological Museum:

It is best to set the plain facts plainly forth, and the following letter of prices Current containing latest quotations for various parts of the human body Suffices to blow the coroner's theory into the air. The following are the prices which we are paying at present for anatomical subjects :-

For one corpse complete £3 5s.

For one thorax 5s.

For one arm, one leg, one head and neck, and one abdomen, <u>net.</u> 15s.

> These prices referred to pickled dissecting-room subjects. The organ removed by the murderer [i.e. the Ripper] can be had for the asking at any post-mortem room, twelve hours after death.

This made the alleged bloody bounty of £20 apiece for the Ripper's hard-won wombs a shade inflationary.

> Another variation on the scientist-as-killer motif was the argument, intricately reasoned in the press, that the murders were being committed by a 'Scientific Sociologist,' who was conceptualised as a social reformer gone berserk … A rational man … would seek to obtain the maximum of effect for the minimum expenditure of money and life, and seize, in Bismarck's terminology, the 'psychological moment' to deliver a decisive stroke … No ordinary killing would do since it would not impress the public. There had to be something so shocking it could not be ignored. Mutilation was therefore an absolute necessity.

Of the conscience-stricken crusader, Fisher adds, 'In the name of science and with the use of its methods to achieve his ends, the image of the murderer had become a malignant cross between Jane Addams and Dr Jekyll.' What is, in Fisher's terms, 'the paradox of serial murder is that characteristic that makes it most beyond our capacity to understand, repetition at the same time provides the key to the public's ability to apprehend it'.

It is the repeated killing that is rebarbative, resistive to the grasp of normalcy. If, however, the murders are not so happenstance, but connected in some apprehensible fashion, they can present with at least a kind of logic, albeit desperately off-line, which can be utilised in terms explicative if not justificatory.

As, in any series of murders, time progresses and the investigators do not, faith in the rational declines, investigative procedures, police experts, scientific method are all denigrated, become casualties, and the 'public will turn to supernatural explanations for the crimes and superhuman methods of finding the killer'.

Fisher demonstrates three ways in which belief in the supernatural is expressed from the standpoint of collective reactions to serial murder: belief that the killer's behaviour stems from demonic, satanic, or otherworldly forces; belief that the killer is the possessor of superhuman powers; belief that the case will ultimately be solved only by miraculous means.

There can be no denying the culturally universal, archetypical imprint upon the collective psyche of the concept of evil, pantheistic images of witches and vampires, werewolves and demons, accompanied by beliefs in a heterogeny of monsters, and demonic and satanic possession.

'Perhaps the most common appeal for supernatural assistance during a serial murder investigation involves the introduction and use of psychics.' There is also, though less and less nowadays, the belief in the efficacy of prayer, supplication for divine intervention and deliverance – 'the good-evil duality embedded in religious teachings'. The hard-pressed populace 'may see the hand of Providence in the fortuitous circumstances that lead to a killer's arrest'.

Fisher finds that 'strong supernatural undercurrents enervated the public's reaction to Jack the Ripper … Reference to ghosts, spirits, and the occult were used to explain the killer's actions, suggest how he might be captured, and even predict the site of the next slaying.'

Spiritualists, the late nineteenth-century analogues of our contemporary psychics, were entreated to turn their extrasensory powers of perception on to the quest for Jack the Ripper.

The *Pall Mall Gazette*, sounding the trumpet and shaking the tambourine, proclaimed,

> There is some sense … in the suggestion that the Whitechapel murders afford the practitioners of occult science (or religion) an unexampled opportunity to prove and advertise the genuineness of

their pretensions. If spiritualists, clairvoyants, and thought-readers all 'lie low and say nuffin',' we may at least conclude that, whatever spirits present at their séances, public spirit is notably absent. Interviews with Carlyle and Shakspeare [*sic*] may be all very interesting, but a short conversation with one of the six spirits so recently sent to their long abode … would for practical purposes be worth more than a volume of trans-Stygian Carlylese. Clairvoyants … might set to work upon Jack the Ripper's letter and determine whether it be genuine or a hoax. Why does the Society for Psychical Research stand ingloriously idle?

'The gauntlet,' remarks Fisher, 'lay where it was thrown.'

When both the earthly powers of the police and the supra-orbital powers of the psychics have likewise proved useless, a fearful and frustrated public tends to demand of itself a reason why the killer continues unknown and unapprehended. And the answer lies, the afflicted populace decides, in the killer himself. It must be something that he does, some ability that he possesses, which both permits him to murder whom, when, and where he chooses, and concomitantly protects him.

It is at this precise psychological point that the process of transference begins. Transference is the importation of their qualities of omniscience and omnipotence from the respectable seekers to the disreputable sought.

Fisher elaborates:

Transference as a collective response bears many similarities to processes that occur on a psychological level. One of the paradoxical outcomes of hostage crises occurs when the captives begin to identify with the aggressors. This process, named the 'Stockholm Syndrome' after an incident during which authorities were startled to see hostages embrace their captors after a long siege was broken, culminates when the captives transfer complete trust to the hostage-takers. On a personal level, transference represents a mechanism for captives to live with the constant fear that engulfs them in the situation and is a means to elicit empathy from captors who have complete power to decide their fate.

This can occur at a community level, the serial killer holding captive the collective conscious. The communal strategy then resorted to is to smother fear by deliberate identification with the progenitor of that fear.

The transference finds expression in several ways. 'The killer can be seen as exceptionally intelligent, carefully planning the next crime … The killer might also be described as having special physical abilities … And of course supernatural powers, once thought vested in psychics, are ultimately attributed to the killer … The cumulative effect of transference results in the killer taking on larger-than-life dimensions in the public mind.'

In the Ripper's case the process of transference was, typically, 'an outgrowth of fear and mystery. Fear inspires a search for meaning, while mystery virtually assures that none will be found.' The principal mystery enshrouding Whitechapel Jack was how he contrived such uproarious violence within an encapsulating silence, while perpetrating his crude butcheries in the teeming centre of an area where the streets were alive with by-passers night and day, where alerted police and eye-peeling vigilantes patrolled in ever-expanding cohorts, and where every window of houses bursting at the seams – with seven and more tenants to a room – was a potential eye. Notwithstanding, Jack performed his slaughterous pentathlon in, literally, deathly silence.

Apropos this, George R. Sims, wearing his Dagonet hat,[6] writing in the *Referee*, 21 October 1888, told his readers,

Last Saturday night, having ascertained that Jack had sent a postcard to the authorities, informing them that he meant to do two more murders, I determined to turn amateur detective and go upon the war-path … I left home at nine in the evening dressed as a ship's engineer, accompanied by Albert Edward, who was made up as a foreign sailor. It was nearly ten when we arrived in Whitechapel, and we had no sooner turned into the murder district than we found things remarkably lively. Once or twice, as we walked along, we spotted the private detectives and amateur policemen, who were out on the same job as ourselves.

We had not been surveying the busy scene many minutes – what a scene Whitechapel-road is on Saturday night! – before we heard a cry, and instantly there was a rush towards a gateway. It was only two ladies quarrelling; but as we hurried up a small boy saluted us with a grin and exclaimed, "Ere ye har, guv'nor! This way to the murder! Triple murder up this court!' There was a roar of laughter, and, true state of the case being ascertained, the crowd dispersed.

The border line between the horrible and the grotesque has grown very fine in Whitechapel of late. There has probably been a revulsion of feeling, and the inhabitants have relieved their overstrained nerves by laughing. Certainly last Saturday night, although another murder was confidently expected, the general body of sightseers and pedestrians were making light of the matter. Along the pavement, which for many a mile is hedged with shooting-galleries and various arrangements based upon the six-throws-a-penny principle, plenty of hoarse-voiced ruffians were selling a penny puzzle in which the puzzle was to find Jack the Ripper. Jack was upon every tongue, male and female, last Saturday night. The costermonger hawking his goods dragged him in; the quack doctor assured the crowd that his marvellous medicine would cure even Jack of his evil propensities; and at the penny shows, outside which the most ghastly pictures of 'the seven victims,' all gashes and crimson drops were exhibited, the proprietors made many a facetious reference to the local Terror. Just past the Pavilion Theatre we came upon a gentleman who was standing in the roadway and banging on an empty bloater-box with a big stick. As soon as he had obtained an audience he delivered himself as follows … 'I haint Duglis 'All, and I haint Jack Dickinson, but my brother's the 'ead jockey in a big racin' stable and my infermation's the best as money can buy, though I sell it in Whitechapel for a penny. I belong to Whitechapel and I like to do my neighbours a good turn. I haint Johnny the Ripper. I'm Johnny the Tipper. (Roars of laughter in the crowd.) Yus; Johnny the Tipper, what give yer Tennybrooze (for the Seesirwitch), and here I've got the winner of the Cambridge at 20 to 1, and it's one penny.'

As soon as the humour of Whitechapel had begun to pall we left the main thoroughfare and plunged into the back streets and labyrinthine network of courts and alleys. We visited the spots where the murders were committed, and about midnight we had Buck's-row entirely to ourselves. How on earth a murder was committed here without attracting the slightest attention is a great mystery. The houses are so close to the spot – there are so many chances against a secret crime being committed – the place was such an unlikely one for a deliberate assassin to select! Albert Edward and I tried to work the murder out and get a theory, but we failed utterly … There was not a soul in sight. We had not stopped by the gate where the murder was committed two seconds before a dozen people were about us as if by magic. Two policemen came up, goodness knows where from, and flashed their lanterns on us, and the rest of the company, who were evidently amateur watchmen, eyed us suspiciously … Everywhere we went that night in the hope of dropping on Jack the Ripper we found that the police were on the alert, and that plenty of amateur detectives were hiding round the corners. From personal observation I should say that there was not a corner of Whitechapel, no matter how obscure, that was left unwatched last Saturday night. All night long the police were about, and we saw them come again and again, and enter dark passages, and turn their bull's-eyes on to dark corners. If Jack had tried another experiment last Saturday, it would have been almost impossible for him to get away. Probably he knew it; at any rate, he didn't come near enough for any of us to put the salt upon his tail with which we were all provided.

Soon after midnight the principal thoroughfares in Whitehall began to clear rapidly. The stalls packed up, the shops closed, and the people went to their homes. The ladies, I noticed, who were out late walked in twos and threes. At midnight we were outside a public-house not far from Mitre Square, and we noticed the men as they came out got together and walked towards home in company.

We stayed in Whitechapel till three in the morning. We crept into back yards, and we hid ourselves down side streets; we adventured ourselves into some of the most lonely and desolate-looking spots it has ever been my lot to witness; but we never remained long in undisputed possession. A policeman was on to us directly. I can bear personal testimony to the marvellous vigilance exercised by Sir Charles Warren's merry men on that Saturday night at least. At three o'clock in the morning we agreed that there was no chance of getting Jack that night, and, after a little friendly converse with a policeman or two, we turned our weary steps towards home.

Thus, Sims bears witness to the correctness of Joseph Fisher's observations. Fisher is not, however, correct in stating that the murder of Annie Chapman was committed 'in the early evening between 5.30 and 6.00 p.m. when it was still light'. It *was* light, but it was the early morning light, around 5.30 a.m., when Annie's light was extinguished.

Explanations for the 'mysteries' are advanced. Fisher points out that 'neck wounds as deep as those on the victims would have made crying out impossible. An attack from behind would have limited the amount of blood spilled on the killer, as would mutilation after the death blow had been delivered. But while medical professionals at the time appreciated these facts, they failed to convince the general population.'

Jack's 'dissections', together with his theft of bodily organs, certainly set the killer apart. There was a dubious presumption that Jack the Anatomist knew exactly what he was so apparently deliberately doing, where to find the desired organs, and how to extract them without meaningless cuts. Not so. 'All this was believed despite the fact that one physician who examined the body of Annie Chapman testified before the coroner's inquest that the killer possessed no special training or expertise. Nevertheless, this solitary voice of reason was ignored. The public chose to believe instead that "not one man in a thousand could have played the part of Annie Chapman's murderer".'

Inseparable from any manifestations of multicide within the community is the pendant media circus. It is so today; it was so in 1888. 'A self-fuelling engine of public opinion is created. Fear, uncertainty, and morbid curiosity lead to a demand for more news, delivery of which generates a higher level of anxiety and interest. The intensity of public feeling is ratcheted ever upward.' It is windfall time for the newspapers: reciprocal windfall time for some of their readers. For, as in the 1995 Fred and Rose West case, where exploitation in the shape of payment from television crews and others for provision of viewing vantage points in Cromwell Street, and the supplying of welcome cups of tea and various other refreshments proved 'nice little earners', so did the East End indigent, in a bid to capitalise on the sudden influx of well-heeled gawpers, 'set up refreshment stands to cater to the curious ... The apotheosis of media involvement [is] when the media become directly involved with the killer.' Although this is of proven occurrence in a number of modern instances, whether or not it actually happened with Jack the Ripper is a continuing source of fierce debate. What unquestionably did happen was that the Ripper letter of 25 September 1888, whether bogus or not, triggered the writing of shoals of further letters to the newspapers, the police, the various vigilantes, Sir Charles Warren, and the Home Secretary.

'Letters were sent to papers outside London such as one received by a Belfast paper claiming that the Ripper had moved his operation there. The net effect was to spread the Ripper terror throughout the Kingdom.'

Fisher appears to take the letter to Mr Lusk seriously, describing it as 'the only communiqué experts believe to be authentic' and adding, seemingly oblivious of the subsequent dismissal of the alleged Eddowes kidney and of the medical concept of a so-called 'ginny kidney', that 'the letter [*sic*] contained part of what examining doctors called the "ginny kidney" of a forty-five-year-old woman, which seemed to fit the description of Catherine Eddowes, from whom it was presumably taken'. And then asks, 'Could it be that the press in its desperate scramble for readers crafted fictitious letters from the killer, created copy, and in the process prodded the real killer to break his silence?'

How grievous a part, Fisher sets out to assess, did the 'Red Terror' represent in community dissolution? How great a responsibility had the ever-present fear in the wearing away of the fabric of the community and the dissolving of the connective bonds that held it together? Individual fear expresses itself in a kaleidoscope of individual mechanisms. Collective fear manifests in myriad changes on the level of contacts and interpersonal relations and interactions, producing in the process enormous impact on social cohesion and serious cracks in the structure of communal solidarity.

'This is never more evident than when a murderer lives within a community and emerges periodically to destroy others. Repeated killings underscore the continuing threat, the fact that the killer is still present and dangerous.'

A tragic truism is that, as Fisher shrewdly perceives, 'fear of the serial killer also magnifies the divisions that exist within the community. Since the killer is viewed as an outsider and a stranger, as those who are different are categorised as a threat. Intolerance, bigotry, and scape-goating increase, as does the use of racial and ethnic stereotypes. A common by-product of a serial murderer at large is an upswing in anti-Semitism, racial conflict, and gay bashing.'

In the specific instance of the Whitechapel murders, the search for scapegoats came to a convenient end in its unenlightened alighting upon the group of recent East End immigrants, the pogrom-fleeing Jews. No longer now need Cockney brother suspect brother, neighbour distrust neighbour, no longer need one view every person met in the street with quills-raised suspicion; henceforth incapacitatory unease could be comfortably and comfortingly canalised along the anti-Semite channel.

There can be no denying that the newspapers, for purposes of their own, fanned the holocaustal flames, giving voice to the rumours, and credence to the outlandish superstitions upon which the edifice of anti-Semitism was raised. Jews were shocked when suddenly confronted by a new wave of persecution. Without provocation, Jews were attacked in the streets. One of the first men suspected of being the Ripper was John Pizer, a Jewish shoemaker.

Fisher sums up:

There was never a shortage of suspects, self-identified, picked up by the police, or pointed out by the public. Arrests for 'suspicion' were commonplace, but in every instance the detainee could account for his actions and was quickly released. There was also no dearth of theories about who Jack the Ripper might be … The list went on and on, limited only by the imagination of the theorist and rarely hindered by fact. In the century following the murders, the search for Jack the Ripper's identity has been unflagging, and the suspects named and the rationale for their guilt have been no less creative, or at times any less far-fetched, than they were at the time.

It is Fisher's finding that 'there is something that does not ring true' about the list of what he designates as 'the most popular candidates for the dubious honour of being Jack the Ripper as well as the basis for their presumed guilt.' The names he knocks off the list of 'likelies' are George Chapman, Dr Neill Cream, Frederick Deeming, Dr William Gull, Prince Albert Victor, James K. Stephen, and Montague J. Druitt – 'most are infamous criminals or well-educated men from the upper classes whose lofty status, even noble birth, presumably insulated them from discovery'. And, at a practical level, he points out that 'it may be that only the notorious or prominent members of Victorian society left enough documentation about their lives that could be mined for clues. Given the findings of recent systematic studies of serial murder, however, it seems doubtful that anyone on the list was actually Jack the Ripper.'

Neither does he accept Alice McKenzie as a Ripper victim, considering her murder 'sufficiently distant in time and different in commission so as to make its link to the other murders quite unlikely'.

For Joseph C. Fisher, as for 'most Ripperologists and certainly for the public at large, the gory reign of Jack the Ripper ended with the butchery of Mary Jane Kelly'.

2
The Shaping of Jack the Ripper

Whitechapel Jack began as an amoeba. Shapeless. The pseudopodia appeared, to give him many shapes. All lethal. Entity he had none; until it was decided – was it by the police or press? – that the murders were not isolated acts of savagery, but living links connected in a chain of death.

'The epicentre of the social tremors,' writes Oliver Cyriax, 'was the state of the victims' bodies … Such savagery was new, in wild excess of any requirement to extinguish life, beyond the previous high-water mark of pointless violence recorded in the Ratcliffe Highway murders seventy years previously.'

The constabulary, baffled, played deadly serious games of blindman's buff. The cartoonists caught them at it. The public prints made mockery of official frustration. Above the high collars of the top brass, faces turned port-wine red. A goutish irritation spread.

Starved of news – the police were giving nothing away, for nothing was all they had to give – hag-ridden journalists, provoked into irresponsible enterprise by snarling news editors snapping viciously about their kicking heels, invented tales and suspects.

Police and public also invented suspects. These unfortunates were being arrested, or 'buckled' as the contemporary slang had it, all over the place; and as regularly released.

There was, for instance, 'Leather Apron'. Wonderful, evocative nickname. True patronymic: Pizer. John Pizer. Aged thirty-eight. Polish-Jewish. Shoe-trimmer by vocation. By avocation, prostitutes' bully, levying blackmail against the street women, whom he terrified; and if his demands for protection money went unmet, he applied violence to them. Although known to habitually carry a sharp knife, and from time to time to flourish it in menace, he had never actually cut or stabbed anyone, but punished with his boots and fists. Arrested in the early hours of 10 September 1888, he proved invincibly innocent *qua* Ripperish activities, and was in due course released to attempt to levy a legalised variety of 'blackmail' – tortious action – against newspapers that had enthusiastically reported with premature incaution upon him. The indications are that his success in that venture is to be accounted in very short restitutionary measures.

Only the day before the netting of 'Leather Apron', that is on Sunday 9 September, William Henry Piggott, a fifty-eight-year-old sea-cook, had been arrested at Gravesend, in Kent. The man had unwisely drawn attention to himself in the Pope's Head Tavern, loudly and proudly proclaiming his misogyny and exhibiting a suspiciously injured hand. The disconcerted landlady summoned the police. From a local fish shop they retrieved a paper parcel, left there by Piggott, which yielded a ripped and bloodstained shirt. Piggott's hasty explanation united torn shirt and damaged hand. He had, he said, seen, at 4.50 a.m. that morning, a woman in Whitechapel fall down in a fit. When he had stooped to her aid, she had bitten his hand, whereupon, in agony and aggrievement, he had fetched her one. Then, as two policemen approached, he had fled. A telegram brought Inspector Abberline down on the Monday morning train, and Piggott was escorted back to Commercial Street Police Station. It transpired that he was not the Ripper after all, but in his own interest he was shunted off to the Whitechapel Union Infirmary, where he received a month's treatment for *delirium tremens*.

A third suspect, arrested a couple of days later – 12 September 1888 – was Joseph (or Jacob) Isenschmid, the Mad Butcher.[7] Born around 1850 in Switzerland, but of so many years' residence in England that he designated himself 'The King of Elthorne Road', at No. 59 of which Holloway, North London, thoroughfare he had set up in business as a pork butcher. This man was recommended, on somewhat insubstantial diagnosis as it proved, by two Holloway GPs, Drs Cowan and Crabb, to the specialist attention of the police, who, in turn, recommended him back to the attention of the medicos – and ultimate internment in Grove Hill Lunatic Asylum, at Bow. So far as Ripperine involvement went, he was adjudged not guilty, but insane.

A last lucky – or, rather, unlucky – dip in the suspect tub brought up one Charles Ludwig, who was actually introduced into the frame by his own foolish behaviour. He was 'buckled' in the small hours of 18 September. At around 3 a.m. that Tuesday morning, this forty-year-old German *friseur*, of respectable aspect but disreputable mien, involved himself in a fierce confrontation with the proprietor of a coffee stall in Whitechapel High Street, who was refusing to serve him. Infuriated, Ludwig's glazed but alcoholic eye fastened in totally unprovoked resentful malice upon bystanding eighteen-year-old Alexander Finlay or Freinberg, whom he fancied was watching him. Ludwig pulled out a knife – just about everybody in the East End seemed to be carrying a knife somewhere about his or her person at that time – and pugnaciously demanded of his ill humour's scapegoat, 'What are you looking at?' Finlay, wishing no truck with this staggering knife wielder, and with that discretion which proverbially betters valour, moved swiftly away.

The *Daily Telegraph*, after interviewing Finlay, reported the incident thus:

Alexander Finlay ... employed at the ice-cream works of Mr Assenheim in Petticoat-lane is able to throw rather more light on the case than appeared from his testimony at the Thames Police court ... he says that the first he saw of Ludwig was about a quarter to four o'clock. Prisoner [Ludwig] was then at the top of Commercial-street in company with a woman, whom he was conducting in the direction of the Minories. 'I took no notice of this at the time,' added Finlay, 'except to remark to the coffee stall-keeper, "There goes a swell with a racketty [*sic*] one." ... In about a quarter of an hour, however, the woman ran back in a state of fright ... Within five minutes the prisoner [Ludwig] came up and asked for a cup of coffee at the stall where I was standing. He, at all events, was drunk, and would only produce a half-penny in payment for the coffee which was given him. I suppose he noticed me looking at him, for he suddenly turned round and asked in broken English, "What are you looking at?" I replied that I was doing no harm, but he said, "Oh, you want something," and pulled out a long penknife with which he made a dash at me ... He retreated after making the first dash [and I] called to a policeman [PC John Gallagher] who was near by and had him arrested ... I heard at the police-court this morning he [Ludwig] pretended not to understand English, but his English when he addressed me was plain enough, though broken.'

Ludwig had, it turned out, in the previous week pulled a knife on a prostitute, one-armed Elizabeth Burns, in Three Kings' Court, a walled-in yard off the Minories.

But Charles Ludwig was not the Ripper either.

Yet another suspect was revealed by police officer Robert Sagar, sergeant in the City Police in 1888, who took part in the Ripper investigations and of whom Major Henry Smith wrote, 'A better or more intelligent officer I never had under my command.' Sagar retired in 1905, by which time he had reached the rank of detective inspector. His obituary appeared in the *Brighton and Hove Herald* of 6 December 1924, where reference is made to his statement – said to have been written in his memoirs, which, incidentally, have never been traced – that 'we had good reason to suspect a man who worked in Butcher's Row, Aldgate. We watched him carefully. There is no doubt that this man was insane, and after a time his friends thought it advisable to have him removed to a private asylum. After he was removed there were no more Ripper atrocities.'

Clearly then, it was not only the indigent and the defenceless who were looked upon askance. William J. Fishman, a leading authority on nineteenth-century social history, and himself a native of that East End of London, concerning which he writes with such depths of knowledge and feeling, tells us, 'Suspicion fell on local doctors, and rumours had it that such notable practitioners as Dr Barnardo and the London Hospital surgeon, Frederick Treves, were both under surveillance.'

Another statement, in equal measure intriguing and puzzling, is made by Fishman: 'Speculation on identity persisted and rumour was rife ... Suspicion of evil in high places was *currently* [my italics] fed by the nocturnal activities of the young Duke of Clarence.'

But make no mistake, during that trickle of weeks in 1888 a number of different factions had each their special agenda. There were those who used the murders as bloodied staves with which to belabour the police and the government. There were those warring newspapers who used them as greedily grasped circulation boosters. Cyriax has captured that particular segment of the prevailing bellicosity neatly. 'London's Whitechapel resembled,' he writes, 'an area under siege. Eight newspapers followed the story daily, magazines picked it up, and the penny dreadfuls magnified its reverberations.'

There were also those of social conscience who took the crimes as a text around which to preach the gospel of their belief in the need for wide-ranging reform. The one thing that united them all was ignorance – total ignorance – as to the identity of the roving mutilator. For the simple truth is that, from beginning to end, from then to now, neither the police nor anyone else knew or knows who Jack the Ripper was.

There was never any official consensus. Robert Anderson was convinced that the culprit was a Jew, whereas his chief, Sir Charles Warren, took a diametrically opposed view and was at pains to refute anti-Semite accusations.

In this respect, an interesting contemporary opinion was expressed by Margaret Harkness. A socialist, feminist and novelist, she was the daughter of the Reverend Robert Harkness, curate of Trinity church, Great Malvern, Worcestershire. She was thirty-four at the time of the Whitechapel murders and extremely familiar with the East

End of London. Under the name of John Law she published in 1889 a novel, *In Darkest London: Captain Lobe, Salvation Army*, wherein she 'completely exonerates the Jews'.

Fishman both writes of, and quotes from, the book:

> A dying slaughterer confesses to the Salvation Army officer that he is the Ripper, and explains the evil dynamic that drove him to commit murder. 'People must eat and someone must kill beasts; but to kill makes a man like a cannibal, it gives him a thirst for blood, and I got to feel at last that nothing would quench my thirst but human blood. Human flesh.' His blood lust reached saturation point when he 'could not go on butchering' and sought some kind of sanctuary in the ghetto. 'I hid myself here among the Jews who hate blood and never spill it. I'm not a Jew, I'm a gentile.' This accords with the peculiar horror entertained by Jews of any mutilation of the human body before or after death, an act strictly forbidden by Talmudic Law.

Fishman observes, 'Whoever the Ripper was, his deeds had ramifications both locally and beyond their time or place.'

There were other notions of even more bizarre order. They ranged from the quasi-mystical suggestion that Satan or Cain might be revisiting the earth to George Bernard Shaw's wry hint that the crimes were the unconventional social work of an assiduous reformer determined to draw attention to the appalling conditions governing the lightless lives of the poor in the East End of prosperous nineteenth-century London. They included theories that the culprit was a vampire, an escaped gorilla (shades of Edgar Allen Poe), a butcher, a slaughterman, a woman disguised as a slaughterman, a Malay, a seaman, a ship's doctor, a secular religious fanatic, or an unbalanced cleric, an escaped lunatic, an illegitimate son of British royalty, a policeman (this idea was cleverly utilised by Thomas Burke in his masterly short story, 'The Hands of Mr Ottermole', in his book *The Pleasantries of Old Quong* (1931)), and, most popular of all, a mad doctor.

Those with a taste for greater specificity later selected Swinburne, Gissing, Walter Sickert, William Gladstone, the Reverend Samuel Barnett (founder of Toynbee Hall), and a perfectly innocent member of the late Bertrand Russell's family. With no more justification a trio of known criminals, Dr Thomas Neill Cream, Frederick Deeming, and Mrs Mary Eleanor Pearcey, came under popular suspicion.

Walter Sickert told a tale of a pale young veterinary student, living in Mornington Crescent, who paralleled in real life Mrs Belloc Lowndes' fictive lodger, as portrayed in her novel *The Lodger* (1913).

Salvation Army Commissioner David C. Lamb is reputed to have entertained queasy suspicions concerning the implication of a highly skilled signwriter in the Whitechapel murders.

Conan Doyle was quite sure that the Ripper was a man who disguised himself as a woman.

Ripper alarms were still being sounded as late as September 1889, when a mutilated female body – a torso lacking head and legs, identity never established – was found under an archway in Pinchin Street, Whitechapel. Again, in February 1891, a woman, Frances Coles, was discovered, in Swallow Gardens, also in Whitechapel, with her throat cut. Gradually, the echoes of the dread name died away – at least in the context of active assassin. The odd thing is that, long after the blood of his last real, or fancied, victim had dried, the memory of the Ripper himself remained perennially fresh.

V. S. Pritchett (1900–97), Man of Letters, recalls in the first volume of his autobiography, *A Cab at the Door* (1969), how, as a small boy, perhaps about 1909 or 1910,

> the terror began to be whispered about our school … We would be standing, a row of us, in the stinking school jakes, happily seeing who could pee the highest, when the whisper would start: Jack

the Ripper was about in Camberwell. What did he do? He took girls' knickers down and slit them up the belly: better informed boys said 'up the cunt'. We left school in terror, and for me, with an agonised responsibility, I had the duty of collecting my sister from a girls' school in the next street and Jack the Ripper was known to wait there. For weeks the boys talked of nothing else. I believed it, yet did not believe it.

From time to time the story of the Ripper's atrocities would be revived in newspaper or magazine articles, or appeared as a spinal chapter in this or that book of classic murder cases retold. These had much to say, but nothing of significance to add.

There were exceptions.

Stewart Evans, scouring down literary byways, encountered, with positively Walpolean serendipitous good fortune, a hitherto unhailed Ripper suspect in an article by W. H. Jago entitled 'The Medical Evidence Stated – Who was the "Ripper"?' in the *Union Jack* magazine's *Detective Supplement* No. 39. London, 27 January 1923.

According to this Mr Jago's information,

It so happened that the police actually arrested the man [the Whitechapel murderer]. It was not until some twenty years afterwards, however, that the identity of Jack the Ripper was established, and by that time interest in the crimes had died down.

The first step in the train of evidence had been known for some years before its importance was fully appreciated. Whilst discussing the conduct of a certain patient the ward-orderly was able to give the following piece of information to the medical officer in charge of one of the criminal lunatic asylums. [The only criminal lunatic asylum then in existence was Broadmoor.]

The orderly had for some years been able to foretell the oncoming of the patient's 'fits', a bit of knowledge which was of great utility in view of the fact that the patient was an exceedingly violent epileptic. The orderly had noticed that two or three hours before the actual fit took place the patient would become very restless, wander, muttering to himself, up and down the ward. After about an hour of this conduct he would ask for a piece of paper and a pencil, and when these had been given to him he would sit down at the table and draw. The drawings were invariably of women's figures in various attitudes, and drawn with great care. As soon as the drawing was completed the man would draw a line somewhere across the figure, but would use the pencil with such force that it frequently tore through the paper. Immediately he had drawn that last line he would have a fit.

The orderly, knowing that the man was going to have a seizure, would make preparations to prevent the man from hurting himself or those around him.

Through lack of appreciation that these drawings might be of importance, the orderly had destroyed them, especially as the man had never asked for them, or even given any sign afterwards that he was aware that he had drawn them. The medical officer, however, gave instructions that they were to be given to him in future, for there was just a possibility that they might serve to clear up certain details about the man's case.

In the course of a few weeks the doctor was able to collect about a dozen of these drawings. He then set about arranging the evidence from all available sources. The asylum records showed that the man had been in the institution for nearly twenty years. Originally he had been sent there for observations as to his mental condition, having been arrested for a very violent and unprovoked attack on a woman in a public-house.

It was evident from the beginning that the man was a dangerous epileptic lunatic, and as no relative had come to claim him he was detained in the asylum as being a danger to the public if not under proper control. The police had not been able to trace his antecedents, while the man himself, being extremely morose and taciturn, as is so common in the epileptic, had obstinately refused to give any account of himself. Nothing special in what he had said or done in the asylum had given a clue to his past, until the investigation of the drawings.

The first point that was obvious in the drawings was that they had been executed by a person with more than average skill. In fact, the accuracy of the details aroused a strong suspicion that the man had an expert knowledge of human anatomy. There was presumptive evidence that the man had been a professional artist. Incidentally, it may be here mentioned that it is well known that eccentricity and even mental instability is frequently found amongst artists of the Bohemian type. But why did the man make the last, and quite unnecessary, mark on the drawing, and with such force as to rip the paper?

The word 'rip' suggested a theory to the doctor. Was this man the once famous 'Ripper'? Working on this theory, the doctor collected all the medical evidence from the various coroners' records of the series of Ripper crimes. He was able to note that the date of the man's arrest and incarceration in the asylum was only a few days after the last murder had been committed. If the man was indeed the Ripper, this would account for the reason why the crimes had ceased so suddenly, and also provide a clue as to why the police had failed to find the criminal.

The doctor then made a series of drawings and carefully inserted a line showing the position of the mutilations that had been perpetrated on the corpses. On comparing these lines with the rips on the man's drawings he found that they corresponded too accurately to be mere coincidence. In other words, the man must have somehow gained an exact knowledge of the nature and position of the wounds.

How did he come by this knowledge? He certainly did not gain it from the public Press, or even from the evidence given by the medical witnesses in the coroner's court, for only the vague statements, such as 'an incised wound,' occurred in the reports of the evidence. The exact details were available only to someone having access to the doctors' post-mortem reports. Furthermore, the murders had been committed in various parts of London – mostly North London – and until the time when the doctor started his inquiry the reports were scattered about in several coroners' districts, so that until the doctor had collected the reports there could only have been one person with a knowledge of all the mutilations, and that was the murderer himself.

No further action was taken in this case, for a certified lunatic cannot, by law, be tried.

This case also illustrates a favourite error of the amateur criminologist. Whenever bones or fragments of a body are found the first explanation suggested is that they were once the property of a medical student who has taken an unusual way of disposing of them. This 'medical student' idea is a survival of the days of the 'body-snatchers', who flourished before the passing of the Anatomy Act. The medical experts would be able to tell in a very short time if the body had been used for anatomical purposes.

3
The Men on the Killing Ground

The Confounding Fathers

The anguish of puzzled alarm which gripped Victorian England in consequence of the series of peculiarly savage murders in and about the bailiwick of Whitechapel provoked a positive frenzy of bewildered speculation among all classes of society.

Indeed, the monarch herself was not proof against the sinister allure of the 'Hunt-the-Ripper' vogue. Queen Victoria's sober and practical thoughts on the subject were embodied in a letter which Her Majesty caused to be addressed to the Home Secretary, Henry Matthews, on 13 November 1888:

> Have the cattle boats and passenger boats been examined? Has any investigation been made as to the number of single men occupying rooms to themselves? The murderer's clothes must be saturated with blood and must be kept somewhere. Is there sufficient surveillance at night?

In the year 1888 the Commissioner of the Metropolitan Police was Sir Charles Warren. His grandson, Watkin W. Williams, author of *The Life of General Sir Charles Warren* (1941), has said, 'I cannot recall that my grandfather ... ever stated in writing his personal views on the identity of Jack the Ripper. It was a subject about which he very seldom spoke. My impression is that he believed the murderer to be a sex maniac who committed suicide after the Miller's Court murder – possibly the young doctor whose body was found in the Thames on 31 December 1888.'

Sir Charles submitted his resignation on 8 November 1888, the eve of Mary Kelly Day. It was not, as has been widely and erroneously believed, in any way connected with his handling of the Jack the Ripper crisis. It was his publication, without prior Home Office authorisation, of an article, 'The Police of the Metropolis', in the November, 1888 issue, No. 23, of *Murray's Magazine*, that was the cause of his departure.

He was succeeded by James Monro. Little love was lost between them. Monro's reign was short, he, in turn, resigning in 1890. He clearly stated that the police had no positive clues as to the identity of the Ripper. But he is reputed to have executed a highly private memorandum, in which he incorporated all that he knew, deduced, and conjectured. This eventually passed into the hands of his eldest son, Charles, who said that his father's theory had been 'a very hot potato', never revealed the name of his father's suspect, and seems to have complied with his parent's advise to 'burn the stuff and try to forget it'.

The Assistant Commissioner of the Metropolitan Police in 1888 was Dr (later Sir) Robert Anderson. In his memoirs, *The Lighter Side of My Official Life* (1910), he avers, no bones about it, that the Ripper was 'a low-class Polish Jew'.

He writes,

> I am almost tempted to disclose the identity of the murderer and of the pressman who wrote the letter [which is preserved in the Police Museum at New Scotland Yard] ... But no public benefit would result from such a course, and the traditions of my old department would suffer. I will merely add that the only person who ever had a good view of the murderer unhesitatingly identified the suspect the instant he was confronted with him; but he refused to give evidence against him. In saying that he was a Polish Jew I am merely stating an ascertained fact. And my words are meant to specify race, not religion. For it would outrage all religious sentiment to talk of the religion of a loathsome creature whose utterly unmentionable vices reduced him to a lower level than that of the brute.

Certain statements made by Anderson in his memoirs, initially published serially in *Blackwood's Magazine*, produced on their appearance, on 4 March 1910, an instant and angry protest from the *Jewish Chronicle*.

Three days later – 7 March – the *Globe* printed an interview with Anderson in which he hastily declared, 'I should be the last man in the world to say anything reflecting on the Jews as a community, but what is true of Christians is equally true of Jews – that there are some people who have lapsed from all that is good and proper … It is a notorious fact that there is a stratum of Jews who will not give up their people.'

The trade edition of Anderson's memoirs came out shortly after their *Blackwood's* serialisation. The comments that had aroused the indignation of the *Jewish Chronicle* were retained, if somewhat modified. Anderson maintained his belief that the murderer 'and his people were certain low-class Polish Jews; for it is a remarkable fact that people of that class in the East End will not give up one of their number to Gentile justice'.

That Anderson did not subscribe to the belief that the Ripper met his end by drowning is evident from a statement that appears in his *Criminals and Crime* (1907):

> No amount of silly hysterics could alter the fact that these crimes [the Whitechapel murders] were a cause of danger only to a particular section of a small and definite class of women, in a limited district of the East End; and that the inhabitants of the metropolis generally were just as secure during the weeks the fiend was on the prowl, as they were before the mania seized him, or after he had been safely caged in an asylum.

Having regard to the dogmatism of Anderson's assertion, it is illuminating to examine conclusions arising from researches on this score carried out by Melvin Harris and Stewart Evans. They turn to the work of Major Arthur Griffiths, who, after serving with the 63rd West Suffolk Regiment, had, in 1870, at the age of thirty-two, entered the prison service. He occupied successively the positions of assistant deputy governor of Chatham Prison, deputy governor at Millbank Prison, 1872, transferring thence to Wormwood Scrubs, before, in 1878, being appointed Her Majesty's Inspector of Prisons, in which capacity he served until 1896. More importantly from our point of view, he was a friend of both Robert Anderson and Melville Leslie Macnaghten, who had been appointed Assistant Chief Constable, CID, Scotland Yard, in June 1889, was promoted head of the CID in 1903, and knighted in 1907.

In *Days of My Years* (1914), Macnaghten has this to say of the Ripper:

> The man, of course, was a sexual maniac, but such madness takes protean forms … Sexual murders are the most difficult of all for police to bring home to the perpetrators, for 'motives' there are none; only a lust for blood, and in many cases a hatred of woman as woman … I do not think there was anything of religious mania about the real Simon Pure, nor do I believe that he had ever been detained in an asylum, nor lived in lodgings. I incline to the belief that the individual who held London in terror resided with his own people; that he absented himself from home at certain times, and that he committed suicide on or about 10 November 1888.

Although he did not actually meet any of Macnaghten's three suspects – Kosminski, Ostrog, and Druitt – Major Griffiths was the first author to describe them, in his *Mysteries of Police and Crime* (1898).

'It would,' said Stewart Evans, 'be of the greatest relevance to know exactly what Major Griffiths had to say in relation to Anderson's claims, if indeed they were communicated to him, and why he accepted the insane doctor [Druitt] and not the Polish Jew [Kosminski] as the most likely "Ripper".'

'The answer,' Evans then tells us, 'can now be given … Yes, we do know that Anderson, as well as Macnaghten, voiced his thoughts on the suspects to Griffiths.'

What Evans and Melvin Harris uncovered in their researches was an article, 'The Detectives in Real Life', which had appeared in the *Windsor Magazine*, in May, 1895, written by Griffiths under the *nom de plume* Alfred Aylmer. The tell-tale paragraph runs,

More dissatisfaction was vented on Mr Anderson at the utterly abortive efforts to discover the perpetrator of the Whitechapel murders. He has himself a perfectly plausible theory that Jack the Ripper was a homicidal maniac, temporarily at large, whose hideous career was cut short by committal to an asylum.

Comments Stewart Evans, 'At this earlier date, 1894 or early 1895, Anderson's "definitely ascertained fact" was only a "perfectly plausible theory". The wording of Griffiths' essay leaves it patently clear that parts of it were used in the 1898 book. Interestingly, it also shows that Griffiths obtained his information from *both* Anderson *and* Macnaghten. This, of course, may be directly linked to the statement made by Ex-Chief Inspector Littlechild in his letter of 23 September 1913, to George R. Sims: "I knew Major Griffiths for many years. He probably got his information from Anderson, who only *thought he knew*."'

The Acting Commissioner of the City Police, in whose area one of the murders, that of Catherine Eddowes, was committed, was Major [later Sir] Henry Smith. In his memoirs, *From Constable to Commissioner* (1910), he writes,

> There is no man living who knows as much of those murders as I do … I must admit that, though within five minutes of the perpetrator one night, and with a very fair description of him besides, he completely beat me and every police officer in London, and I have no more idea now where he lived than I had twenty years ago.

The description to which Sir Henry is referring is that given by 'a sort of hybrid German'. The man in question was a commercial traveller named Joseph Lawende. He, together with two companions, had left the Imperial Club in Duke Street at 1.35 a.m. on 30 September 1888, and as he was going past Church Passage, which leads into Mitre Square, he saw a woman, whom he later identified, by her clothing only, as Eddowes, talking to a man at the entrance to the passage. Lawende described him as 'young, about middle height, with a small fair moustache, dressed in something like navy serge, and with a deerstalker's cap'.

That description was subsequently slightly amplified to embrace the further, and sometimes conflicting, facts that the man was about thirty years old, 5 feet 7 or 8 inches in height, dressed in a pepper-and-salt loose jacket, grey cloth cap of the same colour, was of shabby appearance, fair complexion and wore a reddish neckerchief tied in a knot around his neck. He had the look of a sailor.

To discover this total lack of accord between the three men – Anderson, Macnaghten, and Smith – who must by definition have had access to all the known facts, is as disconcerting as it is disappointing. But the evidence of this very absence of secure top-level intelligence surely provides us with the information that the authorities had no real culprit in their sights.

On his retirement in 1913, due to ill-health, Macnaghten was succeeded in the June of that year by Basil Thomson as Assistant Commissioner (Crime); Thomson remained in that office until 1919. His view of the Whitechapel murders is recorded in his book, *The Story of Scotland Yard* (1935), in which he states, 'The belief of the CID officers at the time was that they were the work of an insane Russian doctor and that the man escaped arrest by committing suicide at the end of 1888.'

This is echoed by Sir John Moylan, Receiver for the Metropolitan Police District (subsequently Assistant Under-Secretary at the Home Office), in his *Scotland Yard and the Metropolitan Police* (1929), where, with an added dimension of certitude, he affirms, 'It is now certain [that he] escaped [justice] by committing suicide at the end of 1888.'

And that disposes of all the significant official top-level opinions and avowals publicly stated in the forty-seven years between 1888 and 1935.

There remain two medical men of the period who must be mentioned, neither of whom, however, had any official connection with the case.

The first is Dr Lyttleton Stewart Forbes Winslow, a distinguished alienist, who developed an almost obsessional interest in the murders. 'Day after day and night after night I spent in the Whitechapel slums,' he records in *Recollections of Forty Years* (1910). Indeed, it has been said that so omnipresent was Forbes Winslow, that at one time the detectives began seriously to wonder if *he* were not the Ripper.

The conclusion to which Winslow came was that the killer was 'a homicidal lunatic goaded on to his dreadful work by a sense of duty ... [He] possibly imagined that he received his commands from God ... After each murder had been carried out and the lust for blood appeased, the lunatic changed at once from a homicidal religious maniac into a quiet man with a perfect knowledge of what he was doing, oblivious of the past ... The assassin was ... a young man ... a well-to-do man.' In the end, Winslow believed that the news of his researches had frightened the Ripper off, that he left the country, returned to his native Australia, and by 1910 was settled in Durban. Forbes Winslow died in 1913, his optimistic 'I have every reason to hope I shall be the means of bringing his capture about' unfulfilled.

The second medical man is Dr Thomas Dutton, of Westbourne Villas, Bayswater, allegedly friend and counsellor of Inspector Abberline. Dutton is credited with the compilation of three handwritten volumes, 'Chronicles of Crime', spanning sixty years of his criminous observation and experience. He died in his seventy-ninth year, in November 1935, at his then home in Uxbridge Road, Shepherd's Bush, and, unfortunately, his 'Chronicles', if, indeed, they ever existed, have disappeared. Not, however, before a portion of his notes on the Ripper case had, by fortunate fortuity, been transcribed by Donald McCormick. From these it would appear that Dutton had suggested to Abberline that if he were looking for a foreigner as author of the Whitechapel atrocities he should turn an eye towards Russians and Poles. The doctor was convinced that the Ripper did not actually live in the East End, but was more likely to be found south of the river, in some such area as Lambeth, Walworth, or Camberwell. He eventually fixed upon a suspect, Dr Pedachenko, or Konovalov, a Russian barber-surgeon, working in Walworth, at Delhaye's hairdresser's shop, Westmoreland Road, who, he suggested, could well prove to be Chapman/Klosowski's double. The Pedachenko/Konovalov theory is complex and will be discussed later when we come to consider the plethora of solutions devised by the ingenuity of what may be termed the amateur contingent.

The Confounded Rank-and-File

The uncertainty pervading the upper echelons of founding fathers in their ivory tower filtered all the way down to the confounded other ranks, pounding the pavements.

Thus, Detective Inspector Frederick George Abberline, who was in charge of the killing-ground investigations, failed to come up with any suspect at all. It was not, in fact, until fourteen years later that Abberline's fancy is alleged to have alighted upon a prime suspect – the Borough Poisoner, George Chapman, a Pole whose real name was Severin Antoniovich Klosowski. When, in October 1902, Inspector George Godley arrested Chapman for the murder of a barmaid, Maud Marsh, Abberline is *supposed* to have said to him, 'You've got Jack the Ripper at last!'

The case for Chapman the Ripper is developed with some ingenuity – and some errors of fact – by Hargrave Lee Adam in his Introduction to the *Trial of George Chapman* (1930), which volume in the *Notable British Trials* series he edited. Chapman's guilt is discussed by ex-Superintendent Arthur Neil, who, as a detective sergeant, played a minor role in the Chapman case, in his book of recollections, *Forty Years of Man-Hunting* (1932), written after his retirement as one of the 'Big Four' of the Yard.

Frederick Porter Wensley, who as a young policeman completing his first year of service was drafted to Whitechapel in 1888, and who later rose to the rank of Chief Constable of the CID at Scotland Yard, was certainly in a position to know the contents of the Ripper file, yet in his book, *Detective Days* (1931), he has absolutely nothing to say as regards the identity, real or theoretical, of Whitechapel Jack.

Another of the stalwarts of the period, Detective Sergeant Benjamin Leeson, writing his reminiscences, *Lost London* (1934), is refreshingly forthright:

> I am afraid I cannot throw any light on the problem of the 'Ripper's' identity, but one thing I do know, and that is that amongst the police who were most concerned in the case there was a general feeling that a certain doctor, known to me, could have thrown quite a lot of light on the subject. This particular doctor was never far away when the crimes were committed … Many stories and theories have been put forward, but, with one exception, I doubt if any of them had the slightest foundation in fact. The exception to which I refer was that of George [*sic*] Klosowski *alias* Chapman … But nobody knows and nobody ever will know the true story of 'Jack the Ripper'.

Ex-Chief Inspector Walter Dew is somewhat more positive, albeit in his negativity. He, too, was a detective officer in Whitechapel in 1888. In *I Caught Crippen* (1938), he writes, 'I was on the spot, actively engaged throughout the whole series of crimes. I ought to know something about it. Yet I have to confess I am as mystified now as I was then by the man's amazing elusiveness.' The one thing of which Dew felt certain was that the killer was neither a doctor nor a medical student – 'Not even the rudiments of surgical skill were needed to cause the mutilations I saw.' And Dew does not consider that there were any real grounds for believing that Chapman had anything to do with the killings.

Not, perhaps, from time immemorial – 1189 according to the *calends* of the lawyers – but from a time well before the memory of any living Ripperologist, the ascription of supremacy in all aspects of the contemporary Hunt the Ripper chase has gone to the undoubted favourite runner in the police stakes, Inspector Frederick George Abberline. Without wishing to appear objurgatory, it has to be said that the distinction, it transpires, is somewhat less than justified, for, as Nicholas Connell and Stewart Evans revealed in their most illuminating and groundbreaking book, *The Man Who Hunted Jack the Ripper* (1990), there was one whose efforts in that direction must surely be rated as highly, higher even. And that one is Detective Inspector Edmund Reid, who, in July 1887, replaced Abberline, who had been uplifted to the Yard, as Local Inspector of H (Whitechapel) Division, under Superintendent Thomas Arnold, who retired in 1892, having stayed on a few years after what would have been his due retirement date in the hope of nabbing Jack. He, incidentally, was of opinion that only four of the murders – those of Polly Nichols, Annie Chapman, Catherine Eddowes, and Mary Jane Kelly – were the work of the Ripper.

Hitherto, Reid the hunter had been a figure almost as misty as Jack the hunted, but the publication of Connell and Evans' book dispelled the mist. Reid emerges from its pages as a very considerable character, latterly tending most amusingly to the eccentric. On a purely biographical level the book is a delight. We, however, must in our context be concerned to evaluate it in terms of its contribution to Ripperological studies, in which respect it is of indubitable primary importance.

For all his acuity and devotion to duty, Reid signally failed to 'buckle' the Whitechapel murderer. 'I have been asked,' he said,

> to tell the story of the 'Ripper' series … here are the only known facts. The whole of the murders were done after the public houses were closed; the victims were all of the same class, the lowest of the low, and living within a quarter of a mile of each other; all were murdered within half a mile area; all were

killed in the same manner. That is all we know for certain … My opinion is that the perpetrator of the crimes was a man who was in the habit of using a certain public house, and of remaining there until closing time. Leaving with the rest of the customers, with what soldiers call 'a touch of the delirium triangle', he would leave with one of the women … Having satisfied his maniacal blood lust he would go away home, and the next day know nothing about it. One thing is to my mind quite certain, and that is that he lived in the district … But this I will say at once. I challenge anyone to produce a tittle of evidence of any kind against anyone. The earth has been raked over and the seas have been swept to find this criminal 'Jack the Ripper', always without success.

So much for the conflicting opinions and conclusions of those who were actually involved in the case.

Connell and Evans' book is extremely useful in its summation of the general hierarchical structure at Scotland Yard, a link-by-link exposition of the 1888 chain of police command.

Overall head of the CID was James Monro, Assistant Metropolitan Police Commissioner. Unfortunately, he did not get on well with the Metropolitan Police Commissioner, Sir Charles Warren. In consequence, in August 1888, Monro resigned. He was replaced on 31 August 1888 by Dr Robert Anderson, Barrister-at-Law, who had been working in the Prison Department and was now appointed Junior Assistant Commissioner of Police.

Senior Assistant Commissioner was Alexander Carmichael Bruce, appointed the same day as Anderson. In the absence of Anderson, Chief Constable Colonel Bolton Monsell stepped into the gap.

In charge at Central Office, CID, was Chief Constable Adolphus Williamson. A sick man, he died in 1889, and John Shore was brought in as Superintendent in his stead.

Under Shore, at the Yard, were five chief inspectors – Greenham, Neame, Butcher, Littlechild, and Swanson – and fourteen inspectors. The local inspectors, at Division, and their men, dealt with most of the routine crime in their respective manors.

In the case of the Whitechapel murders, however, the Yard was called in, and three inspectors were sent to conduct the investigation – Inspector First-Class Frederick George Abberline, and Inspectors Henry Moore and Walter Andrews.

In overall charge of the Ripper case at Scotland Yard was Chief Inspector Donald Sutherland Swanson. In charge on the ground was Superintendent Thomas Arnold, who was the head of H Division (Whitechapel).

Reid was personally involved in all the Whitechapel murder investigations, with the exception of those into the deaths of Mary Ann Nichols – which took place in the territory or manor of J (Bethnal Green) Division, Reid's old stalking ground, where he had been replaced by Local Inspector Joseph Helson – and that of Catherine Eddowes, whose slaughter was enacted upon City of London Police preserves. Reid's remit was, though, to include the horrendous despatches of Alice McKenzie, of the Unknown of Pinchin Street, and of Frances Coles.

It must be noted that Reid's biographers have also transported firmly down to earth, with a resounding and convincing thump, the heretofore somewhat insubstantial Fairy Fay. After a most tenacious and impressive paperchase, which comes to an end at *Reynolds News* on 29 October 1950, the fey one is brought to book as Margaret Hames, fifty-four-year-old widow, savagely attacked, but not murdered.

Another interesting discovery along the way was that of the possible identity of Mary Jane Kelly's mysterious sometime lover, 'Mr Morganstone' of Stepney Gas Works. They traced two siblings, Morgestern, Adrienus L., aged thirty-three, and Maria A., aged twenty-six, both described in the 1881 census as gas stokers, both born in Alphen, Priel, in the Netherlands, both living (in 1881) at No. 43 Fulham Road.

4

The Medicine Men of the East

The Ripperine cohort of physicians, surgeons, and post-mortem-knife-plying pathologists of the East End constituted a second heavyweight investigative branch on the ground; an official adjunct of the police. Of immediate importance were the doctors on the spot – those with hands-on experience, as you might say – in the cases of the five main-line victims.

They were, listed alphabetically, Frederick William Blackwell, Thomas Bond, Frederick Gordon Brown, Rees Ralph Llewellyn, George Bagster Phillips, William Sedgwick Saunders, and George William Sequiera. Those magnificent seven were assisted, either at the scene of the crime or at the post-mortem examination, by, among others, Drs Percy John Clark, Edward Johnston, and Alexander Oberlin MacKellar (Dr Bagster Phillips' assistant). Roderick MacDonald, though medically qualified and practising in the East End, was involved only as the coroner conducting the inquest on Mary Jane Kelly.

Dr Rees Ralph Llewellyn (1849–1921) had been called from his surgery at 152 Whitechapel Road, at 4 a.m. on 31 August 1888, to examine *in situ* the body of Mary Ann Nichols. He also carried out the subsequent post-mortem on her at the dead-house of the Workhouse Infirmary in Old Montague Street, which did service as the Whitechapel Mortuary. The murder had, he decided, been committed at the spot in Buck's Row where the body lay. He observed facial bruising, the possible result, he thought, of a blow from a fist, or it could have been caused by the pressure of a thumb and fingers. He saw body wounds, inflicted he calculated by a knife, strong-bladed, moderately sharp, used violently and in a downwards direction. No part of the viscera was missing. The throat had been spectacularly cut, practically severing the woman's head from her body. There were several incisions in the abdomen. Apart from the suggestion, which he afterwards withdrew, that the murderer – not as yet attained to the distinction of a multicide – was possibly a left-handed person, he had no contribution to make as to the persona of the creature who was presently most magnificently to effloresce into yours truly, Jack the Ripper.

The next medic to enter upon what was to become the increasingly sanguinary field was Dr George Bagster Phillips (1834–97), whose residence and surgery was at No. 2 Spital Square, Spitalfields, and who was, and had been for twenty-three years, the Metropolitan Police H Division (Whitechapel) police surgeon. First called out to Hanbury Street at 6.10 a.m. on 8 September 1888, to pronounce upon the savaged corpse of Annie Chapman, he was to become the most widely experienced of the Ripper doctors, himself either conducting or otherwise attending the post-mortems of four out of the five putative victims.

But he got off to a bad start, making what was surely a mistake when he announced upon his arrival at the scene of the murder at 6.30 a.m. that the woman had been dead for at least two, and possibly three, hours.[8] The trouble was that John Richardson, who lived at 29 Hanbury Street, had been out at 4.45 a.m. sitting on the steps leading down into the backyard, beside which Annie Chapman was later discovered, and there had been no body there at that time. Then, at 5.25 a.m., next-door neighbour, Albert Cadosch, at No. 27, had had occasion to go into the yard at the rear of his house, and had heard words – the only one of which he had been able to catch being a decisive 'No' – passing between some persons apparently in the backyard of No. 29. And he had, on going back into his yard again at, he calculated, about 5.28 a.m., heard a noise as of something falling against the communal back fence.

At around 5.30 a.m., another witness, Mrs Elizabeth Long, had seen a man and a woman, whom she had recognised as Annie Chapman, talking in Hanbury Street, near No. 29. She heard the man say, 'Will you?' and the woman replied, 'Yes.' Since this may well have been the most likely genuine sighting of the Ripper, her description is worth noting. She thought that the man was a foreigner. He looked like a foreigner and was dark-complexioned. Unfortunately, she saw only his back, but had the impression that he was over forty years of age. He was a little taller than the woman. Annie Chapman's height was 5 feet. He was of shabby genteel appearance, and was wearing, she thought, a dark overcoat and a brown deerstalker hat.

If the evidence of Richardson, Cadosch and Mrs Long was correct as to the respective times, then Dr Phillips' estimate of the probable time of death must have been incorrect.

Grumbling the while about the gross unsuitability of the premises, he performed the autopsy on Annie Chapman in the workhouse shed, which did dubious service as the Whitechapel Mortuary. His conclusion was that the woman's breathing had been interfered with prior to her death. He found her face to be swollen, as was her tongue, which protruded between the front teeth, but not beyond the lips. These were both signs of suffocation. The murderer had, Phillips thought, taken hold of the woman by the chin, produced rapid insensibility by asphyxiation, lowered her to the ground and then cut her throat, which was dissevered deeply. Indeed, the muscular structure appeared as though an attempt had been made to separate the cervical vertebrae. Death arose from syncope or failure of the heart's action, consequent upon loss of blood via the throat wound. The body was terribly mutilated, but Phillips was satisfied that the various mutilations had been perpetrated *post mortem*. He displayed reluctance to divulge details to the coroner in open court, but finally reported that missing from the body were parts of the abdominal wall, including the navel, the uterus and its appendages, the upper part of the vagina, and the posterior two-thirds of the bladder. Having, like Dr Llewellyn in the case of Mary Ann Nichols, noted that the cutting of the throat had proceeded from left to right, he had, initially, likewise suspected the killer of being left-handed, but later had second, doubting, thoughts about this. He expressed an opinion as to the chosen instrument of despatch. Not an ordinary knife. It had to be a very sharp one. Thin, narrow blade, at least 6 to 8 inches long. Doing his best to particularise about the lethal weapon, he opined that the wounds observed could have been inflicted by a knife of the sort used for post-mortem dissection, although the ordinary surgical case might not contain such a knife. The sort of knife used by slaughtermen or butchers might, if well ground down, produce such wounds, but the knives plied by those engaged in the leather trade would not have fitted the bill. They would not have been long enough in the blade. He inclined to view the excision with one sweep of the knife of all of the killer's desiderata as indicative of the possession of considerable theoretical anatomical knowledge and remarkable anatomical expertise. Along these lines, then, he indicated lay the direction in which to search to find the Whitechapel murderer.

Dr Frederick William Blackwell (1851–1900), of 100 Commercial Road, enters the list with the killing of Elisabeth Stride, solely because he and his assistant, Edward Johnston, were the medical men most readily available to render assistance at the Berner Street tragedy.

Blackwell is quoted in *The Times* of 3 October 1888: 'At ten minutes past 1 on Sunday morning [30 September 1888] I was called to 40, Berner Street. I was called by a policeman, and my assistant, [Edward] Johnsson [*sic*], went back with him. I followed immediately I had dressed. I consulted my watch on my arrival, and it was just 1.10 [a.m.].'[9]

He at once made his examination, pronounced Elisabeth Stride dead, and then stood by to await the arrival of Dr Phillips.

Blackwell concluded his testimony,

> There was a check silk scarf round the neck, the bow of which was turned to the left side and pulled tightly. There was a long incision in the neck, which exactly corresponded with the lower border of the scarf. The lower edge of the scarf was slightly frayed as if by a sharp knife ... The blood was running down in the gutter into the drain. It was running in an opposite direction to the feet. There

was a quantity of clotted blood just under the body … I formed the opinion that the murderer first took hold of the silk scarf, at the back of it, and then pulled the deceased backwards, but I cannot say whether the throat was cut while the woman was standing or after she was pulled backwards. Deceased would take about a minute and a half to bleed to death.

Dr Phillips, arriving at 1.20 a.m. at Leman Street Police Station, and borne hastily thence to Berner Street, where Elisabeth Stride lay dead, made a preliminary examination at the scene of the crime. The following day Phillips shared with Dr Blackwell, who did the actual dissecting, the performance of a post-mortem on her at St George's-in-the-East Mortuary, in Cable Street. He was very much struck by the appearance over both of the deceased's shoulders, but especially the right one, under the clavicle and also in front of the chest, of a bluish discolouration, for which he subsequently watched, and had since seen on two occasions. This led him to believe that the deceased had been seized by the shoulders and forced to the ground, where her assailant, crouching at her right side, cut her throat. The 6-inch incision, inflicted from left to right, partially severed the left carotid artery, and Stride died of the resultant haemorrhage, coupled with the division of her trachea.

As regards the weapon, Phillips did not think that it would be a knife anything like as long as 9 inches. Neither was there any indication here of the use of a pointed knife. He moreover drew attention to the great dissimilarity between this case and that of Chapman, where the deceased's neck had been severed all round and cut right down to the vertebral column, the vertebral bone being marked, and an evident attempt had been made to separate the cervical vertebrae. In fact, Chapman's neck had been mutilated in precisely the same way as, two months later, Mary Jane Kelly's would be. In the case of Stride, the murderer would not necessarily, said Phillips, be bloodstained. The commencement of the wound and the injury to the blood vessels would be such as to direct the resultant stream – and stream it would be – of blood away from him.

Dr Blackwell's views concurred with those of Phillips. He also confirmed Phillips' observations regarding the presence and significance of the bruising or pressure marks caused by two hands pressing on the dead woman's shoulders.

Dr George William Sequiera (1859–1926), the first medical man on the scene in Mitre Square to view the body of Catherine Eddowes, was a mere bit-part player in the Ripper drama. Called on stage at 1.55 a.m., Monday 1 October 1888, from his nearby surgery at No. 34 Jewry Street, Aldgate, it was he who pronounced Eddowes extinct. He remained, Hippocratic guardian of her cadaver, until Dr Frederick Gordon Brown (1843–1928), the City police surgeon, who had been summoned, put in an appearance.

At the second inquest hearing, on 11 October 1888, Dr Sequiera, in response to questions from Henry H. Crawford, the City solicitor, testified that although the body had been found in the darkest corner of Mitre Square, there would have been sufficient light to allow the murderer to commit his crime without the aid of any additional illumination. He did not think that the perpetrator had any great anatomical skill, nor designs upon any particular organ. He accounted for the absence of noise by his belief that death must have been instantaneous after the severance of the windpipe and the blood vessels. Finally, judging from the condition of the blood, he had decided that life had been extinct probably no more than a quarter of an hour.

Dr Brown arrived at the crime scene at 2.18 a.m. After viewing Eddowes' body *in situ*, he ordered its removal to the City Mortuary, Golden Lane, where the post-mortem would be performed. At Brown's suggestion, Dr Bagster Phillips attended. Brown considered the fancy knife-work in this case to betoken a good deal of knowledge as to the position of the organs in the abdominal cavity and the way of removing them. He envisaged the instrument of destruction employed as sharp, pointed, knife-like, and some 6 inches long. The first wound which it delivered was to Eddowes' throat. His view was that she was lying on the ground at the time of its delivery. Her throat had been cut from left to right, the larynx being severed below the vocal cords. All the deep cervical structures had been cut through to the bone, knife-notchings marking the intervertebral cartilage. The cause of death was haemorrhage from the left carotid artery. Mercifully, the mutilations were, he was glad be able to say, *post mortem*. Missing, carried off by the murderer, was the uterus, along with some of its ligaments, and the left kidney. Not removed were the cervix of the womb and the vagina, both uninjured. He inclined to the view that the mutilator exhibited such a degree of knowledge and dexterity as might be characteristic of someone accustomed to the butchering of animals. No traces of any sexual connection having taken place were found. Brown also noted that the woman's hands and arms were bronzed. A cold, clinical observation, but it has always seemed to me that one of the most pathetic symbols of the Ripper horrors are the suntanned arms of chirrupy little Catherine Eddowes, newly returned from her 'holiday' in the hop-fields of Kent.

Present as an observer of the whole of the Eddowes post-mortem, Dr William Sedgwick Saunders (1824–1901), of 13 Queen Street, Cheapside, was the public analyst for the City of London. He did not think that the killer had displayed any anatomical skill, and, moreover, said that he had seen nothing to lead him to believe that he had had any particular design upon any particular organ. Saunders subsequently looked for, but failed to find, poison in the contents of Eddowes' stomach – 'I received the stomach … I carefully examined it and its contents more particularly for poisons of the narcotic class with negative results, there not being the faintest trace of these or any other poison.'

Dr Bagster Phillips was called by the police at eleven o'clock on Friday morning, 9 November 1888, and a quarter of an hour later was entering Miller's Court to view the thoroughly butchered Mary Jane Kelly. His inquest testimony, given on 12 November 1888, was reported in *The Times* of 13 November 1888:

> I went to the room door leading out of the passage running at the side of 26, Dorset Street. There were two windows to the room. I produce a photograph which will enable you to see exactly the position. Two panes in the window nearest to the passage were broken, and finding the door locked I looked through the lower of the broken panes and satisfied myself that the mutilated corpse lying on the bed was not in need of any immediate attention from me.

It is a likely misreading of this portion of Dr Phillips' testimony that has given rise to the notion that the photograph he produced at the inquest was a photograph of the mutilated Kelly that had been taken from outside the room through the broken pane, rather than an exterior view of the room that showed only the 'two windows to the room'. Further contributing to the false idea that the crime-scene photographs had been taken through the window was the report that appeared in *The Times* and the *Star* on 10 November 1888, which stated,

> [Superintendent Arnold] ordered one of the windows to be entirely removed … While this examination [of the mutilated Kelly] was being made a photographer, who, in the meantime had been sent for, arrived and took photographs of the body, the organs, the room, and its contents. Superintendent Arnold then had the door of the room forced.

As far as I am aware, there are only two extant photographs of the mutilated body, both of which were taken from a position inside the room, but it would seem probable that more were taken.

Continuing with Phillips' testimony, *The Times* advised that, finding the door to No. 13 Miller's Court locked, it was not until 1.30 p.m., when, the door being forced, he entered the room.

The mutilated remains of a female were lying two-thirds over towards the edge of the bedstead nearest to the door. She had only her chemise on, or some under linen garment. I am sure the body had been removed subsequent to the injury which caused death, from that side of the bedstead which was nearest to the wooden partition, because of the large quantity of blood under the bedstead and the saturated condition of the palliasse and the sheet at the top corner nearest the partition. The blood was produced by the severance of the right carotid artery, which was the immediate cause of death. This injury was inflicted while deceased was lying at the right side of the bedstead.

The lengthy and laudatorily scrupulous post-mortem had been carried out at Shoreditch Mortuary in the presence of Dr Thomas Bond (1841–1901). A surgeon at Westminster Hospital, Bond functioned also as divisional police surgeon to A or Whitehall Division of the Metropolitan Police. Enjoying the very considerable confidence and regard of Assistant Commissioner Robert Anderson, Bond's involvement in the Whitechapel murders was in the main consultative – although he was, it is true, actually summoned to Miller's Court to inspect Mary Jane Kelly's cadaver. In that instance, his *post mortem* observations were made in the victim's room, at 2 p.m. on the day of the discovery of her death.

He reported, 'The viscera were found in various parts – *viz:* the uterus & kidneys with one breast, under the head, the other breast by the rt. foot, the liver between the feet, the intestines by the right side, & the spleen by the left side of the body.'

The stomach was attached to the intestines. The right lung remained in the thoracic cavity, its lowest part broken and torn away. The left lung was intact. The pericardium was open below, the heart missing from the pericardial sac. Fostering ambiguity, Bond fails to mention any final cardiac disposition. He did, however, make it clear that the uterus had not been taken away by the killer; neither was it gravid. The neck was cut through the skin and other tissues right down to the vertebrae – the fifth and sixth cervical being deeply notched.

Bond also submitted, at Anderson's request, a general report on the murders of Nichols, Chapman, Stride and Eddowes, although in these cases his experience was confined to the scrutiny of the medical notes that had been written by other doctors. In conflict with Dr Phillips, he believed that 'all five murders were, no doubt, committed by the same hand'.

He then moves on to generalisations:

[In the cases of Nichols, Chapman, Stride, and Eddowes] the throats appear to have been cut from left to right. In the last case [Kelly], owing to extensive mutilation it is impossible to say in what direction the fatal cut was made, but arterial blood was found on the wall in splashes close to where the woman's head must have been lying. All the circumstances surrounding the murders lead me to form the opinion that the women must have been lying down when murdered and in every case the throat was first cut. In all cases there appears to be no evidence of struggling and the attacks were probably so sudden and made in such a position that the woman could neither resist or cry out. In the first four cases the murderer must have attacked from the right side of the victims, in the Dorset Street case, he must have attacked in front or from the left, as there would be no room for him between the wall and the part of the bed on which the woman was lying.

The murderer would not, in Bond's opinion, necessarily have been splashed or deluged with blood, although there must certainly have been some degree of smearing of his hands, arms and parts of his clothing. In every case, except that of Elisabeth Stride, the mutilations were of the same character and made it clear that in all of them the object was mutilation.

Bond did not think the inflicter to have been informed by any scientific or anatomical learning. His hazard as to the instrument employed was 'a strong knife at least 6 inches long, very sharp, pointed at the top and about an inch in width. It may have been a clasp-knife, a butcher's knife, or a surgeon's knife. I think it was no doubt a straight knife.'

Somewhat chancing his arm in those pre-FBI psychological-profiling days, Bond presented a profile of the Ripper as he envisaged him:

The murderer must have been a man of physical strength and of great coolness and daring. There is no evidence that he had any accomplice. He must, in my opinion, be a man subject to periodical attacks of homicidal and erotic mania. The character of the mutilations indicate that the man may be in a condition sexually that may be called satyriasis. It is of course possible that the homicidal impulse may have developed from a revengeful or brooding condition of the mind, or that Religious Mania may have been the original disease, but I do not think that either hypothesis is likely. The murderer in external appearance is quite likely to be a quiet, inoffensive looking man probably middle-aged and neatly and respectably dressed. I think he must be in the habit of wearing a cloak or overcoat or he could hardly have escaped notice in the streets if the blood on his hands or clothes were visible. Assuming the murderer to be such a person as I have just described, he would probably be solitary and eccentric in his habits, also he is most likely to be a man without a regular occupation, but with some small income or pension. He is possibly living among respectable persons who have some knowledge of his character and habits and who may have grounds for suspicion that he is not quite right in his mind at times. Such persons would probably be unwilling to communicate suspicions to the police for fear of trouble or notoriety, whereas if there were a prospect of reward it might overcome their scruples.

Dr Bond was of an importance in the Ripper medical saga equivalent to that of Dr George Bagster Phillips, and it comes as something of a shock to learn that his tragic death at the comparatively early age of sixty was the result of suicide. At a quarter to seven on the morning of Thursday 6 June 1901, Bond jumped from the window of his residence, 7 The Sanctuary, Westminster Abbey, London W.

Reynolds News, 9 June 1901, reported that the doctor's bedroom was on the third floor, a height of some 40 feet from the ground. Thomas Goldsmith, a porter at Westminster Hospital, said that he was going on duty at 6.45 a.m. when he saw what he thought was a bundle of clothes being thrown out of a third-storey window. Immediately afterwards he heard a shriek, and on running to the spot he saw Dr Bond lying unconscious in the area. He was breathing, but only lived about a minute.

Dr Bond, who had not been at all well of late, had a country residence, the Old Marsh Farm, Dunster, Somerset. He held a high reputation in his profession and was extremely popular. Apart from his work in connection with the Whitechapel murders, he had given evidence in several important trials, including that in 1881 of Percy Lefroy Mapleton, the murderer of Isaac Frederick Gold on the Brighton Railway, and he had also carried out the post-mortem on Miss Elizabeth Annie Camp, victim in the unsolved murder of 1897 on the Waterloo-bound train from Feltham, Middlesex.

Giving evidence at the inquest held at Westminster by Mr J. Troutbeck, Mr John Norton, of Queen Anne's Mansions, said that for some years Dr Bond had been in indifferent health and had suffered great pain from an internal malady. He had been in the habit of taking morphia, which had made him extremely emotional, and he had indeed said that some time or other he would jump out of the window. For this reason two nurses were engaged to attend him. He had been addicted to the morphia habit since August 1900, and had been under constant medical care. His mind had apparently become unhinged, as witnessed by the fact that he had taken a great dislike to one of the nurses simply because she had endeavoured to persuade him not to take morphia.

The night nurse who had been in charge of Dr Bond during the early hours of Thursday morning said that he had suffered some pain, but was calm and spoke to her several times in a very rational and sensible manner. He had taken a grain of morphia at eleven o'clock on the Wednesday night, but had had none after that. On the Thursday morning, while Dr Bond was apparently peacefully sleeping, she had left the room for a minute, but heard the rustle of a curtain and became alarmed. She ran back into the room, found that there was no one there and that the window was open. She then discovered that the doctor had leapt through the window into the area 45 feet below.

Dr Bond, only partially dressed, landed on his head. Death must have been almost instantaneous. Several passers-by ran at once to the doctor's assistance and he was carried over to the Westminster Hospital, just opposite. Dr Welch, the house physician on duty there, said that nothing could be done for him. His brain was not lacerated. Interestingly, it was recorded at the post-mortem examination that Bond's brain was small in size.

The coroner, in summing up, said that Dr Bond had been one of his oldest personal friends. He had known him for thirty years. The doctor had suffered painfully for a lengthy period and there could be no doubt that the morphia that he had taken to alleviate his sufferings had had an influence on the brain, which had resulted in this most unfortunate occurrence. The jury found that the deceased committed suicide while temporarily insane.

We will come next upon five additional victims of murder, who, although included in the official file designated 'Whitechapel Murders', may or may not have had a last encounter with Jack. The doctors prominent on the scene with this enigmatical group are – with the exception of the otherwise omnipresent George Bagster Phillips and Thomas Bond – Matthew Brownfield, Charles Alfred Hebbert, G. H. Hillier, Timothy Robert Killeen, Alexander Oberlin MacKellar, and Frederick John Oxley.

The putative victims, in demise order, were:

Emma Elizabeth Smith. Died in the London Hospital attended by house surgeon Dr G. H. Hillier, who subsequently conducted a post-mortem on her. Inquest: 7 April 1888. London Hospital. Coroner: Wynne Edwin Baxter.

Martha Tabram. Post-mortem conducted by Dr Timothy R. Killeen, who had originally been called out from his surgery at 68 Brick Lane to examine the body *in situ* at the Old Montague Street Workhouse Infirmary. Inquest: 23 August 1888, at the Working Lads' Institute, Whitechapel Road. Conducted by George Collier, Deputy Coroner for the South East Middlesex.

Rose Mylett. Post-mortem conducted by Dr Matthew Brownfield. Further post-mortem examinations by Drs Alexander Oberlin MacKellar, Charles Alfred Hebbert, and Thomas Bond. Inquest: 21 December 1888.

Alice McKenzie. Post-mortem examinations by Drs George Bagster Phillips, Thomas Bond, and Frederick Gordon Brown. Inquest: 17 July 1889. Coroner: Wynne Edwin Baxter.

Frances Coles. Inquest: 15 February 1891, at the Working Lads' Institute, Whitechapel Road, Coroner: Wynne Edwin Baxter.

Emma Elizabeth Smith was the first victim listed in the police files. She died of peritonitis two days after she was assaulted on 3 April 1888, by three street robbers. Dr G. H. Hillier, house surgeon in attendance at the London Hospital when she was admitted, said that a portion of her right ear was torn, and that there was a rupture of the peritoneum and other internal organs, caused by a blunt instrument.

Martha Tabram, regarded by many as the Ripper's first victim, was brutally attacked on 7 August 1888, her body having been penetrated by thirty-nine puncture – not 'ripping' – wounds. The question as to what weapon had inflicted those wounds, a topic of long-standing argument and confusion, warrants a closer look, if for no other reason than to illustrate how those facts of the case that were clearly defined at the time devolved into fiction decades later. The surviving documents describing the murder are brief. A first mention appeared in *The Times* on 8 August 1888: 'There was one large wound over her heart, while several other injuries of the nature of stabs were on her body … The injuries on the deceased are, it is stated, not unlike bayonet wounds.'

On 9 August 1888, an inquiry was held respecting the murdered woman. The testimony of Dr Timothy Robert Killeen, the only doctor summoned to the murder scene, and who had also performed the post-mortem, was reported in *The Times* of 10 August 1888. He had pointed out which parts of the body had been penetrated, and suggested by what means the penetration had been effected.

> The witness [Dr Killeen] did not think all the wounds were inflicted with the same instrument. The wounds generally might have been inflicted with a knife, but such an instrument could not have inflicted one of them which went through the chest-bone. His opinion was that one of the wounds was inflicted by some kind of dagger, and that all of them had been caused during life.

There was no testimony from Dr Killeen at the second, and final, inquiry on 23 August 1888. A summary, dated simply 'September 1888', of all the inquiries made by the police into the murder of Martha Tabram, was compiled by Chief Inspector Donald S. Swanson. The only reference therein to Dr Killeen and his findings was as follows: 'Dr Keeling [*sic*] of 68 Brick Lane was called and examined the body and found thirty-nine wounds on body, and neck, and private part with a knife or dagger.'

Contemporary newspapers report these details variantly:

> One wound had been caused by a sword-bayonet or dagger, and the others by a penknife. (*Pall Mall Gazette*, 10 August 1888).

> The woman when found presented a shocking appearance, her body being covered with stab wounds to the number of thirty-nine, some of which had been done with a bayonet. (*Pall Mall Gazette*, 24 August 1888).

> That the stabs were from a weapon shaped like a bayonet, is almost established beyond doubt … [There were also] thirty-eight injuries, some of which almost seem as if they were due to thrusts and cuts from a penknife. (*Echo*, 10 August 1888).

> In the witness' opinion [Dr Killeen] the wounds were not inflicted with the same instrument, there being a deep wound in the breast from some long, strong instrument, while most of the others were done apparently with a penknife. The large wound could have been caused by a sword bayonet or dagger. (*Lloyd's Weekly Newspaper*, 12 August 1888).

> The fact that the wounds appear to have been inflicted with a bayonet has turned suspicion on to soldiers … One can buy bayonets by the dozen in Petticoat Lane, which is not a stone's throw from the scene of the tragedy. (*Star*, 11 August 1888).

Whatever one might reasonably have expected from the doctors of the time in terms of expert medical conjecture, fleet-footed Jack, although assuredly presenting as a case suitable for – or perhaps unsuitable for, but certainly requiring – treatment, seems, notwithstanding, to have presented, *in absentia*, no widely acceptable grounds upon which it was possible, or safe, to base a secure diagnosis.

With so much division and basic disagreement manifest among those doctors on the spot, with hands-on experience, as you might say, who one would have thought to have been in the indisputably best position to know, it is, perhaps, hardly surprising to find that the earliest consideration to exercise and divide the doctors at large was the sanity-insanity issue.

In the *Lancet* of 15 September 1888, a full fortnight before the so-called 'double event', the opinion was editorially expressed that the theory that the Whitechapel murders

> are the work of a lunatic appears to us to be by no means at present well established … As far as we are aware, homicidal mania is generally characterised by the one single and fatal act, although we grant this may have been led up to by a deep-rooted series of delusions. It is most unusual for a lunatic to plan any complicated crime of this kind. Neither, as a rule, does a lunatic take precautions to escape from the consequences of his act … The truth is, that under the circumstances nobody can do more than hazard a guess as to the probable condition of mind of the perpetrator of these terrible tragedies. Until more evidence is forthcoming, it appears to us to be useless to speculate upon what can only at present be regarded as problematical.

An editorial in the *British Medical Journal* of 22 September 1888 also indicated the inadvisability of jumping to the conclusion that it was an insane murderer who was responsible for the Whitechapel killings. The suggestion of a copy-cat element was punted – that is, that there was one sane and one insane killer. The most important issue from a medical point of view was that of diagnosis. Medicine does not recognise any specific type of mental disorder that can be described as 'homicidal mania'. That is a layman's unfounded concept. So what medically accepted forms of insanity could be considered likely to give rise to such a series of savage murders? Eminent psychiatrists of the ilk of Henry Maudsley and C. C. H. Mare acknowledged the existence of 'forms of impulsive insanity in which murder was the common tendency'. In these cases, however, there was as a rule a special antipathy, the insane correlative of love, the tendency of a loving husband to kill his wife, the doting mother to destroy her offspring, or, as Oscar Wilde put it, 'each man kills the thing he loves'.

In the Whitechapel killings nothing of this kind is discernible. There are cases of epileptics who have displayed characters of a murderous and impulsive destructiveness, but this is due to recklessness and a bland disregard of consequences.

That same 22 September 1888, the *Lancet* published a letter addressed to the editors by Dr Lyttleton Forbes Winslow. He opened with the confession that he was 'more or less responsible for the original opinion that the individual who committed the wholesale slaughter in Whitechapel was a lunatic'.

He continued,

> The horrible and revolting details, as stated in the public press are themselves evidence, not of crimes committed by a responsible individual, but by a fiendish madman. You go on to add that 'homicidal mania is generally characterised by one single and fatal act'. Having had extensive experience in cases of homicidal insanity, and having been retained in the chief cases during the past twenty years, I speak as an authority on this part of the subject. I cannot agree with your statement … Homicidal lunatics are cunning, deceptive, plausible, and on the surface, to all outward appearance, sane; but there

is contained within their innermost nature a dangerous lurking after blood, which, though at times latent, will develop when the opportunity arises. That the murderer of the victims in Whitechapel will prove to be such an individual is the belief of Your obedient servant.

Dr Batty Tuke, a specialist in lunacy connected with the Saughton Hall Asylum, Edinburgh, takes a different view. A paragraph from his pen in the *British Medical Journal* of 17 November 1888, states,

It would not be hard to imagine the commission of an isolated act of this character by an insane person, but the whole circumstances of the commission of these crimes. save one, are outside insanity. If they have been committed by a lunatic, his is a case which, in this country, is without parallel or precedent. I have said the circumstances of these crimes are outside insanity, save one, that circumstance is, of course, the horrible nature of the act, but are we to deduce insanity from the revolting nature of the crime alone, when all the other circumstances point away from it? Why should we underestimate the power of strong human wickedness and overestimate that of weak human insanity? For my own part, I can more easily conceive these crimes being the result of savage wickedness than of insane mental action. There is a consciousness in the first idea which there is not in the second. Moreover, there is an incentive to wickedness productive of crime analogous to those now under consideration, which only those very intimately acquainted with the dark records of medical jurisprudence know of. This is not the place to speak of it, and I can only allude to it in order to indicate that there are incentives to crime unappreciable by the great mass of the community.

That November (1888), the *Journal of Jurisprudence* (Edinburgh) published a critique:

On the subject of the murders the London public has produced a great quantity of egregiously foolish utterances, in the different shapes of rumour, comment, and so-called suggestion, than could well have been collected from a similar number of people in any part of the world. It has also, as a matter of course, blamed the police, while at the same time it has, doubtless with the best intentions, done probably as much as in it lay to increase the difficulties in the way of detection. All his was to be looked for. It constitutes one of the most formidable difficulties with which the police are confronted in a case of the kind. All the skill and all the effort of a great system of police have utterly failed to connect any one with a series of atrocious murders, committed not in solitary places, but in one of the most densely populated districts of London; not in the recesses of some lonely wood, but on the public streets of the largest city in the world. It was the very atrocity of the Whitechapel murders that gave rise to the theory of their being the work of a madman. It is not a novel line of reasoning. The mutilation of the bodies of those wretched women in East London. taken by itself, is no indication whatever of insanity on the part of the perpetrator or perpetrators of the deeds. It is said that the hypothesis of insanity as an explanation of these startling crimes, is borne out by the apparent absence of anything like an adequate motive. But this failure is no ground for inferring insanity, and it would be dangerous so to regard it. Apparent absence of motive is no criterion.

The craftiness of the author, or authors, of these deeds is astounding, and the highest tribute to it is the fact that all attempts at detection have been made in vain hitherto. There is, first, cool and deliberate preparation. There is then a careful selection of time and place – darkness and seclusion. There is the choice of a class of victims which, of all others, can most readily and as a matter of ordinary course be decoyed away alone to a secluded place of the kind, and at such an hour. The actual execution of his foul purpose must have been swift and dexterous, and shows coolness of hand and steadiness of purpose. Then all traces of the crime must have been removed from the assassin with great skill and foresight. The perfect circumspection which has characterized his subsequent movements, and has secured complete concealment for him hitherto, has been skilful in the extreme, and must have been previously devised. Lastly, the daring shown in the repetition of the atrocities (assuming them for the moment to be the work of one hand) is only to be equalled by the caution shown in refraining from any too foolhardy attempt to repeat them when detection was imminent. These things are all markedly in the direction of disproving insanity. Dr (Isaac) Ray, in contrasting the sane criminal with the insane remarks: 'The criminal lays plans for the execution of his designs – time, place, and weapons are all suited to his purpose, and when successful, he either flies from the scene of his enormities, or makes every effort to avoid discovery. The homicidal monomaniac, on the contrary, for the most part, consults none of the usual conveniences of crime, he falls upon the object of his prey, often-times without the most proper means for accomplishing his purpose, and perhaps in the presence of a multitude, as if expressly to court observation, and then voluntarily surrenders himself to the constituted authorities.'

In December, 1888, in the *Journal of Nervous and Mental Diseases*, Dr Edward Charles Spitzka of New York, published 'The Whitechapel Murders: Their Medico-Legal and Historical Aspects'.

There are, Spitzka pointed out, very few cases in the literature that, approximate to that of the Ripper.

None are exactly like it. Long series of murders on women, done in the same manner and committed from evidently similar motives are on record, but they were all committed in comparatively deserted localities … At Gainsville, and near Austin, Texas, ten murders, terribly similar in every detail, were committed in 1887. The first blow was with an ax [sic], and afterwards the bodies [were] so mutilated that they fell apart on being lifted up. The killing was uniformly done in bed, the victim was, as a rule, dragged into the yard and there hacked to pieces. Most of those destroyed were colored servants. In his tenth case he [the murderer] failed to complete his task, the victim escaping with her life. The perpetrator has not been discovered.

Frankly, the tale of Texas Jack does not add up satisfactorily. Extrapolating from a somewhat untidy bundle of allegations, one is led to conclude that, between the years 1882 and 1888, an indeterminate number of females were murdered over the area of some 300 miles separating Gainsville in northern Texas from Austin and San Antonio in the south.

Evans and Gainey came to the independent conclusion that the killings were not all the work of a single murderous hand, and in the matter of motive selected rape and robbery. They cited as their source 'a leading Southern newspaper in the USA', the *Atlanta Constitution*.

Some clarity is imported to this tangled matter by Steven Saylor's work of fiction *Twist at the End* (2000), wherein he lists the real names of the eight victims and details of their murders, committed in Austin, Texas, between December 1884 and December 1885.

Across the Atlantic, the 8 December 1888 issue of the *Illustrated Police News*, Boston, Massachusetts, voiced the following:

The fact … that the murders of Jack the Ripper are not committed from any merely selfish motive, like the desire for gain, is an … indication of mental and moral deformity suggestive of downright insanity. He butchers his victims in the most horrible manner and with seeming anatomical knowledge, but he does not rob them. All he wants is to kill them and in such a way as most to excite terror, revulsion and horror in the community. He therefore seems to be a criminal lunatic, inspired perhaps by the mad purpose of crushing out the social evil, for all his victims have been women who belonged to the ranks of the abandoned. Instead of repenting of his murders, very likely he glories in them as heroic deeds performed in the cause of social purity.

Taking year's end stock, the *Lancet*, of December 1888, editorially pronounced:

> The year just closing has, in addition to the usual tally of medico-legal experiences, been marked by a series of crimes (the Whitechapel murders) of unexampled barbarity – crimes rendered all the more notable by their repetition, and that, too, in a crowded part of the metropolis, and by the failure hitherto to detect their diabolical perpetrator. Even yet the public mind has not recovered from the terror which they occasioned.

Nor had it. To this very day faint ripplings of the horror of that ancient autumn of terror are still perceptible to those gifted with the sensitivity to perceive.

5

The Early Scribes

While the blood was virtually yet wet on Jack's knife, a handful of enterprising publishers were preparing to produce chronicles of him and his ghastly activities. One of these men of print was George Purkess, proprietor of the *Illustrated Police News*. He it was who issued one of the first Ripper books – *The Whitechapel Murders: Or the Mysteries of the East End*. It came out in six parts, a total of forty-eight pages, and included accounts of the murders of 'an unknown woman', and Martha Tabram, but not that of Mary Jane Kelly, before whose murder the partwork had been issued. It concluded, therefore, with the murder of Catherine Eddowes. Apart from its infrastructure of true facts regarding the details and sequence of the killings, the work is one of pure fiction of the venerable penny-dreadful genre. 'A man, with a dogskin cap drawn over his eyes, and wearing bushy whiskers, was speaking in whispers to a woman who was in the shadow of the wall. They were close to the arched entrance to George Yard. Presently the woman seemed to yield to his solicitations, and the two passed in.'

The man is imaginatively described: 'He was about the ordinary stature, stout, and had on a dogskin cap … and wore a heavy shoddy cloak with a hood. He associated with no one, but some hours after dark he would appear out of some secret den and glide along the street like a ghost.'

We are led to the secret place, the lair. It is an empty warehouse in chancery:

> Here he struck a match and lit a lamp, which revealed to the eye a large, dreary old warehouse, with a fireplace near which was a mattress with dirty fetid bed-clothes, a box which served as a table, and a few articles necessary to the preparation of food. The man threw off his outer garments and, lighting a pipe, cast himself upon the dirty bed, where we leave him.

Three thousand miles away, across the Atlantic, in New York, was another astute man of business, Richard K. Fox, who had begun his career as business manager of the *National Police Gazette*. Printed on distinctive pink paper, the *Gazette* had obliged the merely curious and the incurably prurient alike with lively, highly spiced reports of the carryings-on in dens of vice, the doings of shady politicians, and crimes of passion gone wayward and straying into murderous blind alleys. It prospered and reaped a tidy fortune.

The *Gazette's* treatment of the Whitechapel horrors was thin. It was, moreover, scornful of the efforts of London's police:

The failure of the British bluecoats to run down this demon, whoever he may be, shows a want of efficiency that amounts to downright stupidity. The London police seem to be way behind the police of other great cities both in this country and in Europe ... The fact that the mysterious London criminal, who has been so long laughing in his sleeve at the police of that great metropolis, has confined himself to one section is another point which tells strongly against the British bluecoats, for that very fact certainly should make their task of detection easier.

However, in the 15 December 1888 issue of the *National Police Gazette* it was announced that a 'thrilling and graphic history' of the Whitechapel murders, 'elegantly illustrated', was now ready. Price 25 cents. Consisting of thirty-eight pages of text and ten of sketches, the booklet added four more murders to the Whitechapel Fiend's discredit – those of Emma Smith, Martha Tabram, an unnamed woman (subsequently identified as Jane Beetmore) found, on Sunday 23 September 1888, lying at the roadside at Birtley, south of Gateshead, and that of a woman (never identified) whose decomposing remains were discovered on 2 October 1888, at the site of a planned new Grand Opera House on the Thames Embankment which never materialised, and which became the site of the rising New Scotland Yard Building.

Also published in New York, in December 1888, was *The Whitechapel Murders: Or, On the Track of the Fiend* by Detective Warren – thirty three-column pages, well illustrated with line drawings. This account covered from the attack on Emma Smith and the killing of Martha Tabram to the murder of Mary Jane Kelly, but collapses terminally into a totally fictitious tale of a gun-toting chase of the Fiend, who evades capture by plunging into the Thames.

Philadelphia is the scene of a third American publication around 1888, *'Leather Apron', Or the Horrors of Whitechapel, London, 1888*. Compiled by Sam'l E. Hudson, this is a more substantial – seventy-six pages – but no more accurate production. Hudson starts off with a reference to the mysterious murders of sailors whose savagely gashed corpses were found on the bulkheads and in the water of Liverpool's Canada Dock. The number of such bodies is said to have totalled 'more than half a score'. The baffled Liverpool police force never discovered the perpetrator. Moving on to the Whitechapel atrocities, which he lists as eight – the canonical five plus Emma Smith, Tabram, and the remains of the unknown woman buried by the Thames – Hudson finds himself unable to hazard the name of any possible culprit.

There was also issued in 1888 *The Curse upon Mitre Square, A.D. 1530–1888*, by John Francis Brown. This booklet concerned itself with the provision of the details of a number of historical events with which the square had been associated. Its last dozen or so pages are devoted to the ill-starred happenings of 1888.

Around 1889, there issued forth anonymously *The Whitechapel Atrocities: Arrest of a Newspaper Reporter*. Published in London, it retailed the experiences of a twenty-five-year-old journalist who contrived to get himself arrested twice in one day – Saturday 24 November – as the suspected East End assassin. The first arrest was not too alarming. He was hustled off to Leman Street Police Station, whence he was swiftly released. The second arrest proved considerably more disturbing. He was carried off to Commercial Street Police Station. He was subjected there to lengthy, searching interrogations regarding his activities during the four previous nights, which he had spent in Spitalfields, questioning its denizens and observing their lives, habits and customs. Having convinced the authorities that all that he had done was done on journalistic assignment, he was duly warned to mind his future movements in that neighbourhood, before being escorted back to his home by two stern police officers.

Pure fiction was the 1889 Chicago publication, *The Whitechapel Mystery: A Psychological Problem ('Jack the Ripper')*. The author was Dr N. T. Oliver, a *nom de plume* adopted by E. O. Tilburn. It was issued as No. 14 of the *Globe Detective* series. Mesmerism played a large part in what was essentially a tale of vengeance. A brother whose innocent sister had been seduced into a life of degradation and ultimate death determines to take fifteen lives, one for each year that his sister had been forced to live in sin.

Also published in Chicago, in November 1889, *The Whitechapel Murders: Or an American Detective in London*, came from the pen of A. F. Pinkerton – no connection with the celebrated American family of private investigators, probably adopted as a pseudonym by one of the stable of Laird & Lee's writers. His chosen victims are Nichols, Chapman, Stride, Eddowes, Kelly, Tabram, Emma Smith, and the innominate decomposed one unearthed beside the Thames. In an appendix he dismisses Tabram and Smith as Ripper victims. Disappointingly, he makes no stab at identifying the Whitechapel knifeman.

When, in the mid-1950s, foraging in the Library of Congress in Washington, D.C., for records of pre-1900 murder trials, the American crime historian and bibliographer, the late Thomas M. McDade, turned up a handwritten card in the old catalogue upon which was inscribed: 'Hayne, W. J. *Jack the Ripper, or Crimes of London. A Full and Authentic Account of the Mysterious Whitechapel Murders*. By a London Detective (anon), a work published by the Utility Book and Novel [*sic*] Co., Chicago, in 1889.'

There were, stamped in red on the upper right-hand edge of the card, the words 'Temporary entry'. And in the left-hand margin were two pencilled notes, 'nt. fd. Nov. 7, 06' and 'Not found 1/4/72'. At the lower edge, also written in pencil, was '66, 14p incl. Pl. 16'– 1889: 196g.'

On a second handwritten card in the old card catalogue was written: '*Jack, the ripper, or the crimes of London*, 1889. See Hayne, W. J.'

The current printed catalogue of the holdings of the Library of Congress does not contain the information displayed on these two cards. Of the work itself there was no sign and, in those books of reference in which it was referred to, it came to be described as 'stolen from the Library of Congress'. All that is known of W. J. Hayne is that he was a Chicago printer and engraver. No copy of his book had ever appeared.

That was until 1 February 2002. On that date a single copy surfaced on eBay. Put up for internet auction by a seller in Chicago, it was described as a paper-bound pamphlet of under eighty pages. Its illustrated front wrapper read, '*Jack the Ripper, Or the Crimes of London*. H. A. Hamlin, Publisher, Chicago.' The title page read, '*Jack the Ripper, or the Crimes of London. Full and Authentic Account of the Mysterious Whitechapel Murders*. Fully illustrated. By a London Detective. Published by Utility Book and Novelty Co. Chicago, Ill.' The name of Hayne was nowhere mentioned. Speculation burgeoned on the grapevine: was this, could this possibly be, the missing Hayne title?

On Friday 8 February 2002, the item was knocked down at £1,600. The composition of this auctioned item lines up pretty well with the bibliographic detail supplied on the old catalogue card from the Library of Congress. Of its eighty pages, sixty-six are occupied with accounts of the murder of Tabram, and of the five canonical cases, and the Thames-side decomposed torso case. The final fourteen pages are devoted to a selection of non-Ripperine 'Crimes Which Have Never Been Explained'. The booklet is copiously illustrated.

There are, however, some discrepancies. The Library of Congress catalogue card does not record the presence of seven unnumbered pages of advertisements for titles from Hamlin's list at the back of the booklet, neither does it mention H. A. Hamlin as the publisher, whose name appears on the front cover.

Provenance-wise, there is inscribed near the corner on the inside of the rear cover, 'Edina Roberts. 602 West Van Buren Street, Chicago, Illinois.' Research discloses that upon her death in the mid-1940s her books were sold to a Chicago bookseller whose stock was disposed of after his death in the late 1990s, and it was the purchaser of the booklet, who, unaware of its scarcity and potential value, put it up for sale on the internet.

Finally, among the early works is a two-in-one volume bearing the somewhat over-weighted title *Full and Authentic Account of the Murder by Henry Wainwright, of His Mistress Harriet Lane and An Extended Account of the Whitechapel Murders by the Infamous Jack the Ripper*.

Issued around 1895 by the Beaver Publishing Company of Toronto, it was the first and flagship volume in a new series, *Chronicles of Crime and Criminals*, whose avowed intent it was that 'the truth will be strictly adhered to, and every story given can be relied upon as strictly authentic'.

The first seventeen pages of the composite volume recount the details of five cases of murder and dismemberment, three in London, one in Paris, and one in Norwich.

The remaining pages are virtually a reprint of *The History of the Whitechapel Murders*, as published seven years before by Mr Fox of New York.

It was not only in England and America that early scribes were at work conscientiously recording every scrap of information – and misinformation – that they could garner about Whitechapel Jack.

Witness the testimony of the renowned journalist of the day, George R. Sims. In an article, 'My Criminal Museum: Who Was Jack the Ripper?', in *Lloyd's Weekly Newspaper*, 22 September 1902, he wrote,

> I have, while travelling abroad purchased in various languages pamphlets and booklets on Jack the Ripper, more or less of the catchpenny order … In 1889, a year after the last of the murders, I was in a little town in the south of Italy … I bought … the red-covered penny dreadful … *Jack Il Terrible Squartatore Di Donne*, which gave detailed and lurid account in Italian of the crimes of the Whitehall fiend.

In the dawn days of the first post-Ripperine century the Danes took a hand in the Whitechapel guessing game. It was, as a matter of fact, a Danish judge, Carl Muusmann, who, in 1908, published *Hvem Var Jack the Ripper? En Dansk Forhorsdommers Undersogelse* (*Who Was Jack the Ripper? A Danish Judge's Investigation*) with an illustration by Rasmus Christiansen, and published by Forhen A. Christiansens Forlag (Hermann-Petersen).

Its title notwithstanding, the principal concern of Muusmann's 102-page book seems to have been with the tale told to him by Hr Kattrup, who was Borgmester, mayor, and an assistant chief constable of Sorø, a town in Zealand, some 45 miles from Copenhagen; that is to say it is not so much to do with any personal investigation that he had made into the Jack the Ripper crimes as with 'What the Borgmester told the Judge'.

It centres upon the murder of a twenty-year-old prostitute, Karoline Metz, at No. 36 Calle de Corrientes, in Buenos Aires, on 25 July 1876. Two days before that (i.e. 23 July), a traveller, Alois Szemeredy, moved suddenly from the Hotel de Provence to the Hotel de Rome, claiming that he had had money, rings and other valuables stolen from his room at the Provence.

Two years later, this same Szemeredy was arrested for the murder of Karoline Metz, put on trial, found guilty, and sentenced to death. He appealed, and, in September 1881, his appeal was allowed. He was acquitted and released.

Immediately upon his return to Budapest, however, he was rearrested as an army deserter. He contrived, by skilful simulation of the Ganser syndrome[10] to hoodwink the doctors into declaring him insane, and tuck him cosily away in an asylum, instead of being forced to endure the rigours and discomforts of prison life.

It was not long thereafter that he was released into the care of his relatives, an arrangement which did not at all suit him, and he promptly sought, and found, a doctor who would declare him to have recovered his complete sanity.

Interviewed in 1886 by the consul-general of Vienna, Dr Gotthelf-Meyer, Szemeredy affirmed that as a young man he had been a medical student and had served as an army doctor in Europe, and later in a similar capacity with the Argentinian forces. He had claimed to be a Hungarian-American. A rumoured past history had him also employing his bogus medical qualifications practically, arranging the timeous demise of rich relatives for impecunious heirs in waiting. It was somewhat picturesquely said that the route of his travels from one South American farm to another was marked along its length by an avenue of tombstones.

In view of Muusmann's conviction that Szemeredy was the Whitechapel slaughterer, Dr Gotthelf-Meyers' description of his appearance two years before the first strike of the Ripper's knife is of interest and significance. 'A tall, thin man, about forty-five years old. His face had a healthy tan. He had brown, smoothly brushed hair, a thick and unusually beautiful moustache covering the mouth completely. The lips were very sensual. The eyes were small and gimlet. The hands were big, sinewy and well-shaped.'

But was Szemeredy ever in London? To this vital question the Austrian police president in Vienna gave a bizarre reply. Producing two police forms completed by Szemeredy, he said that in both forms he calls himself an American surgeon, he gives his age as forty-nine, his religion as Catholic, his condition as single, and, on the second form, he filled in his proposed destination as America. As to 'whether he went to England instead to commit the crime detected in Whitechapel on 12 September [*sic*], I cannot say, but it is curious that on his later visit to Vienna, in 1892, he described himself as "a sausage maker".'[11]

From 11 February 1892, an unknown murderer had been ravaging Vienna and was responsible for the same sort of cloud of fear overhanging the city as had hung over London during those terrible autumn days of four years before, when Jack the Ripper was plying his unpredictable knife.

Then, a merciful relief. A cutting from the Copenhagen morning newspaper of 3 October 1892.

> Vienna, 1 October, 1892
>
> In Prezburg a man named Szemeredy who is supposed to have committed the murder and murderous attacks from the beginning of the year to this date having kept all Vienna in fear, has been arrested.
>
> The police is [*sic*] of the opinion the person arrested who has already given a partial confession is identified to the once notorious woman-killer from London: Jack the Ripper.

Szemeredy, arrested and charged with murder and robbery, hanged himself on 1 October 1892.

The Borgmester lights his pipe and smiles. He harbours no discomfiting doubts that Szemeredy, 'who is of a vagabonding nature and an adventurer who has travelled around the world as an international swindler and thief, is the long sought after Jack the Ripper who has finally fallen into the arms of the police'.

The judge is, perhaps, well … rather more … judicial.[12]

After the publication of Muusmann's book there followed a five-year silence. Jack had slipped out of fashion. Having said which, one must never forget the effect produced when, in 1913, Mrs Marie Belloc Lowndes brought out a purely fictional reprise of the Ripper case in the form of a novel, *The Lodger*, which was a much elongated version of a short story that she had contributed to *McClure's Magazine* (New York) in 1911. As a full-length novel it was a runaway success in both London and New York, and subsequently passed through some thirty-one editions in eighteen languages.

So far as books or smaller works dealing exclusively with Jack the Ripper are concerned, the best part of a decade was now to pass blank-paged until in the 1920s a threepenny pamphlet, *The Whitechapel Horrors: Being an Authentic Account of The Jack the Ripper Murders*, made its appearance under the imprint of the firm of Daisy Bank Publishing, of Manchester. Tom Robinson, its author, had been living in Whitechapel in 1888, so was able to import a first-hand, knife-edged knowledge – at least of the prevalent atmosphere – to his writing, although factually his contribution would seem more dubious, since he allots a seven-body count to Bloody Jack, including Emma Smith and Martha Tabram among his indubitable victims. Initially quite rightly sceptical as regards the authenticity of the Dear Boss letter, he later very much moderates his original opinion, and finally confesses to not having the faintest inkling as to who Jack's alter ego may have been.

William Le Queux, that most unreliable of reporters, who seems to have been at least touched with the Münchausen syndrome, published, in 1923, his volume of reminiscences, *Things I Know About Kings, Celebrities and Crooks*. Reverting to the days when he was on the staff of the *Globe*, and he and his fellow-journalists, Charles Hands and Lincoln Springfield, practically lived as a trio in Whitechapel, confecting lurid and picturesque accounts of their sporadically peripatetic neighbour, homicidal Jack, he 'reveals the actual identity of Jack the Ripper'. Who he? Why, he is none other than Dr Alexander Pedachenko, 'the greatest and boldest of all criminal lunatics'. Who says that it was him? Rasputin. What credence should we give to this? None! But once introduced Jack the Russian stuck fast. And multiplied, as we shall see.

6

Hardback Pioneers

It was not until 1929, forty-one years after the butchering of what is generally believed to have been the Ripper's last victim, poor Mary Jane Kelly, that the first full-length English hardback book to be devoted entirely to a study of the Whitechapel murders appeared.

This was *The Mystery of Jack the Ripper: The World's Greatest Crime Problem*. Written originally as a newspaper or magazine article, it was subsequently expanded into a book, published in 1929 by Messrs Hutchinson. My friend the late Joe Gaute described it as 'one of the first books to come on to my desk', when he joined the publishing house of Hutchinson. Little did he then realise how powerfully it was to initiate and influence the content of myriad future works of like genre, each of which has, over the years, set out to provide its own copyright solution to the dust-gathering conundrum.

Its author was Leonard Matters, an Australian, born in Adelaide on 26 June 1881. He began his journalistic career as a thirteen-year-old messenger boy on the *Perth Daily News*. By the age of twenty, he had graduated to chief Parliamentary correspondent. He fought as a volunteer in the second South African Boer War. He worked in Argentina, where he was managing editor of the *Buenos Aires Herald*. He travelled the world extensively as a freelance, and ended up in Britain, where he became the London representative of *Hindu*, South India's largest-circulation English-language newspaper. He also joined the Labour Party, and served as MP for Kennington, London, 1929–1931. He died on 31 October 1951.

Matters hadn't a clue as to Jack's identity, but, with admirable ingenuity, a journalist's imagination and a liberal powdering of chutzpah, conceived a theory which presented a superficial plausibility. His candidate-elect, straight from the realms of cloud-cuckoo-fairyland, was a Jekyll-and-Hyde medico, the 'Satanic Dr Stanley'. The motive supplied – revenge. Dr Stanley, an eminent London surgeon, had centred all his hopes upon the achievements which he envisaged for his only son, Herbert, a brilliant medical student. Tragically, the young man died of syphilis, contracted from Mary Jane Kelly. Thereafter, the bereaved father, his mind unhinged by grief, set out obsessionally to track down the woman Kelly. His method was to prowl the East End, enquiring of various street women as to Mary Jane's whereabouts, and, lest she should betray with subsequent gossiping the mission that he was pursuing, silencing each woman afterwards by killing her. After four failed attempts, it was eventually the fifth, Catherine Eddowes, who told him where to find Kelly. He visited her at 13 Miller's Court and in a furore of vengeance literally tore her apart. His mission successfully completed, the murders abruptly ceased. Here we are firmly ensconced in the territory of the imagination; witnesses to that which never was o'er land or sea, for not a shred of evidence can be adduced for the existence of the vengeful Dr Stanley. The entire artefact is a pretty exercise in romantic embroidery.

The American writer, Edmund Pearson, transatlantic clone and boon friend of the redoubtable William Roughead, was, in his *More Studies in Murder*, remarkably scathing about Matters' book, opining, 'The deathbed confession of Matters' culprit elect, "Dr Stanley", bears about the same relation to the facts of criminology as the exploits of Peter Rabbit and Jerry Muskrat do to Zoology.'

There was published in Paris in 1935 *Jack l'Éventreur: Scènes Vécues.*[13] The fruit of the pen of Jean Dorsenne, its basic facts derived from the French and English newspapers, it was no more than a fancifully wrought thriller, colourful, rhetorical, episodic, and slightly naive. It presented a selection of real facts and reality-based theories, but, essentially an artefact, lacked modern accuracy, and there is in it considerably more than a leavening of invention and dramatic licence, as well as an unfortunate confusion of names and dates. The framework is a dialogue, more of a monologue, between the first-person narrator, an enthusiastic thirties pioneer Ripperologist, and, in richly reminiscent mood, a surely fictive former Chief Constable, identified solely as G. W. H., living now in rose-embowered retirement in Yorkshire. After pouring scorn upon Leonard Matters, the ex-Chief Constable proceeds to add his own measure of mystification by stating that he had searched the records of doctors practising in London in 1888 and found one whose career seemed similar to that of 'Dr Stanley': his son, too, had died young, and he, the doctor, left the country towards the end of 1888, and was never heard of again. Other characters introduced are Hans Hochkiss, a boatman in Bombay, who made a deathbed confession of having been Jack the Ripper, killing women in Texas as well as in London, and Count Sardrouji or Sardrouk, pulled dead out of the Thames, who had among his possessions a pickled kidney.

The French had their own Jacques the Ripper. His name was Joseph Vâcher. Between 1894 and 1897 he murdered at least eleven people – five adolescent girls, five teenage boys, and a woman he disembowelled. This wandering vagabond and one-time soldier was born in Beaufort, near Lyons, in 1869. He exhibited early the serial killer's typical sadistic overture, breaking goats' legs for pleasure, before graduating to harming humans. The bloodied road which Vâcher had chosen to follow led to the Champs de Mars, in Bourg-en-Bresse, where, on the grey, heavy-clouded morning of bone-chilling sleet of 31 December 1898, the guillotine's knife put a sharp end to Vâcher's life. For months before his execution he had been the subject of extended study by Professor Alexandre Lacassagne, head of the department of Legal Medicine at the University of Lyons, trying to penetrate the complex of his thought processes. But, for all his most strenuous efforts, Lacassagne failed to solve the mystery of what motivated Vâcher.[14]

The year 1935 saw the appearance of R. Thurston Hopkins' book *Life and Death at the Old Bailey*, which contained two important new items for the gleaning.

The first is very likely a reference to Tom Bulling, a London journalist of the 1880s,[15] employed by the Central London News agency in 1888:

> It was perhaps a fortunate thing that the handwriting of this famous (Dear Boss) letter was not identified, for it would have led to the arrest of a harmless Fleet Street journalist. This poor fellow had a breakdown and became a whimsical figure in Fleet Street, only befriended by the staffs of

newspapers and printing works. He would creep about the dark courts waving his hands furiously in the air, would utter stentorian 'Ha, ha, ha's,' and then, meeting some pal, would button-hole him and pour into his ear all the 'inner story' of the East End murders. Many old Fleet Streeters had very shrewd suspicions that this irresponsible fellow wrote the famous Jack the Ripper letter, and even Sir Melville L. Macnaghten, Chief of the Criminal Investigation Department (CID) had his eye on him. Sir Melville, writing in 1914, remarked: 'In this ghastly production I have always thought I could discern the stained forefinger of the journalist – indeed a year later I had shrewd suspicions as to the actual author.'

The second refers to a poet of whom Hopkins writes that he was 'one of Mary Kelly's friends'. Hopkins' long paragraph vignette opines that George Hutchinson's description of the man he saw Mary Kelly take back with her to Miller's Court fits his poet friend, to whom he gives the name of 'Mr Moring'. But the poet, his 'poor devil-driven opium-smoking' haunter of the taverns around the East End', had black lank hair and the dark face of the typical bard, and was 'a man of such extraordinary gentleness' that he could not have been the one to commit such a dreadful series of murders.

Regarding the identity of Hopkins' poet: in 1888, twenty-two-year-old Ernest Dowson was both assisting his father in the family's failing East End docking (as in mooring!) business and fast establishing himself in the influential aesthetic whirl which was to reach its apogee in *The Yellow Book*. Arthur Symons wrote of him that 'there never was a simpler or more attaching charm, because there never was a sweeter or more honest nature.' Symons also said, 'Under the influence of drink, he became almost literally insane, certainly quite irresponsible. He fell into furious and unreasoning passions … he seemed always about to commit some act of absurd violence.' A curious love of the sordid grew upon him, he drifted about in whatever company came his way. Putting the pieces together, one asks, can Mr Moring be Hopkins' thinly disguised Ernest Dowson? And was Mary Kelly the 'friend' satisfying his sexual preference? Such is Mr Hopkins' dark little conundrum.

The next chronological production was a 1937 pre-Paperback Revolution paperback. The work of Edwin T. Woodhall, 'a detective turned author', it was titled *Jack the Ripper: Or, When London Walked in Terror*. He offered us Sex-Change Jack, his Ripper being presented as a Russian damsel in distress, Olga Tchkersoff, who, like Matters' Satanic Dr Stanley, is out for revenge, her prostitute sister having been brought to a sticky end. It need not detain us long. Badly written, shoddily researched, grossly inaccurate, it contributes nothing of importance.

The Jill the Ripper theme is also the somewhat feeble hypothesis at the heart of William Stewart's 1939 offering, *Jack the Ripper: A New Theory*. Stewart, a Brixton artist turned author, cherished a sadistic midwife, her name unknown, as the Whitechapel Fiendess. He is a little vague as to her precise motivation, but makes a brave try with the theory that the midwife had at some time been imprisoned for carrying out abortions. Information had been laid against her by a prostitute whom she had once helped out of a little difficulty, and she was revenging herself against women of the same class as her betrayer. Again, the solution, carefully thought out as it is, stems from the intricacies of imagination, and is without a jot of supporting evidence.

As it came to pass, these two books – Woodhall's and Stewart's – were, as we shall see, a fount of much misinformation, which was in due course to appear in later works by other, copyist, authors.

It is to the dedicated fossicking of that intrepid researcher Andy Aliffe that we owe the revelation of George Bernard Shaw's marginalia on Jack the Ripper. He discloses that in March 1939, William Stewart, because of sundry references which he had made to Shaw in its pages, despatched to G. B. S. a proof copy of his book. In the fullness of time Shaw returned the proof, embellished with succinct marginal notations.

On the title-page Shaw wrote in that famed and crabbed hand, 'It does not matter now who committed the murders. The revival of the subject may possibly excite somebody to repeat them, and cannot do any good that I can imagine. I have made a note on page 140. G. B. S. 17/3/39.'

On page 140 Stewart had written, 'He [Shaw] professed, with true Irish unaccountability, to hold the view that the reason of the murders was to focus attention on the appalling condition of the poor in the East End.'

Shaw ran lines through the text and wrote in the margin, 'Utter nonsense. My article was on the East End charities, and not on the murders, though it used them as an illustration.'

And on page 141, Shaw crossed out Stewart's text – 'How … Shaw thought that Jack the Ripper would be identified by the creation of a Shavian Utopia is a mystery surpassing in profundity that of Jack the Ripper' – and wrote in the margin, 'The article had nothing to do with the identification of Jack the Ripper.'

In *The Harlot Killer*, his 1953 collection of thirteen reprinted semi-fictional tales of Jack the Ripper, written between 1911 and 1951, thus did Allan Barnard, the volume's editor, set the stage for 'Flash-Knifed Jack':

> London's East End in 1888 was one slovenly, crowded district pushed against another, each made up of short, dead-end streets and alleys which ran like dry moats alongside its shabby buildings. Deep in the most miserable part of all this lay Whitechapel, adjoining Spitalfields and Bethnal Green, more than a square mile of poverty and degeneracy, a Babylon of criminals and near-criminals, drunkards, vagrants, thrill-seekers, and the innocent poor, a squalid bazaar of prostitutes come from all over England.

In 1959, Donald McCormick published *The Identity of Jack the Ripper*. The solution that he proposed postulated a Russian killer, Dr Alexander Pedachenko. The sources of his inspiration appear to be fourfold.

Firstly, he has consulted – indirectly – certain private writings of Sir Melville Macnaghten, whose public utterances on the subject, contained in his book of memoirs, *Days of My Years*, we have already considered. In February 1894, however, reacting to a series of articles published in the *Sun* newspaper, in which a mentally deranged fetishist named Thomas Cutbush was unequivocally identified as the Ripper, Macnaghten, apparently smarting at the injustice of the assertion, sat down and wrote a seven-folio memorandum for official eyes only, which he then slipped into the unclosed Ripper file at the Yard.

Seemingly, eyes other than those of officialdom were permitted to see the memorandum, for in his *Mysteries of Police and Crime* Major Arthur Griffiths, amateur criminologist and a friend of Macnaghten's, was able to print almost verbatim the material part of the text, omitting only the actual names of three possible suspects mentioned by Macnaghten.

Griffiths writes,

> The police, after the last murder, had brought their investigations to the point of strongly suspecting several persons, all of them known to be homicidal lunatics, and against three of these they held very plausible and reasonable grounds of suspicion. Concerning two of them the case was weak … One was a Polish Jew, a known lunatic, who was at large in the district of Whitechapel at the time of the murders, and who, having afterwards developed homicidal tendencies, was confined to an asylum. The second possible criminal was a Russian doctor, also insane, who had been a convict both in England and Siberia. This man was in the habit of carrying about surgical knives and instruments in his pockets; his antecedents were of the very worst, and at the time of the Whitechapel murders he was in hiding, or, at least, his whereabouts were never exactly known. The third person was of the same type, but the suspicion in his case was stronger, and there was every reason to believe that his own

friends entertained grave doubts about him. He also was a doctor in the prime of life, was believed to be insane, or on the borderland of insanity, and he disappeared immediately after the last murder, that in Miller's Court, on 9 November 1888. On the last day of that year, seven weeks later, his body was found floating in the Thames, and was said to have been in the water a month.

McCormick selected Suspect No. 2, the Russian doctor, from this trio.

His second source, albeit subsidiary, was that curious book by William Le Queux, *Things I Know about Kings, Celebrities and Crooks* (1923). In it, Le Queux, who had assisted the British Government as a secret agent in the First World War, claimed that he had discovered the manuscript of a book written – in French – by Rasputin, entitled 'Great Russian Criminals', in which it was disclosed that the Whitechapel murderer was a Dr Alexander Pedachenko, who had served on the staff of the Maternity Hospital at Tver, and lived on the second floor of a building in Millionnaya Street, in the central district of St Petersburg. He had gone to London, where he lived with his sister in Westmorland (*sic*) Road, Walworth. From there he sallied forth at night, took an omnibus across London Bridge, and walked to Whitechapel, where he committed his secret crimes.

Le Queux, claiming to quote from the Rasputin manuscript, writes,

> London was horrified by the evil work of a mysterious criminal known as 'Jack the Ripper,' who killed and mutilated a number of women of ill-repute in the East End of the capital. The repetition of the appalling crimes mystified the world. The true author of these atrocities was a member of the Jubilee Street Club, the Anarchist Centre in the East of London. One night in the club the identity of 'Jack the Ripper' was disclosed by a Russian, well known in London, named Nideroest, a spy of our secret police. The identity had been revealed to him by an old Russian Anarchist, Nicholas Zverieff. The mysterious assassin was Pedachenko, according to Zverieff – whose record appears in the reports of the Secret Police – aided by a friend of his named Levitski, and a young tailoress, called Winberg. The latter would approach the victim and hold her in conversation and Levitski kept watch for the police patrols, while the crimes and mutilations took place. Levitski, who had been born in London, wrote the warning post-cards signed 'Jack the Ripper' to the Police and the Press. It was through Levitski that Zverieff knew the truth. Our Secret Police … had themselves actively aided and encouraged the crimes, in order to exhibit to the world certain defects of the English police system…
>
> It was, indeed, for that reason that Pedachenko, the greatest and boldest of all Russian criminal lunatics, was encouraged to go to London and commit that series of atrocious crimes … Eventually, at the orders of the Ministry of the Interior the Secret Police smuggled the assassin out of London, and as Count Luiskovo he landed at Ostend, and was conducted by a secret service agent to Moscow. While there he was, a few months later, caught red-handed attempting to murder and mutilate a woman named Vogak and was eventually sent to an asylum, where he died in 1908. After the return to Russia of Levitski and the woman Winberg the Secret Police deemed it wise to suppress them, and they were therefore exiled to Yakutsk. Such are the actual facts of the 'Jack the Ripper Mystery' which still puzzles the whole world.

Le Queux's reputation for veracity has not survived untarnished.

McCormick's third source was Dr Thomas Dutton's diary for the year 1924, which he claims that he was fortunate enough to see in 1932, before the doctor's papers disappeared. In it, Dutton had, so says McCormick, noted: 'What Le Queux should have found out was that Pedachenko worked as a barber-surgeon in Westmoreland Road, Walworth, in 1888.'

Fourthly, and finally, McCormick asserts that the late Prince Belloselski showed him a copy of the Russian Secret Police bulletin, the *Ochrana Gazette*, dated January 1909, containing this item:

KONOVALOV, VASILY, alias PEDACHENKO, Alexei alias LUISKOVO, Andrey, formerly of Tver, is now officially declared to be dead … A man answering to the description of the above who was wanted for the murder of a woman in the Montmartre district of Paris in 1886, of the murder of five women in the East Quarter of London in 1888 and again of the murder of a woman in Petrograd in 1891 … Known to disguise himself as [a] woman on occasions and was arrested when in woman's clothes in Petrograd before his detention in the asylum where he died.

On the face of it, McCormick's solution has much to recommend it, but, as with the other most likely solution, propounded by Tom Cullen, in his *Autumn of Terror* (1965) – seconded by Daniel Farson, in his *Jack the Ripper* (1972) – which solution we shall presently examine, the final clinching evidence simply does not come up to proof.

Robin Odell's *Jack the Ripper in Fact and Fiction* (1965) and Tom Cullen's *Autumn of Terror*, published within a matter of days of each other, provided, like the Ripper on 30 September, a double event.

With *Autumn of Terror* we seem at first to be on firmer ground. By some means which are not entirely clear, Cullen succeeds in producing, like a conjurer's rabbit out of a Victorian gibus, the name of Montague John Druitt. The context is that official and secret memorandum of Sir Melville Macnaghten's. Cullen supplies the names that Major Griffiths was obliged to suppress. The Polish Jew was Kosminski. The insane Russian doctor was Michael Ostrog. The third person was M. J. Druitt, who is described in Macnaghten's alleged words as 'a doctor of about 41 years of age and of fairly good family … [whose] body was said to have been in the water for a month, or more – on it was found a season ticket between Blackheath and London. From private information I have little doubt but that his own family suspected this man of being the Whitechapel murderer; and it was alleged that he was sexually insane.'

Primed with this completely new information, Cullen set forth in quest of Druitt.

PART 2
THE TERRIBLE HARVESTER:
THE PROPOSED IDENTITIES OF
JACK THE RIPPER

They sought him here, they sought him there,
They sought the Ripper everywhere,
Was he …

7

Jack the Wig: Montague John Druitt

The emergence upon the scene of Montague John Druitt, Barrister-at-Law and prime Ripper suspect, is, like the widespread belief that Jack the Ripper committed suicide after the murder of his supposedly fifth victim, Mary Jane Kelly, attributable to the sole agency of Sir Melville Macnaghten. Although in the official memorandum that he wrote in 1894 there is nothing to single this man out from the three possible suspects whom he named therein, it has been severally stated that Sir Melville's daughter, Christabel, the Dowager Lady Aberconway, had retained in her possession a variant and seemingly somewhat fuller version of those notes.

In 1959, Lady Aberconway showed them to Daniel Farson, who was at that time engaged in research for a television programme about Jack the Ripper. Whereas in his official memorandum Macnaghten expressed no personal conviction as to the pre-eminent guilt of Druitt, it is alleged that in his private papers on the subject he did so most vehemently. Both Daniel Farson and Tom Cullen ascribe these strong sentiments to him:

> I enumerate the cases of 3 men against whom Police held very reasonable suspicion (Druitt, Kosminski and Ostrog). Personally, after much careful & deliberate consideration, I am inclined to exonerate the last 2, but I have always held strong opinions regarding the no. 1, and the more I think the matter over, the stronger do those opinions become. The *truth*, however, will never be known, and did indeed, at one time lie at the bottom of the Thames, if my conjections [*sic*] be correct.

Whether or not Lady Aberconway showed these notes also to Cullen is not recorded, but he certainly came up with Druitt's name. It may be that he did so by approaching the problem from another angle, by seeking the identity of any man whose body was taken from the Thames on or about the last day of 1888 (as reported in Major Griffiths' *Mysteries of Police and Crime*). In any event, he succeeded in tracing reports in the *County of Middlesex Independent* of 2 and 5 January 1889 concerning the death by drowning of a man, subsequently identified as Montague John Druitt, whose water-soaked corpse was found floating in the Thames at Chiswick. The pockets of the deceased were loaded with a number of stones.

The *Southern Guardian* of 5 January added the details that Druitt, a barrister, was identified by his brother, a Bournemouth solicitor, who said that the dead man had recently been employed as an assistant at a school in Blackheath, and that he had left a letter addressed to Mr Valentine, the principal of the school, in which he alluded to suicide. On his body was found a cheque for £50, together with the sum of £16 in gold. The jury returned a verdict of 'suicide whilst of unsound mind'. The funeral took place at Wimborne Cemetery, Dorset, on the afternoon of 3 January 1889.

Working from these clues, Cullen proceeded to establish the historical facts of Montague John Druitt's life. He was born at Wimborne on 15 August 1857, the second son of Wimborne's leading surgeon, William Druitt. At the age of thirteen he won a scholarship to Winchester College, where he made his mark as a first-rate cricketer and debater. In 1876, he was awarded a Winchester Scholarship to New College, Oxford.

The early concept of Druitt as a failed barrister turned to schoolmastering has proved false. The truth is that he had been employed since 1880, when he came down from Oxford with a Class III BA *Lit. Hum.*, as an assistant at a private school, or 'cramming shop', run by George Valentine at 9 Eliot Place, Blackheath, cramming boys for entrance examinations to the universities, the professions, and the Army.

It was while continuing to act as an assistant master at Blackheath that Druitt decided to read for the Bar, borrowing against a £500 expected legacy from his father to finance his studies for a second career. He was admitted to the Inner Temple on 17 May 1882, was called on 29 April 1885, went into Arthur Jelf's Chambers at 9 King's Bench Walk, and joined the Western Circuit and Winchester Sessions. The following September his father died, leaving him very little money from an estate of £16,579.

In 1887, Druitt was recorded as a special pleader for the Western Circuit and Hampshire, Portsmouth and Southampton Assizes. Special pleaders were members of an Inn of Court who devoted themselves mainly to the drawing of pleadings and to attending at Judges' Chambers. The special pleader would also give verbal or written opinions upon statements submitted to him. That his legal career was far from unsuccessful is shown by the fact that at his death he left estate valued at £2,600, which amount was well in excess of his father's legacy to him, plus a posthumous inheritance of £1,083 from his mother, and his earnings as a dominie.

He had last been seen alive on Monday 3 December 1888. Shortly after his suicide, his mother, Ann Druitt, was admitted to Manor House, an upper-class private asylum under the proprietorship of Dr Harrington Tuke at Chiswick. She died there, aged fifty-nine, on 15 December 1890. The cause of death shown on her death certificate is 'melancholia' and 'brain disease, 21 months'.[1]

All this makes sad reading, but where is the necessary connection with Whitechapel and the Ripper murders? Cullen is reduced to theorising. Did Druitt, perhaps, answer a call of conscience to do social work in the East End, as so many of his cohort modishly did? Was he by chance, to be found at Toynbee Hall? There is no evidence on this score. And the murder motive? A kind of mercy killing! Groping, Cullen suggests that the young man, his mind 'pushed to the edge of insanity by the sights around him in London's East End', overwhelmed by a sense of hopelessness and futility, might, out of 'a passion for righteousness', or a sense of sin, have conceived it as his mission to call attention to these evils – and, his mind warped by 'the mercy which can be angry as well as pitiful', have seen it as his plain duty to strike down his pathetic victims. Then, the good deed zealously done, hurry back, bloody of body and cleansed of heart, to the privacy of his chambers in King's Bench Walk, all of 2 miles away.

It won't do. It simply won't do. Cullen himself admits that his hypothesis leaves a trail of questions – explicit and implicit. What were the contents of the letter Druitt left behind? Did it contain a confession of murder? Can Druitt be *shown* to have had connections with

Whitechapel? Why did Macnaghten suspect him so strongly? Questions were to hang in the air for another seven years before, as we shall see, Daniel Farson came confidently forward to answer some of them.

Seizing the opportunities presented by the publication of revised editions of their respective books, Robin Odell, in 1966, and Donald McCormick, in 1970, brought their critical acumen to bear on Cullen's conclusions.

Odell's immediate objection was that the Druitt solution is based on the unquestioning acceptance of the theory that Jack the Ripper committed suicide. It is not, he maintains, confirmed by the behaviour of the police as a whole. The only warrant for thinking suspiciously about a man called Druitt lies in Sir Melville Macnaghten's notes, and we have no data regarding the nature of the private information that convinced him.

Donald McCormick's rejection of the drowned barrister theory follows along much the same lines as Odell's. He points out that Cullen turns up no new evidence – other than that at the time of the Ripper crimes a man named Druitt was still occupying his chambers in the Temple, within walking distance of the East End. Further, McCormick states categorically that on the occasions of the murders of both Mary Ann Nichols and Annie Chapman, Druitt was living in Bournemouth. His authority for this is 'a London doctor' (unnamed). This doctor, McCormick tells us, knew Walter Sickert, the artist. The London doctor's father, also a doctor, was at Oxford with Druitt. The London doctor's father believed that the story about Druitt's being the Ripper arose because the young barrister was blackmailed by someone (unnamed) who threatened to denounce him to the principal of the school at which he worked as Jack the Ripper; whether as a heartless hoax, or as a cruel method of extorting money from him, was not specified. There was nothing seriously wrong with Druitt, but he suffered from insomnia and blackouts, and these threats preyed on his mind. He may, under severe stress, have given a garbled account of the threats to his relatives. The gold on his body could have been intended to pay off the blackmailer. Sickert is said to have told the nameless London doctor that the name of the young veterinary student who lodged in Mornington Crescent and was suspected by his landlord of being the Ripper was something like Drewett or Hewitt. Sickert also said that he told the story to Macnaghten one day at the Garrick Club, and that Sir Melville was convinced it must be Druitt because he had relatives living in Bournemouth, just as the veterinary student was said to have had.

8

Jack the Witness: George Hutchinson

The late Brian Marriner, writing in the October 1966 issue of the quarterly crime magazine *Murder Most Foul* (London), presenting what was essentially a very personal point of view at that time, named Jack the Ripper.

'Your actual Jack the Ripper,' he announced, 'was George Hutchinson.' His witness statement passed muster with the police of 1888, but read today against a background knowledge of serial killers, it 'reeks with guilt'.

George Hutchinson, a twenty-eight-year-old labourer, several weeks unemployed at the time of the Miller's Court murder, a man who lived at the Victoria Working Men's Home, a Commercial Street lodging-house, a mere 300 yards from Kelly's crib, a man who knew Mary Jane comparatively well, the man who was the last known person to see her alive, was also the witness who did not come forward to the police until three days after Kelly's death.

Finally, he made his statement, after walking into Commercial Street Police Station at 6 p.m. on Monday 12 November 1888, the day of the Kelly inquest.

This tardiness he explained by saying that he had only visited a police station at all because a fellow-lodger had thought that it would be advisable. But it is nonetheless a fact that by this action Hutchinson made the transition from potential suspect (fingered by Sarah Lewis) to valued voluntary witness, throwing in for good measure a minutely delineated description of a Jewish-looking gentleman – changed in contemporary published reports to 'foreign-looking', influenced perhaps by police-inspired sensitive politic reasons.

It was Marriner's belief that Hutchinson, wearing 'a mask of sanity', would have looked quite ordinary, quite normal, but four questions give him pause:

> Why did Hutchinson spy on Kelly and her companion for a full three-quarters of an hour at 2 a.m. on a dark, wet, cold November morning?
>
> Why, if he had such an obsessive interest in Kelly that he spent so long spying on her, was he seemingly indifferent to her terrible fate?
>
> Why had he walked past his lodging-house to meet her?
>
> Why was he able to give such an incredibly detailed description (down to the colour of his eyelashes) of a man seen at night, albeit with the aid of a gas lamp?

Was Hutchinson's a true story?

Marriner hazards two possible explanations for his having lied in such meticulously concocted detail. It could have been to explain away his own presence in the vicinity, where he had been seen loitering outside Miller's Court by the witness Sarah Lewis. Or it could have been to get publicity and the consequent chance of earning a few shillings by giving interviews, which he did, to newspaper reporters. In this context, Marriner points out the odd fact that, although there was quite a considerable cash reward on offer for information leading to the capture of the killer, Hutchinson, down on his luck, out of work, seems nevertheless to have balked at the idea of putting himself forward for the reward money. He also points out that all the Ripper murders were committed within easy reach of the Victoria Home. He is sufficiently fair, though, to further point out that Abberline, a policeman of vast experience, who was the officer on the ground, who interviewed and interrogated Hutchinson on a number of occasions, and whose eyes were not susceptible to wool, actually said, 'I am of opinion that his statement is true.'

Graciously acknowledging that, although he (Marriner) has not seen among the dozens of books and hundreds of articles written about Jack the Ripper one that names Hutchinson as a prime suspect, 'Paul Begg mentions the possibility in his *Jack the Ripper: The Uncensored Facts* (1988).' But even so, admits Marriner, Begg 'finally puts the case against Aaron Kosminski [*sic*].'

Unabashed, Marriner concludes with an invitation: 'Read Hutchinson's statement again. They are the words of a ruthless, cunning killer: the words of Jack the Ripper.'

9

Royal Jack: The Duke of Clarence

In November 1970, the Ripper guessing game took a new and completely unexpected turn when a retired surgeon in his mid-eighties, Thomas Edmund Alexander Stowell, published an article, 'Jack the Ripper – a Solution?' in the *Criminologist*.

He took the precaution of denoting his suspect only by the letter 'S' – presumably for 'Suspect' – but from the amplificatory descriptive material the identity of the man has been accepted as Albert Victor Christian Edward, Duke of Clarence, who, but for his early death in 1892, would have succeeded to the throne of England.

The basis for this extraordinary nomination was said to be the private papers of Sir William Withey Gull (1816–90), physician-in-ordinary to Queen Victoria, which were entrusted to Stowell by Sir William's widow. Stowell claimed that Gull had recorded in them that S., that is to say the Duke, had not in fact died of influenza, as had been publicly given out, but that he had been kept in a private asylum near Sandringham, suffering from 'softening of the brain due to syphilis', and prior to his incarceration, he had for some years been in Sir William's professional care.

Stowell states that on more than one occasion Gull was seen in Whitechapel on the night of one of the murders, and hazards that he was there for the purpose of certifying the murderer insane in the event of his being caught, so that he might be put under restraint and an international scandal be averted. He adds that Gull's ubiquitous presence did not go unmarked, and that he was the illustrious surgeon who, the rumour-mongers whispered, was the Ripper. And the old story of the medium, Robert James Lees, conducting the police to the 'impressive mansion in the West End' which was the house of a 'fashionable and highly reputable physician', is revived.[2] Was it, Stowell asks, 74 Brook Street, Grosvenor Square, the home of Sir William Gull? Had the secret of his sinister patient leaked out? Or had the roles of doctor and patient become confused, so that the one was mistakenly held responsible for the irresponsible deeds of the other?

The stir of publicity following Stowell's revelation prompted his swift refusal to confirm that the Royal Duke was the suspect he had in mind, and, before the matter could be pursued further, on 8 November 1970, Stowell died. His son, distressed by the whole business, let it be known that he had destroyed all of his late father's papers on the subject, and there the matter had perforce to rest.

Few responsible criminologists saw in Stowell's contribution the true solution which he believed that he had provided.

Two years later, in 1972, Michael Harrison produced a biography of the Duke of Clarence – *Clarence: The Life of H.R.H. the Duke of Clarence and Avondale, (1864–1892)* – in which he makes it perfectly clear that the Duke could not have been the Ripper.

But Harrison thinks he knows who was. It was, he says, the Duke's homosexual friend, lover perhaps, and tutor, James Kenneth Stephen, first cousin to Virginia Woolf and Vanessa Bell, and second son of Sir James Fitzjames Stephen (1829–94), the High Court judge who presided over the trial of Mrs Maybrick in 1889, and who himself suffered latterly from some form of dementia.

Harrison's arguments for James the Ripper make up in aerial ingenuity for what they lack in down-to-earth substance. He claims that there were ten Ripper murders, and links them with a bawdy ballad, 'Kaphoozelum', known to Stephen, and containing the, for Harrison, significant lines:

> Struck down each year and tolled the bell
> For ten harlots of Jerusalem.

So, with much more recondite comparative analysis of the jingles whose authorship has, on somewhat shaky ground, been attributed to the Ripper, and the published poems of J. K. Stephen, Harrison develops his theory of internal rhymes and correlated external reasons.

He suggests that the jilting of the infatuated Stephen by the inconstant Eddy finally broke a mind that was already fragile, and that the East End murders were symbolic blood-sacrifices of women (for was it not women who had finally seduced his beloved Eddy away from him?) at the altar of his ruined passion.

One small corrective.

Harrison has written that Mary Jane Kelly's funeral was paid for by the Reverend Harry Wilson, Vicar of St Augustine's, Stepney, who was 'uncle to both Henry Francis Wilson, the friend of Eddy, and Harry Wilson, the solicitor. Once again a Wilson, on behalf of that mad Ripper whose identity all the Wilsons seem to have known, stepped in to do what small thing he could to make amends for crimes that he could have done nothing to prevent and that, in all justice, they could not seek to punish.'

In conversation with me, Stephen Knight had said that Kelly's posthumous benefactor was in fact Henry Wilton, who had been verger of the parish church, St Leonard's, Shoreditch, since 1849, and also keeper of the Shoreditch Mortuary.

The contemporary newspapers tell the same story.

The *Star*, 13 November 1888, reported:

> The burial of the victim of the murder-maniac has been settled by several private persons coming forward to pay the expense. A local undertaker has offered to make the coffin and superintend the arrangements without fee, and two of the jurors are prepared to pay for a hearse and coach if the undertaker's offer is accepted.[3]

The *Echo* of 19 November 1888 said, 'The funeral was conducted by Mr H. Wilton, of Shoreditch, whose premises adjoin the church.'

The Times, on 20 November 1888, noted, 'Henry Wilton … is bearing the cost of the interment. If the public wish to bear any share in the expense they can send their subscriptions to Mr Wilton at the church. Should there be a surplus a tombstone would be erected.'

And the *East London Advertiser*, 24 November 1888, stated,

> But it remained for Mr H. Wilton, the sexton attached to Shoreditch Church, to put sympathy into a practical form, and as no relatives have appeared he incurred the total cost of the funeral himself. Mr Wilton has been sexton for over 50 years and he provided the funeral as a mark of sincere sympathy with the poor people of the neighbourhood, in whose welfare he is deeply interested.

Harrison's book is essential reading, but it does not seem possible to accept his *recherché* conclusions with anything approaching the confidence that its author reposes in them.

10

Jack and Jill the Ripper: The Midwife

At the end of August 1972, in a series of articles in the *Sun* newspaper, ex-Detective Chief Superintendent Arthur Butler lifted the veil to reveal … Jill the Ripper. Not a lone she-wolf, but provided with a male partner. Butler's proposition was that a local woman abortionist living in or near Brick Lane, Whitechapel, accidentally killed four women in the course of procuring abortions, and that she disposed of their bodies by wheeling them, Mary Eleanor

Pearcey fashion, in a perambulator to the spots where they were found. The bodies were mutilated *post mortem*, in the particular way in which they were, in order to disguise the fact that a bungled abortion had taken place. The fifth woman, Elisabeth Stride, unmutilated, does not fit the pattern, an inconvenience surmounted by Butler's submission that she was not in fact a Ripper victim. By way of compensation, he adds two more women – Emma Smith and Martha Tabram – to the tally of Ripper killings. These twain were murdered, not by Jill, but by Jack, her noxious accomplice, to silence them because they knew too much.

This was far from being the first time that a Ripper of the species described by Kipling as 'more deadly than the male' had been punted.

William Stewart pioneered at full book's length the novel notion of Jack the Sadistic Midwife back in 1939. It has, as a matter of record, been sporadically reported, and widely believed over the years, that Conan Doyle had thought it likely that the Ripper was a midwife. This is not quite correct. Michael Coren presents the facts more accurately in his 1995 biography of Doyle. 'He thought that the culprit might have dressed himself as a midwife and thus gone unnoticed through the streets of the East End of London because it was expected that a midwife would rush from house to house covered in blood, carrying a surgical bag.' Coren adds: 'He (Doyle) even went a step further opining that the murderer could be a woman.' Coren does not supply a source for this step further, but appends the observation that, 'This Jill-the-Ripper hypothesis had caused Doyle more than a little embarrassment.'

It is surely only fitting that the creator of Sherlock Holmes should have shown an interest in the three-pipe-plus problem of the Whitechapel Fiend, for the Ripper crimes took place in the very year that Holmes made his first bow between hard covers, in *A Study in Scarlet*.[4]

It was on Friday 2 December 1892 that Doyle, in company with his brother-in-law, Ernest William Hornung, creator of Raffles; the amateur gentleman cracksman, Dr Gilbert, the medical officer at Newgate; and Jerome K. Jerome, celebrated author of *Three Men in a Boat*, paid a visit to the Black Museum at Scotland Yard. And there, in the ill-lit, chill and cheerless basement room that housed the grisly collection of relics of decades of crimes and criminals past, among the hangmen's noosed ropes and death masks of the hanged, the burglar's tools of trade, the captured counterfeiter's apparatus of his art, the bludgeons, guns, and secret poisoners' phials, the artefacts of sudden and unceremonious death, the exhibits that captured Doyle's interested fancy most were a letter and a postcard, written in red ink and signed 'Jack the Ripper'.

Thirteen years later, on 19 April 1905, Doyle was to walk very much closer to, indeed in the veritable footsteps of, the Ripper. This satisfying adventure came about because of his membership of Our Society, originally designated The Crimes Club, a select private dining club for those cherishing a deep interest in what the late William Roughead would have called matters criminous. That dark, wet and gloomy Wednesday afternoon a party of club members, which included H. B. Irving, the actor and author son of Sir Henry Irving; Dr Samuel Ingleby Oddie, the future Central London Coroner; Dr Herbert Crosse; Professor Churton Collins, occupant of the Chair of English at Birmingham University and a walking encyclopedia of criminological information; and Conan Doyle met at the Police Hospital in Bishopsgate. Ingleby Oddie had arranged with Dr Frederick Gordon Brown a visit to the scenes of the murders. Brown, one of the doctors called to Mitre Square to examine the body of Catherine Eddowes, had actually performed the subsequent post-mortem upon her. He, along with three City of London Police detectives familiar with the details of the crimes, was to conduct the expedition.

A mere seventeen years since the high rip rubric days of slick-knifed Jack, Whitechapel had changed little. Visiting one after another the scenes of the ancient carnage, the Crimes

Clubmen could not help but note that they all presented the one characteristic of being dark, obscure, secret places, yet each provisioned with easy exits and ample cover.

Churton Collins, that 'louse on the locks of literature' as Tennyson characteristically rudely and unjustly dubbed him, recorded in his diary what, on this privileged visit, he and Doyle saw in Mary Kelly's death place – No. 13 Miller's Court.

> This was a dismal hole … It consisted of one very small room, with a small window, a fire, a chair and a bed. It was sombre and sinister, unwholesome and depressing, and was approached by a single doorstep from a grimy covered passage leading from Dorset Street into a courtyard …
>
> Dr Gordon Browne [*sic*] was inclined to think that he (the murderer) was or had been a medical student, as he undoubtedly had a knowledge of human anatomy, but that he was also a butcher, as the mutilations slashing the nose, etc., were butcher's cuts. There was absolutely no foundation, in his opinion, for the theory that he was a homicidal maniac doctor, whose body was found in the Thames, tho' that is the theory at Scotland Yard, because (1) the last murder, possibly the last two murders, were committed after the body was found, he was strongly of opinion that the last two were Ripper murders; (2) the murderer was never seen near enough for any trustworthy identification, and Dr G. Browne [*sic*] was absolutely of opinion that they still remain an unsolved mystery. He thought the murderer suffered from a sort of homicidal satyriasis – that it was sexual perversion. The trunk found in Finsbury Street in September 1889,[5] which he inspected, had the same incision as was characteristic of the Ripper murders, but it may have been an imitation, and it may have been one of the dynasty of murders – he could not say … The inscription about the Jews, 'The Jews are the men that will not be blamed for nothing,' was probably genuine, as a portion of the Apron covered with blood, etc., on which the fiend had wiped his hands after the Mitre Square murder was found on the ground just beneath it.

The Miller's Court murder scene had been photographed by the police with the terribly savaged cadaver *in situ*. Doyle and his fellow-pilgrims were shown this fading sepia picture of the Ripper's last disembowelled victim. Oddie, later describing 'the mass of human flesh which had once been Mary Kelly', wrote, 'Let it suffice for me to say that in my twenty-seven years as a London coroner I have seen many gruesome sights, but for sheer horror this surpasses anything I ever set eyes on.'[6]

Oddie considered that

> the most reasonable theory to my mind is that the man was a homicidal lunatic with some anatomical knowledge, acquired either as a butcher or a medical student, who obtained physical gratification from murdering women and slashing their bodies about with a knife. As his insanity increased he became suicidal and probably jumped into the Thames, just as 'a man unknown' of whom so many are fished out of the water by the Thames Police. That he was insane is, I think, certain. The very ferocity and frenzy of his methods point to that conclusion, as do the slashings of some of the bodies and organs and the disposition in some cases of viscera and small articles … Did he live in Whitechapel? Most probably not, but he may well have gone there by daylight to examine the locality with a view to his coming exploits … There seems little doubt that the real explanation lies … in some insane medical man, possibly a Russian Jew, living in the East End, who was a lust murderer, a Sadist, whose insanity increased until it culminated in the wild orgy of Dorset Street and was followed by his own suicide in the Thames.

Having been there, seen it, done it (the tour), what were Doyle's ideas about the perpetrator? The Reverend John Lamond, D. D. produced a biographical memoir of his friend Sir Arthur in 1931. Doyle had died on 7 July 1930. In it Lamond wrote,

> It is now public knowledge that 'Jack the Ripper' was apprehended and lodged in a mental institution through the clairvoyance of the late Mr R. J. Lees – a case that completely baffled the authorities of Scotland Yard, even when the leading detectives of Europe were called in, and a munificent reward had been offered. It was only when Mr Lees applied himself to the case that the murderer, a leading West-End physician, could be traced and arrested. After that arrest, the murders that had paralysed the East End of London suddenly ceased.

That is, of course, complete nonsense. Perhaps the circumstance that Lamond was himself a dedicated spiritualist may account for, although certainly not excuse, the proffering of such unevidenced rubbish. Despite its location – in the pages of an eminently respectable biography by an eminently respectable author – it does not necessarily represent Doyle's more sober considerations on the matter. Fortunately, we do know what Doyle thought before the fulminatory virus of an undiscriminating strain of spiritualism ran to fever in his blood, for, in an interview – 'Conan Doyle in His Study: Theory of Sherlock Holmes Concerning the Whitechapel Murder' – in the Cincinnati *Commercial Gazette*, of 10 June 1894, Sir Arthur, speaking on both his own and Mr Holmes' behalf, revealed what was in his mind.

'I am not,' he is reported as saying,

> in the least degree a sharp or an observant man myself. I try to get inside the skin of a sharp man and see how things would strike him. I remember going to the Scotland Yard Museum and looking at the letter which was received from the police, and which purported to come from the Ripper. Of course, it may have been a hoax, but there were reasons to think it genuine, and in any case it was well to find out who wrote it. It was written in red ink in a clerky [*sic*] hand. I tried to think how Holmes might have deduced the writer of that letter. The most obvious point was that the letter was written by some one who had been in America. It began 'Dear Boss,' and contained the phrase, 'Fix it up,'[7] and several other phrases which are not usual with Britishers. Then we have the quality of the paper and the handwriting, which indicate that the letter was not written by a toiler. It was good paper, and a round, easy, clerky [*sic*] hand. He was therefore a man accustomed to the use of a pen. Having determined that much, we cannot avoid the inference that there must be somewhere letters which this man had written over his own name, or documents or accounts that could be readily traced to him. Oddly enough, the police did not, so far as I know, think of that, and so they failed to accomplish anything. Holmes' plan would have been to reproduce the letters in facsimile, and on each plate indicate briefly the peculiarities of the handwriting. Then publish these facsimiles in the leading newspapers of Great Britain and America, and in connection with them offer a reward to any one who could show a letter or any specimen of the same handwriting. Such a course would have enlisted millions of people as detectives in the case.

According to Martin Booth, author of *The Doctor, The Detective and Arthur Conan Doyle* (1997), not many Ripperologists have been aware of the involvement of Dr Joseph Bell, of Edinburgh, Conan Doyle's teacher in his medical student days and the original model for Sherlock Holmes, in the investigation of the Ripper murders. Irving Wallace confirms in *The Sunday Gentleman* (1965): 'Dr Bell went after an impossible crime, as others attack difficult crossword puzzles.'

Ely M. Liebow, providing further details in his biography, *Dr Joe Bell: Model for Sherlock Holmes* (Bowling Green University Popular Press, 1982) informs us that:

> Late in 1888, according to the *Edinburgh Evening News*, Dr Joseph Bell tried his hand in solving the biggest puzzle of them all. The identity of Jack the Ripper. Joe Bell was fascinated not only by the Ripper's letters to the London papers as well as the handwriting itself but also by the killer's maniacal delight in sending such things as human kidneys to the police.[8]
>
> According to the *Edinburgh Evening News*, Joe Bell spoke of the Jack the Ripper murders to a journalist friend, and related how he and another friend who liked solving deep problems, went about the unmasking of the Whitechapel Fiend. 'There were two of us in the hunt, and when two men set out to find a golf ball in the rough, they expect to come across it where the straight lines marked in their mind's eye to it from their original positions, crossed. In the same way, when two men set out to investigate a crime mystery, it is where their researches intersect that we have a result. He and his anonymous friend, taking into account all the Scotland Yard suspects and at least two additional suspects from Scotland, deduced the murderer; each wrote a name on a piece of paper; put the paper in an envelope; and then exchanged envelopes. Evidently both men had the same name (never revealed!). Dr Bell immediately notified Scotland Yard. A week later, the murders came to an end. Was this coincidence? Did Dr Bell and his unnamed friend have something to do with solving the case? – or stopping the carnage?

One cannot think so.

It is possible to make an educated guess as to the identity of Bell's unnamed friend. I strongly suspect that it was Dr Henry Duncan Littlejohn.

Littlejohn (1828–1914), who was appointed Edinburgh's first Medical Officer of Health in 1862, had been extra-mural lecturer in medical jurisprudence since 1854, and Bell had, as a medical student, attended his lectures. Over the years, Littlejohn had built up a vast knowledge of, and expertise in, medico-legal matters. He was created a knight in 1895, before, two years later, being elected to the Chair of Medical Jurisprudence at Edinburgh University.

Bell wrote, presumably referring to Littlejohn's forensic work for the Crown, 'Dr Littlejohn is the medical adviser, and he likes to have a second man with him … and it so happens that for more than twenty years we have done a great deal together, and it has become the regular thing for him to take me into his cases with him.'

One can reveal that Littlejohn and Bell shared a great triumph in the part they played in bringing about the successful conviction of the cruel and calculating Eugène Marie Chantrelle, the odious Edinburgh uxoricide. When, on 31 May 1878, the morning of his execution, 'the dapper Frenchman … appeared on the scaffold, beautifully dressed and smoking an expensive cigar … Dr Littlejohn was there in accordance with his duty. Just before being pinioned, Chantrelle took off his hat, took a last puff on his cigar, and waving his hand to the police physician, cried out, "Bye-bye, Littlejohn. Don't forget to give my compliments to Joe Bell. You both did a good job in bringing me to the scaffold."

11

Jack the Cricketer: Montague John Druitt

Montague John Druitt is summoned back stage centre as the prime suspect in Daniel Farson's *Jack the Ripper*, published in October 1972. In fact, Druitt had been known to, and eyed with suspicion by, Farson as long ago as 1959, six years before Tom Cullen produced him to public print. Undeterred by Cullen's legerdemain, Farson laboured quietly on for another seven years, and the results of his researches were presented in this, the, up to that time, most horrendously illustrated of all the Ripper books.

In it, Farson was able to reveal – from a report traced to the *Acton, Chiswick & Turnham Green Gazette*, 5 January 1889 – the contents of a letter left behind by Druitt. He writes, 'Since Friday I felt I was going to be like mother and the best thing was for me to die.'[9] From the same source it emerges that Druitt had been sacked from the Blackheath School. The reason for his dismissal is not given, but it must have been something serious, and Farson speculates that it might have been in connection with homosexual practices, although there is nothing to substantiate this.

Farson is able to supply, too, the hitherto missing link with the Whitechapel district, for he has discovered from an examination of the Medical Register that Druitt's cousin, Dr Lionel Druitt, was living at 140 Minories in 1879. There is also some rather more tenuous evidence from an ex-head librarian of Poplar, unnamed and now dead we are informed, claiming that he had once seen an M. J. Druitt, in either an old directory or a voters' list, as living in the Minories.

But what Farson regards as his supremely important piece of new evidence is the information that he received from a Mr Knowles that a Dr Lionel Druitt, resident in Australia, had written a personal reminiscence entitled 'The East End Murderer – I Knew Him', which was privately printed by a Mr W. G. Fell, of Dandenong, in 1890. *The Medical Register* for the germane period confirms that Dr Druitt was in Australia in 1887. In 1886, he was practising at 122 Clapham Road, his last English address. Unfortunately, Farson's Ripper dossier, containing Knowles' letter, was stolen from Television House in 1959, and with it the address of his correspondent was lost.

However, in 1961, Farson went to Dandenong Ranges, and at Drouin met an elderly lady, Miss Stevens, who remembered Dr Lionel Druitt, who, she said, was practising there in 1903. He had died at Mentone, Victoria, Australia, in January 1908.

Of the vital document there was no trace. If one day a copy of Dr Lionel Druitt's Will-o'-the-wisp publication should turn up, it might well provide those details which the family gave privately to Sir Melville Macnaghten, and which so convinced him of the identity of Jack the Ripper. Let us remember, though, that even if they were to be brought to light, the suppositions of Dr Druitt, like 'what the soldier said', are not evidence. They would not necessarily, as Farson piously fears, bring closure to the file. They did not close it 125 years ago, for long after Montague John Druitt had been laid to rest in his grave at Wimborne the police were still actively seeking Jack the Ripper.

A *reprise*.

Of all the named suspects put forward over the years 1888–1972, the two most likely candidates would seem to have been Konovalov/Pedachenko and Montague John Druitt. In neither case, however, was the evidence submitted sufficiently substantial to warrant conviction. Too many critical factors lack veridical confirmation; too many persuasive arguments melt away at the point of proof, and in default of new but pressing evidence the verdict must perforce remain an open one.

It may well be that, with modifications, the view originally expressed by Sir Robert Anderson back in 1895 that the criminal was one of the immigrant population – very likely Polish, possibly Russian – comes closest to the truth. The killer could well have been a sexual psychopath, if not, indeed, actually psychotic: a man, perhaps, of the type of Peter Kürten, the Düsseldorf multicide. His deviation would have been that he achieved orgasm-equivalent, or actual orgasm, from the act of mutilation and the plunging of his hands into the warm, moist viscera of a newly slaughtered woman. These are unpleasant waters to fish. His name, even if we knew it, would in all likelihood mean nothing to us, for he would surely have been as anonymous in life as he has become in *post mortem* legend.

The publication of Daniel Farson's book in 1972 did not, as he half-regretfully suspected that it might, prove the end of the affair.

The trail goes winding remorselessly on.

Farson himself had more to say. When, in September, 1972, his book had been presented in pre-publication serialisation in the *London Evening News*, he had received nearly 100 letters. Some of these seemed to him to merit notice in a 'Postscript' to a 1973 paperback edition.

One letter in particular from a Mr Edhouse, of Kentish Town, received in March 1973, was of very considerable interest. The writer had undertaken some research of his own regarding the octogenarian Mr Knowles, who had written to Farson about the Lionel Druitt document, 'The East End Murderer – I Knew Him'. Mr Edhouse, checking the death certificate of Montague John Druitt's mother, Ann, had noted in its column seven the entry 'Emily Knowles present at death, Manor House, Chiswick'.

Mr Edhouse suggests that Emily Knowles was a woman who looked after Mrs Ann Druitt at the Manor House Lunatic Asylum, and was privy to certain vital information imparted to her by her patient after Montague John Druitt's last visit to his mother. Mr Edhouse further suggests that this information was conveyed by Emily Knowles, or by a member of her family, either to Dr Lionel Druitt directly, or else to William Druitt, who confided it to Edward Druitt, who, upon his arrival in Australia, passed it on to Dr Lionel Druitt.

Further research at Somerset House disclosed that an Arthur Knowles, of Hackney, died, aged eighty-four, in June 1959. 'His death,' comments Farson, 'now explains why I never heard from him again.' And he concludes, 'The combination of these facts makes it more evident than ever that such a document as "The East End Murderer" really did exist.'

Another correspondent, Alan Prentice, provided what Farson regarded as significant evidence concerning the phrase 'Dear Boss', contained in some of the alleged Ripper communications. It had hitherto been generally interpreted as an Americanism, but in *The Times* of Friday 16 November 1888, Mr Prentice discovered the following report:

THE WHITECHAPEL MURDERS

The police received another letter from 'Jack the Ripper' yesterday. It began 'Dear Boss,' and went on to explain that the writer always addressed his cousin in those terms. He threatened to commit another murder in the locality on Wednesday next (21 November 1888), on which occasion he would inflict injuries on his victim identical with those inflicted on his last.

Could it be, asks Farson, that this was how Montague Druitt referred to his older cousin, Lionel?

Mr Prentice writes: 'One can see now in retrospect that this report could have alerted the Druitt family that the murderer was one of their own kith and kin.'

And a Mr K. Shawman wrote to Farson: 'A prostitute was in fact assaulted in her room by a man she had invited there. He attempted to cut her throat but ran off after she screamed. The woman's name was Amelia or Ann Farmer. Her address was in George Street, Whitechapel, and the attack occurred on Wednesday 21 November. You will notice that the assailant had returned to the lodgings with Farmer and would therefore have been quite able to perform another Mary Kelly type operation as promised in *The Times* letter.'

Would this, Farson wonders, have been Jack the Ripper's sixth murder, if his nerve had held?

Farson received what he described as 'exciting new evidence' in a letter from a Mr Frederick Martin Lambert Pocock, one of whose relatives owned a fried fish shop next to the railway arch in the Minories, which his mother used to visit. Mr Pocock states that a man named Druitt had an attic room on the third floor, and that after the murders this man used to burn a lot of rubbish in the furnace in the cellar where the fish was fried – 'under the pans and stewed eel copper'. Pocock adds, 'Some of the women he murdered used to use the pub on the corner opposite the Royal Mint.' According to this same correspondent, the man Druitt was suspected at the time. Mr Pocock's mother was 'accosted by a man at the Aldgate East end of the Minories and she suspected him of being the Ripper. When she mentioned the incident to her relatives at the fried fish shop, her description was surprisingly like the lodger in the attic room above.' Since, however, Mr Pocock was not born until around 1892, his 'exciting new evidence' is, unfortunately, only hearsay. Notwithstanding, Farson feels that 'if his recollection is correct, this is the most conclusive proof so far of Montague Druitt's association with the Minories after Lionel Druitt had left'.

In the January 1973 issue of the *Cricketer*, Irving Rosenwater published an article based on a somewhat specialised investigation of his own, 'Jack the Ripper – Sort of a Cricket Person?' Having read Farson's book and found the case made out against Druitt a compulsive, though not a conclusive, one, Rosenwater decided to pursue the suspect's cricketing career and connections. He begins by contradicting the assertion that Druitt played at Lords, then proceeds to reconstruct his cricketing movements during the crucial late summer of 1888. That season he embarked upon his usual programme of matches for Blackheath, with which team he appears to have been associated since 1882, playing against, among others, the Incogniti, the Royal Artillery, the MCC, and the Band of Brothers.

On Saturday 1 September, the day after the murder of Mary Ann Nichols in Buck's Row, Druitt played for Canford against Wimborne, in a small match at Canford, in Dorset.

At 11.30 on the morning of Saturday 8 September, some six hours after the estimated time of the murder of Annie Chapman in Hanbury Street, Druitt was playing for the Blackheath Cricket Club against the Brothers Christopherson, on the Rectory Field, Blackheath.

And yet, despite the fact that Druitt was a member of the MCC and the Incogniti, and played for the Gentlemen (of both Dorset and Bournemouth), Rosenwater supports Farson's thesis – 'On the evidence now disclosed, it will require a courageous and learned man to say that the Whitechapel murderer was not Montague John Druitt, cricketer.'

Montague's brother, Edward, two years his junior, also a keen cricketer and a regular officer in the Royal Engineers, departed for Australia early in 1889, for employment in connection with the Queensland Defence Forces, and Rosenwater suggests that it was Captain Druitt who acquainted Dr Lionel Druitt, who had emigrated to Australia in 1886, of the family's suspicion of the part which his cousin Montague had played in the savage events of 1888.

Another amateur criminologist who zealously pursued the Druitt trail and made his findings available to Farson was David Anderson. It was he who discovered the most informative report of Montague John Druitt's death in the *Acton, Chiswick & Turnham Green Gazette* of 5 January 1889. He it was, too, who succeeded in tracing specimens of Druitt's signature on the documents he signed when he was admitted a barrister of the Inner Temple. Graphologists, comparing Druitt's handwriting with that of the alleged Ripper letters, assured Mr Anderson that they had no doubt that Druitt wrote them. Anderson also provided an interesting, not to say tantalising, footnote. In the *Kentish Mercury* of 2 November 1888, he turned up a report of the finding, near Wimborne station, on the morning of Thursday 1 November, of the mutilated body of Mr Champness William Edwards, Wimborne's stationmaster. He had, Anderson reports, 'been hacked to death, and neither the motive nor the killer was ever found'. But, says Anderson, Druitt was at Wimborne on 2 November.

The fascinating possibilities hinted at by David Anderson evaporate when one reads the following account from *The Times*, Friday 2 November 1888:

> The body of Mr C. W. Edwards, stationmaster of Wimborne, was picked up on the line about 300 yards from Wimborne Station early yesterday morning with half the head cut clean off. The body was lying in the six foot way, with the head across the up line. The deceased's pipe and spectacles were found lying near. He had been at Wimborne Station about eight years, but had relinquished his duties there on Wednesday night, having been appointed stationmaster at Bournemouth West, whither he would have proceeded after his marriage, which had been arranged to take place tomorrow. He was very popular in the town, where a subscription had been set on foot for the purpose of presenting him with a public testimonial. About 7.30 on Wednesday evening (31 October) he walked down the line, the nearest way to a farmhouse where he was invited to spend the evening. He is believed to have been run over by the 8 o'clock up London train.

A case of what, in another context, Edward Hyams has called killing no murder.

The next book to be published, Alexander Kelly's *Jack the Ripper: A Bibliography and Review of the Literature* (1973), listed 250 major publications issued on the subject up to the end of October 1972.[10] It also contained an eleven-page 'Introduction to the Murders and Theories' by Colin Wilson, who states that in none of the inquests on the victims of Jack's cold steel embrace did the doctors who carried out the post-mortems look for signs of male sperm. They did. There was none.

Wilson notes that both Mary Ann Nichols and Annie Chapman had teeth missing, and the description of Elisabeth Stride also reveals the absence of teeth in the lower jaw. This same curious feature was presented in the case of the Thames Nude Murders (1959–1965), in which the victims of the undisclosed killer, nicknamed Jack the Stripper, were also prostitutes. Medical evidence of the presence of semen in the throats of several of the corpses indicated that they had performed an act of fellatio immediately prior to death. But to compare the dental states of the prey of the Ripper and the Stripper, and draw speculative conclusions from it is meaningless, for whereas the Stripper deliberately knocked the women's teeth out – very likely with fellatio in mind – the Ripper's victims were semi-edentulous as the result of neglect and extractions.

Now Colin Wilson is a friend of mine of very long standing. I admire his industry and his capacity for abstract thought. What does, however, disconcert me somewhat is the extent to which, over the years, his views concerning the identity of Saucy Jack have kept changing. He started off in 1960, when he published his novel based upon the case, *Ritual in the Dark*, 'guessing' that Jack was a homosexual sadist harbouring a hatred of women: that is a sexual psychopath. By 1969, however, in *A Casebook of Murder* he diagnoses the Whitechapel murderer as being 'probably a full-blown psychotic, the kind who believes that voices speak to him from the air: that is, a person suffering from schizophrenia, mania, psychotic depression, or an organic psychosis'. Which does he mean? He is of the opinion that the Ripper was 'a sex-pervert of many years' experience', who had worked up morbid fantasies, which included disembowelling women. He was not, however, specifically interested in the genitals. His fantasies were all about 'cutting bellies'. It was the womb itself, the seat of life, that fascinated him. Says Wilson: 'I would draw only one inference: that this destruction of the womb indicated a suicidal tendency in the Ripper; it was the place that bore him about which he felt ambivalent.' It is far more likely, suggests Wilson, that the Ripper was an upper- or middle-class young man with some powerful grudge against the world or his family, than that he was a crazy Russian doctor or barber-surgeon.

He returns to the subject in his *Order of Assassins* (1972), where he firmly announces, 'In my own opinion Druitt is the likeliest suspect for the Ripper murders.' Then, in the next breath, he delivers the opinion that Michael Harrison has 'advanced the most convincing theory to date' – in suggesting that the 'S' of Sir William Gull's papers was James Kenneth Stephen. And Wilson retails an interesting fact communicated to him by Harrison: 'Stephen was also indirectly connected with the school at Blackheath at which Montague John Druitt was a master.' Could it be, Wilson wonders, that Druitt and Stephen were friends? Was this, perhaps, why the police suspected Druitt of being the Ripper? In his 1973 preface – 'Introduction to the Murders and Theories' – to Alexander Kelly's *Bibliography*, Wilson is palpably veering Stephenwards.

Two years later, in his Introduction to Donald Rumbelow's *The Complete Jack the Ripper* (1975), he has come round unequivocally to regarding J. K. Stephen as a more likely suspect than Druitt.

Finally, in *The Mammoth Book of Jack the Ripper*, edited by Maxim Jakubowski and Nathan Braund, to which he contributes 'A Lifetime in Ripperology', Wilson announces, 'I have little doubt that Jack the Ripper and James Maybrick were the same person.' At least he did not accept Thomas Toughill's ridiculous candidate, Frank Miles.

12

Jack the Poet: James Kenneth Stephen

'Certain additional facts have come to light since I finished my book *Clarence* (1972),' writes Michael Harrison in *The World of Sherlock Holmes* (1973). It transpires that Harrison has found reference to his Ripper suspect, James Kenneth Stephen, in the first volume of Professor Quentin Bell's *Virginia Woolf* (1972), which confirms him in his opinion.

Stephen was apparently in the habit of carrying a sword-stick with him – that is to say, Stephen went around London and Cambridge (where he was a Fellow of King's) constantly *armed*. Not only armed, but seemingly prepared to wield his sword!

Harrison reads in Bell's pages of how on one occasion Stephen ran into the Stephen cousins' house at 22 Hyde Park Gate, drew his blade and thrust it into – a cottage-loaf. An innocent bit of horse-play? Let us not be naive. To quote Harrison: 'In those days, the anthropomorphic – female – character of the cottage-loaf was even more evident by reason of a "top knot" added to the "second layer" of the loaf. Obviously, in its origins the cottage-loaf is a representation of the female human figure, and into the "bulging bosom" of the cottage-loaf Stephen plunges the sharp point of his sword. What could more clearly symbolise his wish to kill all females?' A wish, moreover, says Harrison, openly expressed in his poems.

And that is not all. Stephen was a homosexual as well as a misogynist. Jack the Queen?

Harrison continues: 'There is not only the obvious female shape to explain Stephen's attack on the inanimate piece of baked bread; there is the subconscious reaction to a pun meaningful to one familiar with the secret language of the contemporary homosexual underworld, in which a "cottage" was a public urinal (usually of the cast-iron, kerb-edge kind) and a "cottage-loaf" was a male prostitute who loitered – or "loafed" – about such malodorous places. It looks as if the male prostitutes of the East End of the old Queen's reign had a lucky escape.'

The year 1974 brought the publication of the script of a radio programme, *Who Was Jack the Ripper?*, by Michell Raper, put out on BBC Radio Four on 1 June 1972. No new suspect is produced, but the script contains the rather curious assertion that Druitt was 'a social reformer among the poor, which gave him an excuse for being out and about in Whitechapel at odd hours of the night'.

It also contains the text of a letter written by Sir Charles Warren to a Home Office colleague:

> I wish to state that I am fully prepared to take responsibility for adopting the most drastic and arbitrary measures the Secretary of State can name which would further the securing of the murderer – however illegal such measures may seem – provided Her Majesty's government will support me. However, I must observe that the Secretary of State cannot authorise me to do an illegal action and the full responsibility will always rest with me for anything done. I have also ascertained that even such actions as searching houses without a warrant etc. might be adopted, though we would not be justified at present in doing so great an illegal act. Three weeks ago I did not think the public would acquiesce to any illegal action, but I think they would now welcome anything which showed activity and enterprise.

The sentiments expressed in that letter seem to make it plain that, despite latter-day suspicions that have been attached to his behaviour and motivations, Sir Charles was clearly not taking part in any cover-up operation.

13

Jack the Mage: Roslyn Donston Stephenson

In 'Was Jack the Ripper a Black Magician?' in the January 1973 issue of *True Detective*, Leonard Gribble put forward the sensational, and to my mind untenable, proposition that the Whitechapel killer was a black magician. He, very sensibly, disavowed personal responsibility for this esoteric construct, which he allocates to 'someone known to me as a student of occult matters, though not a practitioner of them, who had at one time been friendly with the notorious Aleister Crowley'.

There was, this unnamed informant avers, a medical specialist of good family, who, like 'Dr Stanley' before him, was bent upon avenging the death of an only son, who died 'a raving idiot', in a private asylum, as the result of contracting a virulent sex disease.

This occult avenger's first victim was Martha Tabram, stabbed thirty-nine times – that is three times thirteen, an occult formula we are told. The subsequent black magic sacrifice murders became more complicated, and were aligned so that their commission coincided within minutes with various phases of the moon in the autumn of 1888.

The mutilations, progressively escalating in extent, followed 'a precise sacrificial pattern established by certain procedures of a black mass, in which personal possessions of the human sacrifice are arranged in cabbalistic designs', as alleged in the case of Annie Chapman. They were also deliberately contrived so as to make up the segments of a pentagram, and reached their climax in a 'power pentagram', fashioned from the extirpated organs of health and reproduction from Mary Jane Kelly's body.

On 9 November 1888, the pentagrammatic apogee was reached, the special lunar phases lending potency to sacrifice went into decline, and the murders ended. A further point of occult significance is that lines drawn between the closely proximal loci of the murders, including, of course, that of Martha Tabram in George Yard Buildings, link up to form an elongated pentagram.

The double event of 30 September is also cited as a confirmatory factor: 'It was the very fact of the Ripper being interrupted when about to mutilate Elisabeth Stride's body that made it necessary for him to find a substitute victim without delay, unless the potency of the ultimate pentagram's spell was to be destroyed. So he went hunting for Catherine Eddowes before the moon's influence changed.' This also accounts for there having been six, instead of the pentagram number five, victims. The murder of Elisabeth Stride could not count in any occult calculation dependent upon lunar influences because the requisite ritual mutilation pattern had not been achieved. Mary Jane Kelly's murder was, therefore, the effective fifth in the true pentagram sequence, and with it the mystical pentagram was closed.

Gribble was told that Jack the Ripper's identity was known to Aleister Crowley, but that he would not divulge it. He could not, he said, challenge the protective spell of the pentagram, behind which safeguard the homicidal occultist was working.

The attribution of orgiastic murder to black magic motivation is a common one, as demonstrated by the case of the Manson murders in the United States. Charles Milles Manson led a murderous, sex-and-drugs-based, dune-buggy-disseminated, Californian cult – The Family, a Hippy commune in the Mojave Desert. He was found guilty of inciting the murders of nine people, including that of the well-known film actress Sharon Tate, wife of film director Roman Polanski, in 1969. The Family was thought to have been responsible for a total of some thirty-five free-range killings. Manson was sentenced to life, which he served in San Quentin.

It is surprising that Aleister Crowley himself (1875–1947) has not yet been proposed as a precocious Jack, an oversight which, doubtless, some future theorist will correct.

In *The Confessions of Aleister Crowley* (1969), edited by John Symonds and Kenneth Grant, Crowley writes,

> One theory of the motive of the murderer was that he was performing an Operation to obtain the Supreme Black Magical Power. The seven women had to be killed so that their seven bodies formed a 'Calvary cross of seven points' with its head to the west. The theory was that after killing the third or fourth, I forget which, the murderer acquired the power of invisibility, and this was confirmed by the fact that in one case a policeman heard the shrieks of the dying woman and reached her before life was extinct, yet she lay in a *cul-de-sac*, with no possible exit save to the street; and the policeman saw no sign of the assassin, though he was patrolling outside, expressly on the look-out.

There is no clue as to which seven women Crowley had in mind. Is he beginning with Emma Elizabeth Smith and including Martha Tabram? Or beginning with Martha Tabram and concluding with Frances Coles? In the first instance, invisibility would have been achieved after the murder of Mary Ann Nichols or Annie Chapman. In the second, it would have been after the murder of Annie Chapman or Elisabeth Stride. In any event, it is all much too vague to be able to decide whether the policeman missed the killer of Annie Chapman, Elisabeth Stride, Catherine Eddowes or Alice McKenzie. We must exclude Mary Jane Kelly because she lay in a room, not a *cul-de-sac*.

Equally unsatisfactory is Crowley's story of the authoress, Mabel Collins,[11] and her weird friend. This man had been an officer in a cavalry regiment, a doctor, and many other things in his time. He also claimed to be an advanced magician. He took an enormous interest in the

Ripper murders and would discuss them with Miss Collins and her friend, Vittoria Cremers, giving them pantomimic imitations of how the murderer might have accomplished his task without arousing the suspicion of his victims until the last moment. Mrs Cremers pointed out that his escape must have been a risky matter, 'because of his habit of devouring certain portions of the ladies before leaving them'.

What about the blood on his collar and shirt? No difficulty there, was the reply. Any gentleman in evening dress had only to turn up the collar of a light overcoat to conceal any traces of his supper.

Time passed, Mabel grew weary of her strange gentleman friend. But getting rid of him was a problem because he had a bundle of highly compromising letters written by her. Mrs Cremers, usurper of his position in Miss Collins' affections, volunteered to recover the damaging letters. In the man's bedroom was a tin uniform case. He kept it under his bed, to which it was attached by cords. Neither of the women had ever seen the case open, but Vittoria suspected that this was where he kept the letters. Resourcefully, she got him out of the way for a day or two by the simple expedient of sending him a bogus telegram, went intrepidly into his room, untied the cords, and drew the case out from under the bed. To her surprise it was very light – as if empty. She picked the lock. Opened it. It contained no letters. There was nothing in it, except – seven white evening-dress ties, all stiff and black with clotted blood.

The late Bernard O'Donnell, an extremely capable and highly respected Fleet Street crime reporter, had produced a 372-page manuscript entitled 'Black Magic and Jack the Ripper', or, alternatively, 'This Man Was Jack the Ripper', completed in 1958, in which he named the strange character referred to by Aleister Crowley, and the companion of Miss Collins and Mrs Cremers, as Roslyn D'Onston, author of *The Patristic Gospels* (1904).[12]

O'Donnell's investigation, begun in 1930, had been initiated by the late Hayter Preston, at that time art, book and dramatic critic on the old *Sunday Referee*, who had suggested to O'Donnell that he should undertake enquiries into the identity of Jack the Ripper. 'I can put you on to a woman who knows the whole story – at first hand, too,' he told him. 'Not only did she know the Ripper personally, but at one time she lived in the same house with him.'

That woman was the Baroness Vittoria Cremers, widow of Baron Louis Cremers, at one time attached to the diplomatic corps at the Russian Embassy in Washington. O'Donnell found her, 'a rather diminutive figure, with short-cropped grey hair and a pair of dark, quizzical eyes', living at 34 Marius Road, Balham.

The story she had to tell began in the year 1886, when she was resident in the United States. One day, browsing in a New York bookshop, she picked up a copy of a thirty-one-page theosophical essay entitled 'Light on the Path'. It described itself as 'A Treatise Written for the Personal Use of Those Who Are Ignorant of the Eastern Wisdom, and Who Desire to Enter Within Its Wisdom. Written down by M. C. fellow of the Theosophical Society. Published in London in 1885 by Reeves & Turner.' So profound was the impression it made upon her that she joined the American Theosophical Society.

In 1888, the personal affairs of Vittoria Cremers, now a widow and preferring to call herself Mrs Cremers, necessitated her coming to England, and shortly after her arrival she presented herself at the headquarters of the Theosophical Society in London, at 17 Lansdowne Road, Holland Park, where she was promptly enrolled by the formidable Madame Helena Petrovna Blavatsky, and given the job of looking after the business side of *Lucifer*, the society's monthly magazine.

Now the associate-editor of *Lucifer* was none other than Mabel Collins, that 'M. C.' whose work Mrs Cremers had so deeply admired, and whom she had long cherished the ambition to meet personally. It turned out that Mabel Collins, who, apart from writing on theosophical themes, was a novelist and fashion writer on the *World*, was living at 34 Clarendon Road, the garden of which backed on to the garden of 17 Lansdowne Road, where Mrs Cremers had now taken up residence. The two women met and became close friends.

O'Donnell had finished his manuscript in 1958, but it had never been published. The late J. H. H. Gaute, then at Harrap's, had turned it down, the reason given being its too discursive structure. I was permitted to examine it and present the first public account of its thesis in my *A Casebook on Jack the Ripper* (1975). By agreement with O'Donnell's son, Peter, the publishing rights to the manuscript were acquired by Melvin Harris.

On the afternoon of 1 December 1888, Mrs Cremers found Madame Blavatsky and two prominent theosophists, Dr Archibald Keightley and his cousin, Bertram Keightley, poring excitedly over an article which they, wrongly as it transpired, believed to have been written by the Earl of Crawford and Balcarres, in the *Pall Mall Gazette*, the London evening newspaper edited by W. T. Stead. The author of the article was the first person to make the suggestion that Jack the Ripper was a black magician.

Of this article O'Donnell subsequently wrote:

In one of the books by the great modern occultist [Alphonse Louis Constant], who wrote under the name Éliphas Lévi, *Dogme et rituel de la haute magie* [1861], we find the most elaborate directions for working Magical spells of all kinds … He gives the fullest and clearest details of the necessary steps for evocation by this means, and it is in the list of substances prescribed as absolutely necessary for success that we find the link which joins modern French necromancy with the quest of the East End murderer. These substances are in themselves horrible and difficult to procure. They can only be obtained by means of the most appalling crimes of which murder and mutilation of the dead are the least heinous. Among them are … candles made from human fat … and a preparation made from a certain portion of the body of a harlot. This last point is insisted upon as essential, and it was this extraordinary fact that first drew my attention to the possible connection of the murderer with the black art. Further, in the practice of evocation, the sacrifice of human victims was a necessary part of the process. And the profanation of the cross and other emblems considered sacred, was also enjoined. Leaving out the last murder committed indoors … we find that the sites of the murders form a perfect cross. To those persons to whom this theory may seem somewhat far-fetched, we would merely remark that the French book referred to was only published a few years ago; that thousands were sold; that societies have been formed for the practice and study of its teaching and philosophy; and finally, that within the last twelve months an English edition has been issued.

In 1889, Mrs Cremers had to return to America, and it was March 1890, before she found herself in England once again. She stayed with a Mrs Heilmann, at 21 Montague Street, Russell Square, just round the corner from the British Museum. Mabel Collins had, she knew, left Clarendon Road, and moved to York Terrace, behind Madame Tussauds, but when she called to see her friend she was told that she had gone off to Southsea to work on a new novel.

The next day, Mrs Cremers was on a train for Southsea. She found Mabel Collins quartered in a somewhat seedy house in an unexpectedly drab and shabby street. After the exchange of greetings, Mabel Collins suddenly asked her, 'Do you remember an article in the *Pall Mall Gazette* about Rider Haggard's *She*? It was signed "D.O.", if you remember.'[13] Mrs Cremers remembered it vaguely. She had not read it.

Excitedly, Mabel Collins went on to tell her that she had written to its author, care of the *Gazette*. 'Well, after some weeks I received a reply. It was only a few lines saying that the writer was ill in hospital, but as soon as he was better he would write and make an appointment.' And, sure enough, in due course a letter had arrived from a Dr Roslyn D'Onston making an appointment. 'A marvellous man, Vittoria. A great magician who has wonderful magical secrets.'

Mabel Collins had become infatuated with him and, it transpired, was living with him there in Southsea, and presently D'Onston himself 'materialised' in the room.

Mrs Cremers described him to Bernard O'Donnell as 'a tall, fair-haired man of unassuming appearance. A man at whom one would not look twice.' The sum total of her estimation of him was 'nil – absolutely nil – gentle, uncannily silent in all his movements, one who would remain calm in any crisis. Physically, tall. Not an ounce of superfluous flesh on him. Military bearing unmistakable, and a suggestion of strength and power. His face had a queer pallor. Not a particle of colour anywhere. Upper lip hidden by a fair moustache. Hair thinning at the sides. Teeth slightly discoloured' – from pipe-smoking, she thought.

'But it was his eyes that impressed me most. They were pale blue, and there was not a vestige of life or sparkle in them. They were the eyes which one might expect to find set in the face of a patient in the anaemic ward of any hospital.'

One other feature impressed Mrs Cremers about D'Onston. His appearance of super-cleanliness. His clothes, although obviously old and worn, appeared to have suffered from assiduous brushing rather than wear and tear. A nice, inoffensive, absolutely nil creature, she decided.

D'Onston possessed the recipes for certain beauty creams and potions, and the two women put up the money for their manufacture, formed a company, which they named the Pompadour Cosmetique Company, and took premises in Baker Street, just opposite the fictional residence of Sherlock Holmes.

The office consisted of one large room and a small back room on the first floor, and a flat on the third floor, occupied by Mrs Cremers. D'Onston, who seemed to have no financial resources of any kind and nowhere to live, moved into the small first-floor back room, which Mabel furnished for him.

Although Mrs Cremers lived in the same house as D'Onston and was in regular daily contact with him, it was Mabel Collins, whose lover he undoubtedly was, who knew him better than anyone else, and it was to her that he confided the story of his shattered romance with a woman named Ada.

He had, he claimed, as a young man, held a commission in the Army. He came from a fairly well-off yeoman family, and it was generally understood that he would marry the daughter of a wealthy neighbouring family who was very much in love with him.

However, on one of his jaunts to town with some of his brother officers, he met a woman of the streets named Ada. He began to visit her regularly, fell in love with her and, Gissing-like, determined to marry her and take her away from her miserable life.

Understandably, his family was appalled. His father cut off his allowance. Always a gambler, D'Onston lost a lot of money at the tables one night, and, unable to pay his debts, was forced to seek his father's help. His father agreed to discharge those debts – on one condition: that he undertook to end his association with Ada and marry the heiress. Reluctantly, D'Onston agreed.

And so it was that D'Onston and Ada parted, but not before they made a solemn pledge that, whatever happened, dead or alive, they would meet at midnight on the anniversary of their parting at the place where they had first met – the middle of Westminster Bridge.

Then … tragedy. Within an hour of D'Onston's departure, Ada walked to Westminster Bridge and threw herself into the river.

True to his vow, D'Onston kept his tryst with the dead woman on Westminster Bridge. He leant over the parapet where Ada had flung herself to her death twelve months before. As the chimes of Big Ben sounded, 'he heard the click-clack of heels coming towards him. He saw nothing, no one, but he knew that Ada. too, had kept her promise.'

Mrs Cremers' reaction to this highly coloured story when Mabel Collins confided it to her was, 'Fiction! He was imagining things.'

Later, she was not so sure.

There were other stories. Stories which D'Onston himself told to Mrs Cremers, of things which happened to him as a doctor with Garibaldi's army in Italy, and as a prospector in one of the minor Californian gold rushes. Stories which revealed a coldness and callousness in the man, a cynical disregard for the sanctity of human life. He even, in an unguarded moment, let it drop that he had been married, and conveyed to Mrs Cremers the uneasy suspicion that he had murdered his wife.

Generally speaking, though, of his real self, his true identity, he disclosed nothing, and Mrs Cremers was convinced that D'Onston was only an assumed name.

Once, she asked him why he signed his articles 'Tautriadelta', remarking that it was a strange signature.

'A strange signature, indeed,' he replied, 'but one that means a devil of a lot if you only know. A *devil* of a lot.'

'But what does it stand for?' she persisted.

'Before the captivity,' he said, 'the Hebrew *Tau* was always shown in the form of a cross. It was the last letter of the sacred alphabet. *Tria* is the Greek for three, while *Delta* is the Greek letter D, which is written in the form of a triangle. So the completed word signifies "Cross-three-triangles". There are lots of people who would be interested to know why I use that signature. In fact the knowledge would create quite a sensation. But they will never find out, never.'

Another odd memory of Mrs Cremers'. 'I remember going into D'Onston's room one afternoon. The first thing that caught my eye were some dirty pieces of candle burning on the mantelpiece. They were at the side of the clock in a sort of bunch. "Good God, D'Onston," I exclaimed, "where on earth did you get those filthy-looking candles?" "I made them," he answered quietly. "It is an experiment."'

It was one morning shortly after this incident that Mabel Collins came into the office in Baker Street and told an astounded Vittoria Cremers, 'I believe D'Onston is Jack the Ripper.'

Mabel Collins never revealed what it was that had led her to this dramatic conclusion, All she would say was that it was 'something he said to me. Something he showed me. I cannot tell even you. But I know it, and I am afraid.'

There came a day when Mrs Cremers was to believe it, too.

Vittoria Cremers' version of the discovery of the bloodstained ties differs from that reported by Aleister Crowley. According to what she told Bernard O'Donnell, D'Onston and Mabel Collins had parted, but he was still living at Baker Street, although the cosmetic business was failing and was soon to be wound up.

For some time Mrs Cremers' mind had been plagued by an increasingly intense curiosity to find out who and what D'Onston was, and this idea that he was Jack the Ripper decided her upon a course of action which, normally, would have been abhorrent to her.

On the few occasions when she had been into his room, she had noticed a black enamelled deed box. He had told her that he kept a few first editions and some of his private papers in it. One day when D'Onston was out, Mrs Cremers went into his room and, using an old key she had which fitted the box, opened it. It contained, as he had said, books, but not a single paper or document. Its only other contents were a few black ties of the old-fashioned style with ready-made knots tied in them. Lifting one out of the box, she found that on the underside of the tie, and also at the back of the knot, there was a sort of dull stain, and the tie was quite stiff and hard in those areas, as though something had congealed on it. She examined each of the ties, and on each of them found this self-same soiling.

It was sometime in July 1890 that Vittoria Cremers received what she was always to regard as final proof that Roslyn D'Onston was Jack the Ripper. On this particular day he came into the Baker Street office, sat down and opened up a copy of the *Westminster Gazette*. 'Have you heard that Jack the Ripper is going to start operations again?' he asked. 'It's in the paper again tonight and it was in the papers this morning.'

'Do you think there's anything in it?' she asked.

'No,' said D'Onston with emphasis. 'There will be no more murders.' Then … 'Did I ever tell you that I knew Jack the Ripper? You know that when Mabel first wrote to me I was in hospital. That was just after the last of the murders. I was living in the Whitechapel neighbourhood then. I was taken seriously ill and had to go into hospital. It was there that I met him. He was one of the surgeons, and when he learned that I had also been a doctor we became very chummy. Naturally, we talked about the murders, because they were the one topic of conversation. One night he opened up and confessed that he was Jack the Ripper. At first I didn't believe him, but when he began to describe just how he had carried out the crimes I realised that he was speaking from actual knowledge, and was speaking the truth. At the inquests it was suggested that the women had been murdered by a left-handed man. All those doctor fellows took it for granted that Jack was standing in front of the women when he drew the knife across their throats. He wasn't. He was standing behind them. The doctors at the inquests made a point of mentioning that the women did not fall but appeared to have been laid down. This is about the only thing right about their evidence. Everybody was on the look-out for a man with bloodstained clothing, but, of course, killing the women from behind, my doctor friend avoided this. When he took away those missing organs, he tucked them in the space between his shirt and his tie. And he told me that he always selected the spot where he intended to murder the woman for a very special reason. A reason which you would not understand.'

At the end of the summer of 1891, Mrs Cremers closed the Baker Street office, and the Pompadour Cosmetique Company went out of business. She returned to live at Mrs Heilmann's in Montague Street, Bloomsbury, and D'Onston vanished from her life. Vittoria Cremers died in 1937.

Bernard O'Donnell set to work to find out all that he could about the man who called himself Dr Roslyn D'Onston, and who, according to Mrs Cremers' account, had virtually admitted to her that he was the Whitechapel murderer.

The quest for Roslyn D'Onston was to prove a task almost as Sisyphean as that for the Ripper himself. However, diligence, tenacity, and patience yielded a small dividend of clues.

First of all, there were D'Onston's published writings. Four articles and a book. Two of the articles were published in the *Pall Mall Gazette*.

The first of these, which had appeared on 3 January 1889, was entitled 'The Real Original of "She" By One Who Knew Her', and was signed 'R. D.' It had been written as a follow-up to a two-part article by another hand, which he had read in the *Gazette* a few months previously. This had been the story of a mysterious white woman known as Ayesha, the possessor of uncanny magical powers, whom the contributor had met in Africa. D'Onston wrote of his experiences with another mystery woman, the sorceress

Subè, whom he had known, also in Africa, and whom he compared with the 'She' of Rider Haggard's novel.

The second article, published on 15 February 1889, 'What I Know of Obeeyahism By the Author of the Original of "She"', dealt with D'Onston's further mystical experiences in Africa, and was signed 'Roslyn D'Onston'. In it he confronts the Obeeyah woman, Subè, and, using a talisman given to him he claims by Bulwer Lytton, annihilates her.

The subject matter of both of these articles was magic, and in them D'Onston made it obvious that not only did he believe implicitly in black magic, but that he also practised it. His confession of faith, his credo, ran, 'Magical powers – especially those of necromancy – are absolutely possible, absolutely true, absolutely accomplished.' Incidentally, in the first of these two articles he let fall an autobiographical morsel – that he had been 'connected, in some form or other, with the slave trade. That by the way.'

So, two things were established to O'Donnell's satisfaction. D'Onston was most certainly around at the time of the Whitechapel murders, and, indeed, publishing a very curious article within less than two months of the commission of the last of them. Equally certainly, he was a confirmed believer in black magic.

The third article, 'African Magic', was published at Mrs Cremers' instigation, and with Madame Blavatsky's approval, in *Lucifer*, in November 1890, and was signed 'Tautriadelta'. It contained the significant observation that 'the necromancer must outrage and degrade human nature in every way possible. The very least of the crimes necessary for him (or her) to commit, to attain the powers sought, is actual murder, by which the victim essential to the sacrifice is provided.'

The fourth and most important article, 'A Modern Magician', appeared in W. T. Stead's spiritualist magazine, *Borderland*, in April 1896, and once again the Hermetic name Tautriadelta was employed. The article was introduced by Stead, and what he wrote proved to O'Donnell that he and Mrs Cremers were not alone in their suspicion. Stead declared,

> The writer of the following extraordinary fragment of autobiography has been known to me for many years. He is one of the most remarkable persons I have ever met. For more than a year I was under the impression that he was the veritable Jack the Ripper, an impression which I believe was shared by the police who at least once had him under arrest, although, as he completely satisfied them, they liberated him without bringing him to court.[14]

The particular value of this article was that it provided a certain amount of biographical data. D'Onston told in it how, since the age of fourteen, he had been deeply interested in 'Occult Science', and how, as a young medical student of twenty-three, he had been initiated by Sir Edward Bulwer Lytton and become a neophyte of the Hermetic Lodge of Alexandria,[15] accepting that the Initiate must subjugate himself to his Master, and, by the performance of the 'work' or tasks imposed upon him, overcome all weaknesses of body and mind. From this article we learn, too, that when he was eighteen D'Onston was studying chemistry in Munich – before proceeding to Paris to read medicine – under Dr James Allan, a Scot who had previously been an assistant to Baron Liebig, and, in company with a fellow-student, Karl Hoffman, had carried out successful experiments in connection with doppelgänger phenomena.

D'Onston writes,

> I became obsessed with the idea that the revelation of the doppelgänger phenomena would make me an instrument of the Gods; henceforth, on occasion, I would destroy to save, I would become as Hermes, son of God … 'For they who would slay and save must be armed with a certain strong

and perfect will, defying and penetrating with no uncertain force. This Herpe, the sword that destroyeth the Harlot, by whose aid the Hero overcometh and the Saviour is able to deliver.

D'Onston also admits here having studied black magic under Lytton, and tells of his service as a doctor in Italy with Garibaldi's army, and of a visit to India in order to study the methods of the fakirs.

Melvin Harris confirms that, in August 1860, D'Onston did indeed volunteer to go with the British Excursionists to Italy, where he fought as part of the Southern Italian army, serving as a lieutenant, but latterly awarded the honorary rank of major in recognition of his medical work in the field.

Having digested all this and registered its implications, Bernard O'Donnell was considerably surprised to discover the nature of D'Onston's only full-length book, *The Patristic Gospels* (1904), an holistic translation of the New Testament. It is in fact a highly religious work, completed, its author writes, with 'the undeniable aid of the Holy Spirit'. A strange sentiment, you may think, to come from the pen of the man who wrote those most 'unholy' effusions in the *Pall Mall Gazette*, *Lucifer*, and *Borderland*.

The Patristic Gospels took him, D'Onston informs the reader, eleven years to write. That means that he must have begun work on it in 1892 or 1893, so that the magic left hand was composing paeans in praise of devilry at one and the same time as the right hand was devoutly scrivening a pious comparative and critical analysis of the four Holy Gospels – a truly remarkable feat of mental ambidexterity.

It is a work of profound scholarship, achieved under extremely difficult circumstances, not only during a period described by its author as 'one long fight against pain and paralysis', but also in the face of crippling poverty. There is an extraordinary parallel between Baron Corvo[16] and Dr D'Onston – Corvo, struggling against overwhelming penury, obsessed with Roman Catholicism and the priesthood, yet lacerated by his homosexual fantasies and desires; D'Onston, similarly impoverished, driven to all manner of seedy shifts to keep body and soul together, determinedly beavering away at his religious book, yet all the time tortured by the desire to attain to the supreme pinnacle of black magical power. Two shabby figures flitting, unbeknown to one another, across the horizon of the London of the eighteen-nineties, perhaps even working at the same time in the old gaslit Reading Room of the British Museum, each oblivious of the other's existence, each securely encased in the lonely egotism of his esoteric quest.

W. T. Stead, the innovative editor of both the *Pall Mall Gazette* and *Borderland*, had died in 1912 in the sinking of the *Titanic*, but Mrs Cremers had had an opportunity to ask him to tell her what he knew about D'Onston, and Stead had admitted knowing virtually nothing.

O'Donnell's next step was to pay a visit to Grant Richards, the publisher of *The Patristic Gospels*, who proved scarcely more informative. Yes, he remembered D'Onston – 'A weird, uncanny creature. Gaunt. Sallow. He would come into the office and sit in silence without uttering a word until I could see him, and then he would hardly open his mouth beyond asking for an advance of payment on his book.'

Richards never had any address for him. D'Onston would just drop in and collect any royalties due to him. 'He came in two or three times after the book came out to collect money, and then he simply vanished.' Grant Richards never saw him again.

O'Donnell decided then to follow the clue of the bloodstained ties. Oddly enough, he had known of their alleged existence long before Mrs Cremers had mentioned D'Onston's name to him. In 1925 O'Donnell had written a series of articles for *The World's Pictorial News*, dealing with the life and adventures of Betty May, one of Jacob Epstein's models, who, through her marriage to a young Oxford undergraduate, Raoul Loveday, came under the sinister influence of Aleister Crowley, and spent some time at his Abbey of Thelema, at Cefalù, in Sicily.[17]

Betty May wrote,

> I must tell you how one day I was going through one of the rooms in the abbey when I nearly fell over a small chest that was lying in the middle of it. I opened it and saw inside a number of men's ties. I pulled some of them out, and then dropped them, for they were stiff and stained with something. For the moment I thought it must be blood. Later I found the Mystic and asked him about the ties. He was in one of his kindly moods. 'Sit down,' he said, 'and I will tell you about them.' He then went on to say that these were the relics of one of the most mysterious series of murders that the world had ever known. They had belonged to 'Jack the Ripper!'
>
> '"Jack the Ripper" was before your time,' he went on. 'But I knew him. I knew him personally, and I know where he is today. He gave me those ties. "Jack the Ripper" was a magician. He was one of the cleverest ever known and his crimes were the outcome of his magical studies. The crimes were always of the same nature, and they were obviously carried out by a surgeon of extreme skill. "Jack the Ripper" was a well-known surgeon of his day. Whenever he was going to commit a new crime he put on a new tie. Those are his ties every one of which was steeped in the blood of his victims. Many theories have been advanced to explain how he managed to escape discovery. But "Jack the Ripper" was not only a consummate artist in the perpetration of his crimes. He had attained the highest powers of magic and could make himself invisible. The ties that you found were those he gave to me, the only relics of the most amazing murders in the history of the world.'

I (R. W-E.) have in my library Aleister Crowley's own copy of *Tiger Woman*, liberally encrusted with his caustic marginalia.

Two women who did not know each other had separately told the story of the ties to O'Donnell. Both of them had known Crowley. The next obvious line to pursue was that which led to the person of the Master Therion, the Beast 666. Fortunately, Crowley was one of O'Donnell's friends. O'Donnell had in fact 'ghosted' Crowley's Sunday newspaper story, 'The Wickedest Man in the World', for him.

O'Donnell asked him, 'What happened to the ties in that old box of Jack the Ripper's that Betty May told me about when I was doing her story?'

'I destroyed them,' replied Crowley. 'When I left the Abbey in Cefalù I had to get rid of a lot of things.'

How did you get hold of them?'

'He gave them to me.'

'So you knew him,' said O'Donnell. 'Who was he?'

'Oh! – just another magician,' said Crowley. He added that he had been one of the black variety and that he had seen very little of him. 'I didn't get on very well with him. He had no sense of humour. He died round about 1912 or 1913, I think.'

And, to his intense disappointment, that was all that O'Donnell could ever get Crowley to say on the subject.

But the conversation, however unsatisfactory, had established two things: that Crowley was convinced that the Ripper murders were the work of a black magician, and that that magician was the man who had given him those bloodstained ties – the ties that Mrs Cremers had seen in D'Onston's black tin box forty years before; the ties that Betty May had described to O'Donnell five or six years prior to his hearing Mrs Cremers' story; the ties which Aleister Crowley now confirmed had been in his possession.

O'Donnell concluded that it seemed fair to assume that the owner of those ties – whom both Crowley and Mrs Cremers were convinced was Jack the Ripper – was one and the same man, Roslyn D'Onston; the same D'Onston who, hiding behind the name Tautriadelta, W. T. Stead had also suspected of being the veritable Jack.

Next port of call, Somerset House. O'Donnell searched the registers of births from 1836 to 1845 inclusive, looking under D'Onston, Roslyn, Rosslyn, and Ross. Drew a blank. He then searched the register of deaths from 1904 to 1930. Another blank. Grant Richards had mentioned that D'Onston had once said that he intended to go and live in France. Perhaps he had done so. Perhaps he had died abroad. Or perhaps, an even stronger possibility, Roslyn D'Onston was a completely false name.

O'Donnell tried to track down his quarry through a report of the inquest on his beloved Ada, but without having her surname it was hopeless.

There had been an action brought by D'Onston against Mabel Collins for the return of some of his letters. The case had come up at Marylebone some time in the early nineties. The most rigorous search through the newspaper files failed to disclose any reference to it.

D'Onston had claimed to be a doctor of medicine. O'Donnell checked with the British Medical Association and with the General Medical Council. There was no Dr D'Onston. One interesting small point: in the Catalogue of Authors, at the British Museum Reading Room, O'Donnell noticed that someone had inserted in ink beside the printed name of the author of *The Patristic Gospels*, the letters 'M. D.' Since there was no mention of any medical status attached to the name of Roslyn D'Onston on the title-page of the work, it could only be assumed, said the Superintendent of the Reading Room, that it was D'Onston himself who interpolated the 'M. D.' in the catalogue on some later occasion.[18]

And there, so far as Bernard O'Donnell was concerned, the search for the true identity of Roslyn D'Onston had perforce to end. But he felt that he had succeeded in building up a case to answer. His crowning achievement was the decipherment of Tautriadelta. Not in its literal meaning, for D'Onston himself had revealed that, but in its mystical significance. It seemed, in its way, a discovery of the order of Ventris' decipherment of Linear B – except that in this case one should perhaps call it Linear ABCDE, for the decipherment of Tautriadelta depends upon the lineal conjunction of five points to form the most powerful of all magical symbols, the pentagram. It consists of three overlapping triangles. Cross-three-triangles. And if you draw straight lines between the five loci of the five Jack the Ripper murders, you will in so doing construct a pentagram. Thus, Tautriadelta, D'Onston's Hermetic name, literally marks the five scenes of the Ripper crimes.

O'Donnell's theory was a beautiful, careful, admirably ingenious piece of inductive logic. It certainly persuaded ex-Chief Constable Frederick Wensley, who, sitting in the garden of the house to which he had retired at Southgate, near Palmers Green, in the northern suburbs of London, told him, 'Yours is the only solution of the mystery which stands up to all the facts as I knew them.'

I am afraid, however, that there are some facts which Chief Constable Wensley either did not know, or else had in old age forgotten. There were, among the papers in the Home Office files, three documents which not only cast an unflattering beam of cross-illumination on Bernard O'Donnell's proposed solution to the mystery, but finally established the true identity of Roslyn D'Onston.[19]

On 24 December 1888, a man named George Marsh, describing himself as an unemployed ironmongery salesman, of 24 Pratt Street, Camden Town, presented himself at Scotland Yard at seven o'clock in the evening. He stated that about a month previously he met a man named Stephenson at the Prince Albert public-house in Upper St Martin's Lane, and fell into casual conversation with him about the Whitechapel murders. Since that time he had been meeting Stephenson two or three times a week, on each occasion always discussing the murders in a confidential manner.

Marsh made a statement to the police:

> I have told him that I am an amateur detective and have for weeks been looking for the culprit. Stephenson explained to me how the murders were committed. He said that they were the work of a woman-hater, that the murderer would induce a woman to go up a back street or into a room, and to excite his passion would bugger her and cut her throat the same time with his right hand, holding on with the left. He illustrated the action, and from his manner I am sure that he is the murderer. Today, Stephenson told me that Dr Morgan Davies, of Houndsditch, is the murderer, and he wanted me to see him. He drew up an agreement to share the reward on the conviction of Dr Davies. I made him [do so] under the influence of drink, thinking I should get some further statement, but in this I failed. Then he left me to see Dr Davies, and also to go to Mr Stead of the *Pall Mall Gazette* with an article for which he expected to get two pounds. He wrote the article in the *Pall Mall Gazette* about the writing on the wall about Jews. He got four pounds for that. Stephenson has shown me a discharge as a patient from the London Hospital. He is now living at the common lodging-house at 29 Castle Street, St Martin's Lane, W.C., and has been there three weeks.
>
> His description is: Age 48. Height 5 feet 10 inches. Full face. Sallow complexion. Moustache heavy, mouse-coloured, waxed and turned up. Hair brown, turning grey. Eyes sunken. When looking at a stranger generally has an eyeglass. Dress – grey suit and light brown felt hat, and all well worn. Military appearance and says he has been in forty-two battles. Well-educated. He is not a drunkard. He is what I call a regular soaker – can drink from eight o'clock in the morning until closing time but keep a clear head.

Two days later – 26 December 1888 – this strange gentleman described by Marsh presented himself at Scotland Yard. His name was … Roslyn Donston Stephenson. He came, he said, to draw the attention of the police to the attitude of Dr Morgan Davies, of Castle Street, Houndsditch, to the Whitechapel murders, adding that his suspicions against him were principally in connection with the murder of Mary Jane Kelly, committed indoors. Three weeks ago he had been a patient at the London Hospital. He was in a private ward (Davies), with a Dr Evans, suffering from typhoid, who used to be visited almost nightly by Dr Davies. The murders would then be the usual subject of conversation. Dr Davies always insisted that the murderer was a man sexually effete, that he could only be aroused by some strong stimulus, such as sodomy. He was very positive on this point, saying that the murderer possessed the women from behind, *per anum*.

Stephenson stated,

> At the time Davies could have had no information, any more than myself, that the post-mortem examination revealed semen in the woman's rectum, mixed with her faeces. Many things seemed to me to connect him with the affair. For instance, Davies himself is a woman-hater, although a man of powerful frame and, judging by his sallow face, of strong sexual passions.
>
> One night when five medicos were present disputing his argument that the murderer did not do these crimes in order to obtain specimens of uteri, but that it was the lust of murder developed from sexual lust, Davies acted in a way that fairly terrified those five doctors. He took a knife, buggered an imaginary woman and cut her throat from behind. Then, when she was apparently laid prostrate, ripped and slashed at her from all directions in a perfect state of frenzy. It was only

a few days ago, after I was positively informed by the editor of the *Pall Mall Gazette* that Mary Jane Kelly had been sodomized, that I wondered how did Davies know? Another point. Davies argued that the murderer did not want specimens of uteri, but grasped them and slashed them off in his madness, as they were the only hard substances which met his grasp when his hands were madly plunging into the abdomen of his victims. I may say that Dr Davies was for some time a house physician at the London Hospital, that he has lived in the locality of the murders for some years and has lately taken a house in Castle Street, Houndsditch. He professes his intention of going to Australia shortly should he not quickly make a success in his new house.

Stephenson added that he had mentioned all this to 'a pseudo-detective named Gorge Marsh' with whom he had made an agreement to share any reward which he might derive from his information. The agreement read as follows:

24 Dec. 88
I hereby agree to pay to Dr R. D'O Stephenson (also known as 'Sudden Death')[20] one half of any or all rewards or monies received by me on a/c of the conviction of Dr Davies for wilful murder. Roslyn D'O Stephenson M. D.
29 Castle Street, W.C., St Martin's Lane.

The third document, dated 26 December 1888, is addressed by Inspector Thomas Roots to Chief Inspector Swanson. It states:

When Marsh came here on 24th I was under the impression that Stephenson was a man I had known twenty years. I now find that impression was correct. He is a travelled man of education and ability, a doctor of medicine upon diplomas of Paris and New York, a major from the Italian army – he fought under Garibaldi, and a newspaper writer. He has led a bohemian life, drinks very heavily, and always carries drugs to sober him and stave off *delirium tremens*. He was an applicant for the Orphanage secretaryship at the last election.

We now know that Roslyn Donston Stephenson, giving his profession as author, died on 9 October 1916, aged seventy-six, in Islington Infirmary, Highate Hill. The cause of death was (1) carcinoma of the oesophagus, (2) gastrostomy. He is buried in an unmarked grave in Finchley Cemetery, London.

Before abandoning the theory of Jack the Black Magician, it must be mentioned that another of its most enthusiastic protagonists was the late Arthur Diósy, a well-known author, lecturer, linguist, student of the occult and criminologist, who was one of the many 'Special Writers' engaged by the newspapers of the time to make on-the-spot investigations into the Whitechapel murders. Diósy was commissioned to do so on behalf of the *Star*. He later confided his views to his friend, S. Ingleby Oddie, the Central London Coroner. Oddie subsequently wrote in his autobiography, *Inquest* (1941): 'He [Diósy] thought the murders were the work of some practitioner of "Black Magic".' According to him, among the quests of these people in the East is the *elixir vitae*, one of the ingredients of which must come from a recently killed woman. Diósy got quite excited when he heard of the bright farthings and burnt matches which he said might have formed the 'flaming points' of a magical figure called a 'pentacle' at each angle of which such points were found, and according to ritual certain 'flaming' articles had to be thus disposed. Diósy said later that he had paid a visit to Scotland Yard to place his theories before the authorities, but had been received without enthusiasm, as one can well understand.

14

Jack the Poisoner: Dr Thomas Neill Cream

Under the editorship of Nigel Morland the *Criminologist* had always been ready to provide an outlet for the discussion of the latest Ripper theory, and it was in the *Criminologist*, in November 1970, that the late Thomas E. A. Stowell offered '"Jack the Ripper" – A Solution?', which was the first publication of his Clarence theory.

Morland reported in '"Jack the Ripper" – A Final Word', in the *Criminologist*, autumn 1971, that copies of the alleged handwritings of the Ripper had been submitted to Professor Cecil L. Wilson, Professor of Analytical Chemistry at Queen's University, Belfast, and Document Examiner to the Northern Ireland Ministry of Home Affairs, for comparison with letters in the handwriting of the Duke of Clarence. His conclusion was that all the evidence on the basis of the handwriting was against the identification of Jack the Ripper with the Duke.

In the summer 1974 issue of the *Criminologist*, Donald Bell, a journalist resident in Montreal, offered '"Jack the Ripper" – The Final Solution?'. Bell's candidate was Dr Thomas Neill Cream. The selection was scarcely novel. Indeed, Cream's name frequently crops up in the literature of suspicion, always, however, to be discounted, as is that of Chapman/Klosowski, and for the same reason; the criminological axiom that poisoners do not turn into butchers, and vice versa. This was a proposition to which, and in my view perfectly reasonably, Bell was not prepared to subscribe – the immutability of the *modus*. The briefest scan of latter-day serial killers proves the point. They have become versatile.

The principal circumstance which has always been held to invalidate Cream's claim for serious consideration is that on 1 November 1881, at Boone County, Illinois, a jury found him guilty of the murder by strychnine of an elderly epileptic named Daniel Stott, and sent him to the state prison at Joliet for the term of his natural life. As it turned out, he served only nine and a half years, being 'officially' pardoned' by Governor Joseph W. Fifer, of Illinois, about July 1891, and he is known to have been in London by October 1891.

It has always been assumed that in 1888 Cream was languishing in Joliet, but Bell suggests that it is at least possible that this was not so. In those days Chicago was shot through with corruption, and prisoners were sometimes able to buy their way out of jail, or make deals for the restitution of their freedom.

According to the criminologist Hans Mattick, Director of the University of Illinois Center for Research in Criminal Justice, 'the potentiality to buy one's freedom was far greater in those days than it is today. There were repeated scandals in the parole system, and wardenship of prisons was offered on a political power basis. It's conceivable that there could have been some hanky-panky, and Cream may have bribed someone and been set free in 1888'.

The fact that, except for a small paragraph in the *Joliet Daily News* of 13 June stating that he had been pardoned the previous day, Cream's 'official' release went unreported in the Chicago newspapers could have been indicative of an official cover-up. It seems logical to assume that if Cream really had been set free on 12 June there would be at least a few words somewhere in the Chicago press, for he was known even then as a notoriously mad doctor. Bell notes that 'Cream later told Scotland Yard officers that he was released on 31 July 1891'.

Cream's father had died in 1887, leaving him $16,000, a sum which could easily have yielded the necessary bribe money. Angus McLaren writes in *A Prescription for Murder*, 'Money could accomplish everything … to the purchase of pardon and freedom … [which] no doubt goes some way in explaining why … Daniel Cream was successful in having Governor Joseph W. Fifer declare [his brother] Thomas Neill Cream a "fit and proper subject for executive clemency".'

Suppose that, in one way or another, Cream had succeeded in getting out of Joliet. Where more natural for him to flee to than London, a city which he knew well, for, in the late 1870s, he had lived there and attended a course of lectures at St Thomas' Hospital?

There are quite a striking number of similarities between Cream and the Ripper. Both chose prostitutes as their targets; both wrote bizarre, exhibitionist letters; both killed for the sheer pleasure of killing; the Ripper seems to have been fascinated by the uterus, whereas Cream was interested in obstetrics and carried out abortions. And some of the descriptions given of the Ripper tally most snugly with that of Cream.

George Hutchinson described the man he saw with Mary Kelly on the night of her death – about 5 feet 6 inches tall, aged thirty-four or thirty-five, dark complexion, dark moustache, curling up at the ends. Wearing a long, dark, astrakhan-trimmed overcoat, white collar, black necktie with a horseshoe tiepin, button boots over which were dark gaiters with light buttons, and most eye-catchingly a massive gold chain across his waistcoat.

Cream's official height was 5 feet 9 inches. He was thirty-eight years of age in 1888. His moustache was dark and twirled at the ends. And he sported a horseshoe tiepin. A photograph of him, taken as a student at McGill University, actually shows him wearing it.

One further fact for the winnowing. Cream wrote a thesis at McGill on chloroform. Bell says, 'What is peculiar about all the Ripper's victims is that none of them was heard to scream, or make an audible sound ... The answer is simple: they were obviously chloroformed quickly and expertly – who knew more about the drug than Cream?'

Bell also tells us that 'it has been suspected for years around McGill's medical faculty that Jack the Ripper was once on the rolls', and in 1935 Stephen Leacock wrote to Charles Martin, a former Dean of Medicine, 'I suppose you know that it is practically certain that Jack the Ripper was on our rolls as Dr Neill Cream.'

As for the sudden cessation of the murders after the bloodbath at No. 13 Miller's Court, Bell contends that Cream left England. On 21 November 1888, a letter was delivered to the magistrate at the Thames Police Court.

Dear Boss,
It's no use for you to look for me in London because I'm not there. Don't trouble yourself about me until I return, which will not be very long. I like the work too well to leave it alone.

The postmark was Portsmouth, and Bell believes that Cream went there to find a ship for America. He returned to London in 1891, and took up again the work he liked so well, only this time using a different method – poison instead of the knife.

A last puzzling occurrence.

In June 1892, Mr A. Braxton Hicks, the coroner holding the inquest on Matilda Clover, received a letter: 'Dr Neill is as innocent as you are ... If I were you I would release Dr T. Neill or you might get into trouble. – Juan Pollen alias Jack the Ripper. Beware all. I warn but once.'

Did Cream send the letter himself? It would be in character.

In '"Jack the Ripper" – The Handwriting Analysis', in the *Criminologist*, summer 1974, Derek Davis, who specialised in the examination of handwriting in forensic disputes, presents his report of a comparative analysis of specimens of the alleged writing of Jack the Ripper and a holograph of that of Cream's. Previously, the Canadian graphologist Miss C. M. MacLeod, in 'A "Ripper" Handwriting Analysis', in the *Criminologist*, August 1968, had analysed the handwriting of two alleged Ripper letters – the 'From Hell' letter to Mr Lusk and the letter addressed to Dr Openshaw, postmarked 29 October 1888 – and opined that the

Lusk letter was the most likely to be genuine. Davis, scrutinising later the same two samples, reached, after due consideration of hundreds of calculations, the verdict that Cream wrote both, using as much disguise as possible on each occasion.

Bell presents his case with a high degree of ingenuity and some formidable special pleading, but it does not seem to me to add up to an acceptable indictment of Thomas Neill Cream.

15

Jack the Prince: Prince Albert Victor

The Ripper studies of the 1970s were dominated by the works of Stephen Knight; and, indeed, his directional findings were to initiate two decades of regal obfuscation.

Following Wenceslaus-like in the good Stephen's steps, that transatlantic private eye (retired if not retiring) Mr Frank Spiering brought his not inconsiderable imaginative powers to bear upon the Stowell-spawned case of Prince Jack. His book of that title came out in New York in 1978. There has never been a British edition.

Having kicked off his gumshoes and exchanged the notional rattle of rapid-fire for that of a chattering typewriter, Spiering first turned successful scriptwriter and then fantasist solver of real-life mysteries, such as those of Jack the Ripper and Miss Lizzie Borden. She of the axe.

Fascinated by the vapourings of Thomas Edmund Stowell, he crossed the herring pond and, aided by an innominate friendly Brit in the Metropolitan Police, 'was able to gain access' to what he identified as the sealed and secret contents of the Scotland Yard and Home Office cabinets. Actually, they were produced to him quite routinely in the Record Office. There can be no doubt that Spiering deliberately chose for effective literary purposes to surround the narrative of his field researches in London with a threatening MI5 atmosphere and a sinister 007-style mystery.

What Spiering actually said in his book was that he had been in the Record Office reading:

> The handwritten memorandum of Inspector Abberline detailing his plan to use George Hutchinson, who had seen Marie Jeanette Kelly's killer on the morning she was murdered … At 9 p.m. on the evening of the day I perused the file, I received an unusual telephone call at my hotel from the office of the Home Secretary. They wanted to know exactly why I wanted to see the file. I carefully explained that I was doing a book on mass murderers and in no way intended to write more than a few pages on the most famous mass murderer of all. This explanation seemed to satisfy them, but I felt a slight trace of anxiety when they asked why I wished to copy a document from their file. I explained that since I was not allowed to make notes of the file's contents (I was not even permitted a pencil and paper), that I needed the actual wording of the document in order to be certain that whatever I might quote from it was correct. After a few moments' pause I was told that I could have a copy of the document. It would be sent to me. The following day I paid for the document to be reproduced. But, as I anticipated, I never received it. Suspecting that once the Home Secretary's Office was fully alerted to my methods of obtaining information, that they might attempt to thwart me in some way, on the day that I had studied the file, during the lunch hour period, I had approached a young man left alone on duty at the Photostat machine and slipped him a few pound notes to make a quick copy of the document

for me. I explained that I was leaving by plane that night for New York. Although he related that it was against the normal procedure, he quietly photostatted the document.

David May, writing in the *Sunday Times* of 13 August 1978 an article entitled 'Jack the Ripper Rides Again', provides an explanation. The Home Office telephone call to Spiering was made by a conscientious official who, trying to deal with his application for access to the files as speedily as possible, was granting him the requisite permission over the telephone. Moreover, the Home Office has preserved a minute received from the Record Office which conveys Spiering's thanks. He had, in fact, simply been allowed access to the same files as had been seen by two other authors of books about Jack the Ripper.

Spiering writes, 'Perhaps before the file is officially opened to the public, this document too will disappear with all the others. In consideration of that possibility, it is reproduced below in its entirety.'

And that 'entirety' reveals nothing of any special significance whatsoever. Dated the twelfth day of November 1888, referenced to Papers 52983, signed by F. G. Abberline, Inspector, and T. Arnold, Police Superintendent, it is simply a plain everyday report as to the holding of an inquest on Marie Jeanette Kelly at Shoreditch Town Hall before Dr MacDonald, MP, Coroner. It does, admittedly, refer to an important statement made by George Hutchinson, whom Abberline says he has interrogated and that he believes what he tells him; namely, that he had known Kelly for about three years, occasionally given her a few shillings, and had been surprised to see a man so well dressed in her company on the night of her death. Hutchinson had said that he was confident that he could identify the man, and arrangements had been made for two officers to accompany him round the district that night with a view to finding the man, if possible.

It came to nothing.

Spiering's hunter's luck held good. In November 1977, in his home territory of New York, he located an old portfolio in the New York Academy of Medicine that not even the conservators of the Academy had known was there. Bound into this ancient brown leather tome, with untitled spine, had been a wodge of holographic writings by Dr William Gull. A strange discovery. Stranger still, this volume seems since to have completely vanished.

Melvin Harris wrote to the Academy for further particulars, and requested photocopies of the Gull papers. The librarian, Mr Brett A. Kirkpatrick, replied that to the best of his knowledge the library did not contain a portfolio with notes of Sir William Gull's, but added, 'In a library the size and age of ours, it is possible that a set of notes bound with a larger work or other works could have gone unnoticed by our catalogers, but it is highly unlikely.' He further stated that 'Mr Spiering was never able to remember or reconstruct the catalog entry he submitted for retrieval from our stacks and in which he allegedly found the notes by Gull. Thorough searches by staff also proved fruitless.'

No matter, the important thing is that Spiering read and, presumably being allowed pencil and paper this time, transcribed the vital message of those notes. It was, 'On 3 October I informed the Prince of Wales that his son was dying of syphilis of the brain. Under suggestion, using the Nancy method,[21] my patient admitted to the details.'

Prince Jack is Spiering's bizarre creation out of Michael Harrison out of Stowell, electing 'to boldly go' for the conjoint Clarence–Stephen theory, and take one gigantic step forward – in the wrong direction. Now Prince Eddy is Jack the Knave, with James Kenneth beside and behind him. The prince wields the knife, and J. K., a known dab hand as poet and epistoler, writes the rhymes and letters.

Spiering claimed that he had interviewed members of the staff at Buckingham Palace and Scotland Yard officers. Yet as Melvin Harris, always a fair, but never a word-mincing, commentator, points out, 'A meticulous search shows that nowhere in the book is a single sentence quoted from any palace or police official that backs up his story, so we can eliminate them at once as sources.'

In 1978, prior to publication, Spiering issued a sort of ultimatum to the queen. He would undertake to stop the impending publication of his book if she was prepared to hold a press conference and reveal what she knew of her great-uncle's acts of murder and of the extraordinary mode of his death.[22] The fact that this seems to have been no more than a publicity stunt is reinforced by a statement from Buckingham Palace that the Royal Archives would be opened to Mr Spiering, as they had been opened to, and examined by, other researchers. His reaction – 'I don't want to see any files' – appears to confirm one's suspicions.

So it comes about that, notwithstanding the late Nigel Morland's glowing testimonials:

Of Spiering personally: 'He is a dedicated writer, a man who puts authenticated research above everything else.'

Of his book: 'I am very impressed. He has probed into the Ripper case, probed with a mind unimpressed by baseless facts, and while I fear he is going to revive the whole violent controversy he will do so unintentionally. This book is an important one and, I suggest, the last word on Jack the Ripper.'

One harbours grievous misgivings.

I cannot say that I have a very good feeling regarding the book. Morland's *encomia* worry me. I would hesitate to go so far as the American critic Dale L. Walker did, describing it as 'concocted Grade Z fiction', but incontrovertibly in my view, there is more of fiction than of fact about it. To be fair, though, Spiering himself confessed that what he had written was 'mainly a reconstruction of what *I* feel did happen, based on everything I read officially and unofficially'.

It is, in other words, admittedly hemi-fictive. As such, it is a good read. Smoothly written. Nicely put together. Interesting. I think it only right that such details should be noted and applauded. Books do not write themselves! But, considered as a matter of historic – plausible even – possibility, one has of necessity to issue a warning. Do not be beguiled by the superficially handsome. Do not rely on *Prince Jack* for any veridicality. Even the full-page portrait of Sir Charles Warren is not. It is a photograph of Major-General Sir Hector Macdonald, the famous 'Fighting Mac'.

In the telling of his tale Spiering also makes a cardinal error. He has Prince Eddy, sadistically excited by watching the slaughter of beasts in the Jewish abattoir in Aldgate High Street, steal a butcher's leather apron as a sort of fetishist companion piece to the knife with the long cutting blade, which he has stolen barely a week before from Barber's Yard horse slaughterers in Winthrop Street, hard by Buck's Row. The apron is donned by Prince Eddy as an *aide-'grimoire'* (to conjure forth, or juggle with, the *magie noire* blood ritual concept) to his imaginative satisfaction, and he leaves it behind him in the backyard at 29 Hanbury Street.

Melvin Harris nails the lie *instanter*. 'The apron and its ownership were fully investigated by Coroner Wynne Baxter on the first day of Annie Chapman's inquest. Mrs Richardson, the cat's meat woman, testified that the apron belonged to her son, John.'

To sum up, Melvin Harris wittily concludes, 'At the start we are promised … "the enigmatic outlines of Jack the Ripper are filled in and a royal figure emerges". But instead of that boldly sketched portrait we find nothing but a collection of worthless Yankee Doodles.'

16

The Legal Ripper: Montague John Druitt

Let us now take a look at the hundredth milestone year's eve septimal submissions.

In *The Ripper Legacy: The Life and Death of Jack the Ripper* (1987), Martin Howells and Keith Skinner concentrate on Macnaghten's Suspect No. 1 (at least No. 1 out of the three whom he proposes as more likely than Thomas Cutbush to have been the Ripper) and in so doing achieve some very useful demolition work.

They have traced what Daniel Farson took to be a rare pamphlet, 'The East End Murderer – I Knew Him' by Dr Lionel Druitt. It turned out to be an article in an Australian newspaper supplement. The piece was about an East End London landlady, along the lines of a 'Jack the Ripper was My Lodger' type of story, in the *St Arnaud Mercury* of 29 November 1890, and was reprinted from the *New York World*. They have established that Dr Lionel Druitt did not live in the remote Dandenong Range of Australia, whither a certain indomitable Dan, resolutely peripatetic and stoutly travel-booted as Negley, his father, had valiantly trekked in pursuit of his – bogus as it proved – literary legacy, but in Dandenong Road, in Oakleigh, a thriving industrial suburb of Melbourne.

Mr W. G. Fell, allegedly the printer who was responsible for the issuing of the privately printed pamphlet, was nothing more than a red herring, dredged up from an old man's distorted recollections, and the Macnamara Document of which they had heard being offered for sale for £500 in a Melbourne public-house in the 1920s actually referred to the Melbourne murderer, Frederick Bayley Deeming, late of Rainhill, near Liverpool, achiever of homicidal celebrity for his tucking away beneath the family hearthstone at Dinham Villa his family, wife and four children. It was said that, while awaiting hanging for another hearthstone burial, another wife resurrected, at 57 Andrew Street, Melbourne. Deeming confessed to two alleged Ripper murders, but as a matter of record he had been in South Africa in 1888. Yet another department of odd coincidences entry: one of the many aliases used by Deeming during his Australian visitation was Druin.

Howell and Skinner's researches also yielded the significant contribution that Ann Druitt, Montague's mother, was not a patient at the Manor House Asylum, Chiswick, until eighteen months after her son's suicide. Prior to that – from July 1888 – she had been at Brooke House Asylum, Clapton, less than 2 miles north-east of Whitechapel.

The authors stay enthusiastically with what Christopher Wordsworth styles the 'Wykehamist batsman, failed barrister and sacked schoolmaster' solution. They work very hard at it. They provide rich, cogent argumentation. They assert, rather eccentrically, a cover-up job by Druitt's solicitor brother, William, of Bournemouth. He, they say, gave flawed testimony at the inquest, held at the Lamb Tap, in Church Street, Chiswick. He stated that he was Montague Druitt's only living relative, whereas there were actually two other brothers and three sisters. He also stated that he had found a suicide note among his dead brother's possessions.

The authors comment, 'Druitt's family believed him to be the murderer, and yet his brother was supposed to possess information (i.e. the suicide note) which clearly pointed to his innocence. How can this be, unless this vital piece of evidence is fabricated?' In this, as elsewhere, the authors seem, in attempting to take the evidence against Druitt further, to end up going too far themselves, relying on a heterogeny of assumptions.

Their thesis is: Druitt was a homosexual. He had connections with the Cambridge Apostles, who, aware that he was the Ripper, and backed by shadowy Establishment

Apostles, occupying now some of the highest places in the land, murdered him. They lured him to Chiswick, poisoned him, dumped his body in the Thames, primed as that of a suicide, and, inexplicably, with all the river's meandering length to choose from, selected the crazily close proximity to their Thames-side meeting place, the 'chummery'[23] at Chiswick, for the jettisoning. Their motive? To ensure that there would be no discovery, arrest, and trial, no besmirching public association between the Apostles, their noble and gracious friend Prince Eddy, and their whilom companion, Montague John the Ripper, who had also been on terms of intimate friendship with Prince Albert Victor.

If this were indeed so, it is remarkable that the Ripperwise ever-alert Donald McCormick, who in one of his other literary personae, Richard Deacon, had published *The Cambridge Apostles: A History of Cambridge University's Elite Intellectual Secret Society* (1985), has given in it no hint of any of this. Neither, indeed, have Messrs Howells and Skinner travelled anywhere beyond the boundaries of a dubious possibility in an attempt to link Druitt, the Apostles and Eddy that would surely entitle them to honorary membership of the Speculative Society.[24]

It is a pity that in a book so well researched the authors had to provide a solution at any price. The permanent value of their *Ripper Legacy* to future researchers will lie, not in the conclusion, but in the map of the road which they travelled before taking the final false turning. One must always distinguish between facts and reasons. Not to do so is a common disability among Ripper researchers.

17

The Binomial Ripper: Kosminski or Cohen

Before proceeding to the examination of Martin Fido's *The Crimes, Detection and Death of Jack the Ripper* (1987), which set itself the task of putting the second of Macnaghten's named likelies, Kosminski, under the microscope, we must take note of the totally unexpected emergence, some months after the publication of Fido's book, of a most puzzling piece of conflicting data.

Like manna supplied to the Israelites out of the Sinai Peninsular sky, there descended from the nimbus clouds stacked over Peaslake, in Surrey, what appeared to be a miraculous fall-out of new and significant primary-source testimony lending strength to the suspect stature of Kosminski, as being, in high police quarters, the officially backed pretender to the true identity of elusive Jack.

This – reported in the *Daily Telegraph* of 19 October 1888 – was no less than a holograph note or two scribbled by Chief Inspector Donald Sutherland Swanson, the man who really was in total practical overall charge – under Robert Anderson, it goes without saying, and over Abberline – of the Whitechapel murders investigation. We were being accorded a privileged peep into the mind of one who, all his life, had viewed police work as a branch of the OGPU or KGB – 'decidedly a secret service' were his exact words – and kept a tight upper, and lower, lip. So tight, in fact, that he would not discuss the case even within the sternly disciplined Scots bosom of his own family.

He did, however, or so it would seem, permit himself a sufficiency of private unbuttoning to confide his pencilled secrets to the margins and endpapers of a copy of the autobiography of his old chief, Sir Robert Anderson, *The Lighter Side of My Official Life* (1910). When Swanson died, aged seventy-six in November 1924, this volume passed to his surviving family, with whom it remained, unread, until the death, around 1980, of the second of

Swanson's daughters, the maiden aunt of the old detective's grandson, James Swanson. It was then that his Scots grandfather's books and papers came to him.

Anderson had written in his autobiography that 'the only person who had ever had a good view of the murderer unhesitatingly identified the suspect the instant he was confronted with him, but he refused to give evidence against him. In saying he was a Polish Jew I am merely stating a definitely ascertained fact.' Swanson had pencilled in, 'Because the suspect *was also a Jew*, and also because his evidence would convict the suspect, and witness would be the means of murderer being hanged, which he did not wish to be left on his mind.' On the other side-margin was pencilled in, 'And after this identification, which suspect knew, no other murder of this kind took place in London.' And at the back of the book Swanson had written a longer note: 'Continuing from page 138, after the suspect had been identified at the Seaside Home where he had been sent by us with difficulty in order to subject him to identification, and he knew he was identified. On suspect's return to his brother's house in Whitechapel he was watched by the police (City CID) by day and night. In a very short time the suspect with his hands tied behind his back, he [*sic*] was sent to Stepney Workhouse and then to Colney Hatch [Friern Barnet Asylum] and died shortly afterwards – Kosminski was the suspect – D. S. S.'

As we know, the name Kosminski was not a new one. It had been introduced, it will be recalled, in 1965, when Tom Cullen published Macnaghten's notes for the first time in his *Autumn of Terror*. Armed with the full text, Martin Fido decided to go after Kosminski and did some remarkable and extremely onerous pioneering research, wading laboriously through workhouse, infirmary, and asylum records in pursuit of Macnaghten's mad Polish Jew, Kosminski (no forename given) and, as he thought, possibly the same individual as Anderson's unnamed Polish Jew.

In the end, virtue and persistence rewarded, Fido found one Aaron Kozminski, a twenty-six-year-old Polish Jew, a hairdresser, living with his brother, Wolf Kozminski, whose address was 3 Sion Square, Commercial Road. After treatment at Mile End Old Town Workhouse, Aaron Kozminski was admitted to Colney Hatch on 7 January 1891. He was transferred to Leavesden Asylum,[25] 2½ miles north-west of Watford, in Hertfordshire, in 1894, and died there in 1919.

Most tantalisingly, Aaron Kozminski only half fits the facts given by Swanson about his Kosminski. However … Fido succeeded in tracing another Polish Jew, who did seem to fill the Swanson bill. He was a twenty-three-year-old tailor, of Leman Street, Aldgate East, brought to the Whitechapel Infirmary on 12 December 1888, and admitted to Colney Hatch on 21 December 1888. He died there on 20 October 1889. The one slight drawback is that his name was Aaron David Cohen aka David Cohen. To further complicate matters, Martin Fido, never one to permit himself to be baulked by such trivia, is convinced, has convinced himself, that David Cohen is really Nathan Kaminsky!

'Who he?' do I hear you ask? Well, Nathan Kaminsky was a twenty-three-year-old, unmarried, Polish Jewish bootmaker, no known next of kin, living at No. 15 Black Lion Yard. He was admitted to Whitechapel Workhouse Infirmary on 24 March 1888, and was diagnosed to be suffering from syphilis. He was discharged at the beginning of May 1888. He was, Fido argues, the right age for a sexual serial killer, the right race for Anderson's Polish Jew, and the right occupation for Macnaghten's Kosminski (in the jottings for his 1894 report Macnaghten is said to have included the note that Kosminski's occupation was the leather-aproned one of 'a tanner or cobbler'). Infection with syphilis proved an active sex life among the local prostitutes, and supplied a conscious motive for hatred of street-women. Moreover, the location of Black Lion Yard was virtually at the centre point of the five murders, fitting all the clues provided by the murders themselves. But … the name of Kaminsky is never entered on the lists of pauper lunatics; never appears in the records of any asylum. Neither is there anywhere any record of his death.

How can Fido bridge the gap between Cohen and Kaminsky? His grand unscrambling acrobatic, which exonerates Kosminski and Aaron Kozminski, and reconciles the identities of a guilty Kaminsky/Cohen, depends upon several acts of faith and hope on his part, and a considerable donation of charity on the part of his reader.

The first of his submissions, which requires an effort to swallow, is that the nasality of the Victorian East End Jewish accent was such as could easily have produced the mishearing of 'Nathan' as 'David', and the 'Kamin' of trisyllabic 'Kaminsky', with the 'sky' syllable lost in a combination of Yiddish mumbling and lunatic rambling, could present as the more familiar 'Cohen'. Fido has, he tells us, since been informed that 'Cohen' was the usual 'John Doe' name that petty officialdom doled out to Jews whose names were unpronounceable, hard to spell, or generally uncertain.

The second *actus fidei* requires acceptance of the postulated explanation that the Metropolitan Police investigated Nathan Kaminsky aka Aaron Davis or David Cohen, and the City Police investigated Aaron Kozminski aka Kosminski, each force poaching on the other's manor to do so.

Fido thinks that the City Force's witness, Joseph Lawende, was spirited away to the Met.'s Seaside Home at West Brighton (not opened for convalescent officers until March 1890, so this, he admits, is a mystery), there inconspicuously to identify their suspect, Kaminsky/Cohen. Lawende refused to testify against him, so the Met. did the best they could in the circumstances by having said suspect, in Sir Robert Anderson's words, 'caged in an asylum'.

Plausible enough, except for that seemingly insurmountable business of the Seaside Home.[26]

In an ingeniously argued speculative paper, 'Kosminski and the Seaside Home: An Answer', Stewart P. Evans exhibits his persuasive theory as to how the long-standing confusion regarding this episode in Ripper history has arisen.

'For years the armchair theorists have struggled to explain the anomalies of the statements, admittedly flawed, made by Anderson, Macnaghten, and Swanson.' Here, Evans purposes the advancement of 'a totally viable and legally correct explanation for what happened. It is, of course, not proven, but it is the explanation most consistent with the facts, and with what the various police-officers wrote.'

It is, he believes, the likeliest representation of the veritable scenario in relation to the seriously suspected Aaron Kosminski.

'We know From Macnaghten's writings that he knew of Kosminski and that there "were many circs. connected" with him that "made him a strong suspect".' Notwithstanding, he adopted Druitt as his likeliest candidate.

On the other hand, 'every indication is that, for Anderson, Kosminski was the preferred suspect'.

'To take this study a stage further, we must,' says Evans, 'now look at the "Swanson Marginalia"' and what is plain here is 'that there can be absolutely no doubt that Macnaghten, Anderson, and Swanson are all referring to the same Kosminski. Likewise, there can be no doubt that the Kosminski referred to is one Aaron Kosminski.'

Research, Evans points out, has revealed enough of the facts about Kosminski to permit of certainty of this identification. And those facts he supplies. Since they differ to some extent from those supplied by Fido, I think they had best be given in full.

Aaron Kosminski was born in 1864 or 1865. He came to England in 1882. He was twenty-three or twenty-four in 1888, and was unmarried. His occupation was that of a hairdresser.

On 12 July 1890, he was admitted from 3 Sion Square, Whitechapel, to Mile End Old Town Workhouse, where he was adjudged to be able-bodied, but insane. That, at the age of twenty-five, was his first attack of insanity. On 15 July 1890, he was discharged from the workhouse into the care of his brother-in-law, whose forename was Wolf.

Seven months later, on 4 February 1891, he was readmitted – this time from 16 Greenfield Street, Whitechapel – to Mile End Old Town Workhouse. Examined there on 6 February by Dr Edmund King Houchin, of 23 High Street, Stepney, he was declared of unsound mind, 'and a proper person to be taken charge of and detained under care and treatment'. That same day a committal order was issued, and on 7 February 1891, he was admitted to the County Lunatic Asylum at Colney Hatch.

He was held there for the next three years, being described on 13 April 1894, as 'demented and incoherent', and on 19 April 1894, was discharged thence to Leavesden Asylum, where he died on 24 March 1919.

Evans proceeds next to assess the strength of the status of Kosminski as a suspect. He begins with Anderson's view, which seems to have rested mainly upon the result of witness identification. He then reminds us that 'for the identification to have been conducted, suspicion must have first have existed that Kosminski could be the killer,' even though 'that suspicion was insufficient on its own to warrant arrest or charge'. It is most likely therefore, he concludes, that information was laid 'that he could be the Ripper.' But, whatever the suspicion was, if Anderson and Swanson are largely correct, and there is nothing to show they are not, it was deemed that an attempt at identification should take place.

Macnaghten, as we have already seen, also knew of Kosminski, who he said was 'detained in a lunatic asylum about March 1889'.

It is Evans' soundly based deduction that, 'from all the known evidence, the witness used for identification must be Lawende. Indeed, he was used a week after Kosminski was committed to Colney Hatch Asylum in an attempt to identify James Thomas Sadler as the Ripper.'

Recognising that the great mystery in all this is the alleged identification of Kosminski by the witness at the Seaside Home, Evans asks, 'How are all the apparent anomalies and contradictions addressed?'

Admitting that there are 'some patent, and understandable, errors in the writings of the various police officers,' he goes on to offer 'a common sense and most likely scenario'.

He writes,

> The identification took place between 12 and 15 July, 1890, at the time of Kosminski's first attack and short stay at the workhouse, and whilst he was in the custody of the workhouse officials. (It would have been impossible to do after he had been committed to an asylum). The Clarendon Villas, Brighton, 'where he had been sent by us with difficulty …On suspect's return to his brother's house in Whitechapel he was watched by police (City CID) by day and night. 'In a very short time the suspect … was sent to Stepney Workhouse and then to Colney Hatch and died shortly afterwards,' (Swanson).

The only real errors identified by Evans are, 'Macnaghten's mistake as to the first date of incarceration ("about March 1889"), Swanson's misnaming of the workhouse and his idea that he had died.' Anderson's sole error was his suggestion that the identification had been carried out *after* the suspect 'was caged in an asylum'. To be fair, though, he 'was writing some nineteen years after the event and was concealing the identity of the suspect'.

There is, asserts Evans, 'a totally credible scenario that fits most, if not all, of the known facts, and is totally plausible'.

It is this: in October 1888, house-to-house police inquiries resulted in a long list of possible suspects – Anderson's criterion: 'Every man in the district whose circumstances were such that he could go and come and get rid of his bloodstains in secret.' Aaron Kosminski would have been on that list, but with no other suspicion attaching to him.

In July, 1890, when Kosminski suffered the first attack of insanity, which resulted in his being sent to the workhouse, it is very probable that the police would have been involved in his removal there. Or else it may have been that someone communicated to them the fact that Kosminski had become insane and that they harboured serious suspicions of his being the Whitechapel murderer. The police would then have found his name on their 1888 house-to-house suspects list.

Now as to the identifying witness. There was clearly only one person who came anywhere near the status of a witness with the potential to identify the suspect. That person was Joseph Lawende.

What must also be taken into the equation is the certain fact that no identification proceedings of any kind would have been permitted in the case of a person who had been committed to an asylum. Neither, for that matter, could such a one, that is to say a patient in an asylum, have been either charged or put on trial. All of which irrefutably suggests that the identification attempt must have been made during the period when Kosminski was being temporarily held in the workhouse, and would not until the lapse of a further six months be committed to Colney Hatch. The police would then have had to have arranged for Kosminski to be taken down to Brighton by a staff member of the Mile End Workhouse.

'What I believe happened,' affirms Evans, 'is that the Metropolitan Police arranged for Kosminski to be sent to the Seaside Home. Swanson tellingly uses the word "sent", and also the word "difficulty". The difficulty was probably encountered in getting the workhouse staff to escort Kosminski to the Seaside Home.'

The City Force's suspect, Aaron Kozminski, satisfied them as to his innocence, but was subsequently committed to the asylum by his relatives when his behaviour became intolerable.

Since *both* suspects ended up in Colney Hatch, it is perfectly conceivable that the respective accounts and allocations of ancillary details to names might just possibly have become confused, and by a similar feat of mental prestidigitation, since Mr Fido presents us with a binominate Ripper, and since two may be reasonably held in this case to be one, I find myself able to accept, at least the notion of, his innominate Ripper. In other words, a Yiddisher rose by (practically) any other (unknown) name smells just as sweet a guilty choice.

Fido elects for three beasts with one back – Kozminski, Kaminsky, and Cohen.

To recapitulate: Fido's ultimate thesis seems to be that Anderson's Polish Jew was Macnaghten's Kosminski, who was either Aaron Kozminski, who does not fit the facts, or Nathan Kaminsky, who *does*, but whose name was wrongly registered as David Cohen. All that this proves is the truth of the allegation that the top-brass police thinking was in irreconcilably stark disarray.

If we accept the suggestion that the Whitechapel murderer was indeed a criminal lunatic of whatever degree, then it must surely be that it is along the Fido line that we come nearest to the truth. The veritable Jack seems to be there – but in the next room. Sadly, however, the microscope slips out of focus, our eyes blink and blur, and when we look again the image has vanished. Frankly, I am not at all sure that we should be looking for a psychotic. The Ripper may well have been a psychopath, but not a deranged person.

Martin Fido's book is a valuable contribution, most engagingly written. He falls into some errors, but the plain truth – although it is never plain in a case so complicated and patchily and variantly documented as this – is that, in such a context, papal infallibility remains a Romish wish-think, and good old Christian Science 'error' is bound to creep sinfully in. But some errors are mortal sin errors, whatever the teleological value of that statement, and Mr Fido commits none of that really serious kind. To confuse his perineum with his peritoneum is uncomfortable rather than reprehensible, and a very understandable and excusable lay mistake. Neither is the rendering of ensiform as enform and enciform cartilage a significant error – outside, that is, clinical practice! His book has been, without doubt, a thoroughly worthwhile addition to Ripperature.

18
The Dundonian Ripper: William Bury

Although it was not until 1988 that William Henry Bury was paraded in a full-dress volume as a potential Ripper, he had actually been drawn to the attention of Ripper researchers by Euan Macpherson, of Montrose, in 1986, and, ninety-seven years before that, he had been suggested in the *New York Times* of 12 February 1889 as a likely Ripper, who had murdered his wife because she had suspected his identity. Thereafter, his name had been forgotten, and it was not until the publication of Macpherson's article 'Jack the Ripper in Dundee', in the *Scots Magazine*, in January 1988, that a case was adequately presented as to the possibility that tidings concerning Jack the Ripper might hail from that douce city of Northern Britain.

William Henry Bury was not a Dundonian born. The youngest of a family of three, he first saw the grime-stained light of day in Wolverhampton in 1859. He had migrated to London, and, at the age of thirty, abandoned the business that he had built up in East London as a sawdust merchant, quit his home at 3 Spanby Road, Bow, and, on Saturday 19 January 1889, with his wife, Ellen, boarded a boat for Dundee.

On their arrival there, the couple lodged first in rooms at 43 Union Street, with a Mrs Jane Robertson, before moving, on 29 January, into a basement flat at 113 Princes Street. According to Macpherson's article, Bury went, on Monday 4 February, into the shop a few doors along Princes Street kept by a Mrs Janet Martin, and purchased a length of rope. Exactly one week later, on Monday 13 February, he walked into the Bell Street Police Office saying that his wife had committed suicide.

A completely different version of events is given in *The Scots Black Kalendar* by T. M. Tod, published fifty years earlier, in 1938. Here it is said that, 'according to the police witnesses, Bury had rushed into the police office on a Sunday evening, and exclaimed, "I'm Jack the Ripper, if you go to my house you will find the body of my wife, which I have cut up and placed in a box."'

Both accounts agree upon the sequel.

Bury's confession was at first ridiculed, but as he persisted in it, the police decided to go along and take a look. Apparently to his great surprise, Bury found himself being detained while they checked his peculiar story.

Police Lieutenant David Lamb proceeded to the slaughter at No. 113. He entered Bury's basement, and there, sure enough, was Ellen Bury's savaged body, just as her husband had said, stuffed into a large wooden case. She had marks about her throat, as if she had been strangled. Her abdomen displayed a number of viciously deep, Ripperish stab-wounds. The police surgeon was summoned. He confirmed that Mrs Bury's injuries were inconsistent with her having committed suicide.

Bury was tried before Lord Young at Dundee Circuit Court on 25 March 1889. The court sat continuously for thirteen hours, and it was by the eerie flicker of candlelight that, at around ten o'clock at night, he was found guilty, convicted, and sentenced to die within Dundee Prison on 24 April following, upon which date Bury was duly hanged by Berry.[27]

But what does all this have to do with Jack the Ripper? Well ... when Lieutenant Lamb went to 113 Princes Street, he saw there a rear entrance to the tenement block. On the shabby old door was chalked, 'Jack the Ripper is at the back of this door.' A dark stairway led down to the Burys' apartment. At the turn of the stair was scrawled on the wall, 'Jack the Ripper is in this sellar.' The scribblings were assumed to have been done by some over-imaginative bairn. Anyway, Bury was never questioned about them. Neither was he ever questioned about his movements in London during the autumn of terror.

There is an incident, though, which ought perhaps to be weighed in evidence. Since his advent in Dundee, Bury had become a regular of a public-house situated at No. 129 Princes Street, a few yards from his new home. And there he had struck up an over-the-ale friendship with a man named David Walker, a house painter by trade. Walker testified that around noon on Sunday 10 February, Bury had visited him at his home. Walker was still in bed. They had chatted for a while, then Walker had tossed him the copy of the *People's Journal* which he had been reading, saying, 'Look and see if there's anything about Jack the Ripper, you that knows the place.' Bury reacted in a very odd way. He seemed thoroughly startled and upset, and threw down the paper.

It is also a fact – no more than a coincidence perhaps, but a fact nonetheless – that after Bury's departure from the East End of London no further Ripper murders took place. Moreover, there is evidence that Bury was a man of violence who slept with a knife under his pillow. On one occasion the Burys' London landlady, Elizabeth Haynes, had burst into their room after hearing Mrs Bury's screams for help, and seen Bury holding a knife to his wife's throat. It is true, too, that Bury had had the *opportunity* to commit the Ripper murders. He was living very close to the area where they were taking place.

While awaiting execution, Bury sat down and wrote a detailed confession, and there was forwarded to the Home Secretary a document which was said to have included some startling revelations regarding the Whitechapel murders. The statement was never made public.

One should, I think, further mention that Bury's mother went insane when he was only six months old.

And she died in Worcester County and City Lunatic Asylum, at Powick.

19

Jack the Artist: Walter Sickert

By every tenet of logic Frank Spiering's book should have written an end to the 'Highest in the land' rubbish.

It did not.

The royal bloodline, growing ever thinner, more tenuous, stretched – and stretched credulity – right on up to 1992.

It was in the faltering royal tradition that, in 1990, Jean Overton Fuller offered us *Sickert and the Ripper Crimes.*

This 'verry parfit gentil' lady, riding, wimple and all, on to the field of bloody conflict atop the crooked-legged battle-mare, Florence, under the run colours of the disarrayed Sickert company of knights pursuant, seemed destined for a redoubt.

I can vouchsafe for her as a very kindly, rather fragile, but tenaciously straight-dealing, person. I do, however, suspect that she would not be overly difficult to hoodwink. It might well be that in her honest innocence she would tend towards accepting all people as being as true in themselves and their motives as she was herself.

Our paths crossed in the '60s – her Guilford Place and my Doughty Street, Bloomsbury, days. It was just after she had published her fascinating study of 'Vickybird',[28] *The Magical Dilemma of Victor Neuburg*, which I had reviewed.

Would that I could be as enthusiastic about her contribution to Ripper studies. Albeit she has made some good points. The tale she has to tell is third hand. She was told it in 1948 by her mother, Violet, who was an artist and had become friends with another artist, a Mrs Humphrey Holland, *née*, in 1862, Florence Pash. Florence had been a friend of Walter Sickert, and also, so she claimed, of Mary Jane Kelly.

Jean Overton Fuller's book puts Sickert forward as the sole murderer. But the royal company is in there, hanging about in the wings. Miss Fuller has swallowed the Hobo bait whole. She believes Joseph to be the son of Walter and the grandson of Prince Eddy and his morganatic bride, Annie Elizabeth Crook.

It is not Florence Pash, but Jean Overton Fuller's mother, who has concluded that Sickert was the killer. She bases that gigantic assumption upon the belief that Sickert had seen the bodies of *all* the Ripper victims, and later, from memory, painted pictures of them.

Florence Pash told of the existence of these canvases, so different from his usual quiet, tertiary tonal studies; paintings of bleeding, mutilated corpses at which she could hardly bear to look.

That, the Fullers, mother and daughter, decided, could mean only one thing. How could he possibly have done this unless he had been present at all the murder sites? It was upon this somewhat shaky basis that they concluded that Sickert must have been the Ripper.

The analytical formula would seem to be: Florence tells Violet. Violet manufactures assumptions. Violet tells Jean. Jean leapfrogs to conclusions.

Miss Pash did not subscribe to the Sickert-is-Jack-the-Knife theory. What she believed was that Sickert *knew the identity of the Ripper*, and that he painted cryptic clues into some of his pictures. The supreme clue was in his painting *Ennui*, in which there is a picture within the picture. It hangs on the wall and is a portrait of Queen Victoria. Perched upon her left shoulder is a seagull. A GULL – get it? Another painting, *La Hollandaise*, is said to be of Mary Jane Kelly, as in death, while that entitled *Blackmail, Mrs Barrett*, is of Mary Jane Kelly in life. Good fanciful stuff.

If Florence Pash is to be believed, and it is in my submission a very big if, Sickert had at one time employed Mary Jane Kelly as a nanny, to look after Alice Margaret, and had been subsequently blackmailed by her. Kelly is supposed to have written to him saying that she and three of her East End fellows would blow the gaff on the royal marriage and Alice Margaret if Sickert did not cough up. He communicated this threat to the appropriate quarter and an end was forthwith put to Kelly, her friends, and their blackmail venture.[29]

Incidentally, Miss Fuller makes a nice point as regards Kelly's alleged residence in a convent. She informs us that in the slang of Elizabethan literature, 'nun' was often used to mean 'whore', and 'convent' a 'brothel'. When Hamlet said to Ophelia, 'Get thee to a nunnery', there is a doubt as to in which sense he meant it, lost upon a modern audience.

Florence Pash was convinced that she herself was in danger of her life because of her close knowledge of the Clarence affair. She was certain that an attempt had been made to kill her. It had happened one day in February 1892. She had been taking six-year-old Alice Margaret out for a walk and intended to bring her back to her home with her for tea. It was as they were coming from St Martin's Lane towards Trafalgar Square. They had just passed St Martin-in-the-Fields and were making for Charing Cross station. They were stepping off the curb at the place where the road broadens out at the junction with the Strand near Charing Cross when a coach came, furiously driven, straight at them. Florence jumped swiftly back, trying to lift the child with her to safety on the pavement, but the coach mounted the footway and Alice was hit by one of its wheels. The child, who was probably the target anyway, had to be taken to hospital.[30]

One severe worry as regards the reliability of Florence Pash's testimony is that she apparently trotted out as sober truth the long-discredited story that Sickert had received a hush-money bribe of £500 – in the shape of ostensible payment for an abysmally failed picture – from Lord Salisbury, to insulate his silence about the Masonic conspiracy.

However, in *Noble Essences* (1950), the fifth volume of his autobiography, Sir Osbert Sitwell describes Sickert as retailing the identical anecdote, not in relation to himself, but to the painter A. Vallon, living in great poverty at Dieppe, for whom Salisbury felt sorry and was determined to help with disguised charity. The picture in question, a river scene at Dieppe, was relegated to the attics at Hatfield.

Miss Fuller confesses, 'I do not believe in the three in a coach rumbling through Whitechapel to pick up and kill. Whoever the Ripper was, he went alone, on foot.' Neither was it on Hobo's word alone that she came to accept his ducal pretensions. As she records, Florence Pash claimed to have known of, and believed in, those high connections as long ago as 1892.

The whole of Jean Overton Fuller's tale is, to be sure, a puzzlement. One can only echo the sage advice of the authors of the *A to Z*, which is to treat with extreme caution pending the provision of valid corroborative evidence. And William Beadle, who can always be relied upon to produce a nice descriptive line, has observed, 'The highest level on which this can be put is Chinese whispers.'

20

Joe the Ripper: Joe Barnett

Paul Harrison's *Jack the Ripper: The Mystery Solved*, was the second full-length book of the year 1991.

He started off, Harrison tells us, by analysing the motives for the crimes and arriving at the conclusion that the sole possible motive was jealousy.

His second conclusion was that, without doubt, Jack the Ripper was a psychopath. So the search was on for a jealous psychopath. Scarcely a rarity.

With no more than that to go on, and with, commendably, no specific suspect in mind, Harrison decided to tackle the problem initially by conscientiously researching into everybody else's suspects, hoping to turn up some extra powerful confirmatory factor that had somehow been missed. But in the end all that he was left with were the broken dreams of other researchers.

Paul Harrison was by occupation a Ministry of Defence police officer. He said that he continually reminded himself that 'a policeman's logic would pay dividends provided

I continued to be thorough in my research techniques'. He worked slowly and doggedly on.

The first suspect that he examined was the man Cross, who stumbled upon the Buck's Row cadaver. He does not venture a Charles or George, nor is Charles Cross in the index. However, no matter what his Christian name, he was soon eliminated.

Harrison then looked into the lethiferous potential of John Richardson – he of the leather apron – son of Amelia Richardson, the lessee of 29 Hanbury Street, and completely exonerated him.

His third, and, as it proved, definitive, choice was Joseph Barnett, that self-same live-in lover of Mary Jane Kelly's as Bruce Paley's accusing finger had been levelled at well over a decade before.

Introvert Irish-Cockney, scion of a hard-working, devout, Roman Catholic, immigrant, East End family, he had by the age of twenty-eight lost both his parents and his job as a fish porter at Billingsgate, and relied upon sporadic portering at Spitalfields Market. Astute, intelligent, streetwise, insecure, Joe Barnett, something of a recluse, moved from lodging-house to lodging-house. An unsatisfactory way of life. But that was all to change.

On Friday 8 April 1887, as he was heading home to his Thrawl Street lodgings, he was approached by a propositioning prostitute in Commercial Street. She was Mary Jane Kelly. For Joe Barnett it was love at first sight. They moved in together. A stormy on-off relationship ensued. The ongoing bone of contention was Barnett's determination to get Mary Jane to give up prostitution, and Mary Jane's not to. Joe Barnett became a kind of lower-rung-of-the-ladder George Gissing.

Paul Harrison's 'solution' to the mystery, which has baffled the world for more than a century and a decade, is that Barnett killed four[31] of Mary Jane's practising prostitute friends in as designedly horrific and headline-grabbing a manner as possible, so that their gruesome mutilations and grisly deaths, met plying their part-time trade, would frighten her off the streets, back into his arms.

This dramatic strategy worked, but only for a while. 'The final fuse was ignited by Kelly when she ejected him from the love-nest and declared that their relationship was over.' Driven, 'love to hatred turn'd', in frenzy he proceeded, literally, to destroy her, as he believed she had wilfully destroyed him. If she would not have him, nobody else should have her. 'Barnett's whole rationale for murder was to force a woman into his arms and reform her character. Once that objective had failed, he had no further reason to kill.' The crimes ceased.

Harrison matched his Joseph Barnett against the FBI's magic profile formula. 'Fact after fact fell into place as in a jigsaw.' He felt well pleased. He had caught not Jack, but Joe the Ripper.

Then … four years later, Bruce Paley, having expanded his original idea to book length, brought out *Jack the Ripper: The Simple Truth* (1995). There was not, as a matter of fact, a great deal of difference in the way that Paley and Harrison dealt with Mary Jane's lover and the blood-guilt, which they alike alleged was his. The difficulty was that each had identified a completely different man, with a different *curriculum vitae*, and a different psychological make-up, as Joe.

Harrison claimed that a Joseph Barnett, one-time Billingsgate fish porter, born at 127 Middlesex Street, Whitechapel, on 23 December 1860, was Jack the Ripper. He never married – at least there is no record of his having done so – although he had a son by a local woman with whom, for a time, he lived. Like a retired Great Train Robber, he ran not a flower, but a fruit stall. He lived latterly at 202 Old Ford Road, Bethnal Green, and died, aged sixty-six, on 15 March 1927, of lymphosarcoma of the cervical and mesenteric glands. He was survived by a son, D. Barnett, of the same address.

Paley's evidences were said to apply to a Joseph Barnett born at 4 Hairbrain Court, Whitechapel, in 1858, the son of John and Catherine Barnett, who had fled the poverty and famine of their native Ireland. There were four sons – Denis (1849), Daniel (1851), Joseph (1858), and John (1860) – and one daughter, Catherine (1853). Both Daniel and Joseph worked as fish porters at Billingsgate Market. Like Harrison's Joseph, Paley's Joseph never married, and he, too, lived with a common law wife, Louisa. The couple do not appear to have had any children. His later occupation was that of dock labourer. He died, aged sixty-eight, on 29 November 1926, at 106 Red Lion Street, Shadwell, of (1) bronchitis and (2) oedema of the lungs.

Further research, carried out by Mark Madden, and published in *Ripperana* (No. 6, October 1993) and *True Detective* (November 1993), 'Jack the Ripper and the Irish Connection', has established beyond peradventure that Paul Harrison's Joseph Barnett was not the lover of Mary Jane Kelly. It is to the Joseph Barnett investigated by Bruce Paley that that sad distinction is due.

Paul Harrison's identificatory error in no way negates the general value and interest of what he has to say, nor should it be regarded as simply a reworking of Paley's thesis. Rather like Charles Darwin and Alfred Russel Wallace, both of whom more or less simultaneously hit upon the notion of the role played by natural selection in the evolution of the species, Bruce Paley and Paul Harrison are each entitled to separate credit for their independently arrived at joint conclusion.[32]

Bruce Paley's book is quite rightly praised by Colin Wilson in his Introduction to it for the way in which Paley has succeeded in capturing the atmosphere of Whitechapel at the time of the murders, and that of the London of the late nineteenth century.

21

Jack the Two-Backed Beast: Prince Albert Victor and James Kenneth Stephen

Given Dr David Abrahamsen's long list of academic qualifications, his many years of experience in the field of forensic psychiatry and the ten years of dedicated Ripperological study to which he can lay claim, it would not, perhaps, have been unreasonable to hope that what he had to say would be well worth listening to. He has, after all, interviewed and examined such killers as Nathan Leopold, a noted murderer of 1924, whom he catechised in 1941, and David Berkowitz aka Son of Sam (1977), and served as an expert witness in the investigation of Lee Harvey Oswald. Instead, he has produced *Murder and Madness: The Secret Life of Jack the Ripper* (1992), which Paul Begg, pulling no punches, described as 'the worst book ever written on the case'.[33]

The plain fact of the matter is that Abrahamsen – still in the outworn royalist mode – harks back to the, by this time discredited, theory advanced by his medical confrère, Stowell, and progresses, if that be the correct verb, thence to the further royal dalliance of Michael Harrison's *Clarence* (1972).

For his, Abrahamsen's that is, money, the Ripper is a beast with two backs. He becomes, to filch a psychiatric term, 'fixated' on the royal back of Prince Albert Victor and the commoner back of James Kenneth Stephen. He is never thereafter able to see beyond Eddy and Jem, working together in homosexual homicidal harmony to wreak the havoc.

There can, rather sadly, be no doubt of the good doctor's industry and dedication. In his pursuit of 'the historical, literary, psychiatric-psychocriminal and pathological material' he was bulldog-tenacious in the face of, his own words, 'daunting frustrations'. He availed himself of the resources in London of the Wellcome Institute for the History of Medicine, the British Library, and the British Museum, and, at the London Hospital Medical College, sought the advice of Professor J. M. Cameron, the pathologist, and Bernard G. Sims, the forensic odontologist.

In New York, where he lives, he paid visits to the New York Public Library and the library of the New York Academy of Medicine. He consulted Dr William Eckert, of Wichita, Kansas, who, in 1981, contributed 'The Whitechapel Murders: The Case of Jack the Ripper' to the *American Journal of Forensic Medicine and Pathology*. Vol. 2 No. 1, 1981.

And parcels soared back and forth over the Atlantic, keeping the respective post offices in profit. He received two parcels from the Public Record Office in London containing 1,643 prints of 'the complete files of Jack the Ripper', plus a *tranche* of copies of ancillary inquest documents despatched by the City Archivist at the Guild Hall.

Then, convinced that he had nothing less than the contents of 'never-before-released files' and 'heretofore secret information from Scotland Yard' – for which belief there was, alas, no basis – Dr Abrahamsen set to work. He read every item of information, every scrap of gossip.

Now he made his cardinal error: alighted upon his suspects and proceeded to fit the facts to them. As a psychiatrist, he turned his pince-nez on his suspects' childhoods, and found … what he expected to find. No matter. It is in his role of psychiatrist that we are most interested to hear what Dr Abrahamsen has to say. He is blurbed to us as one of America's leading experts on the criminal mind, the psychiatrist who psychoanalysed the Son of Sam.

To begin with, he is critical of other books about the case – 'most of the literature is in the nature of what might be called descriptive thrillers, which have never sought to explicate the psychodynamics of this cruel drama'.

Thus forewarned, we expose ourselves to a lengthy, sententious, jargon-ridden treatise, leading, at 201 pages' end, precisely nowhere.

Abrahamsen tells us that we may safely conclude that Jack the Ripper did not like women. The extent of his feelings of inadequacy was manifested in the violent disfigurement and disembowelment of their bodies. We may conclude that Jack the Ripper was sexually attracted to corpses.

In psychiatric-speak, Jack continued his cathartic series of assaults – *vulgatim:* went on ripping 'em up. Abrahamsen makes the sound point that the Ripper had no interest in his victims as individuals. There was nothing personal in it. They were merely a selection of representative scapegoats. It is also an odd realisation that not one of his victims, with the exception of Mary Jane Kelly, actually knew the name Jack the Ripper. It was not released into the public domain until *after* the night of the double event, 30 September 1888.

It is not long before, inevitably, our psychiatrist invokes sex. 'The sexual force,' we are told, 'often manifested as revenge, jealousy and envy, is the power that mobilizes, stimulates and maintains the impulse to murder.'

Says Abrahamsen: 'The behaviour of Jack the Ripper exhibits all the signs of sexual perversion. A perverted person is one who is consumed by a painful sexual dichotomy of desire and self-image. It is frequently the result of a poor sexual identity. In the case of Jack the Ripper and Son of Sam, both men experienced a sense of passivity or even castration in their relationships (or lack of them) with their mothers.'

On what authority does he say this? What does he know about the mother of Jack the Ripper? What he is in fact doing here is putting the cart before the hearse, displaying a background knowledge that betrays tailoring to a particular suspect or suspects.

It is a psychiatric commonplace that perversions are psychological expressions of castration, and that deviations – such as sodomy, bestiality, pederasty and paedophilia – are products of the sexual inventiveness consequent upon the need to overcome a sense of castration and passivity. The prevailing psychodynamic is the imperative to seek out inordinate risks to challenge and repair a 'wimpish self-image'.

Abrahamsen naively confesses his methodology. 'I began by extracting certain names from the litany of suspects. Then I applied the psychobiological elements of behaviour, accompanied by the psychohistorical hints along the murky road to the murders.'

And lo, he came up with Eddy and Jem.

Recalling that Michael Harrison originally suspected his Clarence of the commission of the murders, but later changed his mind and designated as the culprit James Kenneth Stephen, who had been the prince's tutor at Cambridge, Abrahamsen comments, 'Harrison painted a clear picture of the historical background, but his theories lacked psychological insight … It is an analysis of the psychological parameters that enabled me to discover that the Ripper murders were perpetrated by Prince Eddy and J. K. Stephen. That realization came years after wading through the police compilation of misanthropes.'

Indeed, Abrahamsen admits that he had been convinced all along that the clue to the Whitechapel murderer's identity remained buried in 'the hulking mounds of investigative reports'.

It was the death of Elisabeth Stride that caused him to abandon the idea that the Ripper stalked his victims independently. On that occasion the murderer was forced to flee in the midst of his *post mortem* desecration ritual, because someone was coming. Examining in closer focus the details surrounding the Ripper murders, Abrahamsen was 'persuaded that the Whitechapel escapades involved an accomplice, a helper, who was posted to warn when somebody was approaching'.

As one confirmation after another emerged from his research, Dr Abrahamsen found that 'the identities of the murderers began to unfold before my eyes'.

But first, let us hear his general conclusions as regards the Ripper. He was, we are told, a necrophile and committed necrophiliac murders. The molestation, mutilation, and desecration which Jack the Ripper carried out was clear indication of his special enthusiasm, fondness, for the corpses of his victims. 'To be blunt, the Whitechapel murderer was sexually in love with the lifeless bodies, which was the reason for the mutilation. He could not give them up, surrender them to somebody else. He wanted to possess their bodies. He put his mark on them to show that they belonged to him and him alone. He was now their master.'

Abrahamsen goes on to explain all about necrophilia. It is, he says, a rare disorder, recognised since olden times. The innocent-seeming fairy story of Sleeping Beauty is in reality an example of necrophiliac fantasy. The necrophiliac murderer desires a sexual object – man or woman – unable to reject him, requires a glacial lover to accept, without negative response, the kiss of death. Scientifically speaking, the normal – or, better word, usual – pattern for the necrophile is first to render the intended helpless, either by physical assault or the administration of some toxic aliment or poison that will produce unconsciousness, and then to despatch him or her while in that state.

That was the mode of Jeffrey L. Dahmer, late of Milwaukee, Wisconsin, who admitted to having killed and dismembered seventeen boys and young men during a thirteen-year *fest* of *lustmord*, between 1978 and 1991.

The dead body provides the necrophile with the highest form of gratification. He is overwhelmed by maximal destructive and sadistic impulses. Study of the necrophiliac acts of modern serial killers cross-illumines valuably the psychopathology of Jack the Ripper. His mode was to strangle, then ply the knife and mutilate.

'Deep in his mind,' Abrahamsen elucidates, 'he had felt rejected by women, which is another way of saying he was afraid of them. His fears turned into desire and perverted love for his victims, once dead. In some cases such disturbed love goes as far as cannibalism, where one drinks the blood or eats the flesh of the victim, as has been reported in the case of Dahmer. To some extent, such was the case of Jack the Ripper.'

Speaking out of a wide experience of forensic psychiatry, Abrahamsen felt it to be likely that the Ripper might have performed anal intercourse with some of his victims. 'It is the type of intercourse practised among homosexuals. In such a position, the murderer was strategically placed to strangle his victim into unconsciousness before completing the ritual of cutting her apart. To Jack the Ripper, the end result of murder superseded the importance of sex. He did not rape his victims. It was not to his liking. Instead, he substituted his knife for his own act of rape.'

Having been alerted by Stowell and Harrison to the Ripperish potentials of Prince Albert Victor and James Kenneth Stephen, and having reached the independent theoretical estimation that the crimes had to be the work of two people – who knew each other very well, were kindred souls – and believing that exhaustive police investigation had established that neither of the perpetrators actually resided in the Whitechapel area, but more likely came in from a short distance away at or around the weekend, which was the time when the murders were committed, Abrahamsen arrived at a certain tentative conclusion.

The next logical step was to examine the psychological credentials of his chosen brace of suspects, to determine whether they had the characteristics to be expected of the Whitechapel murderer. If they did, their personalities would show signs of sexual perversion and disorder. He delved first into the character of Jem Stephen. There was no difficulty in discovering the basic documented facts of his birth, non-marriage, and death, but fleshing out was another matter. The second son of Mr Justice Stephen, the learned author of *A History of the Criminal Law of England*, and the judge who was to preside over the trial for murder of Mrs Maybrick in 1889, he was educated at Eton, where he was the pupil of that redoubtable Uranian, Oscar Browning, and at King's College, Cambridge, where he was elected a member of that exclusive sodality, the Apostles, an elite whose philosophy embraced the doctrine of Higher Sodomy. Incidentally, Jem's supreme skill and endurance when playing the Eton wall game evidenced his possession of the considerable physical strength required of any serious candidate for the sanguiferous coronet.

Abrahamsen had almost given up hope of learning much more when, by serendipity, he stumbled upon Arthur Christopher Benson's *The Leaves of the Tree: Studies in Biography* (1911). It was a series of short biographies of men whom Benson had known at Eton. There emerged from its pages a figure with 'a very big head', whose 'terrific eyes could,' Abrahamsen wrote, 'conjure up frightening or terrifying reaction'. His body 'showed signs of rigidity and stiffness while walking, which, to me, indicated a rigid, inflexible personality'. He found it a significant point that at Eton the fifteen-year-old Jem was a hero among the smaller boys, and here speaks the programmed psychiatrist: 'The reasons were deeply rooted in his sexual fantasies. As a matter of fact, J. K. was very fond of small boys and played with them, not innocently and not naively. The love for such children expressed his pedophilia.'

In *Memories and Friends* (1924), a book which escaped Abrahamsen's attention, A. C. Benson penned another portrait of Stephen, this one of him as he remembered him in his Cambridge days:

J. K. Stephen was a young man of quite extraordinary brilliance and power. One sees the old days in a golden light, no doubt, but yet I do not think I ever heard talk of such range and quality as his; he could be serious, dry, severely intellectual; but he also had a sharp and keen-edged wit, together with a broad, fanciful, and quite irresponsible humour. He enjoyed almost more than strenuous discussion the society of appreciative, friendly, perceptive men, in whose company his talk could ebb and flow with his restless mood.

Quite unjustly, as I believe, Abrahamsen casts a stone at Stephen about his comportment in regard to his six-year-old cousin, Virginia Woolf.

In a memoir, 'A Sketch of the Past', in *Moments of Being: Unpublished Autobiographical Writings* (1976), Virginia Woolf tells of how she was sexually interfered with … 'There was a slab outside the dining-room door for standing dishes upon. Once when I was very small Gerald Duckworth lifted me on to this, and as I sat there he began to explore my body. I can remember the feel of his hand going under my clothes, going firmly and steadily lower and lower. I remember how I hoped he would stop; how I stiffened and wriggled as his hand approached my private parts. But it did not stop. His hand explored my private parts too. I remember resenting, disliking – what is the word for so dumb and mixed a feeling? It must have been strong, since I still recall it.'

The culprit, her eighteen-year-old half-brother, Gerald Duckworth, is clearly enough here named, but Abrahamsen writes: 'Virginia Woolf could not forget her own sexual experiences as a child. In her work she alludes to being fondled by certain family members, an experience we now characterize as sexual abuse … When she became sexually excited, she felt even more guilty and ashamed. The consequences of these feelings contributed to her depression and resultant attempts at suicide. Might one of the family members who fondled her also have been a perpetrator of the Whitechapel murders? The thought is a confounding one.'

No. The thought is a confounded one!

The character of Jem's father, the judge, is said to have been marked by aversion to any display of feeling. This produced a stern, as well as an intellectually highly competitive, home environment. Abrahamsen speaks of Jem's early severance from his mother – although he fails to supply chapter and verse – as having 'instigated his hostile feelings towards women', and quotes in evidence of this misogyny a poem, 'In the Backs', from J. K. Stephen's book of verses, *Lapsus Calami* (1891), in which the versifier sees a woman while 'strolling lonely in the Backs':

> I should not mind
> If she were done away with, killed, or ploughed
> She did not seem to serve a useful end:
> And certainly she was not beautiful.

Abrahamsen comments, 'The term "ploughed" has significant connotations when interpreted as meaning the forceful breaking through or cutting of the woman's body.' No doubt. But what it actually meant in university parlance was nothing more bloodthirsty than to fail an exam – as, 'He was ploughed.' This imputation of violent misogyny is to ignore Quentin Bell's authoritative testimony in *Virginia Woolf: A Biography* (1972), of Jem's descent in pursuit of womankind. He came, in 1889, violently to desire Stella Duckworth, Virginia Woolf's twenty-year-old half-sister, and violently to pursue her. The children were told to say that Stella was away, staying with relations in the country, whenever cousin Jem came a'calling.

But our not-so-tame psychiatrist persists: 'In my opinion it was J. K.'s relationship, or his lack of a relationship, with his mother that initiated his frustration and disappointment and laid the foundation of his hatred of women.' He was, in Abrahamsen's view, emasculated by his mother's rejection of him.

Turning then to look into Clarence's life, Abrahamsen failed to find any detailed study of his psychological and sociological development. There was a dispiriting dearth of reliable material about Prince Eddy's childhood. That did not deter the determined Dr Abrahamsen. 'Fortunately, careful analysis of Eddy's family, the roles of his mother and father and their style of bringing up their children, helped me to decipher the young prince's feelings, reactions and character traits during his formative years.'

The decipherment led him to conclude that the relationship between the prince, his devoted, egocentric, mild-mannered yet dominating mother, and his critical, competitive, frequently hostile father, was one of deep-seated conflicts. A recipe for disaster. Like Peter Pan, Eddy remained a child emotionally, intellectually, and sexually – passive, frightened, and cloaking his dependency with impulsive bravado.

Abrahamsen diagnoses dyslexia as the cause of all the troubles that he lists as besetting Prince Eddy – backwardness, learning disability, his apparently being shut off from his environment, and his inability to take part in sophisticated conversation. Moreover, his mother's 'emotional gyrations militated against Eddy's chances of a normal childhood'. Consciously or unconsciously, Alexandra retarded her children's emotional and intellectual development in order to prolong their dependency. To compensate for lack of manly demeanour, Eddy 'became a great hunter … In concert with other members of the aristocracy, he had become a professional killer.'

In October 1883, the young prince went up to Cambridge. J. K. had been selected to be his tutor and was also elected a Fellow of King's. After the prince came down in June 1885, J. K. was still able, according to Abrahamsen, to 'keep Eddy under his domination', and it is, he also says, a fair assumption (why? one asks) that they saw much more of each other than was realised.

Then, in the winter of 1886/7, while paying a visit to Felixstowe, J. K. sustained a very nasty head injury. Abrahamsen repeats A. C. Benson's version of how the accident occurred. 'There was an erection over a well, a pumping mill, worked by a small windwheel. Jem Stephen clambered up the ladder to examine it, and either by accident or in attempting to take hold of the revolving sails, received a blow to his head which half stunned him.'

Quentin Bell, however, in *Virginia Woolf*, states that the nature of the accident is not certainly known. In the Stephen family it was said that he was struck by some projection from a moving train. In any case, Abrahamsen considers it extremely questionable that he was made mad by the mishap. His expert view is that Stephen had shown symptoms of serious mental disturbances with temper tantrums since childhood, and all kinds of eccentricities, combined with depression and typically aggressive manic behaviour. He was 'periodically manic depressive, with an abnormal and impulsive mind' – whatever that means. Although Jem seemed to recover completely, and Abrahamsen will opine no further than that the blow to the head might have worsened his mental condition, his family and friends always believed that it had coloured his behaviour for the rest of his life.

In the natural order of things, the prince, his university days behind him, would have had to become more and more involved in the public life and duties of royalty, and J. K., feeling the progressive thinning of his influence and slipping of his grasp, grew, as the shadows between lengthened, insanely jealous, and fell to plotting the performance of feats that, by their enormity, would link Eddy indissolubly to him.

Abrahamsen next ranges J. K. and Eddy side by side and extracts from the comparison that:

> Both had been reared in family background circumstances of competition and unrest.
> Both shared miseries in their home lives.

Both exhibited a manly façade, but neither was emotionally able to love a woman. Both, in fact, disliked women.

While J. K. was haunted by the 'absence' of his mother, Eddy's problem was a gallivanting father. Both situations resulted in 'distorted sexual identification and low self-esteem'. It was, pronounces Abrahamsen, natural that they should feel an attraction for each other. Eddy revered J. K. as a witty, gifted Cambridge scholar. He was indeed highly intelligent, restless, manic-depressive, impulsive and aggressive. J. K. found Eddy, who was, in contrast, slow, dependent, impressionable, backward, listless and pliable, an attractive, effeminate young man, whom, despite his rank and station, he could easily dominate. 'Eventually they shared a common base of feelings and what appeared to the untrained eye as great differences in their personality and character were in fact the makings of an emotional intermeshing – like a key in a lock.'

With what justification one is at a loss to say, Abrahamsen declares that 'both had it in mind that women, and in particular prostitutes, deserved to be killed'. He doubts, he says, whether J. K. needed to use much persuasion to get Eddy, who loved to hunt and kill, to join him in wiping out these women they jointly found so threatening.

The psychiatrist has it all beautifully worked out – in his own fancy, to his own satisfaction. 'It seems reasonable to think that the two men met at J. K.'s parents' home – 32 De Vere Gardens, Kensington – and from there took the underground railway from Kensington High Street directly to Whitechapel. The journey took less than an hour, and, around ten or eleven o'clock, they were ready to start their hunting. So began the onslaught of two men, each muffled in his own egocentricity, prowling the streets of Whitechapel in search of victims on whom they could vent their accumulated frustration and hate.'

Abrahamsen conjures forth a *Grand Guignol* scenario for the murder of Mary Jane – or, as he calls her, Marie – Kelly. He suggests that, on the evening of Thursday 8 November 1888, Eddy succeeded in escaping from the private asylum where Gull had put him after the discovery of his connection with the four previous Whitechapel killings, and made his way straight to the Stephens' home in De Vere Gardens.

He and J. K. then boarded the Kensington–Whitechapel train. Perhaps both of them went with Kelly to her room. She would if approached by a couple have surely been thrown off any suspicion that she had run into the Ripper.

Abrahamsen then follows up with this grotesquery ... that Eddy and J. K. may have dressed themselves in women's clothes. These, or at least female undergarments, they have brought with them. 'Many homosexuals carry and/or wear women's underwear, particularly while having sexual intercourse. Women's underwear stimulates sexual orgasm.'

He thus paints for us a truly awful flame-lit Boschean picture. Bathed in the blazing red glow of a massively stoked-up fire, burning so fiercely in the tiny grate as to melt the spout off the kettle, two appalling transvestite figures sexually aroused and scantily clad in provocative women's underwear, glistening with blood, slash and rip, in an orgasmic crescendo of Sadeian lust, their gloating way through their crimson-gloried mutilation ritual.

Abrahamsen writes,

One man left the building about 6:00 a.m., and was heard walking away. The door was locked behind him. I suggest that – possibly helped by J. K. before he walked away down the passage between 5:00 and 6:00 a.m. – Eddy put on Marie's dress and shawl, shaving off his moustache and taking pains and time to create a convincing replica of the victim. Leaving the room, he carefully closed and locked the door after him in order to delay the discovery of the mutilated body and to allow ample time for his escape. Dressed like Marie, he played the role of a transvestite, a frequent homosexual pattern of behaviour, with a success that was measured by the encounter with Mrs Maxwell between 8:00 and 8:30 that morning.

And this is the man who talks in tones of contempt of 'descriptive thrillers'!

He sums up: 'Such behaviour may seem farfetched to a lay person, but it is commonplace to a well-trained psychiatrist or psychoanalyst.'

Following a further sojourn in the asylum after the unpicking of Mary Jane Kelly, Eddy was, with careful nursing and exemplary care, sufficiently restored to be able, for a while, to resume some of his princely duties, and to give the outward appearance of good health.

J. K. was not, as we shall presently see, to be so fortunate.

Getting on for a year after the start of the Whitechapel rampage, Prince Eddy was, in July 1889, reported to have been seen in the famous male brothel at 19 Cleveland Street. One is scarcely surprised to learn that His Royal Highness evaded arrest in a police raid, but it has been reliably stated[34] that he is certainly referred to as 'P. A. V.' in the file on alleged patrons of No. 19 kept by the Director of Public Prosecutions. Promptly that autumn, the discredited prince was packed off to India.

Seeking James Kenneth Stephen, Dr Abrahamsen's research led him to St Andrew's Hospital, Northampton. He found that Stephen had been confined there from November 1891 until his death a couple of months later.

Abrahamsen was fortunate enough to be made free of Stephen's medical notes. The contents of his file included a most curious self-written mental evaluation, couched as if it were written about him by somebody else – but actually composed by Stephen himself. Regarding it, Abrahamsen confides: 'The tone of arrogance typifies a person with pronounced sexual and narcissistic personality disorders. J. K. was attempting to refute the existence of the emotional and mental illness that had gripped his life. But the more he strove to appear normal, the more obvious his abnormality became. His situation had become desperate and gloomy, reflecting the depressive phase of his illness. J. K. would not accept what had happened to him.'

Abrahamsen claims to have shown that the two men whom he identifies (on no sound basis whatsoever) as James Kenneth Stephen and the Duke of Clarence had been present at the murder scenes of the Ripper's third, fourth and fifth victims. Stowell, he reminds us, interpreted the description of the person wearing a deerstalker hat as characteristic of 'S' when dressed to kill. He also claims to have demonstrated that an intimate relationship had blossomed between Jem and Eddy, which, because of its homosexual bent, had to be kept a tight secret. The existence of such a homosexual link between the two has never been established. Abrahamsen has just perpetrated two gigantic, un-factually bolstered assumptions.

There is an almost elegiac tone to Dr Abrahamsen's account of the down-pouring sandglass of the last days of the bifurcate Ripper. 'Within two years after the Whitechapel murders, J. K.'s mental aberrations had become even more apparent. And Eddy, too, was being treated by Gull upon his return from India.'

In the library of the Wellcome Institute, where he had come in search of the medical files of Sir William Gull, Abrahamsen could, to his astonishment, discover no clinical notes about his royal patients. Nowhere could he find one word about Prince Eddy. 'I made the reasonable deduction that certain material had been deliberately removed from the files.'

Thus, all the information that we have on Eddy's illness comes from secondary sources. We have no reports from his attending physicians. Notwithstanding, Dr Abrahamsen maintains that Eddy did present the symptoms of syphilis. Lightning abdominal pains were, he insists, symptoms of neurosyphilis, not pneumonia; and he was known to have walked with a stiff gait, generally assumed to have been caused by gout! Stephen, on the other hand, exhibited no symptoms of syphilis – neither *tabes* nor GPI – and his pupils were equal and reacted to light.

Even in illness, J. K. and Eddy were in lockstep. Having shared a life of mutual emotional disturbance, now they would share a death of mutual derangement.

Eddy died on 14 January 1892. Stephen died on 3 February 1892.

There are aspects of Dr David Abrahamsen in which I see a veritable reincarnation of Dr Forbes Winslow; all the blather about rumour and gossip that linked Eddy and Stephen with the Ripper, for instance, savours of the wildness of Winslow. As indeed William Beadle has apprised us, these rumours, that gossip, never existed until Thomas Stowell brought his case against Clarence into the arena.

Of Abrahamsen's other fifteen books, of his work as a psychiatric saviour, I know nothing, but I do know that in this book he has, in fine, done little more than propel Frank Spiering's lunatic theory forward, with a functional change of personnel, in that Stephen has now become the prime mover, no longer simply the scribe. The partnership persists, but with Stephen's blood-guilt grafted on.

Interestingly, my old friend the late Harford Montgomery Hyde, who had written first-rate books on the Cleveland Street scandal, Oscar Wilde, and the whole relevant period, told me that, all things considered, he thought J. K. Stephen to be the most likely of the named suspects to be the Ripper. Hyde, once a Mason, was, understandably, strongly opposed to Knight's thesis of a Masonic background to the mayhem. It would, he said, have been fundamentally contrary to everything he knew of Masonry and Masonic practice. He had a great deal of respect for the secret society's code of ethics.

What is, it seems to me, of especial value in Dr Abrahamsen's book, is its inclusion of James Kenneth Stephen's full medical history.

22
Tom the Ripper: Thomas Cutbush

Admittedly the year 1993 was dominated by the publication of the Diary and all the kerfuffle surrounding that event, but there were other books. John Wilding published his *Jack the Ripper Revealed*, which 'revelation' did not, I am sorry to have to say, seem to be anything like the final truth, although it was not without regal affinities to Knight's *Final Solution*, of seventeen years before. The book begins well with a sound account of the sequence of Ripper murders; then, like the proverbial curate's egg, it is only good in parts.

Mr Wilding's Ripper is yet another twin-backed beast – dorsally composed of those of Montague John Druitt and James Kenneth Stephen. Neither is a new aspirant. Stephen has played the front half of the beast in a previous pantomime. Around this allegedly maleficent pairing, the author weaves a credulity-straining tale, flashing forth clues of positively painful ingenuity – codes and ciphers, analogues and anagrams. Thus, the chalked writing on the Goulston Street wall, 'The Juwes are The men That Will not be Blamed for nothing' (he gets the so-often misrepresented inscription absolutely right), breaks down and rebuilds, letter by rearranged letter, into the message 'F. G. Abberline. Now hate M. J. Druitt. He sent the woman to hell.'

This anagram game can be quite amusing. One well-known Ripperologist discovered that 'James Maybrick' reassembled yields 'Barmy Jack is me.'

John Wilding introduces us also to Edward VII's East End love nest, above a butcher's shop in Watling Street. When the inner fires failed, or more frequently, had been quenched, His Royal Highness would clamber back into a fresh suit of clothes and rush forth to indulge his alternative favourite pastime of watching satisfying conflagrations!

Wilding's book I respect as an ingenuous exercise in ingenuity rather than an excursion into the fiefdom of fact. I rate it a good roistering boys' yarn. *Ripperana* (No. 7, January 1994) recommends it 'for dedicated crossword buffs only'.

The second alternative Ripper book, published in 1993, was *Jack the Myth: A New Look at the Ripper*, in which the mythopoeic A. P. Wolf takes a close look at unidorsal Thomas Hayne Cutbush, an aptly named young man with a known fetishist proclivity for stabbing or jabbing women in the *gluteus maximus* – Jack the Jabber – who was a Ripper suspect. The twenty-two-year-old nephew, so said Macnaghten, of Metropolitan Police Superintendent Charles Cutbush, he was plainly insane and was committed in April 1891 to Broadmoor Criminal Lunatic Asylum, where his condition, never good, seriously deteriorated over the years. He was described as 'violent, dirty and very destructive at times'. He died there in July 1903.

An especial lupine attitude is here imported into Ripperology, whereby it is seen as an extended indulgence in pornography – and violent pornography at that. Ripperologists in general, and Colin Wilson in particular, come in for some slashing knife-work, worthy of the old eviscerator himself.

I quote: 'To take but one lurid example which has the impotent killer substituting his penis for a knife [surely this should be the other way round!] and then thrusting it into the reproductive organs of his victims as an act of sexual finality ... Was Mary Jane Kelly buggered before being ripped to pieces?'

Again I quote: 'Did the Ripper cut the throats of his prostitute victims while they were bent over in front of him exposing their backside for sex or did he lay them on the ground, have them raise their skirts for sexual intercourse and then plunge his knife into them?'

And one more quote: 'In describing the Ripper about his task of killing Annie Chapman, Colin Wilson equates the killer's behaviour with that of a dog copulating with a bitch on heat. Mary Jane Kelly's murder has blood spurting over walls and Wilson postulates that the Ripper must therefore have been naked when he discovered the "ultimate thrill", a 3-month-old foetus in the victim's womb.'[35]

As an aside to the main story, Colin Wilson throws in a case where the victim's intestines were torn out through her vagina.

If one author relates the rumour that sperm was found in the anal passage of Mary Jane Kelly, then it is immediately shot down by another, because it ruins his own well-thought-out theory that the Ripper was unable to achieve an erection and used his knife instead. This illustrates the sort of stuff that is the Ripperologist's bread and butter.

Having disembarrassed himself of all this, Wolf comes, as one who seeks equity must, with clean hands to the task. His book is most interesting in that it views the Ripper from a refreshingly new perspective. Wolf brings to bear data derived from an examination of the twentieth-century serial killer, and uses it to construct a psychological profile of the innominate one in the best *Silence of the Lambs* tradition.

Such latter-day instructional masters as Ted Bundy, David Berkowitz, Richard Chase, Edward Gein, William Heirens, Joachim Kroll and our own, our very own, Peter Sutcliffe, are pressed into service. The author's unusual slant and provocative theorisings, backed up by the provision of such useful foregoing type-specimens, seem to hit home quite convincingly.

Wolf disputes the concept of the Ripper as a sex killer, choosing to believe that Elisabeth Stride was murdered by her former live-in lover, Michael Kidney, known to have been of the ilk of violence, but would extend the Ripper murders canon to include, as a dummy run, that of Martha Tabram.

No new data is on offer to bolster the guilt of Cutbush. There is the usual 'insinuendo' that because he was the nephew of Superintendent Cutbush of the Yard, there was a 'one of us' cover-up. It remains unconvincing.

A look at Wolf's novel analytical methodology is instructive, and can, I think, prove only beneficial to those who may perhaps have hitherto taken too strong an intellectual root in the received mythology.

In 1993, behind all the smoke and smother, the hype and snipe of Jack the diarist, quietly, modestly, something infinitely more important was taking shape.

It was in the month of February 1991 that Stewart Evans, a Bury St Edmunds police officer with an incurable curiosity about Jack and all his funny little games, answered a telephone call that was to revolutionise both his thinking on the case and, in a way, his life. At the other end – Richmond, London – of the line was an elderly man whom he had never met. 'You won't have heard of me,' he said, 'but I have some Jack the Ripper letters for sale, and I wondered if you were interested.'

The caller was Eric Barton, a well-known book dealer with an uncanny knack of getting hold of unique *objets de crime*. Stewart Evans had heard of him. Stewart Evans *was* interested. Within a week he was holding in a hand trembling with excitement the document that was henceforth to be known as the 'Littlechild Letter', and that was to reveal the first genuine previously unknown police suspect of any calibre to emerge since the discovery of the Macnaghten report put the names of Druitt, Kosminski and Ostrog in the frame for consideration.

In August 1991, Stewart Evans paid me both a visit and a compliment. At a time when it was his top-most top secret, he confided to me the name of the Littlechild suspect. He also laid before me for my inspection his newly acquired treasure. It was a letter, written on 23 September 1913, by former Detective Chief Inspector John George Littlechild, head of the Special (Irish) Branch, James Monro's Secret Department at Scotland Yard at the time of the Whitechapel murders, to his friend the celebrated journalist and author George R. Sims, who was also, as it happened, a friend of Sir Melville Macnaghten.

The name of Littlechild's suspect was Tumblety. Littlechild had written, 'Amongst the suspects, and to my mind a very likely one, was a Dr T ... He was an American quack named Tumblety and was at one time a frequent visitor to London and on these occasions constantly brought under the notice of police, there being a large dossier concerning him at Scotland Yard. Although a "Sycopathia [*sic*] Sexualis" subject he was not known as a "Sadist" (which the murderer unquestionably was) but his feelings towards women were remarkable and bitter in the extreme, a fact on record.'

Stewart Evans and his friend and colleague, Paul Gainey, a former journalist who had joined the Suffolk Police as a press officer in 1991, were to spend two busy years carrying out a thoroughgoing investigation into the life and times of Dr Francis Tumblety, who, in 1995, would be, as we shall see, the subject of their exceedingly important, fresh-ground-breaking book, *The Lodger*.

23

Robert the Ripper: Robert Donston Stephenson

The late Melvin Harris, celebrated debunker, hoax abolitionist, dab hand in the detection of deviousness, merciless expositor, and scourge of the careless, entered the lists sledgehammer in hand to crack walnuts. Instead, in his *Jack the Ripper: The Bloody Truth* (a title which, incidentally, I gave him), he produced a gigantic coconut of his own. He came to mock and, to no one's surprise greater than his own, stayed to appraise, and most astutely, the Ripperish merits of Dr Roslyn D'Onston aka Robert Donston Stephenson, mage, medical practitioner (of sorts), and drunken, drug-taking journalist, who suffered the C-change of a Christian conversion, and survived, newborn, to write learnedly on the patristic gospels.

Harris' visitation in search of 'the bloody truth' proved to be of the greatest value – for eighteen-nineteenths of the way a demolition, or, as he, quite reasonably, might have preferred to hear it styled, a ground-clearing job. An exceedingly capable one, too.

Especially satisfying is his final uprooting of that more-than-hardy perennial, Robert James Lees, medium *extraordinaire* (*très*), who was for long credited with having psychically tracked the medicine-man Ripper down to his West London lair.

Lees, it should be emphasised, was no culpable liar, but a man whose fantasy visions were so potent as sometimes to submerge reality for him: the strong wish became parent to illusory fact. Thinking could make it so. The dream was made flesh. That the flesh was insubstantial is clearly demonstrated by Harris' quotations from Lees' diary for 1888:

> Tuesday, 2 October: Offered services to police to follow up East End murders. Called a fool and a lunatic. Got trace of man from the spot in Berner Street.
> Wednesday, 3 October. Went to City police again. Called a madman and a fool.
> Thursday, 4 October. Went to Scotland Yard. Same result, but promised to write to me.

In January 1931, Lees died and the *Daily Express* despatched a highly experienced reporter, Cyril Morton, wily, resourceful and not overly scrupulous when it came to getting a story (I speak of him from personal knowledge, having had dealings with him on Fleet Street in the late 1950s), to worm – by hook, crook, or chequebook – the secret of the Ripper's identity out of Lees' daughter, Eva, to whom Lees was believed to have divulged it. Sphinx-like, she resisted all bribes and entreaties. Most likely because she was a sphinx without a secret.

Morton's crafty reportorial eye had, however, espied among a bunch of press clippings on Miss Eva's table one from the *Chicago Sunday Times-Herald* of thirty-six years before, and he had duly entered its date in his notebook. On his return to the office, Morton sent for that issue, and the original article, appropriately doctored, updated, and punted as a recently discovered secret document, was republished as a scoop two-parter in the *Daily Express* of 9 and 10 March 1931. A spurious authenticity was subsequently conferred upon the *Express* version of the *Chicago Sunday Times-Herald* story with its endorsement by ex-Detective Sergeant Edwin T. Woodhall, 'Late of Scotland Yard', in his ridiculous book, *Crime and the Supernatural* (1935).

Harris also catches the tampering Dr Forbes Winslow, red-handed and forgery-fingered, altering the date on an alleged Ripper letter addressed to him on 19 October 1889, from 1889 to 1888, and pinpoints the learned alienist as the first – but very far from the last – of the Ripper hunters to be corrupted.

It is in the nineteenth, and very last, chapter of *The Bloody Truth*, 'The Magician from the Mists', that is paraded forth for the first time the enigmatic and undeniably extremely odd, I would go further, sinister, Dr Roslyn D'Onston, whose candidacy derived from the rootings around of the late Bernard O'Donnell.

However, it is Melvin Harris who, having tracked down and had view of O'Donnell's manuscript, has, over an eight-year span of considerable personal research, extensively amplified O'Donnell's work, and in his Ripperological trilogy – *Jack the Ripper: The Bloody Truth* (1987), *The Ripper File* (1989), and *The True Face of Jack the Ripper* (1994) – gradually built up his own powerful indictment of Robert D'Onston.

In *The Ripper File*, what may be regarded as the intermediate report on the Magician from the Mists is once more confined to the ultimate chapter of the book. It is entitled 'A Passion for Darkness'. The preceding chapters are mainly atmospheric, contemporaneous reconstructions of the canonical five Whitechapel murders. 'A selection of some of the Victorian newspaper reports that helped to form, and distort, public opinion, fuel fears and create myths.' That may sound as if it is a purely cosmetic book, that it goes no further than skin-deep. Do not be deceived. The book's clear message is that journalists made the running from start to finish. A journalist it was, Melvin Harris believes, who, penning a bogus letter to the Central News Agency, gave Jack the Ripper his very name. Contemporary journalists kept the public at a white heat of fear throughout that long-ago autumn, and for a century and more thereafter journalists have 'concocted Ripper hoaxes to fill their columns and pockets'. To crown it all, the Ripper himself was, in Harris' submission, a journalist.

Harris confesses, 'I once felt that we would never identify the killer yet finally I came to name D'Onston Stephenson as the only man who can be taken seriously as the Ripper. He alone, of all the suspects, had the right profile, the opportunities, the motives, and the ideal cover. His background, his personality, his skills, his frame of mind, all fitted him for the fateful role.'

Harris warns, however, that 'all references to D'Onston in works prior to mine should be disregarded. The earlier material is grossly inaccurate and has now been superseded. Any pieces written on D'Onston by Aleister Crowley should be read for their curiosity value only, and not taken seriously.'

Two years on from his first Ripper book, Harris has learned a great deal more regarding the biographical details of his suspect, but has still not managed to unearth anything remotely resembling *proof* of D'Onston's blood-guilt.

By 1994, when he published *The True Face of Jack the Ripper*, he had honed his case against D'Onston very sweetly, and he gives here the sources for much of the material included in his two previous books.

'My first verdict on the Whitechapel mystery was,' he tells us, 'an open one. None of the contending theories stood up to close scrutiny, so the killer was probably someone unknown and unsuspected.'

But, after studying the FBI method of serial-killer profiling, Harris became aware of a slight change of emphasis – 'The killer *could* have been suspected at one time but may well have been able to give a convincing display of total innocence.'

Harris thereupon set to work, and, using the documents of the time, applied up-to-the-minute Quantico methods to produce a Master Profile which threw up Roslyn D'Onston as, on thirteen essential points, a very persuasive suspect.

In July 1888, D'Onston, living in Brighton, is allegedly suffering from neurosthenia[36], which is a state of great nervous power and excitement, for which the prescribed treatment is rest, light diet, no stimulants and fresh air, for which latter good old bracing 'Dr Brighton' had, even in those days, been long celebrated. But what does D'Onston do? He turns his ailing back upon salubrious, invigorating ozone-supercharged Brighton, and betakes himself off to the acrid, sooty, sulphur-laden air and grim and grimy atmosphere of Whitechapel, where, on 26 July 1888, he books himself a private bed in that notorious palace of pain and emirate of death, the London Hospital – for, if you please, a rest cure!

He remained in that hospital for 134 days (26 July to 7 December 1888), his time there coinciding, incidentally, with that of the residence, in his basement rooms in 'Bedstead Square', of John Merrick, the Elephant Man. Coinciding, too, with the entire span of the activities of Jack the Ripper (31 August to 9 November 1888).

During his spell as an in-patient, D'Onston established a reputation for being restlessly ambulant, frequently vanishing and equally frequently popping up all over the place. No one could ever at any time be absolutely sure where he was or wasn't. Nocturnal prowling on his part became by repetition remarked and unremarkable, accepted as natural, indeed, in the case of this particular ever-restless neurosthenic patient.

It would not, it follows, have been especially difficult for him therefore to have slipped, unmissed, out of the well-boscaged, poorly railinged hospital perimeter, and, as Harris points out, the first murder, that of Polly Nichols, took place just two minutes' walk from the hospital, and the others were also all committed within quick and easy reach of D'Onston's rest-cure bed.

'The Kelly murder was in a class of its own,' says Harris. The butchery was concealed within the privacy of a house, so an exit could be made at any time. No need to rush along backstreets to the hospital. The return to base could be taken at a brisk walk. And, as always, the hospital grounds provided plenty of cover for a clean-up, even a change of clothing.

In Harris' view, D'Onston's illness was 'certainly faked. The symptoms, excitability, tension, sleeplessness, are easy to assume or induce.' He concludes, 'The hospital [was] an ideal staging-post for D'Onston's series of premeditated killings.'

Conjured out of the mists by Harris' persistent pursuit, D'Onston the Magus emerges as an incorrigible embroiderer, but one whose threads nevertheless are of genuine, not artificial, silk; or, put another way, a small fire of truth is to be found flickering behind all his vasty smokescreens.

Myself, I do not feel that Harris' proof comes up to his conviction. But that, of course, in no way devalues the considerable importance of his very solid contribution to the ongoing effort to reach 'the bloody truth', and the absolute indispensability of his superbly researched trilogy to anyone plagued by a serious desire to sally forth and do likewise.

By way of postscript. My friend Melvin Harris informed me that what kept D'Onston in the London Hospital for a second – seventy-four-day – stay in 1889 was a severe attack of chloralism, the consequences of excessive use of the sleeping draught chloral hydrate. He also confided the quite extraordinary intelligence that it was the celebrated 'Mrs Satan', otherwise Victoria Woodhull, who, around the year 1893, converted Robert Donston Stephenson to Christianity.[37]

24

Jack the Jew

So far as the bewildered and fear-struck indigenous East End nominal Christians were concerned, it was the Russo-Polish wandering Hebraic immigrés who bore the major brunt of suspicion.

Had the mob seen it, the chalked inscription, which had appeared on the black facia of the right-hand jamb at the entrance to Goulston Street Dwellings, beside the short passageway to the common stairs that led up to Nos 108 to 119,[38] might have triggered a home-grown pogrom.

Written in a rounded schoolboy hand, the inscription read,

The Juwes are

The men That

Will not

be Blamed

for nothing

It was while patrolling his Goulston Street beat at 2.55 a.m. on Sunday 30 September 1888 that the sharp eye of PC Alfred Long, of the Metropolitan Police, was the first to spot the inscription. He copied it into his notebook.

A good example of the sort of unexpected difficulties with which one is beset in the reinvestigation of the Whitechapel murders is provided by the disparities encountered in trying to establish so seemingly simple a matter of fact as the words written on the wall.

The following seven variations occur in the literature:

A. 'The Jews are the men that won't be blamed for nothing.' (Smith, 1910).
B. 'The Jews are the men who will not be blamed for nothing.' (Macnaghten, 1914).
C. 'The Jews are not the ones to be accused for nothing.' (Ingleby Oddie, 1941).
D, 'The Jews are not the men to be blamed for nothing.' (McCormick, 1959; Odell, 1965; Camps, 1966).
E. 'The Juwes are the men that will not be blamed for nothing.' (Cullen, 1965; Jones & Lloyd, 1975).
F. 'The Juwes are not the men to be blamed for nothing.' (Farson, 1972).
G. 'The Juwes are not the men that will be blamed for nothing.' (Rumbelow, 1975).

The spelling of the word 'Juwes' set the investigators thinking. Many police were Freemasons and they recalled that in Masonic circles the 'Juwes' are the three men who, according to Masonic tradition, murdered Hiram Abiff, the Masonic Grand Master and builder of Solomon's Temple. Their names were Jubela, Jubelo, and Jubelum. A search was made for them after the crime. They were found. And each lamented:

Jubela: O that my throat had been cut across, my tongue torn out and my body buried in the rough sands of the sea …

Jubelo: O that my left breast had been torn open and my heart and vitals taken thence and thrown over my left shoulder …

Jubelum: O that my body had been severed in two in the midst, and divided to the north and south, my bowels burnt to ashes in the centre and the ashes scattered by the four winds of heaven …

The three murderers were brought before Solomon, who, in his wisdom, decreed it meet and just that each should be executed in the manner in which he himself had described.

Note. Annie Chapman's intestines had been taken out of the body and placed on the shoulder. Catherine Eddowes' abdomen was exposed, the intestines drawn out to a large extent and placed over the right shoulder. A piece of the intestine was quite detached from the body, and placed between the left arm and the body. There was a strong ritual element surrounding the treatment of Mary Jane Kelly's corpse.

Now, two questions are posed. Was the Ripper a Mason? If he was, he would have to have been a fairly senior one to know about the three Juwes, for the information and secret signs and responses that accompany it are part of the ceremony of introduction to the Third or Master Mason's Degree of the Order. Sir Charles Warren, the man who ordered the writing to be cleaned off the wall, was a Mason: a very high-ranking one. Was *that* the reason why he had the writing removed?

This statement is not exactly right. It was Superintendent Thomas Arnold, the officer in charge of H Division, Whitechapel, who, immediately making up his mind that the writing on the wall had nothing to do with the murder, and fearful that its reference to the Jews would, in the already overheated anti-Semitic climate prevailing, be likely to prove inflammatory, had an inspector with a wet sponge standing by when Sir Charles Warren arrived to see it.

Superintendent Thomas Arnold reported,

I was apprehensive that if the writing were left it would be the means of causing a riot and therefore considered it desirable that it should be removed having in view the fact that it was in such a position that it would have been rubbed by the shoulders of persons passing in and out of the Building. Had only a portion of the writing been removed the context would have remained. An Inspector was present by my directions with a sponge for the purpose of removing the writing when Commissioner arrived on the scene.

Warren appeared at 5 a.m. He agreed with Arnold and gave the order that the somewhat cryptic message should be there and then expunged. There were those officers – of the City Police – who felt that the writing ought at least to have been photographed before it was washed off. Sir Robert Anderson was later to describe the erasure of the wall-writing as an act of 'crass stupidity'.

Warren reported to the Home Office:

The most pressing question at that moment was some writing on the wall in Goulston Street evidently written with the intention of inflaming the public mind against the Jews, and which Mr Arnold with a view to prevent serious disorder proposed to obliterate, and had sent down an Inspector with a sponge for that purpose telling him to await his arrival. I considered it desirable that I should decide this matter myself, as it was one involving so great a responsibility whether any action was taken or not. I accordingly went down to Goulston Street at once before going to the scene of the murder: it was just getting light, the public would be in the streets in a few minutes, in a neighbourhood very much crowded on Sunday mornings by Jewish vendors and Christian purchasers from all parts of London. There were several Police around the spot when I arrived, both Metropolitan and City. The writing was on the jamb of the open archway or doorway visible to anybody in the street and could not be covered up without danger of the covering being torn off at once. A discussion took place whether the writing could be left covered up or otherwise or whether any portion of it could be left for an hour until it could be photographed, but after taking into consideration the excited state of the population in London generally at the time the strong feeling which had been excited against the Jews, and the fact that in a short time there would be a large concourse of the people in the streets and having before me the Report that if it was left there the house was likely to be wrecked (in which from my own observation I entirely concurred) I considered it desirable to obliterate the writing at once, having taken a copy ... of which I enclose a duplicate.

Undoubtedly, the erasure of the chalked message was wise. Warren and Arnold's timely action may well have diverted what could have developed into a serious life-threatening riot. The pity of it is that before its obliteration the writing on the wall was not photographed.

25

American Jack: Dr Francis Tumblety

We come now to the *magnum opus* of the year 1995, shamefully and undeservedly overshadowed in a grotesque accident of time by the dubious *Diary*.

Stewart Evans and Paul Gainey's *The Lodger: The Arrest and Escape of Jack the Ripper* was that rarest of Ripper books, one with something really fresh and solid to offer. Dr Tumblety *existed*. Dr Tumblety *was* the prime suspect of one of the most practical contemporary career police officers at the Yard *at the time*. Dr Tumblety's personal characteristics and behaviour pattern present a series of, I suppose we had better call them 'coincidences' – correspondences really – which would seem to defy mere chance.

Here are some to be going on with:

He cherished a most virulent hatred of women in general and prostitutes in particular.
He boasted proudly of his collection of pickled wombs.
He used aliases.
He was in London at the material times of the killings.
He had been the subject of police enquiry before his arrest.
After his arrest and flight, the murders ceased.

Obviously, we are on to *something* here. 'How many coincidences do you need?' asks Stewart Evans.

'In any investigation,' writes A. P. Wolf in *Jack the Myth*, 'whether brutal murder is discussed or simple theft, there may well be a certain amount of coincidence present and often it can be quite safely dismissed as that – circumstantial events that inexplicably coincide. But when there are just too many, then any investigator should pause for thought and ask himself what exactly is going on?'

Having spent a great many years working on the Oscar Slater case, I am myself no stranger to the most outrageous flexings of the long arm of coincidence, and one thing which I have learned to appreciate is that coincidence can be a two-way mirror.

The instant effect of the Littlechild Letter was to direct a laser beam at current Ripper studies. It summoned a totally new, never before even heard of, suspect to the scene; it indicated categorically that there had been no contemporary police interest in Montague John Druitt; it cast serious doubt upon the credibility of Dr Robert Anderson; it identified the very probable source of the letter that had christened the Whitechapel murderer Jack the Ripper.

And that was only a beginning.

Evans and Gainey have, with exemplary diligence, managed to piece together the exceedingly fragmented seventy-year life, and reconstruct the multifaceted personality, of this man who was at first no more than a meaningless name in a letter.[39]

Born, 'as near as can at present be ascertained', in 1833, near Dublin, Tumblety, while still a young child, was brought by his Irish family to Rochester, New York – that same locus where those other mountebanks, the finger-and-toe-cracking Fox sisters, set spiritualism tapping its way to a thumping success. At the identical time that the foxy Fox girls were selling their new religion, the precocious fifteen-year-old Irish-American Frank Tumblety was turning a fast buck peddling pornographic literature on the canal boats.

His first taste of medical practice was doing odd jobs as a teenager for the dubious Dr W. C. Lispenard, MD, consulting physician and surgeon in Dr E. J. Reynolds' large and long-established hospital for the treatment of private diseases on the French system, and specialising in dealing with the intricacies of 'female complaints' – Consulting Office and Operating Rooms, corner of Mill and Market streets, upstairs. Here was sold Dr Reynolds' 'Patent French Safe', warranted a safe and sure preventive against pregnancy and disease, and here were counselled young men who 'by indulging in secret habits, have contracted that soul-subduing, mind-prostrating, body-destroying vice'. Office hours from 7 a.m. to 9 p.m.

Young Francis Tumblety's father, James, died in 1851, and the eighteen-year-old lad left home and made his way to Canada. There, following in Lispenard's disreputable medical footsteps, he built up a reputation as a quack or 'Indian herb' doctor. By the time he was twenty-four, he had become well known as an abortionist in the Quebec–Toronto area, and in 1857 was arrested for attempting to procure an abortion for a seventeen-year-old prostitute, Philomene Dumas. Defended by two astute Irish lawyers, Devlin and Drummond, Fenian sympathisers, who alleged a police frame-up, he was released when no true bill was returned against him.

Three years later, while he was practising at St John, New Brunswick, an inquest found him guilty of gross malpractice, administering irritant medicines which resulted in the death of his patient, James Portmore. This time found guilty of manslaughter, he fled the city. He had, shortly afterwards, to flee again – from Pittsburgh, Pennsylvania, leaving behind two severely troubled female patients.

By 1861, he was practising in Washington, D.C. It is very likely that it was during this period of his life that what has been reported as his disastrous marriage took place. The story is that when he was 'quite a young man' he had fallen desperately in love with a very pretty woman who was some years his senior. The honeymoon was barely over when he discovered that his wife had been, and still was, practising as a prostitute. From love of her to hatred of all womankind he turned.

It was in St Louis, in 1865, that he was arrested on suspicion of being concerned in the plot to assassinate President Abraham Lincoln. He was held briefly in Washington's Old Capitol Prison. No connection could, however, be proved, and he was set free.

His first descent on the Old World seems to have been in 1869, when the thirty-six-year-old 'doctor' visited Ireland, and then England, where he stayed at the rather splendid Langham Hotel, in London. He returned to the States, sailing from Liverpool.

Tumblety was back in Liverpool in 1874, and set up in business there as a herbal doctor. It was in this capacity that he became acquainted with a young man of twenty-one who was a martyr to neuralgic pain in the head and face. This young man was Thomas Henry Hall Caine, who was to achieve very considerable literary distinction as a novelist. Young Caine was apparently facultatively bisexual, and an affair was soon flourishing between him and the misogynistic, homoerotic Tumblety. But, by the turn of the year, Tumblety, true to habit, had managed to make Liverpool too hot to hold him, and took once more to his winged heels.

Cosily settled in at No. 5 Glasshouse Street, on the Piccadilly fringe of London's Soho, by January 1875 he must have – as the old proverb had it that he should not – thrown stones, for he was swiftly away for stays in Cavendish Square and the Strand, and the Midland Hotel, Birmingham, before, in September, he was scooting off across the herring pond once more.

The restless odyssey went on. It was back in England in 1878, and thereafter took place twice-yearly visits to London, where he had an office throughout the early 1880s. Around June 1888, Dr Francis J. Tumblety sailed back to Liverpool from America. He was assuredly well ensconced 'somewhere in London' by Friday 31 August, when Ripper-shed blood fell on the cobbles, for that was also the day on which Tumblety committed an offence of gross indecency with one Arthur Brice, in London. And that was not his first detected act of the kind. Twice more he was to be caught out. On Sunday 14 October 1888, his fellow participant in forbidden homosexual activity in London was James Crowley. On Friday 2 November 1888, a week to the day before Mary Jane Kelly's horrendous demise, Tumblety was once again indulging his taste for gross obscenity, this time with John Doughty, in London.

The doctor's sins finally caught up with him on Wednesday 7 November. That was the day he was arrested. The police were then obliged either to take him before the Court within twenty-four hours or release him on police bail. He was apparently bailed to surrender on 14 November which he did, and was put up before Mr James L. Hannay, the magistrate at Marlborough Street Police Court, on the gross indecency charges, and was remanded on bail in the sum of £300.[40]

Between 20 and 24 November, Tumblety fled England, taking a ferry from the Channel ports to Boulogne, whence he travelled to Le Havre, and there, on 24 November, under the alias Frank Townsend, embarked on the French steamer, *La Bretagne*, for New York.

The oddest thing of all in connection with Dr Tumblety is the total absence of his name, not only from the newspapers, but also from all the official documents – not a single mention in the police papers, the Home Office files, not even in the highly confidential progress reports supplied regularly by the police to the Home Office.

Evans and Gainey combed the Public Record Office files in vain. They sought without success for the large dossier on him that Littlechild had said existed at Scotland Yard. It had vanished. His name exists nowhere amid the acres and acres of bureaucratic paperwork. They shrewdly interpret this curious lacuna as symptomatic of the occurrence of an incident which the authorities would rather not remember.[41] What incident? The loss of their prime suspect? What could have been more disastrous? What more potentially destructive? What more deserving of a conspiracy of silence? They had had him in their hands … and they had let him go! What would the press and public have made of it if they had got wind of it? The gravity of the police error in permitting the bailing of Tumblety from Marlborough Street Police Court would have swung back and forth as lethally as one of those iron balls on a chain that the demolition men use to such effect. It would have demolished the reputations of senior officers, smashed to smithereens those of lesser fry, weakened irreparably the flying buttresses of Scotland Yard, and reduced bright-prospect careers to brick-dust. This was surely – if there ever was one – the time for a complete cover-up. Batten down the hatches. Keep mum. Careless talk costs livelihoods. Let there be smog.

What, say Evans and Gainey, is clear through the fog that has descended around Tumblety is that the detectives investigating his movements considered him dangerous; dangerous enough to pursue to New York.

Not that you will find any surviving official record of that pursuit, either. We have to clutch at straw clues. Evans and Gainey have managed to get a strong grasp on those intentionally fragile clues, and have been able to reconstruct what they believe to be the deliberately hidden scenario. They tell us that, on his previous visits to London, Tumblety had usually stayed at hotels. 'We believe that after his return in 1888 he had changed his lifestyle and took up lodgings at 22 Batty Street.'

Batty Street was snugly in the heart of Ripperland, ideally situated in relation to the sites where the murders took place, and he had engineered there a safe bolt-hole, calculated to provide him with easy access to the killing field and a proximate lair in which to go to ground.

In the early hours of Monday 1 October 1888 – shortly after the murders of Elisabeth Stride and Catherine Eddowes – a German woman, Mrs Kuer, who took in lodgers at her home, No. 22 Batty Street, St George's-in-the-East, was disturbed by the late return of the American gentleman, a doctor, who had engaged one of her rooms. In the morning, the landlady, her suspicions aroused, had her husband check the lodger's room. He saw there a sinister-looking black bag. He opened it and found therein a long sharp knife and a pair of bloodstained shirt cuffs. Next day the lodger left, never to return.

Evans and Gainey are perfectly certain that the 'American Doctor' lodger in question was Dr Tumblety. They are of the opinion that Elisabeth Stride was the victim of a domestic dispute, nothing to do with the Ripper. *He* had been busily occupied at around 1.40 a.m. in Mitre Square. It took between ten and fifteen minutes to walk from there to Batty Street. Imagine, they write, the killer's consternation when, fleeing homewards from Mitre Square, 'he made his way back to his lodgings in Batty Street to find the police swarming around the area. Another killer had murdered Liz Stride earlier that night in Berner Street – very near his lodgings. He had been virtually ensnared completely by accident.' No wonder he fled his lodgings! He must have thought that the police were rapidly moving in on his address after the Mitre Square murder. 'Now he turned his back on those lodgings to take up residence elsewhere, with the police, for the first time, already on his trail.'

Evans and Gainey have put together a persuasive sequence of police activity centred upon the enigmatic Tumblety in this country, and they have also researched connected events in America. They tell us that in the course of the week following the killing of Stride and Eddowes, that is 1–7 October 1888, a 'certain member of the CID' was sent to Liverpool to commence enquiries to trace the movements of a 'certain mysterious personage' who had landed in Liverpool from America. It was found that he had already left Liverpool for London some time before.

A Man from America – not necessarily *the* Man from America who concerns us (although Evans and Gainey incline to the belief that it *was* Tumblety under one of his myriad alter egos) – had stayed at a well-known first-class hotel in the West End (the Charing Cross Hotel). He had departed suddenly, leaving behind a black leather bag containing, as well as wearing apparel, letters, documents, chequebooks and prints of an obscene nature.

We are further informed that, in October 1888, Scotland Yard contacted the San Francisco Police, asking them if they could supply a sample of Tumblety's handwriting. They could – and did. What is interesting is that a request should have been addressed to that city, for it indicates that the Yard must have been making far-flung enquiries and had obtained wide-ranging intelligence regarding him.

The *New York Times* of 19 November 1888, reporting the arrest of Tumblety in London on the previous Thursday (14 November), on suspicion of complicity in the Whitechapel murders, was quite wrong. There is absolutely nothing to indicate that his arrest was in connection with anything other than the gross indecency charges, 'What the article does indicate is that the London detectives did not have enough evidence to charge Tumblety with the murders,' write Evans and Gainey, 'and were no doubt relying on obtaining an admission which was not forthcoming.'

On Sunday 2 December 1888, Tumblety arrived in New York. Two detectives from the New York Police Department had been despatched to wait at the gangway-side, identify him as he left the ship, shadow him, and set a watch on his lodgings, which proved to be at 79 East Tenth Street, where he was staying with a Mrs McNamara, an old friend of his. He had lodged with her before. He had at one time had a business at No. 77 East Tenth.

Chief Inspector Thomas Byrnes, head of the Detective Bureau of the New York City Police Detective Department, told the *New York Times*, 4 December 1888, that there was no charge whatever against Tumblety. He had had him followed for the sole purpose of securing his temporary address. 'I simply wanted to put a tag on him so that we can tell where he is. Of course he cannot be arrested for there is no proof of his complicity in the Whitechapel murders and the crime for which he was under bond in London is not extraditable.' The newspaper account continues: 'Mr Byrnes does not believe that he will have to interfere with Tumblety for anything he may have done in Europe, and laughs at the suggestion that he was the Whitechapel murderer.'

Comment Evans and Gainey: 'It is possible that Byrnes may have been making light of Tumblety to deflect press interest.'

There is talk in the *New York World* of an English detective parading up and down Fourth Avenue and Tenth Street, and in his 'headquarters', a saloon bar on the corner, confiding in the barman. Said that worthy: 'He wanted to know about a feller named Tumblety, and I said I don't know nothink at all about him, and he sez he wuz an English detective and he told me all about them Whitechapel murders, and how he came over here to get the chap that did it.'

According to Evans and Gainey's reasoning, this nameless detective must have been sent over from England by the Yard as soon as it was realised that Tumblety was on the run. If he had left from Liverpool, the probability is that he would have arrived in America well before Tumblety, who had been forced to travel via France, although the American press reports suggest that the English detective may have arrived on the same ship as Tumblety.

Tumblety slipped quietly away from No. 79 East Tenth Street in the small hours of 5 December 1888. A fortnight went by. On 20 December Inspector Walter Andrews, one of the three original Ripper hunters despatched by the Yard to Whitechapel, arrived in Montreal from Toronto. After conferring with the police chief, he left that night for New York. Evans and Gainey consider it most probable that Andrews had been assigned the task of investigating Tumblety as a suspect from an early stage. 'Now he was chasing him across the globe in a last-ditch attempt to retrieve the situation. While the press talked increasingly about the murders, Andrews' American journey went almost unnoticed.' Andrews was the Yard's Russian speaker, and may have been charged with following up all leads relating to foreigners.

Andrews himself stated that twenty-three detectives, two clerks, and one inspector were employed on the Whitechapel murder cases. He also stated that the police were without a jot of evidence upon which to arrest anybody. He added that there were some half-dozen men working in America and that 'American detective agencies have offered to find the murderer on salaries and payment of expenses. But we can do that for ourselves, you know.'

Finally, on the last day of 1888, the English press caught up on the state of play. The readers of the *Pall Mall Gazette* were informed,

> Inspector Andrews, of Scotland Yard, has arrived in New York from Montreal. It is generally believed that he has received orders from England to commence his search in this city for the Whitechapel murderer. Ten days ago Andrews brought hither from England, Roland Gideon

Israel Barnet, charged with helping wreck the Central Bank, Toronto, and since his arrival he has received orders which will keep him in America for some time. The supposed inaction of the Whitechapel murderer for a considerable period and the fact that a man suspected of knowing a good deal about this series of crimes left England for this side of the Atlantic three weeks ago has, says the [*Daily*] *Telegraph* correspondent, produced the impression that Jack the Ripper is in that country.

No result of those enquiries was ever published. No more was ever heard of Tumblety.

In his letter to Sims, Littlechild wrote that he 'was never heard of afterwards. It was believed he committed suicide but certain it is that from this time the "Ripper" murders came to an end.'

Taking their investigations over to America, Evans and Gainey discovered that Tumblety lived on for another fifteen years. In 1901, he was in Baltimore, and it was there that he made a will in which he, far-famed for his vitriolic hatred of such creatures, bequeathed $1,000 to the Home for Fallen Women of Baltimore.

Two years later, on 28 May 1903, he died – a Roman Catholic, ultimately groomed and garnered for salvation by the nuns who ran the institution – in St John's Charity Hospital, St Louis. Among the personal property that he had with him in the hospital they found two imitation gold rings, value three dollars. When, on Friday 8 September 1888, Annie Chapman was murdered, her womb was taken away by her killer. So were two imitation gold brass rings.

The Littlechild Letter also casts a fascinating illuminatory shaft upon the manner in which the killer was transformed from the 'Whitechapel Fiend' – the name by which he was known prior to the publication in the *Daily News*, on 1 October 1888, of the text of the 'Dear Boss' letter – into 'Jack the Ripper', which was used for the first time ever as the signature appended to that letter. With regard to the term 'Jack the Ripper', it was generally believed at the Yard that Tom Bullen[42] of the Central News Agency was the originator, but it is probable that Charles Moore, who, as his chief, was the inventor. It was a smart piece of journalistic work. Poor Bulling occasionally took too much drink. Frankly, one cannot fail to see how he could help it, knocking about so many hours and seeking favours from so many people to procure copy. One night when Bulling 'had taken a few too many he got early information of the death of Prince Bismarck and, instead of going to the office to report it, sent a laconic telegram, "Bloody Bismarck is dead." On this, I believe, Mr Charles Moore fired him out.'

To sum up. Evans and Gainey regard the circumstantial evidence for Tumblety's being responsible for the murders of Nichols, Chapman and Eddowes as overwhelming, especially in the light of their identification of him as the Batty Street lodger. In each case, they say, the womb appears to be the target, although in the dissecting out of Mary Ann Nichols it seems likely that he was disturbed. As to Tumblety's guilt of the murder of Kelly, they are less secure. They note the inconsistencies between the *modus operandi* of her despatch – throat-cutting and strangulation – and the circumstance that the heart, and not the uterus, was purloined. They add, 'A good case has been made for her ex-lover, Joseph Barnett, being her killer, although his responsibility for the other murders was very unlikely. She bore all the signs of a copycat murder, someone having killed her, then deciding to make it look like another Ripper murder by inflicting the gross mutilation.'

In a nutshell, it is their belief that Tumblety killed four (perhaps only three) of the women over ten (perhaps only four) weeks in London, and then returned to America to escape the police. They conclude, 'There certainly was more than one killer at work in the East End of London in 1888, but if Jack the Ripper actually existed, then he was Dr Tumblety.'

Nicholas Warren half-suspects that Tumblety and Dr Hamilton Williams, a Fenian who had practised in Demerara, British Guyana, and who bought in Bond Street, London, the amputating knives used to assassinate the Irish Secretary, Lord Frederick Cavendish, and his undersecretary, Thomas Burke, in Phoenix Park, Dublin, on 6 May 1882, could be one and the same person. Warren points out Tumblety's known use of aliases, his Irish sympathies, and his visits to England prior to 1882. In this context there is a most tantalising reference by Douglas G. Browne, who had access to the Scotland Yard files in the 1950s, in his resultant book, *The Rise of Scotland Yard* (1956), to Sir Melville Macnaghten's appearing to identify the Ripper with the leader of the plot to assassinate Arthur James Balfour, who had been appointed Irish Secretary on 7 March 1887, at the Irish Office. 'An unexplained statement and, possibly, Macnaghten's true belief as to the identity of the Ripper,' says Warren.

Evans and Gainey also point out that there were exactly similar series of prostitute murders in Kingston, Jamaica, in late December 1888, and Managua, Nicaragua, in early 1889, both of which were unsolved. There is no evidence to connect Tumblety positively with these murders, but at that time he was on the run, his whereabouts unknown – and he had been a visitor previously to both the Caribbean and Central America.

26
Looking-Glass Jack: Lewis Carroll

That it was the grievously disordered libido of the Reverend Charles Lutwidge Dodgson, otherwise Lewis Carroll, that begat Jack the Ripper is the burden of Richard Wallace's *Jack the Ripper: 'Light-hearted Friend'* (1996).

The merest hint that Lewis Carroll, the author of *Alice*, friend of bishops, academic mathematician, Anglican deacon, Oxford don, was also the Whitechapel fiend, raises eyebrows in amazement, throws up hands in half-amused disbelief, and, at the extreme, triggers guffaws of scornful incredulity, to the accompaniment of widespread sussuration regarding Wallace in Blunderland.

But wait. Mr Wallace, of Melrose, Massachusetts, a former computer programmer and systems analyst – and therein surely lies a clue – who is now a social worker specialising in the provision of psychotherapy to help children who have suffered severe physical, emotional, or sexual, abuse, is deserving of the courtesy of a hearing.

He tells us, 'The solution I shall be presenting is very much a psychological one. It is based on the symbolic meaning to be found in the details, not one depending on hard, physical evidence.' Which is just as well, for there was virtually no contemporarily observed hard, physical evidence to include in the equation. 'It was,' writes Richard Wallace, 'Stephen Knight who really began to see symbolic patterns in the murders.'

But he and Knight arrive at very different conclusions.

Wallace believes that if there is a strength in his book, it is the identification of a suspect with motive. That motive was a vengeful catharsis. Dodgson, whose life Wallace has raked through in great detail – indeed, he has written a previous full-scale biographical study, *The Agony of Lewis Carroll* (1990), which should really be regarded as essential preliminary reading for the proper evaluation of this second volume – was,

Wallace concludes, a man filled with rage, seething with frustration, a bred-in-the-bone conformist in angry secret revolt. The precipitants of his lifelong sustained furies are identified as his loving father and mother's 'seductive and coercive parenting practices that attempted to mould him into a reduplication of his father, or, rather, into an extension of his father's wishes for himself', and his – postulated by Wallace but unproven – homosexual rape at the age of fourteen by some forty-two boys in the dormitory of his public school, Tom Brown's Rugby, during the course of his first year as a boarder there.

Wallace diagnoses: 'It was during this period that I am increasingly convinced that he suffered what we would recognize today as a psychotic break from which he never recovered … He became a psychopath[43] who focused first on secretive antisocial acts and eventually on multiple homicides and mutilations.'

It was, in Wallace's psycho-scenario, Dodgson's inner life that constituted motive. And that inner life is revealed – *as Wallace sees it*. The means of its encoding, he maintains, was a word game, in which Lewis Carroll is known to have excelled, self-concealment and self-disclosure by anagram. We are back in the latitudes of Wilding![44]

Wallace breaks words and sentences down into their constituent alphabeticals, and proceeds to reconstruct the brick-piles of letters into some exceedingly unedifying edifices. Thus the Carrollian nonsense of the 'Marchioness of Mock Turtles' is transmogrified into the smut-laden nonsense of 'O fuck mother's incest morals'. Even the innocuous-seeming title of one of Carroll's books, *Phantasmagoria and Other Poems*, can be *reductio ad absurdum*, 'Ah, pants and orgasm hero poet am I.' It is as if one were seeing the writing backwards through the looking-glass of the computer.

Take for more intricate instance the first stanza of the Jabberwocky poem from *Through the Looking-Glass*:

> Twas brillig and the slithy toves
> Did gyre and gimble in the wabe:
> All mimsy were the borogoves,
> And the mome raths outgrabe

Here is Wallace's version:

> But I beat my glands til,
> With hand-sword I slay the evil gender
> A slimey theme; borrow gloves,
> And masturbate the hog more!

We seem to have lost three alphabetical bricks somewhere along the way!

A shade worrying too, playing the anagram game, is the odd word, or rather phrase, out of the following:

> Dodgson, disguised as a clerk,
> bought a knife, took trains,
> stayed in his London house.
> He'd help the Fates.
> How?

> Hump from behind,
> Cut a whore in the face,
> masturbate,
> wash up.

'Wash up' is a phrase of American usage and of unlikely occurrence in the writing of a nineteenth-century English don.

Richard Wallace leaves us, Carrollwise, with a conundrum. He asks: From which 'discreet piece of material', published by Lewis Carroll after 1888, is the following anagram reconstructed?

> I strangled Nichols, Chapman, Stride, Eddowes. I gave each a moment to confess her gay sins. I cut the throats left ear to right, and I removed uteri, Feisty whore Mary Ann Kelly flayed around. He and I mutilated her cunt. I mangled her face; I dismembered breasts, ears, heart, a thigh. We masturbated with glee on them. All victims' wounds were awfully messy – a mushy, sticky slime. Scotland Yard and Whitechapel police are no match for our sly foiling game. I hate my mother. I stay mainly a yellow, selfish, sly, coy child. He, Thomas Vere Bayne, I, Charles Lutwidge Dodgson, reign as Jack the Ripper. Lewis Carroll.

Where, we may ask, would the Reverend Dodgson come upon a word like 'feisty', which is nowhere to be found in the full twelve volumes of the *Oxford English Dictionary*? In the *Dictionary of Americanisms on Historical Principles*, the first recorded publication of the word appears fifteen years after Dodgson's death. How did he come to be calling Mary Jane Kelly by the name of Mary Ann Kelly? Albeit she was alternatively referred to from time to time as Mary Janet, Mary Jeanette, or even Black Mary, Fair Emma, or Ginger, so the *A to Z* informs us – but never as Mary Ann.

Who was Thomas Vere Bayne? He was Dodgson's lifelong friend. The two had known each other as schoolboys at Daresbury and Warrington, in Cheshire. They came together again at Oxford, where they were both dons. Of anyone less likely than Thomas Vere Bayne to display Ripperish traits it would be difficult to conceive.

In fine, Richard Wallace, whose scholarship with regard to Lewis Carroll his life and times is not to be lightly dismissed, has developed an audacious, complex, and extremely resourcefully supported theory, which nevertheless does strike me as being rather similar to the ugly sister painfully squeezing her foot into *la Cenerentola*'s slipper. Mr Wallace's slipper, too, is a slipper of glass, but I am sorry to have to confess an inability to see through it so much as the outline of the Dodgson-Carrollian foot.

So goes the hundred-and-I-don't-know-how-manyeth suspect, limping off, his reputation stained, defiled, by contact with his, I don't know how many hundreds of, thus tainted precursors. I have, throughout all of my life, seen the Ripper suspects' long, long trail a'winding past. Incongruously, it always reminds me of a Ripleyan 'Believe it or Not' illustration recalled from my boyhood. It showed an immensely long procession of soup-plate-hatted Chinamen tailing back into the timeless, limitless distance, and the reader was informed that, such is the staggering number and fecundity of the little yellow men, that if at the time of the birth of Christ that procession had begun to file four abreast past you, that line would still be 'crocodiling' past one today. I sometimes feel that that is the way of it with the candidates for the scarlet immortality of Ur-Ripper. I wish those who take over my seven decades' vigil the wisdom that comes from unimpassioned involvement.

27

The Reverend Jack: Reverend John Moses Eppstein

Barely had the Reverend Charles L. Dodgson taken wing than there landed upon my doorstep the clamant persona of the late Reverend John Moses Eppstein.

The vehicle of his transportation to me was Peter Fisher's stylish October 1966 production, *An Illustrated Guide to Jack the Ripper*.

Mr Fisher, we are told, has been collecting information and illustrations of the Jack the Ripper crimes and Victorian London for more than twenty years.

Robin Odell, to whom the author acknowledges an especial indebtedness, has, with his customary Ripperwise sound sense and sensibility, placed an educated finger on the pulse of the enterprise, identifying in his Introduction a need at this period of Ripperine overkill, under-thought, and theoretical silt-up, for a macropedia. And pointing up the macropediac function of this illustrated guide.

The gathering together within the confines of a single cover of so many contemporary line drawings and photographs does indeed supply a two-dimensional external reality to the mind-pictures that each of us have constructed as a sustenant backcloth for the pageant of historical events.

Moreover, with Charles Booth and Jack London put into the witness box of history to limn Victorian Whitechapel – 'a strange place filled with strange people' – the vagaries of one's sociological graspings are solidified.

Fisher remains convinced that the Ripper was an integral part of the dreadful Whitechapel and Spitalfields community: consider the intimacy of his acquaintance with the maze of narrow streets, courts and alleyways; consider his extraordinary ability to approach his alerted, streetwise victims without arousal of suspicion or alarm.

Some writers have put forward the dummy figure of a local beat policeman to fill the easy familiarity comfort bill – but that is to discount 'evidence of the general hatred or dislike for the police'.

Well, then, a doctor? Unlikely, in Mr Fisher's view, for local prostitutes did not normally come into close contact with doctors, since in those pre-NHS days it cost money to see a medical man. Again, a doctor would be dressed sufficiently 'like a toff' to have set a potential victim's hackles of self-preservation up.

A common slaughterman? Possibly. But again Mr Fisher feels that, because rumours of police suspicions of their involvement of a murderous slaughterman were running amok, the ladies of the streets would be likely to give a bloodstained, death-stenching slaughterer the widest possible berth.

But a clergyman – ah! that would be a very different bundle of worms. A clergyman might be *expected*, in a purely professional capacity of course, to approach even the lowliest streetwalker. A 'man of the cloth' would be trusted and respected. Fisher believes that the parcel or shiny black bag, which it has been variously and variantly stated – with what firm basis one takes the liberty to wonder – that the Ripper had been observed to carry, contained 'nothing more innocent-looking than a religious cassock'. And this, he is quite certain, is the reason that Jack was able to get away so easily: he slipped his cassock over his bloodstained 'work clothes'.

It is all headily persuasive stuff. No obvious maniac prowling the streets, blood-dripping knife in hand, eyes ablaze. No furtive slaughterman, leather-aproned, stiff with blood. No patent-leather-booted toff, picking a delicate walkway between the garbage-choked gutters and the delicious channels of free-flowing animal blood.

We are looking for the minister of the lamb of God, whose sweet spilled blood taketh away the sins of the world. *Agnus dei qui tollis peccata mundi.*

And Mr Fisher does not fail us in this religious quest. Below the crown of thorns, beneath the blood of the pierced hands, feet and side, in the shadow of the Saviour, he finds the crouched destroyer. Angry. Angry. Angry. A red mist across the white of his eye. He names him John Moses Eppstein.

This man, ordained deacon in 1858, priest in 1862, was at one time Head Missionary of the London Jewish Society. Between 1867 and 1885, he was a missionary in Turkey, the one place in the entire Victorian world where ritual slaughterings and throat-cuttings, so much a *modus operandi* of the Whitechapel murderer, were carried out unhindered. 'This,' writes Peter Fisher, 'could be an explanation of all the reports of Jack the Ripper being a foreigner.'

During the late nineteenth century, Christ Church, Spitalfields, initiated a policy of close co-operation with other religions, and among those with whom they developed a strong connection was the Jewish Episcopal Church, in Palestine Place, where the Reverend Eppstein was a lecturer. We are informed that he lectured also, quite frequently, at Christ Church, and at the United Methodist Free Church, in Hanbury Street, which was situated directly opposite No. 29.

Mr Fisher uncovered, literally, the evidence of these lectures in parish registers of the period, which he disinterred from beneath a pile of rubble in Christ Church, and confirmed them by reference to entries in the Christ Church parish magazine of the relevant period.

'It all adds up,' he says, 'to an impressive accusing finger against Eppstein.'

But, he claims, his researches into Crockford's *Clerical Directory* were to furnish him with an even more interesting connection.

'Directly under the entry for John Moses Eppstein (incidentally John is often changed to Jack) is an entry for his son, William Charles Eppstein. And William Charles Eppstein was the curate at St Mary's, Spital Square, between 1887 and 1889. The chain of events is getting stronger. Obviously, with his son working in the district, there would have been more reason for regular visits and thus acclimatising himself to the highways and byways of the district.'

Having formulated his theory, Mr Fisher does not proceed forward with any further substantiating evidence for the validity of his Damascene flash. Perhaps in a future edition …

28

Jack the Ghost

So extensive and intensive has been the attention paid over the last seventy years to virtually every aspect of the subject of Jack the Ripper and the Whitechapel murders, that the areas available for really speculative investigation have come to seem dauntingly limited.

Pamela Ball has, however, contrived a novelty. She has brought to bear three decades' worth of work experience as a psychic therapist, healer, and medium, to the cultivation of a Ripper patch of her own.

In the Preface to *Jack the Ripper: A Psychic Investigation. The Compelling Paranormal Search for the Killer's True Identity* (1998), she clearly defines her self-set parameters – 'The intention in writing this book was not to add to the barrage of argument and counter-argument that has steadily flown back and forth, but rather to see whether a different approach to the conundrum, using psychic tools of investigation, would shed new light on the mystery.'

'Different' is certainly the right word. She proposes a direct confrontational technique. She will speak with the killer's victims; she will bandy words with the putative killer. Her investigative tools of choice, all informed by her recondite supranormal methodologies and long practice of occult skills, are astrology, clairvoyance, clairaudience, psychometry, dowsing, mediumship or channelling, and consultation of the Akashic Records, conjointly deployed in an esoteric ensnarement to net the phantasmic Jack.

Pamela Ball is far from being the first to seek an answer in the seance room or at the ouija board, but she is the pioneer provider of a book-length public record of her mediumistic sessions of psychic probings. She and her fellow-researchers, Fiona Ball, Andrew Ball and James Eden, made up a team of four seekers in the Dark Circle.

While personally thanking her associate-workers, she acknowledges 'the help we receive from the "other side"'. She also makes a point of informing her readers that by 'deliberately limiting my exposure to the circumstances surrounding each victim's death the sessions would be uncontaminated by any preconceptions formed through prior knowledge'.[45]

She complains that in the beginning she had nothing concrete with which to work psychically:

> Only towards the end of the investigation was I able – through the generosity of several distinguished Ripper experts – to examine important artefacts: a knife (courtesy of Donald Rumbelow) said to have been left by the side of Annie Chapman's body, a diary thought to have been kept by James Maybrick (made available by Smith Gryphon and Shirley Harrison) and a shawl long believed to have belonged to Catharine [*sic*] Eddowes at the time of her murder [which she was permitted to handle by Andy and Sue Parlour]. I tend to view with suspicion objects that are said to have a 'history'.

The touching evidence provided by the knife was that it had never been touched by Jack the Ripper – that is, if psychic vibrations are to be relied upon.

The notorious Maybrick diary provided, if spirit sources are to be accepted, a somewhat variable history. Unsurprisingly, Pamela Ball's first sensation on handling the diary was one of nausea, a feeling which had been reported also by a number of non-psychic Ripper researchers! Nausea, she said, 'mixed with a very odd feeling of foreboding. It was not a sense of evil, but a kind of broodiness.' The kind of broodiness presignatorily manifest to the hatching of strange tales, perhaps?

Moreover, the book's vibrations were not, we are told, those of James Maybrick. Again, no surprise, since dowsing by Pamela Ball had disclosed the dating of the writing of the pages as 1891, 1892, and 1895, and James Maybrick had died in 1889. The paranormal solution of this riddle was, it transpired, that James Maybrick junior[46] transcribed the journal, which supported Pamela Ball's 'initial feeling that the diary had been copied into its present form'.

As to whether James Maybrick had been associated with the Ripper murders, the dowsing pendulum gave negative answers in the cases of all the unfortunate women except one – that of Elisabeth Stride. It was only after this session that Ball came to believe that he was in some way connected with the murders.

The shawl alone proved psychically solid, if that is the right word. It called forth an almost electric reaction in Ball's hands. Over the months she became extremely aware of Eddowes' vibration. She found it curious that poor vagrant Kate, who wore every item of clothing she owned, should possess so perfect and clean an item as the shawl.

If the claims of this other-worldly book are to be credited, the received psychic intelligence is that it all began with Martha Turner or Tabram. Way back in 1863, Martha had been working in an institution for the insane when a boy child was born there. For some reason which Ball does not seem able to specify, this baby's very existence had to be hushed up. Her extrasensory perception has, however, alerted her to the circumstance that Martha Tabram had been inadvertently drawn into some kind of intrigue which centred upon the birth of this baby, and that her knowledge put her in danger. The psychic record further suggests that all the victims, collectively or individually, shared this knowledge, and that it put all of them in danger. Unfortunately though, a slight drawback, the psychic team has failed to establish whether the Ripper's victims actually knew one another.

As the investigation proceeded, the theme of intrigue and suspicion became increasingly evident. It seemed to run through the whole dreadful business. But, despite making every effort that could be made, everything remained vague, undefined. Ball felt strongly that Catherine Eddowes knew something. All that the psychic probings brought to light was that on the night of her death she was hurrying to meet someone. An appointment in Samarra – with Jack?

As for Mary Jane Kelly, Pamela Ball is convinced that she came to realise that information she held was dangerous and that she was existing in a state of fear before her death. Ball and her team admit to suspicion of Joe Barnett.

Grasping somewhat wildly for reasons to make sense out of the insistent idea that Kelly's murder, although the last in the series, was actually the catalyst for the precedent others, the team took a look at those theories which suggested some significance between the sites and the murders. Ball frankly admits that while the modern sites of the Ripper murders left her vibration-less and cold, she had early on instinctively felt those sites did indeed form the shape of an arrow pointing to the seat of government at Westminster.

That was the transition from the embryonic royalist theory to the political-motivation theory achieved. The psychic team concludes that the women may have been caught between an 'embattled establishment on the one hand and the forces for social and political change on the other'. And, elaborating: 'The most divisive issue in British politics at the time of the murders was the Irish question, which had polarized opinion both in Parliament and the country ... The conflict between East and West London became part of the wider political struggle for freedom and justice.'

A tantalising thought, perhaps, but to what purpose? As we are next informed that, with the exception of Polly Nichols, none of the Ripper's victims were political agitators. Mary Kelly and Joe Barnett did have Irish connections, but neither was ever identified as a Nationalist activist.

Although, astrologically, three of the suspects – James Maybrick, Robert Donston Stephenson, and Joe Barnett – showed the potential to murder, only one exhibited the potential for mutilation – Barnett. And who was it whose psychic profile and vibration most closely fitted the perception that, according to psychic revelation, all but one (Elisabeth Stride) of the women had of their killer? Joseph Barnett.

'Again and again, the murderer's coldness and dissociation while committing his crimes came across, and this dissociation was present when we made contact with Barnett himself ... We came to the conclusion that he was the most likely candidate so far.'

The odd victim out, Elisabeth Stride, was, we are assured, in all probability killed by James Maybrick.

And yet ... all along the shadow of a feeling persisted, clung to the psychic researchers, that Barnett, rather than acting in his own right, was being directed by someone else; and that someone was perhaps the man referred to in the seance sessions simply as 'The Catcher' – a 'ubiquitous figure who seems to have kept his finger on the pulse of what was going on in the East End, who would know who could be manipulated and who could not'.

The team thought it likely that this mysterious character was an information gatherer sent there by the social reformers – people like Josephine Butler or William Stead. They thought that he was a disseminator of negative information, and was used to generate fear and panic in the area by unscrupulous people in authority. They were sure that 'The Catcher' was none other than James Maybrick.

The team does not venture to pronounce upon the 'Dear Boss' letter and other communications. To a certain extent bet-hedging, all they deliver themselves is that – 'If they are genuine … [they] certainly show Jack's need to make a flattering statement about his cleverness. In poking fun at the police in this way, Jack seems to be intimating that he is above the law. This could point to Maybrick, to Donston Stephenson, to Tumblety, to Bertie, and perhaps to Gull, all of whom had a high degree of arrogance in their make-up.'

It is Pamela Ball's psychically generated belief that it was with Annie Chapman's grotesquely orchestrated slaying that the pattern for the rest of the killings was set. 'The manner of her murder captured the interest of the public and perhaps gave the murderer the idea for how to conduct the rest of the campaign he was primed to undertake by Maybrick. Both she and Polly Nichols may have been part of the initial smokescreen to hide the motive for the Tabram murder.'

The most intriguing, not to say controversial, part of this odd book is the section 'Silent Witnesses', wherein are purported to be reproduced sittings or sessions of actual psychic conversation exchanged between July and December 1997 with each of the victims of the Ripper, and with two of those suspected of actually having been the Ripper, namely Maybrick and Druitt.

Maybrick was both difficult to contact and not at all forthcoming when he finally was contacted. Druitt was considerably more co-operative, and clears up the mystery of his alleged dismissal from Mr Valentine's Blackheath school. He had been suffering full-blown migraine attacks, complete with the dazzlements of fortification spectra, and nursing the concurrent fear of inheriting his mother's madness. As the result of sheer emotional overload, he broke down in front of the boys whom he was teaching and was excruciatingly embarrassed and absolutely appalled by his own behaviour. He was not dismissed, but took with his headmaster a joint decision that it would be best if he were to resign.

Pamela Ball writes,

> What seems to have been happening during the contact session was that the privacy barrier that operates with my clients in the present day was also working on this occasion, coupled with Druitt's own need to keep his sexual orientation a secret. It did not feel as though he had ever revealed his homosexuality, but relationships were certainly uppermost in his mind. I was very aware that it was not his influence over the boys that was a problem – in other words, there was no hint of paedophilia – but [only] his mishandling of what was happening to him.

Of the kidney sent to Mr Lusk, information received by Ball convinced her that the body part did not belong to Catherine Eddowes.

The contact session with Mary Jane Kelly confirmed that the body found at No. 13 Miller's Court, was, despite latter-day rumours to the contrary, definitely hers, and that her heart *had* been taken away.

In the course of another sitting it emerged that, certainly so far as Mary Kelly's alleged part in it is concerned, 'the Sickert story is a load of rubbish'.

There is no gainsaying the fact that this is a very unusual book. In one respect it is like a gigantic box of Ripper games. Whether or not one accepts the material that it proffers at a serious level depends entirely upon the susceptibility of the reader. Whatever, it is an interesting, novel and exceedingly well-illustrated addition to the Ripperological literary corpus.

Let me straightaway declare myself disinclined to accept the revelations of the dark circle, but equally loath to dismiss out of hand the genuinely held beliefs of others.

Pamela Bell hopes that, in what she believes to have been her contact sessions with the sad victims of the Ripper, she has been able to bring clarity, and she says that she feels that so far as Jack himself is concerned, 'reaching an understanding of him was an important – and valid – part of the investigation'.

29

George the Ripper: George Hutchinson

Bob Hinton, the author of *From Hell: The Jack the Ripper Mystery* (1998), provides a magisterial – I use the adjective advisedly, for Mr Hinton is specifically described on the back cover of his book as 'a middle aged magistrate from South Wales' – account of the Whitechapel murders, which is to say, he looks at the evidence as a magistrate would, and reasons around and about it.

This proves an effective cerebral approach, and it produces a very lively, well-articulated, clearly and logically progressed narrative.

He dismisses the cases against all previous suspects, including Maybrick and Tumblety, but adds three further victims to the canonical corpse count.

The first of these is Mrs Annie Millwood, aged thirty-eight, widow of a soldier, Richard Millwood. She resided in a common lodging-house at No. 8 White's Row, a few yards from Dorset Street. She was struck down on 25 February 1888, by an unknown assailant. The precise location of the attack is not a matter of record, but it was possibly in the narrow alleyway at the side of the lodging-house, which was used as a shortcut to Butler Street. She was taken to the Whitechapel Workhouse Infirmary, suffering from repeated stabbings with a clasp-knife in her legs and lower body. She seemed to make a satisfactory recovery, and was discharged to South Grove Workhouse, Mile End Road, on 21 March 1888. On 31 March however, she suddenly collapsed there and died. It is not known whether she had ever resorted to prostitution, but she was in no regular occupation and had no visible means of support. She was, Hinton is convinced, Jack the Ripper's first – trial-run – victim.

This belief accords with that expressed by Philip Sugden, who wrote in 1994 in *The Complete History of Jack the Ripper*, 'Apparently she [Annie Millwood] was the victim of an unprovoked attack by a stranger and sustained "numerous" stab wounds in the legs and lower body. This incident, like many of the Ripper's known atrocities, took place on a weekend.'

A month later, at about 12.30 a.m. on 28 March 1888, Ada Wilson, a thirty-nine-year-old sempstress was attacked. A man, a total stranger, had knocked at the door of her house, at 9 Maidman Street, Burdett Road, Mile End,[47] demanded money and threatened that unless she gave him what cash she had he would kill her. Upon her refusing, he stabbed her twice in the throat with a clasp-knife. Her screams sent him running off. After a stay of thirty days in the London Hospital, she was discharged.

Hinton suggests that the two unrelated attacks were trial runs. Sugden does not accept Ada Wilson as a Ripper victim. He says: 'Robbery seems to have been the motive for the attack.'

The third attack ascribed by Hinton to the Ripper – and Sugden agrees, but regards her as Jack's second victim – is that on Martha Turner or Tabram, on 7 August 1888.

The attack on Emma Smith, in Osborn Street, on 3 April 1888, is attributed by neither Hinton nor Sugden to the Whitechapel murderer.

Proceeding to a preliminary review of the generally accepted Ripper killings, Hinton, considering the Buck's Row murder of Polly Nichols, thinks it possible that the killer was seen, but not recognised, by the people on the spot.

The magisterial mind presents us with a novel thought as regards the organs missing from the body of Annie Chapman. Could there possibly be, Hinton wonders, another explanation as to the whereabouts of the missing body parts? He thinks so. 'Now if you take into account the number of slaughterhouses in the immediate vicinity of Hanbury Street, add to that the fact that the front ground floor room of number 29 was used as a cats' meat shop, wouldn't you expect that the cat population of the immediate area would be quite large? Accepting that, can't we now come to a more realistic conclusion as to what became of the missing body parts?'

Applying his legal logic to the problem of the 'Dear Boss' letter, Hinton does not feel that that letter came from the killer. It was too neat, too beautifully laid out, too accurate in spelling and punctuation, and there was something missing. That something was *passion*. Excess of neatness – shortage of passion. Compare it, he suggests, with the letters dashed off by David Berkowitz, the Son of Sam, or William Heirens.

As for 'the reference to trying to save "some of the proper red stuff in a ginger beer bottle,"' he comments, 'This is ridiculous,' and one is led to suppose the letter to be a fake. 'It is possible that it was written by a journalist, although I would have expected a more blood curdling effort from a member of the press. My personal guess is that a bored ledger clerk (red ink wasn't the sort of thing that just anyone had a supply of lying about the place) decided to spend an interesting afternoon.'

Hinton also suspects that – taking into account an old habitude obtaining in the country that Israel Schwartz came from, if you were questioned by the *Polizei* – the descriptions that Schwartz produced for the authorities of the men encountered by him in Berner Street were tailored to please. For this reason, Schwartz's testimony is simply not to be regarded as entirely reliable. It didn't ring true. It is not that he meant to deceive, but that he said whatever he thought the police wanted to hear. For which reason, Schwartz's description of the two men he saw is not evidentially sound.

He does not, moreover, think that Stride was a Ripper victim, but is convinced that her late consort, Michael Kidney, killed her. He notes also that although spoken of as a quiet sober woman, she was, when under the influence of the demon drink, a different person, frequently appearing before the local magistrates for disorderly conduct.

Coming to Catherine Eddowes, Hinton nurtures revolutionary, though not original, thoughts.

> Why had the killer taken the womb and kidney? Well to be perfectly accurate there is absolutely no proof that he did. The only thing that is known for certain is that they were missing from the body … if you are kneeling down pulling the entrails out and slashing at them, small pieces might easily be thrown over your shoulder … For example, a kidney looks like a kidney, but if you step on it, it merely looks like a bloody smear. Similarly with a piece of womb overlooked in all the fuss, who knows what the hungry cat, dog or rat population might have done with it. I cannot readily reconcile the popular picture of the Ripper scurrying away from the scene with his gruesome trophies, with a man who is so fastidious that he cuts away a piece of his victim's apron on which to clean his hands.

As to whether the kidney sent to Lusk had actually been taken from Eddowes' body, Hinton chooses to hedge his bets.

'Although the absence of embalming fluid made it highly unlikely the kidney came from a corpse destined for the dissecting theatres of a teaching hospital, it did not preclude the origin being one of the many corpses autopsied. So did the Lusk kidney come from Eddowes or not? We simply do not know one way or the other, and there are insufficient clues to favour one solution over another.'

What he definitely does not believe is that the 'Juwes' message on the Goulston Street wall was written by the hand of the Ripper. Neither, he points out, is that long mainstay of conspiracy theorists that Sir Charles Warren himself ordered the writing to be obliterated from the wall strictly true. It was Superintendent Thomas Arnold who urged the necessity of expunging the offending words, and 'Sir Charles, to his great credit, realised that such a decision should correctly be made by himself and not a subordinate. This does show the Commissioner to be a man of great moral courage, it would have been easier for him not to get involved in this matter, thus having a handy scapegoat should things go wrong.'

Amusing is Hinton's aside that noisy police boots may have helped the Ripper's 'luck'. Police-issue boots of the day were of the same type as those in use in the Army – with metal studs driven into the soles to improve wear. 'Unfortunately it also made the boots extremely noisy, and the presence of an approaching police officer could be signalled when the constable was still a fair way off … In the Eddowes case this fact may have given the killer the extra vital few minutes he needed to make good his escape.'[48]

In *The Autobiography of a Counter Jumper* (1929), William Frederick Fish tells the story of his participation in the formation, in 1888, of 'The Jack the Ripper Syndicate', a 'private limited liability company' of twenty men. Each contributed 3*s* 6*d* 'for the purchase of ten pairs of rubber-soled sand shoes', to be worn on alternate evenings by ten of the members employed in 'a genuine *bona fide* attempt, mind you, which was made to assist the police, and, incidentally, to claim the reward … amounting to some thousands of pounds … Money was the root principle of all our efforts. And, sad to say, failure, as disrupting tensions developed amongst the men.'

It is Hinton's contention that Catherine Eddowes may not have been a prostitute. 'What if Kate Eddowes wasn't a prostitute? At first that idea seemed ludicrous; of course she was a prostitute everyone said she was. And herein lies the error. You should never accept a statement or a concept without checking it out, that is the first thing you learn when you start to investigate. So I started to check and I found that not only was there no firm evidence to suggest that she was a prostitute, but there were a lot of indicators to show she wasn't.'

There was, however, the report of Inspector James McWilliam, City of London Police, dated 27 October 1888, which stated, 'She had lived with [James] Kelly for seven or eight years, prior to which she had lived with a man named Thomas Conway, a pensioner for about twenty years & had three children by him – two sons & a daughter, but Conway was eventually compelled to leave her on account of her drunken and immoral habits.'

And while Sugden reported in his *Complete History* that friends and acquaintances had insisted that Eddowes was not a prostitute, protestations by Eliza Gold, her sister, James Kelly, her lover, and Frederick Wilkinson, deputy of the lodging-house she lived in, their statements are of questionable objectivity and perforce carry little conviction.

But if she were not a prostitute, why then, asks Hinton, 'was she where she was, and why was she murdered? It was searching for these answers that finally led me to the man I believe was Jack the Ripper.'

For Bob Hinton, Mary Kelly is the key that unlocks the infinitely greater enigma and mystery of the identity of Jack the Ripper. Tackling some of the strange problems and happenings that twine about her murder, he comes first to Caroline Maxwell and her 'vision'. She it was who testified that she saw Kelly alive, but considerably unwell, at 8.30 on Friday morning, 9 November 1888.

Hinton reasons,

> The only possible explanation for this statement is that Mrs Maxwell was confused about the days, and it was Thursday not Friday morning that she had the conversation with Mary. There is a very small indication to this being the case. Mrs Maxwell says that when asked why she was up so early, Mary replied, 'I have the horrors of drink upon me, as I have been drinking for some days past.' This would seem to suggest that Mary had been on a bender for a number of days and this was the result. Yet if we believe Joe Barnett that on the Thursday evening she was completely sober this doesn't make sense. However if Mary's pub crawl had ended Thursday morning and not Friday morning it now makes sense.

As to the riddle of the 'big fire' in Kelly's room on the night of her murder, Hinton notes,

> The solder in use at that time turned liquid at about 160 degrees, however it did lose adhesion at about 140 degrees, but even these relatively low temperatures are well outside what can be obtained by a fire using old clothes as fuel … Basic physics tells you that a hotly burning fire consumes fuel at a faster rate, therefore, for [the fire] to be burning fiercely someone would have to be stoking it with more fuel, and this didn't happen. How then did the kettle lose its spout? Again the logical answer is very simple, we are all assuming that the spout was lost on that night, and yet there is not one shred of evidence to support that. There was a fire in the grate, a kettle has lost its spout, everyone assumes the two things happen concurrently, and yet all the evidence points to this not being the case … The logical answer [is that] the kettle lost its spout some time previously.

Hinton's theory brings to mind that there are those among modern students of the case who think that the scale and fierceness of the fire has become exaggerated. The spout of the little kettle did not, they point out, *melt*; all that happened was that the solder fixing the spout to the body of the kettle disintegrated. This would require considerably less than the postulated *furnace* heat.

As for the 'locked room' mystery, Hinton offers, 'According to Abberline the lock was of the "spring bolt type". This means that it operated in the same manner as a Yale type lock, in other words the door could be fastened securely by merely pulling the door to, the bolt would be shot home automatically.'

Hinton elaborates:

> The type of lock that I believe was fitted to the door was a type known as a Night Latch. These locks had been in use since Georgian times … In appearance it looks just like a normal warded lock, the only clue to its being a spring bolt type is that there is no key-hole on the inside. The inside face of the lock has two knobs, one is milled at the edges and turning this draws back the bolt, and the other slides vertically and is used to fix the bolt in an open position. From the outside you have the normal escutcheon over the key-hole, and thus from the outside it is impossible to tell what type of lock it is.

Locks of this type were 'all able to lock the bolt back in the unlocked position. Mary Kelly had absolutely nothing of value in her room … Surely the logical step for her to take if she had lost her key, would be simply to leave the door "on the latch", once inside she could release the bolt and lock herself in. This is a far more logical and likely scenario than Mary Kelly balancing precariously, often drunk, on a window sill trying to open the door [with her hand thrust through a broken pane] without slicing her arm off.'

With reference to the allegedly missing heart, Hinton writes,

> Dr Bond states 'The pericardium was open below and the heart absent.' What this doesn't tell us is whether or not the heart was absent from the body, or absent from the scene of the crime. As Dr Bond is writing post-mortem notes his only concern is that state in which he found the body, not the circumstances of the crime. That being the case, I have always interpreted his notes to mean the heart was missing from the body, and not necessarily missing from the room. In fact there is some evidence to show that this is so, as other reports speak of the body as being 'complete in all respects'. But this is another point about which it is not possible to be certain.

This is to ignore the fact that in the cases of all the other major corporeal organs removed, Bond carefully records their various locations in the room, but he makes no reference whatsoever to the location of the heart. This surely indicates the probability that it was missing from the room.

In the naming of George Hutchinson as his suspect, Hinton avers that his is the first nomination of that candidate for the distinction. It is actually not. Hinton has formulated the identical guilt theory as that previously proposed by Brian Marriner in 1996.

Listen to Sarah Lewis who testified that at about 2.30 a.m. on 9 November the day of Mary Kelly's murder, she had seen, standing in the covered entrance to Crossingham's Lodging-House, across Dorset Street, and looking up the narrow alleyway to Miller's Court, a man 'not tall, but stout – had on a black wideawake hat. I did not notice his clothes.'

It was, says Hinton, George Hutchinson – 'Unbeknown to Sarah Lewis, she had caught sight of Jack the Ripper.' And forthwith Hinton theorises. Hutchinson concocted a story that would put him legitimately by the alleyway leading into Miller's Court around that time. In full-flowering bravado he presents himself at Commercial Street Police Station at 6 p.m. on 12 November 1888, to tell his tale.

That tale was that he had told his tale – of having seen a man go into Kelly's room with her that night – to a policeman whom he had stopped in the street (who was never traced), that said policeman had not been very interested, and had sent him packing.

Hinton's selected one is the George Hutchinson who was born on 10 December 1859. His father, Joseph, was a licensed victualler. In 1881, he was working as a barman in the John of Jerusalem public-house, No. 1 Rosoman Street, Clerkenwell. In 1888, he is living at the Victoria Home for Working Men, Nos 39–41 Commercial Street. All traces of him are lost some two years after Kelly's murder.

Melvyn Fairclough, in the 1992 second edition of his *The Ripper and the Royals*, included a picture of an individual whom he designated as being 'George Hutchinson'. The picture bears the following caption: 'George Hutchinson (1866–1938), who gave the police a detailed description of the last person seen entering Mary Kelly's room. This photograph, the only one in existence, is published here for the first time.'

'Unfortunately,' Hinton informs us, 'I believe [Fairclough] has the wrong man entirely. For a start [Fairclough's] George Hutchinson's full name is George William Topping Hutchinson, and this is not the name [my selectee] is referred to either in the [news]papers, understandably, or in his statement, not understandably. It is common practice in [police] statements to refer to the person either by the whole of the person's name, or at the very least by his first name and all initials.'

Hinton continues, noting that his George Hutchinson signed a two-page statement, recorded by Sergeant Edward Badham, twice on each page – 'George Hutchinson' on the first, and 'Geo Hutchinson' on the second.

Further confirmation: Fairclough's George W. T. Hutchinson, twenty-two years old, is the wrong age, whereas Hinton's George Hutchinson, 'referred to in all the papers that gave his age as being 28', the right age.

Concludes Hinton: 'It is difficult to see how such a mistake could have been made; there is a great deal of difference between someone who is just 22 and someone who is 28.'

Obviously, Mr Hinton was unaware that Mr Fairclough had honed his research skills in the service of *Diary* adherents.

Hinton characterises Mary Jane Kelly as a user, one who used other people to make her own life easier. He thinks that she directed her charms on George Hutchinson, who, he believes, was an obsessional – a stalker. Hinton's imagined scenario of what turned George Hutchinson into Saucy Jacky goes like this:

> By the beginning of 1888 it was obvious that Mary Kelly didn't want anything to do with George Hutchinson … In [Hutchinson's] statement to Abberline he describes his previous relationship with Kelly as 'having given her some money in the past'. Hardly a basis for happy coexistence. To anyone else this coolness would indicate that Kelly didn't 'fancy' him, but to Hutchinson's obsessive personality this could only mean one thing – someone was preventing them from getting together!

So … who could that be? Hutchinson got it in one. Of course. It was obvious. The prostitutes were to blame. However, he believes Hutchinson killed Eddowes because she was blackmailing him.

One reads in the *East London Observer* of 13 October 1888,

> A reporter gleaned some curious information from the Casual Ward Superintendent of Mile End, regarding Kate Eddowes, the Mitre Square victim. She was formerly well-known in the casual wards there, but had disappeared for a considerable time until the Friday preceding her murder. Asking the woman where she had been in the interval, the superintendent was met with the reply, that she had been in the 'hopping'. 'But,' added the woman, 'I have come back to earn the reward offered for the apprehension of the Whitechapel murderer. I think I know him.'
>
> 'Mind he doesn't murder you too,' replied the superintendent jocularly. 'Oh, no fear of that,' was the remark made by Kate Eddowes. Within four-and-twenty hours afterwards she was a mutilated corpse.[49]

Do the facts support Hinton's averral that Eddowes was blackmailing Jack the Ripper? Hinton does not believe that she approached Hutchinson and bluntly accused him, but possibly she might have sought him out and dropped a hint, and he might have slipped her a few pence and promised her more later.

Hinton's belief in the guilt of Hutchinson rests in part on his assumption that Abberline's clearing of Hutchinson in his report to Warren was done for the simple expedient of keeping any suspicions he may have had to himself. An unsuspecting suspect was what Abberline wanted, and the prevention of any additional murders. Lacking evidence, he could not hold Hutchinson. But for two weeks Hutchinson 'was accompanied by two detectives. The official reason for these two police escorts was "in case Hutchinson should recognise the man he saw" [going home with Kelly] … It is more believable that the two officers were there to prevent a suspect offending again.'

But the greatest objection to the Hutchinson as the Ripper theory is that the vastly experienced Abberline did actually interrogate Hutchinson regarding his statement, and was happy that he was telling the truth.

Mr Hinton has written a very confident, subtle condemnation of George Hutchinson, but there are a number of rickety bridgings over partially concealed gaps, which bedevil his selected territory. To be fair, the author constantly reminds his reader that it is all pure speculation, that there is no proof, but he has the capacity to captivate and (at least temporarily) to blind with brilliant flashes of insight. For, make no mistake, Bob Hinton leads us, blinking, on inspirational excursions into new areas and intellectually pleasing pastures. His book is provocative and thought-provoking, but a long way from being conclusive in its conclusion. Were I sitting as a magistrate, I would not send Hutchinson down on these adductions.

Not so Stephen Wright. Founder, in 1996, of the modest, unpretentious, biannual *Whitechapel Journal*, and self-styled proponent of the American view of 'the Brits' classic Victorian multicide',[50] Wright had stated his conceptualisation of 'Mr Ripper' as a person 'somewhat ordinary, perhaps having a mild manner, but with a hidden ferocious side'. 'Dare I,' he asks, 'a Ripper expert, confess that I really do not know who Jack the Ripper was?'

He did seem pretty certain though that he knew who he was not. Not Chapman. Not Ostrog. Not Tumblety. He was pretty certain, too, emphatic indeed, that the diary of Jack the Ripper was not. Less certain as to whether or not James Maybrick was Jack. What he does come up with in *Jack the Ripper: An American View* (1999), is George Hutchinson, whom he labels a 'new suspect'. He is not.[51]

It is possible to pick a great many factual holes of varying sizes in Mr Wright's account – rights and wrongs, as it were – but they are honest mistakes, not the carefully angled E & OE account of a special pleader. It would be churlish to describe this hard-worked-at book as anything other than a brave effort.

Perhaps it is meet at this point to make mention of the American George Hutchinson who was thought to be the Ripper. No relation to the British suspect of that name, he makes his very brief entrance onto the stage by virtue of the following report published in the *Ottawa Journal* on 16 November 1888:

> Seven or eight years ago, George Hutchinson, an inmate of [Elgin (Illinois) State Hospital] the asylum here, delighted to visit the hospitals and slaughterhouses, and made many peculiar toys from bones. He was an expert with the knife, he escaped from Elgin but was captured at Kankalee and placed in the asylum there [Kankalee (Illinois) State Hospital]. He escaped from that place and afterwards murdered a disreputable woman in Chicago mutilating her body in a way similar to the Whitechapel cases. He was returned to Kankalee but afterwards escaped and has been at large for three or four years. It is thought he may be the Whitechapel fiend.

He wasn't.

30
Never-Was Jack

What is one, hand on heart and anxious not to wound, to say about Peter Turnbull's contribution, *The Killer Who Never Was* (1996)? Let us get the worst out of the way, over and done with. It is an appallingly careless book, its capricious orthography exceeded in caprice only by its crass inaccuracies and inadequate proofreading. Thus, for example, we are presented with Nicholls for Nichols, Eddows for Eddowes, Abbeline for Abberline, Diemsschütz for Diemschütz, Farnier Street for Fournier Street, and Marie Antoinette Kelly.

There are also some frightful howlers – loud as the veritable 'workhouse howl!' herein described most illuminatingly: 'The Workhouse Master would dread to hear that particular ferocious scream, really worthy of wild beasts … commonly known as the "workhouse howl": a fight had broken out amongst the younger women.'

The selection of Turnbullesque 'howls' or howlers present us with Israel Lipski misnamed as Crispin. Elisabeth Stride is said to have been grasping a fistful of cashew nuts, whereas in truth it was a bag of delicate, breath-sweetening cachous that she clutched in her left hand. The Ten Bells public-house is suddenly, and for no sober rhyme or reason, decimated (in the non-literal, loose sense of that word) to the Five Bells.

All this is a pity, a great pity, for there are a number of good things in the book; but, so low is the threshold of Turnbull's dependability that one is always having to cross one's fingers before retailing his uncorroborated anecdotes.

In many respects this is a kind of chapbook or commonplace-book, assembled more or less exclusively from contemporary sources. In it one *reads* the contemporary newspapers as they come out. One *attends* the inquests as they are held. In this context, Mr Turnbull mounts a sustained attack upon Coroner Baxter – not, perhaps, unmerited – and accuses him of playing shamefully to the gallery, and deliberately extending the duration of the inquest hearings in a pandering to his self-importance. One *shares* in the post-shock debate, live.

Provided are some nice touches; word-pictures that linger. Mrs Prater walking to the Five (!) Bells to buy some rum for her breakfast; Thomas Coram from the coconut warehouse picking up a knife in the Whitechapel Road with a bloodstained handkerchief wound round its handle, and PC Drage, to whom Coram, whose blood had run cold, reported his grisly find, stating that he, the constable, would undoubtedly have seen the knife had a horse not elected to fall down just opposite the precise spot; Dr Barnardo, that same doctor of the Barnardo's Homes celebrity, telling of the visit he had paid to No. 32 Flower and Dean Street, and how in that lodging-house kitchen he had talked with the frightened women there about the murders of the Whitechapel Fiend. And how, later, he had recognised in the mortuary the savaged remains of one of the very women with whom he had chatted in the kitchen. It was the body of Elisabeth Stride.

Turnbull believes it to be 'almost certain' that the style 'Jack the Ripper' had street currency well before the 'Dear Boss' letter and subsequent associated postcard were received by the police, thus implying that Tom Bulling was not the originator, but merely the disseminator, of that wonderful 'trade name'.

Another of Turnbull's contentions is that the murdered Stride was not first discovered by Diemschütz – 'What is certain is that the alarm was raised by a man named Gilleman, who ran up [to] the upstairs room of the working men's club and disrupted the merry making. Mr Gilleman, Maurice Eagle [another Turnbullism: it should be Morris], and two others went to the yard, viewed the corpse, and then ran off in divers directions in a determined effort to find a constable … Perhaps some four or five minutes later Louis Diemschütz [*sic*] arrived at the yard.' Neither is Turnbull of the opinion that Elisabeth Stride's murderer was disturbed in the act.

Ventilated, too, by Turnbull, is what he regards as the scandal of the violent posters. What 'contributed to the hysteria as much if not more than the newspapers were the billboard hoardings advertising the newspapers. The penny dreadfuls were published on Saturdays, the posters advertising the forthcoming issues appeared midweek … They were lurid, life-size depictions of naked or near-naked women with knives sticking in the chests, and glued to every available fence or wall space.' They were brilliantly coloured and their sheer number was a constant, inescapable visual stimulus to mass fascination – and mass fear. On them, the Whitechapel Fiend was represented as a Gothic half-human creatures painted red from head to toe.

All of this offbeat background material is great fun, but, as the pages mount, one must eventually ask, what is Mr Turnbull about? Easier asked than answered.

O what a tangled web we weave,
When first we try to undeceive!

His main thesis, as well as I can disentangle it, would seem to be that all five of the so-called Jack the Ripper murders were committed by different unrelated assassins. He believes that in four of them horse slaughtermen were the culprits. Elisabeth Stride he considers likely to have been the victim of Michael Kidney.

This means that the Ripper was 'The Killer Who Never Was' of his title – as much an artefact as Major William Martin, of the Royal Marines, the original 'Man Who Never Was'.[52]

What is one to say about Peter Turnbull's book? Well, warts and all, it is, I think, a rewarding read. He has culled from sources which others have neglected. He is very clearly his own man. In the words of the Alpha to Omega, 'In 1970 this would have been a fascinating and valuable book. In 1996 it is a curiosity.' A quarter of a century beyond its sell-by date? I do not agree. I think that it is still both a curiosity *and* a fascinating and valuable book.

31
Jack the Medic: Sir William Gull

It might reasonably have been thought that, in the wake of the vehemency of Mr Joseph Sickert's *Sunday Times* retraction of thirteen years before, not only was the golden royal vein worked out, but also that it had proved to be fool's gold that they were excavating anyway. But no. It was with considerable surprise that, in November 1991, one received tidings of the imminence of a new book bearing Mr Sickert's *nihil obstat* and *imprimatur*. Hobo, wearing his Joseph's coat of many colours, turned as often as that of the Vicar of Bray, was back in business. Funny business. Like the voice of the turtle, he was heard again in the land, in unembarrassed full spate. His mouthpiece, or ventriloquial dummy, this time was a Mr Melvyn Fairclough.

This latest book of Sickertiana, *The Ripper and the Royals*, was, impenitently and unashamedly, once more regally biased, and in it the eminent physician Sir William Gull is metamorphosed into Jack the Ripper.

I greeted it:

Old Hobo Sickert has sold another batch of tickets for yet another Netley's Mystery Coach Tour, with, this time round, Mr Melvyn Fairclough in the driver's entrepreneurial seat. If you are of a mind to be taken for a ride, I have no hesitation in recommending that you go along for the scenery – but, remember, it is of the two-dimensional variety, length and breadth, but precious scant depth.

The road this latest Jack the Ripper excursion travels does not, I am perfectly certain, lead to the clear centre of the century-old mystery. We have been along it before in the company of Stephen Knight. The familiar landmarks, albeit viewed from a just slightly different perspective, flash by – Annie Elizabeth Crook, her daughter by Prince Eddy, Duke of Clarence, Alice Margaret Crook, John Netley, the sinister coachman, and Sir William Gull, the murderous physician.

But, as the road unwinds, new and alien features are presented to the beleaguered traveller's eye; Netley's veritable notebook – sharing a shelf surely with Hitler's and Maybrick's diaries, Inspector Abberline's long-lost, long unsuspected to exist, diaries, and Dr Dutton's *Chronicles* – Queen

Alexandra's Prince of Wales' feathers hat decoration; and an actual photograph of Prince Eddy, *redivivus*, eighteen years after his official death, alive and well in 1910. We have, too, a new leading conspirator, Lord Randolph Churchill. No byway is neglected, even the Monster of Glamis (Prince Albert Victor!) and Peter Sutcliffe, Saucy Jack's Yorkshire blood-brother, are inducted into the astonishing scenario.

The coincidences, fortuities, and serendipities fall upon us thick and fast. They bewilder with their insolence. It is not always by any means clear whose voice we are hearing articulating the fatuities, inviting our belief, insulting our credulity; that of Hobo Sickert or of the bemused author. This is, as might be expected of a furniture restorer – Mr Fairclough's everyday avocation – a very polished job. But it *is* only a veneer. It is a shame that so much dedication and ingenuity should have been directed to so trumpery an end. Regard this book as being in the nature of a Graham Greene 'entertainment', a *jeu d'esprit*. Do not take it seriously. It lacks even a modicum of proof, a scintilla of confirmation, for any of its brazenly confident claims.

Mr Fairclough did not like what I had written. He liked even less my comparison of his book with *The Jack the Ripper A to Z*, which had come out around the same time, and which I was simultaneously reviewing.

I continued:

Very different from the foregoing kettle of red herrings is the magisterial offering of the most respectable and respected 'Ripperological' trinity, Messrs Paul Begg, Martin Fido and Keith Skinner. Their book is indeed encyclopaedic and provides an up-to-the-minute and generally useful account of the present state of our knowledge concerning the Whitechapel murders.

Turning, as handy yardstick, to the entries regarding the Ripper and the royals, the satisfactory opinionative information is forthcoming that 'it is to be regretted that overall extreme caution is recommended in examining any story emanating from or otherwise associated with Mr Sickert.' Indeed, one cannot even be sure that Hobo Joe *is* Mr Sickert. He *claims* to be the illegitimate son of Walter Sickert and Alice Margaret Crook (Mrs Gorman), and the grandson of Prince Eddy, but authorities on Walter Sickert and Prince Albert Victor have not accepted that claim. In 1978, whilst continuing to claim descent from Walter Sickert and Prince Albert Victor, Joseph Gorman Sickert confessed to the *Sunday Times* that the story of the Masonic conspiracy was 'a hoax, I made it all up'. Hobo subsequently retracted this confession. He also revealed his possession of some diaries, which he said Inspector Abberline had given to Walter Sickert in 1928 for transmission to Alice Margaret Crook (by then Mrs Gorman).

These are purported to contain 'the key to the whole ghastly affair'.

In his preface to the second edition of *The Ripper and the Royals* (1992), Melvyn Fairclough, quite understandably and acceptably, grasped the opportunity to respond, as he saw it, in kind:

Both books [Fairclough's and the *A to Z*] were reviewed together by Richard Whittington-Egan – according to the *A to Z* 'the doyen of British true-crime writers' – who hailed the *A to Z* as 'the magisterial offering of the most respectable and respected "Ripperological" trinity …'As for my book, he advised potential readers 'not [to] take it seriously,' endorsing the *A to Z*'s view that 'extreme caution is recommended in examining any story emanating from or otherwise associated with Mr Sickert.' Whittington-Egan thus appears to have changed his mind radically since he wrote his foreword to Stephen Knight's book sixteen years ago, judging that Knight presented 'a most cleverly worked out – brilliant even – solution.' Why the U-turn? Did he, like his mediaeval namesake, hear the Bells of Bow pealing out 'Turn again Whittington.' Or was it, perhaps that my book, by offering more evidence than Knight's and solving the Ripper mystery for good and all, did precisely the opposite of his wishes as stated in the foreword: 'I don't want the answer found, the guessing game to end.'

Joseph Sickert let it be known, *urbi et orbi*, that there had been a quarrel *in medias res* with Knight. He came to distrust him and the literary partnership had been effectively dissolved ere the end of the book had been reached. With Sickertian aid withdrawn, Knight had been forced to write speculatively. While he still maintained that it was Gull who actually killed and mutilated four of the victims, he was, we are told, simply acting under orders, and the real responsibility lay elsewhere. The revised triumvirate consists of Lord Randolph Churchill, John Netley, and Frederico Albericci. Who is he? you may well ask. He was an Italo-American pickpocket, 'Fingers Freddie,' Sir William Gull's whilom and wily footman.

Joe Sickert's family tree also opens up further now, spreading its branches wider to display some handsome new leaves. Alongside the royals appears the poet Dryden (Colin Thubron will be pleased, or more certainly surprised, about that!). The connection is through the Crook line. It is, moreover, now revealed that Annie Elizabeth, who we have hitherto been wrongly regarding as merely a humble shop assistant, was in reality something very different. Her lineage spidered out to trap in its remoter web-lines such illustrious relations as Lord Salisbury, Lord Arthur Somerset, Sir Charles Warren, and James Kenneth Stephen, Virginia Woolf's uncle.

While shuffling the genealogical cards, it even came out that Mary Jane Kelly might have been descended from the kings of Ireland. Indeed she might – for what Irisher isn't? And Adam and Eve, too, I shouldn't wonder! Mary, by the way, has been rumoured to have escaped the Miller's Court Aceldama, a previously unknown friend, Winifred May Collis, having all-unknowingly understudied for her. Kelly herself fled to Canada.

And if one is amazed by the foregoing revelations, how about this? If, as here implied, Prince Eddy's younger brother, who became King George V, was, ironically, not really one of the positive troop of infants alleged to have been spawned widespread by Edward VII, but was, as was whispered, the tangible expression of a tender passage between the neglected Alexandra and Grand Duke Nicholas of Russia, why then, the rightful King of England was – Joseph Sickert!

It is to three notional leather-bound volumes, written between 1892 and 1915, the Abberline Diaries, that we are indebted for most of the new and startling information. The alert reviewer in *Ripperana*, No. 2. pp. 15–16, drew attention to sundry infelicities in the great detective's epochal diaries. Abberline, apparently not knowing his own name, therein rendered it 'G. F. Abberline' instead of Frederick G. Abberline; quaint orthographical performances – *lapsus calami* – 'Clarance' for Clarence, J. K. Stephen rendered 'Steven'. An inexplicable making of the same errors in the discussion of the backgrounds of Jack's victims as have been perpetrated by some later investigators lacking Abberline's opportunities. It is a curious mental state exhibited by the diarist, in such marked contrast to that of the veritable Abberline of 1893, giving a lucid interview to the representative of the *Pall Mall Gazette*, wherein he acknowledges that he has heard all the popular theories, and unceremoniously dismisses them.

The other questionable *bonnes bouches* proffered by *The Ripper and the Royals* include the alleged photographs of John Charles Netley, George Hutchinson, and the Duke of Clarence in 1910, eighteen years after his official death and burial. The photographs of Clarence's sketchbook and the purse that he is said to have given to Alice Crook are dubious, as are the pictures of Queen Alexandra's ostrich-feather fan and her Prince of Wales' feathers hat decoration, presented as they are as treasured Sickert family memorabilia.

Having admittedly dealt somewhat excoriatingly with Mr Fairclough in my review, I would like to put it on record that I considered the quality of his circumambient historical research to be good and thorough. It was his susceptibility to theoretical suggestion and outrageous persuasion that I criticised. I could not, and never have been able to see Sir William Gull as Jack the Ripper the medic in any capacity, either direct or by association. By that action which speaks louder than the shrillest words, Mr Fairclough has since come to endorse my scepticism. He has now – going from bad to worse some would say – moved all his furniture into the staunch Maybrickian camp. He thus admits to having been gulled.

32

Jack the Cobbler: Edward Buchan

The year 1990 was generally inert, but it saw the appearance of four interesting articles, two in the *Criminologist* and one each in the *Journal of the Police History Society* and the *Cricketer*.

The first of these, in the spring 1990 issue of the *Criminologist*, was 'The Ripper: A Layman's Theory', wherein the author, Mason Jay, plumps for 'a clean-shaven female impersonator in drag' as Whitechapel Jack; so different from the black-bearded, mad Jewish immigrant, whose tantalising image was projected before every East-End-hunting policeman's eyes.

The autumn 1990 issue of the *Criminologist* provided Roger Barber with a platform for his 'Did Jack the Ripper Commit Suicide?' This was a promotional job for a completely new suspect, one Edward Buchan, a shoemaker of 37 Robin Hood Lane, Poplar,[53] who did away with himself by cutting his throat one Monday morning. It so happened that that particular Monday 19 November 1888, was the day of Mary Jane Kelly's funeral – and Buchan's twenty-ninth birthday.

Mr Barber quotes Martin Fido quoting Professor Luigi Cancrini of Bologna University, who considered that the Ripper murders 'evinced an explosive crescendo of increasing theatrical violence which would culminate in a complete breakdown'. And Fido opined that Cancrini would have expected death by suicide rather than by exhaustion.

Mr Barber further takes cognisance of Colin Wilson's view, expressed in his *Casebook of Murder* (1969) – 'I would draw only one inference that this destruction of the womb[54] indicated a suicidal tendency.'

And, finally, Barber is buttressed by the statement made by F. Kraupl Taylor in *Psychopathology: Its Causes and Symptoms*, that in cases of mental delirium, the person 'may cause injury and even death to others; self-mutilation and suicide are possible'.

Thus emboldened, and dismissing the solitary cited suicide within four weeks of the last murder – Druitt's drowning, the given reason for which was his fear that he might go mad like his mother, and the further implied reason being that of his unsavoury dismissal from George Valentine's Blackheath school – Barber sought another timeous suicide, finding it in that of Buchan. The young man was of the right age, that is to say of about the age that those generally held to be reliable witnesses – Israel Schwartz, Joseph Lawende, and Thomas Bowyer – testified to.

But was he Jack the Ripper? Barber supplies: 'He could well have been. The lack of factual evidence available suggests that we shall never definitely know who the psychopath was.'

Then Barber chances his arm. 'Psychological evidence alone shows that Edward Buchan is the likeliest candidate to appear.' Really? Does it? As old Professor Joad used to say, *it depends what you mean* by 'alone'.

Another novel candidate was canvassed by Jon Ogan in the *Journal of the Police History Society*, Vol. 5, 1990. His name was Oswald Puckridge.[55] Ogan's argument in his paper, 'Martha Tabram – the Forgotten Ripper Victim', is that Puckridge (1838–1900) was the murderer. And, indeed, on 19 September 1888, Sir Charles Warren addressed a letter to the Home Office in which he intimated that a man named Puckridge had been released from an asylum on the previous 4 August. 'He was educated as a surgeon – he has threatened to rip people up with a long knife. He is being looked for, but cannot be found yet.'

It was Philip Sugden who subsequently established that this was likely to be the son of John Puckridge, a Sussex farmer, and his wife, Philadelphia, born at Burpham, near Arundel, Sussex, on 13 June 1838, the fourth of five children. Sugden and Neal Shelden discovered that Oswald Puckridge became a chemist and that he was subject to frequent attacks of insanity. He had been a patient at Hoxton House Private Lunatic Asylum, in Hackney, East London, since January 1888. He was discharged from there in the following August.

Five years later, found wandering in Queen Victoria Street, in London, he was sent to Bow Street Infirmary on 9 August 1893, where he remained until 18 August.

In February 1896, he was taken into custody at Bridewell Police Station, and was readmitted to Bow Infirmary on 5 February. He was discharged nine days later – on 14 February – before being finally despatched, categorised as 'a Danger to others', to the City of London Lunatic Asylum, at Stone, Buckinghamshire. He was set at liberty once more on 9 July 1896.

He died on 1 June 1900, of broncho-pneumonia, at the Holborn Workhouse, where he had given his occupation as that of a general labourer. He and his wife, Ellen, *née* Buddle, had a son, Edward Buddle Puckridge, born at Deal in 1870, who had become a grocer and provision dealer. To him Puckridge left effects amounting to the value of £300.

Like many another, the Puckridge candidacy for Ripperhood seems to have perished for lack of any further sustenant data.

33

Jack the Chiseller: James Kelly

In 1997 James Tully, who tells us that he became 'hooked' on Jack the Ripper in the early 1950s, published *The Secret of Prisoner 1167: Was This Man Jack the Ripper?*, his study of the same Kelly that his 'good friend John Morrison' had brought to his attention. But, he continues, 'John [had] put together a good story … Unfortunately, most of what he stated as being factual was nothing of the sort.'

Undeterred, and nothing if not open-minded, Tully set about an examination of Mr Kelly's credentials, and, after nine years' hard labour, is able to provide a completely new *curriculum vitae* for him.

Morrison and Tully took their departure from the same platform, but continued their separate journeys to the same destination along very different lines.

Tully's James Kelly was born in Preston, Lancashire, on 20 April 1860, to unwed, fifteen-year-old Sarah Kelly and John Miller, who had deserted her and her soon-to-be-born son. The child was brought up by his grandmother in Liverpool. He seems to have left school when he was thirteen and been apprenticed to a Liverpool firm of upholsterers. He was then sent over the water to New Brighton, on the opposite bank of the Mersey, where he spent some time at a commercial school. At seventeen, he was found a position with a Liverpool pawnbroker; a situation which did not suit him. It was at about this time that, albeit very gradually, the first symptoms of mental instability began to manifest.

At the age of eighteen he left Liverpool for London, to pursue there his old trade of upholstery. Thus, in 1878, ten years before the Whitechapel serial murders, James Kelly first pointed a toe on

Saucy Jack's cobbled killing ground. His work as an itinerant upholsterer took him incessantly out and about so that he came to know the alleys and courts, covered passageways and dingy lanes of the slaughterings considerably better than the palm of his hand.

A Roman Catholic, forbidden by his religion to indulge in sexual intercourse outside the bounds and bonds of the sacrament of matrimony, Kelly had had neither women friends nor sexual experience in Liverpool, but free, untrammelled, in East London, he is said to have left his virginity with a prostitute, and, in deference to the Locardian doctrine of interchange, taken away a dose of VD with him.

Tully's telling of the story of the murder for which James Kelly was despatched to Broadmoor is totally diverse from that presented by John Morrison.

Sarah Ann Brider, rising twenty-two, lived with her parents, a sister, and three brothers, on the fringe of Islington. She worked as an 'Indian envelope folder'. We are not told of the circumstances in which she and Kelly met, but by March 1882 he had become a lodger in the Brider household.

It was at Christmas 1882 that James, at some point, succeeded in seducing Sarah. The fumbling and bussing was not a success, and he took it into his increasingly muddled head that Sarah had a genital malformation unfitting her for an uxorial role. Tully hazards the possibility that the 'malformation' was no more than vaginismus, resultant upon environmental tensions, furtiveness, and rush.

Even so, the effect upon Kelly and his malfunctioning reason was profound. He gloomed and brooded and blamed. Then … *volte-face* … he proposed marriage. Sarah did not jump at it, but, after a pause, agreed.

During the hiatus Kelly discovered that he was sexually diseased. He tried to delay the wedding – without disclosure. But, swept along by events, he accepted his future mother-in-law's choice of 4 June 1883, and on that appointed day the noises in his now frequently pain-shot head turned to wedding bells.

His wider-spreading derangement began to voice suspicions. His misfortunate wife became the focus of all his more violent delusions. She was 'on the game'. Her mother was her procuress. All along, the twain were after his legacy. They were plotters. They had been deceiving him. Now they were laughing at him behind his back. Round and round in the dark squirrel-cage behind his eyes whirred the sharp-edged, brain-lacerating thoughts. The delusional system gelled, came together at a pocketknife's point: he drove it, stabbing, deep and digging, into Sarah's throat.

Sarah Ann Kelly died in St Bartholomew's Hospital on 24 June 1883. The marriage had lasted less than three weeks.

Kelly was put up for trial at the Central Criminal Court – the Old Bailey – on 1 August 1883. He was found guilty with a recommendation for mercy. Three days before he was to hang, he was, following examination by a team of doctors, certified insane, and was admitted, on 24 August 1883, to Broadmoor Criminal Lunatic Asylum, from which he escaped on 23 January 1888.

Forging a link between James Kelly and the Jack the Ripper murders is no easy matter for Tully; so much of the 'evidence' has to be suppositional. Having told all that he had been able to discover of the authentic details of James Kelly's life, he turns to accounts of the murders presented through the mouths of witnesses at the inquests, and concludes by exploring such connections as he perceives between the murder and his suspect. He does, however, acknowledge that many minor mysteries still surround the killings. Despite his efforts, too many gaps bridged by optimistic 'be that as it mays' remain. The story of the murders, so mandatorily oft-told, is, however, neatly encompassed with no *longueurs*, which is in itself no mean achievement.

It is that massive blow which fractured Martha Tabram's breast-bone that brings Kelly into the picture. 'One of the tools which [Kelly] would have used most often … was a ripping chisel … Was the instrument which broke Tabram's sternum a ripping chisel?'

Tully does not specify the linkage between Polly Nichols and the ripping-chisel-wielding Kelly, but it must surely be the nature and orientation of her wounding. Again, it is the *nature* of the wounding that ties in the same assailant, be it Kelly or whosoever, with the slaying of Annie Chapman – the cut throat, left to right, the abdominal and genital mutilations. This time, though, a novel dimension: Chapman's uterus, the upper part of her vagina, and bladder had been taken away. Tully sees Dark Annie as the fulcrum of change.

The evidence of Mrs Elizabeth Long, suggesting that the woman whom she saw at 5.30 a.m. that Saturday morning of 8 September 1888, talking to a man near No. 29 Hanbury Street, was Annie Chapman is questioned by Tully. He thinks also that the sounds Albert Cadosch heard, while still sleep-befuddled, at around 5.20 a.m., might easily have been misinterpreted by him.

Tully does his best to deal with the conflicting statements as to the time of Annie Chapman's death. Dr Bagster Phillips opined it before 4.30 a.m., while witness John Richardson quite categorically stated that the body was not there at 4,45 a.m., when he was in the back yard of No. 29.

James Kelly is absolved from the murder of Elisabeth Stride since Tully does not accept it to have been committed by the author of the three precedent killings (that figure includes the murder of Tabram). Tully frankly suspects Liz's live-in lover, and likely pimp, Michael Kidney, of doing for her.

With the slaying of Catherine Eddowes in Mitre Square in the early morning hours of 30 September or rather 1 October 1888, to be strictly accurate, we are back with the Ur-Ripper; throat cut, left to right, extensive facial mutilations, snip and nick through left and right eyelids, slick and slice off tip of nose, lay open abdomen, liver stabbed and incised, pancreas heroically gashed, uterus and left kidney knifed out and carried off.

Although the sanguinolent and faecally soiled cut-off of discoloured white apron – definitely part of the apron which Eddowes had been wearing – discovered in Goulston Street makes it virtually certain that Jack the Ripper passed that way, it is by no means equally certain that the 'Juwes' message found in seeming association with the apron fragment was veritably written by the fleeing Ripper.

Tully subscribes to the long-standing doubts as to whether the writing on the black-brick fascia was in Jack's hand at all. Noting Detective Constable Daniel Halse's observation that the writing on the wall was in a schoolboy's round hand, Tully thinks that there may well have been 'a youth in the neighbourhood, even perhaps living in Wentworth (Model) Dwellings', who could have shed a great deal of light on the mystery. It should be noted that the wall on which the writing had been scrawled was not visible from the street, it being inside the entrance way to the right just as one entered, as, indeed, *The Times*, 12 October 1888, reported: 'The writing was in the passage of the building itself, and was on the black dado of the wall. He [Halse] assumed that the writing was recent, because from the number of persons living in the tenement he believed it would have been rubbed out had it been there for any time. There were about three lines of writing, which was in a good schoolboy hand.'

The juxtaposition of apron and wall-writing may have been no more than coincidence. There were scrawled writings on walls all over the East End, and who shall deny the possibility, put forward by Tully, that, attracted by the smell of the rag, some animal might have transported it from a remote corner in which it had been jettisoned to the suggestively central position in which it was found?

Two of the stickiest problems of the Miller's Court affair, the grand conflagration and Mrs Maxwell's matutinal vision, are tackled by Tully.

He pioneers the notion that the burning of the clothes had nothing whatever to do with the provision of illumination. On the contrary, it was contrived to provide a cover of darkness, as it were, for the disposal of incriminating stolen property.

Mrs Maria Harvey, who purported to be a laundress, had, as part of a long-established routine, stolen clothes. Having heard on the very well-rooted Whitechapel grapevine that the police were on to her, she whisked the, literally, material evidence, away from her crib in New Court, and took it to her friend Mary's place, where, wise counsel prevailing, the women decided to burn the dangerously identifiable swag.

As to the time of death of Mary Kelly, Tully submits the opinion of his friend, the late Dr F. D. M. Hocking, a forensic scientist who had worked with Sir Bernard Spilsbury. In his view, rigor mortis commences between two and four hours after death, not six to twelve hours as Dr Thomas Bond is on record as stating. By Bond's reasoning, Kelly's death had occurred between one and two in the morning.

In support of Hocking's view, Tully cites *Gradwohl's Legal Medicine*: 'The delay in the appearance of rigor mortis after death can vary considerably. Ordinarily it is about two to four hours. It is complete in another three to four hours and is generally fully established about nine hours after death.'

Accepting the modern forensic estimates, and cognisant of the variables inherent in the range of hours, it is conceivable that Kelly's death could have taken place at about nine in the morning, which could then account for Mrs Caroline Maxwell's breakfast-time encounter with Mary Jane – be she flesh and blood, ghost or doppelgänger – between eight and half-past of that morning of 9 November.

There is, additionally, the consideration of the state of the partially digested fish and potatoes of Kelly's last meal. Hocking recognised that 'any conclusion as to the time of death based on the degree of digestion of food in the stomach is inordinately inaccurate. People vary widely in their rate of digestion.' He would, though, have put partial digestion at one to two hours after eating, not the three to four hours postulated by Bond. Hocking concludes, 'In my opinion, the finding is consistent with the meal having been taken around 8 a.m. – and not about midnight.'

In the complexion of all this, Tully feels understandably affronted by the apparent failure of the police to make any investigation into the verifiable facts of Caroline Maxwell's statement. 'Apart from checking her avowed movements on that morning, one would have thought that Abberline, on being told by her of Mary's vomiting in the street, would have said: "Show me" … surely *some* traces of the vomit should have been there, perhaps even enough to establish whether it contained fish and potatoes.'

But to what end? It was raining that morning, and even if the vomit had not been washed away, it would have been risky to pronounce upon its specific provenance, since fish – from Billingsgate – and potato formed the staple diet of at least half of the people of the district.

One further point. The Abberline legend is attacked: that officer's outstanding ability questioned. Tully describes him as 'a cut above the average policeman of his day … [but] no deductive genius. He was honest, methodical and competent … The sole reason for his secondment to the [Ripper] murder team was the length of time [fourteen years] which he had spent in the area where the atrocities were happening … He was a good, plodding copper, but he had nothing really special to offer, except his local knowledge.' That was why he had been recalled from Scotland Yard to lead the team of detectives on the ground in Whitechapel.

It is, I think, time to redress an error that has been repeated over the years in book after book on the Whitechapel murders and makes its appearance yet again in Mr Tully's pages. It is that at the time of the Whitechapel murders Henry Moore was a Detective Chief Inspector and therefore, by implication, the superior of Inspector Abberline. The truth of the matter is that, whereas Abberline was an Inspector First Class, Moore was then an Inspector Second Class, and acting under the direction of Abberline. Moore would seem to owe his premature promotion to a passage in ex-Chief Inspector Walter Dew's memoirs:[56] 'The officers sent from Scotland Yard were Chief-Inspector Moore, Inspector Abberline, and Inspector Andrews.' Superior in rank to Abberline was Detective Chief Inspector Donald Sutherland Swanson, who was the desk officer at the Yard responsible for the collection and onward and upward transmission of all reports received from officers involved in the Ripper investigations.

At the age of forty-nine, Abberline, with somewhat of a chip on the shoulder, which, in his view, should have carried considerably sooner the epaulet of higher rank, but with a new-minted, notched-up chief inspector's pension in his plain-clothes' pocket, quit the force in 1892, and spent the succeeding twelve years as a private detective. He died in Bournemouth in 1929.

We come now to the crux of the matter. The Crunch. Is there reason to accept the argued candidature of James Kelly for the role of Jack the Ripper?

Tully was not satisfied with the results of his research efforts at Broadmoor. It took him longer to break into the asylum than it took Kelly to break out. The scaling of the outdated confidentiality barrier occupied the better part of six years, even though there was no real cause for continuing privity. There was perhaps nothing surprising, or significant, in the official haltings and hesitations. They were probably no more than habit. Frustration is endemic in dealing with such institutions – par for the course. Often, the obduration is a matter of inherited lineal instinct and ritualised habitude rather than the obstinate deliberacy of reactive stupidity. No conclusion should be drawn from it, least of all that sacred secrets are being devotedly guarded. One must in these matters sidestep the naiveties of a Mr Spiering. Boys will be boys. Bureaucrats will be bureaucrats. Idiots will be idiots.

What are the reasons that dictate James Tully's conviction of James Kelly's guilt? Taking a leaf from the Quantico protocol, he asserts that Kelly's profile fits virtually every profile of serial lust killers, but for one small detail – he was mad. He fits also the peculiar circumstances of the Ripper killings. He was the only insane, convicted woman-killer at large in the East End of London at the period of the murders, and we know that he possessed an excellent knowledge of the geography of the whole of the East End area.

While disclaiming any graphological expertise, Tully feels nevertheless the necessity to tell us that the first thing that struck him upon viewing the Broadmoor file was Kelly's handwriting, with its distinct resemblance to that of the September 1888 'Dear Boss' letter and the Saucy Jacky postcard, postmarked 1 October 1888. Tully seemingly accepts those communications as genuinely deriving from the Ripper's hand, and points to their tell-tale Americanisms, proffering Kelly's period aboard a United States man-of-war as accounting for such usages.

While reviewing the matter of Ripper correspondence, Tully suggests that another possible Kelly connection arises when one considers two supposed Ripper letters posted in Liverpool. Quite so. The only small snag is that nobody has ever been able to trace either of those letters. They are said to have been seen by Dr Dutton, and Donald McCormick implies that they were in the same handwriting as the 'Dear Boss' letter and associated postcard.

The first Liverpool letter is alleged to have been dated 29 September 1888, and was therefore written *before* the *nom de meurtre* was public knowledge, arguing for its authenticity.

The second communication, incidentally, provided the very precise Liverpool address of the Ripper residence as Prince William Street, which was in the Toxteth area of Liverpool.

It is most unfortunate that both of these valuable fragments of epistolic evidence should have so completely vanished. Perhaps Dr Dutton tucked them away between the pages of one of the three volumes of his, also mysteriously vanished, *Chronicles of Crime* for safekeeping.

The fact is that Tully is perpetuating another error which, for more than fifty years now, has migrated from book to book. To unravel some part of this mystery one must have recourse to J. Hall Richardson's autobiographical *From the City to Fleet Street* (1927). Therein you will find the first report of the Liverpool correspondence, which appears thus:

Liverpool

29th inst.

BEWARE I shall be at work on the 1st and 2nd inst. In 'Minories' at 12 midnight and I give the authorities a good chance but there is never a Policeman near when I am at work.

Yours,

Jack the Ripper

Prince William St, L'pool.

What fools the police are I even give them the name of the street where I am living.

Yours, Jack the Ripper.

Richardson introduces the above communication with the statement that 'the Police and Press received many letters from the "Ripper," mostly written in red ink, *and I give one.*'

Note that he refers to the communication in the singular and gives no indication that the above are two separate letters rather than a bipartite one. Note, too, that neither month nor year are indicated, merely the date – '29th inst.'

Richardson had been a journalist, working for the *Daily Telegraph.*

In 1889, after the Pinchin Street murder, the *Telegraph* received a large number of 'Jack the Ripper' letters, and it is quite possible that it is one of these, and not a letter of 1888, that Richardson has got hold of and is quoting.

McCormick's reference to this letter from Liverpool stated, 'On 29 September this assiduous scribe wrote from Liverpool.' And, having quoted what may well be only the *first* portion of the total letter, he adds, 'Some time later this was followed by another brief missive.' This second 'missive' is thus unwarrantedly presented as a separate entity. McCormick cannot plead ignorance of the source of this information concerning the Liverpool communication, for, in another context elsewhere in his book, he quotes from Richardson's memoirs.

But all is well, for McCormick is able to assure us that no less an authority than Dr Thomas Dutton 'confirms that the Liverpool letters were in his [Jack the Ripper's] hand'.

Tully sedulously logs the progression of Kelly's bid for freedom and the lack of progress of those who sought to recapture him.

At 9.15 p.m. in the evening of Kelly's E – for Escape – Day, Monday 23 January 1888, a special messenger was despatched from Broadmoor to Great Scotland Yard, where, in the first hours of 24 January, information of Kelly's abscondence was lodged, and it was suggested that his mother-in-law's house should be watched.

On Tuesday (24th), the Medical Superintendent of Broadmoor, Dr David Nicholson, officially informing the Home Office of the break-out, wrote, in what Tully calls 'an obvious attempt to play down the seriousness of the matter,' that for a long time previous to his escape 'the active indications of insanity had subsided and he conversed rationally. He showed no signs of being violent, or in any way dangerous.'

A week passed. On 20 January the Metropolitan Police requested a photograph of the escapee. Two were duly sent off to the Commissioner that same day.

The hunt went on. Without success.

Filling in the jigsaw of Kelly's thirty-nine 'lost' years of freedom is an impossible task; there just are not enough retrievable pieces. But, according to Tully, there is one convenient certitude: 'All that we know for certain is that Kelly reappeared in the East End of London during the first half of 1888 … What we know is that later that year he was virtually penniless and that, completely unprepared, he left London precipitately and fled to France.'

Unbridgeable gaps notwithstanding, Tully considers that there is a sufficiency of suspicious circumstances to warrant the conclusion at which he has arrived. To Tully it is suspicious that, three days after the killing of Mary Jane Kelly, on 12 November, Charles Edward Troup[57] wrote the following on James Kelly's file:

> Would it not be well to make inquiry as to what steps have been taken to recapture this man? It is not likely he is the Whitechapel murderer; but his offence was cutting his wife's throat, and he escaped last January, it would be well to know what has become of him.

There is no evidence that James Kelly was actually named as a serious Ripper suspect. Quite the reverse. The Home Office directive was to look at all lunatics either released or escaped in 1888, and as such Kelly would naturally have to be looked at. The police would have to act, and inquire on this directive, but they were, as the *Daily Telegraph* reported, in pursuit of more than James Kelly on that eventful weekend:

> Yesterday [Sunday 11 November 1888] the constabulary made complete census of Dorset Street, having special reference to the persons within it on Thursday night. Although it is but a short thoroughfare there are, it is stated, no fewer than 1,200 men who sleep every night in the common lodging-houses with which it abounds.

There is also the decidedly pause-giving reply, on 14 November 1888, by Dr Nicholson, to the inquiry concerning Kelly which he had received from the Home Office.
Nicholson wrote,

> There is nothing whatever in his behaviour while at Broadmoor to indicate that he would be likely to prove dangerous to others. He was melancholic in his tendencies and more disposed to be suicidal at times. I have no reason, from anything I have seen about the condition of Kelly's mind for thinking that the murders in Whitechapel were committed by him.

Strangely, the Home Office file does not contain a copy of their original inquiry to Dr Nicholson – to which the above is his reply – regarding the possibility of Kelly's being the Whitechapel murderer. Indeed, it is only because of the copy of Nicholson's reply preserved in the Broadmoor file that we know at all of the official finger of suspicion pointing at James Kelly.

Does this, Tully asks, imply the existence of a cover-up? It is with this in mind that he observes that, 'although the records now made public are packed with the names of suspects, there is not a single mention of James Kelly, or anything to do with him'.

This, let's face it, could be either extremely significant, or of no significance whatever. It could mean a cover-up. It could mean that there was nothing to cover up.

We are, indeed, afforded a good deal of negative reinforcement by the very lack of anything substantial having survived in official quarters in the way of expressed contemporary suspicion of James Kelly. There is, for example, no record of a search for him having been mounted. There is no record of any circulation of the missing Kelly's description, similar to the all-stations relay of the description of the suspect man said to have been seen by George Hutchinson at the time of the Mary Kelly murder. Had Mrs Brider not complained to her solicitor of the manner in which she had been treated by the visiting constabulary we should know nothing of the police search for Kelly.

That Mr Tully has set down a formidable indictment in circumstantial and suppositional terms is not to be denied. But, 'be that as it may', to quote a favourite locution of his, it goes nowhere towards proving that, over and above the capacity to be the Whitechapel Fiend, James Kelly actually was the 'Red Terror'. Not a scantling of jury-worth evidence has been produced to connect Kelly materially with any of the East End slaughterings, and executive capacity must be translated into actual witnessed execution, or copper-bottomed evidence of such execution, before one starts bandying about the blood-guilt accusation.

It is all too easy to be superciliously dismissive of other people's suspects. I consider that Mr Tully has accomplished some excellent research, and come up with some truly wondrous suppositions, speculations, and persuasively chiming coincidences. If I have one criticism, it is that his dismissal of Mesdames Long and Maxwell strikes me as over-facile and somewhat cavalier. Nevertheless, he is, without prejudice, to be congratulated upon having had a serious stab at identifying Jack the Ripper; but I cannot feel that, in the person of James Kelly, his knife goes home.[58]

34
Jack the Gynaecologist

In August 1982, Jane Elizabeth Caputi submitted to the Graduate College of Bowling Green State University, Ohio, in partial fulfilment of the requirements for the degree of Doctor of Philosophy, a dissertation, 'The Age of Sex Crime'. The title is taken from Colin Wilson's observation that 'it remains fundamentally true to say that Jack the Ripper inaugurated the age of sex crime'.[59]

With Ms Caputi's book, we are into the prickly, penal territory of aggressive, capital 'F' Feminism, where reverse-sexist butchery, every bit as severe as Macho Jack's, is the meted out order of the day. Inevitably, we soon find ourselves being hied briskly off the well-worn Ripper track and transported willy-nilly into the perilous region of the *deserta vagina dentata*.

Caputi writes,

> Sex crime, rape-murder, lust murder: these are new words for a relatively new kind of crime. And accompanying these are new names, or more accurately, nicknames, for that new kind of criminal. Names like Jack the Ripper, the Düsseldorf Ripper, the Blackout Ripper, the Cleveland Torso Killer, Jack the Kisser, Jack the Stripper, the Boston Strangler, Tampa's Red Light District Strangler, Poland's Red Spider. the Michigan Murderer, the Coed Killer, the Strangler of the Andes, the Son of Sam, the Hillside Strangler, the Ted Murderer (Ted Bundy), the Yorkshire Ripper. Why such colorful masks? Why such drama? And why the accelerating procession of such killers marked by territory and remembered by method?
>
> This line of structurally linked criminals points to the existence of … a cycle that acquired a myth and momentum in 1888 with the celebrated crimes of Jack the Ripper.

Jane Elizabeth identifies the Ripper-style mass murderer as the paradigm for modern sex crime. It was, she avers, the killer known as Jack the Ripper who provided the prototype for 'a criminal career founded upon a compulsion to destroy women'. And she proposes what she terms the Ripper formula: 'A single killer, around whom a mystique forms, a series of similar murders, a ritual style of slaughter, a particular victim type, intense publicity, and a specific region that is terrorized.'

But there was an earlier group of sexual criminals who plagued nineteenth-century Europe. They were colloquially known as 'rippers' and 'stabbers'. As a rule they did not kill their victims, but tried to stab them in the buttocks, breast, or genitals as they walked along the streets. Things reached such a pitch – more than fifty victims in the two years between 1788 and 1790 – that fashionable ladies took to protecting their delicacy by wearing copper pans over their posteriors. Copper-bottom securities, you might say.

A celebrated practitioner of such piquerism, proper style and title unknown, was nicknamed the London Monster. Arrested on 14 December 1790, he turned out to be a twenty-three-year-old Welshman, Rhynwick Williams. He was put up for trial at Bow Street Magistrates' Court. The charge brought against him was that of defacing clothing, which carried the possibility of a potentially harsher penalty than either assault or attempted murder. Found guilty on three counts, he was sentenced to two years in respect of each, and sent to prison for six years. After doing his time, he emerged a new-turned leaf, married the mother of his illegitimate offspring, and returned to his respectable old occupation of artificial flower making.

Between 1885 and 1895, following on the heels of the piquerists, there came a sudden and inexplicable explosion of lethal Jack-the-Ripper-formula-type sex crimes – a Moscow Ripper in 1885, the Texas Ripper, killer and mutilator of a number of young Negro prostitutes, in 1887, Whitechapel Jack in 1888, the Nicaraguan Ripper in 1889.

'A philosophical foundation for this modern form of sex crime was provided at the very beginning of the nineteenth century by the Marquis de Sade whose writings offered the first systematic fusion of sex and violence.'

An article in the *Southern Guardian* of 5 January 1889, demanded, 'Suppose we catch the Whitechapel murderer, can we not before handing him over to the authorities at Broadmoor, make a really decent effort to discover his antecedents, and his parentage, to trace back every step of his career, every hereditary instinct, every acquired taste, every moral slip, every mental idiosyncracy? Surely the time has come for such an effort as this. We are face to face with some mysterious and awful product of modern civilization.'

But of course all these things remain mysteries to this day.

Acknowledging that the East End Ripper has become the prime source of speculation, fiction, and legend, essentially achieving the status of a modern myth, Caputi is scrupulous to advise:

> *Myth* is not used here in any superficial or trivial sense. As Eliade[60] has noted, whenever any new human reality, behaviour or institution occurs, it is accompanied by a new myth. The forever faceless Jack functions as the personification of the new phenomenon of sex crime, a social type, a word in the language, a conventional figure in horror, a consummate outlaw … the human mask for sex crime … as metaphor and myth of the age … the sex criminal steps outside the normal parameters of criminal activity and becomes, like the Western outlaw or the gangster, a symbol or myth of the era.

A generally recognised component of myth is its stimulation of the mimetic urge. In the case of the modern sex-crime myth, its attendant fixed imagery and iconography provide imitative potential which solidifies into cultural ritual – an extreme physical symbolism, perhaps, as exemplified by actual mutilation, accompanied not infrequently by calculated public display of the achieved transmutation of thought into the reality of mutilated flesh and blood.

Of the sex killers, Caputi observes, 'Such men are the "logical" products not only of a national myth of regeneration through violence, an ideology in which men are projected as the violent and the transcendent and women into the sexual and the sacrificial, but also a universal ideology or myth of male superiority. Sex crime is one more ritual through which men enact and dramatise their domination.'

Interestingly, according to Caputi, 'the new age of Ripper-style sex crime began precisely at the point of triumph for a new age of gynaecological surgery, a movement that was characterised by the flamboyant, drastic, risky, and instant use of the knife'. Between 1853 and 1883, four operations were invented: clitordectomy, ovariotomy ('female castration'), hysterectomy, and radical mastectomy – the surgical removal of, respectively, clitoris, ovaries, womb and breast. These operations caught on with the force of a fashion and rapidly became standard procedure for the treatment not only of physical complaints, but just as frequently for mental and moral disorders: 'troublesomeness, eating like a ploughman, masturbation, attempted suicide, erotic tendencies, persecution mania, simple "cussedness", and dysmenorrhea.' With all this somewhat bizarre Victorian gynaecological activity in mind, it has been severally suggested that Jack, with his obsessive interest in uteri, might well have been a deranged gynaecologist.

PART 3
POINTS OF VIEW:
THE HISTORICAL BACKDROP
INTERPRETED

35

The Socio-Politic View

The social and political scene of the late Victorian East End, which formed the background against which the dread figure of Jack the Ripper stalked, is that socio-economic climate engendered by those wandering Jews fleeing the pogroms of Russia, and the Polish Jews, who, ever since the dismemberment of Poland by the Imperial predator in 1772, and on throughout a century's succession of xenophobic ukases and schemes implemented to de-Judaise, had, in a mass exodus from the Land of Bondage, been seeking a Land of Promise in East London.

The promise was scarcely fulfilled. The immigrants found themselves, beyond the pale, unwelcome strangers in a strange land. They came with faith and hope, but received scant charity. Their portion was exploitation: menial labour in the sweat shops. Who should blame them, if, by the waters of the Thames, they sat them down and wept?

But, characteristically, they did not. Rallied by Aron Lieberman, one of the radical intelligentsia and a refugee from the Tsarist Secret Police, they banded together to form the first Hebrew Socialist Union.

And there were others, fighting the good fight in what portion of time they could salvage from the long hours of labour. Their names – Morris Winchevsky, Woolf Wess, Rudolph Rocker, the charismatic German goy – run like a litany, or socialist hagiography, through the pages of East End history. They are the Alien Apostles and Radical Prophets, the Libertarian *Arbeter Frainters*.[1]

Well may William J. Fishman[2] write in remembrance, 'As long as there is one cobbled alley, one undeserted tenement left, which recalls the voices and images of the chaverim, I still walk with my father.'

But for the impoverished indigent Christians a major gauge to anti-alienism – *aliter* anti-Semitism – was the current peak of unemployment. In this prevailing climate of poverty, the Jews were thrust into their customary role as scapegoat. Vested interest wielded its assorted cudgels; political demagogues flew the anti-alien kite; restrictionists and exclusionists fulminated in full spate; a medley of opportunists seized eagerly upon the anti-alien ticket.

It was at this critical juncture that the Jack the Ripper murders occurred, provoking an outbreak of Judophobia. The fact that Elisabeth Stride was found outside the premises of the International Workingmen's Educational Association at 40 Berner Street did not help, but even before that the *East London Observer*, on 15 September 1888, remarked in 'A Reign of Terror in Whitechapel' that, consequent upon the murder of Annie Chapman, 'the whole of London was again sent almost crazy by the news of still another tragedy having been enacted, this time in Hanbury Street', and then, under the cross-head 'A Riot Against the Jews', further commented,

> On Saturday in several quarters of East London the crowds who had assembled in the streets began to assume a very threatening attitude towards the Hebrew population of the District. It was repeatedly asserted that no Englishman could have perpetrated such a horrible crime as that of Hanbury Street, and that it must have been done by a Jew – and forthwith the crowds proceeded to threaten and abuse such of the unfortunate Hebrews as they found in the streets. Happily, the presence of a large number of police in the streets prevented a riot actually taking place.

Aroused by an accusation in the *Church Times* that Jack the Ripper was a Russian anarchist, Benjamin Feigenbaum, belligerently anti-religious and a major contributor to the *Arbeter Fraint*, declaimed, 'Such homage from the Holy Spirit! What the almighty watchdog, Charles Warren, could not discover – the Whitechapel murderer – the Holy Ghost has revealed.'

Chaim Bermant[3] is more concerned with the East End as a geographical entity, and with its informing *Zeitgeist*. His is social rather than socialist history, and through these dark pages buzz the four busy Bs of reform – Barnett, Booth, Barnardo, and Burdett-Coutts.

For Mr Bermant the East End is more a state of mind than an ideological battleground. But he, too, recognises the very real peril inherent in the rumour of Jacob the Ripper: 'The nearest thing to an East End anti-Jewish pogrom, prior to the advent of Mosley, took place during the Jack the Ripper murders in 1888.'

The Jews were a secretive people. They kept themselves to themselves. They spoke a strange tongue. They had strange habits. They impressed the local populace as furtive and sinister.

Observed the *Jewish Chronicle* of 14 September 1888, 'Without doubt the foreign Jews in the East End have been in some peril during the past week owing to the sensationalism of which the district has been a centre.'

Indeed, it was for a time unsafe for Jews to show their faces in the streets at all.

The Central European correspondent of the *Standard* did not help matters by filing a story, printed in the paper's issue of 2 October 1888, that in some parts of Germany it was believed that candles fashioned from the uterus gave off fumes that rendered people unconscious, and that these 'thief candles', *Diebslichter*, as they were called, were used by criminals.

A report from *The Times*' Vienna correspondent, also published on 2 October 1888, did not improve matters. It stated that a Jew named Ritter had been arrested near Cracow and charged with the ritual murder of a Christian woman. The prosecution alleged that the accused had believed that having had sexual intercourse with her, he was obliged by Jewish law to kill her. The fact that Ritter was found not guilty did not mitigate 'the evidence touching the superstitions prevailing among some of the ignorant and degraded of his co-religionists [which] remains on record and was never wholly disproved'.

This item elicited instant letters to the editor from two Jewish religious leaders. The Acting Chief Rabbi of the United Jewish Congregations of the British Empire, Dr Hermann Adler, wrote,

> I can assert, without hesitation, that in no Jewish book is such a barbarity even hinted at. Nor is there any record in the criminal annals of any country of a Jew having been convicted of such a terrible atrocity ... The tragedies enacted in the East End are sufficiently distressing

without the revival of moribund fables and the importation of prejudices abhorrent to the English nation.

Dr Moses Gaster, Chief Rabbi of the Sephardi Jews in England, was equally outraged: 'These are superstitions entertained against the Jews from which the Jews turn with horror and disgust.'

But mud sticks, and people continued to believe that a Jew had been responsible for the Whitechapel slaughterings.

For a time it was popularly thought that the murders were being committed by the Old Nichol – a notorious gang of cut-throats hailing from an evil warren of streets, the Old Nichol,[4] in Bethnal Green – but the police subsequently embraced the theory that a Jewish ritual slaughterman, a *shochet*, steeped in Old Testament law, brooding upon the manifold Talmudic denunciations of harlots and harlotry, might have yielded to some religious impulsion to strike down prostitutes.

Following visits paid to kosher abattoirs, two *shochtim* were detained, then released. Dr Frederick Gordon Brown 'examined the knives commonly used by the *shochtim* and satisfied himself that they could not possibly have been used in any of the murders. The *khalef*, as the implement is known, is single-edged and not pointed, whereas the mutilations on all the victims indicated a pointed blade.'

In the prevalent atmosphere of anti-Semitic hostility, there is little doubt that the Goulston Street wall-writing could, and probably would, have proved disastrously inflammatory.

Sir Charles Warren's decision to erase it was not reached without very careful consideration, However, significance was attached by some newspapers to the misspelling of the word 'Juwes', and it was suggested that the lettering had the appearance of being half Hebrew. There was implied criticism of what was regarded as Warren's hasty action in ordering it to be immediately expunged.

In his report of 6 November 1888, to the Home Office, Warren had written of his concern: 'I may mention that so great was the feeling with regard to the Jews that on the 13th ulto. the Acting Chief Rabbi (Dr Hermann Adler) wrote to me on the subject of the spelling of the word "Juewes" [*sic*] on account of a newspaper asserting that this was a Jewish spelling in the Yiddish dialect.'

Dr Adler's letter of 13 October 1888 had stated, 'The equivalent in the Judao-German [*sic*] (Yiddish) jargon is "Yidden". I do not know of any dialect or language in which "Jews" is spelled "Juewes" [*sic*]. I am convinced that the writing emanated from some illiterate Englishman who did not know how to spell the word correctly.'

On 15 October *The Times*, responding to a request from Warren, informed its readers,

> In reference to the writing on the wall of a house in Goulston Street we are requested by Sir Charles Warren to state that his attention having been called to a paragraph in several daily journals mentioning that in the Yiddish dialect the word is spelt 'Juwes,' he has made inquiries on the subject and finds that this is not a fact. He learns that the equivalent in the Judeo-German (Yiddish) jargon is 'Yidden.'

Bermant discovers an Hebraic significance in the incidence pattern of the murders which imported a definite frisson of unease to Jewish observers in the community.

Martha Tabram's murder he accepts as the first of the Ripper series. That killing took place on 7 August, which date coincided with the eve of the first *Ellul*,[5] the month preceding the Jewish New Year and the Ten Days of Penitence. It is a month of supplication and penitence, with the mournful *shofar*[6] sounding a warning of the approach of the Day of Judgement.

Mary Ann Nichols was killed on 31 August, which coincided with the twenty-fourth day of *Ellul*, a time when the pious rise at dawn to say *Seltchot*, penitential prayers.

'A dreadful pattern was emerging and it seemed as if a Jew, overwhelmed by perverted religious passions, had taken it upon himself to act as an avenging angel in the name of the Lord.'

The most sacred days of the Jewish calendar are *Rosh Hashanah*, the Jewish New Year, and *Yom Kippur*, the Day of Atonement, twenty-four hours of fasting and prayer, the tenth day of the month of *Tishrei*.

The Day of Atonement came and went without the spilling of blood.

The New Year celebrations continue over two days. The first of these celebratory days fell on 6 September, and it was some hours after the close of the evening service of the second celebratory day that Annie Chapman met her end.

Stride and Eddowes' murders took place – well beyond the cycle of the Solemn Days – on the 25th of *Tishrei*, one of the few days in the holiest of Jewish months to be devoid of any religious significance whatever. Neither was there any significance attaching to 9 November, the day of Mary Jane Kelly's demise.

Quite apart from the most valuable commentary that Bermant supplies on the controversial aspect of Jack as Jacob the Ripper, his book presents a skilful evocation of the East End atmosphere. If, as the Francophile assures us, the scent of Paris is a subtle blend of flowers, garlic, caporal and that rich French dust that smells so lyrically of itself, then there is surely, too, an authentic aroma of the old East End. It arises from Chaim Bermant's pages. It is compounded of the sweatshop reek of sewing-machine oil, the acrid wisps of ritual candle smoke, the spicy tang of fish – soused, pickled, salted, marinated – the whiff of borscht, of Black Russian ryes, of bagels, matzos, and *cholas*. And, over all, the sour stench of poverty, that smells so unlyrically of itself.

36
The Sexo-Psychological View

The mid-1980s and early 1990s brought the turn of the ultra-serious crypto-socio-sexo-bio-psychological interpreters to apply their sometimes opaque spyglasses to the conscious and unconscious statements of the crimes.

These were the pre-eminently feminist academics, the cut-glass scrutineers, tending to look at things obliquely and pronounce them crooked. One should not, however, scoff. Not only is it banausic, it is also inept, for the intellectual approach, a few blots of outrageous prejudice aside, is not to be underestimated. Was it not, after all, Dr Richard von Krafft-Ebing whose sane and balanced insights set the course straight for the study and appreciation of the relevance of sexual perversion to the commission of gross crimes? It was he who elaborated a careful taxonomy so constructed as to distinguish the perverted Other from the normative Self. Did not Sigmund Freud, Magnus Hirschfeld, and the redoubtable Baron von Schrenck Notzing straighten the crooked mirror that we might glimpse its distorted reflections in the perspective of their true significance?

Christopher Frayling, writing 'The House that Jack Built', in *Rape*, edited by Sylvana Tamaselli and Roy Porter (1986), remarks that the incidents of the autumn of 1888 have, over the long stretch of time, become confounded with the representation of male sexuality with violence, and to such an extent that race memory identifies Jack the Ripper as the rapist stereotype.

But the Ripper was not a rapist in the conventional usage. The repeated penetrations with sweetly keen knife appear to have been his kind of sexual act. Says Frayling, 'The Whitechapel murders, and their constant re-enactment as myth in the mass media, are a key to the understanding of rape as it has been represented in the popular culture of the twentieth century.'

At the time of the East End killings, the work of neither Freud nor Krafft-Ebing had as yet begun to send its widening circle of ripples through the general consciousness of society. Not, however, by any means unconnected with the provision of an accessible Ripper explanation was the fact that at that precise juncture the American actor-manager, Richard Mansfield, happened to be playing a dramatised version at the Lyceum of Robert Louis Stevenson's *The Strange Case of Dr Jekyll and Mr Hyde*, with its expositional offering of the dual nature of man. R. L. S. himself did not at all approve, insisting that it was totally wrong to interpret the conflict between Jekyll and Hyde in sexual terms – 'The harm was in Jekyll because he was a hypocrite, not because he was fond of women,' wrote Stevenson. Nevertheless, the Ripper as a mad doctor remained one of the three contemporary stereotypes, the Victorian image of the sort of man who would be the Whitechapel murderer. Memories of Knox the anatomist and the ghoulish Edinburgh firm of medical provisioners, Messrs Burke & Hare, would atavistically stir, the barber-surgeon Sweeney Todd's[7] fabled razor would flash and glint, polishing 'em off in melodramatic recall, the soft-footed shades of cruelly obsessional vivisectionists would flicker about minds and consciences.

The second popular stereotype was the Ripper as decadent English Milord – 'Perhaps like,' Frayling clarifies, 'De Quincey's connoisseurs, Wilde's Dorian Gray, or the Goncourts' bizarre version of Lord George Selwyn ... the murderer presented in the stock role of the 1820s Corinthian, the man of leisure who visited the Ratcliffe Highway to watch the rat-fighting and the drunken fights, or to find a torture garden which catered for his particular taste in flesh, *La bête humaine* in a democratic setting.'

This will have pleased the French. 'In Paris,' writes Frayling, 'the murders were immediately related to another literary phenomenon which was almost equally chauvinistic – the fictional celebration of "*le sadisme anglais*": "Jack" became easily absorbed into a perverted pantheon of English Milords ... "*Le vice anglais*," if enjoyed to excess outside the confines of public schools could so easily get out of control. Most of the monographs published by Professor Lacassagne's Institute at Lyons had been about French "vampires", necrophiliacs, and sadistic murders, now at last an Englishman could be added to the list.'

Thirdly, the stereotype of Ripper as anarchist, socialist, or philanthropist. This presents no literary correlative, no Stevensonian, Wildean, or Goncourtian model. Here is the Ripper as foreign agitator – Jewish incendiarist, run a close second by Irish revolutionary, Fenian, and, trailing off in their suspicious wake, Orientals, low-class Asiatics, Thugs, anything else that the xenophobic imagination could thrust into the line of fire.

Failing any of the foregoing, supposing, Heaven forfend!, an English Jack, then he must be a socialist or a philanthropist fallen to mania. A scientific humanitarian was W. T. Stead's choice of possible culprit; denizens all of an East End where 'Nancy was regularly murdered by Bill Sikes'.

As Christopher Frayling is careful to underline, 'whichever of the three categories was chosen, it could be linked with a well-defined moral panic' – and moral panics sold newspapers. He justifiably comments, 'What is surprising, on the face of it, is that explanations [one philistine, one pre-Freudian, one racialist] are *still* accepted by self-styled "Ripperologists" and their readers, when there is so much evidence, social *and* psychological to contradict them.' He sees the Ripper as being himself the victim of that syndrome, sometimes afflicting deeply depressed, highly impressionable men, which represents a fallen woman as the one last person – the victim – that they can push around. The broken breaking the broken: the undead slaying the already dying.

It was the contemporary newspaperman's image of the East End, together with the three mental panics provoked by this mental landscape, which provided for the construct that became a personalised, recognisable Jack. Which is to say that the lay-figure of the Ripper was in one sense 'the invention of the hard-working Victorian penny-a-liners,' ventures Frayling. 'Criminologists may write of *Jack L'Eventreur*, or *Giacomo-lo-Squarciatore*, but he only seems to make full sense in an English setting, in the culture which produced the *Mysteries of London*,[8] Sherlock Holmes (who made his first appearance in 1877, and his first independent hardback appearance in 1888), and *Dr Jekyll and Mr Hyde*.'

What of the veritable Jack do we *really* have? Eyewitness descriptions, two or three. But *were* they really eyewitnesses, *do* they really describe? A few highly dubious letters. The odd postcard. A mural fascia, scrawled with chalk writing of questionable authorship. A piece of blood-and-faeces-stained apron, undoubtedly handled by the killer of Catherine Eddowes. An indeterminate number of real-enough dead bodies. The rest is all lacunae – a space in the files, an *absence*, which has been given a name by an enterprising journalist, and a character by successive writers, reporters, and members of the reading public.

'In terms of historical evidence,' avers Frayling, 'he does not exist, so, for all sorts of reasons, he has been constantly re-invented.'

Deborah Cameron and Elizabeth Frazer in their *The Lust to Kill* (1987) bring some interesting and worthwhile points to bear in their discussion of the Ripper. They are careful to emphasise the fact that by 1888 the notions of sexual crimes and sexual murder were securely established, and many accepted the activities of Jack the Ripper as sexually motivated. On the one hand, he was pronounced by adherents to the emerging scientific study of sex to be a victim of mania; on the other, he was furiously denounced as a 'sex beast'. The nutshell distinction being between the opposing discourses of sickness and sin.

To quote the *Pall Mall Gazette*: 'The murderer is a victim of some erotic mania, which often takes the awful shape of an uncontrollable lust for blood. Sadism, as it is termed from the maniac marquis … is happily so strange to the majority of our people that they find it difficult to credit the possibility of mere debauchery bearing such awful fruitage.'

Cameron and Frazer observe,

> This remark draws an implicit distinction between the majority conception of sadism as 'mere debauchery' and a quasi-scientific or medical way of conceiving it, as an abnormal mental condition or 'mania,' something 'uncontrollable' of which the killer himself is a 'victim'. In the case of Jack the Ripper we are seeing the definition of sexual murder at an early and relatively confused stage; the criminal is in a state of transition as educated people assimilate recent scientific developments.

The Victorian 'beast' was a creation compacted of overt class prejudice, riddled with racism, and misinformed by xenophobic and anti-Semite stereotyping. Judith R. Walkowitz, feminist and American professor of history, records in her *City of Dreadful Delight* (1992), the interesting sociological observation, apropos the tense and fragile social ecology prevailing between the rough and the respectable of Whitechapel, that 'Jewish artisan wives regarded the women of the lodging-houses as "nogoodnicks, prostitutes, old bags and drunks" but they still employed Catherine Eddowes and others like her to char and wash for them, to light their Sabbath fires, sometimes even to mind their children.'

The pedigree of the sex beast was shot through with references to peasants, sinister foreigners and working-class savages. The depiction of the killer as a savage had the, at least theoretical, backing of the positivistic criminology of Lombroso, whose contention it was that *l'uomo delinquente* was an atavistic throwback to the less noble savage of humanity's earlier evolutionary days.

The *Pall Mall Gazette*, of 8 September 1888, reporting the murder of Annie Chapman, put it like this: 'This renewed reminder of the potentialities of revolting barbarity which lie latent in man will administer a salutary shock to the complacent optimism which assumes that the progress of civilisation has rendered unnecessary the bolts and bars, social, moral and legal, which keep the Mr Hyde of humanity from assuming visible shape among us.'

Cameron and Frazer consider that 'both the pessimism and the biologism of this view retain their centrality in discussions of sex murder'. They draw attention to 'one of the most uncompromisingly clinical assessments of Jack the Ripper' as being made by Dr Thomas Bond.[9] He profiled the Whitechapel murderer as 'a man subject to periodical attacks of homicidal and erotic mania. The character of the mutilations indicate that the man may be in a condition sexually that may be called Satyriasis.'

Cameron and Frazer comment, 'This medicalization of Mr Hyde and the concomitant discarding of his spiritual dimension, is one of the most important points of resemblance between the case of Jack the Ripper and that of Peter Sutcliffe ...[10] Sutcliffe's trial and discussion of his case revolved around the question, was he mad or just plain bad? Just as much as in the time of Jack the Ripper, the alternatives posed were either sinfulness or sickness.'

In Judith Walkowitz's *City of Dreadful Delight*, the Ripper is, in a way, merely incidental to a book, which, locating a crucial moment in which feminist sexual politics and narratives of sexual danger were formed, maps out a dense cultural grid across which conflicting and overlapping representations of sexual danger circulated in late Victorian London. Even so, the Ripper became 'a pervasive, bloody symbol for violence against women that feminists and other women had to face daily'. Walkowitz identifies the Ripper story as the product of a medley of Victorian cultural factors, such as pure melodrama, latter-day Victorian male Gothic, and the literature of psychopathology. For her, it articulates fears and antagonisms arising out of existing gender, class, and ethnic relations: diversified social constituencies responding to the media organisation by the weaving of their own stories and the superimposition of them upon the emergent *gestalt*. 'Newspaper reports applied Lamarckian theories of urban degeneration to the Whitechapel horrors, diagnosing them as a product of a diseased environment where "neglected human refuse" bred crime.'

Walkowitz enunciates the sociological judgement that the middle classes of London were infinitely more concerned with the pathological symptoms – street crime, prostitution, epidemic diseases – spawned by Whitechapel than with its material problems. Nonetheless, 'expressions of social and epistemological disorientation were coupled with repeated denunciations of the representatives of law and order.'

Also noted by Judith Walkowitz is the curious combining of the middle-class *Times* readers and socialist readers of *Commonwealth* in their stigmatising view of the economically desperate women as violators of their womanhood for the price of a night's lodging; women for whom the ordained wage of sin was death. Beyond the pinched boundaries of a raw-nerved East End, 'the victims became unsympathetic objects of pity – for radicals and conservatives alike'.

It was W. T. Stead, who, in an article entitled 'Murder and More to Follow', in his *Pall Mall Gazette* (8 September 1888) was the first journalist to write of the sexual origins of the murder of Annie Chapman, and invoke the psychological model of Jekyll and Hyde. Here, says Walkowitz, Stead's reference to sadism as a mania from which the killer was suffering drew upon the concepts of sexual sadism and lust murder. which had only recently been introduced into the medical lexicon by the professor of psychiatry at the University of Vienna, Dr Richard von Krafft-Ebing. 'A pioneer of sexology … Krafft-Ebing's professional duties included assessing proof of morbidity or "degeneracy" for sexual offenders brought before the court to determine whether they should be held responsible for their actions.' He published his collected case histories in a medico-forensic study of the abnormal, *Psychopathia Sexualis*, the appearance of which has been described by Jeffrey Weeks in *Sexuality and Its Discontents: Meanings, Myths, and Modern Sexualities* (1985) as marking the 'eruption into print of the speaking pervert, the individual marked or marred by his (or her) sexual impulse'. First published in 1886, when it consisted of forty-five case histories chronicled and commented upon in 110 pages, *Psychopathia Sexualis* had, by the twelfth edition in 1903, grown to report 238 cases in 437 pages. Case 17 is that of Jack the Ripper, who is, incidentally, also accorded an, albeit brief, mention by Magnus Hirschfeld in *Sexual Anomalies and Perversions* (Encyclopedic Press, London, 1938).

Several American medical men concerned themselves with Saucy Jacky's sexo-psychology.

In Chicago, Dr James G. Kiernan put on his thinking cap and came up with some interesting ideas as regards anomalistic practices shedding possible cross-illumination on the assorted fads, fancies and fantasies seemingly besetting the Whitechapel Fiend. Taking down his taxonomical abacus, Kiernan divided sexual perversion into a quartet of classes – 1. Imperative conceptions. 2. Congenital defect. 3. Insanity or Neurotic states. 4. Vice.

In New York, Dr Charles Edward Spitzka played around with the consideration of strange motives – singular antipathy, notions of romantic revenge, pseudo-philanthropic ideas, theories of mystic number associations, any one or any combination of which might be a contributory factor to the system of crazy-seeming massacrings. Spitzka opined that the Whitechapel killer had 'served an apprenticeship on the dead body', either as butcher, medical man, or enthusiastic amateur of the knife, for without reasonable knowledge of pelvic topography the removal of the human uterus is no easy operation.

And there was Dr William G. Eckert's publication in the *American Journal of Forensic Medicine and Pathology* of 'The Case of Jack the Ripper'. Having noted that there was little blood spilt at the scenes of the crimes, except in the case of Mary Jane Kelly, it was his suggestion that Jack may have strangled his victims *before* cutting their throats, which he did on the right-hand side with deep slashes severing the major blood vessels of the neck, and mutilating their bodies. He also makes the observation that little or no effort seemed to have been made to carry out chemical investigations to determine the degree of intoxication of Jack's victims at the time of their deaths. Neither had there been any check to see if any of them had been drugged or chloroformed, which might have accounted for why none of them was heard to cry out or indeed make any significant sound. Taking all things into account, it is Eckert's opinion that contemporary investigators were seriously disadvantaged by 'the absence of adequate equipment for documentation, including photographic examination and the processing of biological fluids or hair which may have been transferred from the assailant to the victim. Chemical analysis would also have been helpful … Serology was in its infancy, and up until that time little was known about the presence of blood groups.'

Walkowitz undertakes an informative comparison between Jack the Ripper and Peter Sutcliffe, his Yorkshire namesake, who, eschewing hardcore pornography or books about Nazism and torture, exposed himself, she points out, as a rather old-fashioned sadist, satisfied by self-stimulation through regular descents upon 'a macabre waxwork exhibit in Blackpool'.

The reference is to the Liverpool Museum of Anatomy, formerly housed at No. 29 Paradise Street, Liverpool, where it enjoyed considerable popularity from the time of its establishment in the 1850s. It was subsequently purchased by Louis Tussauds and put on show, curtained off on the upper floor of his waxworks exhibition on the seafront at Blackpool.

I myself remember it well, having paid regular visits to the place as a boy, and, indeed, in my medical student days. The Museum of Anatomy was, I recall, treated with a tremendous sort of pseudo-reverence allied to a stealthy prurience. The goggle-eyed holidaymakers who drifted furtively in were strictly segregated as to gender. The law of the Medes and Persians ruled. Men and women only – children not at all – were admitted to the far side of the curtain tantalisingly masking the entrance to the anatomical gallery in alternating males-only and females-only sessions, each lasting about ten minutes, its termination signalled by the tinkling of a bell.

With its 'Upwards of 750 Models and Diagrams Procured at the Anatomical Galleries of Paris, Florence and Munich', the Museum of Anatomy's original – and continuing – purpose was cautionary, to warn the, principally working-class, visitor against the evils of sexual profligacy, and display to him (and her) concretely the sin tax exacted by antisocial disease. It was designed to disabuse the self-abuser, illustrating, with a loose-lipped, slobbering, crazy-eyed waxen head of an aged habitual onanist, the wages of solitary vice; and to put a curb upon the libertine by presenting to him (or, again, her) realistic models of scab-encrusted scrotums, soft-chancred penises, ulcerating nipples, wide-splaying rashes of burning venereal sores, feculence and pus, and suppurating vaginas, the wages of non-solitary vice. In the area of normalcy, there was the wall of torsos – female, headless, limbless, scooped open interior ventrally to expose the healthy foetus in its journey through the Nine Stages of Pregnancy.

It must be admitted that, as the dancing-dust-moted sunbeams struck in through the frosted glass, there was an overall freakish ethos of two-headed dogs, six-legged lambs, Siamese-twin cats and suchlike *lusus naturae*. The ultimate teratoid was the life-sized effigy of Thomas Lane, a young man of Sherborne, in Dorset, who died and was found at post-mortem to have developed within him the foetus of a child of six or seven months' growth. 'This model,' a notice pridefully informed, 'is Protected by Act of Parliament.'

Another well-remembered life-sized model was that of a young woman of Victorian days, laid out fully clothed in her coffin. A Gothic-scripted label informed one that she had died as a result of the pernicious fashion fad of tight-lacing. And not far away, always a source of great fascination to visitors, was the full-length Florentine model of Louise Lateau, the young Belgian Roman Catholic girl who exhibited the extraordinary phenomena of ecstatic fits or trances accompanied by the stigmata, which is to say the marks of the wounds displayed on the body of the crucified Christ. Blood would flow from the holes in her hands and feet, from her left side, between the fifth and sixth ribs, and a sweat of blood appeared on her head, where Christ had worn his crown of thorns.

I would never have believed that there could have survived two such wondrous anatomical *reliquiae diluvianae*, but Gordon Burns in his excellent study *Somebody's Husband, Somebody's Son: The Story of Peter Sutcliffe* (1984), describes Sutcliffe's waxworks of pilgrimage as situate at Morecambe, in what was once the old Whitehall Theatre, on the seafront at the west end of the town, and was in 1956 converted into the waxworks premises of Mr George Nicholson, late of Tussauds, Blackpool.

Mr Burns' brilliant evocation sounds uncommonly like my Blackpudlian nirvana:

> Two rather small, dimly lighted and musty chambers … where Time has eroded definition and basted the developing foetuses and glistening ropes of internal organs to a uniform ox-blood colour … Their antiquity is highlighted by the paleness of the simulated flesh and the freshness of the butcher's muslin which provides a 'bed' for the bodies and is neatly tucked and trimmed to just above the bare breasts and just below the pubic area … The chancred lips of a vagina ooze and fester beneath a grey cloud of pubic hair, which itself is surrounded by male sexual organs in varying degrees of rottenness and putrefaction, like half-eaten sausages, decorously framed in muslin.

But, according to Gordon Burns, Mr Nicholson acquired his anatomical exhibits in the mid-1970s 'from a friend and associate of many years, recently bowed out of the waxwork world'.

It is a nice conceit that, nearly a hundred years earlier than Sutcliffe, Jack the Ripper may have stood staring at just such lurid images of dirt and disease in some other museum of wax. And, filled with loathing for the prostitutes and loose-living women, who, as he monoptically saw it, were responsible for the wreaking of such terrible fleshly havoc, embarked upon his saturnalia of destruction, exposing the private parts of public women of the streets. Mutilating them in a way that gives a whole new meaning to the term 'body language'.

37

The Pathologist's View

Like Cullen, Farson, Rosenwater and David Anderson, the late Professor Francis Camps came out solidly for Druitt's guilt. Quite apart from the fact that, as a pathologist professionally concerned with the medical investigation of murder, it was only to be expected that he would be intrigued by the classic mysteries of the Ripper case, Camps had another and more particular reason for involvement. The London Hospital, where, as Professor of Forensic Medicine at the Medical College, he had his department, was not only situated right in the heart of Ripper terrain, but provided the additional associative stimulus of having had a peripheral connection with the events themselves at the time of their enactment.

Indeed, it was Camps who, in 1966, produced, 'thanks to the detective work of my assistant Sam Hardy', some interesting relics of the case from the basement of the London Hospital.[11]

The relics to which Camps referred were a number of contemporary documents: a plan of the scene of the Mitre Square murder, endorsed by the coroner, and some remarkable pencil sketches of the body of Catherine Eddowes, both *in situ* in Mitre Square (made by Dr Frederick Gordon Brown, the doctor called to Mitre Square) and after its removal to the Golden Lane Mortuary (made by Mr Frederick William Foster, architect and surveyor of 26 Old Jewry, who drew the official court plan of Mitre Square), together with a diagram of the woman's face, showing the principal cuts.[12]

In his book *The Investigation of Murder* (1966), Camps takes a new look at the *post mortem* evidence. One of the aspects of this that especially exercises his attention is that the wounds and mutilations inflicted upon the women were accompanied by far less spillage of blood than might have been expected. According to the witnesses' statements, there was very little blood on the pavement in Buck's Row considering the extent of the wounds on Mary Ann Nichols' body. Inspector Joseph Chandler also noted that there was a relatively small quantity of blood in the Hanbury Street yard where Annie Chapman was butchered, and just a few bloodstains on the wall close to the body, none of them larger than a sixpenny piece.

Camps writes, 'This is in direct contradiction with the fact that they were all stated to have died without crying out.' He goes on to say, 'The probable explanation may lie in a comment in a contemporary number of *The Lancet* that it was strange that their faces were congested under the circumstances, which suggests that the absence of a cry was due to strangulation being the real cause of death, a common practice of sexual murderers.'

He then poses a question: 'The police failed to identify or arrest the Ripper in 1888; would they, if he returned, do any better today?'

In 1888 fingerprint identification was not available as a practical science, so, although the Ripper must have left a great many behind, the police lacked the means to exploit them.

After the Eddowes murder it appears that the killer washed blood off his hands at a public sink set back in a close off Dorset Street,[13] and then wiped them on a piece of apron, which he dropped in the passageway leading to the staircase of No. 108 to 119 Wentworth Dwellings, in nearby Goulston Street. Modern forensic technique might have disclosed by blood grouping whether the blood in the water and on the apron fragment belonged to the victim.

A bloodstained knife, with a 10-inch blade, was found in the Whitechapel Road, near the London Hospital. Dr George Bagster Phillips examined it, but doubted if it was the weapon used to kill Eddowes. Modern methods might have yielded conclusive blood or fingerprint evidence.

Then there was the quite extraordinary carelessness displayed in the handling of the corpse in the case of Mary Ann Nichols. Nobody, not even Dr Rees Ralph Llewellyn, the police surgeon called to Buck's Row, seems to have noticed at first the extent and nature of the woman's injuries. The blood was washed off the pavement before any competent person could examine the scene of the murder and assess by its extent the likelihood that the wounds had been made after death, and the body had been removed before a search for possibly vital clues and trace evidence was undertaken. When the body arrived at the Old Montague Street Workhouse Mortuary, it was stripped and washed before Dr Llewellyn came to carry out the post-mortem. The mortuary attendant, Robert Mann, a pauper from the workhouse, who was assisted by another pauper, James Hatfield, testified, 'I shut up the mortuary and went and had my breakfast. When I came back, me and my mate undressed her and cleaned her up a bit and made her tidy.'

Similarly, Annie Chapman's body was divested of clothing and washed before it was examined by Dr Bagster Phillips, and in this case the corpse was taken to a shed in the labour yard of the Whitechapel Union instead of to a properly equipped mortuary. Incredibly, says Camps, it was only there, after the removal of a handkerchief that was wrapped around the neck, that Dr Phillips noticed that the head had been almost completely severed from the body.[14]

Camps is extremely critical of what he calls 'the singular lack of co-operation' between the doctors and the police in assessing the medical evidence, for 'at no stage do they seem to have discussed it … whilst in two cases there was development by the police of theories of their own which were quite irrelevant, if not contrary, to the doctors' findings'.

Here he is obviously referring to the fact that the police had their own theory that Mary Ann Nichols had been attacked from behind, which was not the view of the doctor, and that they also insisted that the murderer of Annie Chapman must have been covered with blood, despite the expressed medical possibility that the injuries had been made *post mortem*.

On balance, Camps is of opinion that, although the Ripper would have had a much more difficult task in eluding the police of today, the likelihood is that he still would not have been caught.

In his view, certain aspects of the Stride and Eddowes murders could be held to lend credence to the belief that at least three of the many Jack the Ripper letters received may have been genuine. Elisabeth Stride's left ear was torn – but this was an old injury and had nothing to do with the murder wounds – and there was an oblique cut on Catherine Eddowes' right ear. In a letter received by the Central News Agency Office some days before these murders, the writer, who signed himself 'Yours truly, Jack the Ripper', had said that he would be at work again in the near future and would cut off the victim's ears and send them to the police. A postcard, addressed to 'Central News Office, London City E.C.', postmarked 1 October 1888, the day after the Stride and Eddowes killings, explained that, as he had been disturbed, he was unable to send the ears as promised.

The third communication was a letter enclosed in a small package addressed to Mr George Lusk, a builder and chairman of the Whitechapel Vigilance Committee.[15] The parcel contained a portion of what proved to be a human kidney. The writer said that he had taken it from a woman, and that he had fried and eaten the other half.

In fact Eddowes' left kidney *had* been cut out and taken away. According to Camps, about an inch of the 3-inch-long renal artery is said to have remained attached to the Lusk kidney, and this matched up with the two inches of renal artery remaining at the site of the detachment in Eddowes' cadaver.

Professor Camps also sees a psychiatric clue in the bizarre way in which 'neatly placed at the feet of the woman [Annie Chapman] was a row of objects – two brass rings, which had been wrenched from the woman's middle finger, a few pennies and two farthings, which had every appearance of having been arranged with care'. And how, in the case of Mary Jane Kelly, a pile of clothes was laid neatly at the foot of the bed – 'a feature common in sexual killings'.

There are, I think, reasonable grounds for supposing that the story of the rings, pennies and farthings laid at Mrs Chapman's feet has been elaborated. Certainly there is no mention of the discovery of any such articles in the original evidence of either Dr George Bagster Phillips or Inspector Joseph Chandler. Both spoke of finding only a small piece of coarse muslin and a pocket comb in a paper case lying at the woman's feet. Dr Phillips remarked that 'they had apparently been placed there in order or arranged there'.

The farthings were first mentioned in the press on 8 September 1888.

In an article in the *Pall Mall Gazette* in September 1888, Oswald Allen, a journalist who actually covered the murder, wrote, 'A curious feature of this crime is the murderer had pulled off some brass rings which the victim had been wearing and these, together with some trumpery articles which had been taken from her pockets were placed carefully at the victim's feet.'[16]

By 1929, when Leonard Matters published the first book on the subject, the 'trumpery articles' had been metamorphosed into 'two or three coppers and odds and ends'. In 1959, Donald McCormick added two farthings – 'Two brass rings, a few pennies and two farthings were neatly laid out in a row at the woman's feet.' It only remained for Robin Odell, in 1965, to supply the gloss of 'two new farthings', and the legend was complete.

THE WHITECHAPEL MURDERS

OR THE

$500
REWARD FOR THE
MURDERER OF

1 UNKNOWN
DEC 1 87

2 MARTHA TURNER
AUG 7 88

3 MARY NICHOLLS
AUG 31 88

4 ANNIE CHAPMAN
SEPT 8 88

PARDON

MYSTERIES OF THE EAST END

LONDON. G. PURKESS' 286. STRAND. W.C.

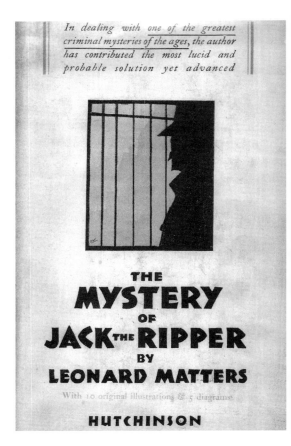

Previous page: 1. *The Whitechapel Murders or the Mysteries of the East End.* 1888. (Author's collection)

Above left: 2. *The Whitechapel Horrors: Being an Authentic Account of the Jack the Ripper Murders.* Tom Robinson. (Author's collection)

Above right: 3. *The Mystery of Jack the Ripper.* Leonard Matters. 1929. (Evans-Skinner Crime Archive)

Left: 4. *Jack L'eventreur: Scénes Vécues.* Jeane Dorsenne. 1935. Translation by Molly Whittington-Egan. 1999. (Author's collection, courtesy of Cappella Archives)

5. *Jack the Ripper or When London Walked in Terror.* Edwin T. Woodhall. 1937. (Author's collection)

6. *Jack the Ripper: A New Theory.* William Stewart. 1939. (Evans-Skinner Crime Archive)

7. *A Casebook on Jack the Ripper*. Richard Whittington-Egan. 1975. (Author's collection, courtesy of Wildy & Sons)

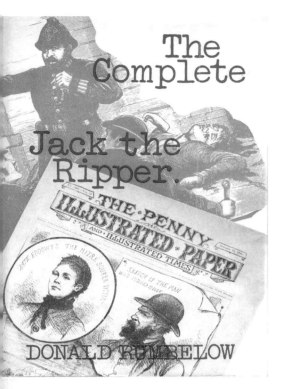

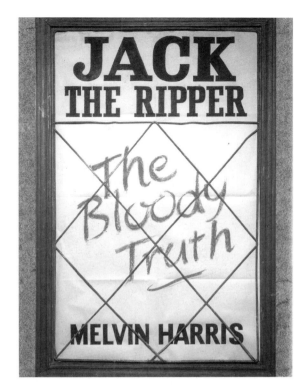

Above left: 8. *The Complete Jack the Ripper.* Donald Rumbelow. 1975. (Author's collection, courtesy of Random House)
Above right: 9. *Jack the Ripper: The Bloody Truth.* Melvin Harris. 1987. (Author's collection, courtesy of Random House)

Above left: 10. *Jack the Ripper: Summing Up and Verdict.* Colin Wilson and Robin Odell. 1987. (Author's collection, courtesy of Random House)
Above right: 11. *The Ripper and the Royals.* Melvyn Fairclough. 1991. (Author's collection, courtesy of Duckworth)

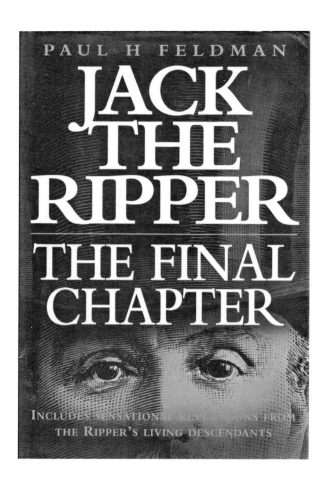

Left: 12. *Jack the Ripper: The Final Chapter.* Paul H. Feldman. 1996. (Author's collection, courtesy of Random House)
Below left: 13. *Jack the Ripper: Letters from Hell.* Stewart P. Evans and Keith Skinner. 2001. (Author's collection, courtesy of The History Press)
Below right: 14. *Jack the Ripper: Scotland Yard Investigates.* Stewart P. Evans and Donald Rumbelow. 2006. (Author's collection, courtesy of The History Press)

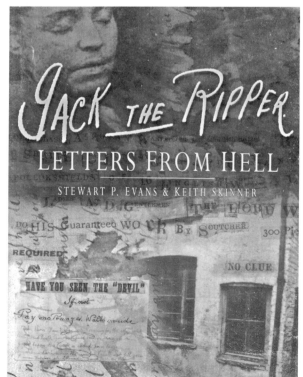

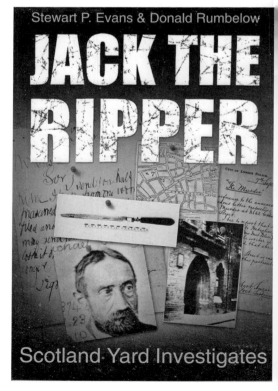

Above left: 15. Tom Robinson. (Author's collection)
Above right: 16. Leonard Matters. (Evans-Skinner Crime Archive)

Above left: 17. Edwin T. Woodhall. (Author's collection)
Above right: 18. William Stewart. (Jean Coram)

Above left: 19. Donald McCormick.
Above right: 20. Robin Odell.

Above left: 21. Tom Cullen.
Above right: 22. Daniel Farson.

Above left: 23. Donald Rumbelow.
Above right: 24. Richard Whittington-Egan.

Above left: 25. Molly Whittington-Egan.
Above right: 26. Stephen Knight.

Above left: 27. Frank Spiering.
Above right: 28. Melvin Harris. (*Who Was Jack the Ripper?*)

Above left: 29. Colin Wilson. (*Who Was Jack the Ripper?*)
Above right: 30. Melvyn Fairclough. (*Who Was Jack the Ripper?*)

Above left: 31. Paul Begg. (*Who Was Jack the Ripper?*)
Above right: 32. Martin Fido. (*Who Was Jack the Ripper?*)

Left: 33. Keith Skinner.
Above: 34. Shirley Harrison. (*Who Was Jack the Ripper?*)

Above left: 35. Philip Sugden. (*Who Was Jack the Ripper?*)
Above right: 36. Paul H. Feldman. (*Who Was Jack the Ripper?*)

Above left: 37. Stewart P. Evans.
Above right: 38. Paul Gainey.

Above: 39. Nichola Connell.
Below left: 40. Nicholas Warren. (*Who Was Jack the Ripper?*)
Below right: 41. Hargrave Lee Adam. (*Thomson's Weekly News*)

Above left: 42. Sir Charles Warren. Metropolitan Police Commissioner. In retirement.
Above right: 43. Sir Robert Anderson. Assistant Commissioner, Metropolitan Police. (*Windsor Magazine*)
Below: 44. Sir Melville Macnaghten. Assistant Chief Constable, CID.
Right: 45. Sir Henry Smith. Acting Commissioner, City of London Police.

Above left: 46. Inspector Frederick George Abberline.
Above right: 47. Detective Inspector Edmund Reid. (*Police Review*)

Above left: 48. Chief Inspector John George Littlechild.
Above right: 49. Walter Dew as a young detective constable.

50. Dr Rees Ralph Llewellyn.

Above left: 51. Dr Bagster Phillips.
Above right: 52. Dr Frederick William Blackwell.

53. Dr George William Sequiera.

Above left: 54. Dr Frederick Gordon Brown.
Above right: 55. Dr Thomas Bond.

56. The discovery of the body of Martha Tabram.

Above left: 57. Buck's Row, where Polly Nichols died.
Above right: 58. Number 29 Hanbury Street, scene of Annie Chapman's death.

Above: 59. Berner Street. Beneath the wheel, beside the iron gate, Elisabeth Stride was found dead.
Below: 60. Mitre Square, whether Catherine Eddowes breathed her last.
Right: 61. Richard and Molly (far left) Whittington-Egan at the spot in Mitre Square where Catherine Eddowes' body lay.

Above left: 62. The entrance to Miller's Court where Mary Jane Kelly dwelt.
Above right: 63. The windows of Mary Jane Kelly's room at No. 13 Miller's Court.

Left: 64. Police examining the room in which Kelly was murdered.
Above: 65. William Stewart's model of Mary Kelly's bedroom.

Above left: 66. Dorset Street, Whitechapel.
Above right: 67. East End street scene.
Below: 68. The London Hospital.

Left: 69. The Jack the Ripper public-house.
Below: 70. Berner Street, Whitechapel.

Above left: 71. Jacob Isenschmid, the Mad Butcher of Elthorne Road.
Above middle: 72. Alois Szemeredy. Buenos Aires murderer and Ripper suspect.
Above right: 73. The entrance to Goulston Street Buildings, where the 'Juwes' writing was.

Above left: 74. Joseph Vâcher, the French Jack the Ripper.
Above middle: 75. Druitt the cricketer.
Above right: 76. Druitt the young athlete.

Above left: 77. Dr Thomas Neill Cream, prescriber of pink pills for pale people.
Above middle: 78. Prince Albert Victor Christian Edward, Duke of Clarence.
Above right: 79. James Kenneth Stephen, Cambridge don and Ripper suspect.

Above left: 80. Joseph William Charles 'Hobo' Sickert or Gorman.
Above middle: 81. Mabel Collins, mystic and mistress.
Above right: 82. Renwick Williams, the London Monster, Piquerist supreme.

Above left: 83. James Kelly, Broadmoor escapee, aged twenty-three.
Above middle: 84. James Kelly, returning Broadmoor escapee, aged sixty-seven.
Above right: 85. Chaim Bermant, eloquent celebrant of East End London.

Above left: 86. John Morrison, obsessed with Mary Jane.
Above middle: 87. Dr Thomas Openshaw, 'The devle with his mikerscope.'
Above right: 88. George Chapman aka Severin Klosowski, Abberline's choice.

89. William Henry Bury.

90. Ingleside, Wandsorth, where Jack's victim Polly worked.

38

The Historian's View

At a time when the classic works by the pioneer Ripper investigators were all published and safely ranged on the reference library shelf, and writing about Jack had become not so much a cottage as a slaughterhouse industry, it was a pleasure to welcome a solid, factual work, one which did not consist of self-serving speculations or out-and-out fantasies mortared together with a paste of scissor-cuttings from the press and the published works of others. Philip Sugden's *The Complete History of Jack the Ripper* hies back to primary sources, including also contemporary newspaper reports, all of which are referenced with a reassuring degree of clarity and correctness.

A police policy of reticence, eminently defensible on the ground that it was a precaution 'to prevent villains being forewarned as to what the CID knew and might do'; or worse, a policy of positive suppression and overt antagonism to the press, led reporters to create news, which could or could not be false. The sad truth is that fiercely competing journalists, badgered by editors and readers for the latest on the Whitechapel murders,[17] were often so starved of facts from official sources that an inevitable market for gossip, hearsay, and uncorroborated and downright invented reports came into being, too many of which were unquestioningly accorded newspaper-selling, spur-of-the-purchase credence. So, although there was a considerable amount of good, sound and honest newspaper reportage, there was also, in cold truth, quite a large segment that was fiction.[18]

'There seems to have been no shortage of informants,' writes Sugden. 'A *Star* reporter investigating the Miller's Court murder in November, 1888, found the locals basking in their new-found importance, anxious to please him and ready to regale with "a hundred highly circumstantial stories," most of which, upon inquiry, proved "totally devoid of truth." Even true anecdotes might be passed from mouth to mouth until they become unrecognizable.'

How well I remember exactly the same conditions prevailing when I was, more than a hundred years later, looking into the case of Fred and Rose West, in Cromwell Street, Gloucester.

The *Star*, always sore pressed to say anything that could be interpreted as favourable to, in my opinion, much-maligned Sir Charles Warren's leadership of the Metropolitan Police, stated, on 1 October 1888:

> Our reporters testify that the conduct of the City police (under Major Henry Smith) offers the most marked and welcome contrast to that of the Metropolitan police force. The men of the latter body are churlish, uncommunicative, and in some cases deliberately deceitful. The City force, which is in some shadowy form under popular control is civil, communicative, and helpful to the press. The question is whether some steps cannot be taken to give effect to the almost unanimous voice of public opinion against the management of the Metropolitan Police.

In his list of minefields of misinformation, Sugden includes the reminiscences of retired police officers and others who had been on the scene. The dangers here arise out of the often unconscious distortions of lengthening memories, or the conscious distortions of the over-eager ghoster. Philip Sugden is blunt about it: 'If you prefer facts to journalism, if you want to know the truth about Jack the Ripper and are tired of being humbugged, read on!'[19]

And read on one should, for the reward is the most comprehensive account of the people and deeds of the London East End of 1888. Sugden does not spare his castigations, squarely blaming, aside from faulty primary sources, 'dishonest research and the sheepish repetition of printed folklore' for the state of disarray in which he found Ripper history.

When, in the 1970s, police and Home Office records on the case became available, Sugden did what many who should have known better did not do. He consulted them – and a great many other ancillary documentary sources as well, such as inquest, court, hospital, workhouse, prison, and genealogical records. The result is a positively pyrotechnic display of exploding canards.

We have now no excuses. We have available here the first entirely authentic accounts of each of the generally accepted five Ripper murders. Sugden would fain extend the tally to six, admitting that of Martha Tabram to the canon. Neither would he, if pressed, exclude 'Clay Pipe Alice' McKenzie, and Frances 'Carrotty Nell' Coles, murdered in 1889 and 1891, respectively.

One gets a good warm feeling when, some two-thirds of the way into this 532-page book, one reads, 'Readers who have stayed the distance now know as much about the Jack the Ripper murders as history can tell.'

Of especial interest is Sugden's construction of in-depth biographical and character studies of the Ripper's sad victims; unfortunates, who, as it turns out, he has found far from being the drabs that unkindly legend has painted them. They are here accorded the courtesy of much painstaking attention and redress.

The long roll of suspects is also intelligently scrutinised. Messrs Druitt and Maybrick are dismissed. So are the royals. A couple of little-known names are introduced, Oswald Puckridge and Nikaner Benelius, a Swedish traveller whose 'behaviour does not seem to have been exactly normal', but of whom there proved to be no reason to harbour suspicions of homicide.[20]

With no knife to grind, no firm evidence to crystallise out any one perpetrator, Sugden does not attempt to put a name to the man whose persona he so clearly profiles. But he does let it slip that if he were backing his fancy in the Ripper stakes his money would be on an outsider named George Chapman, real name Severin Klosowski.

In the second (1975) edition of his *Complete History*, Sugden has added an addendum, since, as he states, 'there were still murky corners of the story waiting to be swept out'.

Firstly, there is the 'particularly intriguing problem [of] the biography of Mary Kelly,' which, 'thanks to a recent discovery by Mr Ron Bernard of Cardiff', suggests that there is 'almost certainly *some* truth in [Joseph] Barnett's narrative' about her. Secondly, Sugden looks at Aaron Kosminski, an interest he attributes to the concurrent research of Mark King on the family of Aaron Kosminski.[21]

Thirdly, he writes of Michael Ostrog, explaining, 'When I wrote the *Complete History* I knew nothing of Ostrog's career after 1888. But this area of his life has now been opened up by Mr D. S. Goffee, who patiently searched out some details of Ostrog's later convictions from contemporary newspapers.'[22]

Ostrog seems to have been a character derived from the same sort of genetic criminal template as the man who plagued the life of Adolf Beck, the mysterious William Augustus Wyatt aka John Smith aka Augustus William Meyer.[23]

Besides being the author of one of the longest books on Jack the Ripper, Philip Sugden is the author also of the most diminutive. It is *The Life and Times of Jack the Ripper* (1996), a veritable collector's piece; a vest-pocket volume reminiscent of those limp-leather or suede-bound miniature books of the sayings of the wise and famous. A classic example of *multum in parvo*, its sixty-eight-page textual compass, plus sixteen full-page illustrations, provides an absolutely first-rate, accurate, brief and to-the-point summation of the entire case.

It was in 1994 also that Paul Begg, Martin Fido and Keith Skinner brought out their revision of *The Jack the Ripper A to Z*. In it, they reported of Dr Thomas Dutton's famously vanished *Chronicles of Crime*, that, at the time of going to press, it seemed possible that the *Chronicles* had been rediscovered as a result of the appeal put out on the 'Diary of Jack the Ripper' video. Alas! in the next, 1996, edition … the rest is silence.

Also under the 1994 star, Patricia Cory issued a privately printed desktop publication, *An Eye to the Future*. Her thesis was a variation on the Masonic theme. Prince Eddy has contracted syphilis as a result of *per anum* activities. Making the best of an exceedingly bad job, the Establishment is endeavouring to establish that His Royal Highness' indisposition was at least acquired through heterosexual channels. Unfortunately, neglectful of what was clearly a patriotic duty, the street women of Whitechapel refused confirmation of the Prince's infection in an East End bordello. Whereupon, high-ranking Freemasons banded together to silence the ring-leading prostitutes by murdering them, and thus terrorising the lesser fry into submission. This strategic procedure was known as the policy of 'An Eye to the Future' – the import of which descriptive terminology being that seeds of bogus clues were to be sown which, in the fullness of time, would flower into the requisite blossoms of deception.

39

The Policeman's View

The publication of Donald Rumbelow's *The Complete Jack the Ripper* (1975) brought forth a work that was an admirable conspectus of all that had gone before.

The book opens with an exposition of the harsh background against which the savagery was played out – outcast London. It is sufficiently daunting. Having conditioned the reader to the required state of acceptance for the horrors that are to come – the bloody knife in Buck's Row and Hanbury Street, the double event in Berner Street and Mitre Square, the grand slaughterhouse climacteric in Miller's Court – he embarks, implacable and persistent, upon the minute circumstantial narration of the five murders, which by general consensus of informed opinion were then held to be indisputably ascribable to the Ripper – hallmarked by method, patented in Hell. The abdomen laid open. The urino-genital attack. The visceral theft.

Thus far he breaks no significant new ground, but rests content to dot the 'i' of previous circumstance and cross the 't' of authorised description. Now, however, the spadework of exhumation done, he is ready to call his witnesses, put his new documents into evidence, summon to the bar his predecessors in the Hunt-the-Ripper trials, and the suspects they dragged behind them. All will be subjected to fierce re-examination.

It has been said, and repeated down the years (as a derisive sign of official ineptness), that the two champion bloodhounds, Barnaby and Burgho, imported by Sir Charles Warren to sniff out the Ripper, had been lost in fog during a test run at Tooting Common. Rumbelow gives a short, correct account of the testing of the hounds in Regent's Park, and also of the Tooting Common disaster.

There is, however, more to the story. It was after the Berner Street and Mitre Square tragedies that Sir Charles communicated with Edwin Brough, 'the well-known bloodhound breeder of Scarborough … and asked [him] to bring a couple of trained hounds up to London for the purpose of testing their capabilities in the way of following the scent of a man'.

The trial runs in Hyde Park, with Warren himself as the quarry and Barnaby and Burgho as the pursuers, were reported, with a somewhat Colonel Blimpish irreverence, on 20 October 1888, by the *Illustrated Police News*, of Boston, Massachusetts:

> Sir Charles Warren, in his tight military dress, and puffing and blowing with his exertions, did not look a very dignified Chief Commissioner, but if he went back to Scotland Yard hot and tired it was certainly with the most novel feeling that he had made a good start with his day's work. He was very mad when the evening newspapers came out with reports of his morning's doings, which, doubtless, were also read and noticed by the murderer.

The circumstances, several weeks later, that led to the non-appearance of the bloodhounds at Tooting Common were given by Edward Taunton, who had been kennelling the dogs in London for Edwin Brough, their owner, in *The Times* on 13 November 1888:

> The origin of the tale regarding the hounds being lost at Tooting while being practised in tracking a man I can only account for in the following way. I had arranged to take Barnaby out to Hemel Hempstead to give the hound some practice. The same day a sheep was maliciously killed on Tooting Common, and the police wired to London asking that the hounds might be sent down. I was then some miles away from London with Barnaby, and did not get the telegram until on my return, late in the evening. Somebody doubtless remarked that the hounds were missing, meaning that they did not arrive when sent for, and this was magnified into a report that they had been lost. At that time Burgho was at Scarborough. Under the circumstances in which the body of Mary Ann [*sic*] Kelly was found I do not think bloodhounds would have been of any use. It was then broad daylight and the streets crowded with people. The only chance the hounds would have had would have been in the event of a murdered body being discovered as the others were, in the small hours of the morning, and being on the trail before many people were about.

Some years later, Edwin Brough published in *The Bloodhound and Its Use in Tracking Criminals*, his view of the 'deterrent influence' of bloodhounds, and in particular their effect on the Whitechapel murderer:

> The deterrent effect of the knowledge that Bloodhounds may be used is a most important factor which should not be lost sight of. It is a very significant fact that at the time of the 'Jack the Ripper' outrages in the East End there were no murders committed for the two months during which Sir Charles Warren had arranged for a couple of Bloodhounds to be kept in London, but directly it was announced that the hounds had been sent back, another of this series of horrible murders was perpetrated.

In reporting the murder of Mary Jane Kelly, the *Echo*, on 10 November 1888, made the following comments:

> There are six two-roomed houses in Miller's Court, all of them owned by a grocer whose shop in Dorset Street forms one corner of the entrance to the court. Mr [John] McCarthy, the proprietor of this shop, has no hesitation in avowing his knowledge that all his six houses were tenanted by women of a certain class. They were let out in separate rooms 'furnished,' that is to say, there is in each of them a bed and a table, and, perhaps, one or two odds and ends, all of the roughest and most trumpery description, since, if the things had any appreciable value in the market they would be certain to disappear. For these rooms rents are supposed to be paid daily, but of course

they will sometimes get a good deal in arrear. This was the case with one of the tenants, who had occupied a ground-floor room on the right hand side of the court for about twelve months. Her name was understood to be Mary Jane Kelly – a young woman of 24, tall, slim, fair, of fresh complexion, and attractive appearance.

While the rooms were known as 'McCarthy's Rents' – an enclave of unfortunates, all beholden to the landlord, McCarthy, for whatever consideration they might receive in the event that they could not come forth with the daily rent – Rumbelow suggests that the term was applied by local custom and usage not to the houses, but to the prostitutes who rented them, and that McCarthy obtained money other than rent (in its normally accepted meaning) from the activities of his 'rents'. This, by the way, could explain how Mary Jane Kelly came to be accorded the privilege of owing her notoriously stringent landlord some seven weeks' arrears for the room that she occupied. She had been kept off the streets for a time by the indisposition of an alleged pregnancy,[24] but he would know that he could rely upon the fact that once she was back in business she would soon be able to make good her debt, plus adequate compensatory interest.

This interpretative contribution is, admittedly, of curiosity rather than evidential value, and the same may be said of Rumbelow's next offering. Between August and November 1888, the period during which the murders were being committed, and, indeed, for some considerable time thereafter, the police were receiving an ever increasing volume of letters from an ever increasingly disturbed general public. At the height of the panic the official postbag was swollen to the extent of an estimated 1,000 letters a week.

Rumbelow prints a selection of some of the more *outré* theories and impractical suggestions put forward by well-meaning, but ill-thinking, correspondents. Included in this epistolary maelstrom were a number of missives purporting to be written by the Whitechapel murderer himself. The majority of them Rumbelow dismisses. But there were two that gave him pause: the 'Dear Boss' letter, dated 25 September 1888 (the most celebrated of the lot), and the equally celebrated postcard, franked 1 October, both of which were reproduced in facsimile on a Metropolitan Police poster published on 3 October 1888.

On reflection, Rumbelow is not disposed to regard either of them as genuine. Neither did Robert Anderson nor Melville Macnaghten, both of whom took the view that they were the creations of an enterprising journalist, with Macnaghten adding, 'But whoever did pen the gruesome stuff, it is certain to my mind that it was not the mad miscreant who had committed the murders.'

In default of any evidence to the contrary, we must surely accept that they were hoaxes. The claim put forward by some writers that the postcard displays apparent foreknowledge of the double event of 30 September is based upon a misreading of the postmark, which is actually 1 October, the day *after* the killing of Stride and Eddowes.

On the other hand, Rumbelow thinks that the letter dated 16 October 1888, sent to Mr Lusk with the kidney, and the jeering letter, postmarked 29 October, directed to Dr Openshaw, may well have been genuine. These are views that I do not share with him, for even supposing that one or both of them came from the pen of the killer, a presumption which I am not prepared to uphold, what does it tell us? What evidential value are we to place upon them? None. The class tone could as easily be the result of guile as the product of ignorance. It is therefore useless, Rumbelow contends, to compare the normal writing of selected Ripper suspects with the writing of the Lusk and Openshaw exhibits.

Handwriting under stress can become totally unrecognisable, a point well demonstrated in the case of Peter Kürten,[25] who admitted to having been influenced by the Ripper and to having also sent murder-letters. His wife testified, 'When the murder-letters were printed in the papers he showed them to me, and I never noticed any similarity between his writing and what I saw in print.'

Is there no personal description of the Ripper? Was this creature of the darkness so phantasmic, so ethereal in all but the terrible consequences of his visitations, that no human eye ever beheld him? The eye-witness testimony that Rumbelow supplies offers a bewildering multiplicity of alleged personal descriptions. The only trouble is that you can scarcely find two accounts that correspond.

He is dark, says one witness, fair, says another. And so it goes on: stout, thin, clean-shaven, moustached, He speaks with a soft, cultured voice, a harsh, foreign accent. He wears a deerstalker hat, a round, peaked cap. He carries a long, thin parcel. He carries nothing. He is twenty-eight, thirty-three, forty.

It is this very abundance of adjectival, and poverty of substantive, material which has opened the field to such a wealth of speculative materialisations. Rumbelow dismisses the meretricious claims to the bloodstained crown of laurel with valid argument.

In disposing of the widely approbated legend of a 'mysterious lodger', buttressed by the artist Walter Sickert and propagated by Mrs Belloc Lowndes' novel, Rumbelow puts into evidence a statement made to the police by that most dedicated of contemporary Ripper hunters, Dr Lyttleton Stewart Forbes Winslow. It reveals that the doctor, by his own admission, was in possession of no useful clues, no special knowledge. All that he had was hearsay evidence, given to him, a year after the murders started, by a Mr E. Callaghan, who, in April 1888, had 'rented a large bed sitting room in his house,' 27 Sun Street, Finsbury Square, to Mr G. Wentworth Bell Smith, 'whose business it was to raise money for the Toronto Trust Society'.[26]

Chief Inspector Swanson investigated. Mrs Callaghan told of her lodger's obsessive writing on religious matters, his late comings and goings, the fact that he insisted on washing his own shirts, and how she had found bloodstains on his bed.

Mr Callaghan related how 'the household regarded him as a lunatic because of his delusions about "Women of the Streets," who he frequently declared should be drowned'.

In Swanson's final report on the matter, dated 23 September 1889, he stated that he was unable to find a record of any information having been given to the police by the Callaghans regarding their lodger. Forbes Winslow's grandiose claims to have found Jack the Ripper, repeated in 1910 in his *Recollections of Forty Years*, were revealed to be patent nonsense.

Rumbelow provides a double event of his own – the first publication of Dr Thomas Bond's general report on the Whitechapel murders, which he had sent to Anderson, and the previously unpublished full text of Melville Macnaghten's confidential memorandum on the case. In Rumbelow's submission, these two documents constituted the main basis upon which most of the arguments for or against the respective theories advanced (up to 1975) have to a considerable extent relied. The crucial importance attaching to the Macnaghten memorandum was, of course, the naming of three strongly possible suspects – Kosminski, Ostrog, and Druitt.

Of Kosminski, Rumbelow says nought. He identifies Michael Ostrog as 'a Russian doctor, and a convict, who was subsequently detained in a lunatic asylum as a homicidal maniac;' an elusive figure around whom a highly complex web of theories has been spun. He does not believe he is the Polish Jew referred to as the culprit by Robert Anderson. That individual Rumbelow distinguishes as John Pizer, cognomen Leather Apron, who was arrested, accused and acquitted. Nor does he accept Donald McCormick's suggestion that Ostrog may have been Severin Klosowski, better known as George Chapman. The psychological profile simply does not fit.

Of William Le Queux's proffer, that of Dr Alexander Pedachenko, the character reputed to have surfaced in 'Great Russian Criminals', the document allegedly written by Rasputin and handed to Le Queux by the Kerensky government, Rumbelow writes,

> The genuineness of the Rasputin papers are [*sic*] open to doubts on several counts. They were written in French, which Rasputin, according to Prince Belloselski, 'was certainly not fluent enough in … to dictate a narrative in that tongue. If he dictated this at all it must have been in Russian.' Once the doubts have been raised then they harden into near certainty that the papers were faked, particularly when A. T. Vassilyev, who was the Tsarist police chief, states in his book, *The Ochrana*, that Rasputin's apartments were immediately searched after his death for compromising documents and that none were found.

The late C. W. Shepherd, who had ghosted three of Le Queux's books, when asked by Rumbelow if he had ever seen the Rasputin papers, replied that while he was visiting Le Queux, Le Queux had pointed out the Rasputin documents to him. He [Shepherd] said, 'I saw them in a terrific-sized envelope, sealed and plastered with signs and codes and all sorts of things.' Unfortunately, Le Queux never opened it in his presence.

Rumbelow adds,

> One doubts him [Le Queux], just as one doubts the genuineness of the Rasputin papers. So what the Russian sources eventually boil down to is a collection of papers that only came into existence after 1906 – eighteen years at least after the murders, and the source for them was a well-known liar, [Johann] Nideroest … They [the Rasputin papers] have to be dismissed from the case.

Rumbelow's surmise is that the pages may well have been faked for the propagandist purpose of showing the Tsarist government in the worst possible light. Nideroest was well known in London around 1905–15, as a casual journalist, who had been more than once exposed as a concocter of bogus stories, and was regarded as an unmitigated and unscrupulous liar. He was not, in fact, a Russian, but a German-Swiss. In 1909, the police gave evidence that although he was a member of the Russian and Lettish Social Club, he was not an anarchist, and that the information that he had been selling to the newspapers about bombs being made in Whitechapel was all nonsense.

There is not a kopeck's worth of evidence to suggest, let alone establish, that Macnaghten's Ostrog and Le Queux and McCormick's Pedachenko were the same individual, although it is of interest to note that in his *A History of the Russian Secret Service* (1972), Donald McCormick (writing as Richard Deacon) states that the *Ochrana Gazette* gave Mikhail Ostrog's aliases as Vasilly Konovalov, Alexey Pedachenko and Andrey Lusikovo [*sic*].

Theory seems, in the course of thirteen years, to have hardened into fact – a 'fact' which Rumbelow does not find himself able to accept. He maintains, and I am in total agreement with him, that the existence of Pedachenko, under any of the given names, remains unproven.

Mr M. J. Druitt, the last of the three Macnaghten-named suspects, also fails to make the grade with Rumbelow: 'The one obvious thing that is missing is any shred of evidence that Montague John Druitt was Jack the Ripper.'

At this juncture Rumbelow imports a 'legend' of his own – 'Jack the Ripper's knife'. It was, he explains, given to him by a Miss Dorothy Stroud, who, in 1937, was an assistant to the editor of *Sporting Life*, Hugh Pollard. It was he who gave her the knife, one of a pair.

Pollard had been a partner of Robert Churchill, gunsmith to Scotland Yard, and Rumbelow thinks it very likely that Pollard had also been one of the Yard's extramural forensic experts, that he was given the knives to destroy, but, unable to resist the temptation, kept them instead as historic criminal relics.

Musing quixotically, Rumbelow writes of the knife: 'Although this is very circumstantial, it is the sort of evidence which, if found in Druitt's room, might have turned a hunt for a potential suicide into a search for Jack the Ripper.'

The knife reappears over two decades later, when it is placed in the hands of psychic, Pamela Ball.[27]

The principal value of Rumbelow's book is that it gathers together all the theories of any consequence that, up to the time of its publication in 1975, had been formulated by previous writers on the subject. His analysis of these theories is sympathetic, but where a witness does not come up to proof, Rumbelow has no hesitation in saying so. This is a most useful clearing of the ground.

Pictorially, the book provides a good number of contemporary images, including the first *post mortem* photographs of 'Clay Pipe Alice' McKenzie and Frances Coles, neither of whom Rumbelow regards as Ripper victims. The facial resemblance between Druitt and the Duke of Clarence is revealed by juxtaposed photographs of the two men.

Rumbelow's presentation as to the mechanics of Saucy Jack's methodology of attack strongly supports Professor Camps' belief that the contemporary medical men, seizing upon the all-too-obvious, wrongly accepted that the cut throats were the attack of the first instance. Dearth of blood, other than under Polly Nichols' body, the fact that Annie Chapman may have managed to call out, something which she certainly could not have done had her vocal cords been instantly slit, and sundry curious bruisings which were observed about the faces of the corpses all strike him as indicative of the extreme possibility that the women were first strangled.

Refreshingly, Rumbelow does not strain to conjure a new suspect out of the worse-for-wear gibus, but rests discontent with the plethora already supplied.

'I have always had the feeling,' he writes in a neat and classic observation, 'that on the Day of Judgment, when all things shall be known, when I and other generations of "Ripperologists" ask for Jack the Ripper to step forward and call out his true name, we shall turn and look with blank astonishment at one another as he does so and say "Who?"'

40
The Fictive Detectives' View

Donald Rumbelow was a serving police officer; the ostensible presenters of Elwyn Jones and John Lloyd's *The Ripper File* (1975), the book which grew out of the television programme, are those never-serving police officers, the strictly fictitious Detective Chief Superintendents Barlow and Watt. But do not be misled, in all other respects this book is rigorously non-fiction, and the device of employing Charles Barlow and John Watt as archetypal twentieth-century narrator-commentators proves both effective and inoffensive.

Their statement of intent is put into the mouth of John Watt – 'No theories or guesswork – there's been a sight too much of that already – just the facts. Plain, old-fashioned detective work … Who was there? Who saw what? Who said what? Read the statements, compare what they say. After all, murder is murder, in 1888 or 1978.'

So … they proceed, by way of case stated, to apply the police techniques of 1975 to the *ancien problème*, but, frankly, fare no better than their predecessors of 1888.

They begin by reading through the files on each of the five murders, then pause to ask themselves: what do we know about Jack the Ripper? The answer: precious little.

At the inquest on the first victim, Polly Ann Nichols, Dr Llewellyn gave evidence that her killer was probably left-handed and possessed some knowledge of anatomy. Dr Bagster Phillips, who performed the post-mortem on the victim of the second murder, Annie Chapman, confirmed the Ripper's anatomical knowledge. To this could be added the fact that an eyewitness (Mrs Elizabeth Long) who had seen Annie Chapman talking to a man described him as 'dark, over forty, taller than Chapman', who was just over five feet.

Barlow was looking puzzled. Why, he was wondering, had the Ripper waited so long before striking? He had killed Chapman around half-past five in the morning when it was already light and the streets were filling with work-bound people. To this could be added the fact that no one saw anybody who appeared anything like a maniacal murderer, which would seem to bear testimony to the Ripper's having been a totally respectable-looking figure. It is possible that he might have been wearing a long, dark overcoat to hide bloodstains.

The fifth inquest, that on Mary Jane Kelly, caused our fictive detectives some concern. To begin with they wondered why it was not conducted by the same coroner, Wynne Baxter, as those on Nichols, Chapman and Stride. (That on Catherine Eddowes, who had been killed in Mitre Square, was held by the London and Southwark Coroner, Samuel Frederick Langham. He, incidentally, had always thought that the Ripper managed to vanish so swiftly and completely from the scene of his crime because he had discovered some means of getting down the manholes and escaping via the sewers.) Wynne Baxter had a reputation for asking awkward questions. It struck them as odd that, after five murders in ten weeks, all clearly by a clever and dangerous criminal, the inquest should be transferred to another coroner, Dr Roderick MacDonald, on the grounds that the body is lying in his district.[28]

Then, what does Dr MacDonald do? He calls a couple of witnesses.

Mrs Maxwell turns up with her story of seeing Kelly and chatting to her in the street hours after everyone else is agreed that Kelly is supposed to be dead.

> Then we come to the medical evidence – our old friend, Dr Phillips, who doesn't like giving all the facts at inquests unless Wynne Baxter is there to drag them out of him. And all he tells us is that the body had been moved on the bed and she had had her throat cut!
>
> It's no wonder the *Daily Telegraph* wrote that editorial complaining about the way the whole thing was rushed through. What's more, because that inquest was wrapped up so quickly we shall never know what kind of a show George Hutchinson would have put up. The inquest was over before he even had time to come forward: a couple of statements, two irrelevant medical facts, a little chat from Abberline about waiting for doggies – and bang! All over! Everybody go home! And this was Jack the Ripper's fifth killing!

Certainly, the inquest on Kelly reads like a put-up job, and so, indeed, it could have been, in order to keep the horrific details out of the newspapers and avoid the panic's getting to over-boil point.

'Hideous malice, deadly cunning, insatiable thirst for blood – all these are the marks of the mad homicide. The ghoul-like creature who stalks through the streets of London, stalking down his victims like a Pawnee Indian, is simply drunk with blood and he will have more.'

Such immoderate journalese was wreaking havoc. Mrs Mary Burridge was standing at the door of her home at 132 Blackfriars Road, reading an account in the *Star* of the terrible goings-on in Whitechapel. She was so much affected that she retired to her kitchen, where she fell down in a fit. That was on a Saturday. She regained consciousness for a short time on the Monday, but then relapsed and died.

The other side of the coin is the occupants of the houses adjoining No. 29 Hanbury Street charging an admission fee of one penny to several hundreds of people anxious to view the very spot where Annie Chapman was done to death.

The crop of available facts for the fictive detectives was not luxuriant. One fact that emerged as pre-eminently obvious was that at that time a real policeman's lot was not a happy one. In a single year twenty-seven of them died, 'mainly through exposure to the elements', and 191 had to be taken off the beat because of sore feet.

The Metropolitan Police was, moreover, understaffed. Whereas the population of Metropolitan London added up to 5,490,576, the police numbered only 14,261 – 30 superintendents, 837 inspectors, 1,369 sergeants, and 12,025 constables.

The Yard had a new broom as Commissioner, Sir Charles Warren. James Monro was in charge of the CID. Monro, who did not get on with Warren, resigned and was replaced by Robert Anderson. Since 30 September 1888, under Inspector Abberline, Inspectors Reid, Moore and Nairn, Sergeants Thick, Godley, McCarthy and Pierce had been engaged upon the Whitechapel murders.

Each officer had to make, on average, 30 inquiries a week, and 1,400 letters were received, many of which had to be followed up.

In Whitechapel at the time of the murders 62 houses were brothels. There were 233 Common Lodging-Houses, with 8,500 people dossing in them, of which an estimated 1,200 were prostitutes. Quite apart from the not inconsiderable criminal element, the people of Whitechapel were difficult to deal with because of the general sense of Sword of Damocles panic that hovered permanently above them. The smallest incident could be suddenly transformed by crowd hysteria into an occasion of threatening gravity.

On 9 September 1888, for instance, Inspector Joseph Helson reports,

> The crowds in Spitalfields during the day have been causing great difficulty. This morning two men were arrested for minor offences. On each occasion a large crowd formed and rushed after the police shouting 'The murderer's caught'. Another man, injured in a quarrel, was carried to the station on a stretcher. A crowd formed outside the station and declined to disperse. A further arrest was made of a man for whom there had been a warrant out for some time. People came pouring out of the market, from the courts and out of the public houses … They were shouting that he was 'one of the gang' and they were going to lynch him. A very large crowd gathered and the constables present had their work cut out to prevent the man being torn to pieces. The barrack doors of the station were closed the moment the man had been brought in. A number of constables had to be stationed outside to prevent the mob rushing the doors. In addition, a gang of youths began a march down Hanbury Street. They were shouting 'Down with the Jews … It was a Jew that did it'. They were dispersed, but, despite this, several fights occurred. A large number of men were held in reserve and rushed to wherever trouble began. However, as night fell, the numbers of mobs expressing open antipathy to the Jews grew in number and a request had to be forwarded to headquarters for more men …

Barlow and Watt turn up the reminiscences of ex-Chief Inspector Walter Dew, who had been a young Detective Constable in Whitechapel in 1888:

> The whole area was in a panic after they found Annie Chapman's body. The day after the murder I was in Hanbury Street taking statements from people when I saw a man called 'Squibby' standing in the crowd. I knew he was wanted. I also knew that every time he was arrested it took half a dozen policemen to bring him in, and usually by the time they had got him to the station he hadn't got a rag of clothing left on his back, and half the police weren't fit for duty for a while again. I was standing

with another detective called Stacey when I saw Squibby. But the moment I saw him, he saw me. He dashed across the road and ran off down Commercial Street. Stacey and I went after him – drawing our truncheons – plain clothes men carried truncheons during the Ripper murders. But seeing us dash off, the crowd started shouting 'Jack the Ripper! Jack the Ripper!'

Soon there were hundreds of people yelling out and coming after us. I was passing Fashion Street when a big fellow tried to trip me up but I hit him with my truncheon and he fell into a baker's window. Squibby got into Flower and Dean Street, went into the front door of a house, over a back wall and into the house next door with Stacey and me after him. Finally we grabbed him as he was getting out through a window. We were both done in by now and I thought we were going to be really in for it, trying to take Squibby in. But instead of starting to fight, he was shaking like a leaf. Then I realized why. It wasn't us he was scared of – it was the crowd. They were all round the house by now shouting that the Ripper was in there and for us to bring him out so they could lynch him. Messages had been sent to the stations around and eventually when the crowd died down a bit we went downstairs and found scores of policemen clearing a space in front of the house.

But when we got Squibby out, the crowd went mad again. They rushed us and tried to break through the cordon and get at Squibby. In the end we put him in a four-wheeler and went on in that, with the police forming a cordon all round it. But that wasn't any good either, and they almost turned the cab over several times. Finally, an inspector called Babbingon said we would be better off on foot. The whole of Commercial Street was filled with a yelling mob by now but the police formed a cordon all the way to Commercial Street station. In the end we managed to fight our way into the station. The doors were shut, but the mob stayed outside for hours trying to get in. Nothing we could shout made any difference to them. Squibby was a changed man after that though. As far as I know he never resisted arrest again.

Painstakingly, Barlow and Watt plod on, thumbing through police reports, folios of eyewitness statements, sheaves of contemporary newspaper cuttings. They even manage – such is the magical prestige of television – to coax open the officially closed Scotland Yard, Home Office, and Director of Public Prosecutions Office files. Alas, with scant dividend upon their invested powers of persuasion.

Like Mr Rumbelow, they do not hesitate to release the three prime suspects – Chapman, Pedachenko, and Druitt – from the custody of suspicion, but, quoting from the *East London Advertiser* of 1 December 1888, they introduce a new suspect, Nicolai Vassilyeff, Vasili or Vassily, who, says the *Advertiser*, was identified by a Russian newspaper of the period as the murderer.

Said to have been born in Tiraspol, in the Ukraine, province of Kherson, in 1847, Vassilyeff studied at the University of Odessa. Having become a fanatical anarchist, he migrated to Paris in the 1870s. There he developed a mania: that fallen women could only atone for their sins and obtain redemption by being killed. Accordingly, as the instrument of their redemption, he murdered several Parisian prostitutes, in conditions similar to those of the Whitechapel murders. He was placed under restraint and then committed to an asylum. Shortly before the first of the Whitechapel murders he was released, and is said to have proceeded to London. Thereafter he was lost sight of.

Vassilyeff takes his place beside Pedachenko and Ostrog to complete an insubstantial Russian trio. Ostrog, however, is no longer insubstantial. His existence is supported by a very substantial criminal record.

For all their scrupulous re-examinations, careful analyses, their equipment of sagacity, accumulated acuity and professional know-how, our notional modern detective superintendents are as bothered and bewildered as their forerunners of a century ago when seeking to put a name to the putative Ripper. They admit defeat.

PART 4
THE FIRST CENTURY:
THE CENTENARY OF THE
WHITECHAPEL MURDERS

41

The Bloody Centenary

The 1980s brought Saucy Jacky's centennial year.

In 1988 the bells rang out.

How quickly a hundred years pass. It is a discovery one makes as one grows older; the shrinking of the spaces between Christmases. When I was born, the last Ripper victim had been in her grave only thirty-six years. Now, already, time for the centurial stocktaking. And in the brief course of that hundred years (including leap – to conclusions! – years) – 5,200 weeks, 36,523 days – how great has been the yield of fact and fancy gatherings.

Jack the Ripper. A name to conjure with. And in that name some very strange conjuring tricks, slick prestidigitations, have been performed; the production of a royal duke out of a Masonic silk-hat; and out of sundry bee-ridden bonnets has emerged an astonishing assemblage of bizarre characters.

So what, in this centenary year, could have been counted as new? Absolute candour might close the discussion at this point, but kindly light must lead the trepid reader on through the reopened alleyways of Ripper territory to see what was *offered* as new. A nice legal distinction, and like many of the law's subtle hair-splits, not quite fair. For the seven celebrant centenary volumes (six of them actually published in 1987, the publishers breaking the habit of a commercial lifetime by producing their wares a year *early*, instead of the usual six months late) brought a great tidying-up, a grand new sweep of correction and clarification on minor points of major interest.

The occasion evoked some fine writing, as well as some lamentably bad scribbling, by contemporary newspaper journalists.

Among the best, this of innominate Jack, contributed by John Carey, to the *Sunday Times*:

> Like Dracula or Santa Claus or Robin Hood, he belongs to our cloudy pantheon of immortals, and we are unwilling to see him deposed. We need him. He is Death in pantomime garb: one of the figures we use for coming to terms with our ultimate terror. His semi-fictional nature is what makes him acceptable. Popularised through films, stories and book-illustrations, he has the harmless garishness of romance – a cartoon image pinned protectively over the festering shambles of the Whitechapel corpses ... His jaunty name was invented for him. Its fairy-tale ring (evoking Jack the Giant Killer) helps to remove him from the human sphere.

However, as regards the Ripper's unmasking, our seven hundred-year authors 'all rake together the same blood-soaked evidence, but reach no consensus'. No matter. As, in the *Observer*, Christopher Wordsworth observed, 'The hunt is meeting … to draw those charnel coverts once again.' An observation to be weighed against Colin Wilson's sage remark that 'a problem for the modern writer on the subject is to produce a new suspect'.

To parody the super-tramp, W. H. Davies,

> What is this life, if after care,
> There's no new Ripper name to share?

Happily, none of the septet yielded to the mega-temptation. Four of the seven new books were really retrospections, surveys of the old battlefield rather than innovatory research volumes. Two examined in depth the credentials of Macnaghten's nominees, Druitt and Kosminski. The seventh staked the claim of a previously improperly explored candidacy, that of Dr Roslyn D'Onston.

Television producers, ever watchful for the main chance, did not neglect the centenary celebration. There were three efforts in the autumn of 1988: Christopher Frayling's *Shadow of the Ripper*, shown in early September on BBC 2; *The Secret Identity of Jack the Ripper*, a two-hour documentary, aired in the United States and Canada in late October; and the made-for-television film *Jack the Ripper*, written by Derek Marlowe and David Wickes, televised on ITV on 11 and 18 October.

In the course of those first hundred years a number of suspects were brought to book – Montague John Druitt, Roslyn Donston Stephenson, William Bury, the Duke of Clarence, James Kenneth Stephen, Sir William Gull, Walter Sickert, Kaminski, Aaron Kosminski, David Cohen, Joseph Barnett, George Hutchinson, Michael Ostrog, Francis Tumblety and James Maybrick. No one of them has been universally accepted as Whitechapel Jack.

To acknowledge the historic occasion with suitable subtlety and low-key celebration a gallant gathering of nuclear Ripperologists assembled at the Golden Heart, a Victorian tavern in Commercial Street, in the golden heart of Whitechapel, on the anniversary evening of 9 November 1988, 100 years to the day since the butchering of sweet Mary Jane brought the frightful serial murder series to its close.

Among the Ripperologically illustrious present were Tom Cullen, Martin Fido, Robin Odell, Donald Rumbelow and Keith Skinner. To mark the commemoration, each of them was presented with a special necktie, bearing the date 1888 and a five-knife motif.

42
The Hundred Years' War of Words

Naturally, in his *Jack the Ripper: One Hundred Years of Mystery* (1987), Peter Underwood, celebrated as the author of volumes innumerable on psychic matters, lends a sympathetic pen to the 'puzzling and remarkable' story of Robert James Lees, accepting it as fact.

Although the tale, 'The Capture of Jack the Ripper', was first printed in Chicago in 1895, Mr Underwood writes, 'It has recently come to light that there is overwhelming evidence that the story was widely known in London as early as July 1889.'

In support of his claim he cites a letter sent to Scotland Yard, dated 25 July 1889:

> Dear Boss
> You have not caught me yet you see,
> with all your cunning, with all your 'Lees',
> with all your blue bottles.

The signature is 'Jack the Ripper'.

Underwood does not give a source for his recently discovered overwhelming evidence, but his argument closely echoes Stephen Knight's tale in 1976. Both authors believe that the mention of 'Lees' is proof that the Robert James Lees story of the discovery and detention of Jack the anonymous distinguished physician was widely known in London half a dozen years before the addendum of the circumstances of his committal to an asylum by his professional brethren was published in Chicago.

Perhaps. Perhaps not.

Could one not read 'all your Lees' as a sardonic genetic reference to all the psychics who professed that the Whitechapel murders could be solved (but were not) by them?

The *A to Z* remarked that 'no one has ever offered an explanation for the word "Lees" … other than the possibility that it refers to R. J. Lees'.

No one, that is, until Stewart Evans. It was during his research on the many letters ascribed to the authorship of Jack the Ripper that Evans advised me that on making a close examination of an enlargement of the 25 July 1889 letter, he had concluded that Knight's reading of it had been in error. It is Evans' submission that what Knight had interpreted as 'with all your Lees' should correctly be read as 'with all your tecs', thus giving the sentence a clarity which otherwise it had lacked.

Underwood is at pains to make the point that, in any event, Lees' diary, which is preserved at Stansted Hall, in Essex, which might have been appealed to, 'has long been suspected of "having been tampered with"', something that, he says, Melvin Harris full well knew, because he, Underwood, had told him so 'in person'. Yet in his *Sorry, You've Been Duped!* (1986) Harris never mentioned it. And Elizabeth Longford, author of a highly regarded biography of Queen Victoria, is introduced by Underwood as a critic of both the Lees story and the idea that Lees was ever a medium for the Queen.

But Underwood writes that Longford, Harris 'and others may be forgiven since they were not in possession of the full facts'. To quote, in these slightly bellicose contexts, Underwood's own words: 'It is always easy to see what one wants to see and there are many kinds of truth.' A splendidly pregnant *caveat* for affixion to the walls of all inhabited glass houses.

A Dr Howard was reported in the *Chicago Sunday Times-Herald* in 1895 as being 'one of a dozen London physicians who sat at a court of medical inquiry or as a commission in lunacy upon one of their brother physicians. For it was definitely proved that the dreadful "Jack the Ripper" was no less a person than a physician in high standing – a man enjoying the patronage of the best society in the West End of London.'

The Medical Register for 1888 lists a Dr Howard who spent some time in America around that period. He had an address at the St George's Club in Hanover Square. I am able to shed some further light on Dr Benjamin Howard's alleged revelations.

The following article appeared in the London Sunday newspaper, *The People*, on 19 May 1895:

A STARTLING STORY

Not long ago there appeared in a London weekly a terribly realistic description of a criminal lunatic who was confined in one of our penal establishments. The man had degenerated into an inarticulate beast. He was said to be the fiend known as 'Jack the Ripper.' The article wanted the authority of a leading morning paper to make any serious impression. It was only regarded as a fanciful narrative from the pen of a clever novelist. It may have been true nevertheless, and colour is given to this possibility by a statement which has recently been made in San Francisco by Dr Howard, an Anglo-American physician not unknown in London, and who is, I believe, a member of the Royal College of Surgeons. I knew Dr Howard very well at one time, and always regarded him as a man of intellectual power. He has been telling the Bohemian Club of San Francisco a remarkable story, no other than the true and particular account of the capture and confinement of 'Jack the Ripper,' who was no other than a well-known London physician, now supposed to be dead. For the sake of the profession and for other reasons he was wiped out by a mock death and burial, but at the present time is under restriction as a dangerous lunatic. It was, according to Dr Howard, one Robert James Lees, a philanthropist and advanced labour leader, and a friend of Mr Keir Hardie, who, through his extraordinary clairvoyant powers, led the London detectives to the home of the murderer. Mr Lees is mentioned as still residing at 26, The Gardens, Peckham Rye. At present he is the leader of 'the Christian spiritualists in Great Britain.' A commission *de lunatico inquirendo* established the facts against the criminal who confessed to mental aberrations, during which he lived some other life and awoke to find himself in strange places under strange circumstances. Dr Howard affirms that he was a member of the commission that sent 'Jack the Ripper' to an asylum for the rest of his days. Dr Howard will have to answer for the breach of a vow which he made in common with his colleagues never to reveal what had passed. The story is told with remarkable circumstantiality, and Chicago publishes a portrait of Mr Lees, who might well be interviewed on the subject. If the narrative with which he is credited is true, it is one of the most striking of hypnotic revelations.

On 26 January 1896, Dr Howard addressed the following letter, which is now in my possession, to the Editor and Publisher of *The People*:

> St Georges Club,
> Hanover Sqr, W.
> Jany 26 – 96
>
> Sirs
>
> A number of persons have called my attention to 'A startling story' in your widely read *The People* – May 19, 1895 directly charging me with 'the breach of a vow' – etc. In this publication my name is dis-honourably associated with Jack the Ripper – and in such a way – as if true – renders me liable to shew cause to the British Medical Council why my name with three degrees attached should not be expunged from the Official Register. Unfortunately for the Parties of the other part – there is not a single item of this startling statement concerning me which has the slightest foundation in fact.
>
> Beyond what I have read in newspapers, I have never known anything about Jack the Ripper. I have never made any public statement about Jack the Ripper – and at the time of the alleged public statement by me I was thousands of miles distant from San Francisco where it is alleged I made it. In my absence from London this statement has passed uncontradicted so long that the damage has multiplied beyond private methods of correction.
>
> I am Yours Truly
> B. Howard

This letter was passed to Mr Joseph Hatton, the journalist who wrote the *People* story, and on 31 January 1896, he replied:

Dear Dr Howard,

I took the 'Jack the Ripper' notes from a two-column report in the *Chicago Times*. It was published in such evident good faith that I never thought of doubting it. You will observe that I spoke of you not only with respect but with admiration. I hope at all events that the incident may lead to a renewal of our friendship. Tell me what you would like me to do and I shall only be too glad to comply with your wishes.

I always remember you as an appreciative acquaintance of the dear son whom I lost and of whom you predicted great things.

Won't you come and see me?

Joseph Hatton.

Peter Underwood dismisses Dr Howard's letter, with a Mandy Rice-Davies 'Well he would, wouldn't he?' shrug.

Of borderland interest is Underwood's treatment of the manifestation of alleged ghosts and other paranormal events in connection with the Ripper, among which he reprints the accounts by the venerable Father of Ghost Hunting, the late Elliott O'Donnell, in *Haunted Britain* (1948), of conversations he had in 1895 with several inhabitants of the area.

Underwood's investigative methodology included writing to known Ripperologists in order to acquire first-hand knowledge of current state-of-the-thinking from leading and misleading 'authorities'.

In his pages is embalmed the opinion of my friend the late Joe H. H. Gaute, nearly sixty years a publisher, who hosted his first literary lunch back in 1927, with Elliott O'Donnell as his guest, and who, upon joining Hutchinson's, was promptly involved in the publishing of Leonard Matters' pioneering volume on the case, *The Mystery of Jack the Ripper* (1929). Gaute's rather shaky vote for the Ripper nomination is here recorded as: 'To me, the Ripper has always been a nasty little man in a dirty overcoat, rather like Christie, but that by now who he was will never be discovered. If I was forced to say who was the most likely person, I would probably name Druitt.'

Peter Rowe, LL.B., BA[1] has contributed to Underwood's book an eight-page summary of his thoughts, 'A Cynic's Viewpoint'.

Two of his observations are of particular interest. The first, appearing as it did in 1987, presaged events that came very much to pass in 1993.

It could be that at some future time there might be found some long lost affidavit which amounted to Jack the Ripper's confession. Even if such a document surfaced it would be subject to a great deal of scrutiny before it was accepted as genuine. A straight 'I did it,' followed by a clear signature would not do; we should require some signs that the signatory had some special knowledge which only the real murderer could possess. Mysterious documents, suddenly emerging, are not always what they seem to be.

The second is Rowe's account of the case against James Thomas Sadler in regard to the murder of Frances Coles. He enters a *nolle prosequi*, for, while finding a wealth of circumstantial evidence against Sadler in respect of the Coles murder, he discovered basically none insofar as the earlier Whitechapel killings were concerned.

Underwood even includes an eight-page piece by Sean P. Day: his whimsical recall of his just completed (1978), forever-lost, never-published manuscript, *The Jack the Ripper Bedside Companion*. Open-mindedness can go no further.

Although Peter Underwood personally favours a simple and singular solution to the identity of Jack the Ripper, since he believes that 'simple answers are often the right ones,' he proffers 'an unnamed nonentity who disappeared into the East End of 1888 as mysteriously as he had appeared'.

He nevertheless sponsors two new suspects, Joseph Barnett and James Kelly. Barnett had actually been put forward by Bruce Paley, in 'A New Theory on the Jack the Ripper Murders', which appeared in the April 1982 issue of the London-published monthly magazine *True Crime*, although I had in fact received a manuscript from Mr Paley detailing his suspicions against Barnett a good five years before that. The other, James Kelly, was the very personal selection of the late John Morrison.

In June 1986, I met Mr Morrison. I visited him at his home in Leytonstone, on the Essex border of East London. Then sixty years of age, he had, like so many others since, become a victim of redundancy, and he confessed frankly, 'Mad Jack has kept me sane!' What he meant was that time, which would otherwise have hung heavily on his enforcedly idle hands, and thoughts and resentments, which might otherwise have seriously troubled his head, were all defused of potentially harmful effect by his absorbing himself in a dedicated search for the identity of Jack the Ripper.

Sitting in his Ripper Murder Hunt HQ – the living-room of his house in Goodall Road – surrounded by books and gruesome wallcharts of victims and slaying sites, John Morrison told me how it all began with a dream.

'I dreamt I was in court. They were trying Jack the Ripper. Lord Hailsham was the judge. He called for evidence … and they produced a *Guinness Book of Records*. Next morning I went along to the local library, got hold of a copy of the book. And there it was – the name of Jack the Ripper.'

He had run Jack to earth in the pages of *The Guinness Book of Records*. Only it wasn't Jack, it was James the Ripper aka James Kelly, the man who held the record as the longest-ever escapee from Broadmoor – thirty-nine years.

Morrison set to work to find out all he could about Kelly. This is the story he tells. James Kelly, an Irishman, was living with his wife in Liverpool. It was there that he met a beautiful young Irish girl named Mary. They had a passionate affair and Mary became pregnant. Almost immediately, she adopted her lover's surname, becoming Mary Kelly. It was not long before Kelly's wife learned of his illicit liaison, and there was a violent quarrel in the course of which he killed her. Arrested and charged with murder, James Kelly was lodged in the hospital wing of Liverpool Prison. He stood trial at Liverpool Assizes at St George's Hall, was found guilty and sentenced to hang, but was subsequently reprieved on the grounds of insanity, and committed to Broadmoor Criminal Lunatic Asylum, where he was admitted on 24 August 1883.

Meanwhile, Mary Kelly, desperate to erase all trace of James from her life, fled to London, where, after having an abortion, she went on the streets. Kelly saw Mary's desertion and rejection of him as vile treachery. Her getting rid of their child[2] made it even worse. The thought of her selling herself to other men was worst of all.

Using a pass key made from a corset spring, wife-killer Kelly went over the wall on 28 January 1888; just sixty-five days later, the Ripper slaughter began.

Morrison's account continues. He tells us that Kelly made his way to Liverpool, intending to collect Mary and vanish together to Ireland. But what he found when he got there was that she had gone off with another Liverpool-Irish girl, Marie Harvey, to, it was said, the Irish ghetto in the Whitechapel district of London, where she and Marie were now working as prostitutes. Before leaving Liverpool, Mary had either undergone an abortion, or left their child in the care of the nuns at a local Roman Catholic convent. He was unable to discover for certain which.

It was at this point that James Kelly vowed that 'if his informant was correct, he would find Mary and rip her so-and-so heart out, and that of any of her sister-trash who might get in his way'. And so it was that he headed for London, and in Whitechapel started making enquiries as to Mary Kelly's whereabouts.

In the course of those enquiries, he killed ten women (claims Morrison) before finally tracking Mary to her hovel in Miller's Court. His practice was to slay each prostitute whom he had questioned, in order to silence her. By the time the last of the ten died, a woman named Kate Kelly aka Catherine Eddowes, the police were hot on the Ripper's trail.

For a while the killings stopped. Then Scotland Yard received a letter from Liverpool admitting the murders. James Kelly had gone home. He returned to London in November, went straight to Mary Kelly's Whitechapel hideout, literally ripped her to pieces, and bore off her faithless heart.

Morrison said that the police wanted to raise the alarm, put out a hue and cry for James Kelly, but the Home Office, under Henry Matthews, said no. Why? Because officialdom was embarrassed by its own incompetence in having failed to make the connection between the dangerous homicidal lunatic at large and the Whitechapel massacrings. Police Commissioner Sir Charles Warren was ordered to clam up or stand down. He chose to resign.

Sheer fantasy?

'I have proof,' says Morrison. 'Inspector Chandler's mistress[3] wrote a book about the case. It is disguised as fiction, but it reveals so much of the mechanics and details of the police work that it just has to be the inside story of the truth.'

Another piece of weird Morrison legendry lies behind this.

John Morrison was without question a fanatical enthusiast. I remember him, eyes shining, tongue flailing, rocket-launching into a breathless monologue on the topic that had become the single most important thing in his life. And as, conversationally, one peels back layer after layer of his obsessionist researches, rather like opening one of those ornamental wooden Russian dolls, each shell as it is removed revealing yet another, identical but slightly smaller, hollow doll, until, in the end, at the secret centre, is one small, solid figure – you come at last to his most passionate concern, Mary Jane Kelly, or Marie Jeanette Kelly, as, romantically, he almost always calls her. To him she is, as Irene Adler was to Sherlock Holmes, *the* woman.

It was within the shade of Marie Jeanette that one of his several great revelations shaped itself.

'I stood by Marie's unmarked grave and said mentally "I don't know if you can hear me Marie. But if you can please help me to find your killer." I promised her that if she would help me, then in return I would one day have her grave marked by a fine headstone – and more people would visit her grave than ever frequented the birthplace of the Great Bard!'

Suddenly it started to rain and, leaving the cemetery, Morrison began subconsciously to wander in the direction of a car-boot sale. And there, although he never normally read fiction, he bought two battered suitcases of second-hand books for three pounds. When he got home he arranged the sixty-odd volumes in two small bookcases. 'One book on the bottom shelf was jutting out and, in attempting to push it back with my foot, it fell to the floor, opening at a page which read "Jack the Ripper" ...'

The book in question turned out to be *The Lodger* by Marie Belloc Lowndes.[4]

Morrison says,

I read it and could not help but notice something on the lines of the following: 'My friend from the Yard Joe Chandler told me that the man they were really seeking for the Whitechapel murders was a man who had committed murder in a house in Liverpool, a man who was sent to a lunatic asylum. He escaped just prior to the commencement of the Whitechapel crimes and in so doing he stole all the staff wages, amounting to a considerable sum, in gold sovereigns. We never reported this at the time for reasons of embarrassment.' I then knew that James Kelly was the only person who was able to fit that description.

Let us, purely in the spirit of zealous pursuit of that accuracy which is the best substitute that we can manage for absolute truth, reproduce the passage from *The Lodger*, something on the lines of which Morrison has quoted. It runs,

'Four murders of the kind were committed eight years ago – two in Leipsic, the others, just afterwards, in Liverpool – and there were certain peculiarities connected with the crimes which made it clear they were committed by the same hand. The perpetrator was caught, fortunately for us, red-handed, just as he was leaving the house of his last victim, for in Liverpool the murder was committed in a house. I myself saw the unhappy man – I say unhappy, for there is no doubt at all that he was mad' – he hesitated, and added in a lower tone – 'suffering from an acute form of religious mania. I myself saw him, as I say, at some length. But now comes the really interesting point. I have just been informed that a month ago this criminal lunatic, as we must of course regard him, made his escape from the asylum where he was confined. He arranged the whole thing with extraordinary cunning and intelligence, and we should probably have caught him long ago, were it not that he managed, when on his way out of the place, to annex a considerable sum of money in gold, with which the wages of the asylum staff were about to be paid. It is owing to that fact that his escape was, very wrongly, concealed.'

Apropos *The Lodger*, you will find in Mrs Belloc Lowndes' *The Merry Wives of Westminster*, the following:

I had once sat at dinner next a man who told me that a butler and lady's maid, who had been in his parents' service, had married, and set up a humble lodging-house. They were convinced Jack the Ripper had spent the night in their house before and after he had committed the most horrible of his murders. I told myself that this might form the core of a striking short story. I wrote the story, and under the title of *The Lodger* it was published … Some years ago a Dutch criminologist wrote and asked me to put him in touch with the characters, and he angrily refused to believe I had invented them.

Morrison maintains that Marie Belloc Lowndes' diary is a key piece of evidence supporting his theory. It shows, he insists, that seven well-known people, including Queen Victoria, Oscar Wilde, and Winston Churchill, knew about the cover-up of Kelly's escape by the Government and by Scotland Yard, and that they also knew the identity of the Ripper.

The most curious coda to the classic Kelly escape is recorded in Ralph Partridge's *Broadmoor: A History of Criminal Lunacy and Its Problems* (1953). In 1896, the British Consul at New Orleans was visited by a man who said he was an escaped criminal lunatic who had been detained in Broadmoor during Her Majesty's Pleasure. He wished to surrender and be sent back there. The Consul was instructed by the Foreign Office to coax Kelly aboard the next ship sailing to Liverpool, put him in the captain's charge, and notify the Foreign Office of the vessel's name. A party of attendants from Broadmoor, together with a posse of Liverpool police, would then be at the Liverpool Landing-Stage to meet the ship when it arrived and nab Kelly. But the reception committee clean missed him.

Thirty-one years passed. Then, one February day in 1927 – Saturday the 12th, to be precise – there was a knocking at the Main Gate of Broadmoor. Upon opening it, the gate attendant found an old man outside who said that he was James Kelly and that he wanted to come in. The trouble was that, after the lapse of thirty-nine years, there was no one left who could identify him. They sent for a long since retired officer, who promptly recognised the bent and wrinkled claimant as the genuine fleet-footed Kelly of yore. As an 'at Her Majesty's Pleasure' resident who had never been officially released, Kelly claimed, and was granted, his entitlement to return to Broadmoor for the rest of his life. He was given a new number and duly readmitted. Eighteen months later, on 17 September 1929, he died comfortably there.

John Morrison appears to me to have confused and enmeshed the stories of the real James Kelly and that of the purely fictive criminal lunatic, Mr Sleuth, in *The Lodger*. He also constructs a most curious final link between James Kelly and Marie Belloc Lowndes. He tells us, and it is true, that in 1947, not long before she died, Mrs Belloc Lowndes asked to see a Roman Catholic priest from Broadmoor. Morrison convinced himself that 'she verified what she knew (about James Kelly) with the priest who had heard Kelly's last confession and given him absolution'.[5]

On 3 December 1986, John Morrison kept his promise to the woman with whom, disregarding the restrictive shackles of time and space, it almost seemed as if he were half in love. Over her previously unmarked grave – No. 16, Row 67 – in St Patrick's Cemetery, Langthorne Road, Leytonstone, there was on that day erected a fine marble memorial stone.

> Marie Jeanette Kelly
> Age 25
> The Prima Donna of Spitalfields
> And Last Known victim of
> Jack the Ripper
> Murdered Fri. Nov. 9th 1888.
> Do not stop to stand and stare
> Unless to utter fervent prayer
>
> (Mary Magdalene Intercede)
> Dedicated by John Morrison
> Dec 3rd 1986.

A space had been deliberately left at the bottom of the headstone for something to be added. But only when the guilt of his suspect, James Kelly, has been publicly acknowledged would John Morrison permit *Requiescat in Pace* to be carved upon the foot of Mary Jane Kelly's tombstone. Meanwhile, he had reinstated her, a sort of seedy *Mater Dolorosa*, with her own marked plot of God's acre.[6]

Morrison confided that he had reserved a nearby burial-plot for himself, that in death he might lie beside the dead girl who, because she so loved to sing, he christened the Prima Donna of Spitalfields.

He subsequently published (*c.* 1988) a thirty-eight-page booklet, *Jimmy Kelly's Year of Ripper Murders, 1888*, wherein he tells, after his own fashion, his own story.

John Morrison died in June 2005. He was cremated and his ashes lie in London Cemetery.

So far as Peter Underwood's book is concerned, my personal reaction to it is that the author is palpably fair to everyone. He has entered bravely into a region of high specialisation other than his own. Most Ripperologists know as little about box-headed elementals as Mr Underwood knows about the vertiginous winds and turns of Saucy Jacky and his bedazzled fanciers! I would, however, unhesitatingly recommend his book for its splendid entertainment value.

43
Centennial Spawnings

Terence Sharkey's centurial offering, *Jack the Ripper: One Hundred Years of Investigation* (1987), while commercially a sound and attractively got-up volume, does not contrive to bring us any nearer to the truth about Jack. To be plainly honest, Mr Sharkey's book was the least satisfactory and satisfying of the centennial septet. The best that the author seems able to do is to proffer to the reader what he calls 'a chocolate box' of other people's potential culprits.

This is his appetising invitation: 'The Ripper selection of chocolate-coated candy is the biggest yet. Some are gold-wrapped ... But one man's fancy is another's fiction, and by now the gold-wrapping is frequently tarnished ... There will always be new suspects, silver-wrapped, gold-wrapped, and flavour of the month. But for now, lift the lid and make your choice.'

Sharkey's research implements appear to have been scissors and paste, albeit industriously enough employed and no pains spared in his thoroughly conscientious fossicking, but resulting in a slender book which displays neither cerebration nor consecutive argument in favour of any particular claimant. I present this, I may say, as a statement of fact, and not in any sense as a criticism. It is most assuredly not incumbent upon any writer about the Whitechapel murders to play the name game. And let it be said that Sharkey has very certainly succeeded in doing what he set out to do. He 'evocatively recreates the spine-chilling atmosphere of the darkened alleys of Victorian London and invites you to formulate your own theory about the identity of this notorious killer'.

Colin Wilson and Robin Odell lay the facts before us in an atmosphere altogether less hectic and lurid. They confine their anniversal contribution, *Jack the Ripper: Summing Up and Verdict* (1987), to just that. The verdict is a bit shaky as, indeed, it responsibly has to be, but the summing-up is admirable.

The authors arraign no new suspect before the court of their readership. Odell has, of course, previously nominated an innominate *shochet*: an eminently feasible selection in my view, but awkward of definitive determination.

Wilson furnishes an astute adumbration for a psychological portrait of the likely Ripper, but is unable to fix a name label to the sitter. With benefit of insights provided by modern serial killers of the calibre of Peter Kürten, Albert Fish, Earle Nelson, Neville Heath, Peter Sutcliffe, that redoubtable Alaskan human hunter Robert Hansen, and the awful Joachim Kroll, he makes the point that, whatever else, the Ripper *in absentia* has to be 'a twisted ego' type of sex killer, driven by what James Reinhardt[7] in his *Sex Perversions and Sex Crimes* (1957) calls 'mutilation madness'.

This, Wilson believes, is the psychological reality behind the Whitechapel murders. For him, 'it is difficult if not impossible to call to mind a single case involving "mutilation madness" (by a female killer). Consequently, one is forced to the conclusion that sexual mutilation is a crime of the male sexual pervert, and that the notion of a female Jack the

Ripper is a grotesque impossibility.' It may also indicate that Martha Tabram was, in fact, a Ripper victim after all.

The authors then jointly direct that the entirety of suspects here and heretofore put up be found not guilty. Gulping here and there, the jurors obediently follow the court's *diktat*.

My own summing up: a very sane and sober, bank-balancing type of evaluation of the contending suspects, arriving at the very proper conclusion that none of them bears the proclamatory blood-guilt stains.

Inevitably, on the verge of the liberally spawning centenary year, Donald Rumbelow's modern, parenting volume, anachronistically titled The *Complete Jack the Ripper* – revised and reissued in August 1987 – was unable to take into account new accusations levelled against such of the latest gaol delivery as Joseph Barnett, James Kelly, and William Henry Bury,[8] *qua* postulatory Rippers.

Rumbelow's book, first published a dozen years earlier, still rates as the best all-round conspectus of the field of blood. It is a work minutely detailed – even down to the varicose vein immediately below the knee of chief Metropolitan Police bloodhound Inspector Frederick Abberline's left leg?

Among the many excellences of his achievement, Rumbelow has succeeded in mapping the hitherto unrevealed workhouse pilgrimages and sorry sagas of the wretched targets of Jack's keen knife. Especially full and fascinating is his log of the erstwhile uncertain movements of Elisabeth Stride. His researches were both anticipated and complemented by those of Klas Lithner, published in translation as 'The Swedish Ripper Victim' in the London magazine *True Detective* in December 1987.

Rumbelow turns effective detective on the detective, the heretofore elusive Frederick George Abberline, anatomising him and placing him, for the first time, securely in the frame.

Fallen a victim of Rumbelow's further research is his own secretly cherished suspect, Timothy Donovan, deputy of the common lodging-house at 35 Dorset Street. He has been discovered to have died eight days before the Mary Jane Kelly murder. Rumbelow therefore offers no candidate for Judgement Day's upstanding figure.[9]

The solitary celebratory volume to come out actually in the centenary year was Paul Begg's *Jack the Ripper: The Uncensored Facts: A Documented History of the White*chapel *Murders of 1888*, 1988.

Reviewing it at the time, I wrote,

> After the recent plethora of books on a subject which, to anyone other than the insatiable enthusiast or suspect hobbyist, must seem to be truly played out, the advent of this eighth, to mark, with still bewildered respect, the centennial of the sanguineous innominate's achievement, will surely appear to be unrequiring of remark. All must have been said again and again and again, to the power of seven. However, permit me, as one who has most assiduously attended the accouchements of the precedent septuplets, to assure you that this late delivery – timeous, in fact – merits eightfold attention.

And so indeed it did – and does. For you will find here no wild royalist, or anti-royalist, fantasies. No free play with Masons, their aprons and their trowels. A. Pedachenko is banished to that nowhere place whence he should never have come. His diaconal rights are recognised as highly dubious. Mr Druitt definitively did not do it.

Mercifully, Mr Begg wheels or trundles no new nominee forth. No physician's phaeton flashes through the cobbled arteries of Whitechapel. With Mr Begg we are gratefully in the presence of an author with an eye for detail and referenced sourcing. He provides us with a much and long needed setting of the historical record straight. He has made the correction of mistakes and misinterpretations his especial business. He has concentrated wonderfully upon the plain, and not always so simple, putting right of perpetually repeated error and the reduplicated *lapsus calami* that bedevil and befog the literature. His meticulous renovation dispels the mist of legend and chips away the crusted patina which, over the years, had accumulated needlessly to distort and disfigure the clean lineaments of a classic case.

It is one of the great values of the work that the author begs no questions, he goes right back to the original documentation in his quest for answers. Moreover, he supplies soundly-based analyses to assist in the deciding of what conclusions may or may not be fairly drawn regarding the three major suspect names in the Macnaghten papers. Perhaps the least satisfactory part of the book is that which considers the credentials of Michael Ostrog, but it was to be another three years before Begg, Fido, and Skinner, in the first edition of their *A to Z*, filled in the long sought details of the life and capers of Macnaghten's third 'for instance' nominee. There was an even fuller account in the 1996 revised *A to Z*. Both accounts credit D. S. Goffee and Philip Sugden with the original research. Kosminski was Begg's choice of top suspect, relying very heavily on Anderson. It is because of this nomination that one expects more from him when, as he writes, 'it is necessary to outline and examine a theory advanced by Martin Fido.' This Begg proceeds to do in some detail, but omitting mention of Fido's unique theory that the identification of Kosminski had taken place in the Seaside Home at Bexhill, not Brighton.

Begg's interpretation of the circumstances attendant upon the appointment of an officer to supervise the Whitechapel Murders Inquiry during Anderson's stay in Switzerland is based on a 'document preserved in private hands,' which Begg prefaces with the following comments: 'Before departing for Switzerland, Anderson recommended the appointment of a senior officer to supervise the inquiry into the murders. The man selected to take charge of the investigation into the Whitechapel murders was Detective Chief Inspector Donald Sutherland Swanson'. An essential Ripper-shelf volume for anyone who proposes to give any serious attention to the perennially fascinating series of killings perpetrated in the cauldron or melting-pot of London's over-boiling East End in the high days of the immigrant invasion. This is the book to read if you want to get to know the people in and around the case, if you want to get back to bedrock – but, as the *A to Z* candidly notes, you are nevertheless advised to re-check primary sources, since occasional literals and misdatings have passed the proof-reading.

In *The Man Who Hunted Jack the Ripper* (2000) Nicholas Connell and Stewart Evans, citing the *Commissioner's Report* of 15 September 1888, in private hands,[10] write that

> after a week of familiarising himself with his new office at Scotland Yard, Anderson went off on his month's holiday to Switzerland. He was, he claimed, suffering from the stress of his work, and the leave was taken on his doctor's orders. He left on the day before Chapman's murder, effectively leaving the detectives without their leader. The seriousness of the emerging terror in the East End was, perhaps, not as apparent when Anderson left as it was shortly to become … Sir Charles Warren was distressed and annoyed by Anderson's absence, for he needed a man to take the helm in this important matter.

On 15 September 1888, Sir Charles wrote a report to the Assistant Commissioner (CID): 'I am convinced that the Whitechapel murder case is one that can be successfully grappled with if it is systematically taken in hand. I go so far as to say that I could myself in a few days unravel the mystery provided I could spare the time and give individual attention to it.'

Sir Charles felt that the utmost importance must be attached to putting the whole Central Office to work on the case in the supervisory hands of one man. The man he selected was Detective Chief Inspector Donald Sutherland Swanson.

The man selected by Connell and Evans for especial attention is Detective Inspector Edmund Reid. A hitherto somewhat neglected figure in the Ripper saga, he was actually the officer who succeeded Abberline as the head of H Division (Whitechapel) CID. He was a great character and this biographical study has an interesting tale to tell, although his involvement in the Ripper affair was not of any great significance.

PART 5
THE GREAT HOAX:
THE DIARY OF JACK THE RIPPER

44

The Diary of a Diary

It was in the August of 1992 that two charming visitors beat a path to my precipitous home halfway up the Malvern Hills. They were the writer Shirley Harrison and Sally Evemy, her researcher, come to consult me, under the seal of secrecy, regarding my fellow Liverpool townsman, James Maybrick, who, they excitedly confided, had been … Jack the Ripper.

This, I confess, took me by considerable surprise, but if it were indeed so, I could, blowing my trumpet on a variation of the 'My father knew Lloyd George' theme, announce, 'My grandfather knew Jack the Ripper', for in the old days in my native Liverpool the Maybricks used to come to dinner at my grandparents' home. And, as a matter of fact, my grandfather and grandmother were in the Maybricks' private horse-drawn *charàbanc* party that went to the Grand National on that fateful Friday, 29 March 1889, when that stout-hearted mare, Frigate, with Tommy Beasley up, won the steeplechase, and James Maybrick lost his temper over Alfred Brierley, the admirer of his wife, Florence, and quarrelled embarrassingly publicly with the flirtatious Florie.

The story which was unfolded to me that August afternoon was of the incredible discovery in Liverpool of a journal or sporadic diary, which, in my informants' belief, had been written by Jack the Ripper, and put it beyond reasonable doubt that James was Jack.

The man who brought this unique document to light was a forty-year-old Liverpudlian, Mike Barrett, who lived with his wife, Anne, and young daughter, Caroline, in a Victorian terrace house in Goldie Street, in the Liverpool district of Anfield.[1]

Born and bred in Liverpool, brought up in Maybrickian Aigburth, Barrett went to sea in the Merchant Navy at the age of fifteen. Older and ashore, he earned a living in a variety of ways, including working as a chef, before finding a more permanent berth as the scales man with a firm of scrap-metal dealers in the Vauxhall area of Liverpool.

About the year 1981, he collapsed at work. Kidney failure was diagnosed – perhaps the delayed result of a road accident in which he had been involved as a child. Since his collapse, when he was twenty-nine, Barrett had never worked again, living a somewhat restricted remittance-man kind of life on some £68-a-week invalidity benefit money and the wage his wife brought home from her job as a secretary. He was, however, a would-be freelance journalist and had enjoyed what he saw as the first-footings of a modest success, devising word-puzzles and writing a feature piece about Kylie Minogue for a children's magazine, *Look-in*.

One of his regular house-husbandly duties was to collect Caroline from school. Equally regular was his en route visit to the Saddle public-house, on the windswept corner of

Fountains Road, Anfield, stranded halfway between Liverpool and Everton football grounds. And it was there, in 1987, that he first came to know Anthony Devereux, a retired compositor in his fifties, who had been employed at the *Liverpool Daily Post*.

Over the years Mike and Tony became firm bar-counter friends. Following a less than amiable severance from his wife, Devereux lived on his own, and when, at Christmas-time 1990, he fell and fractured his hip, Barrett would pop in and do his food shopping for him.

It was perhaps, Barrett diffidently offers, as a gesture of gratitude that Tony made him a present. That present, wrapped in a brown paper parcel, was, he says, handed to him one day in May, or perhaps it was June, 1991. Barrett, whose motto is, 'If you tell the truth you cannot get into trouble for telling the truth', remembers: 'I called with some bread and milk he wanted, and we were talking about the racing on the TV. He had this brown paper parcel on his knee when he said, "Here you are. That's for you. Do something with it."'

Barrett bore his parcel home. Opening it, he found a big, black, ledger-like book, quarter-bound in scuffed leather, gold-leaf-banded on its calf-backed spine. Inside, a clutch of the first forty-eight pages – that is to say twenty-four sheets – was missing. It looked as if they had been cut out. On sixty-three of the remaining sixty-four pages was scrawled a jumbled mass of handwriting which he found difficult to read at a first glance, But he was able to decipher the entry on the last page – 'I give my name that all know of me, so history do tell, what love can do to a gentle man born. Yours truly Jack the Ripper.'

Barrett says he thought it was a joke. 'I telephoned Tony and asked him what the hell he was playing at. He said he wasn't playing. I hit him with question after question over the next few weeks, but he wouldn't tell me anything. 'I gave it to you because I thought you may want to do something with it, not ask me questions.' It was impossible for him to write this diary. He didn't have the capability. I asked him who else knew about it. 'No bugger alive today,' he said.

Then, in July, or it may have been early August, 1991, while the Barretts were away on holiday, Anthony Devereux suffered a massive heart attack, and died in hospital, aged sixty. Left as it were in the lurch, desperately on his own, Barrett conceived the notion of hunting for the identity of the Ripper, that is the diarist, in Liverpool, not London. 'I wanted to prove the diary was genuine. The diary mentions Whitechapel in Liverpool as well as Whitechapel in London.'

He began by buying every book on Jack the Ripper that he could find. He noted that Jack had allegedly written letters to the police *from Liverpool*. That was encouraging. He haunted the public library, huddling over Ripper books, squinting at innumerable yards of microfilm of old newspapers. He read anything he could lay his hands on dealing with old-time Liverpool mysteries. One day he found a copy of my book, *Liverpool Tales of Murder, Mayhem and Mystery*, and in it he read of James Maybrick, and Battlecrease House, in Aigburth.

'Only connect,' as E. M. Forster says. Mike Barrett connected. 'I nearly had a heart attack,' he recalled. 'You could have scraped me off the ceiling that night. Battlecrease was mentioned in the Diary … and here it was, brought to life, populated, the house in which James and his wife, Florence, lived with their two children. I had found the connection. I had discovered the identity of Jack the Ripper.'

But how came this diary into the hands of Tony Devereux? Where had it been for the past 102 years? Its author had written, 'I leave this now in a place where it shall be found.' Many were subsequently to conclude that it had been hidden beneath the floorboards in Battlecrease House, which had, as a matter of fact, been lifted by electricians in 1991–92. But that was not Barrett's belief. He reasoned, 'It is well documented that the last time James Maybrick went to his office in Knowsley Buildings, Tithebarn Street, in the centre of Liverpool, was on 3 May 1889, and the final diary entry was on 3 May. My guess is that he wrote it at work, finished it there, and left it there. He spent his last days at Battlecrease House and died there on 11 May 1889.' Knowsley Buildings was demolished in the late 1960s. The diary *could* have been found there and, passing through heaven knows what devious route, arrived eventually in Devereux's hands.

Excited now by his Ripper diary, but not really sure how to proceed, in the spring of 1992 Barrett pulled out a paperback from among the Alistair Macleans in his living-room bookcase, and, seeing that it was published by Pan Books, telephoned that publisher in London – only to be somewhat deflatingly told that he would need to get himself an agent. He was, however, given a name, Doreen Montgomery of the Holborn literary agency Rupert Crew Ltd. And very soon, best-bibbed-and-tuckered, precious parcel in hand, Mike Barrett was boarding the train from Liverpool Lime Street to London Euston.

He found Doreen Montgomery and Shirley Harrison, an author-client of hers, who, all things proving propitious, would be offered the job of more thoroughly investigating, editing, and writing up the diary, waiting at Rupert Crew's office in King's Mews, just behind Theobalds Road. With, inevitably, the 1982 debacle of the forged Hitler diaries in the forefronts of their minds, the two women decided to proceed with caution.

Acting on impulse, off trotted Shirley Harrison with Mike Barrett on the authentication trail. First destination: the British Museum.[2] 'Fascinating,' said Robert A. H. Smith, curator of nineteenth-century manuscripts. 'Quite extraordinary. It looks authentic. But you'll have to take it to a document examiner. We don't have forensic facilities here.'

Not satisfactory. Not unsatisfactory. Indecisive.

In Great Russell Street, opposite the museum, was Jarndyce's, the antiquarian bookseller's. They popped in there. Brian Lake, the proprietor and a specialist in nineteenth-century literature, very properly, echoed Robert Smith's fence-sitting view. 'It looks exciting, but find a forensic scientist to settle its precise date.'

Not satisfactory. Not unsatisfactory. Inconclusive.

Meanwhile, following Barrett's London sortie, the Rupert Crew agency, acting on his behalf, put the 'diary' up for auction. London publishing houses were invited to bid for it, plus the rights of a book, to be written by Shirley Harrison, based on the 9,000-word document, telling the tale of its discovery, investigation and authentication.

The top bidder was Robert Smith, owner of the relatively small firm of Smith Gryphon, who, when he was a commissioning editor with Sidgwick & Jackson, had had a great success with Martin Howells and Keith Skinner's *The Ripper Legacy* (1987).

Smith sent the journal off to Dr David Baxendale, of Document Evidence Ltd, a Birmingham firm employed by a good half of Britain's police forces to detect fraud. Smith asked Baxendale and his team to provide, in particular, details regarding the age of the ink, and for an estimate, if possible, of when the ink had been applied to the paper.

There was no occupation of the fence here. Dr Baxendale viewed the diary with suspicion – and said so.

Although he could find nothing to substantiate the idea that the book had not been manufactured in the late nineteenth century, he was quick to note that the inside of the front cover, which was damaged, had had something which had once been attached to it torn off. He observed also that there was extensive staining of the inside of the book's front cover, to the fly-leaf, and to the stubs of the cut-out pages. Under the microscope, the stains, some of which on the fly-leaf were rectangular, had the appearance of glue.

The discovery of a fragment of paper lodged in the binding cast an entirely new light on the authenticity of the document. The fragment was of a totally different composition from that of the pages of the diary. Coated with a glue-like material, it seemed to be the torn-off edge of a small photograph. It indicated that most probably the pages which had been cut out had had photographs glued to them. Those photographs were, to judge by the rectangular stains, likely to have measured approximately three-and-a-half inches by two-and-a-half inches, which was a popular size for photographic prints from roll film between the First and Second World Wars. The Victorians in their photography used large glass-plate printing.

In fact, the volume had all the hallmarks of having been used as a photograph album, at least thirty years after Jack the Ripper allegedly scribed his homicidal diary in it.

Something else worried Baxendale. A test widely used to date documents is the so-called solubility test. This entails the dropping of a chemical solvent on to the ink. If a document is more than a hundred years old, one would expect the ink to take several minutes to dissolve. The older the ink, the longer it takes to dissolve, because the passage of time causes ink and paper to integrate. When Baxendale tested the ink of the writing in the Diary, it began to dissolve in just a few seconds. He therefore felt justified in expressing the opinion that the document had most likely been written in the course of the past two or three years.

Baxendale was moreover discomfited by the presence in the ink of a synthetic dye, nigrosine, which, he said, had only been used in inks since the 1940s, and by the absence of iron, which was a regular ingredient of Victorian inks.

Possibly most damning of all was Baxendale's conviction that the handwriting showed such variation in fluency and letter formation that he could not accept it as having been naturally written. It was, for the most part, in the looped cursive mode of Victorian copperplate, but from time to time the penman lapsed into that disconnected-plain-letter script style which did not become common until the mid-twentieth century.

And there the matter might have ended had not another scientific analyst, Dr Nicholas Eastaugh, come up with a distinctly more heartening result.

Dr Eastaugh, an independent consultant, was not actually a forensic scientist. He had started out as an artwork authenticator, undertaking the analysis of historical materials at his Teddington studio in South London. He moved on from working on paintings to drawings, and thence to ink and paper. Asked by Robert Smith to conduct an analysis of the Diary's ink, establish its age, and pinpoint precisely when it was applied to paper, he hied himself off to the University of Oxford in order to scrutinise the diary's constituents under the nuclear microscope.

Analysis of the paper revealed no modern fibres, only those of cotton and wood-pulp. He discovered in the ink the presence of a significant amount of iron, which is not found in modern inks. Moreover, the Patent Office provided the information that nigrosine had actually been patented in 1867, and was in general use in writing inks by the 1870s.

Dr Eastaugh became the pro-Diary lobby's chief scientific expert. To summarise, he wrote that 'the results of the various analyses of ink and paper in the Diary performed so far, have not given rise to any conflict with the date of 1888/9. If the Diary is a modern forgery, then it has "passed" a range of tests which would have shown up many materials now used in ink and paper manufacture. However, we must be aware that we cannot as yet wholly rule out, on the scientific evidence as it stands, a sophisticated modern forgery.'

And that was good enough for publisher and author, so far as what might be termed the *physical* attributes of the Diary. What about its *psychic* validity, that is to say the acceptability of its psychological content?

Shirley Harrison contacted Dr David Forshaw, a consultant to the Alcohol and Addiction Unit at the Maudsley Psychiatric Hospital, Denmark Hill, South London. He was asked to give his professional opinion as to whether the writer of the Diary had actually committed the atrocities therein described, or if the journal was merely an aggregate of the sick fantasies of a cynical forger. His preliminary verdict was that the diary's author was indeed writing out of gruesome experience.

He would eventually, after several months' study of the Diary's contents, produce a 15,000-word report, stating that in order to have faked it the writer would have had to have possessed a profound understanding of criminal psychology and the effect of drug addiction. He believed that, whoever it was who had written the diary, was writing out of genuine personal experience, and that the psychological profile of the diary's author was consistent with the psychopathology of a serial killer. Arguing from the basis of its contents, he felt that 'on the balance of probabilities, from a psychiatric perspective, it is authentic'.

The diary was now all set to be launched on its way to the public prints.

Deals were done with Warner Books for the hardback, and Simon and Schuster for the paperback, American rights, and with the TV documentary makers Duocrave for film rights. The men with the calculators were smilingly totting up a future profit forecast hovering around the £4 million sterling mark.

It was the Duocrave buy-in that brought Paul H. Feldman blustering on to the scene. His official style and status was 'Executive producer and director of research'. He was to become a universal Ripperean gadfly, and the most committed and unwavering of Maybrickians, lavish with his time and resources in pursuit of the establishment of his stereoscopically perceived final solution.

Paul Feldman it was, who, in December 1992, had the graphologist Anna Koren fly in from Israel. Graphology concerns itself with the interpretation from the study of a person's handwriting of their character, capabilities, inabilities, inclinations, disinclinations and so forth. Far from being an exact science, it is to a large extent inspirational, more closely allied to such artful 'sciences' as phrenology, astrology, psychometry, palmistry and crystal ballography, than to the sort of dull, down-to-earth, line-by-line, letter-by-letter forensic examination carried painstakingly out by the disputed document examiner.

Anna Koren, Director of the Graphology Centres in Haifa, Tel Aviv, Sydney and London, a member of the American Association of Graphologists and a forensic document examiner for the Israeli Ministry of Social Security Services, must have been wearing her mystic hat as a graphologist when she took her first peek at the disputed Diary. Her ESP factor X must have been humming that day, for, although her English can most charitably be described as basic, and although she was reported as having made no perceptible attempt to read or otherwise assimilate the content of the Diary, she was able, 'off-the-cuff', to confirm to her ecstatic audience 'everything we had come to suspect about James Maybrick'. She was also – from the handwriting – able to describe the author of the Diary as someone with 'psychological disorders'.

Sadly, her later, much later,[3] report proved distinctly less exhilarating. 'Unfortunately I have not managed to reach unequivocal conclusions with regard to the comparison of the letter "Dear Boss", the letter of 6 October,[4] the will of James Maybrick, and the diaries [*sic*] signed by Jack the Ripper. I have invested many many hours into examining these writings during the 9 months that have elapsed since I first saw the Diary in December, 1992 … I have found both similarities and contradictions in the documents and it is impossible for me to reach a verdict.'

Sue Iremonger had also been brought in by Feldman. Trained in both England and Chicago, a member of the World Association of Document Examiners, and a qualified psychotherapist specialising in the psychopathic personality into the bargain, she was not a graphologist. She was, however, expert in the examination of such disputed documents as fraudulent cheques, signature comparisons, and the identification of anonymous notes and poison-pen letters. She found it impossible, as had Anna Koren, to link the handwriting of the Diary with that of either the 'Dear Boss' letter or Maybrick's will. She was of the opinion that the body of the text of Maybrick's will was written by Maybrick himself.

Nothing if not thorough, Feldman sent off photocopies of the two signed pages of Maybrick's probated will, and of his signed marriage certificate, to Reed C. Hayes, of Kailua, Hawaii. A Handwriting and Document examiner, and member of the American Board of Forensic Handwriting Analysts, he was additionally a graphologist and a member of the International Grapho-analysis Society. This 'eminent document examiner' (he is so described by Shirley Harrison) contributed an opinion that it was highly improbable that the hand which signed James Maybrick's marriage certificate was that which wrote and signed James Maybrick's will.

The following March (1993), a glossy brochure intimating the advent of the forthcoming book and film was issued. Beautifully produced, an incarnadined, top-hatted, demi-masked incognito Maybrick glaring crimson-eyed and bush-browed from its shiny black cover, it supplied five suitably selected, appetite-whetting quotations from the journal, cited the approbatory views of seven suitably selected experts, and rounded off its powerful sales-pitch projection with the reassurance that 'over the last eighteen months, image enhancement, laser technology, historical research, extensive ink, paper, and forensic handwriting analysis have all played their part in uncovering the hidden secrets of a unique document. The result: Beyond all reasonable doubt, this document was written at the time of the Whitechapel Murders by the man responsible.'

Very impressive.

The *Guardian* of 24 March 1993 informed the world – or at any rate the world of its readers – '"Explosive" Diary to Uncloak Ripper.' And went on to say that the identity of Jack the Ripper was about to be unmasked 'definitively and incontrovertibly, say the publishers of a forthcoming book, *The Diary of Jack the Ripper*'. Almost 250,000 copies are to be published worldwide. 'The publishers are refusing to divulge details, and MIA Productions, who are to make a three-hour dramatised documentary for television, is even keeping the identities of the cast secret. Said Paul Feldman, the co-producer: "They know how explosive this story is, and have asked us to protect them from the press."'

Injecting a faintly cynical note, the *Daily Mail* of 26 March asked, 'Will They Ever Really Unmask Jack the Ripper?' 'Just when you would have thought,' said the article, 'that Jack's legend was going beyond its shelf life, comes this teasing glimpse of the Ripper as home body – husband and father who burned with spurned passion that led him to commit the six notorious murders.'

And what about the handwriting? 'Anna Koren, a leading graphologist who has read the diary, telephoned at her office in Israel, told the *Daily Mail*: "It seems to me that the handwriting is genuine. It's not fake. The writing is spontaneous and fluent. It looks as if the person who wrote it believed in what he wrote and went through an experience that was real. Everything he wrote in the diary was his emotion. No one could fake that."'

Paul Feldman explained, 'It's not a diary in the sense that it has got the date at the top of each page. It's a journal and he doesn't give his own name. We actually had to work out who wrote the document from the evidence within.'

The *Daily Telegraph* of 19 April 1993, reporting that more than a dozen experts had signed a confidentiality clause before examining the Diary and found themselves unable to say that it was genuine and equally unable to declare it false, quoted Donald Rumbelow: 'We are all trying to shake it at the moment. We are very conscious of the fact that the whole thing may be a hoax. But on what we have seen so far we can't say that it is. It's very exciting. Tests of ink and paper are all being done and they are contemporaneous. But I am still holding back and kicking it around.' The 'more than a dozen experts' not named in the *Telegraph* were named in a piece by Nicholas Warren, 'The Diary of an Extraordinarily Nervous Man', in the July 1993 issue of *Ripperana* – Paul Begg, Dr Nicholas Eastaugh, Melvyn Fairclough, Martin Fido, Dr David Forshaw, Martin Howells, Hannah Koren, Donald Rumbelow, Keith Skinner, William Waddell, Richard Whittington-Egan, Colin Wilson. All were constrained from discussing the diary until after its publication.

As one might have expected, it was the *Liverpool Daily Post* that, on 22 April 1993, revealed – prepublication – the identity of the scrivening Ripper as James Maybrick, cotton broker, late of Liverpool. The credit must go to staff reporter Harold Brough. A journalist colleague of Mr Brough's had told him how, quite by chance, he had got talking to a man on the London to Liverpool train who had told him that he had the Ripper Diary. It had, he said, been left to him by an old man.

'I traced the man on the train,' wrote Brough, 'but decided not to name him.'

However, following the story of the meeting, published in 21 April, *Daily Post*, the man in question telephoned Brough and confirmed that he did indeed own the Diary. Brough's telephone calls that day had also included one from a retired Liverpool schoolteacher who was interested in the Maybrick case. He said that he had been contacted by a London writer, Shirley Harrison, to see if he could help her with a book she was writing about Maybrick. She had also said that a Liverpool man had come forward with a diary. 'He had been given it by an old drinking pal, just like your Ripper man on the train. But her diary was of James Maybrick.' There were then, it seemed, *two* men from Liverpool who had contacted the publishing business in London – 'one clutching the Ripper Diary, the other the diary of James Maybrick – unless they are one and the same'.

Harold Brough commented, 'A cloak of secrecy, as dense as any of the legendary East End fogs, has settled on those involved with the coming sensational publication …'

The next day's *Sun* (23 April), shining through the fog, summed it all up in its own (fortunately) inimitable telegramese – 'Jack the Ripper was Rich, Randy Scouser.' And Kevin Ludden's maculate piece got off to a mandatorily titillatory, racy start: 'The real Jack the Ripper was a wealthy pervert from Liverpool …'

Robert Smith, cautious but apparently sincere, and Paul Feldman, garrulous but businesslike, gave interviews to Peter Guttridge, London correspondent of the *Sydney Morning Herald*.[5]

Said Smith, 'I am totally convinced the journal is genuine. And when they see the research we have done on it, even the most sceptical person will have to take it seriously.'

Said Feldman, 'Of course people who haven't seen the Diary won't believe it. When my researchers and I first got involved we were all very cynical too. But the Diary will convince the world.'

Paul Begg, Mr Feldman's director of research, added, 'In this situation a "Ripper expert" is the least expert of the experts.' He thought that the Diary was genuine. 'On the basis of the extensive scientific analysis, I cannot honestly see any reasonable alternative.'

But Nicholas Warren had an alternative. He declared the Diary a 'palpable fraud'.

In the *Observer* of Sunday 25 April 1993, Brian McConnell, a descendent of Mr William Robert Connell, of Counsel, who was a junior member of the prosecution team at the trial of Florence Maybrick, wrote unambiguously: 'The man named last week as the real Jack the Ripper was alive and not well, 200 miles away in Liverpool at the time the murders were committed in London.'

McConnell will have no truck with the notion of James the Ripper or Jim the Penman. He points out that Dr Arthur Hopper, the Maybrick family doctor in Liverpool, told the Court that he had seen James Maybrick fifteen or twenty times between June and September 1888. A clerk (Thomas Lowry), a bookkeeper (George Smith) and a charwoman (Mrs Eliza Busher) all gave evidence of Maybrick's presence in Liverpool and regular attendance at the office during the material time.

H. B. Irving, editor of the *Notable British Trials* volume on the trial of Florence Maybrick, remarks in his Introduction that it was 'some short time before his death' that the domestic happiness of the Maybrick household became overcast'. Irving continues, 'Mrs Maybrick had, it would seem, some ground of complaint against her husband in regard to a woman, while she herself had conceived an illicit passion for a man of the name of Brierley.'

Brian McConnell observes, 'All this took place six months after the Ripper murders[6] and Maybrick having kept a mistress for a long time, does not seem a likely person to have developed a murderous hate for all prostitutes, as suggested in the diaries [*sic*].'

McConnell quotes Nicholas Warren: 'I believe the diary is a hoax. Claimed to contain matters which could be only known to the Ripper, [it] contains no material about the case which was not known before, and its authenticity has not so far been borne out.'

He quotes, too, Stewart Evans: 'I think the diary is a hoax. It is said to have been subjected to forensic scrutiny since it was found more than two years ago. I do not know what that can prove. Paper made in 1888 can be bought in antique shops and ink used on paper more than two or three years later cannot be easily authenticated or identified.'

Three weeks before – on 7 April 1993, actually – Robert Smith had approached the *Sunday Times* with the offer of an option to take up the serial rights and publish extracts from the Diary for an unreturnable sum of £5,000, which sum would, in the event of the paper's taking up said option, be acknowledged and credited as part-payment of the full and final price tag of £75,000. Moreover, on payment of the £5,000 option fee, the *Sunday Times* would be permitted to conduct its own examination into the *bona fides* of the Diary, the sole requirement imposed being that the representatives of the paper itself, and any other experts it chose to bring in, must sign a preliminary agreement to keep the contents of the Diary confidential.

This was neither unreasonable nor unusual, for, in the special milieu of Fleet Street, any leakage picked up by other newspapers could result in repercussions seriously undermining, if not totally destroying, the value of the property under offer.

Having, not without reluctance and after much discussion, conformed to the condition specified, the *Sunday Times* launched its independent investigation. There were, the newspaper decided, four possibilities: the Diary was a genuine document; it was a modern hoax; it was a fantasy written by James Maybrick; it was a Victorian forgery, perhaps invented in an attempt to secure the release of Florence Maybrick, but never used. The last two options were rapidly dismissed, for the simple reason that the Diary contained certain facts which only the killer could have known at the time, facts which had, however, emerged into the public arena in 1987. The Diary must, then, be either genuine or a modern – i.e. post-1987 – hoax. The *Sunday Times* set out to discover which.

One of the first things that the paper's researchers came, or rather, did *not* come, face to face with was Baxendale's unfavourable forensic report. Robert Smith confirmed its receipt, but said that it contained a number of errors. 'I put it into my bottom drawer and forgot all about it.'

The *Sunday Times*' next quest was for a further sample of James Maybrick's handwriting. Smith had conceded that it would be 'a piece of cake' to dismiss the Diary as a fake if its handwriting did not match that of Maybrick. But unfortunately, he said, there was only one example of Maybrick's handwriting in existence: a signature on a will, that might or might not have been his signature anyway.

This proved untrue. The *Sunday Times* obtained copies of both Maybrick's entry in a marriage register and a two-page will. The handwriting in the marriage register, signed in 1881, proved virtually identical to that of the will, signed in 1889. The handwriting in the Diary bore no resemblance to the handwriting of James Maybrick.

True, the Diary repeats such phrases as 'funny little games, ha ha,' which appear in letters purportedly written by the Ripper to the police, but again, the signature at the end of the Diary is not like any of the signatures on letters to the police.

Far from satisfied, the *Sunday Times* commissioned its own team of experts, consisting of Dr Audrey Giles, former head of the Metropolitan Police Laboratory's Questioned Document Section, Dr Kate Flint, lecturer in Victorian and modern English literature at the faculty of English, Oxford University, and Mr Tom Cullen, a pioneer Ripper historian.

Dr Giles, examining the Diary in her study at Chesham Bois, in Buckinghamshire, had her suspicions aroused by the torn-out pages. She also identified strokes added to the letters 'f', 'y', and 'g', in order to give them the large, rounded loops of copperplate. She was quite positive that Maybrick's will was not written by the author of the Diary. She noted especially that the letters 'J' and 'M' were very different, which, since these were Maybrick's initials, she regarded as significant. She agreed with both Robert Smith and Barrett that Maybrick's handwriting could have been affected by drugs or his emotional state, but said, 'Although drugs, alcohol and stress can influence the size and proportion of an individual's writing, the fine detail and construction will not be altered.'

Dr Flint, embowered within stacks of dictionaries, picked out the odd anachronistic-seeming phrases. 'One off' struck a discordant note. The *Oxford English Dictionary* first dates it to 1934, but the dictionary's editors admit that verbal usage may predate inclusion in the dictionary by as much as nearly half a century. However, the expression 'to top myself' was not recorded until 1958, seventy years after the Whitechapel murders.

Mr Cullen forthrightly declared, 'My impression of the so-called Ripper/Maybrick diaries [*sic*] is that they [*sic*] are forgeries of a not particularly clever character. There appears to be a good deal of stage management involved in the repentance scene at the end, which smacks of good old Victorian melodrama. For the rest, they [*sic*] seem to me to be a farrago of nonsense.'

The researchers discovered, too, the scientific report that Dr Baxendale had prepared for Robert Smith twelve months before, in which he had cast serious doubts regarding the authenticity of the document. His conclusion was duly and significantly noted.

Finally, around July, the panel of experts convened by the *Sunday Times* delivered its conjoint verdict that the Diary was most likely a forgery.

Informed of this finding, Robert Smith threatened to sue for damages if the *Sunday Times* breached its confidentiality agreement. But, as it turned out, it was the newspaper that, on 20 July 1993, went to the High Court seeking to be released from the contractual obligation to preserve confidentiality, on the grounds of fraud, fraudulent misrepresentation, or negligent misrepresentation.

In the meantime, Robert Smith, all oblivious, went blithely ahead with the publishing of a four-page supplement to the *Bookseller* of 23 July, proclaiming that 'THE WORLD'S GREATEST MURDER MYSTERY WILL BE SOLVED ON OCTOBER 7th – with the publication of the Diary'.

Six days later, on 29 July, the *Sunday Times* reported the whole matter to the police, depositing the records of its research results with the International and Organised Crimes Branch (SO1) at New Scotland Yard.

All this was ticking away ominously as a time bomb in the background when, on Friday 30 July 1993, there was published in the *Washington Post* an article that for the British backers of the Diary was to have a calamitous effect.

Its author was David Streitfeld, a *Post* staff writer. His article, headed 'Jack the Ripoff!', began, 'Not since the Hitler diaries – heck, maybe even the Mussolini diaries – has there been such excitement over the discovery of a historical document. Imagine it; the most famous criminal of modern times, the granddaddy of all serial killers, had left behind a journal in which he ranted, explained, confessed … But this week, faced with the publication of a story casting doubt on the authenticity of the Diary, Warner Books said it will cancel the book if questions about the document's legitimacy cannot be resolved.'

Larry Kirshbaum, president of Warner Books, who had in fact been tipped off by Streitfeld in advance – Warner's Warning you might, with deference to William Roughead, call it – had announced that he intended to order the carrying out of additional thorough and independent investigation into the Diary's validity prior to releasing it to the bookstores.

The *Post* put out a dragnet for British Ripperologist quotations. First came Melvin Harris with, 'Are you good at spelling? It's C-R-A-P.' Less scatologically, but equally dismissively, Nicholas Warren designated it 'an obvious hoax'. John Ross, curator of the Scotland Yard crime museum, simply laughed, and commented, 'The whole thing's preposterous. At best, it's another suspect. But we've got suspects coming out of our ears. I get at least two letters a week with another one.'

But the Smith of Smith Gryphon stood marmoreal in face of the onslaught, the tempest blowing through the small, querulous world of Ripperology.

'The opinions of Ripperologists who have not read the Diary and not read our commentary are not worth quoting,' was his calm riposte amid all the peevishness.

Streitfeld went on to provide an example of the kind of debate that was raging back and forth.

A Smith Gryphon pamphlet plugging the forthcoming book says: 'Independent sets of ink tests were conducted in two British universities, using state-of-the-art technology. The ink was very complex, but it passed its tests with flying colours'; similarly with paper … Scientific analyst Dr Nicholas Eastaugh concludes: 'In all the tests that have been conducted, none of them has disproved the authenticity of the diary.' In an interview, Eastaugh was even more doubtful. 'With the current state of the testing, we can't distinguish between its being a document from 1889 and something much more recent – say five to ten years old.' He added that he had for some time been saying that more tests were needed, but that none had been ordered, and he was not happy with the extent of investigation. Referring to the missing pages, apparently cut from the front of the diary volume, Eastaugh commented: 'If you wanted to introduce subjective opinions, then you'd say it's rather suspicious.'

Very rightly, Streitfeld diagnoses, 'At the heart of the Ripper dispute is a comparison of the handwriting in the diary with the two other known examples of Maybrick writing: on his marriage certificate and on his will. The nay-sayers say there's no match, and that disqualifies the Diary from being real right there. Smith said there's no match because the will is a copy done by a clerk.'

Streitfeld's article concludes, 'Fake or, however improbably, real, the fate of the diary will be decided within the next 30 days. As the motto on Maybrick's coat of arms has it: "Time reveals all."'

Kirshbaum had commissioned Kenneth W. Rendell, a dealer in historical documents, to assess the status of the Diary, and Robert Smith, co-operating, flew, on 8 August 1993, to Chicago, bringing with him the Diary itself, as well as a number of what he regarded as crucial key documents, including photocopies of the Maybrick will and marriage certificate.

Rendell and a trio of hand-picked experts were waiting to meet him in the laboratory of one of the chosen experts, Mrs Maureen Casey Owens, former president of the American Society of Questioned Document Examiners and for twenty-five years the Chicago Police Department's consultant in document examination. The second member of the trio was Robert L. Kuranz, a research chemist of more than thirty years' standing and who had a special knowledge of the composition of inks. The third was forgery detector, Dr Joe Nickell. There was a fourth member of the team, Rod McNeil, but he was not there that day. He was the devisor of a test, the ion migration test, which, he claimed, could put a date to the time when ink had been placed on paper. His skills were said to have been employed by both the FBI and the American Secret Service.

Rendell's first reaction, as well as that of Mrs Owens and Dr Nickell, was that the Diary had been written much more recently than at the putative date of 1888, and, indeed, they were subsequently to find nothing which would alter that early impression. Not only did they consider the actual writing style inconsistent with letter formations of the alleged period of its execution, but they noted also a uniformity in the appearance of the ink and of the slant of the writing in going from one section or entry to the next, which was not consonant with the implied writing of those sections or entries at different times. It was, in fact, classically indicative of a forger writing multiple entries at one time. Noted, too, was a suspicion-generating lack of variation in layout. But the greatest surprise of all was the discovery that the text of Maybrick's will was indubitably written by the same hand as that which had signed both it and the marriage certificate; that of James Maybrick. 'This,' said Rendell, 'was an unexpected development, as I had been told that the evidence that it [the will] was written by Maybrick's brother, Michael, was very strong. I was never shown this evidence.'

Neither, it would seem, was he shown Dr Forshaw's evidence in its entirety. Forshaw had submitted a 59-page, 15,000-word report on the Diary. Its final paragraph read, 'The account is feasible and indeed makes sense. However, there are other possibilities; it could be a modern or old fake or the product of a deluded mind contemporaneous with the Jack the Ripper murders.' According to Rendell, this paragraph – which is effectively a totally nugatory piece of rear-covering – had been deleted (imperfectly, obviously) when he first saw the Forshaw report.

Robert Kuranz analysed the ink and endorsed Eastaugh's findings. Some of the ink and paper samples which he had taken from the Diary were sent to Mr McNeil to undergo his ion migration test. In due course he came up with the answer that it indicated a median date of 1921 plus or minus 12 years: that is a time range of from 1909 to 1933. He later formulated a provisional revision to the extent of stating that in his view the ink was put on the paper prior to 1970 anyway.[7]

The general conclusion of the Rendell report was: 'There is no other possibility – the writer of the Jack the Ripper Diary was not James Maybrick … this is a hoax.'

Equally condemnatory of the Diary was Phillip Knightley's summation, published in the *Independent on Sunday*, of 29 August 1993, He considered it puzzling that if, as in the Diary the writer says that he did, Maybrick confessed to his wife that he was the Ripper, she did not use this knowledge as part of her defence at her life-or-death trial for his murder, on the lines of, 'My husband was Jack the Ripper and I feared for my own life.' Nor was there any reference to it in her memoirs, *My Fifteen Lost Years*, published in 1905. As Knightley rightly remarks, 'Even in those days a book entitled *I Was Jack the Ripper's Wife* would have had an enormous sale.' But no, not once in all the fifty-two years of life remaining to her after Maybrick's death did she breathe so much as a hint of it.

Knightley records Nick Warren's pertinent observation that 'there has been no ESDA [Electrostatic Deposition Apparatus] test. This shows the electrical impression carried from one page to the one underneath. This would not last 105 years, so if there is an impression, this would mean that the diary is, as I believe, a forgery.'[8]

Finally, Knightley asks, 'Who is behind it?' There is, he says, nothing in the Diary that was not publicly known by 1987, so this suggests that if it was a fake, it was created after that date. The writer would be someone who had detailed knowledge of both the Maybrick case and the Ripper murders – he would have chosen Maybrick because he had sufficient characteristics to make him a plausible Jack.

It would have required a mere triad, or at the most quartet, of books to acquire the requisite 'expert' knowledge – Martin Fido's *The Crimes, Detection and Death of Jack the Ripper* (1987), *The Poisoned Life of Mrs Maybrick* by Bernard Ryan with Sir Michael Havers (1977), and *Trial of Mrs Maybrick* by H. B. Irving (1912). The fourth, to put the icing on the cake, would have been the new and completely revised 1987 edition of Donald Rumbelow's *The Complete Jack the Ripper*.

In that August of 1993, the *Sunday Times* applied for a speedy trial on the grounds that it was in the public interest that the book, *The Diary of Jack the Ripper*, be exposed before going on sale. Mr Justice Lindsay ruled that there was 'a real possibility that for a period in October, if nothing is done, the public or some of its members, may be deceived'. He ordered a speedy trial. It never came to that. In the second week of September, Smith Gryphon agreed to repay the £5,000 to the *Sunday Times*, make a small contribution to legal costs (£1,500) and release the newspaper, and others, from the confidentiality agreements.

Less than a month before P – for publication – Day, 7 October, 'The Day the World's Greatest Murder Mystery Will Be Solved', and suddenly the slogan had gone sour. So said Shaun Usher in the *Daily Mail* of 9 September 1993.

The bad news for Smith Gryphon was that, despite every effort, brave and foolish, the publisher and his enthusiastic fugleman, the indefatigable, undeflatable Feldman, could make and had made, Warner Books had remained inconvincible and unconvinced. Worse. President Kirshbaum had spoken. Of the Diary, America's publishing sensation of the season, the US rights of which he had bought for a record sum, he had pronounced: 'It's not what it purports to be. Despite the huge sales potential, our credibility means more.' Then, turning the presidential thumb firmly down, he decreed that the entire print run of 200,000 hardbacks should be pulped.

The truth – rarely pure and never simple, as Oscar Wilde epigrammatically remarked – is that the Diary 'got blown out of the water by a spoil-sport called Kenneth Rendell'. But all was not lost. Hyperion, a publishing stable-fellow of Disneyland (which some cynical Ripperology students see as horses-for-courses appropriate), took the book over. Wisely, when publishing they included, *qua* appendix, the Rendell Report.

Usher's article continues: 'Rendell insisted that scientific tests on the "Diary", an impressively Dickensian-looking ledger, showed that the ink on its 92 faded pages[9] wasn't made until a quarter of a century or so *after* the final Ripper outrage.'

Usher reports an agonising Robert Smith response: '"I wasn't very impressed with Kenneth Rendell's report." He says that ink-testing "is not an exact science," that the diary has information only the killer could have known, and "amazed rather than annoyed" at America's perception of a hoax, Mr Smith urges readers to judge for themselves. "Never mind American nay-sayers," he argues, "30 *other* experts have given the diary their approval.'"

Rather unfairly, Usher breaks in with the scarcely neutral or judicial interjection that, 'The most fascinating facet of the Great Ripper Hoax is its demonstration of a particularly unpleasant, insane serial killer's enduring death-grip on the public's curiosity and imagination.' A cheap point – inexpensively made.

And then, in the *Liverpool Daily Post* (26 September 1993), just seven days before the Diary's publication, the final sensation. Michael Barrett tells Harold Brough 'How the Ripper Diary Ruined My Life'.

'Michael Barrett is only 41, yet moves slowly with the aid of a walking stick … He says "Nothing can bring back my health. My life is in total turmoil. I wish I could turn the clock back, that I had never been given that brown paper parcel."'

He lays the blame for the stroke that has left him partly paralysed on his right side fairly and squarely on the stress and strain brought on by living with the Ripper story. The Diary apart, which he frankly admits became an obsession which ultimately took over his life, his two main interests had always been his garden and the Royal British Legion, of which he was the proud standard bearer of the Liverpool Walton branch. His greatest ambition? To have his own small greenhouse. All that was, like his marriage, behind him. 'I have been through hell and high water.' The stress shows in his face: he has aged way beyond the wheel-turns of time. 'I wish Tony Devereux had never bloody well given the Diary to me. I wish I had thrown the wretched thing on the fire,' he says. And means it.

At 11 a.m. on 4 October 1993, at the Arts Club, 40 Dover Street, London, W1, Smith Gryphon staged a press conference and the launch of the Diary. 'The author and the experts will be on hand to answer detailed questions,' said the invitation.

Present – not *exactly* by invitation, but present – was the Great Debunker himself, Mr Melvin Harris. He occupied a back seat, well out of the ambit of the limes. He sat, inconspicuous, silent, poised, waiting. He waited until the press had asked its questions. He waited until the general silence betokened the fact that there were going to be no more questions asked … 'Then I uncoiled myself from my back seat and made two very basic requests: "Where is the expert who will put his reputation on the line and state that this diary is an authentic document written by James Maybrick in 1888 and 1889?" and "Where is there another expert also prepared to put his reputation on the line and state that James Maybrick's will is a forgery?" The silence was uncanny. Mr Smith was left alone on the bridge of the *Titanic*.'

Thursday, 7 October 1993. *The Diary of Jack the Ripper* was published. In vitiation of its previous stance of absolute certainty, it wore upon its front cover, stuck across the words 'The Discovery. The Investigation. The Authentication', a small white label which read, 'IS IT GENUINE? Read the evidence, then judge for yourself.'

I wrote in *Contemporary Review*,[10]

The game's afoot, Watson. Still. Five years after the centennial mark, with its sanguineous froth of celebrant volumes, a haemorrhagic trickle, three new-sponsored pretenders to the bloodstained crown have appeared. The first, and most potentially important, is James Maybrick, alleged author of what is claimed to be the veritable diary, the killing book, of Saucy Jack. Of dubious provenance, scribed in a hectic scrawl which bears no resemblance to known samples of the flowing Victorian fist of James the penman, this vaunted journal seems rather less than satisfactory. Maybrick, himself a murderee – he fell victim to the venerific practices of his young wife (or so a Court decided) – is on the face of it an unlikely nomination for the rôle of Ripper, and I harbour grievous doubts in regard to the validity of his candidature. I cannot go along with his assumption of the authorship of the 'Dear Boss' letter addressed to the Central News Office, which, in my belief, was really a spot of constructive mayhem by a contemporary journalist. I am made more than passing uneasy, too, by the diarist's blithe acceptance of the canard of the rings and farthings in the Annie Chapman-Hanbury Street scenario. Even so, I think that all interested parties should accept the challenge of the stick-on label to the front cover and 'Read the evidence, then judge for yourself.' It is a beautifully produced volume; Miss Shirley Harrison, described as the narrator, has contrived a most difficult task of organisation of the complex duality of material outstandingly well, and there is here some splendid new background information on the Maybricks. Right or wrong, there can be no doubt that the diary already occupies a definite niche on the alarmingly lengthening Whitechapel Murders' shelf.

Precisely a fortnight after publication, the *Daily Express* (21 October 1993) announced that Scotland Yard was to probe. It was to look into the possibility that the attempted sale of serial rights – to the *Sunday Times* – had been fraudulent. Again according to the *Daily Express* (26 November 1993), the Yard officers had concluded that the document was probably a forgery, compiled in Liverpool during the past ten years. But they had also decided that there had been no criminality in either its publication or its marketing. This was effectively confirmed in January 1994, when the Crown Prosecution Service decided against any further action.

We come now to what Sherlock Holmes would surely have called the curious incident of the scratched watch. We have to go back in time to July 1993, just a few weeks before, in the August, *The Diary of Jack the Ripper* went off to the printers. That was when the long arm of coincidence flexed itself most extraordinarily; that was when Robert Smith received a very unexpected telephone call. On the other end of the line was Mr Albert Johnson, of Liverpool. He told him, 'I think I've got James Maybrick's watch.' Smith drove to Liverpool to meet Mr Johnson at his brother Robbie's house.

Albert Johnson, getting on in years, was semi-retired, but still holding down a part-time security job at a local college. He had purchased the watch in question, a handsome gold pocket watch made by Henry Verity of Lancaster in 1846, from a jeweller's shop, Stewart's, over the water in Wallasey, on the Cheshire side of the Mersey. He produced a receipt for the £225 he had paid for it on 14 July 1992. The jeweller is said to have held the watch for at least five years before the sale.

When Mr Johnson opened the watch, he had seen on the inner case behind the works some rather indistinct scratchings. Producing a small magnifying glass, he now invited Smith to take a look at them. Sure enough, scratched at the bottom of the rim was the signature 'J. Maybrick.' Across the centre were the words, 'I am Jack'. Around the edge, five sets of initials – M. N., A. C., E. S., C. E., and M. K.

Realising that the watch could be important, Albert and Robbie Johnson had decided, at the suggestion of their solicitor, Richard Nicholas, to invest a little money in having it forensically tested. They took it to Dr Stephen Turgoose, of the Corrosion and Protection Centre at the University of Manchester's Institute of Science and Technology.

Having examined the watch and its markings with a scanning electron microscope, Dr Turgoose in due course reported his opinion that 'the wear apparent on many of the engravings (i.e. scratchings), evidenced by the rounded edgings of the markings and "polishing out" in places, would indicate a substantial age for the engravings. The actual age would depend upon the cleaning or polishing regime employed, and any definition of number of years has a great degree of uncertainty.'

However, given these qualifications, he would be of the opinion that the engravings were likely to have been executed more than ten years ago, and possibly much longer He was careful to point out, though, that while he had found no evidence that would indicate that the engravings had been originated in the last few years, equally he had found no evidence which would conclusively prove their age. They *could* have been produced recently and been artificially aged by polishing.

The Johnson brothers brought the watch down to London for the launch of Shirley Harrison's book. The press response to the watch was 'a thunderous – and disappointing – silence'. Those few who did mention it found its emergence, a couple of months after the first newspaper reports of the discovery of the Maybrick journal, redolent of 'a conspiracy theory that linked both watch and diary as coming from a common, dubious source'.

Egged on by the pro-Diary faction, the Johnson brothers sought a second opinion. The watch was delivered into the hands of the metallurgist Dr Robert K. Wild, at the Interface Analysis Centre, Bristol University.

He tested it under the electron microscope, using the technique of scanning Auger microscopy (SAM), combined with argon ion depth profiling. He photographed, as had Dr Turgoose, particles of brass embedded within the scratch marks. These slivers were blackened with age.

His report stated, 'The particles embedded in the base of the engraving are brass from the engraving tool. The particle investigated is very heavily contaminated and appears to have been considerably corroded.' This suggested that the particle had indeed been embedded in the surface for some considerable time. He continued, 'Provided the watch has remained in a normal environment, it would seem likely that the engravings were at least of several tens of years ago. This would agree with the findings of D. Turgoose (1993), and in my opinion it is unlikely that anyone would have sufficient expertise to implant aged brass particles into the base of the engravings.'[11]

Ripperana – No. 8, April 1994 – announced its profound surprise on learning that Mr Albert Johnson, who had always protested his strong determination not to make the slightest profit through the ownership of 'such a loathsome relic', and stated his intention to 'donate his chance find to a suitable museum', had reportedly spent £4,000 on having metallurgical tests carried out in an effort to prove the authenticity of the scratchings on his artefact. *Ripperana* points out that, the report of Dr Stephen Turgoose having proved inconclusive, Dr Wild's proved hardly more satisfactory.

Wild wrote, 'The amount of time the watch was available for examination was limited to only a few hours and as a result a thorough investigation was not possible and any conclusions are therefore preliminary at this stage … To give an accurate date to the watch from its surface composition and from the brass particles embedded in the base of the scratches it would be necessary to analyse several standards of known age, encompassing the age of the watch to recent time, of both brass and gold which had been known to have been exposed to similar conditions. This would involve a considerable amount of work.'

His conclusion therefore was that, 'From the limited amount of evidence that has been acquired it would appear that the engraving on the back of the watch has not been done recently and is at least several tens of years old – but it is not possible to be more accurate without considerably more work.'

And so for the nonce matters in uncertainty stand, while 'time has ticked a heaven round the stars', and the little gold Maybrick watch goes tick,tick,ticking on … a still unexploded time bomb.

A time bomb of another kind *was* exploded when, in the *Liverpool Daily Post*, of 27 June 1994, Mike Barrett confessed, 'How I Faked Ripper Diary.'

'Yes, I am a forger,' he told Harold Brough. 'The greatest in history.' Barrett, said Brough, is seriously ill. He decided to confess after his doctor told him that he had only days to live. The story that he told was that he had bought an old photograph album from the auctioneers, Outhwaite and Litherland, of Fontenoy Street, Liverpool, and ripped out all the used pages. He had then bought some ink from a shop at the Liverpool Bluecoat Chambers. He had typed the diary out at home on his word processor. He admitted, 'Tony Devereux had sod-all to do with it. I wrote it. I fooled the world.' Barrett added that he was no novice author. He had written material for the Dundee publisher, D. C. Thomson, for some years. He said that he had worked on the Ripper Diary for five years – 'I decided I would write the story of the century. I bloody well did it.' Having confessed the hoax, Barrett declared, 'I now feel at peace with myself.'

The *Post* reported his separated wife, Anne, as saying: 'This is bullshit. He told me he got the diary from Tony Devereux and that is all I know. He is now trying to get back at me because I left him. The whole thing is an absolute nightmare. But I will fight like a tiger to protect myself and my family against anything he says.'

The publisher, Robert Smith, commented: 'I find it remarkable in view of the thorough investigation by Scotland Yard in Liverpool last year, and the many expert opinions indicating it is genuine.

And the following day, losing no time, Barrett's lawyers put it about that their client was 'not in full control of his faculties' when he made his 'Confession'.

Unimpressed by this recantation was the following Sunday's *Sunday Times*, 3 July 1994, wherein, positively triumphant, Maurice Chittenden, the associate editor, wrote: 'It is the confession of Jack the Ripoff. For months he haunted the publishing houses of London, clutching a dusty black ledger in his hand. Now the man who fooled the book world – but not the *Sunday Times* – by 'discovering' the diary of Jack the Ripper has admitted he wrote it himself.'

Despite warnings that it was a fake, the book still sold 50,000 hardback copies in Britain, was translated into eleven languages, and sold another 50,000 overseas. 'But not a word in the ledger was true.' Continued Chittenden, 'For nearly a year Barrett maintained the book was authentic. However, last week he admitted he spent ten days tapping out the 9,000-word 'confession' on a word processor in his Victorian terraced house in Liverpool.' He transcribed the confession from his word processor, using ink made from a traditional recipe and bought from an art shop. 'I did it because I could not pay the mortgage and I fooled the world.'

The *Sunday Times* report concluded, 'Last night Barrett was in an alcohol treatment unit at Liverpool's Fazakerley Hospital as lawyers and publishers tried to undo the damage … Barrett first confessed to Shirley Harrison, the author of the book based on the diary. She said, "He said he wanted to confess because he is an ill man and believes he is going to die." Later Barrett gave a signed statement admitting his forgery to Harold Brough.'

Eight weeks after the unburdening of Michael Barrett, his wife, Anne, was also to unload her conscience. On 3 August 1994, Shirley Harrison, Sally Evemy, Doreen Montgomery, Robert Smith and Keith Skinner sat around a small tape recorder in Paul Feldman's Baker Street, London, office, and listened to a statement that she had made on tape to Feldman a few days earlier.

She supposed, she said, that she knew it was inevitable that one day the truth about the Ripper Diary would come out. She apologised most sincerely that it had taken so long, but she had had what she felt were justifiable reasons for preserving the fiction. 'I realised some time ago that the snowball effect had intruded deeply in your lives, and this has been a heavy burden for me to carry.'

The Diary, she explained, had never been intended for publication. Not by her. It was, she thought, in 1968–9 that she saw it for the first time. She had discovered it in a large tin trunk at the back of a fitted cupboard in the house where she was living with her widowed father, Billy Graham. In 1950, after the death of Billy Graham's father – her grandfather – her father's stepmother, Edith Formby, had come for Christmas dinner, and she gave Billy Graham a suitcase, which contained, among other things, a diary. Edith Formby told Billy Graham that it had been left to him by his granny.

It would have been about the year 1988, when Anne and her husband, Michael Barrett, whom she had married on 4 December 1975, moved to their own house in Goldie Street, Anfield, that, along with a number of other things that he did not want, Anne's father gave her the diary. She never showed it to her husband. She did not like having the thing in the house, and jammed it away behind a cupboard.

Some time later Mike Barrett started drinking. 'He was desperately trying to write, but didn't seem to be getting anywhere.' He was becoming very fed up and frustrated, and it was making things difficult between the pair of them. 'I thought of giving him the diary then, so that he could use it as the basis for a book. I was hoping he would be able to write a fictional story about the diary.' But she knew that if she gave it to him herself and told him its history, he would be badgering her father, who wasn't getting on too well with his son-in-law, for details. 'So I came up with the plan of giving Mike the diary via someone else. I found some brown paper which had been lining a drawer and wrapped the diary in it, and tied it with string. I took the parcel to Tony Devereux and asked him to give it to Mike and tell him to do something with it, which he faithfully did.'

Following the publication in the autumn of 1994 of the paperback edition of *The Diary*, Mike Barrett surfaced most significantly, and indignantly, in the January 1995 issue (No. 11) of *Ripperana*, 'particularly incensed by the assumption, carried on page 231 of Shirley Harrison's paperback, that he was too unread to come up with lines such as "Oh costly intercourse of death."'

Barrett indeed went on to supply *Ripperana* with the full source of that quotation. It came from a poem, '*Sancta Maria Dolorum*', by Richard Crashaw. He found it in a book, which he had since lodged with his solicitor, *English Poetry and Prose, 1540–1674*, edited by Christopher Ricks, published by Sphere Reference Books in 1986.

> O costly intercourse
> of death's, and worse,
> Divided loves.

The piece in *Ripperana* wittily continues,

> Mr Barrett, his memory unimpaired by Korsakoff's syndrome … has now recalled details of the transaction involved in purchasing the album used for the 'Diary' from the Liverpool auctioneers … He purchased a double lot, consisting of the album and an unusual square compass for the sum of fifty pounds (borrowed from his father-in-law) under the false name 'Mr Williams'. The album presumably contained postcards or photographs of maritime interest, and this unusual lot is likely to have been sold in 1991.

In 1994, the *Sunday Times*, *Ripperana*, and Melvin Harris jointly funded a crucial analysis of six ink samples taken from the original twelve removed from the Diary by Robert

Kuranz in the course of the Warner Books' investigation in Chicago in 1993. The testing was carried out by Dr Diana Simpson, who headed a body known as Analysis for Industry, recommended by the Forensic Science Society. She was asked to test for one substance only – chloroacetamide.

Why? Stewart Evans and Paul Gainey tell us in the paperback edition of their book *The Lodger: The Arrest and Escape of Jack the Ripper* – re-titled *Jack the Ripper: First American Serial Killer*: 'In his confession,[12] Barrett revealed the name of the shop where the ink used in the diary came from. This shop (the Bluecoat Art Shop, Liverpool) confirmed that they had indeed sold a special manuscript ink, made by Diamine, a Liverpool company. It contained iron salts and nigrosine as colouring matter, with chloroacetamide as its preservative. Chloroacetamide is a modern commercial product, first used in ink manufacture in the 1960s. Its presence in the diary would prove beyond doubt it was a fake.'

According to her report of 19 October 1994, Dr Simpson found chloroacetamide present, albeit in sub-microgram levels, after ruling out all possibility of contamination.

Shirley Harrison and Keith Skinner took the Diary to Leeds University, where they commissioned rival tests by the Department of Dyeing and Colour Chemistry. The reported results were that the ink contained neither chloroacetamide nor nigrosine, and that it was *not* Diamine.

Professor John C. Roberts, Professor of Paper Science at the University of Manchester's Institute of Science and Technology, invoked as a consultant arbitrator, examined both reports. One point that he immediately made was that Dr Simpson did not appear to have carried out a control test in order to ascertain whether the chloroacetamide could have been contained in the paper attached to the ink samples. Leeds, he noted, had scraped the ink away from the paper of their test samples. He said that chloroacetamide was *not* a modern, but an old, compound, and that it had been used extensively in the 1880s, although not, so far as we know, in paper. However … 'Even if no reference could be found to its use in paper in 1889, the fact that it existed well before that date would devalue the scientific evidence in support of the fact that the diaries [*sic*] were forged … The argument that it had found its way into the ink or paper by some obscure route can never be completely discounted.'

Then, just to make everything nigrosine-black, up pops Alec Voller, head chemist of Diamine Ltd, who, on 30 October 1995, was shown the Diary for the first time. The ink in which it is written is not one of Diamine's, he declared. In it he detected nigrosine. He noted also an irregular fading and bronzing. These, he said, were both indicators of age. 'The general appearance is characteristic of documents I have seen which are ninety-plus years old, and it is certainly not out of the realms of possibility that it dates back to 1889. Certainly the ink did not go on the paper within recent years.'[13]

This is, as I have had reason to observe elsewhere, where we came in.

What are we to make of it all? It has been conflict, conflict every step of the way, expert contradicting expert. Never mind testing the ink, said one, too much ink – and paper – has been wasted writing about it.

Another, Alex Chisholm, has compiled a masterly analysis of the factual content of absurdities, anomalies, and dissonances which give the lie, he says, to the claim that it has not been possible to demonstrate from internal evidence that the Diary is anything other than genuine.

Chisholm writes,

> Myths and legend, false claims and fantasy, have long distorted the history of Whitechapel murders, from its emergence to the Autumn of 1888, to the lucrative business it has become,

for some, today. But never before have these come together, in conjunction with an ignorance of historical fact, to play so central a role in any work as they do in *The Diary of Jack the Ripper*. The favourite Maybricknick defence has been to retreat behind their paper walls and discharge accusations of subjectivity at their detractors. I feel an explanation of my position may be appropriate. While retaining strong reservations about the possibility of finding the illusory objectivity in any history, I for one did not buy the diary because I believed it to be a hoax. I bought it to read and evaluate its contents in relation to the documented evidence. It is this which forged the belief that anyone conducting a similar evaluation can only conclude that *The Diary of Jack the Ripper* is a work of fiction. To my mind this is not subjective, it is sensible, and it is a sensibility which exposes the approach of diary proponents as subjective in the extreme … I am not a Ripperologist, and if I have a vested interest it is in history against which the Maybricknicks have evidently set their hand … [with their] incessant and inaccurate claims … that their diary is accurate in all essentials, and the willingness to promote the false belief that scientific evidence confirms its authenticity.

On the fact that the Diary was written in an album that had numerous pages missing, Chisholm observes,

It is indeed convenient that the accident, or purpose, of history which relieved the diary of its previous pages has left the structure of the narrative intact. A structure which strategically begins by revealing the plot, in the fashion of a particularly tawdry 'soap.' … Here within the space of the initial eleven lines of the first remaining page [of the diary] we have all the key words, 'Whitechapel,' 'London,' 'whore,' 'revenge,' together with a *mystery* and an individual who is 'too clever' to pay for his actions. I say 'his' because in this introduction we have already been given sufficient information to conclude that the diarist is claiming to be Jack the Ripper. Considering the previous pages have been removed and lost, this stroke of luck simply beggars belief. Yet such preparatory narrative finds ready analogues throughout the text which continually asks the reader to accept, without question, extraordinary feats of precognition.

On the matter of the diarist stating that he had placed Kelly's body parts 'all over the room' and of the other 'clues' he had left, Chisholm writes,

No amount of selective manipulation can conceal the fact the author of the diary was certain where Kelly's breasts had been left. The fact that 'he' was wrong in 'his' certainty provides a clear indication that 'his' information was derived from subsequent literature, and 'he' never saw the inside of Miller's Court, except of course from the perspective of the police photographer. This is further borne out in reference to the bloody initials supposedly left as a clue. 'I left it there for the fools but they will never find it.' Again confidence that the fools will never find it is easily arrived at with the benefit of hind sight. 'Left it in *front* for all eyes to see' confirms that our diarist is patently informed by the main police photographer's perspective. The diarist does not claim to have left it in front of 'them' or the 'fools' but only 'in *front* for all eyes to see.' The wall on which these initials were supposed to have been written was at the right side of the room on entry, to the right side of Kelly. The only thing the initials could reasonably be described as 'in *front*' of being the police photographer's lens. It is here that reference to 'for all eyes to see' appears to be relevant. No more than a few witnessed the scene at Miller's Court and do not merit description as '*all eyes*.' The only way such a statement can achieve any justification is if it refers to the widespread dissemination of the main surviving photograph in subsequent literature.

What about motive or motivation? Unless we accept Michael Barrett's admission that it was written to pay the mortgage, there has been no clear definition. It is, however, unsafe to accept evidence proffered by Barrett. His confessions are too volatile. It is meet to remember the sage observation, quoted in another context, by Nicholas Warren, 'Absence of evidence is not evidence of absence.'

I have been told bluntly: anyone today who believes the journal to be truly the Diary of Jack the Ripper must be regarded as a fool.

45

The Diarist

Paul H. Feldman's *Jack the Ripper: The Final Chapter*, published in September 1997, was essentially a blow-by-blow account of his battle to establish an acceptable, which is to say a Maybrickian, provenance for that most questionable and questioned of documents, the putationary Diary of Jack the Ripper.

'If,' writes Feldman, who has filtered a reputed £150,000 into his substantiating investigation, 'this diary was a fake, then it had not been created by an amateur.' And that, in a somewhat belated-seeming *non sequitur*, he informs his reader, 'is why this book is being written nearly four years after the Diary was first made public'.

Mr Feldman argues with the frenzied ingenuity of a convinced barrister determined to get the accused's neck broken. His entire case turns upon the necessity to create a plausibility of source. Cutting a track through the forest of verbiage – some 400 tight-packed pages of it – is daunting. We are required to cope with tangled genealogical lines, legitimate and illegitimate, which have the complexity of a Chinese puzzle.

Back in 1992, Feldman had been a convinced Druittist. He abandoned that position after being informed by Paul Begg that he, Martin Fido and Keith Skinner 'didn't believe that he [Feldman] could continue to finance research into Jack the Ripper or make a documentary without taking into account the diary found in Liverpool'. This led Feldman to Robert Smith of Smith Gryphon and a business deal which committed him, heart, soul, and purse, to the self-appointed mission of proving the Diary to be all that it claimed to be.

By a mixture of perspiration and inspiration, Feldman arrived at an independent resolution of the secret of the diarist's identity. This conclusion he encoded in a cryptic clue of his own invention – 'Spring time for building houses' – May brick. It was on his faith in this hunch of his proving correct that a business deal was struck with Robert Smith of Smith Gryphon, and Feldman set about the hard task of standing up the Diary – although he frankly admitted, 'I could not yet quite believe that this really was Jack the Ripper's Diary, and yet there was something about it that was frighteningly honest.'

Feldman could not but agree that Dr Baxendale's verdict as to the Diary's credentials had not been exactly hopeful. Encouragement came, however, with the reading of the magic words in Dr Nicholas Eastaugh's report to Robert Smith: 'There is nothing in the ink that is inconsistent with the Victorian date.'[14]

But cause for anxiety was not long in surfacing. Recent arguments had been put that Elisabeth Stride was not a Ripper victim, and less recent arguments had held that the 'Dear Boss' letter of 25 September 1888 had been a hoax. Awkwardly, the author of the Diary was claiming responsibility on both of these disputed counts.

The position now stood like this: crime historians had not been able to prove the Diary false from its factual contents; neither had the few preliminary tests to which it had been subjected put it out of court.

It was at this juncture that a knowledgeable business friend suggested to Feldman that he should call in the professionals. He did so. A graphologist, Anna Koren. She came, she saw, she concurred: it was not a fake. 'Impossible' was the word she used. Music to Feldman's ears. She delivered an exceptionally graphic graphological assessment. The person, she said, who wrote the Diary was, she deduced from the handwriting, disturbed, possibly mentally, was beset by sexual problems, exhibited signs of multiple personality, was a hypochondriac, was associated with drugs and alcohol, and, although externally controlled, was internally a volcano.

James Maybrick to a 'T', claimed Feldman, and, buttressed by Ms Koren's grapho-diagnoses, he embarked upon his crusade, pouring money, energy and enthusiasm into the yawning void of doubt.

Paul Feldman made short work of those scientific experts whose conclusions opposed his views. He could but agree that Dr David Baxendale's was – to use Feldman's own word – 'disappointing', and that it 'appeared to deal three body blows – too fast dissolving ink, the presence of nigrosine, the absence of iron'. As for the learned doctor's observations concerning the physical characteristics of the volume in which the Diary was written, Feldman countered that, 'Any of the diary's owners over the last 103 years (assuming it to be genuine) could have stuck a photograph in it, only to remove it later.'

Dr Audrey Giles had opined that ink blots and smudges had been deliberately contrived to add an appearance of age, and had reported, 'I found no evidence that the diary was written by Jack the Ripper.'

Retorted Feldman, 'I found that last remark astonishing. So much so that I wondered if it was a misquote or had been taken out of context. What evidence had the doctor expected to find? Dr Giles had spent no more than a few minutes examining the document.'

Dr Kate Flint's professional pinpointing of anachronistic expressions elicited the following response:

> I was always prepared to accept that any linguistic anomalies would prove this diary a fake. When I learnt that Dr Kate Flint was not a lecturer in English *language* or linguistics, I suspected an error, again, had been made. I reasoned that, if somebody had taken the trouble to forge sixty-three pages of Victorian language, something as glaring as the term 'one-off' would not have been overlooked. Shirley Harrison, however, discovered the term in engineers' records belonging to Trayners of Kent and dated 1860 – twenty-four years[15] before the Ripper murders, and seventy-four years before it found its way into the *Oxford Dictionary*. Harrison also discovered that 'dictionary research revealed that the expressions "topped," (meaning hanged) and "gathering momentum" were in use before late Victorian times.' This diary had already proved several experts wrong. The discovery by Shirley of the use of the phrase 'one-off' proved the *Oxford English Dictionary* wrong.

American specialist opinion is allotted similar short shrift. The Rendell team, for instance. Dr Joe Nickell, member thereof, remarked, 'We determined the diary was an obvious forgery, based primarily on conclusive handwriting evidence.'

'Conclusive?' echoes Feldman, 'We had asked three different experts to give their opinions, and each of them responded differently … What is conclusive is that there are contradictory statements about the date of the document from people within the Rendell team.'

Particularly outraged is Feldman by Nickell's remarking that 'neither James Maybrick nor any other candidate for Ripperhood could have written a diary a century after the events this amateurish fake purports to describe'.

Rejoins Feldman, 'I am not sure I can understand what the sentence means by 'amateurish'. I am not sure I can understand the sentence! It is a syntactical mess. What I take it to mean is that this document is so palpable a modern fake that no one, such as James Maybrick or anyone else who was alive a hundred years ago, at the time of the events that this amateurish fake purports to describe, and thought of because of their contemporaneity as a possible Jack the Ripper, could therefore have written it.'

Roderick McNeil, of Polson, Montana, carried out one of his 'perfected' ion migration tests on the Diary. The normal drill for such tests is the use of a scanning auger microscopy technique to measure the migratory movements of minute particles in the ink, and to calculate from this measurement the length of time that the ink has been on the paper. Such ion migration tests have, Melvin Harris assures us, been in use by document examiners for more than sixty years, but the only man to posit the feasibility of accurate dating by this means is McNeil, who claims that he has been able to refine the testing technique. This means that, whereas ion migration observation has in the past been used simply to determine the age difference, if any, between two specimens of writing which were held to have existed at an identical time under identical conditions, one ought now to be able to put a date to the time when the ink and the paper first came into contact. Once again, Feldman has an answer. 'As it stands now, no one knows whether the difference in humidity and temperature can affect the dating of a document using an ion migration test … There was, however,' he adds, 'something more telling and important.' And he quotes McNeil's statement: 'It is my strong opinion based on the auger-stms results that the document is not new,' adding, 'There is no attempt by Joe Nickell to explain the findings of Rod McNeil. How convenient. It has been said that Kenneth Rendell had "concerns" over Rod McNeil's tests. Then why did he employ him?'[16]

Of Sue Iremonger Feldman was dismissive. 'Sue Iremonger admitted that she had not studied the effects on handwriting of "multiple personality disorder" … As far as I was concerned, this meant that Sue was not qualified to comment on whether the diary was genuine.'

Sharp to the point as ever, Melvin Harris reminds us that multiple personalities are extremely rare phenomena, 'and when they arise they are readily identified by persistent amnesia and by the great diversity of personalities displayed. In the case of James Maybrick there was nothing at all in his behaviour that justifies the idea of multiple personality disorder.'[17] Harris indicts Feldman for avoiding the real issues and denigrating the work of skilled examiners. 'For Sue was not alone. Feldman fails to tell his readers that her diagnosis was matched independently *by other skilled examiners*, like Rendell himself, like Joe Nickell and like Maureen Casey Owens. Each of these examiners pronounced the Diary to be a fake.'

Kenneth Rendell himself originally concluded that the Diary was written in or around 1921, asserts Feldman. Later he changed his mind. 'He moved from 1920 to 1991, despite the evidence of the team of scientists working for him.'

Melvin Harris takes issue with Feldman on this. 'Rendell did not change his mind. His report was the work of five independent examiners. McNeil stood on his own, and the others doubted whether his tests gave any reliable results.'

On 22 April 1993, the *Liverpool Daily Post* had published the fact that the diary said to be that of Jack the Ripper was now alleged to have been written by Jack's *alter ego*, James

Maybrick. This intelligence prompted one Albert Johnson to get in touch with Harold Brough to tell him that if this was indeed the case, then he owned Jack the Ripper's pocket watch. This fascinating information was rapidly relayed to Robert Smith, who swallowed it hook, line and watch chain. He gave Feldman Johnson's telephone number, and Feldman leapt into action. He made contact with Albert Johnson and his brother, Robert, and on 5 July 1993, they, together with their solicitor, Richard Nicholas, brought the watch to Feldman's house in Hertfordshire for his inspection.

One of the first things that Feldman noticed about it was that within an ornate encircling design on the back of the watch were engraved the initials 'J. O.' 'Why 'O'?' asks Feldman. 'Was this not the watch of James Maybrick? If this was a forgery would it not have carried the initials of the man it was supposed to have belonged to?'[18]

Scanning the scratches on the inside of the back of the watch, he could make out the letter 'H' and what appeared to him to be a date, '9/3'. 'That impressed me a great deal. My research had already gone far enough to convince me of the strong possibility that the diary was genuine. If it was, then Maybrick had claimed his first victim when he had gone to Manchester when it was "cold and damp". The next paragraph in the diary said, "Summer is near the warm weather will do me good". The ninth of March was consistent with both statements.'

That inscription, Feldman decided, was evidentially significant. 'While the *Liverpool Daily Post* had revealed the identity of the author of the diary, it had not revealed the contents. It couldn't. Harold Brough had never seen it. If this had been an attempt to cash in on the diary, Albert Johnson would not have scratched the letter H, or "9/3". The conclusion was indisputable – the watch and the diary were linked. There could be no doubt. Either they were both genuine or both forged by the same person.'

The provenance of the watch was provable back to 1983, when the father-in-law of the jeweller who sold it, who was then in business in Lancaster, recalled a little man coming to his shop and selling it to him. Interestingly, Feldman records, 'Robbie (Johnson) seemed convinced that the watch was genuine but the diary was not.' Conversely, Billy Graham, discussing the Maybrick watch, 'thought it was a load of "bollocks". This was the word Robbie Johnson had used to describe the diary.'

Feldman now introduces a very different and most interesting speculative line. 'I had a hunch, as I did with the diary, that the watch was inherited. I did not know whether it had passed through Albert or Valerie's (his wife) lines of descendants. Robbie had already told me he believed the watch was associated to his family and not Valerie's.'

Albert Johnson confided that it might perhaps have been his grandmother on his mother's side, Elizabeth Crawley, who held the clue. 'But his comment indicated that if there was a connection to his grandmother, then his story of buying the watch from the shop did not add up,' as Feldman shrewdly muses.

Feldman set about checking. He spoke personally to the jeweller who allegedly had sold the watch to Albert Johnson, Ronald George Murphy, proprietor of Stewart's, Seaview Road, Wallasey. He also made contact with Timothy Dundas, of The Clock Workshop, 4 Grange Road, West Kirby, Wirral, the horologist who had cleaned the watch in question and put it back into good working order for Mr Murphy.

Dundas remembered the watch as bearing the maker's name, Verity, in black lettering – the same colour as the numerals – on the porcelain dial. He remembered no engravings on either the outer or the inner back of the watch.

The watch in the possession of Albert Johnson does not have a porcelain face, does not have Verity written in black, or any other colour, on the face, and the numerals are not in black.

Albert's watch is gold ... The back is engraved with the letters 'J. O.' The numbers on the face are gold on gold. The name 'Verity' does not appear on the face. But 'Lancaster Verity' is engraved on the workings of the watch. The marking 'No. 1286', which identifies it from any other, is also engraved on the workings.

Inexplicably in Feldman's view, 'almost two years later on 3 July 1996, Timothy Dundas swore an affidavit that the watch pictured in the Liverpool *Daily Post* with Albert Johnson in September 1993, was the watch that he "repaired"'.

In that affidavit Dundas further states, 'Marks on this watch relating to "Jack the Ripper" have been made on the watch since I examined and repaired it in 1992.'

The Assyrian, Harris, comes down like a wolf on the pro-diary fold. The watch? 'An opportunist hoax inspired by the diary' (*The Maybrick Hoax*, p. 33). It is not a man's watch anyway, says Harris. It is a lady's. After the most professional scanning through his watchmaker's *loupe*, Timothy Dundas saw nothing more than the usual previous repairers' marks scratched on the back of the watch.

But what about the much-vaunted antiquity of the Ripper scratchings? 'The alleged dating is *not* a dating of the scratches,' Melvin Harris insists. 'It is just the dating of two ultra-tiny particles of corroded brass found at two points in these scratches. Those particles could have been shed from a well-corroded brass pointer used to make the scratches, [or] deposited by a contaminated cleaning cloth or buff when the markings were polished and "distressed".'

Feldman's answer to the problem of the Janus-faced watch is: 'It is obvious that two watches must exist.' He tells his reader that further research revealed that, prior to the arrival in 1887 of the nursemaid, Alice Yapp – who brought up the Maybrick children and brought down their mother by opening up a letter written by Florence Maybrick to her lover, Alfred Brierley – the Maybricks' first child, James, had been looked after by a previous nursemaid, Emma Parker. Emma, also known as Rosa, had subsequently married a man named John Over. Ever alert to the tiniest confirmatory possibility, Feldman just wondered: could the 'J. O.' refer to him? If so, that would surely supply a sort of connection, somewhat tenuous perhaps, with the Maybrick family.

That still begged the question: how did the watch jump the gap between the Overs and the Johnsons? Mr Feldman duly erected a bridge. A preliminary difficulty was presented by the fact that Albert Johnson had sworn that he had bought the watch from Stewart's. Not one to be beaten, Feldman theorises: Albert might have been 'sworn to secrecy about the watch, I know Albert would never break that promise'.

'So what grim secret is Albert hiding?' asks Harris. 'Feldman declares that Albert is a Maybrick.' Is it that he would fain spare his descendants knowledge not only of their illegitimacy, but of the Glamis-like secret that they are also the dread Ripper's blood kith and kin?

And what is the clinching evidence that Feldman brings of Albert and Robbie's Maybrickean lineage? It is lineage, literally: two lines on two marriage certificates. Albert Johnson's grandmother, Elizabeth Crawley, had married her first husband, Charles Taylor, in 1888. One of the witnesses who signed the certificate was a William McKay. At the wedding, in January 1896, of Bessie Jane Over, whose mother had once worked for the Maybricks,[19] a signatory witness was ... a William McKay. Feldman ordered copies of both certificates. He triumphantly announces: 'The signatures were too similar to be from different people. Here was a link between Albert Johnson's family and the Maybricks.'

Harris ordered copies of both certificates. He is constrained to report, 'They show that the two signatures were written by *two distinct individuals*.'

Another Maybrickian-Johnsonian link which fails to take the strain involves an entry in a Birthday Book once owned by Olga Maybrick Ellison. The entry reads, 'Mrs Johnson. 160 Goodwin Avenue, Bidston.' Feldman finds reason to believe that Albert Johnson's mother had lived in Goodwin Avenue in the 1960s. Harris checked. *Kelly's Directory* for 1960 showed the family living at Number 160 as Johnstone. 'But directories can sometimes err,' he acknowledges, 'so I consulted the Electoral Registers for the 1960s. These confirmed that *Kelly's* was correct. The family at the crucial address was the Johnstone family; David, Margaret and George. No connection whatsoever with the Johnson family (Alfred and Margaret)[20] who once lived at 57 Goodwin Avenue – in 1960.'

Thus, Pelion upon Ossa, does the weight of trivia rise. Feldman confesses, 'My feeling at the end of 1995 was that Albert had inherited the watch from his family. In order to leave the watch to his family, he acquired the "white-faced" Verity watch with "black numbers" from Stewart's the Jeweller's. This gave him a receipt, which could then be associated with the watch he already owned. He would not then need to pass on to his own descendants the burden of being branded illegitimate descendants of the Maybricks.'

There is just one small point to stick in the craw; why, one wonders, if he was concerned about the feelings of his descendants, would Albert have elected to go public about the watch in the first place? No one knew he had it. No one needed to know that he had it. Albert Johnson's reported (by Feldman) refusal of an offer from an unnamed Texas businessman of $40,000 for the watch would seem to scotch any suspicion of a money-making scam.

But there are other puzzling open questions. Did Albert Johnson buy a gold-faced watch from Stewart's – or was it a white one with the calibrations of time etched in black? Did he buy both black *and* gold, knowing that the gold one had been sold to the shop by his mother? Has the 'J. O.' engraved on the all-gold watch's back any connection with John Over, husband of the Maybrick children's nanny? And was that nanny, asks Feldman, James Maybrick's mistress? Did she bear him any children? The permutations of possibility are legion.

Feldman's final words: 'In the period between autumn 1995 and the spring of 1996, I disclosed all my research to Albert Johnson. He no longer denied he was a "Maybrick", but would not alter his story of how he came by the watch. I will not push Albert, there is no point. Something far more important than money prevents Albert from telling everything he knows and, I am sure, always will.'

Albert and Robbie Johnson were far from being the only 'hidden' Maybricks, whom, in the course of his in-depth saturation researches Feldman uncovered, or flushed out. Other principal players who were duly identified by Feldman as wrong-side-of-the-blanket Maybricks included Anne Graham, her father, Billy, and her grandfather, William!

The first thing Feldman did was to order up copies of the birth, marriage, and death certificates of almost every Maybrick recorded since 1837, the year that certificates were first issued. Hundreds of them. No expense spared. 'St Catherine's House gave me a discount!' confides Feldman wryly. The collation of this mass of certificates threw up a perplexing pattern – or, rather, non-pattern – a series of free-floating bearers of the name who defied linking with any previous or contemporaneously existing Maybricks. Feldman noted that the majority of these enigmatic certificates originated in Huntingdon, and he identified in particular the area of Whittlesey, some 4 miles outside Peterborough.

Next, he made it his business to contact Brian Maybrick, who was the grandson of James Maybrick's first cousin, John. Brian and his son, David, were the only living Maybricks at the time, and Brian, one of whose interests was family history, had never heard a single one of the names that Paul Feldman now disclosed to him.

All of this was excellent genealogical work, but the discovery of lost Maybricks proved in the end to have no relevance to the Ripper linkage. More fruitful in Feldman's submission was what he regards as the evidence for a relationship between the Graham family and the main-line Maybricks.

In July 1994, Feldman conducted a key interview with Anne Graham's eighty-year-old father, William (Billy) Graham. He showed him his album of lost-and-found Maybricks and their kin. Mr Graham recognised none of them. Feldman questioned him about his parents. Of his mother, he knew nothing. His father, he said, was William Graham, who had married for the first time on 27 July 1911. His bride had been Rebecca Jones, a widow who already had six children. She was to bear three more – including Billy – to William, before she died, on 9 October 1918, an early victim of the Plague of the Spanish Lady, the great flu pandemic of 1918–19.

Clearly, there was no connection between the Whittlesey Maybricks and the Liverpool Grahams. Even so, Feldman was hopeful that old Billy might be able to tell him why, after her release from prison in 1904, Florence Maybrick had used the name Graham.: A reasonable possibility seems to be because one of her mother's family names was Ingraham. In 1904 she travelled back to America under the name Rose Ingraham, and when, in 1927, she paid a return visit to England, she came as Elizabeth Ingraham.

'Did she?' said Mr Graham. 'She must have had a crush on the old fellow, eh? (laughs) I don't mid you saying that it is … about him, you know – eh?'

Feldman persisted: 'She called herself Mrs Graham.' Which evoked the response: 'Yes. Dirty old git.'

All this seems to have started the slightly rusted wheels of Mr Billy Graham's mind – or imagination – revolving. He was now suggesting that it was possible that his father, William, was Florence Maybrick's son! William was born in 1878 or 1879. Florence would have been sixteen or seventeen when she had him.

Militating against this is the tale Feldman recounts of how, when in 1897, 'Mary H. Krout, a reporter for the Chicago *Inter Ocean*', visited Aylesbury Prison for an exclusive interview with Florence Maybrick, Florence made the following statement: 'I have seen the children's pictures and Henry has grown so tall …' Trevor Christie included this statement in his book, *Etched in Arsenic*, with the name 'Bobo' replacing 'Henry'.[21] Does a mother normally forget the name of her child?

'Another coincidence – or her other son?' asks Feldman. Is Feldman now allotting twin bastards to Florence in 1878–79?

Far more likely, Mary Krout got her note wrong. Incidentally, the home that William Graham was brought up in already had a child by the name of Henry living there.

Feldman had a question for Billy Graham. 'Do you think all this happened in Hartlepool? Do you think your dad was born in Hartlepool? Billy Graham nodded. Then, hesitantly, "Yes, I think so." Then, gathering certainty, "Yes, yes, that's where … He was a Geordie, because they used to talk about him where he worked … He was a bad-tempered old git, because they used to say, bad-tempered old Geordie."'

It was Anne Graham who, all unknowingly, was to supply the missing link with the name Henry. In November, 1994, she suddenly recalled how when she was a child her father used often to take her with him to a tiny graveyard in Croxteth. She couldn't remember the name of the person on the tombstone that he visited, but she could distinctly remember her father saying, 'He's family,' and she volunteered to go back and take a photograph of the stone. The name on it was Henry Stanley Flinn, born 1858, died 7 March 1927. Billy Graham had suggested that his father was Florence Maybrick's illegitimate son. Could this be Billy Graham's real grandfather?

Research revealed that Henry Stanley Flinn had been a very important Liverpool man, the extremely wealthy ship owner of the Dominion Line. He had married in 1890, but had had no children. 'The bloodline had died out and this,' Feldman incautiously appends, 'was probably due to the high rate of syphilis that ran through the family.' Could he have been the father of Florence's child? It was common at that time to name your first son after his father.

Taking, metaphorically, a deep breath, Feldman addresses himself now to the vexed and extremely vexing matter of the handwriting evidence. In somewhat of an understatement, he allows, 'The handwriting in the Diary, *prima facia*, was a problem.' Another problem was that the writer of the Diary had also, rather disconcertingly one might think, implied his authorship of the celebrated 'Dear Boss' letter of 25 September 1888, sent to the Central News Agency.

Feldman has no option but to admit that 'the handwriting of the Diary bore no visible resemblance to the handwriting of this letter either'. But he seeks with sophistry to gain advantage from the bristling discrepancies: 'Our "forger" makes no attempt to copy the handwriting, or even a signature that appears on the will of James Maybrick or the 'Dear Boss' letter. A modern-day forger would know that the handwriting would be the first thing to be compared.'

Feldman sought out James Maybrick's will, lodged at Somerset House. Its penmanship was nothing like that of the Diary. The two signatures attached to the will seemed to be in the same hand as the text and similar to Maybrick's signature on his marriage certificate.

He then discovered a further, previously unknown, specimen of James' handwriting; the holograph presentation inscription in a bible that he had given to his mistress, Sarah Ann Robertson, on her birthday, 2 August 1865. But alas! what was surely a research triumph turned to sand in his mouth. Feldman's own words: 'It only seemed to confuse.'

One would not quarrel with his conclusion that 'the only conclusive thing about the handwriting evidence was that it was *in*conclusive'.

Of the will itself, Mr Feldman had a good deal to say. 'Let me make it perfectly clear,' he insists, 'I do not dispute that the will currently held at Somerset House is the will that was 'proved' to be that of James Maybrick. Nor do I deny that the words contained within that will were once written by James Maybrick.'

What he also insists upon is that 'there are two, and arguably three, versions of the will'. Finally, he says, there is the proved version at Somerset House, purporting to have been written by Maybrick himself in his own hand, and signed by him on 25 April 1889. Secondly, there is the version transcribed by Alexander William MacDougall in 1891.[22] He states that he personally visited Liverpool District Probate Office for the specific purpose of viewing the will, and describes it as being 'in a large and shaky hand and written on blue paper', replying to which assertion, Feldman counters, 'The description, "large and shaky", may be accurate in describing pages of the diary, but most certainly does not describe the will at Somerset House. Neither does MacDougall's description of "blue paper". The most accurate description is "grey". It could be white that has discoloured with age.'

Five years later, in *The Maybrick Case. A Statement of the Case as a Whole. Being Three Letters Addressed to Sir Matthew Ridley, Bart., MP, Secretary of State for the Home Department, etc.*, MacDougall 'altered his description of the will to "large and sprawling", which could be a fair description of the will that now exists'.

So what, Feldman wants to know, is the relevance of all this? 'The will of James Maybrick has not suddenly become a mystery for the convenience of the believers in the diary ... The will was a question of debate in 1891. MacDougall wrote then: "Now that the document, which is described as a will, purporting to have been signed by James Maybrick in the presence of Geo. R. Davidson and Geo. Smith on the 25 April, 1889, is a very suspicious circumstance".'[23] He goes on to refer to Edwin Maybrick's having been seen coming out of James's bedroom on the night of Friday 10 May 1889, the very eve of his death, with some document in his hand which he had taken in for the dying man to sign, and which document Alice Yapp, described by MacDougall as 'knowing and hearing everything', said was a will.

It was Paul Feldman's belief that Michael Maybrick poisoned his brother knowing him to be Jack the Ripper, and fearing that the revelation would destroy *his* position and social standing.

> Michael Maybrick certainly had a motive to ensure that his brother never recovered. Florence was also a problem. Would she talk? If she had not been arrested, she would have retained custody of the children and been able to continue residing in Battlecrease House, free to say whatever she wanted to whomever she wanted whenever she wanted. The children were under the care of Michael, and Florence, even after the trial, would have been aware of the consequences for her children should Michael be ruined through scandal and shame.

Feldman puts a searching question. If the will dated 25 April 1889 was the only will written and signed by James Maybrick, then what were the brothers attempting to get him to sign on 10 May 1889? Moreover, what was the will that Mrs Briggs was searching for on 12 May, the day after James Maybrick died?[24]

Scrutinising both versions of the will – that at Somerset House and that published by MacDougall in his *Treatise* – Feldman found himself particularly alerted by the misspelling in the Somerset House version of James's daughter's name, Gladys Evelyn, as *Eveleyn*.

'More curious, however, was MacDougall's claim that an "Affidavit of due execution" was filed on 29 July 1889. Such an affidavit is required when a will is rejected by probate. All the newspapers on 30 July confirmed that such an affidavit had been filed the previous day. The will currently at Somerset House bears no mention of such an affidavit.'

Feldman queried this with the District Probate Registrar, Mr C. W. Fox, whose best answer was, 'I agree it is strange that the copy will reproduced in the *Liverpool Echo* refers to an affidavit of due execution, whereas the copies from the Principal Registry do not.'

Most revealing in MacDougall's version, says Feldman, is the wording of the attestation clause: 'Signed by the testator in the presence of us who, at his request and in the presence of each other, have hereunto affixed our names as witnesses, Geo. R. Davidson, Geo. Smith.'

'The words "in his presence" should follow "request". They do not. Such a mistake would cause probate to be rejected. Such a mistake would cause an "affidavit of due execution" to be filed. There was no mistake by the newspaper or MacDougall.'

A possible explanation was provided to Feldman by Mr Clive Dyal, Record Keeper at Somerset House. 'A will was rejected by probate and the trustees were informed that, unless another will was found, the testator (James Maybrick) would have died intestate.'[25] Another will was 'found', and together with an 'affidavit of due execution' was filed with the 'rejected' version at the Liverpool District Probate Register Office. After fifty years, only the 'proved' will would have been sent to Somerset House, all other documents being destroyed.

Melvin Harris offers an alternative explanation. MacDougall transcribed the will incorrectly from the newspapers, which, in turn, had also got the information wrong. But, objects Feldman, MacDougall's version differs from those of the newspapers.

In his thirty-seven-page document prepared for circulation and exposure on the internet, *The Maybrick Hoax*, Harris points out a number of flaws in Feldman's argument regarding

James Maybrick's will. 'This will was written on tough, light blue, legal paper. One sheet, measuring 11 inches by 17 inches, was folded once to create the double-sided pages. Thus, since everything of importance is on one document, there can be no excuse for overlooking any of the wording. Yet the text shown in Feldman only covers the writing on two of these pages.' The contents of the crucial back page are not presented. 'The missing page proves that the will was passed at Liverpool on 29 July, 1889, without challenge. It is the one and only original will.' (*Hoax*, p. 23)

Apart from noting the absence in *The Final Chapter* of the *complete* text of Maybrick's will, Harris is critical of the fact that there is no mention of the very existence, never mind the text, of a certified copy of what he strongly maintains was Maybrick's one and only and proved will. 'This copy faithfully records every detail shown on the handwritten original, including all oddities of punctuation and capitalisation and ampersands. It is extra proof that this will is the very document endorsed on 29 July.' (*Hoax*, p. 23)

The text of the newspaper reports that appeared on 30 July 1889, had been, says Harris, '*read out* to waiting reporters. So their copies lack the visual accuracy of the Certified Copy, but they *independently* confirm the text of the will now at Somerset House. They also provide full proof that the MacDougall version of the will is nothing but a grossly faulty version of these newspaper reports.'

Harris emphasises the unreliability of MacDougall transcriptions. 'MacDougall is so faulty that each time he quotes from *his own* mangled version of the will he gives a *different* rendering.'

Harris' clinching argument is 'the fact that the holograph will carries a red ink endorsement which reads: "Affidavit of search filed. T. E. Paget District Registrar," this confirms that, after search, no other will or codicil was found. Thus there were no other versions in existence and nothing in conflict with the will signed on 25 April, 1889.' (*Hoax*, p. 24)

To countenance the possibility of two wills having been taken to Grant is to believe in something that would be legally impossible.

Picking up Feldman's question about the Sunday morning search at Battlecrease House on 12 May 1889, Harris writes, 'Although there was a temporary panic in the Maybrick house when the will could not be located, no other will was ever signed. And the original of 25 April, was eventually found, safe *in a sealed envelope*. It was afterwards handed to the coroner on 28 May 1889, and read by him and by lawyers.'

Considering the whole matter in somewhat closer focus in *The Maybrick Will – The Crucial Key to a Shabby Hoax*, a five-page document, also prepared for circulation and display on the internet, Melvin Harris sets out the genesis of the disputed will and the course of its subsequent treatment.

On 25 April 1889, James Maybrick wrote out a will. He was in good health at that time and in his office; Paul Feldman's claim that he was at home and ill in bed is contradicted by the trial evidence. No executors were named in that will, so on his death it could not be dealt with by straightforward probate. Since the two brothers, Thomas and Michael, were named in the will as trustees, they applied for a Grant of Administration. This would give them the powers of Universal Legatees in Trust. On 29 July 1889, that will of April was endorsed on the back with the details of the Grant of Administration. Thus, the two-page will carried two distinct documents,[26] written at different times. It also carried the official embossed stamp of the High Court; it carried the signature (in red ink) of the District Registrar, T. E. Paget, and his endorsement which stated: 'Affidavit of search filed'; in other words, no document in conflict with the will had been discovered or was known about.

When the Grant of Administration was made, a certified copy of this will was made as well and its text included the details of the Grant as shown on the rear of the original. It was stamped by the Registry on its embossing machine; it was further stamped twice with the personal hand-stamp of Registrar Paget and then initialled by him.

On 30 July 1889, the day after the Grant of Administration, both the *Liverpool Mercury* and the *Liverpool Post* printed a verbatim account of the text of the will that went to Grant on the previous day. The text of the newspaper reports agreed exactly[27] with the text of the will at Somerset House and its certified copy.

Harris proceeds now to his refutationary argument.

Start from the unchallengeable fact that the clerk making the certified copy supplied a text that agrees in every way with the holograph will. Next accept that the newspaper text is based on the holograph will, and that it contains all the so-called 'missing words' that Feldman, Robert Smith, and Shirley Harrison have been talking about.[28] It is also the sole source for some few extraneous words about the Affidavit of due execution.

Where does MacDougall's text with its missing words come from? His book text is based on this newspaper text and nothing else. His text even repeats the one spelling error[29] found in the newspaper. It also picks up the 'Affidavit' words which can be found nowhere else. But all the manifold errors are his, or an assistant's; they do not represent the text of any will that ever existed. Indeed, in his 'Notice to the Reader' MacDougall actually states that his text is based on newspaper reports. The fact that MacDougall saw the will at a later date is significant only in the sense that it makes his neglect even more serious.

We now have to pose two questions; questions avoided by all those who have misused the MacDougall text.

Question A. They pretend that MacDougall saw a will different from the extant one. Since the text of the extant one was vouched for on 29 July 1889, their plea means that there had to be two versions of this will in open, side-by-side, existence in 1889. But MacDougall does not say this at any time, and he is the sort of man who would have jumped at the chance to make capital out of such a discovery. Neither does anyone else around at the time, whether pro- or anti-Florence, mention such a fantastic anomaly. Is it, as it would appear, Paul Feldman alone who is responsible for this fiction?

Question B. The MacDougall text shows the solicitors' section of 29 July 1889, as integral with the Maybrick section (the holograph text of the will) of 25 April 1889. And this is, of course, how it should be, and how it is on the Somerset House holograph and its certified copy. How is it possible then, logically and legally, for two different wills disposing of exactly the same property, to have been passed for Grant on the same day, to the same Universal Legatee in Trust, and with each of these differing wills endorsed by solicitors Layton, Steel, and Springman, as the very one passed?

This brings Mr Harris to the consideration of Feldman's reference to the Affidavit of due execution and his suspicion because he found that 'the will currently at Somerset House bears no mention of such an affidavit'.

Harris comments that the expectation of finding a reference to such an affidavit arises out of a misunderstanding, or misinterpretation, of 'a snippet of information first found in the newspaper reports of 30 July 1889'. What happened, he goes on to explain, is that the clerk reading out the will to the newspaper reporters was simply providing them with the name of the official supervising the Grant when he told them, 'Affidavit of execution filed by T. E. Paget, District Registrar.'

In fact, those words actually 'negate the very idea that the will had anything attached to it. They state specifically that the affidavit was filed. Just so; all the affidavits involved with this will, together with the Bond, were filed in the Registry.[30] This was standard practice and a legal requirement. In brief, everything on public record does no more than allude to the standard filing procedures and confirms that the will never had any other papers attached to it, since no such attachments were ever needed.'

To be fair, confusion was further confounded by the unfortunate circumstance that in the newspaper reports the statement regarding the Affidavit of due execution was not distinctly separated, as it should have been, from the wording of the Granting statement.

One further point in connection with the will. James Maybrick was insured for £5,000 in two policies with the Mutual Reserve Fund Life Association of New York. One of the policies was for £3,000 and the other for £2,000, this last being drawn in favour of his wife. 'The policy for £2,000 is mentioned in the will at Somerset House. The policy for £3,000 is not,' says Feldman, adding, 'The largest policy of all would not have been overlooked by James Maybrick.'

Melvin Harris corrects:

> The policy for £3,000 is not mentioned because it doesn't need to be mentioned. His will states 'I leave and bequeath all my worldly possessions, of whatever kind or description. Including … Life Insurances … in trust with my brothers …' That wording covers each and every Life Insurance policy left in trust. So he was free to take out a score or more of extra policies without having to give details of any of them. The two policies made out in his wife's name were mentioned only because they were the two things specifically left to her.

Setting the controverted will aside, it was of course fundamental to the acceptance of the Diary as genuine that one should also accept as genuine its author's claim that he had sent letters signed 'Jack the Ripper' – that to include the pioneering 'Dear Boss' epistle of 25 September 1889.

On this issue, Paul Feldman, guard lowered, steps forthright into the bright light of the square ring – 'If the letters were a hoax then the diary must be a hoax as well,' he unambiguously allows. It is, however, his contention that the generally accepted first letter to be signed 'Jack the Ripper' – that of 25 September – was not the first to bear that signature. Citing Edwin T. Woodhall's *Jack the Ripper or When London Walked in Terror* (1937), he quotes,

> After his third victim's death, (that of Annie Chapman on 9 September 1888),[31] the public looked upon these crimes as little short of an uncanny kind of fiendish miracle. It is from this time, soon after September the ninth, that these crimes came to be known as the work of one named 'Jack the Ripper', due once more to the influence of the Press in giving this sinister title extensive publicity. During the brief interval between the fourth (Elisabeth Stride, 30 September) and fifth (Catherine Eddowes, 30 September–1 October) murders anonymous communications began to trickle in to some sections of the Press and police. Many, of course, were useless and simply the work of idle and stupid people. But one particular postcard, written in red ink and received by some Press head office was promptly seized on and at once widely re-quoted by other sensational sections of the Press as the man the police were looking for high and low. The postcard in question was a threat and written in grim poetic fashion as follows:

'I'm not an alien maniac,
Nor yet a foreign tripper;
I'm just your jolly, lively friend,
Yours truly – "Jack the Ripper."

P.S. – Look out next time. I'm doing the job more perfect.'

Authentic or otherwise, from this moment that name of the particular anonymous postcard writer caught on to the public imagination. (Woodhall. pp. 23–24)

Feldman tell us, 'Oddly enough there is a different version of the ditty quoted in the memoirs of Sir Melville Macnaghten:

I'm not a butcher, I'm not a Yid,
Nor yet a foreign Skipper,
But I'm your own light-hearted friend,
Yours truly, Jack the Ripper.

Macnaghten does not identify any date as to the receipt by the police of this postcard with its doggerel. If, indeed, that actually was the source from which he was quoting. Macnaghten joined the Metropolitan Police on 1 June 1889. He refers to the verse as 'one of the first documents which I perused at Scotland Yard, for at that time the police postbag bulged large with hundreds of anonymous communications on the subject of the East End tragedies'. Note the phrase '*at that time*', that is *circa* June 1889. Did 'the above queer verse', as Sir Melville calls it, reach Scotland Yard in June 1889's bulging police postbag? If so, the verse can hardly have pre-empted the letter of September 1888 as the source of the Whitechapel murderer's trade name. Macnaghten published his verse twenty-three years before Woodhall came out with his variant version. I would suggest that it is entirely possible that Woodhall, imperfectly recollecting the original verse, valiantly improvised the first, second, and third lines, and assigned a vague and invented date to the composition.

Feldman won't have that. 'Why were there two versions?' he persists. 'Had the author of the diary singled out the 25 September letter as the first communication signed Jack the Ripper? Was the postcard reproduced by Woodhall the one piece of evidence that proved the diary a forgery?' He is playing tongue-in-cheek Devil's advocate. Three lines later he is pointing enthusiastically to 'an important claim made in the diary where the author wrote: "Michael would be proud of my funny little rhyme ... " This was written just after the diarist's recollection of the Annie Chapman murder, precisely where Woodhall's reference suggested one would find it! So our diarist was aware of the earlier communication.'

I think that Mr Feldman is taking liberties here. Read again the Woodhall passage. He states that during the brief interval between, by his calculations, the fourth and fifth murders – those of Stride and Eddowes – anonymous communications began to drift in. That interval would have been brief indeed; about forty-four minutes! I suspect that the period to which Woodhall may have intended to allude was the interval between the murders of Annie Chapman and Elisabeth Stride, a span of twenty-two days, within which, incidentally, Tuesday 25 September would fall.

Harris proclaims unusually loudly,

I warned Feldman that Woodhall himself was a rogue who altered the text of documents to suit himself; that he cared little for the truth and was nothing more than a tall-story merchant. That I would endorse *anything* written by that man is not only incredible but a blatant lie ... Anyone who believed in Woodhall's postcard yarn could rightly be judged as a wholly incompetent investigator and a worthless historian. Because *this postcard never existed*. Woodhall is claiming that his postcard was noted and quoted in the press of the day, yet he doesn't name a single paper that featured it. Where are the press cuttings of the time that quote this poem? There are none.

Feldman makes the further point that

at the same time as he was penning his recollections of the double event, the diarist decided to 'include my funny little rhyme that will convince them that it is the truth I tell'. This was extraordinary. In 108 years of Ripper books, not one author had ever commented on the fact that there were two versions of this poem, let alone attempt to explain why. Only the diary told us. Only the diary gave the answer. Not only were two versions of the rhyme sent, but the entries in the diary were precisely where the obscure historical evidence indicated that they should be.

Melvin Harris cannot let all this go unchallenged. Feldman had written, 'Throughout the diary the author resents the ability of Michael to compose verse.' Says Harris,

His (James') brother Michael never wrote verse or lyrics. Yes, he was a famous, popular and prolific light composer of the day, but the lyrics of all the many songs associated with his name were written by other people. But the fakers didn't know this. In their ignorance they invented the idea of this rivalry on James Maybrick's part – 'If Michael can succeed in rhyming verse then I can do better, a great deal better he shall not outdo me.' This invention allowed them to introduce verse into the diary. They felt the need to do this because they were under the illusion that the Ripper had taunted in verse.

It has been suggested by many authors that the 'Dear Boss' letter of 25 September, and the 'Saucy Jacky' postcard of 1 October 1888, which was posted on the same day as that on which the 25 September letter was published, were both hoaxes, and that anyone could have sent that postcard, having simply copied the style and content of the letter. No, says Feldman with customary vehemence, no, this could not have been an imitative hoax. Why? Nothing simpler. Because a facsimile of the 'Dear Boss' letter was not published until 3 October; yet the handwriting matched that of the letter. 'Well it would, wouldn't it, if the same journalistic joker wrote both.'

For his own peculiar reasons Feldman needs to establish that the letter condemned by Robert Anderson as a fake was *not* the 'Dear Boss' communication, but the Lusk letter. To this end, he calls into evidence the testimony of Bill Waddell, former curator of the Black Museum. '(He) told me that to the best of his knowledge the 25 September letter was never in the Black Museum. Even the facsimile was not put there until 1921, when the museum was refurbished.'

Robert Anderson, in 'The Lighter Side of My Official Life', a series of articles in *Blackwood's Magazine*, wrote in March 1910, 'I will only add that the "Jack the Ripper" letter which is preserved in the Police Museum at Scotland Yard is the creation of an enterprising journalist.'

Feldman argues that 'the 25 September letter and "Saucy Jacky" postcard sent to the Central News may have, over the years, become confused with another letter paired with another postcard'. He is referring to the Lusk letter, card and kidney. He avers that it was the Lusk letter that Sir Henry Smith was defending against Anderson's attack. Smith wrote, 'A facsimile of the writing of the purloiner of the kidney … had appeared in an evening paper … and I instantly laid the letter before him (Sir James Fraser).'[32]

'It is obvious,' opines Feldman, 'that Smith (despite his arrogant claim that he knew more about the Ripper than any living man), writing twenty-two years after the murders, relying on memory alone, mistakenly lumped together the "purloiner" of the "Lusk" kidney and the facsimile of the letter and postcard sent to Central News. He must have been confusing the "Lusk letter" with that of 25 September, since the "Lusk letter" was never published in facsimile form. Nevertheless, it is clear that Smith believed that the kidney, and therefore the "Lusk letter", were sent by the Ripper.'

There follows a most convoluted piece of sophistry. Feldman informs his reader that after Smith published his book,[33] Anderson defended himself against Smith's attack. He refuted Smith's contention that the 'Dear Boss' letter was not a hoax. 'Since Smith argued for the "Lusk letter" it must have been the "Lusk letter" Anderson argued against, and not the 25 September letter. If Anderson had been referring to the 25 September letter when stating it was the work of a journalist, he would have been, in effect, criticising his own officers for having the facsimiles made and circulated.'

Not only Smith, but also Inspector Dew, Feldman would have us believe, suffered from confusion.

> In his memoirs,[34] Walter Dew, a former Detective Constable in H Division who worked on the Ripper case, reproduced the text of the 25 September letter in his chapter on the Ripper. He then, curiously, claimed: 'The man who wrote that letter was illiterate.' This must have been very confusing for his readers, since they could see from the text that it was not 'illiterate', that it was written in a neat hand and employed reasonably good grammar. We might expect an illiterate to misspell words … But no, there was not one spelling mistake. Was Walter Dew confused? Clearly this letter was not that of an illiterate. The 'Lusk letter' certainly was. Had Dew's publisher made the error of publishing the letter that was in the Black Museum then (1939)?

Having, to his own satisfaction at least, 'established the likelihood that the letter dated 25 September 1888, signed "Jack the Ripper" was indeed sent by the Whitechapel murderer,' Feldman felt that the letter files of both the Metropolitan and the City Police needed careful scrutiny. From out of this scrutiny emerged a letter 'which was apparently written by the author of the letter dated 25 September,' which Feldman was to label as 'beyond all reasonable doubt … sent by Jack the Ripper'. Dated 5 October 1888, it was addressed 'Dear Friend', and began: 'In the name of God hear me I swear I did not kill the female whose body was found at Whitehall.' This reference was to the torso found on 2 October, in the foundations of the Scotland Yard building. The letter continues:

> If she was an honest woman I will hunt down and destroy her murderer. If she was a whore God will bless the hand that slew her, for the woman of Moab and Median shall die and their blood shall mingle with the dust. I never harm any others or the Divine power that protects and helps me in my grand work would quit forever. Do as I do and the light of my glory shall shine upon you. I must get to work tomorrow treble event this time yes yes three must be ripped will send you a bit of face by post I promise this dear old Boss. The police now reckon my work a *practical* joke well well Jacky's a very *practical* joker ha ha ha. Keep this back till three are wiped out and you can show the cold meat.

Feldman finds this convincing. 'If you were a hoaxer and the newspapers had written that Jack the Ripper had killed again, then such a hoaxer would have claimed ownership [*sic*] of that murder. The police had never considered this crime to be the work of Jack the Ripper but a hoaxer could not have known that. Only two people would have known that this murder was the work of a different hand: Jack the Ripper and the murderer of the Whitehall victim!'

I find it difficult to believe that Mr Feldman can offer such an argument as a serious proposition.

Then there is the persuasion presented by the letter, the existence of which is here, in Mr Feldman's pages, for the first time revealed. Its provenance, dating back to late 1908, is that it is said to have been serendipitously discovered by a Mr Peter McClelland at the Public Record Office. The story is that, permitted access to the original Home Office Ripper files, he gently opened with his thumbnail a report folder, the edges of which had become stuck together over the years, and out dropped this letter. Mr McClelland himself has also dropped out since the event and has proved impossible to trace.

However, the serendipitous letter remains. It is dated 17 September 1888, and reads,

Dear Boss,
So now they say *I am a Yid* when will they lern Dear old Boss? You an me know the truth dont we, Lusk can look forever hell never find me but I am rite under his nose, all the time. I watch them looking for me an it gives me fits ha ha I love my work so I shant stop until I get buckled *and even then* watch out for your old pal Jacky.
Catch me if you can
Jack the Ripper
Sorry about the blood still messy from the last one. What a pretty necklace I gave her.

Feldman thinks that this letter 'furnishes the pedigree for the "Lusk letter", how it came to be written and who wrote it. A journalist looking at it could easily have copied it both in style and content.' He also believes that the 17 September letter and that of 25 September must both have been sent by the same person. 'Why? Because apart from the police and a few people at Central News no one knew about the expression "Dear Boss" or the name "Jack the Ripper" until the 25 September letter was first published on 1 October. No one, that is, except the journalists who copied it to create the "Lusk letter". And of course the man who sent it – Jack the Ripper.'

When looking at the alleged Ripper-written letters Feldman and the members of his research team focused, he tells us, upon those letters which were initialled by Chief Inspector Swanson, and, however Feldman chooses to interpret the contents of these letters and, whatever we may decide regarding those interpretations, what surely must count to his credit is the fact that he observed that 'Swanson initialled' letters existed as a distinguishing category. *Honor ad illum qui honorem meret.*

One of these letters Feldman found especially suggestive. Dated 8 October 1888, headed Galashiels, addressed 'Dear Boss', it brought tidings of the Ripper's being on the road to the tweed factories, and promised to let the Innerleithen Constabulary know when he was about to start his 'nice Little game'. With James Maybrick well in the forefront of his mind, Feldman writes, 'Galashiels and Innerleithen lie close together in the Scottish borders. Their main industry in the 1880s was tweed weaving. Not tweed made exclusively from wool, such as Harris tweed, but a cheaper version made from a mixture of wool and cotton. Cotton merchants ... would have sound business reasons for visiting the area.'

There are several further matters which require comment.

There is the problem of Mary Jane Kelly's heart. Feldman asks, 'Was the heart taken away by the murderer?' Then admits, 'If it was, then our diary was a fake – "I took none of it away with me."'[35] He then temporises: 'Whether the heart was removed from the body, found by the doctors and put back or removed by the murderer, who took it away with him, was not made clear by Bond, who merely stated that it was absent from the pericardium …'

Melvin Harris is curt about this. 'The diary says of Mary Kelly "no heart no heart" and Feldman puzzles over this, but the fakers have simply picked up the words "He cut out her heart …"from Underwood page 75.'

We move next to Feldman's fruitful contemplation of the official police list of Catherine Eddowes' clothes and possessions. He alights on the item '1 Tin Match Box, empty'. And comments,

> Our diarist had written, 'damn it the tin box was empty.' Not only was the complete police list never published at the time, but the existence of this list was not even known about until Donald Rumbelow and Martin Fido published it in their books in 1987. The seven words that our diarist wrote meant that the diary either had to be a modern forgery or we were looking at a document that nobody ever felt would be discovered, the emotions and words written by the perpetrator of the Whitechapel murders … The anger displayed by the author of the diary when discovering that the tin box was empty fascinated me. Not only had we discovered a new anomaly in Ripperology, but I believe our diarist was suggesting a reason for it. Did Abberline keep the box back because he knew it belonged to the Ripper? Did that box show traces of drugs?

Harris' observations on the foregoing: 'Fido's page 70[36] printed the police list of Eddowes' belongings and this provided our fakers with some telling references. These were items found in the police list and Feldman creates a little drama around one item: the empty tin matchbox. There *is* no mystery. If the diary had used the words: "Chamber pots, rubber, lunatics for the use of", you would at once have recognised the old military inventory style. And "tin match box, empty" is written in that style because it is nothing but a quote from the police list, which was not in print until 1987.'

Harris finds Feldman creating another mystery. Feldman writes, 'Another significant item on the published list was "the red leather cigarette case". It seems hardly likely that a woman in penury who, that very morning, pawned her boyfriend's boots, would own a leather cigarette case with metal fittings.' Harris goes on to explain, 'In 1888 such cases, with nickel fittings, were a very cheap market line, They were of little value to start with, but when the leather grew scuffed and stained with use, they would hardly be worth a farthing.'

Feldman again: 'At 12.45 on the morning after the double event, a policeman on his beat found a knife lying in Mr Christmas's shop doorway in Whitechapel Road, a few hundred yards from Stride's murder,' recounts Feldman.

> The knife was short – about 2 inches long according to the *Evening News*, reporting it the following day, 1 October – and at Stride's inquest Dr Bagster Phillips claimed that this knife could have killed Stride … My research on this knife led to corrections made in *The Jack the Ripper A to Z*. The authors had previously reported that this knife was found two days *before* the night of the double event. This confusion, among other doubts, had led modern Ripper commentators to question whether Elizabeth Stride had been a victim of the Whitechapel murderer. The police in charge of the investigation at the time seemed to be in no doubt whatsoever. Once again, this extraordinary diary had made us think. The diarist made no attempt to conform with the latest

theories. He even made reference to "the whores knife". The diarist knew Stride was a Ripper victim. Would a forger have flown in the face of modern thinking, putting his work at risk, by boldly accepting Stride as a victim? I think not.

Harris rejoins: 'The "whores knife" of the diary has nothing to do with Stride; it refers to Eddowes' "White Handle Table Knife" as listed by the police. Their list runs in this order: Knife; cigarette case; matchbox; The fakers chose those items, along with the "sugar and tea", for no other reason than to create their crude rhymes.'

Finally, Feldman makes reference to the existence of Mrs Maybrick's diary. 'The diary, which was in three small volumes, tied together with a blue silken cord, was taken by a gentleman[37] who declined to give his name to Messrs Triscler and Co., the Ludgate Circus publishers. He said that he was a relative of the Maybrick family, and had found the books in a box of Mrs Maybrick's at Battlecrease House.' This diary was first heard of in September 1889. The manager of Triscler's, who examined it and was of the opinion that it was genuine, noted that the writing in each of the three books, although said to be that of the same person, was different. The first book contained Mrs Maybrick's childhood reminiscences, the second those of her girlhood, and the third those of her married life. Unable himself to make an offer in the absence of the head of the firm, the manager suggested that it might be worthwhile approaching Mr Stuart Cumberland, editor and proprietor of the *Mirror* newspaper.

Feldman quotes a letter from Liverpool addressed to Mr Cumberland:

Sir,

  You call yourself a thought-reader and claim to know all about the blood-thirsty scoundrel 'Jack the Ripper'; but up to the present I have seen no sign from you respecting the innocent woman who lies in agonised suspense in Walton gaol … You can have visions about the Whitechapel murderer, but poor Mrs Maybrick in your idea is apparently unworthy of a dream. It ought all to be clear to you, but perhaps you don't want it to be so…

  A lover of justice.

'A letter from Liverpool connecting Florence Maybrick with Jack the Ripper?' he trumpets. 'Surely this means that someone at the time knew the truth about James? That person was obviously very frustrated that no one else could work it out – "It ought all to be clear to you …"'

Harris, in replying to this intemperate speculation, brings his wide knowledge of hoaxes and hoax masters and mistresses to bear. Stuart Cumberland, he informs us,

was much more than an editor. His real name was Charles Garner, and under that name he had worked with the great showman W. Irving Bishop, 'The World's Most Eminent Mind-Reader.' From Bishop he learned the art of 'contact mind-reading', a technique that allows the expert to find hidden objects, and solve all manner of baffling problems. And he then perfected one of Bishop's acts which linked magic with crime; this was the celebrated Murder Game, which was acted out in theatres and large private houses. In his absence an imaginary murder would be staged. On his return to the scene of the 'crime', he would unfailingly find the victim, the killer, and the hidden murder weapon, even when blindfolded. These amazing feats, coupled with his other uncanny acts, skills that made him into a formidable flesh-and-blood lie-detector, led many people to imagine that he was a clairvoyant and utilised psychic powers. This begot the idea that he could act as a psychic detective, and that is why the correspondent from Liverpool waxed so indignant. That irate Liverpudlian was dismayed because Cumberland would not take time to use his special psychic methods to discover the truth about the Maybrick murder case.

One of a number of crucial questions posited in the Diary's kite-flying context is – was Florence Maybrick even in England in the 1877–1879 period? To this end, Feldman offers an article that he unearthed from the *Liverpool Echo* of 9 August 1889. In it is stated that the residents of the village of Kempsey, near Worcester, 'recollect that twenty years ago, that is *c.* 1869, Mrs Maybrick, then a little girl (she would have been seven or eight years of age) lived there at "The Vineyards" with her sister[38] and mother, Madam Du Barry. After a residence of about two years, they suddenly left.'[39]

Very well, let us accept that Florence was in England *circa* 1869, that certainly does not lend credence to the idea that eight or nine years later she was in Hartlepool dallying with twenty-year-old Henry Flinn – the meanderings of an eighty-year-old man dying of cancer apart, there is really nothing to substantiate this, although Feldman tries hard ... 'An affidavit of John Baillie Knight',[40] dated 17 August 1889, states, 'I first met the Prisoner about two years previous to her marriage in or about the year 1879 at the house of my Aunts, the Misses Baillie.' They lived in London.

Further support came from Trevor Christie's private notes, which were obtained from Wyoming University. He wrote, 'The Baroness and her children came to the US in 1879 to settle the Chandler estate.' Christie's source was the *New York Times*, dated 9 August 1889. The family had indeed arrived from Liverpool that month. Christie also produced a timetable of Florence's movements. It showed that she had been living in England in April, 1879. This would appear to be confirmed by Bernard Ryan, in the book, *The Poisoned Life of Mrs Maybrick*, which he wrote in collaboration with Sir Michael Havers (William Kimber, London, 1977.).

Emboldened, Feldman demands, 'Was Henry Stanley Flinn the father of Florence's child, born to her in 1879?' We have absolutely no evidence of the birth of any such child.

He asks, 'Was his (Flinn's) death in 1927 the reason that Florence came to England?' Again, not a jot or tittle of evidence to suggest so.

Finally, 'Could Florence have used her influence with Henry to get James' cousin a job?'[41] A rhetorical question, surely? Pure arm-chancing.

Feldman is candid: 'We may never know for sure the answers to the questions I've been posing.'

Notwithstanding, by page 309 Feldman can bring himself to write, 'Florence, we have learnt, had relationships with several men.' Fair enough. There is no reason to doubt the truth of this statement. Though, equally, there is no reason to accept it. But he continues: 'There was an illegitimate child at the tender age of sixteen.' This second sentence is disgraceful. Pure – impure – speculation has in the course of the turning pages crystallised into fact! We have been offered absolutely no proof of any kind that the young Florence ever gave birth to a child. All that tittle-tattle about William Graham being Florence's son by Henry Flinn, Billy Graham being her grandson, and Anne Graham or Barrett being her great-granddaughter is total speculation – and ill-witnessed, ill-informed, not very convincing, speculation at that.

Feldman knew that James Maybrick had had at least five illegitimate children, but nobody had ever suggested in the last hundred and more years that James's wife had given birth prior to her marriage, and he thought it significant that 'the Maybrick one', 'she', and 'dirty old cow' were variant ways in which Billy Graham would refer to her.

Changing tack, trying to discover anything further that he could about the history of the Diary, Feldman remarked, 'So Edith[42] never told you where this [the Diary] came from when she gave it to you?' 'No,' said Billy, adding that she had said something about his ganny (granny).

Feldman is able to supply some information about Billy Graham's 'ganny', Elizabeth Formby. She had, according to her grandson, run a laundry at No. 10 Peel Street, near the Dingle, whither Battlecrease House used to send the household washing to be done. Anne Graham had the impression that Elizabeth Formby was the local 'fence', and that when servants wanted to steal items they would get them out of the house by wrapping them up in the washing. Was James Maybrick's diary perhaps smuggled out and into Ganny Formby's hands by this route? Who in Battlecrease House would have secreted it in the dirty washing? Alice Yapp perhaps?[43] Possibly Alice Yapp, Florence's enemy, who may, suggests Feldman, also have been James's on-the-premises mistress, and, according to Billy Graham, Elizabeth Formby's close friend, who accompanied Yapp to the Maybrick trial. Providing convenient linkage, Billy also claims that it was Elizabeth Formby who gave him the Diary.

Billy joined the Army in 1933, and spent the next ten years serving abroad. He came back to England in 1943, and that, he says, is when he first saw the Diary. He spoke of Granny Formby's having two sisters – or perhaps stepsisters – who 'belonged to shipping owners, the Flynns [*sic*] ... They used to come down [to visit] – they lived over in Birkenhead in a place called the Woodlands. They had their own carriages – a horse and carriage, you know – and they used to come over in that. They used to leave her a few shillings before they left and now and again they would write to her.'

Billy's sister, Mary Graham, confirmed that she knew of the Flynns, but was unable to tell where they fitted into the family tree. She had, in fact, worked for one of the Flynn sisters, Mrs Elizabeth Borrows, who owned a tobacconist's shop. She was an illegitimate Flinn. The informant on her death certificate was William Graham, described as 'cousin'. There were legitimate Flinns who lived in Birkenhead, and there were Flinns who owned auction rooms in nearby Rock Ferry.

Approaching the last pages of his long apologia for, and battle to establish the provenance of, Diary and diarist, Paul Feldman demands, 'If the Diary is a fake, tell me how it was done. Tell me who did it. Tell me when. Where did the information *within* the document come from?

Melvin Harris answers: 'There is nothing factual in the diary text that is new. Every incident in it was derived from writings present in popular form years before the diary surfaced. Indeed, all the Ripper material was present in two books.'[44]

As to the how, who, when of the Diary, that is for each reader to discover and decide for himself, searching diligently between the lines.

To sum up, then.

What Paul Feldman's book is: an heroic expenditure of time, money and energy.

What Paul Feldman's book is not: a safe and satisfactory conviction of James Maybrick as the Ripper.

PART 6
DREADS AND DROLLS:
A MEANINGFUL MISCELLANY

46

The Knight's Tale

The year 1976 – on the eve of which year the survey of the field of blood provided by the first edition of my *Casebook* came to a close – was to mark a kind of watershed, a dirty-water shed some would say, in the progress of serious Ripper studies. It heralded the reinforcement of the grotesque royal line, or tangent, canard.

The publication in the July of Stephen Knight's *Jack the Ripper: The Final Solution* was destined to influence detrimentally the course of Ripper research for the succeeding decade, not only leading directly to a *cul-de-sac* series of nonsense publications, but also, because of the book's immense, world-spanning success, fostering a widely held misconception, which it is still, in many areas of popular thinking, difficult to redress.

We must, I think, in view of the fact that it was the brilliant, but perfervid, imagination and, it has regretfully to be said, none-too-scrupulous enthusiasm of my poor friend Stephen Knight that was responsible for so much that followed, take a closer look at the genesis of his book and that of Knight, for, tragically dead at the age of thirty-three, he has himself become an integral part of Ripper history.

It was the enormous sensation created by the publication of Stowell's article, '"Jack the Ripper" – A Solution?' in *The Criminologist* in November 1970 that really awakened a general far-flung interest in Jack the Ripper. As the late Nigel Morland recalled in 1978,

> The Third World War did not break out in November 1970, but newspaper headlines in every country could not have been bigger or blacker, *WAS JACK THE RIPPER OF ROYAL BLOOD?* The question was repeated again and again. Our office telephone rang day and night for over a week. Cables, letters, personal visitors poured in on us. Newspapers, magazines, radio networks, and television companies never let us alone and *The Criminologist* achieved more unwanted publicity in a month than it could have bought for a million dollars. That is the story, and to *The Criminologist* article [continued the journal's scarcely penitent editor] I must blame the huge flood of 'Ripper' books, films, and such of the past seven years.

Titillating by the toothsomeness of the royal scandal of Stowell's semi-revelations, the Ripper and all his works and romps became an 'in' subject for the seventies, and without doubt it was this new height of public inquisitiveness that gave the BBC the idea of putting out a television drama-documentary titled, with laudable restraint of imagination, 'Jack the Ripper', *simpliciter*.

Early in 1973 a four-strong investigation team, consisting of Paul Bonner (who, with Leonard Lewis, would eventually produce the programme), Ian Sharp, Karen de Groot, and Wendy Sturgess, went most effectively to work.

All the customary and conventional databank sources were visited, revisited and ransacked. The British Library and various other libraries were swept. Old newspaper files and cuttings' libraries were quartered. There was a grand garnering from magazines and journals of sheaves of features, articles and informative paragraphs on the subject, ranging from the ridiculous to the absurd. The Public Record Office was raked through. Scotland Yard and Home Office dossiers were, by special permission, opened and scanned.

In the course of the investigative groundwork, a luncheon was arranged with 'one of the highest in the land' – Scotland that is, Yard. The identity of this official grandee remains to this day secret, but over the post-T-bone coffee and brandy, a name was whispered through the cigar-haze, a tip given to hospitality providers. Bonner and Elwyn Jones. And thus it came about that Mr Joseph William Charles 'Hobo' Sickert was discreetly introduced into the ensuing charade.

The show, beautifully scripted by my old and sadly missed friend, the late Elwyn Jones, and John Lloyd, on air on Channel 1, pleasingly diverted the nation on Friday evenings for six weeks, from 15 July through to 17 August 1973. It was in the final episode that Mr Sickert was fitted into a six-minute slot to tell his unbelievable story.

Among those who did not believe it was a young journalist named Stephen Knight, who, working on the *East London Advertiser*, in whose bailiwick the original atrocities had been enacted, was despatched one month later – in September 1973 – to interview Mr Sickert at his home in Kentish Town.

Hobo spoke of his boyhood memories of the talk of his putatinary father, Walter Sickert. I say 'putatinary' advisedly, for there is no secure evidence of that boasted illicit relationship. Joseph Sickert was one of the few people whom I have ever met who campaigned for his own bastardy.

Anyway, having stated most emphatically to Knight that he *was* the illegitimate son of Walter Sickert, he went on to say that when he was fourteen years old his father had told him this strange story about the Ripper murders.

At that time Knight's plan was simply to write a newspaper feature, but his shrewd eye descried considerably more mileage in the tale that Hobo had to unfold, and when, four hours later, Knight emerged, blinking and bewildered, into the strong, day-lit reality of the workaday North London streets, he felt, he confessed, stunned by that first personal encounter with Mr Sickert and his torrential recitative to the music *du temps perdu*.

The truth is, as Martin Fido has pointed out, that 'Knight was surprised to find the old gentleman transparently honest, and apparently convinced by his father's weird story. Such fantasies are contagious.'

Setting out to check the details, Knight gradually began to feel persuaded, experiencing the convenient dissolution of disbelief and ancillary hardening of the arteries of conviction. Then came bold resolution – to adopt, adapt, and enlarge the astonishing tortuous tale. He proceeded forthwith to convert Hobo Sickert's ramshackle cairn into a cunningly crafted folly tower. Like most journalists, he knew a good story when he invented one.

It is essential, therefore, that something should be said of the Knight's tale, with its infinity of theorisings and legless postulations, which, like its Chaucerian analogue, may be gently but firmly relegated to the taxonomic pigeon-hole, fictive. Knight's book derived, and let there be no mealy-mouthing about it, *directly* from Hobo's ingenuity the linked notions of royalty and the Freemasons, and took on board supporting evidence generously made available by the BBC team.

To reiterate, the tangential royal line was drawn from the point S (for Stowell) to pass through the BBC television drama-documentary, via Sickert, to Knight. He, let us be clear, imported neither the royal coat of arms nor the Masonic emblem to the Ripper saga; begat out of Stowell and Sickert, they were first introduced into the bloodied arena of the Whitechapel killings by the BBC. What Knight, finding them already in place, did, was embrace both insignia and elaborate their conjoint pattern on the banner, which his bestselling book waved all over the world.

From this time forward undiscerning royalophiles and purblind regiphobes cherished a beguiling notion to toy with, embrace, or out of hand reject, according to inclination: the Ripper as a royal! It is a conceit which, with the general royal-conscious populace, caught on, and, like toffee to a blanket, stuck.

For the next thirteen months Knight courted the goodwill of the BBC team, fiercely interrogated Hobo, and himself investigated vigorously in his spare time. As his notebooks filled, it seemed to him that more and more confirmatory evidence, gleaned from birth and death certificates, parish records, rent books, workhouse registers, medical histories, police files, and so on, was falling into place. And from these sources was conjured forth the canvas upon which he proceeded to embroider.

He saw the Ripper as the beast with three backs – Sir William Gull, John Netley, the psychopathic coachman, and, according to information supplied by Joseph Sickert, Dr Robert Anderson.[1] But this last nominee stuck in his craw: he found himself deeply distrusting Sickert's assertion that Anderson had been present at the murders.[2]

Inexorably, Knight came to the conclusion that Walter Sickert must have been the third man. This, not unnaturally, did not at all please Joseph Sickert, to whom it was revealed only at the eleventh-and-a-half hour before publication, and he was persuaded at the time, or so it seemed, to accept it.

Not so. Knight's Ripper historian peer, Tom Cullen, in a review in the *Hampstead Express and News* of 16 July 1976 – which could have borne the cross head 'Knight of the Wrong Knives' – was frankly contemptuous. 'Until Knight's book appeared an escaped gorilla was the most improbable candidate … There would be no point in treating a farrago of nonsense like this seriously were it not for the fact that it will be believed by tens of thousands of people.'

Eschewing verbal mincing, Cullen continued, 'This book is in fact a coconut-shy in which such easy targets as the Establishment, the Royal Family, Freemasonry, the Bohemia of Tite Street, Chelsea, are offered at a penny a throw … The author has done a disservice to crime writers whose works are the result of painstaking efforts to arrive at the truth. The temptation now will be to outbid Knight in the fantasy stakes. Briefly, Knight has given murder a bad name.'

And it is, indeed, a matter of sad record that, for all his enthusiasm and assiduity, the sum total of what Knight managed to establish was mainly confirmation of what the BBC team had uncovered, namely that once upon a time a flesh-and-blood Annie Elizabeth Crook *had* lived at No. 6 Cleveland Street – it was written on her daughter Alice Margaret Crook's birth certificate; that there really had been a carman named John Charles Netley, born in May 1860, whose death was reported in the *Marylebone Mercury and West London Gazette* of 26 September 1903,[3] as the result of the wheel of the horse-van he was driving – his employers were Messrs Thompson & McKay, carmen to the Great Central Railway Company – having hit the stone post of a pedestrian street island. Netley had been catapulted from his driving seat on to the roadway, where he was kicked in the head by one of the horses and a wheel of the van went over him.[4] Inquest held 23 September. Verdict: accidental death. There is absolutely no evidence linking this John Charles Netley with the demon driver of the Whitechapel hearse-coach legend.

Knight also claimed to have found confirmation of an alleged attempt by Netley to run down the three-and-a-half-year-old Alice Margaret Crook. He relies upon a paragraph in the *Illustrated Police News*, 6 October 1888.

> Shortly after four o'clock on Monday afternoon [1 October] a little girl was run over by a hansom cab in Fleet Street, opposite Anderton's Hotel. The child was placed in the cab and conveyed to St Bartholomew's Hospital in an insensible condition, one of the wheels having passed over her body. From the serious nature of her injuries the little sufferer is not likely to recover.

Quite apart from the proven fact that Alice Margaret Crook turned up with her mother just three months later at Endell Street Workhouse, Covent Garden, evincing no signs or symptoms of what would have been a very gross injury, further newspaper searching has disclosed that the little victim of the hansom accident was actually a nine-year-old girl named Lizzie Madewell.

For all his dedicated bloodhounding, Knight came up with nothing about the Duke of Clarence, nothing about a secret marriage, nothing about the Freemasons, nothing about the involvement of Sir William Gull or Lord Salisbury. It ought, incidentally, to be pointed out that, although among the confusions of posterity the credit, or discredit, for the introduction of the Masonic conspiracy theory has been allotted to Knight, it was not in truth his original conception, but that of the writers of the BBC drama-documentary of 1973.

Knight wrote to me on 29 November 1976, 'I am enclosing the only copy of Mr Wood's[5] article that I have. I point out that it is the only one in case, thinking it is a duplicate you either destroy it in disgust or frame it as a fine example of how to out-nasty a nasty, I have produced a notebook-full of scrawl as a result of reading the piece, but as yet they [*sic*] do not mean very much.'

As it happened, Mr Wood had kindly included me in his list of those to whom he had privately circulated copies of his utterly damning, twenty-five-page rebuttal of Knight's theory; a document wittily titled 'Jack the Ripper: By Appointment'.

> In the latest Ripper theory ... Stephen Knight has pandered to popular taste. A love of Gothic fiction permeates his book, which includes ritual murder, Royal births, high-class skulduggery, kidnapping, true-love, private asylums, Court intrigue, and the rattle of dimly-lit coaches on cobbled stones. All the ingredients for a chunky novel are there, but Mr Knight has tried to convince us that the story is fact.

Thus Simon Wood's epigraph.

Thereafter, without any bush-beating nonsense, he proceeds to the dismemberment. This rational, sweet-reasoned, utterly and devastatingly irrefutable dissection, performed without anaesthetic of any kind, was not made public, in the fullest sense, for another eleven years, until, in March 1987, Wood published a revised and somewhat abbreviated version of it in the first number of his now unhappily defunct magazine, *Bloodhound*.

'Crime fiction comes in many forms,' he began, 'but when it masquerades as fact ...'

What followed was a completely objective, coldly clinical analysis of data uncovered and supplied by Alan Neate, the Keeper of Records at the Greater London Record Office. It was, moreover, the precisely same material that Mr Neate had provided for Stephen Knight, and upon which Knight had based the arguments of his book. Only the interpretations of Knight and Wood – and possibly the span of their sight – were at variance.

Rejecting the devices and stratagems, undersights and oversights of selective reportage, Wood proved beyond peradventure that Knight was, as the Christian Scientists say, a soul in error. A number of key factors in the Sickert-Knight story were rendered nugatory. Research in the Royal Archives yielded nothing that would indicate the existence of any sort of relationship, such as that postulated by Knight, between Princess Alexandra and the Sickert family. Wood was able to show that in 1888 neither Annie Elizabeth Crook nor Walter Sickert could have been occupying the given premises in Cleveland Street – Nos 6 and 15, respectively – the buildings in question having been demolished in 1887. Neither could, as Knight maintains, Annie Elizabeth Crook and Elizabeth Cook, both – but at different periods – occupants of No. 6 Cleveland Street, be one and the same person. The building in which Annie Crook lived in 1885 was razed when, between 1886 and 1888, Nos 4 to 14 Cleveland Street were pulled down. The former No. 6 was replaced by a block of flats, known as Cleveland Residences, and it was here, at this new No. 6, that Elizabeth Cook occupied the basement flat in 1888. She remained in residence there until 1893. The continuance of occupancy lovingly envisaged by Stephen Knight vanishes in the brick-dust. None of Walter Sickert's biographers make any reference to his having had a studio at No. 15 Cleveland Street. He did, however, have one at No. 15 adjacent Fitzroy Street ... but that was more than three decades later.

Wood also demonstrated incontrovertibly that Annie Elizabeth Crook was not a Roman Catholic. Thus dissolves the alleged cardinal reason for Establishment shock-horror at Annie and Eddy's alleged covert nuptials.

He found not a single strand of evidence to suggest that Annie Elizabeth's mental and physical decline was due to anything other than natural misfortune; nothing to do with Sir William Gull. There is ample surviving medical data to show that rather than being the sharp-edged legacy of the devilishly plied surgeon's knife, her undoubted epilepsy was far more likely to have been inherited from her epileptic mother, Sarah Ann Crook. Nor is it true that Annie Elizabeth spent from mid-1888 until the end of her days continually confined in hospitals and mental homes.

It is nevertheless a fact that her life was a sad pilgrimage from workhouse to workhouse, infirmary to infirmary, with sorry interstices of living in shoddy, two-shilling-a-week rooms in even shoddier streets of outcast London. No way for the mother of a royal princess, even an illegitimate one, to live, or to be royally permitted to live.

That high-born lady, Alice, married in 1918, when she was thirty-three, a forty-five-year-old fish-curer named William Gorman. Said in some quarters to be impotent, he did very well, all things considered, fathering five children – one of whom, one suspects, was Joseph William Charles Gorman or Sickert – in the course of a long and fruitful marriage, which ended only when death did them part.

Knight's statement that the St George's Club of Hanover Square ran a hospital at 367 Fulham Road, wherein Annie Elizabeth Crook died, was shown by Wood to be completely false. No. 367 was the address of the Fulham Road Workhouse, maintained by a statutory Poor Law authority, the St George's Board of Guardians, up to 1913, but by 1920, when Annie Elizabeth did indeed die there, maintained by the City of Westminster Board of Guardians.

Simon Wood ends his remarkable article not so much in triumph as on a note of sad whimsicality: 'A few years ago I met Stephen Knight and dismantled his theory ... He listened intently and remained smilingly unrepentant, but in a postscript he [Knight] wrote:

"Other evidence, which requires deeper investigation ... has also come to light. I am in the process of examining this and expect some conclusions in time for the next edition." Sadly, he never took up the challenge.'

The first to publish the name of Sir William Gull, who figures so prominently and bloodily in the Knight's tale, in connection with the Whitechapel murders was Thomas Stowell, in his article in *The Criminologist* in 1970. Previously there had been no more than the dropping of variously veiled hints concerning his possible involvement. Both the Peckham spiritualist medium Robert James Lees and Dr Benjamin Howard are said to have been party to non-specific statements which nevertheless pointed a very heavy finger of suspicion towards Queen Victoria's physician-in-ordinary.

The whole question of the veridical status of Robert James Lees, and the value to be placed upon the various and varying accounts of the psychic trail, which he has been widely credited with following to the heart of the matter of identification, has been most thoroughly examined and reliably dilated upon by Melvin Harris in *The Face of Jack the Ripper* (1994).

Dr Benjamin Howard supplied his own written refutation of the Chicago canard,[6] but when Knight was shown a copy of Howard's furious letter his response was couched in the usual words of his standard denial-formula prelude, 'I am not surprised.' At what he was not surprised this time was the existence of such a letter, for Dr Howard 'could hardly admit to having broken Masonic secrets'.

The spinal American story, 'The Capture of Jack the Ripper', in the *Chicago Sunday Times-Herald* of 28 April 1895, recounted how, when the Whitechapel killing business was all over,

> it was absolutely proved beyond peradventure that the physician in question [never actually named] was the murderer, and his insanity fully established by a commission *de lunatico inquirendo*, all parties having knowledge of the facts were sworn to secrecy. The doctor – still not named – was at once removed to a private insane asylum in Islington, and he is now the most intractable and dangerous madman confined in that establishment. None of the keepers know that the desperate maniac, who flings himself from side to side in his padded cell and makes the long watches of the night hideous with his piercing cries is the famous 'Jack the Ripper.' To them, and to the visiting inspectors he is simply known as Thomas Mason, alias number 124.

Knight goes a'burrowing and comes up with the tidings that, sure enough, there was an asylum, St Mary's, in Islington. True, its records had been destroyed, but there had been an Islington pauper named Thomas Mason, who died in 1896 at exactly the age Gull would have been, had he (Gull) not died in 1890. Knight further confides to his readers that a bogus funeral was enacted in 1890, and a coffin filled with stones was lowered into what purported to be Gull's grave at Thorpe-le-Soken, in Essex. As to what happened when Gull (under the false identity of Thomas Mason) really died in 1896, he does not pretend to be able to offer enlightenment.

Now all this is assuredly nonsense, as, indeed, is the notion of the ailing, stroke-burdened, dextrally hemiplegic (albeit perhaps mildly), intermittently aphasic, seventy-two-year-old knight-physician rattling about Whitechapel in a closed carriage, feeding poisoned grapes to ageing street-walkers, before slicing them to final silence.

It is pure – impure is perhaps a better word – speculation. There is nothing to substantiate it, any more than there is anything to indicate that the real Thomas Mason (1817–1902), a retired bookbinder, of Bookbinders' Alms Houses, Balls Pond Road, Islington, who died of *bronchitis senectus* in Islington Infirmary, was ever in the lunacy ward – he is not on the

Pauper Lunatic Returns for the years 1888 to 1896 – or been shown to have had the remotest connection with Sir William Withey Gull.

A postscript: Lord Salisbury, the Prime Minister and alleged prime mover in the Masonic conspiracy and enlister of Gull, was not a Mason.

Much distaste, disgust, anger even, has resulted from the introduction by Knight into his book of that esoteric volume *The Protocols of the Learned Elders of Zion,*[7] which he invoked in order to link Masonry with the Ripper murders. It is his contention that out of their state of genuine fear for their very future, Britain's rulers turned for guidance to that secret code of conduct embodied in the so-called protocols.

William Beadle wrote angrily of Knight's *Final Solution* that it was 'an abomination. In part it relied upon history's most infamous faked book ... a grotesque forgery which carried within itself the seeds of a far more appalling final solution. Knight's work ... in linking itself with the *Protocols* is contaminated by them.'

Beadle goes on: 'In order to indict the Masons, Knight was forced to rely heavily on the aforementioned *Protocols of the Elders of Zion*, which can justifiably be described as a sort of Nazi handbook for attacking Jews and Masons. Allegedly written by Zionists seeking world domination.' It was in fact an anti-semitic forgery.

We owe our clearest exposition of the *Protocols* to the scholarly work of Melvin Harris. He tells us that the whole thing is based upon a political satire. The so-called protocols are blatant fiction – and appallingly bad fiction at that. They were never known to Gull or any of the Freemasons of the 1880s, for the eminently simple reason that they did not then, as such, exist.

It was a French Roman Catholic lawyer of philosophic turn, Monsieur Maurice Joly, living in the Paris of the 1860s, who laid their foundation. A man strongly liberal in his political ideals, he was necessarily and seriously at odds with the despotism of Napoleon III. It was this antagonism which pricked him to the composition of a satirical attack, written with iconoclastic tongue in iconoclast's cheek, much as Lytton Strachey's mischievous *Eminent Victorians* (1918) was, on the modes of the dictatorial emperor.

In 1864, under the anaesthetising and tranquillising title *Dialogues aux Enfers Machiavel et Montesquieu*, the cynical, opportunist, Machiavellian views on manipulation are given tangible expression. Picked over and plumped up, augmented by sundry additional works of fiction, the Jolyian japes were compacted into the *sul serio Protocols*. Its exact origin is a matter of dispute, but the forgery is said to have been concocted in Paris around 1897, at the height of the Dreyfus affair. Responsible for it were agents of the Ochrana, the Tsarist secret police. Its purpose was to justify the pogroms. At first mimeographed and restricted in circulation to diplomatic circles, in the way of such poisons it rapidly spread throughout the whole of Europe. Sergei Aleksandrovich Nilus, a fanatical Russian, self-styled mystic and believer in the impending coming of the Antichrist, included crude and muddled protocolic passages in a pamphlet, published in Moscow in 1905, which was used to stir up anti-Semitic feelings.

The first printed version of the *Protocols* was produced in Germany in 1919. An English edition followed early in 1920. By the mid-twenties, the *Protocols of the Elders of Zion* had become Europe's best-selling book after the Bible. It fed Hitler's personal paranoid fantasies, providing, as he, jaundice-eyed, saw it, secure proof of the existence of a world-wide Jewish plot, and he cited the *Protocols* as justification for his extermination programme.

Both Martin Fido and Paul Begg have made telling points in their commentaries upon Knight's theory.

Fido considered the political climate:

Socialist and freethinking attacks on royalty are cited as evidence that the monarchy was in danger and a secret Catholic marriage might have brought it down. This (together with the monarchy's importance to Freemasonry) is put forward to explain Salisbury's complicity. But the Major political concern of the period was the Irish question. The monarchy was far more secure than it had been when Victoria and Albert rescued it from the dismal disrepute into which George IV's self-indulgence and William IV's inarticulacy had brought it. Salisbury was now a reds-under-the-bed conspiracy-monger.

Paul Begg had this to say on the Masonics:

They [the 'Juwes'] featured in British Masonic rituals until 1814, but they were dropped during the major revision of the ritual between 1814 and 1816. By 1888 it is doubtful if many British Masons would even have known their names [Jubela, Jubelo, and Jubelum]. In the United States, however, the names were and are used. But in neither country were Jubelo, Jubela and Jubelum known officially or colloquially as the 'Juwes.' They were always referred to as 'the ruffians'. 'Juwes' is not and never has been a Masonic word, nor has 'Juwes' or any word approximating to it ever appeared in British, Continental or American Masonic rituals.

Patrick Ensor, in the *Guardian* of 7 July 1976, described Knight's story as that of 'an Establishment plot that makes Watergate look amateurish'. And, in what exemplifies the critical acumen of a former boon-fellow-about-Fleet-Street of mine, that argute, witty, distinguished amateur herpetologist and professional *littérateur*, the late Maurice Richardson, laconically observed *en passant* the Knight's tale to be 'so transcendentally preposterous that it deserves a room to itself in the Münchausen Museum of Pseudologia Fantastica'.

Why, then, did I write a Foreword to so shaky a propositional book? I stand by every carefully chosen word of that Foreword … but I will break a rule and tell a tale out of school. Persuaded both by my friendship with the late Stephen Knight and the iron-within-velvet insistence of the publisher whom we shared at that time, the late J. H. H. Joe Gaute of Messrs Harrap's, against my better judgement, I did so – and found myself in the midst of an uproar.

I wrote two Forewords actually. The first, wherein I had expressed not wisely but too well sundry doubts and dubieties, and proclaimed that I was not to be counted among the 'Gullibles', upset all concerned. Friendly pressures were brought to bear. Would I, perhaps, think again – and a little more charitably? I did. I felt obliged to tincture my scepticism with a homeopathic trituration of amiable credulity. I dropped the principal offending sentence – 'You must not include me among the "Gullibles"' – and substituted for the discerning intelligence such phrases as I felt would surely convey to it the hidden agenda of my misgivings. And I believe they did.

In any event, I have thus far learned of only one who failed to catch my drift, Mr Melvyn Fairclough. I wrote with genuine admiration of the ingenuity that had gone into the construction of an artful artefact. Pharisee that I was as regards Knight's confection, by way of compensation for not being able, hand on heart, to blazon enthusiastically his 'solution', I was very happy to be able to rediscover to him the precise location of the anonymous scribe's 'Juwes' chalked message in Goulston Street in time for him to furnish the first-ever photograph of the site in his book.

It is a matter of record that those parts of the Sickert-Knight story which it has been possible to test have proved to be untrue. It is a tale bedevilled by lies, half-truths and meaningless truths.

In the *Sunday Times* of 18 June 1978, Joseph Sickert came out of the closet of his make-believe Peter Pan-ish Never Never Land and confessed of his Grand Ripper Revelation; it was a hoax. It was a whopping fib. The only segment of the sorry saga to which he still stuck, Araldite tight, was that of his ducal ancestry. 'As an artist [and picture restorer] I found it easy to paint Jack the Ripper into the story I had been told about Prince Albert Victor and my grandmother by my father when I was six years old.'[8]

Hobo now confesses that 'things have got out of hand,' and he wants to 'clear the name of my father'.

Stephen Knight, the paper reports, 'could not be contacted this weekend'. But on 2 July 1978, Knight came galloping full tilt, glass-armoured (Melvin Harris' bright image) into the *Sunday Times* arena. He was 'not surprised' (there goes that phrase again!) that Sickert was now trying to denounce the contents of his book. 'He threatened to do this after I had told him that I believed his father, Walter Sickert, had been directly involved in the killings.' This, said Knight, was what had

> so incensed and troubled Joseph Sickert. He at first begged me not to publish my findings about his father. I had to refuse. He told me then that he would find some way of exonerating him even if it meant denying the whole story. I had been prepared for this, and before showing him the last chapter I had secured a signed statement from him that I had recounted his father's original story with complete accuracy. Beyond that, of course, the new evidence I had uncovered spoke for itself.

As Philip Sugden has well noted, 'what is disconcerting about the whole episode, however, is the attitude of Stephen Knight himself. His research is now known to have uncovered evidence which proved that the story was untrue. Yet he shamelessly chose to suppress it.'

Knight's theory, in sum, was 'a colossus built on sand'. Whatever shortcomings may be imputed to him, one must not yield to the always too easy temptation to write a man off because his conclusions conflict with your own, and in your view do not lie congruous with the ley lines of intuitive reason.

Stephen Knight made, *obiter* as it were, important contributions to knowledge concerning the Ripper case. He gave the twentieth century its first intimation of the curious testimony of Israel Schwartz regarding the man who threw Elisabeth Stride down upon the Berner Street footway; he revealed Abberline's report on Polly Nichols, Swanson's report on Catherine Eddowes, Sergeant White's report of his interview with Matthew Packer, and the fact that Sir Charles Warren's handwritten notes of Packer's statement are preserved in the files. That he may not always have recognised the real worth of the nuggets of his finding does not detract from their intrinsic value.

As to his narrative, his theory, which I have advisedly dubbed 'The Knight's Tale', it was surely just that. Fiction. In the Stevensonian sense, a rattling good yarn.

47

The Ninth Decade

Almost ninety years gone by ... but the effort to understanding has gone on ... and on ...

Commencing with the issue of 16 December 1977, and continuing for sixteen instalments, to 14 April 1978, there appeared in the *Police Review* (London), an impressive series of articles under the collective title, 'The Whitechapel Murders: Jack the Ripper', by William Vincent, the pseudonym of Peter Rowe, former superintendent in the City of London Police, and subsequently a member of the legal staff attached in the Court of Appeal, Criminal Division.

The narrative opens:

> While there was an abundance of professional prostitutes there were many who were little more than amateurs. They were known as 'the unfortunates,' perhaps having been widowed or abandoned by husbands, or merely been born into circumstances of poverty. The word 'unfortunates' was an apt one and the women tended to call themselves by it.
>
> For them 'home' was a bed in a large, dirty lodging house; perhaps 'bed' was only a mattress or some straw – provided they could find a few pence to pay for it. Selling their bodies could provide those few pence, or alternatively, they might find a man willing to share his bed with them for a night – if they were lucky that arrangement might become a semi-permanent one.

This is followed by a straightforward recounting of the acts of violence inflicted upon twelve of these women, of the world they inhabited, and the terror that the people of that world lived in as a consequence of those acts. Mr Vincent's is a worthy achievement, an honest tale honestly told.

The last volume to appear in this decade was *Will the Real Jack the Ripper* (1979) by Arthur Douglas. Although a mere seventy-two-page limp-back, it would be a grievous mistake to underrate it. Essentially a pedagogic work, bristling with puns and ingenious wordplay, it is the dominie marking in schoolmasterly fashion the errors and omissions, the discrepancies and disparities, in the compositions of other Ripper authors, scrawling witty comments in red ink in their margins. On the positive side, Douglas most convincingly dismisses all heretofore identificatory hazards, and asserts the continuing inviolable anonymity of the Whitechapel murderer.

The book is written in bravura style, studded with some very nice literary touches, and graced by such felicitous and pictorially evocative sentences as, 'There are some, also, who would find significance in the dates of and the intervals between the murders, as if each act were a blood-red bead on an astral abacus', and such engaging images as that of Jack as 'the man who removed the coverings from the legs of Victorians' tables and chairs'.

His final apophthegm, with which, three decades on, I would not quarrel, is: 'So when all is done and said, the one incontrovertible truth that is known about the identity of Jack the Ripper ... is that the identity of Jack the Ripper is not known.' Which, like Douglas's book, is a sort of circular argument.

One other thing which we may safely assume is, as Mr Douglas in his happy and homely fashion puts it, that 'Jack the Ripper knew every inch of Whitechapel ... as surely as the London cab horse knew its way back to the rank and a welcome nose-bag.'

The plan of the book is to take each slaying and display it starkly, strictly factually, to the reader in the present tense. Each episode is then followed up with a scrupulous account of its subsequent investigation and down-the-years encrusting theoretical accumulation. Without question, the book fulfils its function designate as a 'dramatic, thought-provoking primer for budding Ripperologists'.

Eight years were to pass before there was another book published on the great East End knifeman and the 'funny little games' he played in Whitechapel.

48

The Buff Envelope

Apart from the premature publication of the centennial volumes, the year 1987 saw a bit of a build-up of excitement about the forthcoming anniversary, complete with merry quips about having a ripping time, telling ripping yarns, and the odd dour comment about too many books on the subject ripping us off, and suchlike examples of pop wit and wisdom.

Among the most notable peripheral commentators was the critic who, when he heard that Druitt was an excellent batsman who played regularly for Blackheath – on the Rectory Field and many another willow-and-ball venue – delivered himself of the balanced judgement that 'chaps like that ... don't spend their time off the pitch eviscerating women, and sending them through the post. It just isn't cricket.'

The big event of 1987 had to be the arrival at Scotland Yard in November, via a Croydon pillar box, of a large, plain brown envelope, bearing a two-penny and an eighteen-pence stamp. Sent anonymously, it contained a sheaf of long-lost homing Ripper documents. They were the original handwritten 'Dear Boss' letter, in red ink, addressed to the Central News Office in September 1888, and signed 'Jack the Ripper' – the first usage of the *nom de sang*; Dr Thomas Bond's preliminary post-mortem report on Mary Jane Kelly's body as found *in situ*; some notes on the post-mortem examination of the body of Mary Ann Nichols; a draft pardon for accomplices willing to testify; and, fourthly and finally, nothing to do with the Ripper, a separate usurpation, some police notes on the Crippen case.

What were believed to be the complete surviving files on the Whitechapel murders had been passed from Scotland Yard CRO to the Public Record Office and made accessible to the public in the 1970s. When these documents had been extracted, purloined, it is not possible to say. Forensic examination of the envelope and its contents failed to yield any evidence as to the sender.

The November 1987 issue of *True Detective* contained a long and very interesting article from the pen of Nicholas Warren, a young surgeon who, very shortly, was to come to play an important part in the affairs of Ripper research. In this article, 'Jack the Ripper: The World's Greatest Mystery', he looked back over the precedent ninety-nine years at some of the main stories and theories that had, in that time, gone to the building of the Ripper legend.

> As the shadows lengthen on a November evening in Commercial Street, Spitalfields, the atmosphere of that dreadful autumn 99 years ago may still be felt. The fogs have abated, the lighting is less eerie, but the narrow byways around the market and Christ Church still exude decay and desolation. A contemporary witness of the 'Reign of Terror' was asked, years later, what he recalled most vividly about the Ripper era. It was, he replied, the dreadful silence.

Travelling far beyond Stephen Knight's so-called 'final solution', Warren examined in meticulous detail the suspicious factors that unquestionably surrounded the alleged beliefs and behaviour of Walter Sickert, who, it is said, in his last years, following a stroke, believed that *he* was Jack the Ripper.

And Mr Warren, possibly tongue-in-cheek, adumbrates a novel scenario which could involve Mary Kelly, Sickert, and the suggestive signposts of his works. Three of his pictures repay keen scrutiny and careful consideration: they are *The Painter in His Studio*, *La Hollandaise* and *Ennui*.

In the first, a self-portrait, the picture shows in the foreground a headless female torso. Portions of the upper limbs are missing. The right thigh is pared to the bone – as at Miller's Court. The left breast is missing. What appear to be intestines are draped over the left shoulder. The second picture depicts a stoutly built nude woman reclining upon a cheap iron bedstead. The nose and ears seem to be missing; the chin is supported by something indistinct. The figure has some indefinable object draped over her left shoulder. There is a broken windowpane – as at Miller's Court. The literal translation of *La Hollandaise* is 'The Dutchwoman', but Nicholas Warren has found that the term may have loose connotations with prostitution. He adds that 'Dutch', in English, indicates something false, a substitute or sham, as in the compounds Dutch gold, Dutch Uncle, Dutch courage, a Dutch auction, a Dutch treat. The Dutchwoman is thus a woman substituted by Sickert, the identifier, for Kelly – a complete sham. The third picture, completed in 1913–14, shows a man and a woman. He is gazing into space. She is staring at the wall. The woman is large and of about the same age as Kelly would have been had she survived the attack at Miller's Court, that is, about fifty years old. Sickert's model for the painting was his maid, named Marie. No photograph of Kelly, in life, seems to have survived. She is, however, described as stout, quite tall, with a square jaw and long dark hair. Marie the maid certainly bears a striking resemblance to Mary Kelly. Both women shared the feature of prominent cheeks, verging on jowliness. Could this be a portrait of Kelly in middle age?

And Warren directs a final good-as-a-wink nod to his reader. There are two versions of *Ennui*. One is in the Ashmolean Museum, at Oxford. The other is at the Tate Gallery, in London. There is an important difference between them. Go to see the Tate Gallery version. 'At first, there appears to be an indistinct feature – a bright streak or painted highlight on the canvas,' he tells us. 'But look carefully! There is definitely something on Marie's left shoulder.'

In the *Sunday Times* of 29 November 1987, John Carey wrote that he did not consider it to have been clearly established that all five generally accepted Ripper victims had died by the same hand. Indeed, Dr Bagster Phillips, the H Division police surgeon, maintained that they had not. Moreover, the widespread popular belief that all five suffered pretty well identical injuries is wrong. Polly Nichols had her throat so deeply cut as almost to decapitate her, and her abdomen was slashed. Annie Chapman's throat was cut deeply, similarly to Polly Nichols', and she was disembowelled and had her uterus removed. Elisabeth Stride's throat was cut, but not deeply, and she had no other injuries – but in her case the killer had been disturbed. Catherine Eddowes had her throat cut, was disembowelled, had her uterus and left kidney removed, and her face mutilated. Mary Kelly had her throat cut, and was thereafter simply taken apart. Her heart was missing.

Given that Alice McKenzie and Frances Coles were made to look like – but were not – Ripper victims, how can we be sure that copycat Ripper killings did not take place earlier than November 1888?

'The idea,' says John Carey, 'that there were several minor maniacs on the loose rather than one star slayer does not conflict with the established facts, but it is extremely unlikely to catch on, because it lacks the glamour of the Ripper myth.'

Just before Christmas 1987, the pub – the old Ten Bells, on the corner of Fournier Street and Commercial Street, Spitalfields, where almost certainly all of the Ripper victims must at one time or another of temporary prosperity have taken a convivial glass – which had in the 1970s been renamed The Jack the Ripper, became the focus of a feminist demonstration. The Legions of Women gathered outside, loudly and angrily claiming that it was making money out of brutality to women. This confused logic hit home to nervously sympathetic ears. Truman's, the brewery that owned the house, averse to any adverse publicity, issued its mandate. Disregarding the wishes and feelings of the licensee, the brewers decided and directed that the premises should forthwith revert to its old style and title, The Ten Bells. It was further advised that the landlady must not continue the sale of the cocktail of her own invention, the Ripper Tipple. Henceforth it was known as the Tipper Ripple.

49

Jack and the Feminists

Things came to a head – a feminine head – in 1988. Dissatisfaction, resentment, had been simmering for some years; as we have already seen, it boiled up and over because of the public-house in Spitalfields, The Ten Bells, standing, since at least 1752, hard by Nicholas Hawksmoor's Christ Church, at the corner of Commercial and Fournier streets. Oral tradition had it that it had been favoured by the regular custom of Annie Chapman and Mary Jane Kelly, and that the latter had had her soliciting pitch right outside it. Out of deference to its long-standing association with Saucy Jacky and those who were to become his victims, in 1976 the name of The Ten Bells had been changed to The Jack the Ripper.

A powerful feminist protest hit Whitechapel. The thinking behind that protest comes clearly through in an article by Deborah Cameron, contributed to the *Guardian* of 15 March 1988. In it, she complains bitterly of the depths plumbed by those producing Ripper computer games, badges, and T-shirts, and, by implication, changing pub names. Self-respecting feminists felt that not only were such products – and actions – in the worst possible taste, but 'to glamorise sexual murder', as they undoubtedly did, was downright harmful.

Ms Cameron, quite understandably, objects to what she sees as the trivialisation of the suffering of women, or its treatment as a 'turn-on', or a joke. She is, again understandably, worried by what strikes her as the casual equation of violence and sex, the thrill of transgression, the contempt for female bodies, the reinforcement of those patriarchal masculine attitudes which 'lead to sexual violence and murder … For some men it seems that the exploits of "Jack" provide a ready-made framework for their own sadistic fantasies …'

Ms Cameron is disturbed by what she interprets as 'this kind of male identification with the Ripper … in what passes for serious writing about the East End murders'.

She accuses such authors of regarding the Jack the Ripper affair as a classic whodunnit, and observes that on the much more significant question of *why*, they take refuge in the popular wisdom of the tap-room.

She comments, 'Something else which comes across clearly in this genre is a schoolboy camaraderie with fellow-enthusiasts which even encompasses the Ripper himself.'

And she ridicules one author's dedication of his complete history of the case – 'To Ripperologists everywhere – not forgetting Jack who brought us together.' Oddly, she forgets to mention the Jill the Ripper theorists.

In the book *The Lust to Kill: A Feminist Investigation of Sexual Murder*, which, in 1987, Deborah Cameron published with Elizabeth Frazer, the authors note that 'the Ripper killings were explained by some commentators as the work of a "sex maniac" ... but this explanation was not universally accepted, with many other hypotheses being seriously suggested. Nowadays by contrast it is very unlikely that the repeated murder and mutilation of prostitutes would be explained as anything other than a sexual crime.'

Cameron and Frazer consider that 'serious writing about Jack the Ripper is untypical of the biographical/case history approach,' and think that it is because he remains the Great Unknown that he 'has attained the status of a popular folk-devil, rather like Dracula or Frankenstein's monster'. They visualise him luridly 'stealing down foggy London streets, with a top hat and swirling black cloak, tapping his cane'.

They quote the *Pall Mall Gazette* of 10 September 1888: 'The murderer is a victim of erotic mania, which often takes the awful shape of an uncontrollable lust for blood. Sadism, as it is termed from the maniac marquis (De Sade) ... is happily so strange to the majority of our people that they find it difficult to credit the possibility of mere debauchery bearing such awful fruitage.'

Cameron and Frazer add,

This remark draws an implicit distinction between the majority conception of sadism as 'mere debauchery' ... and a quasi-scientific or medical way of conceiving it, as an abnormal mental condition or 'mania'; something 'uncontrollable' of which the killer himself is 'victim.' In the case of Jack the Ripper, we are seeing the definition of sexual murder at an early and relatively confused stage; the criminal is in a state of transition as educated people assimilate recent scientific developments.

To quote again the *Pall Mall Gazette*, 8 September 1888:

This renewed reminder (the murder of Annie Chapman) of the potentialities of revolting barbarity which lie latent in man will administer a salutary shock to the complacent optimism which assumes that the progress of civilisation has rendered unnecessary the bolts and bars, social, moral, and legal, which keep the Mr Hyde of humanity from assuming visible shape among us. There certainly seems to be a tolerably realistic impersonification of Mr Hyde at large in Whitechapel.

In Cameron and Frazer's opinion 'both the pessimism and the biologism of this view retain their centrality in discussions of sex murder'.

In his clinical assessment of murders and murderer, Dr Thomas Bond thought the character of the inflicted mutilations indicative of possible satyriasis. Cameron and Frazer see this 'medicalization of Mr Hyde and the concomitant discarding of his spiritual dimension' as 'one of the most important points of resemblance between the case of Jack the Ripper and that of Peter Sutcliffe',[9] the discussion of whose case and trial 'revolved around the question, was he mad or just plain bad? Just as much as in the time of Jack the Ripper, the alternatives posed were either sinfulness or sickness.'

As Judith R. Walkowitz writes in her *City of Dreadful Delight: Narratives of Sexual Danger in Late-Victorian London* (1992),

The social context of the Ripper's exploits, however, have not disappeared from twentieth-century representation, although they, too, have undergone a mythic revision. The Whitechapel murders have continued to provide a common vocabulary of male violence against women, a vocabulary now more than one hundred years old. Its persistence owes much to the mass media's exploitation of Ripper iconography. Depiction of female mutilation in mainstream cinema, celebrations of the Ripper as a 'hero' of crime intensify fears of male violence and convince women that they are helpless victims.

She also comments that in 1888 Doctors James G. Kiernan and E. C. Spitzka 'located the Ripper along a spectrum of contemporary perverts, from female masturbators and "urnings" of both sexes, to the exclusively male perpetrators of "lust murder" and sexual sadism'.

She has praise, too, for 'that great crusader against libertine debauchery, [who] was the first journalist to draw attention to the "sexual origins" of the crime [on Annie Chapman] and to invoke Dr Jekyll and Mr Hyde as a psychological model of the murderer'. This was W. T. Stead, editor of the *Pall Mall Gazette*, author in 1885 of that classic exposure of child prostitution, *Maiden Tribute of Modern Babylon*.

Walkowitz goes on to point out that changing historical circumstances can provoke a different response to these media productions. The case of Peter Sutcliffe, the Yorkshire Ripper, constitutes 'a late-twentieth-century "replay" of the Ripper episode that engendered a different political reaction from contemporary British feminists, who took to the streets to protest the crimes and the media amplification of the terror'.

In the half-dozen years between 1975 and 1981 the good folk resident in Bradford and Leeds were being terrorised by a serial killer whose menace was alarmingly boosted by the media-bestowed name, the Yorkshire Ripper. By the end of 1980, thirteen women had fallen victim to him.

The ensuing panic bade fair to equal that of 1888. The similarities to the circumstances of the hundred years precedent murders were marked. (1) A single mythic killer. (2) A series of ritual slayings. (3) Stereotyped victims (prostitutes). (4) A specific terrorised area. (5) Intense media publicity – 'The press consistently invoked the example of the legendary Ripper to enhance the contemporary power and prestige of the contemporary killer. It not only gave the murderer his name, but it proceeded to cast "him" as a classic Victorian sex beast and to transform the North of England into the foggy gaslight "mean streets" of the Victorian East End. "Bradford on a Saturday night is pure Victorian Gothic … dank slate roofs gleaming, the blackened brick … even the quarter moon obliges. Fitfully disappearing behind windswept clouds," declared the *Evening News Magazine*.' (6) There were even messages to the police, purporting to come from the killer himself, tape recordings, paralleling the 'Dear Boss' letters of the 1880s, and proving, as they most likely were, bogus.

The feminists, seeing and accepting the sexual challenge posed by Jack's Yorkshire cousin, responded spiritedly, gluing up the locks on the doors of sex shops, flinging paint and oil at the screens of cinemas showing films of Ripper-style killings and male sexual violence, removing some £400 worth of pornography from a city bookshop, and sending the volumes' burnt ashes out with press releases.

One sees in the eventual arrest and trial of Sutcliffe a simulacrum surely of how it would have been if Jack the Ripper had been 'buckled' and put in the dock. Sutcliffe challenged medical and legal concepts of insanity. In the heel of it, it was the legal presumption of his sanity that prevailed, and Sutcliffe, pronounced guilty by the jury, was sentenced by the Court to life imprisonment. His claim that while digging graves – he was a lorry driver, but had at one time had a job as a grave-digger – he had received messages from God, upon which he had acted, had failed to convince and was dismissed. However, in March 1984, Sutcliffe was transferred from prison to Broadmoor. He was said to have undergone some form of mental degeneration.

50

The Ripper Profiled

It was back in 1981 – the salad days of the utilisation of a new toy called psychological profiling[10] – that Dr G. William Eckert, director of the Milton Helpern International Center for Forensic Science, first suggested a modern forensic study of the Ripper case, and in due season there was published in the *American Journal of Forensic Medicine and Pathology*, Vol. 2, No. 1 (1981), a paper entitled 'The Whitechapel Murders: The Case of Jack the Ripper'. Its scarcely earth-shattering conclusion was to find it 'quite possible that with modern techniques … more evidence at the scene or on the body might have been uncovered'.

Some years on, on 20 February 1988, the *San Francisco Chronicle* announced that a member of a team of forensic scientists believed that they had come as close as anyone ever would to determining who Jack the Ripper was.

Up spake Dr Eckert again: 'The Ripper case is *the* classic serial murder case that exists in the world. This is the only time it's ever been evaluated applying modern knowledge and techniques, and I believe we will be able to say who is the most probable suspect.'

Eckert's eight-man team included Dr Thomas T. Noguchi, a pathologist and former Los Angeles coroner, three forensic psychologists, a crime laboratory expert from Canada, and two forensic experts, one of whom was a forensic odontologist from the London Hospital. The team was compiling psychological profiles on fifteen suspects, among whom were a kosher butcher, several doctors, a Russian spy, and a lawyer.

A coast-to-coast television event to mark the centenary was screened in America in October 1988. The programme, 'The Secret Identity of Jack the Ripper', put together by Cosgrove Meurer TV Productions, aimed at presenting all the available evidence, taking in the work done by Dr Eckert and his team and offering additionally a criminal investigative analysis, otherwise psychological profile, prepared by experts from the FBI Academy, Quantico. Supervisory Special Agent John E. Douglas prepared the profile. He and Robert R. Hazelwood, also of Quantico, appeared on the programme alongside participating scientists and historians.

The profile indicated the following likely features to be sought in the culprit. He would be male (female serial lust killers are virtually unknown). He would be likely to be between twenty-eight and thirty-six years of age. He would be a local resident. That he was of low social class emerged from the lack of fastidiousness evinced in the murders. He displayed none of the supposed surgical or anatomical skill; what he performed was really nothing more than elementary butchery. That he was probably in employment was suggested by the murders being committed at weekends – Friday, Saturday, Sunday nights. That he was able to commit the crimes between midnight and 6 a.m. was indicative of an absence of accountability in a familial situation. He was indeed likely to be seen by his associates as a loner. There was a definite probability that he had been in some sort of trouble with the police *before* the murders, and that he had been abused as a child – especially by, or with the concurrence of, his mother.

What must of course be recognised is that this profile was based on the sparse facts gleaned from 1888, many of which may not have related to the actual killer at all.

The FBI agents were convinced that the taunting letters to the police were written by an impostor, because the type of individual responsible for the Whitechapel murders 'would not have the personality to set up a public challenge to the police. This was not someone who could hold his own verbally. The physical circumstances of the crimes told us this was someone who could blend in with his surroundings and not cause suspicion or fear on the part of the prostitutes. He would be a quiet loner, not a macho butcher who would prowl the streets nightly and return to the scenes of his crimes.' The mutilation pointed to a mentally disturbed, sexually inadequate person with a lot of generalised rage against women. His 'blitz' style of attack told of personal and social inadequacy.

Special Agent Douglas was sure that, as in the case of Peter Sutcliffe, the so-called Yorkshire Ripper, he would undoubtedly have been interviewed by the police in the course of their investigations. Jack the Ripper would not have committed suicide after the last murder. Generally, when serial murders cease, it is because the murderer came close to being identified, was interviewed by the police, or was arrested for some other type of offence.

Douglas concluded that of all the suspects presented, Aaron Kozminsky fitted the profile far the best. Douglas qualified, however, that while he certainly would not, a hundred years later, be sure that Kozminsky *was* the Ripper, what he *could* state, with a high degree of confidence, was that Jack the Ripper was someone *like* Kozminsky, and he further said that, had this criminal investigative analysis of today been available then, its input would have helped the police to narrow their focus and come up with the killer's identity. For that reason, he would say that by modern standards this case would be very solvable.

Dr Eckert subsequently reported the television treatment in a paper, 'The Ripper Project: Modern Science Solving Mysteries of History', in the *American Journal of Forensic Medicine and Pathology*, Vol. 10 No. 2 (1989).

51
Mr Lusk's Renal Postbag

I have serious misgivings concerning aspects of the Lusk kidney legend. I feel that the case for the organ's having been derived from Eddowes' body has been overstated. It is, in my view, a sufficiently important issue, reflecting as it does most strongly upon the credibility of the 'From Hell' letter, to warrant the digression of a full examination.

The circumstances of the kidney's reception were as follows. On the evening of Tuesday 16 October 1888, by either the 5 p.m. or 8 p.m. mail (contemporary accounts differ as to the precise time) a small parcel was delivered to the home of Mr George Lusk, who lived at Nos 1–3 Alderney Street, Mile End.

This package, measuring 3½ inches square, was wrapped in brown paper, upon which was written, 'Mr Lusk, Head Vigilance Committee. Alderney Street, Mile End.' Inside was a cardboard box containing some meaty substance, which gave off a very offensive odour, and which appeared to be a kidney that had been divided longitudinally.

Enclosed in the box with it was a letter:

From hell
Mr Lusk
Sur
I send you half the Kidne I took from one woman prasarved it for you tother piece I fried and ate
it was very nice I may send you the bloody knif that took it out if you only wate a whil longer
signed
Catch me when you can
Mishter Lusk

At first Mr Lusk was disposed to think that it was just another disagreeable hoax. He had, in fact, in his capacity as chairman of the Vigilance Committee, already been the recipient of several communications purporting to have come from the perpetrator of the Whitechapel murders.

Indeed, only a day or two before the arrival of the kidney, a postcard had been delivered to his home:

Say Boss – You seem rare frightened guess I'd like to give you *fits* but I can't stop time enough to let you box of toys play copper games with me but hope to see you when I don't hurry too much
– Bye-bye Boss
Mr Lusk, Head Vigilance Committee, Alderney Street, Mile End.

Poor Mr Lusk seems also to have been marked down for other unwanted attention, for according to *The Times* of 8 October 1888,

On Saturday [6 October] evening it became necessary to call in the police for the purpose of keeping a look-out for a mysterious stranger who had been prowling round his premises and his son's house with the object, it is believed, of striking through Mr Lusk at the Vigilance Committee. After an interview with a constable and a detective-sergeant, the matter was deemed of sufficient importance to warrant the attendance of an inspector from Bethnal Green, and at 10.30 [he] waited on Mr Lusk and heard his statement of the matter. The description given of this man is as follows: Height 5 ft. 9 in. Aged 38 to 40. Full beard and moustache, matted and untrimmed. Dent on bridge of the nose. Wide nostrils. Florid complexion. Eyes sunken. Dressed in a rusty frock coat. White turn-down collar. Black tie. No watch chain. Deerstalker hat. Left boot broken out at the left side. Carried a brown walking stick with a round top.

According to Mr J. Aarons, the treasurer of the Whitechapel Vigilance Committee, who lived at 74 Mile End Road,

Mr Lusk, our chairman, came over to me last night (Wednesday, 17 October 1888) in a state of considerable excitement. I asked him what was the matter, when he replied, 'I suppose you will laugh at what I am going to tell you, but you must know that I had a little parcel come to me on Tuesday evening, and to my surprise it contains half a kidney and a letter from Jack the Ripper.' To tell you the truth, I did not believe in it, and I laughed and said I thought that somebody had been trying to frighten him. Mr Lusk, however, said it was no laughing matter to him. I then suggested that, as it was late, we should leave the matter over till the morning, when I and other members of the Committee would come round. This morning (Thursday, 18 October), at about half-past nine, Mr Harris, our secretary, Mr Reeves, Mr Lawton, and myself went across to see Mr, Lusk, who opened his desk and pulled out a small square cardboard box, wrapped in brown paper. Mr Lusk said, 'Throw it away, I hate the sight of it.' I examined the box and its contents, and being sure that it was not a sheep's kidney, I advised that, instead of throwing it away, we should see Dr Frederick Wiles, of 56 Mile End Road. We did not, however, find him in, but Mr F. S. Reed, his assistant, was. He gave an opinion that it was a portion of a human kidney which had been preserved in spirits of wine, but, to make sure, he would go over to the London Hospital, where it could be microscopically examined. On his return Mr Reed said that Dr Openshaw, at the Pathological Museum, stated that the kidney belonged to a female, that it was part of the left kidney, and that the woman had been in the habit of drinking. He should think that the person had died about the same time the Mitre Square murder was committed. It was then agreed that we should take the parcel to Leman Street Police Station, where we saw Inspector Abberline.

Since the kidney related to a crime that had occurred within the jurisdiction of the City Police, it, and the letter that had accompanied it, were despatched to Major Henry Smith, the acting head of the City Police.

The *Daily Telegraph* of Saturday 20 October 1888 reported that the City Police authorities were engaged on Friday 19 October in making inquiries with respect to the Lusk kidney. It had been submitted by them to Dr Frederick Gordon Brown, the surgeon to the City Police, for microscopical examination,

> and upon his report will in large measure depend the further steps that may be taken. It may be remembered that it was Dr Gordon Browne [*sic*] who gave evidence at the Mitre Square inquest with reference to the organs missing from the body of the woman Eddowes. He then intimated that only the right kidney could be found and that now submitted to him is a portion of a left kidney, the suggestion being that it forms part of that which was taken away. It is stated, however, that on this point no definite opinion can be pronounced, as these organs vary considerably in the same person, and conclusions based on the condition of the right kidney may very well prove misleading. On the other hand, it is asserted that only a small portion of the renal artery adhered to the kidney, while in the case of the Mitre Square victim a large portion of the artery adhered to the body.

Until recently, a careful search had failed to reveal the whereabouts of either Dr Brown's original detailed post-mortem report on the body of Catherine Eddowes, or his subsequent special report on the Lusk kidney.

It is interesting now to see how, over the years, various writers have added, with what firm justification it has proved elusive to discover, sundry supplementary 'facts' to the somewhat sparse primary data. Thus, while Leonard Matters, writing in 1929, makes no mention of the kidney, and William Stewart, in 1939, merely refers to the existence – in another context – of Mr George Lush (*sic*), Donald McCormick, in 1959, tells the story of the kidney for the first time, but he has Mr Lusk masquerading as 'Mr Lark', and reports that Dr Openshaw put the age of the woman from whom the kidney had been extracted as about forty-five, and the time of its removal as within the last two weeks – i.e. some time since 5 October. Tom Cullen, in 1965, states, correctly, that Openshaw estimated the time of the kidney's removal as within the last three weeks – i.e. some time since 28 September. Also in 1965, Robin Odell repeats McCormick's two-week error, and makes no bones about declaring that 'it was established that the severed portion of the renal artery attached to the kidney sent in the post matched the corresponding part of that artery left in the body'.[11] Daniel Farson, in 1972, has Dr Openshaw believing that the kidney had come from the body of Catherine Eddowes – despite the fact that he reports Openshaw as saying that it had been taken from the body of a gin-soaked woman in the last two weeks – and Eddowes had died nearly three weeks before, on 30 September.[12] Incidentally, in the second edition of Farson's book, Mr Lusk is put off his breakfast by the arrival of the kidney.[13] I find no evidence that Lusk was so late a breakfaster! In 1975, Donald Rumbelow writes, 'The kidney was in an advanced state of Bright's disease, and the one that had been left in the body was in an exactly similar state.'[14]

Tracking back, I have found that the source for most of this is Lieutenant-Colonel Sir Henry Smith's book of memoirs, *From Constable to Commissioner* (1910). Here is what he has to say:

When the body [of Eddowes] was examined by the police surgeon, Mr Gordon Brown, one kidney was found to be missing, and some days after the murder what purported to be that kidney was posted to the office of the Central News,[15] together with a short note of rather a jocular character unfit for publication. Both kidney and note the manager at once forwarded to me ... I made over the kidney to the police surgeon, instructing him to consult with the most eminent men in the profession, and send me a report without delay I give the substance of it. The renal artery is about three inches long. Two inches remained in the corpse, one inch was attached to the kidney. The kidney left in the corpse was in an advanced stage of Bright's Disease; the kidney sent me was in an exactly similar state. But what was of more importance, Mr Sutton, one of the senior surgeons at the London Hospital, whom Gordon Brown asked to meet him and another practitioner in consultation, and who was one of the greatest authorities living on the kidney and its diseases, said he would pledge his reputation that the kidney submitted to them had been put in spirits within a few hours of its removal from the body – thus effectually disposing of all hoaxes in connection with it. The body of anyone done to death by violence is not taken direct to the dissecting-room, but must await an inquest, never held before the following day at the soonest.

There is no denying that, of all people, Major (as he then was) Henry Smith was indisputably in the best position to provide an authoritative account of the medical findings in regard to the Lusk kidney, for it was by him that Dr Brown's report was requested and to him that it was rendered. However, he is writing these memoirs some twenty-two years after the event, and there is internal evidence to show that his memory is none too reliable. He says, for instance, that the postal kidney was received 'some days after the murder'. It was received two weeks and three days after the murder. He says, as we have seen, that it was posted to the office of the Central News, and forwarded to him by the manager of that news agency. He does not so much as mention Mr Lusk, its true recipient. That the organ received was in an advanced stage of Bright's disease, as he maintains, may perhaps be so, but the fact that that also applied to the kidney that remained in Eddowes' body is nowhere reported in any surviving document.

It must be remembered, too, that Bright's disease is not a disease deriving from a single causative factor in the way that, say, tuberculosis is. It is simply a descriptive term, coined by Dr Richard Bright, of Guy's Hospital, about the year 1827, applied to a collection of associated signs and symptoms connected with a class of diseases of the kidney, the most common of which are albuminuria and oedema, accruing from a variety of different aetiologies to produce such diseases as, among others, acute, sub-acute and chronic glomerulonephritis and nephritis. It is likely that the kidneys of very many people, particularly, it could be argued, those of the submerged and destitute classes of the period, whose physical resistance to disease might be expected to present a low profile, would exhibit morbid changes of the type that would fall into the symptom pattern of what in those days was identified as Bright's disease, so the mere fact that the Lusk kidney and Catherine Eddowes' remaining kidney both showed such pathological signs would be by no means conclusive, or even persuasive.

It must be added that Bright's disease is not caused by, or in any way connected with, alcoholism. Neither does alcohol injure or destroy the kidneys, as it does the liver and stomach; and the term 'ginny' kidney, attributed to Dr Openshaw, is medically meaningless. It may perhaps be that, at a time when the popular mind was much occupied with the 'evils of strong drink', inflammatory and degenerative conditions of the kidney were, erroneously, as it has proved, ascribed to it.

I am at a loss, too, to understand how Dr Openshaw was able to make, if indeed he did, so categorical a pronouncement concerning the gender of the person from whom the excised kidney had been taken. There is no distinguishing sexual characteristic stamped in the human kidney. You could not tell whether it came from a man or a woman. Neither would it be possible to estimate, as Dr Openshaw is said to have estimated, the age of a person from a portion of kidney, especially a diseased kidney. I suspect that in these particularities Dr Openshaw has been misreported.[16]

On the other hand, it is perfectly possible, by means of histological examination, to assess, from the condition of preservation exhibited by the cells of the tissue, the approximate time at which a specimen has been placed in spirits.

At a first glance, the statement concerning the attachment of renal artery seems to provide irrefutable proof that the Lusk kidney came from the Mitre Square victim. Closer scrutiny diminishes certitude. The renal artery is, as Smith correctly informs us, on average approximately 3 inches long, although that on the left kidney will be shorter than that on the right, and roughly the thickness of a pencil. Approximately 1 inch remained attached to the Lusk kidney, although it may well have shrunk as the result of immersion in spirits of wine. Now that is just about the amount of renal artery that you would expect to find on any crudely excised kidney, as unless the operator sets out with the deliberate intention of detaching the organ and artery intact, he is likely to divide the artery closer to its distal extremity – that is, away from the aorta and nearer to the corpus of the kidney. The implication that it was possible to match up the fragment of artery on the Lusk kidney with the alleged greater length of artery remaining in the cadaver is not factually supported, for the Lusk kidney was received by Dr Gordon Brown on 19 October, and Catherine Eddowes had been buried in the City of London Cemetery at Ilford on 8 October.[17] Her body would not, therefore, have been available for the making of conclusive comparisons, and she was certainly not exhumed for the purpose.

It is my personal opinion that Smith, or his literary 'ghost', gilded the kidney. One must, in the absence of any further contradictory report, call into evidence Dr Brown's clear and unequivocal statement regarding the identification of the Lusk kidney with Eddowes' missing kidney. 'On this point no definite opinion can be pronounced.'

There was one person, however, who expressed approval of Dr Openshaw and his stalwart efforts. On 29 October 1888, an unknown hand slipped a brief but pungent missive into an East London post box.

Dr Openshaw
Pathological curator
London Hospital
Whitechapel
Old boss you was rite it was the left kidney i was goin to hopperate agin close to your ospitle just as i was goin to dror mi nife along of er bloomin throte them cusses of coppers spoilt the game but i guess i wil be on the job soon and will send you another bit of innerds
Jack the ripper
O have you seen the devl with his mikerscope and scalpul a lookin at a Kidney with a slide cocked up

Meanwhile, at Scotland Yard the police were scanning the brown paper wrapping of Mr Lusk's parcel. Apart from the letters 'OND' – obviously part of the word 'London' – the postmark on it was indecipherable, but the post office officials were of the opinion that the package had been posted in either the Eastern or the East Central district of London. The fact that it bore only one postmark suggested that it was posted in the district in which it was received, the Eastern District, for letters and packages travelling from one postal district to another usually bore the postmarks of both.

A further point which emerged was that the package was too large to have been dropped into an ordinary postbox, and it seemed likely that it had been despatched from Lombard Street or Gracechurch Street, at both of which post offices there were receptacles of unusually wide dimensions. The packet bore two penny stamps and had been posted in the ordinary way. Had it been sent by parcel post, the place of despatch would have been traceable, and there would have been further possibility that one of the officials might have remembered the sender.

The police also decided that there was little doubt that the 'From Hell' letter and the postcard previously received by Mr Lusk were in the same handwriting and noted that these two communications differed in every respect, other than in the use of the word 'boss', from others signed 'Jack the Ripper'.

The *Daily Telegraph* of 20 October 1888 reports a statement made on the night of Friday 19 October by a Miss Emily Marsh, whose father carried on business in the leather trade at 218 Jubilee Street.

> In Mr Marsh's absence Miss Marsh was in the front shop, shortly after one o'clock on Monday last [15 October] when a stranger, dressed in clerical costume, entered, and referring to the reward bill in the window, asked for the address of Mr Lusk, described therein as the president of the Vigilance Committee. Miss Marsh at once referred the man to Mr J. Aarons, the treasurer of the Committee, who resides at the corner of Jubilee Street and Mile End Road, a distance of about 30 yards, The man, however, said he did not wish to go there, and Miss Marsh thereupon produced a newspaper in which Mr Lusk's address was given as Alderney Road, Globe Road, no number being given. She requested the stranger to read the address, but he declined, saying, 'Read it out,' and proceeded to write something in his pocket-book, keeping his head down meanwhile. He subsequently left the shop, after thanking the young lady for the information, but not before Miss Marsh, alarmed by the man's appearance, had sent the shop-boy, John Cormack, to see that all was right. This lad, as well as Miss Marsh, gave a full description of the man, while Mr Marsh, who happened to come along at the time, also encountered him on the pavement outside. The stranger is described as a man of some forty-five years of age, fully six feet in height, and slimly built. He wore a soft felt black hat, drawn over his forehead, a stand-up collar, and a very long black single-breasted overcoat, with a Prussian or clerical collar partly turned up. His face was of a sallow type, and he had a dark beard and moustache. The man spoke with what was taken to be an Irish accent. No importance was attached to the incident until Miss Marsh read of the receipt by Mr Lusk of a strange parcel, and then it occurred to her that the stranger might be the person who had despatched it. His inquiry was made at one o'clock on Monday afternoon, and Mr Lusk received the package at eight p.m. the next day. The address on the package curiously enough gives no number in Alderney Road, a piece of information which Miss Marsh could not supply. It appears that on leaving the shop the man went right by Mr Aaron's house, but did not call.

I cannot see any especial significance in the fact that the address on the package gave no number in Alderney Road, for it is plainly stated that the address read out by Miss Marsh from the newspaper did not give any number, so that anyone reading any copy of the newspaper for the purpose of obtaining Mr Lusk's address would not be in possession of the number. The detail about the Irish accent is, however, interesting. It was not the first blush of suspicion against the Irish. Sir Charles Warren had frankly admitted that he thought that the author of the 'Juwes' writing on the wall was an Irishman. Certainly, the double-negative construction presented idiomatic Hibernian undertones – 'I'll not be after being blamed for nothing' – and the spelling of Mr as 'Mishter' Lusk had Hibernian overtones.

Strangely enough, it was an Irishman, twenty-eight-year-old Patrick Joseph Byrne, who, seventy-one years later, proved capable of the commission of an atrocity of comparable calibre, when, on 23 December 1959, he decapitated and ferociously mutilated Stephanie Baird, aged twenty-one, at the YWCA Hostel in Wheeleys Road, at Edgbaston, Birmingham.

It is worth quoting the statement which Byrne made to the Birmingham City Police on 10 February 1960 for the light it throws upon the Ripper-style mentality and disordered thought processes:

> She screamed and then I put my hands round her neck. She went backwards inside the room with me squeezing her throat, and then fell backwards. Her head bumped on the floor and I was lying on top of her, kissing her and squeezing her neck at the one time. I heard a couple of noises in her throat, but kept on kissing her. I was fully sure she was dead then because I had the whole power of my back squeezing her throat … I started licking and biting her all over … There was a table knife in there. I got the knife in my right hand, then caught hold of her right breast and carved the knife round it. It was hard to cut round the skin, but in the end I got it off. I was very surprised and disappointed it came away flat in my hand. I just looked at it and then flung it towards the bed. I scored her round the chest with the knife and then started to cut down the stomach to have a look at the womb.

He goes on to describe how he tore one of her stockings off and slashed down her legs with the knife and tried to cut out her vagina:

> But the knife would not cut very well. I then went back to her head and, grabbing her hair, I pulled her up and could see her back. I scored her back with the knife a few times, but it didn't go very deep. Her back seemed beautiful before and I felt I wanted to score it. I lay her back on the floor and I saw the front of her throat become very plump. I ran the knife across the front of it and it parted very easily. I started on the back of the neck then, catching hold of her hair and pulling her head close to my bare chest. I kept on cutting away. It surprised me how easy the head came off … I had it by the hair and I stood up. I held it up to the mirror and looked at it through the mirror. It was then I noticed a saucepan at the back of the room reflected in the mirror. A thought came into my head tremendously quick to put the head in the pan. Just after I had done some of the mutilations, I stood up and wrote a note with a biro on some paper on the dressing table. I can't remember the words I used, but I wanted everybody to see my life in one little note. When I got out of the room I was pretty frantic and I went round the back. I don't remember getting there, but the next thing I saw was another lighted window in the other block of cubicles. I was very excited, breathing heavy and thinking I ought to terrorise all women. I wanted to get my own back on them for causing my nervous tension through sex. I felt I only wanted to kill beautiful women.[18]

Professor Camps makes the point that recent advances in the methodology of handwriting identification and the chemical analysis of ink and paper would today be very likely to establish whether or not the letter and postcard addressed to the Central News Office, and the postcard and 'From hell' letter to Mr Lusk, emanated from the same source.

Robert Jackson writes in *Frances Camps* (1975), 'Camps himself did not accept the theory that the killer must necessarily have been a doctor or a man of medical training

… Any surgeon who operated in this manner would have been struck off the medical register.'

Camps discarded both the Duke of Clarence and Sir William Gull as suspects, and 'with his knowledge of the workings of the criminal mind, came down in favour of the Farson theory'.

As to the question of what became of Jack the Ripper, Camps emphasised that 'sadistic killers of this type do not burn out or retire. The explanation for his disappearance after the killing of Mary Jane Kelly can only, he thinks, be supplied in terms of emigration, incarceration – in prison or mental hospital – or death.

52
Pictures of the Dead

According to the authors of the *A to Z*, it was in the spring of the centenary year, in the pages of the *London Evening Standard* of 21 April 1988, that the first public mention was made of the existence of the Abberline diaries.

Although at that time no one, except Joseph Sickert, whose property the alleged diaries were, was known to have actually seen them, the *A to Z* authors committed themselves, in their 1994 revised edition, to the statement that '*Prima facie* they [the diaries] appear to be forgeries' – and no *post facto* cause has emerged to displace that appearance. Rather the reverse.

Sundry Abberline diary entry extracts were exclusively disclosed in Melvyn Fairclough's *The Ripper and the Royals* (1991) – which work, incidentally, was openly sponsored by Joseph Sickert – and the *A to Z* authors having thus had the opportunity to read there those extracts, observed that details given about the Ripper's victims in the alleged Abberline diary give every sign of derivation from an article by Neal Shelden, 'Victims of Jack the Ripper' in *True Detective*, January 1989. A kind of confirmation seems afforded by the meticulous reproduction in the diary extracts of certain minor, admitted, Sheldenian errors. A major error, however, was the reversal by, presumably Abberline, of 'his own forename initials'. Fairclough has since admitted that he 'no longer believes the diaries to be genuine'. The strong presumption is that they were the work of the skilled artist Hobo Sickert or Gorman.

What you might call the 'Big Bang' of the year 1988 was the Press Association story of 17 August that 'within the last few months an album of photographs, believed to have been used for lectures, was found among the effects of a deceased senior police officer. His family forwarded them to the Yard.'

They were mortuary photographs of Ripper victims. It was the first time that we had seen three of the faces: that of Polly Nichols with her throat slashed, Annie Chapman, and Elisabeth Stride on a mortuary slab. The other two photographs were a copy of the familiar one of Catherine Eddowes and a previously unknown variant photograph of Mary Jane Kelly on her blood-soaked deathbed.[19]

John Ezard wrote in the *Guardian* (19 August 1988): 'These pictures in a faded sepia album retain the power to move even when displayed under cellophane in the Yard's plate-glass tower block. Three of them show the blanched, life-worn faces of prostitutes butchered in a world of cobblestones and gaslight. They rest on mortuary slabs or in coffins.'

I think that the ability of the modern journalist to write excellent, straightforward and evocative descriptive prose is continually underestimated and consistently undervalued. Many, many journalists use words and turns of phrase like verbal Sheraton.

News came from Canada that same month, via the *Toronto Globe and Mail*, 30 August 1988, that a Canadian group, including literary agent Helen Heller, had been led by their researches to the conclusion that Mary Kelly's landlord, fifty-one-year-old John McCarthy, was the Ripper.

In September, BBC 2 put out under their *Timewatch* banner, a topical 'Shadow of the Ripper' documentary, in which Christopher Frayling delivered himself of a professor of cultural history's academic appraisal of the Jack the Ripper murders. His centennial view of the Victorian horror story was the penetrating observation that it had all been 'got up' by the press. Had contemporary journalists and sequent authors not made such a big deal of the affair, it would most certainly have been forgotten. Instead, by dreaming up solutions, involving royalty, upper-class decadents and sadistic doctors, the killings have been promoted from fact to legend. Rather than asking, 'Who was Jack the Ripper?' we should be asking 'Why do we need to know?' A supportive American academic lady contributed, 'Jack the Ripper can only be understood as part of the social and historical context of class conflict, urban crisis and the challenge of feminism.'

Daniel Farson, writing to the *Spectator* on 10 September 1988 about the *Timewatch* documentary, described most theories of Ripper identity as 'pyramids of guesswork constructed on a single false clue'. Expanding, he went on: 'In this way you can prove that the Ripper was Oscar Wilde or Marie Lloyd.' And, with a winning candour of insight, confessed, 'All the Ripperologists, myself included, are fiercely protective of our individual suspects, like stage-struck mothers.'

Farson also informs us, most interestingly, that the late Professor Keith Simpson told him that he thought it unlikely that the Ripper was a doctor, for his obsession would have been satisfied by his work or noticed by his colleagues. But he did believe that Jack had a medical background.

The Criminologist, in its autumn 1988 issue, carried an article by Colin Kendell, 'Did Mary Kelly Die?' He advanced the thought that her extreme facial mutilation made her identification uncertain, so that Caroline Maxwell, and other witnesses who believed that they had seen her alive later on the morning of 9 November 1888, might have been correct.

Two later pieces in the *Criminologist* – spring 1989 and summer 1990 – confirm the impression that Mr Kendell's well-presented and responsibly argued work conveys. One recognises that he is, however, resting his case on Stephen Knight's *Final Solution*, and striving to work other data into supporting material for his belief in the guilt of Sir William Gull.

On the question of Mary Kelly's survival, Nicholas Warren, in his November 1987 contribution to *True Detective*, dangles a tempting piece of bait – or baiting. Mary Kelly, he reminds us, told some interesting, perhaps tall, stories about her past life. Most persistently she spoke of meeting in the West End of London a young man of certain cultural pretensions and accompanying him to France. Now all these facts about this mysterious young man glove-fit Walter Sickert. He was twenty-eight in 1888, burning with ambition. He maintained West End London premises. He made frequent trips to France, staying for long periods. Could he and Marie Jeanette … There is small harm in an occasional whimsicality.

At the beginning of 1988, a suspect, whom Stewart Hicks, a Norwich accountant and Ripper theoretician or fancier of respected standing, had been nursing since around 1985, was, as the rocket-launchers' lingo has it, 'looking good'. This was a Dr John Hewitt (1850–92). Hicks had reason to think that he was Sickert's unnamed veterinary student. Prior to 1888, Dr Hewitt practised in Manchester, but in that year was confined in Coton Hill Private Asylum, at Stafford. Hicks contacted Colin Wilson and they made the promising discovery that Hewitt had been out and about from time to time during the year 1888.

I well remember Colin Wilson's excitement when, in strictest confidence, he told me all this. But Ripper research is generous with disappointments – if nothing else! – and this proved to be one of them. In 1988, the Coton Hill Asylum papers were placed in the Record Office, and Hicks and Wilson found that the periods when Hewitt had been at large did not chime with the Ripper murder dates.

Joseph C. Rupp, MD, PhD, Medical Examiner of Nueces County, Texas, asked in the winter 1988 issue of the *Criminologist*, 'Was Francis Thompson Jack the Ripper?' Dr Rupp had been reading John Walsh's biography of the poet, *Strange Harp, Strange Symphony* (1968).

Born in Preston, Lancashire, in 1859, Thompson, the son of a doctor, was, by the age of twenty-eight, a failed priest and a failed medical student. He was also a laudanum addict, down and out on the streets of London. That bitter winter of '87, he was befriended by a young prostitute, who, pitying him, took him home to share her food and lodging with her. Then, in the April of 1888, Thompson was rescued by Wilfred Meynell, editor of the Catholic magazine *Merry England*, to which he had submitted an essay and some poems. But this rescue precipitated a life-crisis for Thompson. It meant the breaking off of his relationship with the prostitute who had for so long looked after him. In the end, it was this unselfish girl herself who solved the problem. Quietly, without a word, without a trace, she removed herself, disappeared – for ever. Thompson was desolate. In the slightly adapted words of, perhaps, his finest poem, 'The Hound of Heaven':

> He sought her down the nights and down the days,
> He sought her down the arches of the years,
> He sought her down the labyrinthine ways
> Of his own mind, and in the mist of tears …

During that autumn of terror – August, September 1888 – Thompson was conducting his desperate search through all of hard-cobble-hearted London's netherworld. A note in Walsh's book observes,

> At this time occurred the most bizarre coincidence in Thompson's life. During the very weeks that he was searching for his prostitute friend, London was in an uproar over the ghastly deaths of five such women at the hands of Jack the Ripper. In these circumstances his concern for his friend's welfare would naturally have been heightened. The police threw a wide net over the city, investigating thousands of drifters, and known consorters with the city's lower elements, and it is not beyond possibility that Thompson himself may have been questioned. He was, after all, a drug addict, acquainted with prostitutes, and, most alarming, a former medical student!

In mid-November 1888, Thompson entered hospital for treatment for his addiction. Following his sudden departure from the London scene, the Ripper killings ceased.

So Rupp's case shapes itself. Thompson, in addition to being a drug-addicted associate of prostitutes, and former medical student, was certainly possessed of – or by – a chaotic sexuality. His poetry of the time seethes with underlying rage. Francis Thompson seems to Joseph Rupp at least as good a suspect as any number of others. Perhaps, he asks, a far better one?

I would not be so sure about that. There seem to me to be too many assumptive gaps. A major one: there has not been a scintilla of evidence produced that Thompson ever hunted for his De Quincey lady among the purlieus and stews of Spitalfields and Whitechapel.

Brian Marriner brought down the curtain on the centenary year, penning a neat summary, 'Looking Back on Jack the Ripper', in the December 1988 number of *True Detective*.[20] And it was Brian Marriner again, who, in the January 1989 issue of *True Detective*, opened the year with a lengthy discussion of the suspect status of George Chapman, aka Severin Klosowski, 'The Enigma of George Chapman'.[21] This very capably reviews at length all of the thinnish sheaves of garnered evidence, but has of necessity to leave us feeling, yet again, as one used to feel in the days of continuous cinema performances, this is where we came in.

Brian Marriner died in 1999.

53
A Victimology

That same January 1989 issue of *True Detective* included also Neal Shelden's new-ground-breaking 'Victims of Jack the Ripper', in which he reported the results of his dexterous forays into the backgrounds of the five generally accepted recipients of ungentle Jack's terminal ministrations. By a combination of orthodox genealogical methodology, unique personal doggedness, and pure inspiration, Mr Shelden succeeded in uncovering a great deal about the anonymous lives and hidden personalities of the unfortunate women who were the Ripper's victims.

Mary Jane Kelly proved the most disappointing. No amount of leafing through documents at the General Registrar's Office or examination of the what has been thought to be the appropriate census (Carmarthen for 1881), and the deposited papers of workhouses and infirmaries, brought in a single fact for the winnowing. She was, and remains, what police and social workers who deal with the waifs and strays of the streets call 'a mystery'.

At least Mr Shelden was able to put the record, which had been wrong for a hundred years, right on Catherine Eddowes' age. At the inquest, her sister, Eliza, had said, 'To the best of my knowledge, she was forty-three on her last birthday [14 April 1888].' Mr Shelden is obliged, ungallantly, to give it away that actually, she was, at the time of her murder, forty-six years and five months old.

Let us see what else time has let slip in the matter of the truth about other of Jack's victims.

Mary Ann Nichols has always seemed a very shadowy, one might almost say self-effacing, character; little more than a humped bundle on the cobbles of Buck's Row in the light of the policeman's bull's-eye. Mary Ann was, in fact, London born and bred. The daughter of a locksmith, Edward Walker, of Dean Street, Fetter Lane, she was born in 1845. In 1864, nineteen-year-old Mary Ann married William Nichols, a printer of Bouverie Street, which is where they lived, briefly, when they were first married. They then moved on to live with Mary Ann's father, resident at No. 131 Trafalgar Street, Walworth. Between 1864 and 1870, Mary Ann bore William three children – Edward John (1864), Percy George (1868), and Alice Esther (1870). They moved again in July 1876, this time to a place of their own, Tenement No. 3, Block D, of Peabody Buildings, in Duchy Street, Stamford Street Estate, Lambeth. Two more children were born here, Eliza Sarah (1876) and, the last of the brood, Henry Alfred (1878). By this time things were going badly wrong. Mary Ann had begun to drink heavily and had, on a number of occasions, moved out of the family home, but had always eventually returned. William had taken up with a woman who had assisted at Mary Ann's accouchement with Eliza Sarah. The Nichols separated in 1880. William kept the children, except Edward John, who went off to live with his mother, and did not so much as speak to his father until after his mother's death. William paid Mary Ann a weekly allowance of five shillings (worth then about £12), which continued until 1882, when he discovered that she was earning money as a prostitute. Her lifestyle degenerated. From September 1880 to May 1881, she was in Lambeth Workhouse. After further spells in the workhouse and Lambeth Infirmary, she went, in March 1883, to live with her father, but her constant drinking caused friction and, after a bad quarrel, she left the following May. After another spell in Lambeth Workhouse, she settled into 15 York Street, Walworth, where she lived with a blacksmith named Stuart Drew. The cohabitation lasted until 1887, when, after she had sold some of Drew's possessions in order to buy drink, he left her, and she went back into the workhouse. Mary Ann made a final effort at respectability when, on 14 April 1888, she entered the service of Mr Samuel Cowdry and his wife, Sarah, in Wandsworth.

She wrote to her father:

> Ingleside,
> Rose Hill Road,
> Wandsworth.
>
> I just write to say you will be glad to know that I am settled in my new place, and going all right up to now. My people went out yesterday, and have not returned, so I am left in charge. It is a grand place inside, with trees and gardens back and front. All has been newly done up. They are teetotallers, and very religious, so I ought to get on. They are very nice people, and I have not much to do. I hope you are all right and the boy has work. So goodbye now for the present.
>
> Yours truly,
> Polly
> Answer soon please, and let me know how you are.

In July Mary Ann absconded from the Cowdrys', with a bundle of stolen clothes, valued at £3 10*s*.

So it was back to the workhouse – Gray's Inn Temporary Workhouse – and then, in August, a four-penny bed at 18 Thrawl Street and at The White House, a dosshouse at No. 36 Flower and Dean Street.

Mary Ann's long, sad, lonely pilgrimage came to its end in the small hours of 31 August 1888, on the shining wet cobbles of Buck's Row.

Annie Chapman, the second canonical victim of Jack's keen knife, was, like Mary Ann Nichols, a Londoner, but she was four years older, born, Eliza Annie Smith, in Paddington in 1841. Her father, George Smith, the son of a Lincolnshire shoemaker, followed his father's trade until, in December 1834, he went to London and enlisted in the Second Regiment of the Life Guards. He married Ruth Chapman, the daughter of a shoemaker of Hurstmonceux, in Sussex, in 1846, so baby Annie was plainly an early arrival, making her appearance on the wrong side of the blanket. Annie was ten when the family moved to Windsor, in 1856. The next fact that we have is that in 1869 the twenty-eight-year-old Annie, described as 5 feet tall, stout, well-proportioned, with a fair complexion, blue eyes, dark, wavy brown hair, a large, prominent, rather thick nose, and, later, two front teeth missing from her lower jaw, married John Chapman, at All Saints Church, in Ennismore Gardens, Knightsbridge. They lived in West London until 1882, when they moved back to Windsor. Annie had borne John two daughters, Emily Ruth (1870) and Annie Georgina (1873), and a crippled son, John

Alfred (1880). Tragically, Emily, who suffered from epileptic fits, had died of meningitis in 1882, and it was shortly before her death that Annie started to show signs of restlessness. She abandoned her family and returned to London alone. Allegedly, it was her alcoholism and immorality which broke up the marriage. Right up to the time of his death in 1886, her husband continued to send her occasional sums of money. When the sporadic allowances ceased, things became tough. She managed to scrape a living by hawking her own crochet work, selling matches or flowers, accepting bits and pieces of financial help from men friends and, when all else failed, resorting to prostitution. Neal Shelden describes her as 'clever and industrious. A very respectable, quiet, but sociable woman, who never used bad language, was well educated, and often read in her leisure time.'

It must have been 'the demon drink' that undermined all these vauntedly fine qualities and reduced her in the end to what she became. The *Windsor and Eton Gazette* of 15 September 1888 reported that 'her dissolute habits made it imperatively necessary that she should reside elsewhere'. She was well known throughout the neighbourhood of Clewer and Windsor and was often seen wandering about the country like a common tramp. During 1886 she was living at 30 Dorset Street with a sievemaker known by the nickname of Jack Sievey. It seems that they must have drifted apart, for from around May 1888 she was living mainly at Crossingham's Lodging-House, at 35 Dorset Street.

Elisabeth Stride was the Ripper's third strike. She was the daughter of Swedish farmer Gustaf Ericsson, of Stora Tumlehed, Hisingen Island, Torslanda, near Gothenburg. Born in 1843, she moved in 1860, when she was seventeen, to Gothenburg, where, in February 1861, she found employment as a domestic servant with Lars Frederick Olofsson. She left the service of the Olofsson family in February 1864, and by March 1865 was registered by the police of Gothenburg as a professional prostitute.

The following April, she was admitted to Kurhuset, the hospital in the red-light district near Gothenburg Harbour, for the treatment of venereal disease. She was suffering from venereal warts. While hospitalised she gave birth to a stillborn daughter.

Discharged in May 1865, she was readmitted in August to be treated for a venereal ulcer. Discharged in September, she had to be admitted again in October. The ulcer had not cleared up. She was finally discharged, wart and ulcer free, and in a certified state of general good health, on 1 November 1865.

On 14 November, she was struck off the police register of prostitutes. She had taken a job as a maid with a woman named Maria Wejsner.

Elisabeth's mother had died in 1864, and on receiving, in late 1865 or January 1866, a substantial inheritance, she applied for, and was granted, permission to move to London, and, on 7 February 1866, sailed for England.

On 7 March 1869, giving her maiden name as Gustifson and her address as 67 Gower Street, she married, at the parish church of St Giles-in-the-Fields, John Thomas Stride, and they opened a coffee shop in Upper North Street, Poplar.

We have no hint of the why or wherefore of it, but on 21 March 1877, she was taken by the police from the Thames Magistrates Court, Arbour Square, Stepney, to the Poplar Workhouse.

The year 1878 was that of the great Thames disaster, when, on the evening of 3 September, the paddle steamer *Princess Alice* collided with the collier *Bywell Castle* off Tripcock Point, near North Woolwich, and sank with the loss of more than 600 lives.

Elisabeth Stride claimed that her husband and two children were among the drowned. This proved to be untrue. As a matter of fact, John Thomas Stride died of heart disease in Stepney Sick Asylum on 24 October 1884.

In 1881, the couple were living together at 69 Usher Road, Old Ford Road, Bow, but the marriage was in trouble. In December 1881, Elisabeth was undergoing a nasty attack of bronchitis and was for a time being nursed in the Whitechapel Workhouse Infirmary, and she gave as her home address that of a lodging-house in Brick Lane. After leaving the infirmary, she moved into a lodging-house at 32 Flower and Dean Street.

By 1885, she was living with Michael Kidney, a labourer in his early thirties, at 38 Dorset Street. He was rough of tongue and arm and she brought a charge of assault against him. He drank and she seems to have been overfond of the bottle, managing to amass eight convictions for drunkenness in the final year of her rather short life.

She met death, the lightning flash of a throat-cutting knife, in gloomy Dutfield's Yard on 30 September 1888.

The victim of frisky Jacky's final *al fresco* killing was his fourth selected, Catherine Eddowes. Neal Shelden has done sterling research on her.

Catherine was from Wolverhampton. She was born at Graisley Green on 14 April 1842, which means that she was forty-six when Jack claimed her.

By no stretch of the imagination could her early years be described as jolly. Her father, George Eddowes, a tin plate varnisher, moved with his sizeable family – Catherine had a brother and four sisters, and there were to be four more brothers and two more sisters – to Bermondsey before Catherine was two. Her mother, Catherine, *née* Evans, died of pulmonary tuberculosis in 1855, when her daughter was only thirteen. Two years later her father died.

The young Catherine, or Kate as she was called, was educated at St John's Charity School, Potter's Field, Tooley Street. After their mother's death, most of the children were sent to Bermondsey Workhouse and Industrial School, Kate, however, went on to Dowgate Charity School in the City of London.

According to the 1861 census, Kate was then living with her aunt (Elizabeth Eddowes), her husband, William, and their three children, at 50 Bilston Street, Wolverhampton. Her occupation was given on the census form as 'scourer', although another aunt, Sarah Croot, of 36 Bilston Street, said that Kate worked as a tin plate stamper at the Old Hall Works in Wolverhampton, where Uncle William also worked.

Kate, discovered in 1862 to be stealing, was unable to keep her job at the Old Hall Works, and ran away to live on what was known as 'The Brick Hill', Bagot Street, Birmingham, with another uncle, Thomas Eddowes, who was a pugilist turned boot and shoemaker. She found work in Birmingham as a tray polisher with a firm in Legge Street.

It was some time in 1862 that Kate met, it is believed in Birmingham, a twenty-four-year-old man named Thomas Conway. He had served, under the name of Quinn, as Private No. 350, in the 1st Battalion of the 18th Royal Irish Regiment, and, discharged at Dublin, invalided out with rheumatism, chronic bronchitis, and heart disease, was drawing a military pension. The couple teamed up and are said to have made a modest living by selling chapbooks – which Conway wrote – in Birmingham and the Midlands.

Kate used to give the impression that she was legitimately married to Conway, and had his initials, T. C., tattooed on her forearm. But no trace of any such marriage could anywhere be found. Nevertheless, she presented him with three children – Catherine Ann Conway (1863), Thomas (1868), Alfred George (1873).

The 1881 census shows Thomas, Kate and their two sons living at 71 Lower George Street, Chelsea. Conway was described as a hawker, Kate as a charwoman. Later that year, the Conways separated. He took his sons with him. The rupture was blamed on Kate's drinking; she was slipping into alcoholism, and periodic absences from home, but it is also likely that she was subjected to brutal treatment by Conway, as witness her blackened eyes, and not loath to escape his clutches. She made her way to Spitalfields, where her widowed sister, Eliza, was living. When times were hard, Kate turned to prostitution. At other times, she earned a little money working for the Jewish community in Brick Lane.

It was not long before she joined forces with an Irish labourer-cum-market-porter, John Kelly, with whom she went to live in lodgings at 55 Flower and Dean Street. The liaison lasted. She was still with him in 1888.

Jack was ready and waiting for her in the south-west corner of Mitre Square shortly after the clock struck half-past one on the morning of 1 October 1888.

54
A Child's Guide to Ripperland

On the book front in 1990 there came forth from San Diego the year's solitary but worthy volume; slender – ninety-six pages – becomingly plainly titled simply *Jack the Ripper*, which says all and nothing at all. It is included in a series published by the Greenhaven Press, of San Diego, entitled *Great Mysteries: Opposing Viewpoints*.

Written by a Bedford, Indiana, wife and mother, Katie Colby-Newton, it is veritably 'The Young Folks' Garland of Ripperianiae', targeted at young people and schoolchildren from around ten years of age upwards.

Nicely illustrated, a somewhat garish fairy-tale-type picture on its board cover apart, it is an exercise in comprehensive brevity, deceptively simply written, disguising a great deal of hard work; for simple things are almost always the most complicated to produce.

Mrs Colby-Newton believes that the story is 'more than a mystery. It is a tragedy that ruined far more lives than those of the five women killed by the elusive butcher'. This book, we are told, is written for the curious – those who want to explore the mysteries.

Katie Colby-Newton sets the scene:

> Imagine the city of London in 1888. Imagine the evil-smelling alleyways and courtyards of Whitechapel in the East End. This area, the worst section of the city, has dark streets lighted only by gaslight. The lamps glow dimly yellow in the misty night. Walls, doorways, and windows are only fuzzily visible. Deep threatening shadows take over most of the walkways. The darkness and the dirt can easily hide a murderer. Imagine the constant ocean of noise in the slum: the bustle of delivery wagons rumbling on the way to market; the rattle of the carriages of wealthy men leaving prostitutes and drinking and gambling houses; the gruff conversations of workers on their way to and from jobs in the markets and slaughterhouses, the rattles, clangs, and whistles of a nearby train; the carousing of drunkards.
>
> 'Murder!' comes a cry from a Whitechapel courtyard. The chilling scream goes unheard. It is all part of the night noise. Jack the Ripper, the notorious murderer, escapes again, cloaked and invisible. The noise and the darkness swallow him up.

Then, having sketched in the socio-economic silhouette of the murder map – 'Poverty, degradation, desperation, and despair filled the streets' – she supplies unsparingly the basic details of each of the five core murders.

What kind of person was Jack the Ripper? asks Mrs Colby-Newton, and proceeds to list, 'with the opinions of Dr Thomas Bond and Colin Wilson in mind', the characteristics that the undiscovered killer had revealed.

Dr Bond reported,

> The murderer must have been a man of physical strength and of great coolness and daring. There is no evidence that he had an accomplice. He must in my opinion be a man subject to attacks of homicidal and erotic mania … It is of course possible that the Homicidal impulse may have developed from a revengeful or brooding condition of the mind, or that religious mania may have been the original disease, but I do not think either hypothesis is likely. The murderer in external appearance is quite likely to be a quiet inoffensive looking man, probably middle-aged and neatly and respectably dressed. I think he must be in the habit of wearing a cloak or overcoat or he could hardly have escaped notice in the streets if the blood on his hands or clothes were visible … He would be solitary and eccentric in his habits, also he is most likely to be a man without regular occupation, but with some small income or pension. He is possibly living among respectable persons who have some knowledge of his character and habits and who may have grounds for suspicion that he isn't quite right in his mind at times. Such persons would probably be unwilling to communicate suspicions to the police for fear of trouble or notoriety.

Colin Wilson thinks that Jack the Ripper 'was a sick man, a man twisted with hatred and wracked by sadistic cravings.' He belonged to a group of people whose personalities are dominant – that is, they have to control other people. The Ripper had a need to dominate women. He was not a talented or creative man. He probably had no way to release harmlessly the overwhelming feeling that he must dominate a woman or kill her. Probably Jack the Ripper was not very talented but was frustrated, angry at society, and maybe a 'downstart'. A downstart is a person who works below his or her qualifications. For example, a downstart may be qualified to teach at the college level but can only find a job as a cashier in a grocery store.

With the opinions of Dr Thomas Bond and Colin Wilson in mind, the author proceeds to the presentation of a series of opposing viewpoints regarding the name of the true perpetrator.

A selection of high-profile suspects is identity paraded. Royal Jack is given pride of place, but Druitt, Chapman, Cutbush, Dr Forbes Winslow's Mr G., Wentworth Bell Smith, Robin Odell's shadowy *shochet*, and – the misogynist's choice – Jill the Ripper are also put up.

The author expresses no personal preference in the sempiternal search for the nomination of the elusive butcher. Instead, she asks,

> Were the Ripper murders the crimes of a sick and perverted killer? Were they a cry for attention to the horrible living and working conditions of the poor of London in that late-Victorian era? Were they a political cover-up?
>
> Much of what has been written about this most notorious of killers has been denounced by other 'experts' as being a 'twisting' of the facts. The Ripperologists who travel to London to do their research find that time – 125 years have passed since the killings took place – is only one of their enemies. The police files are frustratingly incomplete. The newspapers of the day often did not report straight facts; they embellished in order to excite the interest of their readers. Did the London police of 1888 solve the mystery of Jack the Ripper, and then suppress the answer? If they did not, can we hope to solve it today? Many people think we can.

To bring the curtain down on the year 1990, Andrew Holloway presented in the December issue of the *Cricketer* an article, 'Not Guilty', in which he produced a most elaborate plot, postulating that Montague John Druitt did not commit suicide, but was in reality the victim of his solicitor brother William's rapacity, his desire to gain control of the family estates. He fed the police with the bogus story of his fear that Montague John was the Ripper, thus diverting and directing their suspicion. He it was who, having drugged or poisoned Montague, dumped his body in the Thames and fabricated the while-of-unsound-mind suicide.

55
Ostrog Unmasked

Described by the austerely magisterial and extremely influential *Times Literary Supplement* as 'well written, scholarly and authoritative', *The Jack the Ripper A to Z* became at once on its publication in 1991 the encyclopedic bible of Ripperology, its trinity of authors – Paul Begg, Martin Fido and Keith Skinner – transformed overnight into a veneration of Ripperological gurus.

How shrewd was Donald Rumbelow's critical judgement: 'This book has to be the anchor of future Jack the Ripper studies.'

I, too, was impressed, writing in the *New Law Journal*,[22]

> Alpha to omega, this book provides an absolutely reliable summation of the current state of the art of the 'Ripperologist'. Venerable chestnuts are roasted and exploded, barnaclings of legends scraped away. New intelligences are imparted; full data, for instance, concerning the mad Russian doctor, Michael Ostrog, hitherto a suspect name to conjure with, the fact that Mary Jane Kelly, Jack's last canonical victim, was not pregnant, and it was her heart, not her uterus, that was borne away.

I most heartily welcome the new generation of Ripper students, extremely capable, resourceful and industrious. I, who had by then been studying the sequence of Whitechapel murders for more than fifty years, who had read every book on the subject, and would, until the advent of the new generation of students, have unhesitatingly opined that we would never know the identity of Saucy Jacky, felt now not so sure.

An undeniably great coup was the unearthing of the details concerning, and even a photograph of, Macnaghten's third man, the hitherto always elusive and rather mysterious Michael Ostrog. He stands here revealed as no Ripper – just a rather sad conman and petty thief.

Ostrog fielded an impressive array of aliases – Bernard Ashley, Dr Barker, Claude Gayton, Claude Clayton, Max Grief Gosslar, Max Kaife Gosslar, Dr Grant, 'Grand Guidon', Stanislas Lublinski, Ashley Nabokoff, Orloff, Henry Ray, Count Sobieski, Max Sobieski, and perhaps some twenty others.

Born around the year 1833, he was thumb-nailed by Macnaghten 'a mad Russian doctor and a convict and unquestionably a homicidal maniac. This man was said to have been habitually cruel to women, and for a long time was known to have carried about with him surgical knives and other instruments; his antecedents were of the very worst and his whereabouts at the time of the Whitechapel murders could never be satisfactorily accounted for.'

This account by Macnaghten is worryingly inaccurate. Nowhere else is Ostrog said to have terrorised or to have behaved habitually cruelly towards women. Never in the course of his thefts and frauds did he display violence or the threat of violence. Nowhere, other than by Macnaghten, is he referred to as a *homicidal* maniac. It is true that he spent several periods of incarceration in lunatic asylums, but when, in 1894, he was closely observed by the prison doctor, Dr Morris, in Reading Gaol, Dr Morris told the Buckinghamshire Quarter Sessions that Ostrog was a 'shammer', not a lunatic. It is true, the *Police Gazette* confirms, that he was, however, regarded as a serious Ripper suspect.

There is some confusion as to his nationality. He is variously inscribed in police records as a Russian, a Russian Pole, and a Polish Jew. The French police say that he himself stated that he had been born in Warsaw in 1835.

The files at Buckinghamshire County Gaol assert that he had had a superior education, record that he gave his religion as Greek Orthodox (although he was probably Jewish), and note his dubious claim to having spent two years with the Russian Army and five with the Russian Navy.

Actually, Ostrog was a wily confidence trickster and a pretty despicable sneak thief. His earliest recorded nefarious activities date back to 1863. He was then, in the guise of a twenty-seven-year-old student, name of Max Grief Gosslar or Max Kaife Gosslar, committing petty thefts at Oriel and New Colleges, Oxford, in respect of which he was given ten months.

The following year he passed himself off in Bishop's Storford as a noble count or prince, who, in order to escape would-be assassins had had to live wild in the woods in Poland. Such was his cunning, his gentle and genteel mien, that he managed to surround himself with many sympathisers.

He next turns up in Cambridge, where he is known as Max Sobieskie. Caught red-handed attempting a crime in a college, he was convicted as a rogue and vagabond and awarded a three-month sentence.

Tunbridge Wells was favoured with his presence, in the role of Count Sobieski, exiled son of the King of Poland, in which role he succeeded in extracting money and property from gullible people, and set off for Exeter, where his sins caught up with him, and he was sentenced to eight months for fraud and felony.

His luck changed and he was acquitted of fraud at Gloucester Quarter Sessions in January 1866.

Around July 1873, Ostrog paid a visit to Windsor, and it was about this time that he succeeded in introducing himself to, and ingratiating himself with, the celebrated urning, Oscar Browning, who was then a housemaster at Eton, and, having been given the run of his library, Ostrog helped himself to two of Browning's valuable books. An interesting and unexpected crossing of two very different life paths.

As already noted, one of Ostrog's twenty-odd aliases was Nabokoff.[23]

It emerged in the second, revised paperback edition of the *A to Z* (1994), that Mr Derryl S. Goffee had independently discovered Ostrog prior to the publication of the first edition of the *A to Z*, in 1991.

The Jack the Ripper A to Z has, since its first issuing in hardback, been reprinted three times in paperback editions. In so live a subject as the study of the Whitechapel murderer, it is absolutely vital to acquire the various subsequent paperback editions of the main hardback works, for they are invariably revised and augmented versions of the original, and therefore indispensable to the serious student, to whom it is of prime importance to be equipped with the very latest intelligence.

In December 1900, Ostrog, under the name of John Evest, was brought to trial at the County of London Sessions, Clerkenwell.[24] A microscope, the property of Colonel James Mulroney of the Indian Medical Service, had been stolen from the London Hospital Medical College. Ostrog subsequently pawned it at a shop in Lewisham. Caught trying to sell the pawn ticket to a neighbouring chemist, he was sentenced to five years' penal servitude.

By this time his health was poor and he was partially paralysed. He did not complete the full term of his imprisonment, being released on licence from Parkhurst on 17 September 1904. He informed the appropriate authorities that he would be earning his living as a doctor, and gave his address to be as 29 Brooke Street, Holborn, which was the St Giles' Christian Mission, a home for discharged prisoners.

He was now in his seventies, grey-haired, aged and decrepit. 'It is probable,' writes Philip Sugden, 'that his sad and wasted life came to an end in some workhouse institution shortly after his release from prison. But no record of Ostrog's death has as yet been discovered. Apparently he died, as he had lived, under an assumed name.

56

Launching *Ripperana* and Floating the *Ripperologist*

Unquestionably, the most momentous Ripperological event of the year 1992 was the founding by Mr Nicholas P. Warren, F.R.C.S., F.R.C.S. Ed., of a quarterly journal of Ripperology, *Ripperana*, a landmark in the progress of Ripper studies.

The first issue came out in July 1992. An editorial announced, 'While mainly concerned with the Jack the Ripper (Whitechapel) Murders of 1888, we aim to cover all classic true murder cases which remain officially unsolved.'

The very first number dug new ground. In a fascinating article, 'The Asylum at Ascot', written by the editor himself, it was revealed that the 'insane medical student, in hiding from his family, who was subsequently confined in a private asylum near Ascot (or possibly Windsor), sought by Colin Wilson since the 1960s, was John William Smith Sanders'.

Sanders, born in 1862, son of an Indian Army surgeon, had indeed enrolled as a student at the London Hospital, in Whitechapel. Research by Paul Begg and Keith Skinner had established that from 1867 onwards, Sanders, who was seriously disturbed and violent, had been in and out of a number of different asylums, but Warren's research disclosed that the so-called 'Ascot Asylum', Virginia Water, Surrey, in 1885, had been 'a private asylum for the genteel'. The disused Victorian asylum, a Gothic architectural masterpiece based on the Cloth Hall at Ypres, is near Ascot and equidistant from Windsor. From the 1891 census – just available – Warren was able to confirm that Sanders had been a resident patient there in 1891, although somewhat curiously described as 'a medical student of Glasgow'.

An interesting footnote. Mr Warren writes, 'During the early summer of 1990, the current author was told of a peculiar rumour … within the bowels of this vast institution was a derelict padded cell. A *graffito* on the door proclaimed it to be "Jack the Ripper's Room". The room in question was slightly below ground level, and lit mainly by daylight through a grille in the ceiling.'

At the time of Warren's writing, the old building, which was listed – that is to say it had a preservation order attached to it – was privately owned by a firm of property developers, and was patrolled by security guards, so that it proved impossible to confirm the presence of the alleged *graffito*.

Ripperana irresistibly reminds one in many ways of that splendid and most informatively useful Sherlockian periodical, *The Baker Street Journal*,[25] in which all manner of recondite matters are ventilated. I think that a point which ought to be made, and made strongly, is how much we are indebted to the usually meticulous, and not infrequently inspired, research carried out by the legions of modest, largely unassuming, largely unsung, amateur (in the true sense of loving) researchers, humbly beavering away, to whom the more flamboyant experts designate, and indeed the whole subject, are beholden for the constant trickle of those, individually perhaps trivial-seeming, contributions to knowledge, which, collectively, add up to a considerable sum.

It is so often that in the course of their case-making for personal theories, which may or may not in the end evoke substantial approval, the excavation which fails to unearth the object desired by the excavator throws up other valuable data. To these lone strugglers, who may perhaps never write a book, but whose triumph and reward is the printing of a research report article in *Ripperana,* or some such prestigeful medium, or possibly a modest attributory footnote in somebody else's book, we should all, I feel, doff our deerstalkers, be mindful of, and liberally acknowledge our very real obligation to them.

In his article 'Dr Merchant Was Not Jack the Ripper', in the spring 1992 issue of the *Criminologist,* Nicholas Warren turned a critical eye on the tale told by former Metropolitan PC Robert Clifford Spicer in the *Daily Express* of 16 March 1931, entitled 'I Caught Jack the Ripper'. Spicer, of course, did nothing of the sort. What he did was, at the height of the 1888 panic, encounter a respectable-looking man in out-of-the-way Heneage Court in the company of a prostitute known as Rosy. The man's cuffs were stained with blood and he had with him a black bag. Spicer arrested him and marched him off to Commercial Street Police Station. There he identified himself as a Brixton doctor, and Spicer's superiors immediately released him, without so much as looking into his black bag.

In a short article, 'Jack the Ripper – The Mystery Solved?' contributed in 1972 to *City,* the magazine of the City of London Police, B. E. Reilly correctly identified the doctor involved, but gave him the pseudonym 'Dr Merchant'. Nicholas Warren set to work to unravel this anonym. A chapman was an old-fashioned travelling salesman, a merchant, and, sure enough, a Dr Frederick Richard Chapman, of 4 Barrington Road, Brixton, had died, aged thirty-seven, in Guy's Hospital, on 12 December 1888, of septicaemia psoas,[26] abscess of spinal tubercular origin. In Warren's professional opinion, 'No one who died from this condition in December 1888 could have been prowling around Whitechapel in search of victims to overpower only a month before.' Mr Warren concludes, '"Dr Merchant" was not Jack the Ripper.'

In the second, October 1992, issue of *Ripperana,* Nicholas Warren reports, without citing sources, that Lord Randolph Churchill was a suspect many years before Stowell published his seminal paper in the *Criminologist* (November 1970). Therein, Stowell claimed that he had seen private papers in the possession of Caroline Acland, the daughter of Sir William Gull. These convinced him that Jack the Ripper was the scion of a noble house of England. Stowell took this to be the Duke of Clarence. He had misinterpreted two clues. First, that the Ripper's family 'had for fifty years earned the love and admiration of large numbers of people by its devotion to public service'. This could hardly apply to the House of Hanover! The second was a passage taken from the physician's diary: 'Informed – that his son was dying from syphilis of the brain.' No royal prince died from neurosyphilis at the relevant time, certainly not Prince Eddy.

Stowell must have been examining the papers of Caroline Acland's father-in-law, Sir Henry Wentworth Acland. During the years 1926–27, Sir Henry's papers were being sorted and catalogued for deposit in the Bodleian Library, at Oxford. Sir Henry was family physician to the Duke of Marlborough. The Marlboroughs had earned widespread admiration for their militaristic public service. The scion of the House of Marlborough was Lord Randolph Churchill, who died on 24 January 1895 – of syphilis of the brain.

The winter 1992 *Criminologist* published what was to be the first of a three-part series of articles by Christopher Smith under the general heading, 'Jack the Ripper and the Alembic Connection'. His suspect is Dr William Wynn Westcott (1848–1925), Coroner for Central London, who was also a keen occultist and a founder member of the Hermetic Order of the Golden Dawn. Among its 200 or so members was numbered W. B. Yeats, passing on from Madame Blavatsky's Theosophists in the hope that with MacGregor Mathers and Wynn Westcott he might find proof that 'the sage Ahaseurus dwells in a sea cavern 'mid the Demonesi'. Wynn Westcott, however, immediately abandoned the Golden Dawn in 1897, seeing the full light of day when the authorities presented him with a straight choice between occultism and coronership. There is nothing to link him with the Whitechapel murders.

Also in 1992, *Fleuve Noir* published in Paris *Jack L'Éventreur* by Stephane Bourgoin, with a Preface by Robert Bloch. This has been assessed in the *A to Z* as 'a sound and sensible overview – taking good account of recent work and endorsing no controversial theories'.

The gingerly accouched Cloak and Dagger Club – irreverently referred to by some as the Smoke and Stagger Club – founded for the purpose of ventilating amid the smoke and fume of a jolly tavern deep in the heart of Ripperland, the Alma public-house, all matters fringe and central Ripperian, took place in 1995.

Between the winter of 1994 and September 1995, there were produced under the editorship of Mark Galloway three issues of the *Cloak and Dagger Newsletter*, progressing in size from an initial pilot issue of ten pages, to a second of twelve, and a third of twenty.

The fourth issue, December 1995, was rechristened the *Ripperologist*, and by December, 1996, the eighth number of the former *Newsletter* had expanded to thirty-two pages, with Paul Daniel listed therein as editor.

And in February 1997, to complete, as it were, the clean-sweeping metamorphosis, the club changed its bimensual venue to an East Commercial Street hostelry, the City Darts, formerly, and more happily, the Princess Alice.

In Paul Daniel's refashioning editorial hands, the *Ripperologist* became a newly-formatted bimonthly, intended to supplement rather than confront its senior sister publication, *Ripperana*. Its now sixty pages exude an air of bristling enthusiasm in which discretion and valour seesaw, about equally balanced.

With the April 2000 issue, Paul Begg assumed the editorship. Under his captaincy the magazine's logging of the Ripperian voyage of discovery continued smoothly and storm-free. Novel research and new discoveries were recorded and commented upon, a platform was provided for the revision and reinterpretation of older events, and articles were published relating to the Ripper, his contemporary environment and the historic happenings of his day. Forthcoming books were announced and, in due course, reviewed. News of what was happening at the club, and to its members, lent the magazine a welcome personal element of warmth.

57

Palmer's Index

Jack the Ripper: A Reference Guide is a work – somewhat reminiscent of Palmer's classic index to *The Times* – by an American student of the Ripper case, Scott Palmer, of San Diego, who presents varied qualifications for the self-imposed task which, at so many thousands of miles remove, he has bravely undertaken.

He has been a funeral director. That gave him several years' first-hand acquaintance with cadavers. He is a practised writer, having written and edited short stories and articles, as well as having written books about the cinema in Great Britain, Australia, and New Zealand. He is also described as a distinguished and high-ranking Freemason.

His Ripper reference guide succeeds in what it sets out to do, which is to provide, in the short and modest compass of some 150 pages, a mini-version of that which takes up 519 close-packed pages in its role model the *A to Z*.

'There has,' writes Mr Palmer, 'been much speculation as to the Ripper's anatomical or surgical skills (or the lack thereof).'

He then goes on to tell the reader that he has in the past

> worked a number of years in a mortuary and am more than familiar with autopsies and the dissection
> of cadavers. I can therefore state with some degree of authority that Jack the Ripper most certainly
> had to have had some medical skills or training. We can see clear evidence of this in the report of Dr
> Frederick Gordon Brown on the body of Catherine Eddowes, the Mitre Square victim ... Eddowes's
> kidney had been carefully extracted, and any surgeon or coroner will verify (as does surgeon N. P.
> Warren in his 1989 article in the *Criminologist*) that the kidney is extremely difficult to expose from
> the front of the body, especially as it is hidden behind a membrane. Other organs were taken from
> victims carefully and wholly – when one remembers that these organs were removed in a very short
> time, most in almost total darkness, one can reasonably conclude the degree of skill necessary to
> do this would be even greater. Someone merely slashing about with a sharp instrument, with no
> knowledge or skill, inside a corpse would only make a mess. It would not be possible to remove these
> organs randomly or accidentally.

As a Master Mason of good standing, Mr Palmer is, he says, 'worthy and well qualified' to be able
to speak authoritatively about 'Freemasonry and its involvement in these murders'.

He accordingly tells us, 'There have been a number of theories having to do with
Freemasonry. While it is true that a great many of the high-ranking police and political
figures in London in 1888 were Freemasons, apparently none of the authors of the books
has himself been a Freemason, otherwise certain inaccuracies (and in some cases stupidities)
would not have been written.'

Mr Palmer's is a brave effort, but it has to be said that its tendering of information is,
necessarily, very considerably less encyclopedic than that of the *A to Z*. The book's 200-odd
entries are distributed under eight headings – Victims; Witnesses; Suspects; Politicians and
Police; Coroners and Doctors; Miscellaneous; Freemasonry; Poems and Letters.

'We will probably,' he concedes, 'never know beyond doubt the identity of Jack the Ripper, but
with the passage of time the interest and fascination increases.'

His book is not designed to draw conclusions as to the Ripper's identity, but is offered as a
work of reference, which endeavours to list all of the principal characters involved, as well as a
number of the minor ones.

Rather more ambitious is *Jack the Ripper: An Encyclopedia* by John J. Eddleston. With 304
pages at his disposal, Mr Eddleston has room to develop a much closer focus on the case. Not
only does he supply profiles of the key police officials involved, but he also scrutinises the police
procedures and investigations, and identifies their blunders and errors. He provides painstaking
descriptions of the locations where the bodies were found, careful life histories of the victims, and
meticulous evaluations of all the chief suspects. He discusses the myths which have grown up
around the case and takes an analytical look at the proliferation of Ripperine literature.

Mr Eddleston does not subscribe to the popular notion that the police of the day were
incompetent. It is his opinion that the reason that they failed to capture the Ripper was that they
were looking for the wrong type of man. They were looking for a slavering maniac, whereas the
Ripper would probably have been a quiet, calculatedly background-merging figure.

Eddleston opines that the Lusk kidney was probably genuine; therefore, he concludes, the
'From Hell' letter to Openshaw may have been genuine, and by inference the 17 September 1888
letter may also have been genuine.[27]

A point that seems to have been overlooked by other authors is the significance of some of the
mutilations carried out on the victims. Only two were subjected to facial mutilations – Eddowes
and Kelly. Facial mutilations are, psychological profilers aver, usually evidence that killer and

victim knew each other. The closer the relationship, the more urgent the need to depersonalise the victim, and consequently the more extreme the mutilation.

Eddleston thinks that Mary Jane Kelly is the key to the series of murders. We are looking for someone who knew her quite well. Two men fit the bill – Joseph Barnett and George Hutchinson.

It was now necessary to establish a connection between one of these two and Catherine Eddowes. The best that he can manage is the woefully tenuous linkage of Hutchinson's knowing Eddowes by sight as a fellow drinker in one of the watering holes which they both happened to patronise.

As John Eddleston points out, although it was manifestly impossible for anyone living in the Whitechapel or Spitalfields area not to have heard about the murder of Mary Jane, it was, again like the curious incident of Sherlock Holmes' dog in the night, George Hutchinson's curious incident that, although he had a strange tale to unfold, he did nothing.

At the inquest on Kelly, held on 12 November 1888, Sarah Lewis testified to having seen a man 'not tall but stout and wearing a black wideawake hat', standing in an entry by Crossingham's Lodging-House, situated at 35 Dorset Street, almost directly opposite Miller's Court.

There could be, as Hutchinson himself must have been the first to realise, no mistaking, from the pinpoint accuracy of Mrs Lewis's description, that he had been the mystery man in the entry.

But, until he read of Mrs Lewis's testimony in the newspaper, Hutchinson had been noteworthily backward in coming forward. Says Eddleston, 'I believe that he had no intention of coming forward.'

However, although the one-day inquest was over and done with, Hutchinson forthwith hustled himself along to Commercial Street Police Station, where he described, down to the colour of his eyelashes, the astrakhan-great-coated, very-thick-gold-watch-chain-hung, handsomely turned-out punter with whom, as he watched, Kelly turned in.

John Eddleston makes it clear:

> I am *not* stating categorically that George Hutchinson was Jack the Ripper. All I can say is that of all the suspects named thus far, he is the only one I can accept. He fitted the 'properties' of our killer, lived close to the epicentre of the crimes, knew the area well and certainly knew Mary Jane Kelly. I would not be at all surprised if Jack proved to be someone else, but that someone must fit the physical and psychological description of our killer even better than Hutchinson.
>
> Jack the Ripper was not a raving lunatic who ended up confined in some asylum. He did not commit suicide, and we need look for no other reason for his stopping than the fact of self-preservation. He was a young local man, strong and stocky, who knew Mary Jane Kelly well and may have been a passing acquaintance of Catherine Eddowes.

58

A Ripperish Who's Who

Camille Wolf, doctor of medicine, specialist dealer in the category of what are somewhat unmelifluously described as 'True Crime' books, had a brainwave: why not an anatomy of the Ripperologists? A book which would identify them and their held opinions.

Ably aided and abetted by her research assistant, Loretta Lay, she set to work there and then to put together *Who Was Jack the Ripper? A Collection of Present-Day Theories and Observations*.

The book duly appeared in 1995. In it, fifty-four contributors from Aliffe, Andy, to Wright, Stephen, are granted, without scold's bridle, their freedom of say. Those sayings proving a curious mixture of facetious *jeux d'esprit* and ultra-serious thump-a-tubbing!

It was, however, a happy inspiration, and it will be amusing for Ripper students of the future, looking at the photographs therein of fifty-three of the contributors (only an image of A. P. Wolf is among the missing) to put faces to the old pioneer Ripperphiles, which is more than they will, I prophecy, ever be able to do to Jack himself.

The odd three out in this venture are Tom Cullen, who wouldn't come out to play; Daniel Farson, who could not be induced to give his autograph; and A. P. Wolf, who would yield up neither likeness nor holographic mark, thus fuelling the suspicion voiced by *Ripperana*, endorsed by others, that he may be a she, an 'established author resident in the Bahamas'.

For some undivinable reason William Beadle, who this same year brought out his *Jack the Ripper: Anatomy of a Myth* (1995), is also among the missing. A pity. He has written what *Ripperana*'s reviewer[28] calls 'a sober overview of the known facts'.

I concur. Indeed, I would go further and designate it an overall exceedingly intelligent and brightly written evaluation of the field, or a portion of the field, for he stops short at the royals and the Macnaghten cohort. If he has erred, and he has occasionally, it has been as a consequence of 'facts' from those whom he may, quite mistakenly, have regarded as his masters. He displays uncommon common sense and a most commendable capacity for trenchant argumentation. I found his book a pleasure to read, although I am bound to say that I am not in tune with his selection of William Bury as a gilt-edged candidate.

The most curious submission is that of A. P. Wolf, who insists that 'Ripper "historians" inhabit a very dark world … over a coffee one [of the historians] might cheerfully ask the other: "So you think her breasts were found on the table and not between her legs?"'[29]

We are presented with a vivid picture: 'A slaughtered woman, ripped to pieces but still with legs intact is laid out for us all to see and where her sex was is now a gaping bloody hole and the "historians" are proud that this is the very first time that their readers have had to feast their eyes on this spectacle of cunningly disguised pornography.' It is, Wolf says, 'the Ripper "historians" who have created the monster that still walks the streets of Whitechapel and the world today. It is a sad legacy.'

On the other hand, Colin Wilson, who confesses that he became interested in the Ripper murders as a child, does not appear to have been adversely affected. I wonder though – for he says that he has only about 5 per cent doubt about the genuineness of Jack the Ripper's Diary!

In his contribution Simon D. Wood takes up the position of the supreme iconoclast … Jack the Ripper

> must have a good schoolboy hand and a piece of chalk for writing on walls. He must have a dark jocularity and a command of vernacular, both English and American, for writing epistles to the Press. He must have surgical knowledge. He must be an Heir to the British throne, a mentally unstable barrister, a Jewish slaughterman, a Tsarist secret agent and a barber. She must be a deranged midwife. He must arouse no suspicion. He must have an intimate knowledge of Whitechapel's streets and alleyways. He must be a Liverpool cotton merchant daft enough to leave behind a hand-written diary and the initials of his victims scratched in the back of a watch. He must have split-second timing. Jack must be nimble, Jack must be quick. In legend, Jack satisfies all these criteria. Yet in truth he satisfies none. Why?

'Simply,' says Simon Wood, 'because there never was such a person as Jack the Ripper and, despite all our best investigative efforts, never will be.'

Wood is the first to admit that there was certainly a person who cruelly murdered Mary Ann Nichols, Annie Chapman and Catherine Eddowes. There was a person who coincidentally killed Elisabeth Stride in Berners Street, and the person or persons unknown who butchered an unidentified female in Miller's Court.

But Jack, he thinks, was merely 'a figure society conjured from thin air in an attempt to give shape and form to the incomprehensible and which was later turned to profitable advantage by various vested interests'.

Nevertheless, Jack is still today very real. He is still out there playing his funny little games. 'But as for putting a name to him … You might just as well try to identify the Bogeyman.'

There is, however, one contributor to this fascinating book who does not hesitate to do just that. He is Jonathan Goodman, and his sole contribution to Ripperology, his sole right to be included in this anthology, is his naming of Jack in his 'Dictionary of the Unknown Famous', *Who He?*, as Peter J. Harpick.

Goodman explains,

> I meant that to poke fun at the 'Hunt the Ripper' game. I assumed that all readers would understand that the name of my 'candidate' was an anagram of the alias, that the potted biography was a fiction – therefore I was surprised to receive a letter from a Ripperologist requesting further information about Peter J. Harpick, and I remain astonished that a dozen other people subsequently wrote me similar letters. I must say, I found it rather hard to compose polite replies.

59

Trow's Plight

Between the covers of *The Many Faces of Jack the Ripper* (1997), its author, M. J. Trow, plights his troth, pledges to tell the oft-told ancient tale as, in a new and modern light, he sees it.

In this pursuit we are escorted first, in the footsteps of that social pioneer from San Francisco, Jack (John Griffith) London (1876–1916), writer of a documentary of starkest urban poverty, *The People of the Abyss* (1903), through that East End London slumland which the horror-smitten American called the Abyss, on one of the shortest, best-managed, topographically and historically informative Jack-the-Ripperland walks to be had.

Our walking companions, Jack London apart, are those seasoned old journalists George R. Sims and Edwin Pugh, with authors Arthur St John Adcock and William J. Fishman to nudge our elbows at appropriate moments.

'Even now,' whispers Fishman, 'in the still hours, as the moon strikes the steeple of old Christ Church, and casts a long shadow over the rickety tenements of Spitalfields, a sudden catch of movement, crouched silhouette in a desolate alleyway, all senses alert, as Old Jack, poised momentarily en route, continues on his way to a rendezvous with murder in the City of Dreadful Night.'[30]

We circle the Abyss, we cross the Ghetto, with its updated aroma of curry and sprinkled flavouring of Asian street names. We are there introduced to the out-at-elbows – and everywhere else – indigenes and immigrant peoples of the Abyss. And, in search of the supreme anti-hero citizen of this mean city, have the pretenders' identities paraded before us, one after one, with no prospective Jack for our delectation singled out.

Many Faces is, essentially, a work of surveillance, covering the old killings and killer's ground with commonsensical efficiency, but without any especial inspiration. It is, in the main, journeyman stuff. No axe or knives to grind. Nor anything new to bring to the assaying. Established facts, well-honed arguments, are, however, restated with sufficient grace and elegance of organisation.

Toying with us, Mr Trow writes, 'In 1891 a little board game for children appeared on the market. It was called "How to Catch Jack" and, with varying degrees of sophistication, people have been playing it ever since!' And, so far as Jack the Ripper is concerned, some play it like children still.

It is precisely because he thinks to have descried an imported flippancy in the bending of old truths, or the invention of new 'truths', to point a finger at a favoured suspect, and apprehended how this has brought sundry self-styled Ripperologists into disrepute with accredited crime historians, that, says Mr Trow, he undertook this book. A situation exists, he believes, in which 'Jack is now the "universal man" of serial slaughter – he is all things to all men' – he is Jack the toff, the 'swell', the caped and top-hatted man-about-town … the idea of the Ripper being a middle- or upper-class gent with a university education, medical training and respectability, is a more delicious prospect than that of his being a peripatetic lunatic from the Abyss.

Trow is sure that the Victorian police missed Jack for the very simple reason that they were looking for the wrong sort of culprit. 'The science of criminology in 1888 pointed to a dribbling lunatic. There is no doubt that two overriding considerations guided the police inquiries at the time – medical skill and insanity.' That was the approbated view of both the natives of the Abyss and the run-of-the-station-house bluebottle on the beat, of the Whitechapel Fiend, whom they were respectively fleeing from and looking for.

No room for superciliousness here, though. Your educated men – like Melville Macnaghten – were shooting equally wide of the mark. M. J. Druitt? Sexually insane. Kosminski? Insane; too much indulgence in solitary vice over too many years. Michael Ostrog? A homicidal maniac.

Trow subscribes to the far from universally accepted view that the Ripper was the world's first serial killer, and accordingly remarks that the authorities hadn't the faintest idea that they were dealing with 'a new kind of criminal'.

Even so, he considers that this factor has been exploited. He cannot share the view of writers, such as the *A to Z* triad, who, he claims, have sought to whitewash the police of the day by pointing out that, in spite of the lack of forensic sophistication, their actions were at all times sensible and thorough. He feels, too, that 'the decision made by the Home Secretary and by the Commissioners of the Met. and the City forces to hold back on any public explanation or discussion of the Ripper murders was not only wrong, but disastrous; it abetted an atmosphere of suspicion at the time and one of conspiracy ever since'. True, as any number of Ripper-inspired authors will happily attest.

In fact, the gamut of police conduct, from political infighting at the summit to the comportment and capabilities of barely adequate bobbies on the beat, with the honourable exception of the middle-management level of detective inspectors and superintendents of the calibre of Abberline and Swanson, constrains Trow, following in the charivarial tracks of Mr Punch, to refer to them as 'The Defective Force'.

Trow has written, 'If conspiracy there was, it was the Metropolitan and City forces, who, through stupidity and missed opportunities, conspired to let Jack go free.' A harsh judgement.

Superintendent Thomas Arnold, of the Met. believed that only four of the customarily nominated five victims had met their ends at the hands of the Ripper, but, sadly, as a result of a piece of bad reportage in 1893, we cannot now be sure whether the superintendent was excluding Catherine Eddowes or Mary Jane Kelly from Jack's tally. The modern tendency is to exclude Stride, who was 'killed with a short, round-ended knife, unlike the pointed weapon of the other murders. There was no sign of punching or manual strangulation. The body was found on its side, not on its back as in the other cases, and, most obviously of all, there were no bodily mutilations.'

The Ripper was no magician, no phantom of the night. He was clever, resourceful, and knew both the areas and the shortcomings of the police very well.

Jostled by his gaol delivery of forty-odd named, and one unnamed, suspects, Trow allocates them for easier processing to seven non-watertight groups – Jews, Doctors, Visitors, Locals, Policemen, Others and Royals; the many faces – and each in turn is dismissed from the DIY dock in which some misguided prosecutor has placed him.

What Trow regards as one of the most interesting pieces of contemporary speculation, Mr Edward Knight Larkins' perception of a *folie à quatre* among the sailors on a Portuguese cattle boat, receives a negative vote.

Mr Larkins, clerk in the Statistical Department of Customs and Excise by avocation, dedicated busybody by vocation, set, in this latter capacity, an eagle's I-spy-eye upon the comings and goings of two Portuguese vessels, the *City of London* and *City of Oporto*.[31] He had decided that crew-member Manuel Cruz Xavier had killed Polly Nichols, and that, in a copycat murder, crew-member José Laurenco had killed Annie Chapman the next time the ship was in. A third crewman, João de Souza Machado, was believed by Larkins to have worked with Laurenco on the murders of Annie Chapman, Liz Stride, and Catherine Eddowes, and he thought that Machado killed Mary Jane Kelly on his own.

Since Larkins was also convinced that it was the Ripper who murdered Alice McKenzie on 17 July 1889, and since Machado was not on the ship at that date, the statistical clerk cheerfully nominated another crewman, Joachim de Rocha, as the killer. Dr Robert Anderson nominated Larkins as 'a troublesome busybody'.

Alois Szemeredy makes his appearance, but is given short shrift. 'The case against [him] would seem to be non-existent.'

Turning his attention to Francis Tumblety, 'the most recent serious suspect to emerge', Trow finds it necessary to issue a number of caveats regarding the case presented by Stewart Evans and Paul Gainey. He is critical of the summary list of fifteen points which the two authors suggest as strongly indicative of Tumblety's guilt, dismissing them since they are, in the main, circumstantial.

Messrs Evans and Gainey do not claim that they are anything other than circumstantial, and are in total accord with Trow's view that they would be insufficient to satisfy the prosecution authorities.

Trow further contends that, whereas Evans and Gainey suggest that Tumblety 'fits many of the psychological requirements; he was a *"psychopathia sexualis"* subject and hated women,' the fact is that 'modern profiling of serial killers is altogether different from Richard [von] Krafft-Ebing's pioneering work of 1886 and Tumblety fails to fit as many of the "requirements" as he does fit.'

Trow challenges also Tumblety's supposed hatred of women; albeit commented on by some contemporaries, 'others who knew him well refused to believe he was capable of such crimes'.

Trow's criticism extends, too, to the assertion that Tumblety 'was in London at the relevant time,' and that the 'police were interested in an American who lodged at Number 22 Batty Street, near Berner Street where Liz Stride was killed, and his landlady discovered one of his bloodstained shirts, which made her suspicious of him. There is of course no evidence whatever that the American's bloodstains belonged to a Ripper victim or that the lodger was Tumblety.'

As for Evans and Gainey's statement that Tumblety 'had the necessary anatomical knowledge evinced by the murderer, and owned an anatomical collection that included wombs "from all classes of women"', Trow responds, 'Tumblety was such an accomplished liar that his credentials are impossible to check … In other words, we have no idea whether he had any anatomical skills or not' – which answer does not address the simple fact that Tumblety *had* owned an anatomical collection that included wombs from all classes of women.

Evans and Gainey point out that Tumblety was arrested within days of the murder of Kelly on suspicion of being the murderer, and that the murders ceased upon his arrest and subsequent flight, a very strong indicator of guilt.

Trow counters: 'The sole "evidence" for this comes from American newspapers … There is nothing in the British press to suggest that this was why Tumblety was held and there is no mention of him whatsoever in the police files. He was actually arrested on 7 November, two days before Mary Kelly was killed. Evans and Gainey assume that he was bailed to wander the streets in search of her [Kelly], but equally he may have been in jail, which obviously rules him out completely.'

Trow's assumption aside, what Evans and Gainey actually wrote was, 'The Central Criminal Court register held at the Greater London Record Office, however, reveals that "Dr Tumblety, physician, 56 yrs, was taken into police custody, initially on 7 November 1888, on a gross indecency offence". This was two days before the Kelly murder and it would seem he was released, on police bail, the same or next day, his arrest on suspicion of the murders following on Monday the 12th.'

Quite reasonably, Evans and Gainey underline the fact that a top Scotland Yard man felt that Tumblety was the killer, a belief he shared with others.

Trow is not reassured. He writes, 'According to [Chief Inspector] Littlechild, there was a large dossier on [Tumblety] at the Yard, but the Special Branch man admits that Tumblety was not considered a sadist. It is certainly odd that no other policeman mentions him and that the London press, who so avidly followed the Ripper case at every twist, should not get wind of the story.'

Tumblety 'used aliases, was always turning up and disappearing again,' wrote Evans and Gainey.

'Probably well over half the people of the Abyss used aliases,' responds Trow, 'let alone shifty American con-men. A slippery, streetwise character as Tumblety undoubtedly was, does not make a serial killer.'

Trow takes on board Evans and Gainey's point that 'Scotland Yard was in touch with the American police about [Tumblety] both before and after his arrest', and it elicits, from him the riposte: 'Just as they were in touch with the French, Austrian and Portuguese authorities on similar wild goose chases and with a similar lack of results.' And, driving home his point, assertively adds, 'Inspector Andrews "was sent with other officers to pursue [Tumblety] to New York". In fact, Walter Andrews was sent to Montreal, Canada, with two bank bombers, Roland Gideon and Israel Barnet [*sic*].[32] He was then directed to New York, but precisely why is unknown.'[33]

Nor was Barnett the 'bank bomber' Trow tells us he was. He helped 'wreck' the Central Bank by fraud, not bombs.[34]

Reaffirming and reinforcing his disbelief in the rectitude of the candidature of Francis Tumblety, Trow maintains that at fifty years of age Tumblety was at least fifteen years too old to fit any of the known Ripper sightings.[35]

Moreover, at 5 feet 10 inches he was too tall, and, as Trow phrases it, he 'would have stood out like a sore thumb among the stunted derelicts of the Abyss'.

But for Trow, the most damning case against Tumblety as Ripper is his extraordinarily high profile, his huge moustache, his ludicrously exaggerated dress, and he concludes: 'The man who kills women in a dingy backstreet is not a self-publicist.' Trow seems somehow to have overlooked Dr Thomas Neill Cream.

On a scale of his own devising, Trow judges the theory put forward in 1995 by Bernard Brown, of the Metropolitan Police, in 'Was Jack the Ripper a Policeman?' – that the Ripper was a policeman who 'was able to come and go like a phantom because he disappeared in the swirling steam of the Underground [Railway] ventilation shafts and used the Underground for a fast getaway' – as a theory 'representing near-lunacy'.[36] Nonetheless, Brown's article deserves a hearing.

The Metropolitan, District, Great Eastern, South Eastern, and the London, Brighton & South Coast companies all ran their trains through the area via Whitechapel. Old maps show the proximity of all the murder sites to a railway line, and in particular to an underground railway station. Buck's Row was just behind Whitechapel station. Hanbury Street and Dorset Street were conveniently close to Shoreditch station, at the northern end of Brick Lane. Berner Street was a matter of yards from St Mary's station, which stood on the south side of the Whitechapel Road. Mitre Square was very handy to Aldgate station. Jack could easily have arrived undetected from St Mary's to Aldgate station on the night of the double event. Incidentally, at the end of Goulston Street, where the fragment of Eddowes' apron and the 'Juwes' wall-writing were discovered, and which was clearly Jack's escape route, was Aldgate East station.

In 1888, underground railways were, Brown reminds us, steam-operated, and there were gratings and grilles installed below the roadway to act as blowholes for the liberation of sulphurous fumes. These would also have served as bolt-holes, allowing the fleeing Ripper access to the network of subterranean tunnels without his having to go via the conventional entrance to a public railway station.

Now all these various railway companies, dock companies, too, for that matter, employed their own uniformed police constables, who, to the uninitiated eye, would be practically indistinguishable from an ordinary policeman.

The possibility of Jack the Copper – the 'Hands of Mr Ottermole' and all that[37] – has been previously canvassed, but the main flaw was always held to be that a Metropolitan policeman could not have entered Mitre Square, within the City of London jurisdiction, without being identified as such, any more than a City policeman could have trespassed unobserved upon the Metropolitan manor. Whereas, an officer of the Underground Railway Police could have come and gone across both Metropolitan and City borders at will, completely unremarked. Brown submits a member of the Underground Railway Police for the role of Ripper.

A novel thought of Brown's is that the word in the Goulston Street wall-writing was not 'Juwes' but 'Jayes', written in defiance and derision by one of the PCs from J Division, who had been unpopularly imported to help out H Division in the patrolling of the Whitechapel patch.

Another interesting piece of 'side think' punted by Brown is his suggestion that the reason for the October lull in the killings, and for the murder of Mary Jane Kelly being the first – Mitre Square excepted – to take place west of Commercial Street, could be that the North Metropolitan Tramway Company had been laying down new tramlines along the length of Commercial Street, night and day, so that horse-drawn traffic would be being diverted down such vital Ripper-runs as Brick Lane, Thrawl, Flower and Dean, Fashion, Church, and Hanbury Streets. The sudden influx and activity would have spoiled these favoured patrols for the local ladies of the streets, but the change could only be beneficial, not only staying the knife hand of Jack the wielder, player of funny little games, but directing pocket-wise the hands of the navvies employed on tramway construction, prospective clients who would prove only too ready to fork out for funny little games of a non-lethal variety!

From the Ripper's point of view, another inconvenience would have been that his usual – according to Brown – escape routes, north to Shoreditch station, south to Aldgate East, had become temporarily too risky. His only alternative was to head west into the City Force area before the alarm was raised, and escape below at Bishopsgate Metropolitan underground station, which lay below the new Liverpool Street terminus.

On 15 November 1888, the chocolate-coloured horse-trams of the Bloomsbury to Poplar route were spanking along the new-laid Commercial Street line. On 20 December 1888, in Clarke's Yard, Poplar High Street, the strangled body of Rose Mylett was found. Was she, as alleged at the time, another Ripper victim? Unlikely.

It is Brown's ultimate submission that Jack the Ripper was a member of the Underground Railway Police. Trow does not agree.

Among Trow's further dismissals are Druitt, D'Onston Stephenson, William Bury, and Sir George Arthur, that odd twenty-eight-year-old ex-Etonian, gazetted to the 2nd Life Guards. A wealthy 'swell' who, in his salad days, went slumming for pleasure, and whose habit it was to knock about Whitechapel in a slouch hat and old shooting coat, he managed to get himself briefly arrested on suspicion of being the Whitechapel Fiend. He subsequently served in Egypt and South Africa, and later in life matured into a well-respected military historian.

Rejected also by Trow as credible suspects are the two Jameses. James Kelly is spared much attention and no credulity. Regarding the second James, Trow writes, 'The sole evidence' linking Maybrick with the Ripper killings is 'the sixty-three-page journal with the black and gold binding.' Trow's dubiety is aroused by its claim that Maybrick wrote at least one of the received Ripper letters – 'We know the real Ripper wrote none of them. It claims that the murderer left two coins at the feet of Annie Chapman. The Ripper left nothing. It claims that Mary Kelly's breasts were displayed on her bedside table. They weren't. It goes without saying that the real killer would have been able to distinguish between what he actually did and what subsequent reporters of his day and theorists since have invented or conjectured.'

The Duke of Clarence, Lord Randolph Churchill, J. K. Stephen, and the 'elaborate tosh' of journalist Stephen Knight are likewise accorded Trow's acquittal. The royals, he declares, were in the frame because of the theorists who reasoned that there had to be an explanation for Jack's not being caught. But he *was* caught, the theorists contend, after the murder of Mary Jane Kelly. Which, according to Trow, led to the cover-up to end all cover-ups.

The nomination of a foreign royal, Leopold II, King of the Belgians, as the Whitechapel murderer is an intriguing one. His candidateship sponsor is Jacquemine Charrot-Ludwidge, a researcher who was employed by Daniel Farson. Leopold, who inherited the throne on the death of his father in 1865, took a personal, certainly callous, probably unhealthy, very possibly sadistic, interest in witnessing the atrocities inflicted upon the African inhabitants of the Belgian Congo. His private life delivered up more than a whiff of scandal. He had, it is said, a house in England. Charrot-Ludwidge, on what evidence it is not disclosed, believes that house to be the one described, erroneously, by the medium Robert James Lees as that of a physician. It was one to which Leopold made unrecorded visits which, however, coincided with the times of the Ripper murders.

In a final endeavour to 'strip Jack naked', Trow gives thought to the problem of defining the serial killer. He makes a valiant attempt to equate Jack's noctambulations with the 'seven operational phases by which the serial killer operates', as outlined by Joel Norris in his *Serial Killers: The Growing Menace*.

There is the first phase, that is the withdrawal into a private world of perverted fantasy and the gradual building up of the simple urge to the irresistible compulsion to the matching of the thought with the act. Then follow the operational phases: (1) the aura phase; (2) the trolling phase, that is the pleasurable prowl and stimulating search for prey; (3) the wooing phase, which is the disarming by charming, the soothing away of the victim-to-be's probable misgivings and possible suspicions; (4) the capture phase follows, it is the time of non-reversible decision, the prelude to the moment of the strike, the pinnacle of pleasure, the crescendo to which all the long weeks or months of stalking and waiting have been leading up; (5) the killing act phase; this is succeeded by (6) the totem phase, which is the taking from the victim of a trophy – the victim's uterus, heart, or kidney would splendidly suffice – whereby to prolong, to stimulate a subsequent action-replay of the grand climacteric; and finally, the post-operative (7) depression phase, during which, all passion spent, the killer endures an abysmally flattening 'low' before the irrepressible *lustmord* starts to recover, build, and charge itself again. It is in this final phase of the cycle that the serial killer can become suicidal.

Comments Trow, 'It is in the depression phase that Jack escaped. This phase can last for hours, weeks, months or years. So rather than combing asylums for patients admitted within months of the event or securing the obituaries for deaths, suicidal or accidental before 1890, we ought to widen the net considerably – and the wider it becomes, the colder the trail gets. I personally believe we will never know the identity of Jack the Ripper.'

Trow feels sure that it is the factor of the indefinite cooling-off time that has eluded the majority of researchers and led them to look in the wrong direction for the Ripper.

Most experts agree, he says, that the true serial killer is a sadist. It is, I think, in this context, well to remember that Jack killed swiftly. All the mutilatory hideousnesses were performed upon non-sentient corpses. This is an unworthy sadist.

Unquestionably it is, I would think, as Trow commits himself to saying, 'at the bottom of Jack London's Abyss that we will find Jack the Ripper – lost in an alien world with which he could not cope. His answer was to lash out, the conscious target of his unconscious bewilderment were five sad women who had never done him any harm.'

How close, asks Trow, can we get to this outsider, this alienated man? His answer is to eschew what he calls the Victorian profile, derived from the writings of Henry Havelock Ellis, for a modern one, and 'substitute for it the "famous triad," the three danger signs in young children': bed-wetting (over 60 per cent of serial killers were still soaking their sheets in their teens); arson, a fascination with fires, delighting in the flare and roar of the flames; sadistic urges from the age of seven or eight, ripping the wings off flies and torturing cats.

Unwittingly, Trow has come up with a profile of Peter Kürten, admitted admirer of the Whitechapel Fiend and proclaimed Monster of Düsseldorf.

There is small doubt, in Trow's opinion, of Jack's having been a psychopath – no conscience, no awareness of wrongdoing. He also thinks that he fits the category of mission-oriented killer. And that is the order of thinking that created the idea of Jack as the deranged social worker, the sincere but unbalanced do-gooder, determined to reform a rotten and oblivious society by any means … a Thomas Barnardo or a Frederick Charrington, who, declares Trow, was 'the oddest philanthropist of the East End … and I am astonished that no one from the loonier ranks of Ripperologists has fingered him as Jack before now'.

Favoured son of the brewing Charrington family, educated at Marlborough, nourished and nurtured in the lap of luxury, Frederick Charrington, striking his own path, embraced – all power to his non-lifting elbow – teetotalism. As his biographer, Guy Thorne,[38] recounts it in Charrington's own words, the catalyst for this move was a scene which Frederick witnessed on a 'memorable evening' outside a family-owned pub, the Rising Sun:

> A poor woman with two or three children dragging at her skirts, went up to the swing-doors, and calling out to her husband inside, she said, 'Oh, Tom, do give me some money, the children are crying for bread.' At that the man came through the doorway. He made no reply in words. He looked at her for a moment and then knocked her down into the gutter. Just then I looked up and saw my own name CHARRINGTON in huge gilt letters on the top of the public-house, and it suddenly flashed into my mind that that was only one case of dreadful misery and fiendish brutality in one of the several hundred public-houses that our firm possessed.

Trow turns up the melodrama in his retelling of this incident. Whereas Charrington had written that the wife was 'knocked … down into the gutter' by her husband, Trow has it that the wife was 'beaten to a pulp by her husband'. A gross and unnecessary exaggeration.

In 1886, in the wake of William Booth, Frederick Charrington established his headquarters on Mile End Waste. He provided coffee rooms, a library, and buildings for the YMCA, the YWCA, and the Band of Hope. He ventured out on to the risky East End ground, wandering the streets, speaking in frank terms to prostitutes and their clients, and having, quite often, to be rescued from their resultant anger by the patrolling stalwarts of H Division – from the about-to-be-enacted promise of a good battering. But he persisted, an implacable enemy of brothels and brothel-keepers, launching an all-out offensive against the houses of ill repute and their operators in 1887, compiling lists of the visitors to the houses of ill repute in a little black notebook. Perhaps that little black book of his should have been consulted by the Ripper-hunting police.

If not a killer with a mission, Jack might equally possibly have been a hedonistic killer – doing them in, ripping them up, 'just for jolly'. Or, alternatively, he could have been a power-seeker, grandee possessor of the will to dominate. Many modern psychiatrists take the view that violent sex crimes, such as rape and murder, have less to do with sexual desire than with the desire to dominate.

There is, to be honest in summary, a pretty fair sprinkling of errors of fact, and what might be termed cumulative marginal oversights, in Mr Trow's book. There are, too, rather disconcerting failures, if not to recognise, at least to identify to the reader, canards as canards. A caveat as regards total reliance must therefore be issued to newcomers to the field into whose hands it may fall.

A curious pervasive atmosphere of anachronism suffuses the book's pages; it is as if the clock on the author's writing-table had stopped at 1990. He pays, it is true, respectful lip service to Philip Sugden's 1994 publication, but then, inexplicably, seems often to fly in the face of Sugden's carefully architected warnings.

The use of the imaginative illustration of the all-seeing reflective eye of the corpse of Mary Jane Kelly as a kind of recurrent text divisional icon is a nice original idea, but the realist does well to remember that the old forensic ophthalmic conceit of the retinal image retention capacity of eyeballs was just that.

Albeit Trow's plight is like a pre-Essenic biblical study taking sparse cognisance of the discovery of the Dead Sea Scrolls, his plain-stated pledge nonetheless merits its distinctive niche in the Ripper ambries. It is: Jack the Ripper lived locally, in either Whitechapel or Spitalfields. He was in his late twenties or early thirties. He was probably single and lived on his own. He was employed, which is why he struck at weekends, and had enough income to be able to vary his clothes. He had surgical skill of a limited type and was probably a slaughterman or a Billingsgate fish market porter. He was probably interviewed by the police, perhaps on more than one occasion. He did not commit suicide, neither was he incarcerated in a lunatic asylum. He was not a Jew. Jack was, concludes Trow, an Irish cockney.

60

Parlour Games

I do not denigrate Andy and Sue Parlour, who, per Kevin O'Donnell, in *The Jack the Ripper Whitechapel Murders* (1997), confess, 'We are being deliberately playful and spinning a yarn.' Even so, they have been deadly serious in their researches, and Kevin O'Donnell, as their scrivenery amanuensis, has brought only intentional flashes of humour to his arduous, if not indeed onerous, task of setting forth to write upon so complex a minefield of a subject in which, he states frankly, he had no interest, or any real knowledge to speak of, 'until about eighteen months ago'.

The Parlours, on the other hand, had no real practice in the writing of books, but they had come to have a powerful interest in Jack the Ripper and his murderous ways. What is more, you could, in a manner of speaking, say that the Ripper was in Andrew William Parlour's blood, for none other than Saucy Jack it was who wiped away his collateral progenitress, Mary Ann Nichols. Polly Nichols' blood may not actually flow through Mr Parlour's veins, although the Ripper's conventionally accepted first victim perches, fair, square, and undeniable, on a parlous side-branch of the Parlours' family tree.[39]

It was, we are told, when the Parlours began to look into their family history and uncovered the Ripperine skeleton in the cupboard that their interest in half-recollected family traditions, and gossip of the old days when the Parlour clan first settled in the Whitechapel area, was rekindled. Now they say, freely admitting that all of this is speculation, that they have weaved an intriguing web – but, 'As soon as we try to flesh out the details of a conspiracy, we are in the land of the imagination. There are too few cast iron facts to build upon.'

As Keith Skinner writes in his Foreword to the Parlour book, 'Whatever the outcome, the compilers of this book bring with their contribution a cheerful and good-natured attitude. In the present climate of Ripper studies this is truly welcome.' There can be no denying that the pervasive atmosphere among the Ripperologists at this time was cantankerous, strongly held opinions being reinforced by strong and harshly worded argumentation, breeding resultant ill feeling.

The Parlours have done well in turning up some new information. In the matter of Elisabeth Stride, for example, oral tradition has it that Stride used to frequent the Gothenburg docks as a prostitute, and that it was an English sailor, whom she met in the course of 'business', who brought her to London in 1866, only to leave her subsequently, when he discovered that she was still conducting sexual liaisons.

A two-sentence entry, dated 30 September 1888, in the Swedish church's diary, written in Swedish by its pastor, Johannis Palmer, arouses interest. It reads, 'In the morning at 1 a.m. Elisabeth Gustafsdotter Stride was murdered in Berner Street. She had often received assistance from the church. (by "Jack the Ripper"?)'

What do the Parlours do with this?

First, their thesis: 'The name "Jack the Ripper" is usually thought to have appeared with the first letter sent to the press, the "Dear Boss" letter and the "Saucy Jacky" postcard. Extracts from these were published on 1 October. But the full reproduction only came on 4 October. The name "Jack the Ripper" was mentioned in some newspapers on 1 October and 2 October along with extracts. We have a diary entry using the name a full day before anyone had printed it.'

Next, their speculative leap: 'It is likely that "Jack the Ripper" was one of the names used for the killer on the streets of Whitechapel, along with "Leather Apron", before the letters were ever sent!'

This is a thoroughly unsafe assumption. There is a strong possibility, likelihood I would suggest, that the phrase '(by "Jack the Ripper"?)' was added after the original diary entry had been made, or, alternatively, that the diary entry was written up, as diary entries so very often are, on the day *after* the date printed at the head of the diary space. In any event, the evidence is unquestionably too weak to warrant so strong and wide-ranging a conclusion.

Which criticism the Parlours presumably anticipated, for they append, 'It is, of course, possible that the Ripper reference was written in the 30 September entry a day later, after reading the newspaper. Given that Pastor Johannis Palmer was noted for his pedantic efficiency on organisational issues and matters of record, it is unlikely. Also the entry goes on after the reference to the Ripper. It was a long entry and the name "Jack the Ripper" was thus not entered later.'

I must profoundly disagree. The good pastor would, I am sure, be just the sort of perfectionist to insert a telling detail – and the reproduction of the entry from the actual diary shows that there was on the contrary ample space for an interlinear addition to be scribed in.

The Parlours also claim to recognise 'a note of uncertainty as to whether Stride really was a Ripper victim in the diary extract'.

Again, one is bound to proffer the alternative proposition, that the tone of what is written is a question plain and simple, rather than a critically posed query expressing implied dubiety.

Let the mark of interrogation stand for what it stands for. I would wish to issue a reminder that the majority of serious students of the case have long accepted Stride as a Ripper victim, and that there were police officers at the time who were perfectly satisfied as to her canonical status. The currently voiced suspicion of Michael Kidney, her abusive lover, is a much later development.

Stride was a frequent visitor to the Swedish Seamen's Mission, located opposite the church in a large three-storey house on the corner of the Square. It was looked after by Sven Olsson, the church's verger or *klockare* (bell-ringer). There was a reading room at the Mission and Stride was a frequent visitor, keeping up with the news from home in the Swedish papers which were provided there. Also provided was alcohol, with the usual legal dispensation to dispense it twenty-four hours a day – but only to Scandinavian seamen. One shrewdly suspects, however, that the intelligent Stride was capable of circumnavigation in this respect. She is, indeed, recalled to this day as a highly intelligent woman, who spoke English with scarcely a trace of foreign accent, and was fluent in Yiddish. Recollected rumour has it, too, that Stride used the Mission as a venue for the picking up of Swedish men, in intimate acquaintance with whom she naturally felt very much more at home than with English clients.

Stride also often partook of the welfare money distributed by the church to the Swedish community. The Parish Register mentions that, in 1880, she was 'helped by the church because of her husband's illness'. In 1888, she had been given a shilling handout and a Swedish hymn book.

There is pathos in the fact that the church stood only two or three hundred yards from the spot in Berner Street where, ten days later, Elisabeth Stride met her violent end.

The busily burrowing Parlours lay claim also to some revelations regarding the perennially elusive Mary Jane Kelly. They have, they believe, traced her 'to a birth in Castletown, Limerick'[40] in 1864, to a John Kelly and an Ann McCarthy. Two brothers are also listed in the Irish records, John Kelly, born 1866, and Peter Kelly, born 1868. This seems very likely to be *the* Mary Jane Kelly, and her mother's maiden name might solve a long-standing problem for Ripperologists, many of whom have wondered why her (Kelly's) landlord, John McCarthy, allowed her to be six weeks behind with her rent. If John McCarthy was related to her mother, possibly being Mary Jane's uncle, that might explain everything. Alternatively, there is Donald Rumbelow's harsher speculation as to why Mary Kelly's rent arrears was tolerated by John McCarthy.

There is a venerable oral tradition that, during her early days as a London novice, Mary Jane Kelly had taken shelter under the wings of the nuns at the Providence Row Night Refuge at 50 Crispin Street, opposite Dorset Street, Spitalfields, where she stayed briefly, was found a place in domestic service, disliked it, absconded, and took to the streets. The Parlours determined that such an oral tradition *did* exist, 'but the elderly nuns who had been told of this much earlier have all died'.

And *was* it Mary Jane who was anatomised at No. 13? The Parlours doubt it. They are exercised, too, as regards the matter of her more-than-once-alleged pregnancy. As they express it, 'a question mark hangs over whether the corpse in 13 Miller's Court was pregnant or not'.

Well, there, at least, their questing minds can be set at rest. In 1987 Dr Thomas Bond's long-lost preliminary post-mortem report was recovered by Scotland Yard. It makes it clear that Mary

Kelly's uterus was neither stolen nor gravid. It lay, with her kidneys and one severed breast, under her head.

Despite the family relationship, the Parlours do not have a great deal to add to what we already know of Mary Ann Nichols, except that they name her mother as Ann King, whereas Sugden accords her the Christian name Caroline.[41]

The Parlours' book includes many photographs from the Parlour family album. Those of Polly Nichols' husband, William 'Inker' Nichols, and her eldest son, Edward John Nichols, are published here for the first time.

The Parlours sole innovatory contribution to the Annie Chapman story is the information, God knows whence derived, that the polished farthings laid at her feet (or, to be factual in the matter, *not* laid there, or anywhere else) were deposited 'with the Queen's head placed uppermost'. A circumstance which the Parlours appear to see as a highly significant clue.

We come now to the Parlours' elucidation of the abiding mystery of Catherine Eddowes' shawl.

To begin, as Dylan Thomas was wont to say, at the beginning … In 1991, Paul Harrison, in his somewhat prematurely titled *Jack the Ripper: The Mystery Solved*, told the tale of how, in late November 1989, following up without alacrity a telephoned tip-off which he had received a year or so previously from London-based Chief Inspector Mick Wyatt, he had repaired ultimately to a video shop in St Osyth Road, Clacton-on-Sea, Essex, whose proprietors, John and Janice Dowler, had in their possession a purported genuine Ripper artefact. This, so it was asserted, was a shawl which had once graced the disgraced shoulders of poor Catherine Eddowes.

Harrison was heartened to find the Dowlers extremely cynical as to the said shawl's *bona fides*. Refreshingly, this did not suggest commercialism or the profiteering motive. The shawl had come into their hands, they said, several years before, when a friend who knew an antique dealer had brought it round and offered it to them. Upon their deciding that, because of its alleged history, they did not want the thing in their home, the shawl was duly removed. But, some days later, it, or rather two small pieces of it, very smartly framed by Arabella Vincenti Fine Art, returned like homing pigeons.

In 1933, Bill Waddell, now retired from his post as curator of the Black Museum at Scotland Yard, wrote, 'Recently I acquired a silk screen printed shawl. It had been in the donor's family for years and a large section has been cut out reputedly by his [the donor's] mother, because she did not like the blood stains on it. I am told that it was the shawl worn by Catherine Eddowes when she was killed.'[42]

In 1966, the framed pieces of the shawl were sold to an antique dealer named Malcolm, in Thetford, Norfolk, who, in an effort to authenticate his acquisition, contacted the Black Museum. Coincidentally, John Ross, the museum's new curator, had arranged for an expert from Sotheby's to examine the main portion of the shawl. The specialist dated it to the early 1900s, which raised the scepticism as to its alleged provenance.[43]

Stewart Evans visited Malcolm on 14 December 1996, and took photographs of the framed pieces of the shawl. Subsequently, Malcolm sold the framed pieces to the Parlours.

Nicholas Warren, discussing the alleged Eddowes shawl, notes that on the reverse side of the framed pieces is the handwritten legend, 'Two silk samples, taken from Catherine Eddowes' shawl at the time of the discovery of her body by Constable Amos Simpson in 1888 (end of September) victim of Jack the Ripper.'

Comments Warren, 'Since this passage is barely punctuated, it is possible – given that the body was actually found by PC Watkins – that the intended meaning was for Amos Simpson to have taken samples at the time the body was discovered (by another officer). Nevertheless, no PC Amos Simpson has ever been traced in surviving Metropolitan or City Police records.'

The first item of new information was that the Dowlers had acquired the framed pieces of shawl in exchange for a rare copy of the first edition of the *Radio Times*.

Next comes the name of the antique dealer from whom the Dowlers got the shawl. He was David Melville Hayes, of Arabella Vincenti Fine Art. The shawl had passed down in Hayes' family, together with the oral tradition of how his great, great-uncle Amos, a police constable, had picked it up in Mitre Square on the night of the murder.

The occupation of the elusive Amos, the record of whose police service no one had so far been able to find, was confirmed by his entry on the birth certificate of his son, Henry.

Further zealous searching through Metropolitan Police records brought to light that he had joined that body in 1868, at the age of twenty-one, was posted, first, to Y Division (Kentish Town), promoted acting-sergeant in 1881, and transferred to N Division (Islington) in 1886. He spent the last dozen years of his police career at Cheshunt, in Hertfordshire, retiring to end his days in his birthplace, Acton, near Sudbury, in Suffolk. He died, aged seventy, in 1917.

The Parlours feel that their documenting of the facts surrounding the shawl in the Black Museum has gone a long way towards establishing its provenance; what has not been established is how Acting-Sergeant Simpson got his hands on the shawl in the first place.

Mitre Square was unequivocal City of London Police territory. As a Metropolitan Police officer, Sergeant Simpson would have been definitely 'off his patch' the minute he pointed a boot there. But the Parlours observe that, at its most southerly part, N Division approached close to the City boundary, near Mitre Square. Might not, they ask, a patrolling Sergeant Simpson have been brought into the Square in answer to the aid-summoning whistle of City Police Constable Edward Watkins?

A family legend has it that Uncle Amos had been on some kind of special duty, which 'simply meant being drafted in from another area to help with a case. This happened frequently in the Whitechapel area to reinforce the police on the streets.'

But still unsolved is the question of how the shawl came into Amos Simpson's hands. Did he remove it from Eddowes' body as she was lying on the ground? Was it as it was being conveyed to the mortuary, or at some time subsequently?

The Parlours are frank. 'We cannot authenticate the shawl.' But they can, they say, 'authenticate that part of the oral family tradition that Amos Simpson was a serving Metropolitan Police sergeant, and that adds a degree of credibility to the provenance of the shawl.'

Even so, there are difficulties, serious difficulties. To start with, nowhere has there been found any record of Catherine Eddowes ever having possessed, or being found with, such a shawl. The police listing of the clothing on the cadaver when it was undressed at the City Mortuary, Golden Lane, specifically described it all as being old and dirty:

A black cloth jacket, edged about the collar and sleeves with imitation fur, and with two outside pockets trimmed with black silk braid and imitation fur.

A brown linsey dress bodice, with a black velvet collar and brown metal buttons down the front.

A green alpaca skirt.

A blue skirt with a red flounce.

A chintz skirt, with three flounces, brown button on waistband.

A piece of red gauze silk – found on the neck.

There is no mention of a shawl, and certainly not a shawl in the remarkably decent condition that the questioned shawl is in.

According to Paul Harrison, 'the description of the dress[44] worn by Catharine [*sic*] Eddowes on the night of her death perfectly matches the piece of shawl in the frame: tiny flowered patterns, containing the colours blue, pink, green, yellow and maroon. It is an almost identical description, but since there is no record of Catharine [*sic*] Eddowes wearing or possessing a shawl on the night of her death we are left to wonder.'[45]

Nicolas Warren rightly remarks, 'Extant descriptions of the pattern … are completely different,' and goes on to quote *The Times* of 1 October 1888: 'Her dress is of dark green print, the pattern consisting of Michaelmas daisies and golden lilies.'

The garment is described in the same terms, on Saturday 6 October 1888, by both the London *Illustrated Police News* and the *East London Observer*. 'Her dress was made of green chintz, the pattern consisting of Michaelmas daisies.'

The Parlours state plainly, 'We do not have any colours of the daisies, and no mention of chrysanthemums or lilies!'

While taking into account the Parlours' 'small way' of strengthening the case for the shawl's genuineness by invoking the familial remembrance of Uncle Amos as 'a very upright and moral man', one must also take into the reckoning that we have it on very good authority that the just man falls seven times a day. If the shawl was filched from the Ripper's fourth victim, Uncle Amos's momentary lapse from his customary path of rectitude may be charitably understood. Equally, he may have strayed from the stern highway of truth, investing the genuine trophy from another murder with the false glamour that would irradiate a Ripper relic.

Next, the Parlours on the conspiracy theory as received via oral tradition.

'The old King (Edward VII),' Andy Parlour's father once said, 'had those women killed.'

Various oral traditions 'seemed to have circulated [in 1888] in the East End', not only about the Queen's son (Albert Edward, Prince of Wales, family name Bertie) but also about other royals.

Andy Parlour now asks, upon what were those whisperings based? Possibly it was the 'close proximity and probable friendship' of the Ripper's five victims, which sets him thinking that maybe there was more than a lustful serial killer on the loose. Perhaps what was going on was a deliberate attempt to silence these five women because they knew something that was dangerous, something acutely sensitive, something that would have damaged the reputation of a gentleman, or of someone higher?

Thus do the Parlours accouche a rebirth of the *ancien royal* conspiracy theory, such as that expounded by Joseph Sickert. In his version the royal was Prince Albert Victor Christian Edward (family name Eddy), the son of Bertie.

The Parlours cast as main players in their conspiracy theory Bertie, Mary Jane Kelly, Druitt and J. K. Stephen, with Sir William Gull as the linchpin.

The Parlours obviously read, and swallowed, the canards of the involvement of Gull with the Whitechapel murders and the cover-up surrounding his alleged death in the 1895 American work of imaginative fiction *The Capture of Jack the Ripper*.

Their acceptance of the Gull canard was powerfully reinforced by the story broadcast by Mrs Emily Porter, great-niece of the psychic Robert James Lee, of how she had learned through her family of the false burial of Gull. The rumour is still whisperedly rife in Thorpe-le-Soken, in Essex, where Gull is buried and the Parlours live.

The Parlours offer a theory of their own as to why the 'Juwes' message was left in Goulston Street. It was, they say, because Goulston Street is linked with Gull. How? By name. Because, in 1849, Gull, had been chosen to deliver the Goulstonian lectures, at the College of Physicians of London; a lectureship founded by Theodore Goulston, in 1632.

Thus do the inventive Parlours play their games.

They are ingenious, managing to find an emergent pattern of significance in the murder sites which implicates 'Parliament, and adds fuel to the cause of the conspiracy theorists'.

They have also 'toyed with Masonic links'. They compare Druitt's death in the waters of the Thames with that of 'God's Banker', Roberto Calvi, president of Italy's Banco Ambrosiano, found murdered in June 1982, suspended from Blackfriars Bridge, above the waters of the Thames.

They see clues indicative of the guilt of J. K. Stephen in the title of his collection of poems, and also in the material of some of them. But one finds no evidence at all to support their adumbrated murderous alliance between Stephen and Druitt. The invoking of John Netley, and even 'Fingers Freddy', as quartering the quartering territory in quest of the appropriate victims, hardly convinces.

They are satisfied that the unrecognisably disfigured body at No. 13 Miller's Court was not Mary Jane Kelly but that of twenty-year-old Winifred Collyer, who lived around the corner from Dorset Street – 'it might be the case that she was the Winifred in Kelly's room on the fateful night, and the source for the "Winifred Collis" in the Abberline Diaries'.[46]

What do I make of the Parlours' conclusions? I think that the links which they have contrived display hard work tempered with hopeful ingenuity, but in the final analysis one must add the word tenuous. I find myself congenitally suspicious of the suppositious, and we have a great deal of, albeit disarmingly charmingly confessed, supposition here, and neonatal theories exhibiting pronounced stretch marks. It is my view that, along the way, the pilgrim Parlours have plucked haphazard a posy of interesting blossoms, but they have been rambling through a sadly barren and basically infertile terrain. The best thing to do with this book is to take it in the spirit of good-natured romp in which it is tentatively offered.

61
Jack's Baedekers

The first attempt at an orderly assemblage of the multifarious writings on the Whitechapel murders was made in 1971 by David Streatfield, former librarian at New Scotland Yard. The work was really a pamphlet, issued in stiff paper covers, the fifty-five pages of which were held together, literally, with thread. It was titled *Jack the Ripper: A Bibliography and Review of the Literature*, and listed some 275 titles, two-thirds fact, one-third fiction, and a miscellany of other items. Colin Wilson had been prevailed upon to provide an eleven-page 'Introduction to the Murders and the Theories'.

The name of the author of the Bibliography was given as 'Alexander Kelly', Mr Streatfield choosing to hide his light under a bushel, and, in what must surely have been perpetrated as a sly insider joke, David Streatfield is fulsomely thanked by Mr Kelly in the acknowledgements 'for help and advice'.

The year 1984 saw the appearance of a fully revised and expanded edition, eighty-three pages, hard covers, which now included some 450 titles, retaining the ratio of fact to fiction, and the Wilson Introduction, as before. But, sad to relate, in this edition David Streatfield receives no thanks from the author for help and advice.

In 1987, the complete factual sections, namely 'Contemporary Records, Facts and Theories, and Biographies', of the 1984 edition of the *Bibliography* were reprinted under the heading 'Bibliography' in *Jack the Ripper: Summing Up and Verdict* by Colin Wilson and Robin Odell. The assemblage is now presented under three headings – 'The Facts and the Theories', 'Fiction and Drama: A Selection', and 'Films, Television and Radio' – in one easy-to-read alphabetical sequence, prefaced by the four-page 'A Hundred Years of Ripperature' by Alexander Kelly. Updating consists of five new titles and a minor editing of a few of the annotations. Selections of fiction, drama, films, television and radio have been much reduced. Curiously, there is no acknowledgement in *Summing Up* that the material is, in essence, a reprinting of the 1984 *Bibliography*.

Eight years on, in 1995, the *Bibliography* has once again been 'fully revised and expanded', this time with the assistance of David Sharp on the 'Movies, Films, and TV, etc.' section. The Wilson Introduction is still included, but, unwisely perhaps, without any emendation of a text now twenty-three years old, for there have in the course of that near quarter of a century been numerous new theories and developments in Ripper studies. This edition of the *Bibliography* stretches now to 186 pages, lists some 925 works, with, again, the identical ratio of fact to fiction. Important titles are highlighted, and there are encrustations of interesting, albeit strictly subjective, annotations. There is a twenty-one-page name, title, and subject index. The book is back to soft covers, a pity, but, all in all, and no matter who claims authorship, the work continues to be a useful contribution.

With considerable panache, Ross Strachan set out from his Ayrshire base some dozen years ago to compile his own Ripper book, but one 'aimed at the collector and not the general reader of Ripper material'. He purposed an illuminating volume, a companion to light the way of that ideal Ripperphile focused in his mind's eye, through the tangled forest of print intimidatingly skirting the murky and tortuous terrain of Whitechapel Jack; a sort of guidebook of the kind made famous by Karl Baedeker, which our great-grandparents used to slip into their luggage before embarking upon the Grand Tour.

Strachan began in essentially practical mode by devoting his time and resources to the zealous quartering of 'more bookshops than I care to remember'. And, in the process, the personal acquisition of, to quote his own words, 'a huge amount of books and ephemera relating to the case'.

Although primarily envisioned as a world-scanning bibliography, the first since Kelly and Sharp's updated 1995 edition of Kelly's original 1973 publication, Strachan's first effort in 1996 was the relatively modest *Jack the Ripper, A Collectors [sic] Guide to the Many Books Published*, containing 145 titles – factual, fiction, and 'other works'.

A revised and updated version followed in 1997. The title count was now up to 189, with a strong emphasis on fiction.

Strachan's next edition, in 1999, was retitled *The Jack the Ripper Handbook: A Reader's Companion* and included in its listing of some 700 items accounts of a multitude of Ripper consumer goods other than books. There is, for instance, a section devoted to the recording of such collectables as Ripper maps, cards, board games, computer games, a Jack the Ripper clock, 'Zippo lighter', fishing lure, belt buckle, Ripperine figurines, coins and tokens, pub signs, and theatre programmes. There are sections also on Ripperish audio tapes, and on music and recordings featuring lyric Jack.

The *Handbook* is said by its author to be 'the most extensive bibliography ever published on the subject of Jack the Ripper'.

The section concerned with the case literature – Ripperature – is split into London and East End titles; factual works on the Ripper; books that contain material relating to the Whitechapel murders and murderer; foreign-language publications; Jack the Ripper in fiction – which contains the main body of the work and is divided into three sub-sections: (1) Fiction, English language, (2) Foreign translations of English-language fiction, (3) Foreign fiction, magazine and 'fanzine' factual, fictional and factional accounts of the Ripper murders; and, finally, comics and graphic novels, in both English and foreign languages. Strachan supplies a wealth of material, including fascinating reproductions – some sixteen – of Ripper book covers.

Such, indeed, is the richness of the *Handbook* that one experiences some difficulty in locating specific volumes in the complexity of twenty taxonomic categories and the thickets of the 'by date of publication' arrangement. It would be a good notion to include a terminal author, title and subject index in any future edition.

62

Jack in the Belfry

Pastor John George Gibson is ushered forth in 1999 as the latest Ripper suspect. He makes his bow in *The Bell Tower: The Case of Jack the Ripper Finally Solved ... in San Francisco*, a factional tale which Robert Graysmith, author of *Zodiac*, *The Sleeping Lady*, *Unabomber* and *The Murder of Bob Crane*, has constructed, using some fact and much imagination.

This is actually no novel offering up of the Reverend John George Gibson as a red-handed minister of religion, for in the celebrated Girl in the Belfry case, he was at the time nominee in chief of 'those who knew the Real Truth' to take the place of William Henry Theodore Durrant, a young medical student and brother of the famed dancer Maud Allen, in the dock.

The story begins at San Francisco's Emmanuel Baptist church, standing – or, rather, which stood, before its universally applauded deliberate destruction at spring's end 1915 – at No. 131 on broad, tree-lined Bartlett Street, and was from its earliest days an ill-wished place.

Built to look like a small cathedral 'amid the hollows, odd lights and drifting fog' of an ancient burial ground, it came to be known as the Gray Cathedral or the Haunted Church on the Haunted Street. 'Rumors of ghosts and orgies' swirled around the bizarre grey eminence, with its sinister, soaring bell-tower, which sprang dramatically from its north-west corner and swayed alarmingly in the wind.

A place unhallowing and unhallowed. Emmanuel's men of God laboured there, it seemed, under a curse. The first pastor cut his throat. The second shot himself. The third murdered the publisher of the *San Francisco Chronicle*.

Then there was John George Gibson, who insisted on being known as, and called, Jack. Born in Edinburgh in August 1859, which Athens of the North he quit twenty years on to attend Spurgeon's College in London, lodging in Camberwell Church Street with a fellow divinity student, Jesse Gibson – same patronym, no relation. It was during these London years, Graysmith tells us, that the two Gibsons gained an intimate knowledge of the East End.

Thus is the Whitechapel link forged.

From 1881, when he emerged from Spurgeon's College duly qualified, until mid-1887, Jack Gibson was serving as a minister of the church at St Andrews University, in Scotland.

Then ... a disconcerting blank until December 1888.

Graysmith ponders the blank ... and speculates. Did not Jack Gibson resemble the person Joseph Lawende saw talking to Catherine Eddowes shortly before her death?

Graysmith supplies Gibson's personal description: thirty-five years old. Exactly 5 feet 9 inches tall. Fair-haired. A small sandy moustache, curling at the ends. Blue-grey eyes, sly and imperious, heavily hooded. Wide, round face. Full-blooded, broad-shouldered, athletic and, although stubby, well-built. His finely rounded neck bore terrible scarring on both sides and he kept a red scarf wrapped around it. He was effeminate in both voice and manner, but spoke like a gentleman.

Citing Sugden,[47] Graysmith quotes triumphantly from Joseph Lawende's description of the man he saw chatting with Catherine Eddowes minutes before her death ... a man thirty years old, 5 feet 8 inches tall, with a fair complexion, fair hair, and a small light moustache that curled up at the ends. He was broad-shouldered, of medium build, round-faced, with a red handkerchief around his neck and carried himself like a gentleman.[48]

Did he not also resemble the official sketch of the Whitechapel murders suspect? And yet more: was not the Ripper possibly an entity of two knives, four hands, which is to say a criminal partnership. Dissolving and dissolved?

Now the audacious suggestion – is it not probable that the two pastors Gibson, John and Jesse, one-time London room-mates, were a team who set about terrorising the East End in 1888 with a 'grand design' which remained undiscovered for over a century? Jack the Ripper and friend, motivated by religious mania, anti-Semitism, and a hatred of prostitutes.

In late December 1888, the duo depart London – Jesse migrated to Canada. Jack Gibson packed up his belongings and quit Britain to seek his mission in the United States.

Graysmith, tracking only Pastor Jack, and not paying attention too punctilious to the calendar, notes that the reverend gentleman's arrival on American shores coincided with the murder, on 23 April 1891, of an aged prostitute of the Whitechapel ilk, Carrie Brown, nicknamed 'Old Shakespeare', in the seedy East River Hotel on the lower Manhattan waterfront. New York newspapers speculated that Jack the Ripper had come to New York, having apparently vanished from Whitechapel after his 9 November 1888 murder of Mary Jane Kelly.

Pastor Jack claimed that at the time of the Old Shakespeare murder he had been serving at a Red Bluff, California, church, although, inexplicably, the records show that he was actually at a church in New Brunswick – but whether the reference is to the New Brunswick in Canada or the New Brunswick in New Jersey, conveniently close[49] to Carrie Brown's Manhattan murder scene, goes unrecorded.

From Red Bluff, where he had remained for three and a half years, he went to Chico, California, for another two and a quarter years. He arrived in San Francisco in the November of 1894. Less than six months after his advent as pastor of Emmanuel church, two appalling murders took place.

On 3 April 1895, Blanche Lamont, aged twenty-one, was found, her strangled, marmoreal-white nude corpse arranged as though in prayer, in the upper reaches of the eerie, wind-swaying belfry. A fearful sight, made all the more horrifying when the body was moved, for, as one chronicler[50] relates, 'while the body was as white as marble as it lay in the cool belfry, when it was removed to the body of the church, where the air was much warmer, it turned almost jet black'.

Nine days later, on 12 April, the stabbed corpse of twenty-year-old Minnie Williams was discovered in a closet in the church library.

William Henry Theodore Durrant, a twenty-four-year-old medical student, ardent member of the congregation, assistant superintendent of the Sunday School, was tried for the murder of Blanche Lamont. Fifty witnesses testified for the prosecution.[51] He was found guilty. But the rumour was strongly bruited that Pastor Jack had been the real killer.

Graysmith persists in a refusal to believe in the guilt of the 'severely devout' Durrant. He remains obdurately convinced of his entire innocence. 'Could such a religious man,' he asks, 'commit atrocities within a church and could he conceivably die with the word "innocent" on his lips if it was a lie?'

Like Abrahamsen, he thinks the Ripper to have been an entity of two knives, four hands, which is to say a murderous partnership, dissolving and dissolved.

He writes, 'The second man brings to mind Pastor Gibson's roommate on [Camberwell] Church Street. He was tall and thin with a very pronounced accent [peculiar to some parts of Canada]. As a reverend, he dressed in clerical costume and had a dark beard.'

Graysmith goes on to compare the Reverend Jesse significantly with the man who inquired of Miss Emily Marsh at her father's shop in Jubilee Street about Mr Lusk's address – 'a man of some forty-five years of age, fully 6 feet in height, and slimly built. He wore a soft felt black hat, drawn over his forehead, a stand-up collar, and a very long black single-breasted overcoat, with a Prussian or clerical collar partly turned up. His face was of a sallow type, and he had a dark beard and moustache. The man spoke with what was taken to be an Irish accent.'[52]

'To think like Durrant, I [Graysmith] must take on his personality and reconstruct his lost diary.' And Graysmith forthwith channels Durrant:

> The answer to [the murder of Blanche Lamont] revealed itself to me [Durrant] in a brightly colored dream ... What I saw from the rafters ... as I looked through the beams into the tower, shook my faith even more and caused me to remain silent ever after. I glimpsed the reddened face of Pastor Gibson, so distorted that I scarcely recognized it. He was crouched in his black robe and was clutching at an ax ... Was she [Minnie Williams] slain by a religious fanatic, so as to be discovered on Easter, the most important Christian event of the year – the Resurrection? It shook my faith in God, believe me. The Pastor [Gibson] represented the church. He was the church to me and I could not bring myself to speak [the truth about Pastor Gibson] to save my life.

While not wishing to detract from so hallucinatory and Godlike a reconstruction of poor Theo as Graysmith has come up with, it is perhaps of interest to read what critic Anthony Boucher wrote of 'that legend which Theo Durrant wove about himself in the last days before his execution':

> There were his dreams in the cell – true prophetic dreams, he swore, of events he could not have known beforehand ... 'I received an intimation in a dream that may prove a magnificent clue ... Spread out before me on a scroll were strange characters that some power enabled me to decipher. The words were a revelation in regard to the perpetrator of the murder with which I am charged.' ... For weeks Theo had been engaged on a manuscript. On each trip to the prison, his father would carry away a few more pages of this magnum opus – which has regrettably never been heard of again.

Durrant was hanged in San Quentin Prison on 7 January 1898. Pastor Gibson survived him by fourteen years. As time, the great effacer, went by, Pastor Jack lived down the ugly rumours. He was still at Emmanuel in August 1908 when his flock arranged a special birthday celebration in his honour. But six months later, in February 1909, he resigned from his fourteen-year pastorate. His given reason, want of sufficient income. The Emmanuel Mission was clearly failing, drying up.

Thereafter, Pastor Jack evaporates as mysteriously as his Whitechapel namesake. He is said to have died in Chicago, around 1912, making a deathbed confession. True or false? Disappointingly, Graysmith's research has accomplished no such revelation.

I do not believe that Theo Durrant was innocent of the Emmanuel Baptist murders, and that the true culprit was the pastor of that ill-wished temple. I do not believe that when the Ripper is called upon to stand before the bar of Heaven and speak forth his name it will be that of the servant of the Lord, John or Jack George Gibson.[53]

What Robert Graysmith's book lacks in ultimate credibility, it makes up for in instantaneous ingenuity. But that ingenuity does not bear scrutiny. The preposterousness of cunningly crafted arguments gradually emerges as the word-clouds which envelop – as indeed the mist and fogs blowing up from the Bay swathed the grey bulk of the church of Emmanuel itself – disintegrate in the gentle breeze of rationality and the sunlight of pure reason.

63
Jack's Enchiridion

For quite a few years Ripperologists had been aware of the existence of Stewart Evans' 'Red Book'. He was wont to carry it around tantalisingly with him. Whenever disputes arose and memory failed, he would have recourse to the consulting of this incarnadined enchiridion, which, with the passage of time, came to acquire the almost mythological status of an oracle.

No longer need envy gnash its green teeth. Published in October 2000, simultaneously in England and America, but under diverse titles – *The Ultimate Jack the Ripper Sourcebook* (British) and *The Ultimate Jack the Ripper Companion* (American), officially authored by Evans and Keith Skinner – Stewart's Red Book became universally available in a hefty, 692-page, liberally illustrated volume, placing a valuable reference tool in the researcher's hands.

In it are printed the entire contents of the original Scotland Yard Ripper files, this vital primary source material usefully augmented with a selection of significant extracts from never-before-seen Home Office files, Britain's Royal Archives, contemporary police notebooks, copies of doctors' and pathologists' reports, sundry revelatory letters, and telling items from newspapers of the time. Interestingly, not to say alarmingly, we are informed that the book contains copies of documents which are now missing from the official files.

What has until now been needed, was, in the words of the authors, 'a survey of all the known facts about the murders, free of modern commentary and interpretation'. And this is what they have set out to provide. It is their belief that they have laid before the reader 'the full factual history of the Whitechapel Murders'.

As Evans and Skinner point out, 'the extant police and Home Office records on the murders, held at the Public Record Office at Kew (South West London) and other archives are vast and impossible to quote in full'. There has, therefore, admittedly been the need to impose a degree of selectivity, but not, they insist, 'in such a way as to affect the value of the relevant source material available'.

To reduce to plain-reading print the mass of handwritten documentation, often virtually illegible, often faded to the veriest limits of visibility, not infrequently damaged to such an extent that Stewart Evans found the task of transcription of the utmost difficulty, is akin, indeed, to one of the labours of Hercules. When the microfilmed material from which he was working became just too intractable, he would, wherever possible, inspect the original document. Literally years were eaten up in the effort.

The opening words of the first chapter draw a careful distinction between what the authors refer to as the Whitechapel murders, which is to say the entire series of eleven killings, from that of Emma Smith in April 1888 to that of Frances Coles in February 1891, and the so-called Ripper murders, which began (arguably) with the killing of Martha Tabram in August 1888 and ended with that of Mary Jane Kelly in November 1888. The authors consider it distinctly possible that only three of the murders may have been the work of Jack's hand.

This is a book of record, not interpretation. Encyclopedic, it is divided into forty-four chapters of varying length, each of which is prefaced by a brief but illuminating note of guidance. The book is an invaluable, indeed indispensable, research tool, and it is the one volume that must not be disregarded by anyone who is planning to undertake serious work on the case.

A chapter on my old fellow Liverpudlian, Frederick Bayley Deeming, the Rainhill murderer, born actually 'over the water' in Birkenhead, is to be found tucked away among the Ripperian chapters. Two letters concerning Deeming from a Mr Charles Barber, of Ardwick, Manchester, one to the Secretary of the Whitechapel Vigilance Society and one to the Home Office, are printed. Barber based his case against Deeming upon a vivid dream which he had had.

I have dreamt of the crime that this so-called 'Jack the Ripper' has done. My dream of the Mitre Square murder is very clear, for I saw him on the job and afterwards take to the ship – namely, the *Alaska*. Sir, you will find what I here make out – the ship was in port on all the dates given: (1) April 3, 1888, (2) August 7, 1888, (3) August 31, 1888, (4) September 8, 1888, (5) September 30, 1888, (6)

November 8, 1888; (7) July 17, 1889, (8) September 10, 1889. When that ship was not in port no crime was reported of this man 'Jack the Ripper.' Again that ship arrived at Queenstown one day last week, which I have dreamt so much about. I made this remark to my friend: 'Oh, the ship *Alaska* has arrived, and we shall soon be hearing something more of "Jack the Ripper" again.' They made but little of it, but when they saw it in the paper they wondered, and said that he must have been on the ship *Alaska*. I cannot give over thinking about it. He is about 5 feet 7 inches, rather stout, a little round-shouldered or short-necked, not much hair on his face, aged forty or over. Saw him again in the early part of the morning of 11 September 1889, in my dream.

Extract from a long statement by Mr Barber:

> While reading over the Rainhill stories and this man Williams, otherwise Deeming, I cannot come to any other belief than he is none other than the so-called 'Jack the Ripper', for I saw him on four or five different occasions in my visions. I will take it upon myself though I don't know Whitechapel, not ever being at the place – I will mark out on a sheet of paper each one of the places where the murders have been committed, and shall be tied blindfolded, and believe me, I can give some very vivid pictures of each murder ... I have seen this man on all the different murders, and after they were committed, for I saw him at the railway station booking to go away.
>
> He was then dressed in black clothes, with a longish coat on, a kind of billycock hat, with a black bag in his left hand. He was against the barriers getting his ticket when I saw him. After this I saw him; this was some time after in July 1889. It was in this way I saw him. I have it that it was at some docks, where there were some large vessels. One of these vessels was ready to start off. It was a fine vessel, with its cords stretched from mast pole to bow and stern, with small flags attached, and I read the name of this vessel, *Alaska*, and just as it was blowing off to start – for I could see the steam blowing off – this same man that I had seen times before came along the docks with a black bag in his left hand, and mounted the vessel by means of a ladder. Then off went the vessel. He seemed to me to be the last person to get on, for I saw no other person get on after him. At this I awoke, saying to myself, 'That is Jack the Ripper.'

Then there is the account of a John Langan, an American (of whom I had never heard) detained in Boulogne. Mr F. W. Bonham, H.M. Consul, had written from the British Consulate in Boulogne to Sir Charles Warren on 10 October 1888, informing him that a man had called at the Consulate that day asking for assistance. The Vice-Consul who saw him thought that he bore a striking resemblance to the sketch portrait in the *Daily Telegraph* (6 October 1888) of the man wanted for the East End murders. The man, down and out, was requesting help to go to South Wales to work in the coal mines. He produced a discharge from a British ship at Glasgow on 10 April 1888, in which he had only shipped at New York on 30 March 1888. As the man said that he had been born in the United States, Bonham had said that he would not assist him, and sent him to the American Consul. Bonham had then procured a copy of the *Daily Telegraph*, and handed it to the police, who arrested Langan as a vagrant. Following ordered inquiries made in Glasgow and at Langan's previous residence at an address there confirmed, he was released from custody and vanishes from the horizon of suspicion.

Naturally, Dr Francis Tumblety makes due appearance, but let it be recorded to Stewart Evans' credit that no attempt is made at special pleading for his conviction.

Epicedium

Now that the hour has struck to bring to an end the writing of this long book about so faraway and long-ago a crime, I am assailed by all manner of insistent thoughts and not-to-be-burked memories.

As one grows older, Time seems to telescope. In curious fashion it both foreshortens *and* extends. Events from the past tend, arbitrarily, sometimes to coalesce, and at other times to increase the distances of space between.

I am thinking now specifically of the small boy who, in the 1930s, deceiving his parents, who believed him to be safely ensconced in the academic groves of the South Kensington Natural History Museum, went trolling off on the Metropolitan Railway to Whitechapel, to meet and question old folk who had actually lived through the historic autumn of terror. The horror recollected in tranquillity of those simple people is something that has stayed with me all through the decades of my ongoing study of the Ripper case.

Such is the vividness of that recollection after all the intervening years that it reinforces the essential truth of my father, the learned attorney's apophthegm that life is just a hen's march!

I am inclined to think that, in a sense, much that is labelled history is no more than a fable for posterity that has been universally and solemnly agreed upon. By this definition, the chronicle of Jack the Ripper does not qualify as history, for search as I might – and did – I failed to find any unified view, any consensus. Instead, I found a multitude of chroniclers selectively using poorly documented evidence, unreliable hearsay testimony and plain supposition, to bolster their own pet theories and contentious conclusions.

This may perhaps serve to answer any charge which maybe brought against me of having been persistently destructive in the criticisms to which I have given voice.

I have felt it to be within my brevet to be on the *qui vive* for any self-serving prejudice or bias by which an author could, all unconsciously, distort the track to his conclusion. Such unintentional auto-trickery can make an event seem both predictable and inevitable. Real danger lurks and hides in the temptation to hunt for and discover links existing between what are actually totally distinct and dissociated factors. One is, of course, concerned to identify truth, but equally to identify for what they are myths and fantasies, so as to be able to weed them out along with misconceptions and errors.

As well as maker of myths and fantasies, the scanning of the biased eye can be the source of innocent or deliberate error. The efficient investigation must take into account the sad circumstance that much information reported, and relied upon, as historical fact is nothing of the sort and has to be regarded with suspicion.

Two vital qualities, I have discovered, as absolute essentials for anyone attempting to write a Ripper book are suspicion and cynicism. Unfortunately, things just do not happen as neatly and obligingly as vested interpretation can make them seem to do. What really happens is that a small number of different and unrelated events, being recognised and duly remarked, gradually synthesise, come together, to reveal in a sudden flash a whole new 'truth', which, alas, is greater than the sum of its parts.

But truth is fickle. Examining the life and times of Jack the Ripper, and more especially their aftermath, is a treacherous endeavour.

What then, as of this year 2013, is the conclusion?

I find no case to answer against any of the accused. They are dismissed. The verdict must remain undisturbed. Some person or persons unknown.

Those sad trollops – Polly Nichols, Dark Annie Chapman, Long Liz Stride, Catherine Eddowes and Black Mary Kelly – have lain in their paupers' graves these one hundred and twenty-five years. And somewhere, too, their slayer now lies buried, his identity safely masked behind the carved name on his stone.

Dead. All dead.

And yet the paradox is that they, the physically mutilated and the mentally mutilate, share an uneasy immortality that has been denied to the worthier great majority, as Evelyn Burnaby was wont to call them.

In their end was a beginning.

They, and the creature who destroyed them, survive, poor pale ghosts, flitting on and on through dark alleys of the mind and mean gaslit streets and courts of memory, to plague the ingenuity of succeeding generations seeking to supply the answer to an overwhelming question. An answer which, in all probability, not even the five victims of the sixth ghost knew …

His name.

Appendix A
Stephen Knight: A Memorial

For all that the late Stephen Knight has been accorded a degree of disapproval, castigation even, by some and sundry researchers who have followed in his blurred prints, it would, I think, be manifestly wrong to estimate his ultimate worth solely upon the basis of *The Final Solution*, and the admittedly unacceptable theory which it propounds and proffers. To be fair, along the way he made a very real and enduring contribution to Ripper studies. The facts which he unearthed when he succeeded in getting both the Scotland Yard and the Home Office files opened up to him must be weighed favourably in the balance. It should be allowed, and remembered, that it is his conscientiously transcribed notes and collated gleanings from these sources which constitute his real legacy to us, not his bit of nonsense with the royals.

It is in this spirit that I offer this small memorial to a pitifully short life to those who knew, and more especially to those who never knew, the young man that it would summon back to remembrance.

Stephen Knight was born, a Wednesday's child, on 26 September 1951, at Hainault in Essex. He attended West Hatch Technical High School, at nearby Chigwell, where, in his own words, he was 'unsuccessfully educated', and told by his teachers, 'Your future lies in ruins before you.' He was inclined to agree when he took his first job as a trainee showroom salesman for the London Electricity Board.

But he had already made up his mind that what he really wanted was to be a journalist, and found himself facing the first – and toughest – assignment that any journalist has first to cope with, getting a foothold in the profession. Determination stood him in good stead. In 1969, aged eighteen, he succeeded in having himself accepted as a trainee junior reporter on the *Ilford Pictorial*, and when that paper folded about his still-wet ears, contrived a desk place on the *Ilford Recorder*. Sacked somewhat prematurely from the *Recorder*, he achieved a smooth, upwardly mobile transition to the *Hornchurch Echo*, where, at the age of twenty, he was promoted to chief reporter. For a month's span in 1973, he worked on the *East London Advertiser*, before rejoining the staff of the *Ilford Recorder*, where he became chief reporter and subsequently feature-writer-cum-dramatic-critic-cum-book-reviewer.

Still restless, he parted company again with the *Recorder*, this time of his own volition, in 1975, to take up a position on the *Travel Trade Gazette*, but was off on his own travels again in 1976, as a full-time, self-employed writer, following the enormous success of *The Final Solution*. He had meanwhile married Margot Kenrick, acquiring two stepdaughters, Natasha and Nicola, and, in 1977, she bore him a baby daughter of his own, Nanouska. The following year, he, Margot and Nanouska took a trip to Australia. In August 1978, from Singapore, *en route*, he sent me a cheerful postcard. Later, he told me that he was scenting the antipodean track of Constance Kent, the young fratricide of Road Hill House, who would, in 1979, stand fully discovered and revealed by Bernard Taylor in his definitive book on the case, *Cruelly Murdered*, as the 100-year-old Miss Ruth Emilie Kaye, who had died, full of redemptive honours – a congratulatory message from the King and Queen no less – after a career of nursing lepers, on 10 April 1944, in a rest home in the municipality of Strathfield, New South Wales.

In 1979 Knight produced his first novel, *Requiem at Rogano*, an Edwardian detective story really, with a supernatural tinge. He did not, I remember, like the publisher's choice of title. He told me that he had wanted to call it *The Heretics of Rogano*. It was generally well received. A satisfactory successor to his Ripper book.

After all this early-flowering success, the year 1980 was to prove his *annus horribilis*. And in a most unexpected way. It began, low key and innocently enough, with Knight seeing an advertisement which appeared in the *London Evening Standard* seeking people who suffered from epilepsy to take part in a BBC *Horizon* documentary on the disease. He answered it because he wanted to have an opportunity of talking about the public's misunderstanding of the illness.

Three years before – in 1977 – he had started to have epileptic episodes. 'When I was ten I was hit on the head by a cricket bat.' The doctors believed that a consequent area of dead tissue discovered in the brain was the causal factor. Recently, his epileptic fits had been steadily increasing in intensity and duration. 'Not knowing why was,' he said, 'rather frightening.'

Martin Freeth, the producer of the *Horizon* programme, was anxious to show viewers a scan of an epileptic brain, and, knowing that the mark left by the cricket bat accident would show up, chose Knight as the guinea pig. The scanner revealed that this necrotic patch had increased to the size of an egg. Within a week a biopsy had established the diagnosis of a cerebral tumour, and he underwent brain surgery in the Maudsley Hospital, at Denmark Hill, South London.

He recovered. 'I was told that there was only about a 5 per cent chance of the tumour ever recurring, as it was very low grade. I translated that as nought per cent and just carried on living.'

And there was a happy sequel.

In his private world things had not been going along too smoothly. Critical differences had blown up between him and his 'Belle Marguerite'. In November 1980, it was announced that Lesley Newson, *Horizon*'s twenty-eight-year-old researcher, and Stephen Knight would marry when his divorce from his separated wife came through. In the event, though, they never did.

With six-monthly scans proving clear, Knight went merrily on to write *The Brotherhood: The Secret World of the Freemasons*, published early in 1984. It was a direct result of his literary Mason-watching, carried out in connection with his Ripper book. His new work, containing as it did many sensational allegations, among them that the KGB had succeeded in infiltrating Masonry, and with its exposure of the power of the square among the guardians, at all levels, of the law, caused a considerable stir – and most satisfactory sales figures.

What proved to be his last book,[54] *The Killing of Justice Godfrey*, another piece of investigative work, also came out in 1984 – in the July. This Knight regarded as his best book. He explained,

When I was thirteen I had the idea of taking an historical mystery and 'solving' it in the form of a short story. I approached my history teacher at West Hatch Technical High School, Chigwell – an man called John Hudson – and asked him if he knew a suitable case. He immediately told me to get Alfred Marks' *Who Killed Sir Edmund Berry Godfrey?* from the library. It was, he said, the greatest unsolved murder in English history. Alas, Mr Marks' turgid prose proved too much for me and I abandoned the project. But the idea stayed with me and when, ten years later, I finished my book *Jack the Ripper: The Final Solution*, and was casting around for a new subject, Godfrey seemed the obvious choice, the three-hundredth anniversary of his death was just three years off. If John Hudson had not hooked me in 1965 it is unlikely this book would ever have been written.

It, too, was well received.

The Brotherhood was dedicated, 'For Ma and Pa, with love.' *The Killing of Justice Godfrey* introduced a completely novel dedication: 'For Barbara Mary Land. Love.' No more for Margot. His marriage had ended in divorce. Lesley Newson had also 'ended', her place taken by a new girlfriend, Barbara Mary Land.

The first disquieting hints that something was going wrong with himself came shortly after the publication of *The Brotherhood*. 'I began to get strange symptoms. I developed a curious kind of word blindness – not being able to say the word I wanted, however simple, and my handwriting started to become very, very bad. I thought it was due to over-medication from the drugs I'd been taking for epilepsy.'

He was in South Carolina, holidaying with Barbara Mary Land, that summer of 1984, when he suddenly realised that the postcards he was writing home were 'indecipherable travesties' of his usual writing. Equally worrying was the fact that he found when he was walking that he was continually stumbling to the right.

'I telephoned my doctor, Peter Fenwick, at the Maudsley.' Dr Fenwick told him that if he was getting headaches he must come home immediately. He was. He flew back the next day.

Knight, who was interviewed in considerable depth by Anne de Courcey, from whose perceptive and sympathetic article in the *Standard* I quote, told her, 'I was so confident I was only suffering from over-medication I'd booked a room at the Gatwick Hilton and a return flight the following afternoon. The first inkling that anything was wrong otherwise was when I was kept waiting while they looked at my scan. It turned out they were comparing it with the previous ones. Then a doctor came into the room and said, "I'm afraid there's a recurrence of the tumour."'

The following day Knight saw Dr Fenwick. 'He knew that I always respond best to the truth. I asked him how long I had got. He said, "We intend to give you another operation followed by chemotherapy. Even if there's nil response to either you will have at least two years." Although I cried at the time and was very upset, we were actually able to have conversation about what those two years would contain for me.'

In July 1984, about 70 per cent of the aggressive cancer tumour was removed by operation. The remaining 30 per cent could not, because of its proximity to speech and movement centres of the brain, be subjected to surgical interference. Chemotherapy for eighteen months was prescribed.

Every six weeks throughout that autumn, winter and spring, Knight went to the National Hospital for Nervous Diseases, in leafy Queen Square, Bloomsbury, where, nearly fifty years before, another tragic young writer, Denton Welch, had been a doomed patient. Brain scans and blood tests in the morning. Chemotherapy in the afternoon. Often, after being injected with iodine to boost the scan's effectiveness, he would feel sick. 'Then I get frightened, because if I'm sick with my head stuck in one position I might choke myself.'

In October 1984, Knight, only thirty-three, was painfully honest with Anne de Courcey. 'They have now told me frankly there is nothing they can do to save my life, only prolong it. The surgeon who did the operation thinks it more likely I have one year than two.'

Knight had heard of the special attitude that was being taken to cancer at the Bristol Centre, where it was treated without drugs or surgery. He visited it and found himself so impressed with the work being done there that he promptly adopted the fruit and vegetable diet which the Centre advocated. 'Apart from the nausea and illness induced by chemotherapy, I feel incredibly healthy,' he announced. 'More so than I've ever been in my whole life – although I still get a yearning for sausage, bacon and eggs.'

But he was too clever a young man to lose sight of the fact that he was 'treading a very slender tightrope between wanting so much to live that I have been trying all sorts of unorthodox therapies, and at the same time trying to realise that if none of them works I will die – and to come to terms with this. I've received such incredible amounts of love, both from expected and unexpected sources, that there are now times when, just for a few seconds, I feel open and accepting to everything. Then I slip back and begin to fret.'

Stephen Knight spent his last days enjoying himself, living with Barbara Land in his house at Leytonstone. It was large enough for them to have friends visiting them constantly. He said, 'I always have plots in my head but at the moment I'm not getting round to writing them. I've visited several healers – there's a whole network of people in alternative work, one of whom leads to another. It's a new world to me, and very exciting. More than anything else, I have taught myself to live in the moment. Even all the blubbering and soul-searching and agonising I did was part of being in the moment. So is thinking, but acceptingly, "I don't know if I shall see another October."'

He did not.

He died in July 1885, while staying with friends[55] at Carradale, in Argyllshire. And that is where he is buried.

When I last saw him, Stephen Knight was calling himself Swami Puja Debal, and explained to me that he was now a follower of the Indian religious leader Bhagwan Shree Rajneesh, having become a Sannyasin after the ending of his marriage. He had his little daughter, Nanouska, with him, and we all trooped into a small café bar hard by the London School of Economics. We drank a dish of tea – Indian, of course – together and Nanouska had an ice cream. He wore, I remember, a strange dark corduroy cap – shaped somewhat like one of those that Burke and Hare, the body snatchers, wear in old engravings – to hide his hairless, bandaged head. He carried with him an air of finality.

Perhaps now he knows the answer to the big question. Whatever, let us remember him with charity. He was human. He erred. He was mortal. Spare him that small slice of immortality which is the warmth of one's fellows' remembrance.

Appendix B
Ripperature: The Literature about Jack the Ripper

The literature about Jack the Ripper and his East End murders is, taking into account a multitude of tributaries as well as the mainstream writings, vast. It is not possible here to pretend to anything approaching completeness, but what we can do is to identify the major seminal, as it were, works in the genre.

To begin at the beginning, which is to say in the year when the blood fell on the Whitechapel cobblestones, there issued forth from the London penny dreadful publishing company of G. Purkess, of 286 Strand, W.C., a forty-eight-page booklet, *The Whitechapel Murders or the Mysteries of the East End*, which must qualify as the first mainly non-fictional account of the doings of the creature who was initially christened the Whitechapel Fiend. After ten decades of virtual invisibility, a limited number of reprints of this pioneer work have become available.

The other contemporary work, this time transatlantic, was Richard K. Fox's *The History of the Whitechapel Murders: A Full and Authentic Narrative of the Above Murders, With Sketches*, published in New York in 1888. As in the case of its English counterpart, this account is compounded of basic fact, but with a goodly topping of fiction. It, too, is available in a recent limited edition reprint.

In 1889, in Germany and Italy there were produced two anonymous works – *The Latest Atrocities of Jack the Ripper*, published in Stuttgart, and *Jack lo Squartatore*, published in Venice. And in 1908, the Dutch writer Carl Muusmann published in Copenhagen *Hvem var Jack the Ripper? – Who Was Jack the Ripper?* – and hazarded the answer that he was American-born Alois Szemeredy. Szemeredy was said to have deserted from the Austrian Army, committed murder and been locked away in an Argentinian asylum in 1885.

It was not until the 1920s that the chroniclers got busy once more with the recording of Saucy Jacky's malfeasances. Tom Robinson, an old-style Fleet Street man, who had actually been assigned to East End investigative reporting while Jack was on the loose about the courts and alleyways, presented *The Whitechapel Horrors: Being an Authentic Account of the Jack the Ripper Murders*, from the Daisy Bank Printing & Publishing Co., Manchester, price 3d. This is a scarce item, but can also be had now in a recent reprint.

But it was the year 1929 which saw the birth, the emergence from Hutchinson & Co., London, of the 'Father of all Ripper Books', the first full-length study, *The Mystery of Jack the Ripper*, by the Australian journalist and one-time Labour MP for Kennington, Leonard Matters (1881–1951). Matters' solution, featuring the vengeful 'Dr Stanley', is, in plain speak, rubbish, but in other respects the book is no mean pioneering achievement.

Strangely enough, the next book on the Ripper came out in 1935 in France. Written by Jean Dorsenne, published in a paperback edition only by *Les Editions de France* (Paris) in their *Le Livre D'Aujourd Hui* series, and titled *Jack L'Eventreur: Scénes Vecues*, it has become one of the extremely rare books on the case. However, a copy came into the hands of Molly Whittington-Egan, who has translated it, and a limited edition in English has been issued (Cappella Archive, 1999).

Another Frenchman, Stéphane Bourgoin, would, fifty-five years later – in 1992 – bring out another paperback-only Ripper work, this time from *Les Editions Fleuve Noir, Jack L'Eventreur*. An unexceptionable retelling of the old story, it adds nothing new, but at least sticks reliably to the generally accepted facts.

To return to the English publishing scene. In 1937 ex-policeman Edwin T. Woodhall was the author of a Mellifont paperback, *Jack the Ripper or When London Walked in Terror*. Again, rubbish in its central thesis, but nevertheless an essential item in the history of Ripper celebration. An original copy of the book is both rare to find and expensive to buy, but a reasonably priced limited edition facsimile reprint was published by P. & D. Riley, Runcorn, in 1997.

In 1939, William Stewart, artist (as he described himself), produced *Jack the Ripper: A New Theory*. The new theory was that Jack was Jacqueline, a malevolent midwife – a notion previously floated by Conan Doyle, but resoundingly sunk by serious students of the case. This book, too, has become scarce and commands a price far in excess of its value as a contribution to genuine Ripperological knowledge.

Two more decades passed. A war was fought. In 1959 another journalist, of dubious credentials as a Ripper historian, Donald McCormick, perpetrated a fantasy entitled *The Identity of Jack the Ripper*. Herein the Russian Dr Alexander Pedachenko was paraded forth as the veritable Ripper. His candidature is immensely unlikely, but the book which sponsors it has become a purse-straining – and draining – collector's *desideratum*.

A shorter interval – six years – and the American journalist, Tom Cullen, comes out with *Autumn of Terror: Jack the Ripper, His Crimes and Times*. A new suspect is here nominated, Montague John Druitt, barrister and schoolmaster. There is a plausibility about this which converts. Convinced Druittists are soon in the ascendant.

Daniel Farson, with his *Jack the Ripper*, is thoroughly ratificatory. So, too, in 1987, with *The Ripper Legacy: The Life and Death of Jack the Ripper*, are Martin Howells and Keith Skinner.

Druitt continued to lead the field until, in Stephen Knight's 1976 input, *Jack the Ripper: The Final Solution*, royalty were introduced, and, predictably, swept the board. It is fairly generally admitted that Druitt and Prince Albert Victor, later Duke of Clarence, were mere theoretical offshoots.

The main-line Ripper books that followed Matters' formal lead were Robin Odell's *Jack the Ripper in Fact and Fiction* (1965) and *The Complete Jack the Ripper* by Donald Rumbelow in 1975. That year saw also the issue of *The Ripper File* by Elwyn Jones and John Lloyd. Essentially a *jeu d'esprit*, it nevertheless contains some interesting material. It has become hard to find.

My own *A Casebook on Jack the Ripper* (1975) set out to dispose of the more bizarre theorisings and underpin the serious main-line literature. It also seized the opportunity of dispelling a number of canards and time-honoured – or, rather, dishonoured – statements of alleged fact.

The American writer Frank Spiering sought to bolster the royalist conspiracy case with *Prince Jack: The True Story of Jack the Ripper* (1978). This was a work of sheer fantasy. 'The True Story' was precisely what it was not.

Modest, but useful, was *Will the Real Jack the Ripper*, by Arthur Douglas (1979). It accomplishes very respectably in its seventy-two pages that which was its object – to provide 'a thought-provoking primer for budding Ripperologists'.

The 1980s witnessed a great efflorescence, a bumper crop, of centennial Ripperature. Martin Fido opened, very capably, the batting with *The Crimes, Detection and Death of Jack the Ripper*

(1987). This was followed by *Jack the Ripper: The Bloody Truth* (1987) by Melvin Harris, who went on to complete a hat-trick with *The Ripper File* (1989) and *The True Face of Jack the Ripper* (1994).

Also seeing the light of print in the *annus mirabilis*, or *horribilis*, according to your Ripperian viewpoint, came, as we have already noted, Howells and Skinner's very skilful Druittist's *apologia*, *The Ripper Legacy*, Colin Wilson and Robin Odell's judicial centennial *Jack the Ripper: Summing Up and Verdict* (1987), and, finally, a couple of *livres d'occasion*, *Jack the Ripper: 100 Years of Investigation* by Terence Sharkey (1987) and *Jack the Ripper: One Hundred Years of Mystery*, by that well-known chaser of phantoms, Peter Underwood (1987).

In the actual centenary year – 1988 – only one volume was published, Paul Begg's *Jack the Ripper: The Uncensored Facts*. This does, however, count as a main-line work.

A hiatus. Then, in 1990, Jean Overton Fuller delivered her pro-royalist – or should it perhaps be anti-royalist? – *Sickert and the Ripper Crimes: An Investigation into the Relationship Between the Whitechapel Murders of 1888 and the English Tonal Painter Walter Richard Sickert*, resoundingly supported by Melvyn Fairclough's *The Ripper and the Royals* (1991). And Paul Harrison, following a new tack, proclaimed, possibly a shade too prematurely, *Jack the Ripper: The Mystery Solved* (1991).

The year 1991 also saw the inauguration of a most important main-line station – *The Jack the Ripper A to Z* – compiled by the illustrious Ripperian trinity, Paul Begg, Martin Fido and Keith Skinner.

The succeeding eight years have seen no lessening in the output of Ripper studies of all shades. Among, unexpectedly, the most offbeat offerings there came from the pen of the well-known American psychiatrist Dr David Abrahamsen *Murder and Madness: The Secret Life of Jack the Ripper* (1992).

The year 1993's yield consisted of *Jack the Ripper Revealed* by John Wilding and *Jack the Myth* by A. P. Wolf, who likened Jack to Hughes Mearns' man on the stair …

> As I was going up the stair,
> I met a man who wasn't there,
> I met the man again today
> I wish, I wish he'd go away.
>
> 'The Psychoed'

But the 'Big Bang' of 1991 was the publication of the alleged journal, *The Diary of Jack the Ripper*, narrative by Shirley Harrison. Its authenticity is today unaccepted by most students of the document, although it has been stoutly defended by Paul H. Feldman, who has presented his argumentation upon its behalf in *Jack the Ripper: The Final Chapter* (1997). Feldman died in 2005.

We were brought right back on the main line with the 1994 publication of Philip Sugden's carefully assembled and generally refreshingly reliable *The Complete History of Jack the Ripper*.

Camille Wolff, doctor of medicine and London crime book dealer, hit upon a new idea when, in 1995, she produced, under the title *Who Was Jack the Ripper? A Collection of Present-Day Theories and Observations*, what was actually a 'Who's Who' of Ripperologists. And that same year saw the publication of an updated edition of *Jack the Ripper: A Bibliography and Review of the Literature* by Alexander Kelly with David Sharp.

Bruce Paley's *Jack the Ripper: The Simple Truth* (1995) simply confirmed Oscar Wilde's maxim that 'the truth is rarely pure and never simple'. William Beadle's *Jack the Ripper: Anatomy of a Myth* provided the interesting thoughts of a very-much-his-own-man author.

The Book of the Year, however, had to be Stewart Evans and Paul Gainey's *The Lodger: The Arrest and Escape of Jack the Ripper* – subsequently retitled *Jack the Ripper: First American Serial Killer*. Herein, for the first time since, in 1914, Sir Melville Macnaghten named his three choices, the reader is presented with a new officially nominated suspect – Dr Francis J. Tumblety. This puts the book in a class of its own among the 'moderns'.

A curious importation from the United States, which arrived in 1996, was *Jack the Ripper: 'Light-hearted Friend'* by Richard Wallace, in which Lewis Carroll is identified as the Whitechapel murderer.

An equally curious importation to some Ripperological students' way of thinking, is the notion, bruited by Peter Turnbull in *The Killer Who Never Was* (1996), that the Ripper was every bit as much a mythologic artefact as Major Martin, the military man who never was.

A handsome end to the Whitechapel crop of '96 was provided by *An Illustrated Guide to Jack the Ripper* by Peter Fisher.

In *The Jack the Ripper Whitechapel Murders* (1997), Kevin O'Donnell wrote up the researches carried out by Andy and Sue Parlour – Ripperian rites or Parlour games, you could say! A most entertaining book, anyway. Also published in 1997 was James Tully's write-up of his researches, *The Secret of Prisoner 1167: Was This Man Jack the Ripper?*, in which he proffers a somewhat unusual suspect – another gentleman from my native heath, Liverpool, to go in tandem with James Maybrick!

An elegant coffee table – or perhaps coffin table would be a more apt description – book, M. J. Trow's *The Many Faces of Jack the Ripper* (1997) is a visually satisfying addition to the Ripper corpus, albeit one may not necessarily agree with the author's suspect selection.

The following year – 1998 – supplied a further four volumes for the sagging Ripper shelf.

From America, John Smithkey III subscribed *Jack the Ripper: The Inquest of the Final Victim Mary Kelly*, the main feature of which is the volume's provision of a generous ration of facsimile documentation.

The next 1998 contribution was a decidedly unusual one: *Jack the Ripper: A Psychic Investigation: The Compelling Paranormal Search for the Killer's True Identity* by Pamela Ball.

Unquestionably more down to earth was Bob Hinton's *From Hell … The Jack the Ripper Mystery*, an entertainingly written and eminently readable piece of work, but with no surprise as to his elected suspect.

The fourth volume to appear in 1998 was *In the Footsteps of the Whitechapel Murderer* by John F. Plimmer. Once again a work with a novel approach. Mr Plimmer, a West Midlands police officer of thirty-one years' standing, retiring in 1997 with the rank of Detective Superintendent, decided to bring to bear upon the Ripper problem his wide experience of modern killer-catching techniques, in order to assess the chances of the Ripper's having been 'buckled' by late twentieth-century methodologies.

A great many books have been written about Jack the Ripper in the course of the last fifteen years, but the majority tend to be repetitious accounts of the murders, which, however well retold, add nothing of any new significance to the dog-eared tale.

There are a few which should not be missed. There is Robin Odell's *Ripperology: A Study of the World's First Serial Killer and a Literary Phenomenon*, from the Kent State University Press, Kent, Ohio, 2006; *Jack the Ripper: Scotland Yard Investigates*, Stewart P. Evans and Donald Rumbelow, Sutton Publishing, Stroud, Gloucestershire, 2006; *Jack the Ripper: Letters From Hell*, Stewart P. Evans & Keith Skinner, Sutton Publishing, Stroud, Gloucestershire, 2001; and *The Complete Jack the Ripper A to Z*, Paul Begg, Martin Fido and Keith Skinner, John Blake, London, 2010.

Lastly, and most importantly, *The Ultimate Jack the Ripper Sourcebook*, Stewart P. Evans & Keith Skinner, Robinson, London, 2000.

Notes

Prologue & Part 1 The Seeding of the Killing Field: The Murders of 1888

1. See *Poppy-Land*. Clement Scott. Jarrold & Sons, 1894, and *Poppyland: Strands of Norfolk History*. Peter Stibbons & David Cleveland. Poppyland Publishing, North Walsham, Norfolk, 1990.
2. Although the invention of the label 'serial killer' is generally credited to Robert K. Ressler of the FBI, it was in fact used by John Brophy on page 189 of his *The Meaning of Murder* (1966).
3. In the *Observer* (London), 3 January 1988.
4. Peter Turnbull in *The Killer Who Never Was* (1966). p. 66.
5. Catherine her Christian name should be, according to the authors of *The Jack the Ripper A to Z*, who have taken that spelling from a reading of her birth certificate. But there are others who dispute that interpretation. See *Jack the Ripper: The Uncensored Facts*. Paul Begg. p. 232, note 1.
6. In 1877 Sims began writing under the pseudonym of 'Dagonet' a weekly column, 'Mustard and Cress', in the Sunday newspaper the *Referee*. He continued to write it for forty-five years, until his death in 1922.
7. Isenschmidt is referred to in all contemporary documents, and by the police, as 'Joseph', but Sugden gives him the Christian name of 'Jacob'. As Sugden is normally most reliable, I think that this discrepancy ought to be registered.
8. At the inquest on Chapman, Phillips conceded that he might have miscalculated the effects of the coldness of the morning and the great loss of blood in his original estimate of the time of death.
9. It was actually ten minutes past 1 a.m. on Monday 1 October 1888.
10. A psychiatric reaction characterised by the patient's deliverance of wrong replies to simple, easily answered questions – How many days in the week? Answer: Eight. How many legs has a dog? Answer: Five. Other symptoms, not difficult to fake, are clouding of consciousness, pseudo-hallucinations, and conversion symptoms.
11. *The Complete Jack the Ripper A to Z* (John Blake Publishing, London, 2010) informs us that from 1890 Szemeredy 'lived in Budapest with a widow, Julianne

Karlovicz, for whom he worked in her pork butcher's shop'.
12. In June 1999, the learned judge's work was not so much translated as rendered into quaint English – as witness blood dogs for bloodhounds. We are nonetheless grateful to the publisher, Adam Wood, and the translator, Rikke Skipper-Pederson, for making the volume available, and readable, ninety-one years after its original, and for the most part, language-locked publication
13. Translated in 1999 by Molly Whittington-Egan as *Jack l'Éventreur: Scenes from Life* (Cappella Archive)
14. See *The Killer of Little Shepherds*. Douglas Starr. Simon & Schuster. London and New York, 2011.
15. Thomas John Bulling (1847–1934).

Part 2 The Terrible Harvester: The Proposed Identities of Jack the Ripper

1. For a full discussion of Ann Druitt's terminal illness, see *The Ripper Legacy: The Life and Death of Jack the Ripper*. Martin Howells and Keith Skinner. p. 188.
2. For Fred Archer's treatment of this story, which had its beginning in the *Chicago Sunday Times-Herald*, 28 April 1895, see 'Human Bloodhound Tracks Jack the Ripper' in his *Ghost Detectives* (1970).
3. The local undertaker referred to is Henry Wilton. He died in 1907 in his ninety-seventh year.
4. Holmes actually made his first bow in *Beeton's Christmas Annual* in 1887, wherein the story 'A Study in Scarlet' first appeared.
5. This should actually be Pinchin Street.
6. *Inquest*. S. Ingleby Oddie (1941).
7. Doyle's recollection would seem to be at fault here, for no such phrase as 'fix it up' appears in the 'Dear Boss' letter. The word 'fix' is used, but solely in the context, 'They won't fix me just yet.'
8. No human kidneys were received by the police. A human kidney was sent through the post to Mr George Lusk, president of the Whitechapel Vigilance Committee, on 16 October 1888.
9. Farson has established that Ann Druitt had become insane in July 1888, *before* the murders, and not, as stated by Cullen, after the death of her son.
10. Alexander Kelly is the pseudonym of David Streatfield,

former librarian at New Scotland Yard.

11. Mabel Collins was the widow of Dr Keningale Robert Cook, who had used her as a spiritualist medium and recorded the phenomena, which she produced in a book that he wrote.

12. His real name was Robert Donston Stephenson.

13. Not 'D.O.' but 'R. D.' for Roslyn d'Onston. The article was 'The Real Original of "She"'.

14. There is no evidence that D'Onston was ever actually arrested, although he did tell Mrs Cremers that on two occasions he was taken in, like so many hundreds of others, for questioning.

15. These events, he states, took place in the spring of the year following the publication of Lytton's *A Strange Story*. That was in 1862, so D'Onston must have been born around 1840. Research by Melvin Harris has revealed that, according to his birth certificate, his baptismal name was Robert Donston Stephenson. He was born on 20 April 1841, at 35 Charles Street, Sculcoates, a district of Hull, in the East Riding of Yorkshire, and was the son of Richard Stephenson, mill owner and a partner in the firm of Dawber and Stephenson, Bone and Seed Crushers and Linseed Oil Manufacturers, and Isabella Stephenson, *née* Dawber. We now know that Roslyn Donston Stephenson, giving his profession as author, died on 9 October 1916, aged 76, in Islington infirmary, Highate Hill. The cause of death was (1) carcinoma of the oesophagus and (2) gastronomy. He is buried in an unmarked grave in Finchley Cemetery, London.

16. Baron Corvo was the *nom de plume* of Frederick Rolfe (1860–1913), English novelist and historian.

17. These articles, expanded, were published in book form, by Duckworth, in 1929, under the title *Tiger Woman: My Story*, with authorship credited to Betty May. No mention is made of Bernard O'Donnell, who had 'ghosted' it.

18. The British Museum Catalogue was freely accessible to the public at the round central desk in the old British Museum Reading Room.

19. These documents inexplicably vanished in the 1970s.

20. This is a gambling term for 'a decision by one throw of the dice, and not by e.g. two out of three'.

21. There were in France at this time two main neurological schools concerning themselves with psychopathology and psychotherapy. The Salpêtrière school presided over by Professor Jean Martin Charcot (1825–95), named after the Salpêtrière Hospital in Paris where he held his clinics, and the Nancy school presided over by Professor Hippolyte Bernheim (1837–1919) and named after its geographical location, the city of Nancy, standing on the left bank of the River Meurthe, 175 miles south-east of Paris. Both schools practised hypnosis. Their techniques differed. Charcot's *grand hypnotisme* was oriented more theoretically, viewing the phenomena of hypnotism as being themselves manifestations of abnormality. The hypnotism practised has been described as a cultured hypnotism, that is to say not natural, but like a cultured pearl. The Nancy school's contention was that hypnosis is no more than a condition of exaggerated suggestibility artificially induced. It was more practical, less theoretical, frankly more interested in the cure of the patient. It was this line of thought and pendant methodology that apparently appealed to Gull.

22. Spiering suggests that Lord Salisbury, very likely in cahoots with the Prince of Wales, had Clarence quietly suppressed with a lethal dose of morphia.

23. At this time, Henry Wilson, a barrister now, an Apostle and one of Prince Eddy's closest friends in his Cambridge days, found himself in the position to be able to carry out an idea he had long cherished – the establishing, in a picturesque little house in Chiswick Mall called The Osiers, of a 'chummery', where a succession of young men, chiefly from Cambridge, would find an ideal substitute for the lonely and uncomfortable lodgings which would otherwise have been their lot. And here, too, would be welcomed other – and older – of Harry's 'chums' – not leading lights of society, not necessarily intellectuals at all, but men who did possess in common certain very definite qualities which were necessary to gain Harry's good graces. Those, at The Osiers, could always be sure of finding sympathetic, cheering, youthful company. A sort of riverside Cleveland Street.

24. The Spec. The celebrated debating society at Edinburgh University. A body iconoclastic, witty and rebellious, election was – and still is – on intellectual merit. Robert Louis Stevenson was a member.

25. Founded in 1870 as the Metropolitan Asylum, for chronic imbeciles of a 'quiet and harmless nature'. Renamed Leavesden Mental Hospital in 1920, still holding a large proportion of patients of subnormal intellect, together with an assortment of chronic mental cases. Closed in 1997.

26. Perhaps the premises had already been acquired, and was therefore available for this purpose, although not yet operational as a convalescent home.

27. James Berry (1852–1913) a Bradford, Yorkshire, police constable turned shoe salesman, who became the public executioner in succession to William Marwood, of whom it used to be gruesomely joked, 'If Pa killed Ma, who would hang Pa?' Answer: 'Marwood.' Berry held the office of hangman from 1884 to 1891.

28. So splendidly celebrated by Arthur Calder Marshall in *The Magic of My Youth* (1951).

29. Rather puzzling is the fact that, having been told back in 1948 by Florence Pash the story of Sickert's involvement in the Whitechapel killings, Jean Overton Fuller makes absolutely no reference to it when writing about Jack the Ripper in her *The Magical Dilemma of Victor Neuburg*, first published in 1965. Neither does she refer to it in the revised second edition of that book, published in 1990, a quarter of a century later. And yet in the November of that same year she brought out her indictment of Sickert.

30. A variant version of this story – told by Knight – sets the locus as Drury Lane. 'Netley charged along Drury Lane in his carriage just as Alice Margaret was crossing the road with an elderly relative who was helping to bring her up. The child was not so badly hurt on this occasion because she was spun out of the way of the wheels when the corner of the carriage struck her. She was taken to hospital unconscious but released after a day, having been treated for concussion. The elderly woman who had been with her later described the driver of the coach to Sickert. He knew at once it was Netley.

31. Or perhaps only three, for Harrison expresses doubt that the murder of Elisabeth Stride was linked with those committed by the Ripper.

32. Although, as a matter of record, neither was actually the first to canvas the proposition of Joseph Barnett as Jack the Ripper in a book. It was first hazarded by Mark Andrews in his novel, *The Return of Jack the Ripper*, published in New York in 1977.

33. *Ripperana*, October 1992, No. 2. p. 26.

34. See *The Ripper Legacy*. Martin Howells and Keith Skinner. pp. 162–3.

35. Happily, I am able to report that this was not so. In spite of rumours to the contrary, Mary Jane Kelly was not pregnant at the time of her murder.

36. No! This is not a misprint. Neur*o*sthenia is the precise opposite of neur*as*thenia.

37. For details of this remarkable woman, *Mrs Satan: The Incredible Saga of Victoria Woodhull*. Johanna Johnston. Macmillan, London, 1967, should be consulted.

38. The precise location of the wall-writing is the subject of dispute. Superintendent Arnold stated that the writing was 'on the wall of the entrance'. Sir Charles Warren spoke of it as being 'on the jamb of the open archway of doorway visible to anybody in the street'. What we are in fact looking at is an arched open entrance with no door. This entrance was surrounded by bricks, about a foot or so in depth. The writing was on the right-hand side of this brickwork jamb.

39. Some of this material came to light after the publication of the hardback edition of *The Lodger* in August 1995, and appears in the addendum to the paperback edition of 1996, which was retitled *Jack the Ripper: First American Serial Killer*.

40. Gross indecency – which term embraces such acts between two persons of the male sex as fellatio, masturbation, or intercrural ejaculation, but not anal penetration, which was a more serious offence – was only a misdemeanour, carrying a maximum sentence of two years.

41. Alternatively, Evans suggested to me, the very real reason why the file on Tumblety referred to by Littlechild is missing is probably because it was a Special Branch file. These are never passed to the Public Record Office, and it may well still exist. Much is made of there being no mention of him in the contemporary files, but neither is there any mention of Druitt, Kosminski or Ostrog.

42. Littlechild made a small spelling error here. The correct name was Thomas J. Bulling.

43. What is Wallace saying? Is he classing Dodgson as a psychotic or a psychopath?

44. John Wilding and his *Jack the Ripper Revealed* (1993).

45. The psychic practitioner claims to have the capacity in certain states of consciousness to make contact with a kind of cosmic picture gallery, a record of the past, present and future of all our lives, and to view, rather in the mode that an ordinary viewer would watch television or a video, the replay of every thought, feeling and action since the world began.

46. History tells us of the existence of no such person.

47. Begg, Fido and Skinner give the address in the *A to Z* (1996) as No. 19 Maidman Street.

48. In *The Times* of 23 July 1888, in a letter to the editor headed 'Silent Soles for Policemen's Boots', Thomas B. Parkinson wrote, 'In Liverpool for some time past the policemen on night duty have worn rubber-soled boots, and are able to move about without advertising their whereabouts by the heavy tramp which announces the approach of our London policemen.'

49. Common sense will dismiss this as obvious nonsense. *If* Eddowes was saying such a thing, she was clearly doing it to impress people. *If* it was true, why tell it to so casual an acquaintance as the Mile End Ward Superintendent? She would surely have confided her secret to people whom she knew better – especially to her partner, John Kelly. Neither the Superintendent nor Kelly was called as a witness at the inquest, and there is no record of the police having been aware, as they certainly would have been, of Eddowes' alleged claim to knowledge of the Ripper's identity.

50. Stephen Wright died, aged seventy-seven, on 18 April 2000, in New York.

51. There is, however, a sizeable swathe of opinion that he intended to rob the punter being entertained by Kelly. Hutchinson was penniless at the time, which explains why he eyed and noted the man's jewellery, and why he waited so long for him to come out of Miller's Court. It also provides an explanation as to why, uneasy with reflected guilt, he hesitated so long before reporting the matter to the police.

52. Major Martin was born of the inspiration of the late Ewen Montague QC, serving at the time, 1942, as a lieutenant-commander in the wartime Navy. With graveyard humour they christened Montague's intelligence ploy 'Operation Mincemeat'. The idea was to float ashore – from a submarine – on the coast of Spain the body of a British staff-officer. He would be made to appear as if he had died after an aircraft had been lost at sea. Attached to his wrist would be a briefcase full of important-looking documents. The Germans had established a thriving and highly efficient espionage network in neutral Spain, and it was a safe bet that the dead British officer's secret papers would, in a very short space of time indeed, be in German hands. Those papers would contain vital misinformation, leading the enemy to believe – if they accepted them as genuine – that the Allied forces had no intention of invading Sicily from North Africa, which, of course, was precisely what the Allies did intend.

It was my old friend the late Sir William Bentley Purchase, the North London Coroner, who, under patriotic duress, acquired the vital cadaver for the intelligence boys. It was the corpse of 'an unknown man', and Purchase told me that, pending its despatch per canister, 30-cwt Ford van and the submarine *Seraph*, he had kept the body in the bath in his chambers in Inner Temple.

The ruse succeeded, and saved many hundreds of British and American lives.

'In the graveyard of the Spanish town of Huelva there lies a British subject. As he died, alone, in the foggy damp of England in the late autumn of 1942, he little thought that he would lie forever under the sunny skies of Spain after a funeral with full military honours … In life he had done little for his country; but in death he did more than most could achieve in a lifetime of service.' Thus did Ewen Montague write the epicedium of 'Major Martin', the unknown man, who, unknowingly, went so gloriously to war. In fact, he is no longer the 'Unknown Soldier'. I am able to reveal that the body was that of a thirty-four-year-old tramp named Glydwr Michael who had committed suicide by drinking phosphorus in a London Warehouse.

53. He was, according to the *East London Advertiser*, of 24 November 1888, which wrongly named him *Robert Buchan*, forty years of age. The *East End News*, of 23 November 1888, had him down as a marine store dealer. It was his father, Horace Buchan, who was the owner of the marine stores at 42 Robin Hood Lane, where the son worked as a sorter for his father, and probably carried on his own trade as a shoemaker in the back shop.

54. Wilson is discussing specifically the mutilation of Annie Chapman.

55. The name is also spelt Puckeridge in some documents.

56. *I Caught Crippen*. Blackie and Son, London, 1938.

57. Tully simply states that the file note was signed by 'somebody there with the initials "C. E. T."' Stewart Evans has identified 'C. E. T.' as Charles Edward Troup, the same man who subsequently chaired the Parliamentary Commission that led to the establishment of fingerprinting as an official police procedure.

58. Sadly, James Tully died on 17 December 2001.

59. Colin Wilson. Introduction to Donald Rumbelow's *Complete Jack the Ripper* (1987). p. 1.

60. Mircea Eliade. *Myths, Rites, Symbols: A Mircea Eliade Reader*, edited by Wendell C. Beane and William G. Doty. New York, Harper & Row, 1976.

Part 3 Points of View: The Historical Backdrop Interpreted

1. The *Arbeter Fraint*, a radical Yiddish newspaper, began publication in London in 1885. It became the *Anarchist* after 1892.

2. *East End Jewish Radicals 1875–1914*. Duckworth, London, 1975.

3. In *Point of Arrival: A Study of London's East End*. Eyre Methuen, London, 1975.

4. We now know pretty surely that there was never any such body as the Old Nichol Gang. Research has failed to reveal any contemporary reference to it. The earliest mention of it occurs in Donald McCormick's *The Identity of Jack the Ripper* (1959). pp. 19 and 26. The circumstance that both William Fishman and Chaim Bermant appear to have accepted as fact but what was surely McCormickian invention is most probably to be accounted for by reason of their both turning, when writing their own books on the East End, to McCormick for (as they believed) reliable information about the days when Jack the Ripper stalked the territory about which they were writing. As a result, they have, in all good faith, perpetuated the McCormick myth. His book is listed in both of their select bibliographies.

5. That is the twelfth and final month of the civil calendar, corresponding to August–September.

6. The Ram's horn sounded on *Rosh Hashanah*.

7. Sweeney Todd was being held aloft well into the twentieth century by the great barnstormer, Tod Slaughter.

8. Here Frayling appears to be referring to a series of penny dreadfuls published from 1846 to 1855 under that title, written by George William MacArthur Reynolds (1814–79), who founded *Reynolds's Weekly Newspaper* in 1850.

9. Bond pronounced the five murders – those of Nichols, Chapman, Stride, Eddowes and Kelly – to be the work of one hand. He did not think that the perpetrator was a vengeful religious fanatic, nor that he was possessed of scientific skill or anatomical knowledge. Contemporaneously with Bond's report was initiated a recycling of Jack as a medical specimen. In November and December 1888, two articles appeared in American medical journals. Dr James Kierman published 'Sexual Perversion and the Whitechapel Murders' in the *Medical Standard*, 4, No. 5. November 1888. pp. 129–30, and December 1888. pp. 170–71. And Dr E. C. Spitzka published 'The Whitechapel Murders: Their Medico-Legal and Historical Aspects' in the *Journal of Nervous and Mental Diseases* 13, No. 12, December 1888. pp. 765–78. Both articles presented prior histories of lust murder, illustrating that the Ripper murders were far from being unprecedented in the annals of crime. Comments Walkowitz, 'Both located the Ripper along a spectrum of contemporary perverts, from female masturbators and "urnings" of both sexes to the exclusively male perpetrators of "lust murder" and sexual sadism. Both relied on newspaper accounts of post-mortem reports of the mutilations and murders to diagnose the criminal: both remained undecided as to "his" legal responsibility, whether his actions were the result of congenital disease, or acquired vice.'

10. The so-called Yorkshire Ripper. Tried at the Old Bailey in 1981.

11. The discovery was the subject of an article by Francis E. Camps, 'More about "Jack the Ripper"', *London Hospital Gazette* no. 1 (April 1966). Reprinted in the *Criminologist*, February 1968; and in *Camps on Crime* (1973).

12. The three pencil sketches are reproduced in *Gradwohl's Legal Medicine*. 2nd edition, edited by Francis E. Camps. John Wright & Sons, Bristol, 1968. p. 63.

13. According to Major Henry Smith in *From Constable to Commissioner*. p. 153.

14. In fact, the injuries, including the severely cut throat, were noted at the scene at Hanbury Street. At the inquest, held at the Working Lads' Institute, in Whitechapel Road, Dr Bagster Phillips registered a most vigorous protest against making public the details of the injuries sustained by Annie Chapman. Wynne Edwin Baxter, the coroner, insisted, however, that he must do so, and, after several ladies and boys who were in the room had withdrawn, and the coroner had delivered a broad hint to the representatives of the press that the detailed medical evidence ought not to be published, Dr Phillips unhappily described the mutilations. No newspaper printed the details. The following report appeared in the *Lancet*, 29 September 1888: 'The abdomen had been entirely laid open: the intestines, severed from their mesenteric attachments, had been lifted out of the body, and placed on the shoulder of the corpse, whilst from the pelvis, the uterus and its appendages with the upper portion of the vagina and the posterior two-thirds of the bladder, had been entirely removed. No trace of these parts could be found.' In view of the fact that the incisions were clearly made, excising the pelvic organs with a single clean cut, avoiding the rectum and dividing the vagina low enough to avoid injury to the *cervix uteri*, Dr Phillips felt that the killer would have to have had considerable anatomical knowledge.

15. Sometimes referred to as the Mile End Vigilance Committee.

16. This article has in the past proved defiantly difficult to trace. This has been the result of misinformation supplied by William Stewart. I have tracked it down. It appeared in the fourth edition of the *Pall Mall Gazette* of 8 September 1888. There is nothing to indicate that it was written by Oswald Allen, but that is not surprising as such reports seldom bore bylines in those days. But what is, perhaps, surprising, is that the article contains no paragraph remotely resembling that quoted by Stewart, and there is no reference whatsoever in it to 'trumpery articles' or of their being 'placed carefully at the victim's feet'.

17. When reference is made to the Whitechapel murders

it is to the eleven murders that are contained in the Metropolitan Police files identified as 'Whitechapel Murders'. The murders, which occurred from 3 April 1888 to 13 February 1891, were of Emma Smith, Martha Tabram, Mary Ann Nichols, Annie Chapman, Elisabeth Stride, Catherine Eddowes, Mary Jane Kelly, Rose Mylett, Alice McKenzie, Frances Coles, and the Pinchin Street torso. On the other hand, reference to the so-called 'Jack the Ripper Murders' presumes the inclusion of only those of Nichols, Chapman, Stride, Eddowes, and Kelly, the five murders which occurred from 31 August 1888 to 9 November 1888, the notorious 'Autumn of Terror'.

18. His misgivings about the accuracy of newspaper reporting in 1888 notwithstanding, Sugden draws heavily on such sources for his *Complete History*.

19. *Complete History*. Sugden. p. 13.

20. In an article headed 'Whitechapel', the *Star*, 19 November 1888, p. 3, noted that, although Nikaner A. Benelius 'has been preaching in the streets, and behaving in a manner which suggests that he is not as fully responsible for his actions as he might be,' he had been 'quite cleared' of any 'suspicion in connection with the Berner Street murder [but, nonetheless] is likely to be arrested every time the public attention is strained to the point of suspecting every man of odd behaviour'.

21. For a discussion by Sugden on Kosminski see Mark King, 'Kozminski', *Ripperana*. January 1995. pp. 12–14.

22. For D. S. Goffee on Ostrog see 'The Search for Michael Ostrog', *Ripperana*. October 1994. pp. 5–12.

23. Adolf Beck was the victim of mistaken identity. He was convicted for larceny in 1896 – for which crime he served five years in prison – and again in 1904, the sentence for which offence was suspended by a court of inquiry which found all the charges against him in both trials to be without foundation.

24. We know now that she was not pregnant at the time of her death, but she might earlier have suffered a miscarriage or been otherwise unwell.

25. Peter Kürten (1883–1931) spent virtually half of his life in prison. He testified on the second day of his trial, 'In prison I began to think about revenging myself on society. I did myself a great deal of damage through reading blood-and-thunder stories, for instance I read the tale of "Jack the Ripper" several times. When I came to think over what I had read, when I was in prison, I thought what pleasure it would give me to do things of that kind once I got out again.' – *The Monster of Düsseldorf: The Life and Trial of Peter Kürten*. Margaret Seaton Wagner. Faber & Faber, London, 1932.

26. Begg, Fido and Skinner, in the *A to Z* (1996), suspect that 'Toronto Trust' is a mistranscription of 'Toronto Truss Society', which had an office in Finsbury Square, and solicited donations.

27. See page 130.

28. In 1877 the coronial district was subdivided, Wynne Baxter retaining the South-Eastern district, which comprised Whitechapel and Bethnal Green, and Dr Rodney MacDonald took on the North-East part of East Middlesex.

Part 4 The First Century: The Centenary of the Whitechapel Murders

1. It was Peter Rowe, who, under the pen-name William Vincent, had contributed to the *Police Review* (London) an impressive series of sixteen articles, 'The Whitechapel Murders: Jack the Ripper', which ran from 16 December 1977 to 14 April 1978.

2. Morrison felt that there was reason to think that the child went full term, was a girl, and was adopted. A man called Daley wrote from Bristol saying that his family had always believed that their great-grandmother was the illegitimate child of Mary Kelly.

3. According to that encyclopedic source of strength and Ripperine lore, the *A to Z*, our likely lad, Inspector Joseph Luniss Chandler, becomes a rather unlikely lad to have enjoyed dalliance with the lady whom Mr Morrison has the delicacy to describe in print as his great friend, but more bluntly to me as his mistress. She was the socially impeccable Mrs Marie Belloc Lowndes, wife of Frederic Lowndes, for many years a respected member of the staff of *The Times*, and a mover in high circles. Inspector Chandler, whose sole participation in the case of the Whitechapel murders was his handling of the body of Annie Chapman, consequent upon his happening to have been the duty inspector at Commercial Street police station at the time of the discovery of the Hanbury Street murder, was demoted to sergeant for drunkenness on duty in 1892. He hardly seems to have been possessed of the requisite social mien to share intimacies – bedroom or otherwise – with the plainly upper-crust Marie. Neither does it seem circumstantially convincing that, because she writes in her celebrated Ripper novel, *The Lodger* (1913), of a friendly young Scotland Yarder, name of Joe Chandler, to quote once more the *A to Z*, 'there is reason to suppose she had received inside information from the Commercial Street inspector, let alone that she bought it for thirty shillings [£1.50] at 6.50 p.m. on 9 November 1888, as Morrison asserts'.

4. I must confess to finding this puzzling, for nowhere in my copy of *The Lodger* is the name of Jack the Ripper mentioned. The character in the novel plainly based upon Whitechapel Jack is The Avenger.

5. In their Foreword to *Diaries and Letters of Marie Belloc Lowndes 1911–1947* (1971), Elizabeth Iddesleigh and Susan Lowndes Marques write, 'In August 1947, she fell ill … Her elder daughter drove her down to her husband's house in Hampshire, and there on 14 November she died, having received the last Sacraments of her Church. The priest who came to administer them was the Roman Catholic Chaplain to Broadmoor Criminal Lunatic Asylum. During her short illness he had become a friend …'

6. It was reported by James Marsh in *Ripperana*, No. 15, January 1996, that John Morrison had erected the headstone of Mary Jane Kelly, (a) over the wrong grave, and (b) without the required authority; anyway the stone was duly removed. Later, the cemetery superintendent placed a refurbished 1890 memorial stone above Mary Jane Kelly's actual grave. John Morrison lodged objection to the new memorial and took measures which led to its replacement by a ceramic cube bearing the words, 'Mary Jeanette Kelly. Aged 25, Murdered 9 November, 1888.'

7. James Melvin Reinhardt, Professor of Criminology at the University of Nebraska, author of *The Murderous Trail of Charles Starkweather* (1960) and *The Psychology of Strange Killers* (1962).

8. Although Bruce Paley's citing of Barnett as the Ripper had actually appeared in *True Crime* magazine in April 1982, John Morrison did not surface with James Kelly until

around May 1986. Euan Macpherson's nomination of Bury, the Dundee Ripper, first saw the light of print in the *Scots Magazine* (Glasgow) in January 1988.

9. Stewart Evans informs me that he has been unable to discover any proof that the deceased Timothy Donovan is the one who was the Dorset Street deputy.

10. The document in question came to light in October 1987. It was in the possession of James Swanson, the grandson of Detective Chief Inspector Donald Sutherland Swanson.

Part 5 The Great Hoax: The Diary of Jack the Ripper

1. Curiously enough, it was at the old Liverpool Wellington Rooms on Mount Pleasant, where, nearly a hundred years before, Florence Maybrick used to attend glittering Victorian balls, and which had since been transformed into the Irish Centre, that Anne and Mike Barrett met. They married in December 1975.

2. Although it seems to have been indicated in some quarters that Barrett's visit to Rupert Crew's took place in March or April 1992, Shirley Harrison appears to place it on 5 June 1992, which was the day when Robert A. H. Smith of the British Museum expressed his original view on the diary. See *The Diary of Jack the Ripper*. Paperback edition. 1994. p. 226.

3. 11 September 1993.

4. This letter was noted in the files by Robert Smith. It had been posted in N. W. London, and Sue Iremonger identified it as being in the same hand as the 'Dear Boss' letter.

5. The story appeared in the *Sydney Morning Herald* of 24 April 1993.

6. Shirley Harrison in *The Diary of Jack the Ripper* states that 'in a later, unpublicised affidavit, Brierley acknowledged that he first met Florie in 1887. It should be noted, however, that at the Maybrick trial witnesses spoke of the affair beginning about Christmas 1888. What Brierley actually says in this affidavit of his of 16 August 1889, is, 'I first met Mrs Maybrick at her own house at dinner about two years ago. I met her in company once or twice between that occasion and November 1888. In that month I went to a dance at her house. I subsequently met her at various dances and became on intimate terms with her and her husband. Mr Maybrick was at home on each occasion on which I have visited or called at the house. I never was improperly intimate with her until our meeting in London on the 22nd March last ... and I verily believe that was the only occasion on which Mrs Maybrick was unfaithful to her husband.'

7. Martin Fido suggests that, in context, it is interesting to read in Robert Lindsey's *A Gathering of Saints: A True Story of Money, Murder and Deceit* (1988), of the parts played by Rendell and McNeil in the mystery of the Mormon documents.

8. In any event the paper of the alleged Diary's pages is too thick for ESDA testing to have any relevance.

9. We may take this as an interesting example of the prevailing standard of accuracy which may be expected and must be allowed for. Here are the variously reported number of pages in the Diary. Shaun Usher (*Daily Mail*): 92 pages. Nigel Bunyan (*Daily Telegraph*), Brian McConnell (*Observer*), John Millar (*Daily Record*), and Harold Brough (*Liverpool Daily Post*): 65 pages. Phillip Knightley (*Independent on Sunday*): 64 or 65 pages. John Mullin (*Guardian*), Bill Mouland (*Daily Mail*), and Kevin Ludden (*Sun*): 64 pages. David Streitfield (*Washington Post*), Philip Sugden (*The Complete History of Jack the Ripper*), and Scott Palmer (*Jack the Ripper: A Reference Guide*): 63 pages. Peter Guttridge (*Sydney Morning Herald*): 62 pages. The correct figure is 63 pages.

10. *Contemporary Review*. Vol. 264. No. 1539. April 1994. pp. 221–2.

11. See 'Surface Analysis of a Gold Watch: Comparison of Original Surface and Scratch Marks', R. K. Wild. 31 January 1994.

12. In the first edition, Century, London, 1995, the date is given as 1974, but amended in all subsequent editions to 'in the 1960s'.

13. Mr Voller was later reported to have had second, or it may be third, thoughts.

14. Melvin Harris, in his thorough and well-supported refutation of Feldman's arguments, points out that all that this means is that the ink is an iron-gall ink showing no traces of modern twentieth-century dyes. 'As such, it is the same type of ink that was used in 1888. It is also the same type of ink that was used in 1908, 1918, 1928, 1938, 1948, 1958, etc. Some such inks are still made today. A sample made today will match the basic profile of any other iron-gall ink, regardless of its age. The chemistry involved is the same today as it was a century or more ago. An iron-gall ink is one of the simplest of all inks.' (*The Maybrick Hoax: A Guide Through the Labyrinth*. Melvin Harris. 1997. Circulated manuscript and put on the internet.)

15. This should surely be twenty-eight years.

16. McNeil was later to acknowledge that his results could have been distorted if there had been any artificial ageing of the document – if, for example, they (*sic*) had been over-aged. In the case of the fake Mussolini diaries they had been made to look older by heating them in an oven.

17. *The Maybrick Hoax*. p. 27.

18. But surely it *did*, as we have seen on page 235, display the signature 'James Maybrick', and around the edge of the rim of the inner case five sets of initials matching those of the five canonical Ripper victims.

19. There is a worrying hiatus here. According to her marriage certificate, Bessie Jane Over was twenty-two years of age at the time of her wedding in January 1896. That means that she was born around 1874. But ... Emma Over did not enter the Maybricks' service until 1881–82, and did not leave to get married until around September 1887, at which time Bessie Jane would have been eleven years old.

20. Albert's mother was Dora *née* Somers.

21. The Maybricks' first and only son was named James Chandler, and was nicknamed Bobo. Christie's source, the *Inter Ocean*, Chicago, October 1897, reads 'Henry'.

22. Alexander William MacDougall, Barrister-at-law, of Hanney, near Wantage, in Berkshire, and Richmond, on the south-west rim of London. He had attended the trial of Mrs Maybrick and been thoroughly disturbed by it, as, indeed, he had been back in 1877 by the trial of the Stauntons in the Penge murder case. He had at that time convened a public meeting in the grand hall of the Cannon Street Hotel in the centre of London, as a result of which an agitation arose which led to the remission of the capital penalty for the four accused. Now,

in collaboration with his friend Dr Lyttleton Stewart Forbes Winslow, a meeting was once again convened at the Cannon Street Hotel, and once again a reprieve, in this case for Florence Maybrick, followed. Convinced that she had been wrongfully convicted, MacDougall continued his campaign for her release, writing a massive treatise on the case in 1891, and producing a slimmer, updated volume in 1896. This time, however, his tactics did not succeed.

23. *The Maybrick Case. A Treatise on the Facts of the Case, and of the Proceedings in connection with the Charge, Trial, Conviction, and Present Imprisonment of Florence Elizabeth Maybrick.* Baillière, Tindall and Cox, London, 1891.

24. On Sunday morning, 12 May 1889, Matilda Briggs, with Michael and Edwin Maybrick and Mrs Martha Hughes, was searching Battlecrease House for the keys of the safe, in which they hoped to find James's will.

25. In such an event, everything would automatically have gone to Florence.

26. (1) The will proper, of 25 April 1889, and (2) the Grant of Administration, of 29 July 1889.

27. Apart, that is, from one word, the writing of 'what' instead of 'whatever' in line 4 – an obvious error of no importance.

28. The words in question – a total of eighteen – are missing from MacDougall's 1891 version of the will. And, for good measure, he imports one word not present in the original holograph version.

29. 'What' for 'whatever'.

30. Thomas and Michael Maybrick had had to be sworn before the Grant could be made. They had had to swear an affidavit of entitlement and intent. They had had to swear an Inland Revenue affidavit, and put up a bond to double the value of the estate. And they had had to pay out all the fees for these services.

31. This date is incorrect. Chapman was killed on Saturday 8 September 1888.

32. Sir James Fraser was Commissioner of the City Police, whom Smith was to succeed in that office.

33. *From Constable to Commissioner.*

34. *I Caught Crippen.* Blackie and Son, London, 1938.

35. The exact diary words are, 'Regret I did not take any of it away with me.'

36. *The Crimes, Detection and Death of Jack the Ripper.*

37. A Mr Miller – at least that is what he called himself.

38. Florence never had a sister. She had an elder brother, Holbrook St John Chandler.

39. Florence's mother, Caroline Elizabeth Holbrook, had married William G. Chandler. He was Florence and her brother Holbrook's father. He died in 1863. The widowed Caroline Chandler took Florence and Holbrook abroad to be educated and before leaving America married a fine, upstanding Confederate officer, Captain Franklin Bache Du Barry. On the vessel bearing them to Scotland he died. For the second time within a year Caroline Elizabeth was a widow. She and her children lived in England for a short while and then crossed the Channel to Paris. Thereafter, she drifted back to New York in the late 1860s. Restless, she returned to Europe, where, in 1872, she married her third husband, Baron Adolf von Roques, a Prussian cavalry officer. They lived in Cologne, Wiesbaden, and St Petersburg, before, in 1879, he abandoned her. The quality of the baroness's life deteriorated. She is said to have led a frenzied existence. 'Flitting back and forth across the Atlantic, she left a trail of scandalous conduct, bad debts

and broken promises in England, France, Germany and the United States.' (*Etched in Arsenic.* Trevor L. Christie. Harrap, London, 1969. p. 32)

40. John Baillie Knight, of 31 Holland Park, Bayswater. A young man who was a distant cousin of Florence.

41. James Maybrick's first cousin, John Maybrick, was employed by the Dominion Line as a senior pilot.

42. Edith Formby, Billy Graham's stepmother.

43. The diary research carried out by Paul Feldman and Shirley Harrison brought to light some fascinating background information regarding Alice Yapp. She was a native of Ludlow, in Shropshire, where she was born in 1860 or 1861. Her parents were said to be well-to-do. On the death of her father, she went into service as a nursemaid. She was courted by a man from a watch and clockmaker's shop in Lord Street, Liverpool, who used to go to wind up the clocks at the house where she was employed before taking up a position at the Maybricks'. Yapp had been expecting to get married in July 1889, but the engagement had been broken off when the clock-winder removed, or was removed, to Montrose. In January 1892, Yapp, then living in Roseberry Avenue, London, gave birth to a daughter, Margery. She gives her name on the birth certificate as Alice Murrin, formerly Yapp, but, says Feldman, did not marry Edward Murrin until June 1904 – twelve and a half years later. By that time she was living in Lewisham. Alice Murrin died at Epsom in 1953, aged ninety-two … After the Maybrick trial newspapers insinuated the existence of an improper relationship between Alice and the late James Maybrick. Feldman 'floats' a 'different possibility': could Alice Yapp 'have been another of James Maybrick's illegitimate children'?

44. *The Crimes, Detection and Death of Jack the Ripper* (1987) by Martin Fido, and *Jack the Ripper: One Hundred Years of Mystery* (1987) by Peter Underwood.

Part 6 Dreads and Drolls: A Meaningful Miscellany & Appendices

1. Assistant Commissioner CID. He was not knighted until 1901.

2. He could not have been, for when Annie Chapman was murdered he was on his way to Switzerland on sick leave, and was still there when Stride and Eddowes met their ends.

3. Department of Queer Coincidences. Item. Stephen Knight's birth date – forty-eight years on.

4. Further Department of Queer Coincidences item. The fatal accident occurred in Park Road, just where it meets Baker Street, outside the *Clarence* Gate of Regent's Park, and Paul H. Feldman, in his *Jack the Ripper: The Final Chapter*, informs us that the scene of Netley's mishap was 'outside Michael Maybrick's front door'.

5. Simon D. Wood was a dedicated researcher who was at that time applying his skills to the matter of setting the historical record right, as he saw it.

6. See page 210.

7. For a bibliography of the literature on the *Protocols* see *Warrant for Genocide.* Norman Cohn. Serif, London, 1967.

8. Elsewhere Hobo dates the retailment to his fourteenth or fifteenth year.

9. The Yorkshire Ripper.

10. Psychological profiling was by no means new, except in the sense that it was enjoying a new wave of awareness

and appreciation. It was a New York City psychiatrist, Dr James A. Brussel, who may really be said to have kick-started – with his psychological investigation of the George Metesky 'Mad Bomber' case (1957) – in the 1950s and 1960s a technique which essentially reached back to Cesare Lombroso and his *L'Uomo Delinquente*, published in 1876. In the early 1970s, largely as a result of the impact of the escalating phenomenon of haphazard serial killing, which was not amenable to solution by traditional tried and time-tested empirical methods of homicide investigation, senior special agents instructing at the FBI's National Academy at Quantico, Virginia, set up the Behavioral Science Unit (BSU), where principles employing psychological structuring were called into practical service. This novel law enforcement tool was supplemented by the FBI's introduction in 1984–85 of their Violent Criminal Apprehension Program (VICAP), a system of central information pooling, whence logged and analysed data regarding homicides from all over the United States is available on tap.

11. *Jack the Ripper in Fact and Fiction*. p. 82.

12. *Jack the Ripper*. p 44.

13. Farson. p. 41.

14. *The Complete Jack the Ripper*. p. 131.

15. Smith's recollection is at fault here. It was, as we have seen, posted to Mr George Akin Lusk.

16. Time has explained my lack of understanding: it has transpired that Openshaw himself categorically denied making the pronouncements attributed to him.

17. Grave No. 49336. Square 318.

18. Patrick Joseph Byrne was tried before Mr Justice Stable at Birmingham Assizes in March 1960. He was found guilty of murder and sentenced to life imprisonment. In July 1960, the murder conviction was quashed at the Court of Criminal Appeal and a verdict of guilty of manslaughter substituted. The life sentence, however, stood, Lord Chief Justice Parker observing that it was the only possible sentence having regard to Byrne's tendencies.

19. Bill Waddell in *The Black Museum: New Scotland Yard* (1992) provides a different version. He writes, 'While going through some old photograph albums that had been used for CID training, I found pictures of the five victims. The scramble to release them to the press was one of the most remarkable experiences of my forty years with the Metropolitan Police.'

20. Since copies of so-far-back numbers may be hard to come by, it should be noted that a virtually identical printing of the article is to be found in Brian Marriner's *A Century of Sex Killers*. Forum Press, London, 1992.

21. A slightly variant, but still satisfactorily full, version is included in Marriner's *Murder With Venom*. Forum Press, London, 1993.

22. *New Law Journal*. Vol. 142. No. 6539. p. 206. 14 February 1992.

23. Which, incongruously perhaps – perhaps not! – sends one's mind flitting off to the great lepidopterist, Vladimir Nabokov, and his pinned and spread-winged Lolita, a superb study in sexual obsession. Humbert and Jack are surely inhabitants of – albeit different parts of the forest – the same sick world.

24. This and the information following is derived from Philip Sugden's *The Complete History of Jack the Ripper*. Robinson, London, paperback edition of 1995. p. 478.

25. *The Baker Street Journal: An Irregular Quarterly of Sherlockiana*. Founded in January 1946. Organ of the Baker Street Irregulars of New York, which society, the inspiration of Christopher Morley in 1934, is the oldest and most prestigious of the American societies devoted to the study and appreciation of Mr Sherlock Holmes and his work.

26. Psoas is the name of the loin muscle.

27. Ref.: HO144/221/A49301C. Although the 'Dear Boss' letter of 25 September 1888 is that which is generally credited with containing the first usage of the name Jack the Ripper, the fact is that that signature is actually appended to this letter, also addressed 'Dear Boss', and dated nine days before. However, Stewart Evans, who has actually seen and handled this 17 September letter, is confident that it is a modern production. He tells me, 'The writing is a juvenile scrawl, modern in appearance, and totally different from all the other correspondence. Also it is written on poor-quality paper in, apparently, blue ball-point pen ink.'

28. Issue of July 1995, No. 13. p. 18.

29. An incidental by-product of this *Who's Who* has been the revelation that A. P. Wolf is not a 'he' but, apparently, a 'she', whose name is said to be Jennifer Lamy.

30. *The Streets of East London*. William J. Fishman. Duckworth, London, 1979. p. 111.

31. The *A to Z* states that Laurenco sailed between London and Oporto on the *City of Cork*. John J. Eddleston states that Larkins suspected sailors from three vessels, the *City of London*, the *City of Cork*, and the *City of Oporto*. Larkins also blamed another seaman, Joachim de Rocha, for the murder of Alice McKenzie. All the seamen were thoroughly investigated. All four were cleared.

32. Inspector Andrews was escorting one man only, but one man who had three given names, Roland Gideon Israel Barnett, as witnessed by the extradition papers and also the *Pall Mall Gazette* of 31 December 1888, which reported, 'Ten days ago Andrews brought hither from England Roland Gideon Israel Barnet [*sic*] charged with helping to wreck the Central Bank, Toronto, and since his arrival he [Andrews] has received orders which will keep him in America for some time.'

33. Trow does not give any references for the quoted portion of his comments.

34. The *Illustrated Police News* of Boston, Massachusetts, 22 September 1888, supplies the true facts.

35. The majority of Ripper researchers agree that there was probably only one sighting which may be reliably regarded as likely to have been genuine, and that that was the sighting in Hanbury Street at 5.30 a.m. on 8 September 1888, by Mrs Elizabeth Long aka Mrs Durrell. On the other hand, the man seen with the woman in Church Passage, Mitre Square, on the night of 29/30 September 1888, could equally well have afforded Joseph Lawende a genuine glimpse of the Ripper.

36. There are two versions of 'Was Jack the Ripper a Policeman?' by Bernard Brown, in the *Journal of the Police History Society*, 10, 1995. p. 3, and subsequently expanded in an article in the quarterly London crime magazine *Murder Most Foul*. October 1996. p. 36.

37. See the short story by Thomas Burke in his book of short stories, *The Pleasantries of Old Quong* (1931).

38. *The Great Acceptance: The Life Story of F. N. Charrington*. Guy Thorne (Cyril A. E. R. Gull).

39. George and Mary Ann Cushway, who kept a lodging-house at 9 Leman Street, Whitechapel, had a daughter,

Mary Ann Cushway, who married a George Nichols. This George Nichols was a cousin of Mary Ann 'Polly' Nichols. The Cushway-Nichols' daughter, Mary Ann Nichols (not to be confused with Mary Ann 'Polly' Nichols) married Benjamin William Parlour. Their son, William Parlour, was the father of Andrew William 'Andy' Parlour, who is the husband of Sue Parlour.

40. There are two Castletowns in County Limerick, Castletown parish, East Limerick, 5 miles north-east of Pallas Green, and Castletown village, 7 miles west of Bruree railway station, South County Limerick.

41. *Complete History*. Sugden. p. 42.

42. *The Black Museum* (1993). Waddell. p. 91.

43. 'A Piece of Eddowes' Shawl,' *Ripperana*. April 1997. p. 8 states that the specialist called in was from Christie's.

44. Eddowes was not wearing a dress as such, but a separate dress bodice, and a skirt. This descriptive error is widely perpetrated and perpetuated.

45. *Jack the Ripper: The Mystery Solved*. Paul Harrison. p. 179.

46. Melvyn Fairclough in his *The Ripper and the Royals* asserts that Abberline's diary for the year 1896 is 'the sole extant source naming Kelly's previously unknown friend Winifred May Collis'.

47. *The Complete History of Jack the Ripper*. p. 247.

48. Sugden, quoting the *Police Gazette*, of 19 October 1888, actually gives a height of '5 ft. 7 or 8 in.' There is no mention of a moustache other than 'moustache fair'. He quotes only 'medium build', refers to a 'reddish neckerchief tied in a knot', and describes the man as having the 'appearance of a sailor'.

49. New Brunswick, NJ, to lower Manhattan is a distance of some 35 miles.

50. *Celebrated Criminal Cases of America* (1995). Thomas S. Duke. p. 119.

51. 'Separate coroners' inquests resulted in verdicts charging Durrant with both murders, and separate preliminary hearings by the police magistrate resulted in his being held without bail for the murders of Blanche Lamont and Minnie Williams. Subsequently indicted by the Grand Jury, it was decided to try him first for the murder of Miss Lamont, though, later, additional evidence came to light which made the case of Miss Williams even stronger than the one on which he was convicted.' – 'The Trial of William Henry Theodore Durrant for the Murder of Blanche Lamont, San Francisco, California, 1895', *American State Trials*. Edited by John D. Lawson. Vol. 15. p. 640. For a detailed account of the trial, see pp. 636–756.

52. *The Complete History of Jack the Ripper*. Sugden. p. 266.

53. Though doubts are sown. Joseph Henry Jackson and Lenore Glenn Offord in their *The Girl in the Belfry* (Gold Medal True Crime Series No. 12, Fawcett, Greenwich, Connecticut, 1957) say, 'Reverend J. George Gibson *was* odd, though this hardly warranted suspecting him of murder. He was a crotchety Scot, a bachelor very much taken up with his own dignity, it is plain that he handled the press badly and that he was stiff and unco-operative when the police questioned him.' Jackson & Offord say of Theodore Durrant that he had no solid alibi for the hour when Minnie Williams was killed, whereas Pastor Gibson, the only other possible suspect, could prove his own whereabouts at the material time.

54. Apart, that is, from his contribution to the posthumous *Perfect Murder* (1987). The book was taken over by Bernard Taylor. To say that he completed it would be to give a false impression. The book consists of seven chapters in 251 pages. Knight wrote only two chapters totalling forty-five pages – Tony Mancini and on the Lower Quinton Black Magic Murder. I was happily able to help him as regards both subjects. Mancini I had met on several occasions and had had long and intimate conversations with him about the Brighton trunk murder. In the matter of the Charles Walton affair, I had met the old man's niece and been privy to the details of certain family secrets from her. I had also known Chief Inspector Fabian and discussed the investigation of the case with him. I knew who had committed the murder.

55. An Englishman whom I know only by his adopted Indian sect name of Chandro, and his Irish wife.

Bibliography

Abrahamsen, David, *Murder and Madness: The Secret Life of Jack the Ripper* (London: Robson Books, 1992)
Account of the Whitechapel Murders by the Infamous Jack the Ripper (Toronto, *c.* 1895)
A London Detective (pseudonym of W. J. Hayne), *Jack the Ripper, or Crimes of London: A Full and Authentic Account of the Mysterious Whitechapel Murders* (Chicago: Utility Book & Novelty Co., 1889)
Anderson, Sir Robert, *The Lighter Side of My Official Life* (London: Hodder & Stoughton, 1910)
Bailey, Hilary, *The Cry From Street to Street* (London: Constable, 1992)
Ball, Pamela, *Jack the Ripper: A Psychic Investigation* (London: Arcturus, 1998)
Barnard, Allan (ed.), *The Harlot Killer* (New York: Dodd, Mead, 1953)
Barry, John Brooks, *The Michaelmas Girls* (London: Andre Deutsch, 1975)
Begg, Paul, *Jack the Ripper: The Uncensored Facts. A Documented History of the Whitechapel Murders of 1888* (London: Robson Books, 1988)
Begg, Paul, Martin Fido and Keith Skinner, *The Jack the Ripper A to Z* (London: Headline, 1996)
Bermant, Chaim, *Point of Arrival: A Study of London's East End* (London: Eyre Methuen, 1975)
Bondeson, Jan, *The London Monster: A Sanguinary Tale* (Stroud: The History Press, 2003)
Brown, John Francis, *The Curse upon Mitre Square, A.D. 1530–1888* (1888)
Cameron, Deborah and Elizabeth Frazer, *The Lust to Kill: A Feminist Investigation of Sexual Murder* (Cambridge: Polity Press, with Basil Blackwell, 1987)
Camps, Francis E., *Camps on Crime* (Newton Abbot: David & Charles, 1973)
Camps, Francis E. (ed.), *Gradwohl's Legal Medicine* (Bristol: John Wright & Sons, 1968)
Camps, Francis E. and Richard Barber, *The Investigation of Murder* (London: Michael Joseph, 1966)
Caputi, Jane Elizabeth, *The Age of Sex Crime. A Dissertation submitted to the Graduate College of Bowling Green State University in partial fulfilment of the requirements for the degree of Doctor of Philosophy August, 1982* (Ann Arbor, Michigan: University Microfilms International, 1982)
Colby-Newton, Katie, *Jack the Ripper* (*Great Mysteries: Opposing Viewpoints Series*) (San Diego: Greenhaven, 1990)
Connell, Nicholas and Stewart P. Evans, *The Man Who Hunted Jack the Ripper: Edmund Reid and the Police Perspective* (Cambridge: Rupert Books, 1999)
Cullen, Tom, *Autumn of Terror* (London: The Bodley Head, 1965)
Dorsenne, Jean, *Jack L'Éventreur. Scènes Vécues,* trans. by Molly Whittington-Egan (Great Malvern: Cappella Archive, 1999)
Eddleston, John J., *Jack the Ripper: An Encyclopedia* (London: Metro Publishing, 2002)
Evans, Stewart P. and Keith Skinner, *The Ultimate Jack the Ripper Sourcebook: An Illustrated Encyclopedia* (London: Robinson, 2000)
Evans, Stewart P. and Paul Gainey, *The Lodger: The Arrest and Escape of Jack the Ripper* (London: Century, 1995)
Fairclough, Melvyn, *The Ripper and the Royals* (London: Duckworth, 1991)
Farson, Daniel, *Jack the Ripper* (London: Michael Joseph, 1972)
Feldman, Paul H., *Jack the Ripper: The Final Chapter* (London: Virgin Books, 1997)
Fido, Martin, *The Crimes, Detection and Death of Jack the Ripper* (London: Weidenfeld and Nicolson, 1987)
Fisher, Joseph C., *Killer Among Us: Public Reactions to Serial Murder* (Westport, Conn.: Praeger, 1997)
Fisher, Peter, *An Illustrated Guide to Jack the Ripper* (Runcorn, Cheshire: P & D Riley, 1996)

Fishman, William J., *East End 1888: A Year in a London Borough among the Labouring Poor* (London: Duckworth, 1988)

Fishman, William J., *East End Jewish Radicals, 1875–1914* (London: Duckworth in association with the Acton Society Trust, 1975)

Full and Authentic Account of the Murder by Henry Wainwright of His Mistress Harriet Lane and An Extended Account of the Whitechapel Murders by the Infamous Jack the Ripper (Toronto, c. 1895)

Fuller, Jean Overton, *Sickert and the Ripper Crimes* (Oxford: Mandrake, 1990)

Graysmith, Robert, *The Bell Tower: The Case of Jack the Ripper Finally Solved ... in San Francisco* (Washington, D.C.: Regnery Publishing, 1999)

Harris, Melvin, *Jack the Ripper: The Bloody Truth* (London: Columbus Books, 1987)

Harris, Melvin, *The Ripper File* (London: W. H. Allen, 1989)

Harris, Melvin, *The True Face of Jack the Ripper* (London: Michael O'Mara Books, 1994)

Harrison, Michael, *Clarence: The Life of H.R.H. the Duke of Clarence and Avondale (1864–1892)* (London: W. H. Allen, 1972)

Harrison, Paul, *Jack the Ripper: The Mystery Solved* (London: Robert Hale, 1991)

Harrison, Shirley, *The Diary of Jack the Ripper* (London: Smith Gryphon, 1993)

Hinton, Bob, *From Hell ... The Jack the Ripper Mystery* (Abertillery: Old Bakehouse Publications, 1998)

Hudson, Sam'l E., *'Leather Apron', Or the Horrors of Whitechapel, London, 1888* (Philadelphia, 1888)

Jones, Elwyn and John Lloyd, *The Ripper File: The Documentary Investigation by Detective Chief Superintendents Charles Barlow and John Watt* (London: Arthur Barker, 1975)

Kelly, Alexander and David Sharp, *Jack the Ripper: A Bibliography and Review of the Literature* (London: The Association of Assistant Librarians, 1995)

Knight, Stephen, *Jack the Ripper: The Final Solution* (London: Harrap, 1976)

Leighton, D. J., *Montague Druitt: Portrait of a Contender* (London: Hydrangea Publishing, 2005)

Linder, Seth, Caroline Morris and Keith Skinner, *Ripper Diary: The Inside Story* (Stroud: Sutton Publishing, 2003)

Macnaghten, Sir Melville L., *Days of My Years* (London: Edward Arnold, London, 1914)

Macpherson, Euan, *The Trial of Jack the Ripper: The Case of William Bury (1859–1889)* (Edinburgh: Mainstream Publishing, 2005)

Matters, Leonard, *The Mystery of Jack the Ripper* (London: Hutchinson, 1929)

McCormick, Donald, *The Identity of Jack the Ripper* (London: Jarrolds, 1959)

McLaren, Angus, *A Prescription For Murder: The Victorian Serial Killings of Dr Thomas Neill Cream* (The University of Chicago Press, 1993)

Muusmann, Carl, *Hvem Var Jack the Ripper? En Dansk Forhorsdommers Undersogelse* (København, 1908)

O'Donnell, Kevin, *The Jack the Ripper Whitechapel Murders* (St Osyth, Essex: Ten Bells Publishing, 1997)

Oddie, S. Ingleby, *Inquest* (London: Hutchinson, 1941)

Odell, Robin, *Jack the Ripper in Fact and Fiction* (London: Harrap, 1965)

Oliver, Dr N. T., *The Whitechapel Mystery: A Psychological Problem ('Jack the Ripper')* (Chicago, 1889)

Paley, Bruce, *Jack the Ripper: The Simple Truth* (London: Headline, 1995)

Palmer, Scott, *Jack the Ripper: A Reference Guide* (Lanham, Maryland: The Scarecrow Press, Inc., 1995)

Pinkerton, A. F., *The Whitechapel Murders: Or, an American Detective in London* (Chicago, 1889)

Robinson, A. F., *The Whitechapel Horrors, Being an Authentic Account of The Jack the Ripper Murders* (Manchester: Daisy Bank Publishing, 1918)

Rumbelow, Donald, *The Complete Jack the Ripper* (London: W. H. Allen, 1987)

Sharkey, Terence, *Jack the Ripper: 100 Years of Investigation* (London: Ward Lock, 1987)

Shelden, Neal, *Annie Chapman: Jack the Ripper Victim: A Short Biography* (Hornchurch, Essex: Neal Shelden, 2001)

Shelden, Neal, *Catherine Eddowes: Jack the Ripper Victim* (Hornchurch, Essex: Neal Shelden, 2003)

Shelden, Neal, *The Victims of Jack the Ripper* (Knoxville, Tenn.: Inklings Press, 2007)

Smith, Sir Henry, *From Constable to Commissioner: The Story of Sixty Years, Most of Them Misspent* (London: Chatto & Windus, 1910)

Spiering, Frank, *Prince Jack* (New York: Doubleday, 1978)

Stewart, William, *Jack the Ripper: A New Theory* (London: Quality Press, 1939)

Strachan, Ross, *The Jack the Ripper Handbook: A Reader's Companion* (Irvine, Scotland: Great Scot Services, 1999)

Sugden, Philip, *The Complete History of Jack the Ripper* (London: Robinson, 1994)

The Whitechapel Murders: Or, the Mysteries of the East End (London, 1888)

Trow, M. J., *The Many Faces of Jack the Ripper* (Chichester: Summersdale, 1997)

Tully, James, *The Secret of Prisoner 1167: Was This Man Jack the Ripper?* (London: Robinson, 1997)

Turnbull, Peter, *The Killer Who Never Was* (Hull: Clark, Lawrence Publishers, 1996)

Underwood, Peter, *Jack the Ripper: One Hundred Years of Mystery* (London: Blandford Press, 1987)

Walkowitz, Judith R., *City of Dreadful Delight: Narratives of Sexual Danger in Late-Victorian London* (London: Virago Press, 1992)

Wallace, Richard, *Jack the Ripper: 'Light-hearted Friend'* (Melrose, Mass.: Gemini Press, 1996)

Warren, Detective, *The Whitechapel Murders: Or, On the Track of the Fiend* (New York, 1888)

Whittington-Egan, Molly, *Doctor Forbes Winslow: Defender of the Insane* (Great Malvern: Cappella Archive, 1999)

Wilding, John, *Jack the Ripper Revealed* (London: Constable, 1993)

Williams, Watkin Wyn, *The Life of General Sir Charles Warren, G.C.M.B., K.C.B., F.R.S. Commandant Royal Engineers* (Oxford: Basil Blackwell, 1941)

Wilson, Colin and Robin Odell, *Jack the Ripper: Summing Up and Verdict* (London: Bantam Press, 1987)

Wolf, A. P., *Jack the Myth: A New Look at the Ripper* (London: Robert Hale, 1993)

Wolff, Camille (ed.), *Who Was Jack the Ripper?* (London: Grey House Books, 1995)

Woodhall, Edwin T., *Jack the Ripper: Or, When London Walked in Terror* (London: Mellifont Press, 1937)

Wright, Stephen, *Jack the Ripper: An American View* (New York: Mystery Notebook Editions, 1999)

Index

Also available from Amberley Publishing

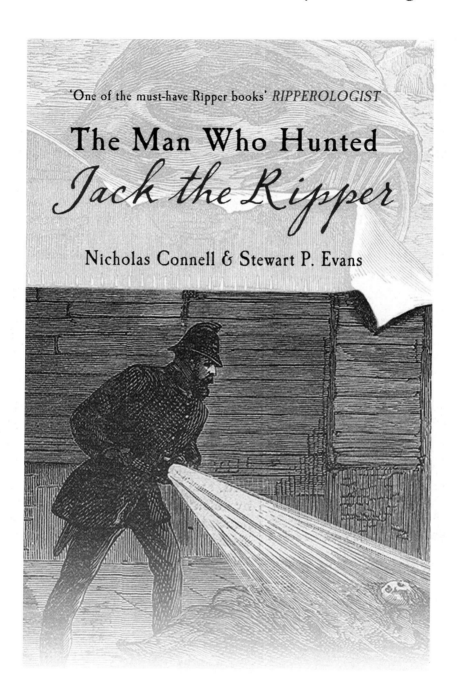

'One of the must-have Ripper books' *RIPPEROLOGIST*

The Man Who Hunted

Jack the Ripper

Nicholas Connell & Stewart P. Evans

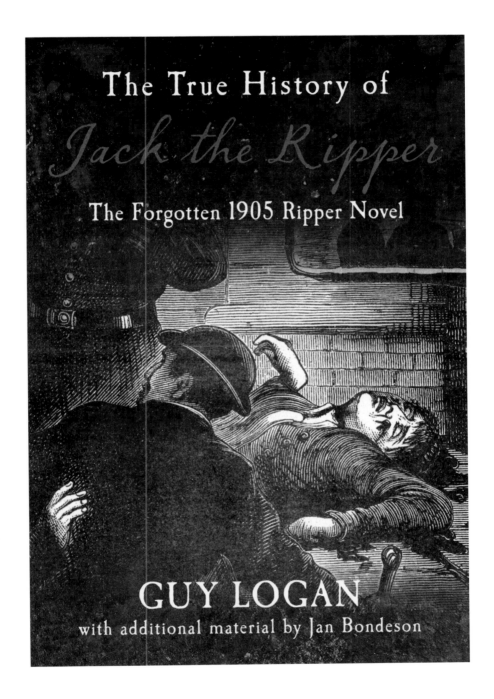

Also available from Amberley Publishing

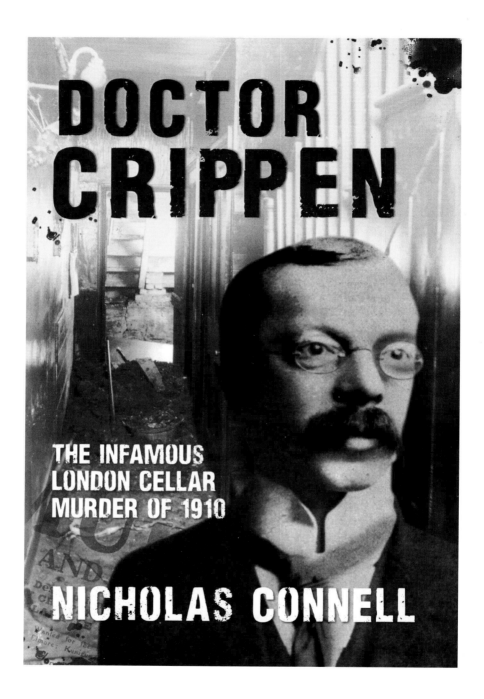

DOCTOR CRIPPEN

THE INFAMOUS LONDON CELLAR MURDER OF 1910

NICHOLAS CONNELL